UNITED STATES JEWRY, 1776-1985

UNITED
STATES
JEWRY
1776–1985

JACOB RADER MARCUS

Hebrew Union College

Jewish Institute

of Religion

VOLUME II

The Germanic Period

WAYNE STATE

UNIVERSITY PRESS

DETROIT

Library of Congress Cataloging-in-Publication Data
(Revised for vol. 2)

Marcus, Jacob Rader, 1896–
  United States Jewry, 1776–1985.

  Includes bibliographical references and index.
  Contents: v. 1. [without special title]—v. 2. The Germanic period.
  1. Jews—United States—History.   2. Judaism—United States—History.
3. United States—Ethnic relations.
E184.J5.M237   1989   973′.04924   89–5723
ISBN 0-8143-2186-0

TO MY DEAR ONES WHO HAVE PASSED FROM TIME TO ETERNITY

My father, my mother, my brother, my sister, my wife, my daughter

THE HISTORIAN WHO WORSHIPS

AT AN ALTAR LOWER THAN TRUTH

DISHONORS HIS CAUSE AND HIMSELF.

—*Henry F. Hedges,*
A History of the Town of East-Hampton, N.Y.

CONTENTS

THE COMING OF THE "GERMANS"

WHO CAME

The Revolution of 1775, important as it was to be to American Jewry in the future, was not in itself important in determining the type of Jewish immigrants who came to these shores. A few Sephardic families continued to filter into North America from the Continent and the Caribbean. The revolt of the blacks in San Domingo, Haiti, compelled a number of Jews to seek refuge in Charleston and New York City. The Sorias, who finally made their home in New York after a series of hair-breadth escapes, boasted that they were Spanish nobility. They survived the black revolution because father Aaron Soria had once befriended a slave Pierre. At the time of the uprising Pierre, now a general, saved the father just as he was about to be executed. Sephardic Jewish history is filled with such romantic, mythical, escapes. Most of the newcomers, however, were Ashkenazim, Jews who followed the German, not the Sephardic or Spanish-Portuguese rite. The largest Jewish ethnic group that entered the United States after the Revolution was German—from Alsace to Posen. Many had migrated from the Rhine Provinces, Wuerttemberg, Baden, and above all, Bavaria. From the Hapsburg Empire came large numbers of Bohemians and Hungarians, and from farther east and north there were substantial numbers of Poles and even a few Russians. The Posen Germans are frequently called Poles by their fellow Jews because Posen was once part of the old Polish republic. Included in the "German" migration up to 1881 are Italians, Dutch, French, and English. Unlike many of the Central Europeans, the French and English did not come to the United States in order to escape disabilities. The only West European for whom life was unbearable at home was the unhappy husband who deserted his wife, or the occasional criminal who sought safety on this side of the Atlantic. In May, 1827, Ikey Solomon—Charles Dickens's Fagin—escaped from custody in London, graced America with his presence, and ostensibly supported himself by trading in watches and trinkets. In reality he was a purveyor of fraudulent debentures and fictitious stock. Hearing that his wife Ann had been transported as a criminal to Tasmania he attempted to rejoin her, was captured, and redispatched back to Australia as a convicted escaped criminal.[1]

Most of the Central Europeans who landed here were young and unmarried. Many came as individuals; whole families with children also migrated. At times, not often, groups from a single village traveled together and established themselves in the same American town. Thus Cleveland Jewry owes its origins in 1839 to a number of Bavarians from the town of Unsleben. The typical Central European Jew who debarked at an eastern American port was poor but no pauper; after 1848 the cultured businessmen and professionals who fled Europe were not without means. Though there were marked social and educational distinctions separating the newcomers, they were in the main a one-class group: nearly all were in some form of trade. There was a substantial minority of artisans, shoemakers, butchers, and bakers; some were domestic servants and a few, farmers. Practically all the Germans, especially the Poseners, were religious traditional Jews. With a few exceptions these men and women were industrious, thrifty, and sober. Above all they were courageous; leave-taking was heartrending: they left behind parents, wives, and children, the familiar synagog, and the hallowed "house of life," the cemetery, where dear ones were buried. In addition the voyage across the seas in the sailing vessels of the first half of the century was a fearful hazard. It is said that 15,000 of the 90,000 passengers traveling on British ships to Canada perished on the way. Here in a strange land, the newcomers had to learn a strange tongue, start a new way of life, eat forbidden food, and desecrate the Sabbath in the desperate effort to survive. Some who came were fortified with "provisions for the road." They carried with them ethical letters enjoining upon them courage, integrity, charity, religious observance, and warning them against dishonesty, drunkenness, gambling, and prostitutes. And don't forget to write home![2]

WHY THEY CAME

Jews like other immigrants left Europe for America because of "push" and "pull." Europe "pushed" them out; America "pulled" them in. In 1847 Giacomo Meyerbeer, the German opera composer, traveled to Vienna. As a nonresident he would be expected to pay a special tax to enter through the city's gates. To spare him that embarrassment—he might not have come—the State made him a *cavalier*. This fiscal discrimination was typical of the petty harassments that "pushed" Jews from Europe. Except for France, Holland, and Belgium, Jews suffered disabilities in all European lands in the first half of the nineteenth century. Even in England a Jew could not sit in the House of Commons till 1858, take a degree at Oxford or Cambridge till 1871, and aspire to be Lord Lieutenant of Ireland or Lord High Chancellor till the 1890's. The period from 1815 to 1848, the Age of Metternich, was a time of reaction affecting all Germans but Jews in particular. It was an age of police spying, censorship, and repression of liberal thinking and expression. In 1845 Bavaria refused to allow its rabbis to attend a so-called "liberal" rabbinical conference. In 1819 anti-Jewish riots occurred in various parts of Germany; Jews were beaten, maimed, and plundered. The uncertainties of post-Napoleonic Central Europe, political and cultural repression, and famine in the countryside induced the unhappy populace to strike out at the traditional scapegoats, the Jews. Post-Enlightenment Europe, cultured and blasé, witnessed a brief revival of medievalism.[3]

Conscious always of French egalitarianism and American republican freedoms, distressed by repressive regimes, by dislocations on the farms due to agrarian changes, and by economic displacements that followed in the wake of an emerging capitalism, the Europeans rose in revolt in 1830 and 1848. The rationalization or modernization of the farms, bad harvests, potato blight, drought, and disease, drove farmers off the soil. Power-driven machines in the new factories put handicraftsmen out of work. In 1844 artisans in Prague attacked a factory where the Jewish owner had introduced a cotton-printing machine; during the 1848 Revolution there was a movement to boycott the Jews in that city, and in Heidelberg the custom tailors stormed Jewish shops which sold ready-made clothing. Distress in the country and in the city compelled German farmers and workers to seek a new future for themselves in distant America and, in turn, affected the Jewish traders and artisans in the towns and hamlets who were dependent on the farmers for their livelihood. Victims of changes on farm and in factory, many Jews, too, were compelled to migrate.

Jewish artisans, petty traders, and peddlers saw little hope for themselves in the new and changing economy. The plight of the Jews was twofold. As Germans, Austrians, Bohemians, Hungarians, and Poles they were subject to all the ills that confronted those peoples. As Jews they had to cope with the Judeophobic unhappy, underprivileged masses, with a new zeitgeist—a new national anti-Jewish political philosophy—with conservative churches and regimes determined to stop the floodtides of nineteenth-century democracy. All three groups, people, church, and state, were caught in a tangled web of tradition that was now linked to the new romantic chauvinistic nationalism. It was a spiritual world that had little tolerance for a son of Israel. Enfranchised in Central Europe in the early nineteenth century by the hated enemy, the French, the Jew was the beneficiary of egalitarianism. He was deeply resented in much the same way that the Negro was to be resented in the United States in the emancipatory decades of the mid-nineteenth century. Equality was unthinkable, unbearable. The eighteenth-century humanitarianism and the cosmopolitanism of the Enlightenment were now to make way for the new nationalism—the concept that religion, people, and government were one; only a good Christian could be a good citizen, a good German. There was no place for the Jew in this new scheme; Jews were here on sufferance: if they were successful they were envied.[4]

Perhaps only the psychohistorian can properly evaluate the massive flood of literary vituperation that poured over the emancipated aspiring Jews of the post-Napoleonic period. They were attacked because they were Jews, because they hoped to be free, because they, too, wished to be thought of as German. Not the worst but the best people, college professors and distinguished theologians, attacked them mercilessly. A scholar in Hamburg writing to a secretary of the Massachusetts Historical Society in 1817 spoke of the poor Jews as a "beggarly and immoral unclean people." Germany, he wrote, would have been ruined if they had continued to enjoy the rights given them by the French invaders. The pamphleteer Hartwig Hundt, while not recommending the murder of Jews, stated that he deemed killing a Jew not a crime but a misdemeanor. The solution to the Jewish problem was to castrate the males, sell the children to the British to work the plantations, and dispatch the mothers and daughters to whorehouses. It is not difficult to understand why in such a climate of opinion thousands of Jews thought of emigration as their only salvation. Let it be clearly understood. Few, if any, states or statesmen of that generation deliberately set out to load the Jews down with disabilities. They wanted at worst to maintain the status quo ante-French Revolution. They wanted to continue the eighteenth-century world of autocracy, privilege, and oligarchy; they hoped that they could turn the errant clock back. Their concept of the status of the Jew was rooted in history and they hesitated to modify it. They believed in ghettos and saw no reason not to cherish their traditional social prejudices against Jews. In Catholic South Germany and Austria the Church was unsympathetic to Protestants and Jews. The Church which had suffered under the French libertarians reacted by maintaining a policy of intolerance toward Jews throughout most of the nineteenth century. Fearful of all forms of modernism and liberalism, Prussia in the 1820's forbade Jews to bear Christian first names and closed down Reform synagogs. The Austrian religionists were convinced that the abolition of guild restrictions and granting Jews the privilege of becoming master artisans would be a blow to Catholicism.[5]

The list of legal, economic, and cultural disabilities imposed on Jews in Central Europe is almost infinite; yet on the whole Jews managed to survive. Very few of the laws were new; most were merely restored after 1815. The State itself was not free: cities, provinces, guilds, estates had vested rights, hoary with age, and the authorities hesitated to abolish them. In many instances it had no desire to do so. If conscription was onerous, the answer was that it affected Christians also. The humiliating oath "according to the Jewish custom"—(*more Judaico*)—exacted in the courts of Jews only—was in use in Saxony as late as 1879. Jews could hold no public position of trust and responsibility; they could not be teachers in the schools or instructors in the universities and if they aspired to be attorneys and practice law they would first have to renounce Judaism and join a Christian church. It was the hope of entering the legal profession and assuming public office that induced Heinrich Heine, the poet, to forsake his faith. Wherever Jews turned they found themselves confronted with disabling laws that circumscribed opportunity. In many provinces, especially in the Austrian empire, they found it difficult to own and farm land and estates. Throughout Central Europe the right to settle in a community was a jealously guarded privilege which was frequently denied to Jews. Even one of the Rothschilds was refused civic rights in the South German town of Baden-Baden as late as 1861. Whole provinces in Austria were closed to Jews, and in 1841 they were not allowed to dwell in one of the suburbs of Prague. Jews bitterly resented the *Familianten Gesetz*, the family restrictive laws of South Germany and Austria which limited severely the number of Jewish marriages well into the 1850's; some Jewish children were compelled to emigrate if they wished to found families. Rabbi Isaac M. Wise of Cincinnati told his disciples that his persistence in performing marriages illegally and secretly got him into trouble with the authorities in Bohemia and was one of the reasons which made it necessary for him to leave the country. That such marriage limitations were on occasion also imposed on the Christian poor was small comfort to a Jewish businessman who saw his family dispersed. With the biblical story of destruction of Jewish babies in the days of Moses in mind, Jews referred to these anti-marriage restrictions as Pharaonic laws.

The right to work was a privilege frequently denied the German and Austrian Jew. Not only was he kept out of the craft guilds but only too often he was forbidden to engage in specific trades and occupations. The Saxe-Weimar of Goethe frowned on Jews who hoped to be bakers, butchers, and innkeepers; the Austrians did not approve of them as millers or apothecaries, and in 1845 the Bavarians forbade them to deal in grain and cattle. For a time, in the 1850's, the Jews of Hungary were not permitted to employ Christian servants, and in 1860 the archbishop of Lemberg threatened with ecclesiastical punishments any Christian who took service with a Jewish employer. And if a Jewish family finally decided that emigration was the least of its problems it was confronted with a payment of a substantial departure or emigration tax; that non-Jews also had to pay this tax on occasion was small comfort. Thousands and hundreds of thousands of Central Europeans, and the Jews among them, hoped in 1848 that the republican revolutions would bring them all liberty and freedom. After a year the revolutions sputtered out and with them the hopes for more liberal regimes faded. Although most German revolutionists were sympathetic to Jews, even then Jews were attacked: in Baden and Upper Silesia the mobs turned against them; Polish nationalists in Posen rejected the Israelites and in Austria and Hungary many Czechs and Magyars were determined, if they should be emancipated, not to share their new freedom with their fellow Jews even though the latter had helped man the barricades.[6]

Yet by the middle 1850's conditions for the Jews improved decidedly throughout Germany and the Austrian Empire. The conservative governments now allied themselves with the rising bourgeois as the English had done in the eighteenth century; it was a new form of mercantilism. And as the businessmen came to power bringing wealth and culture they carried the Jewish merchants and industrialists along with them. They all came into their own. However, if these newly accepted Jews decided against emigration—and they were passionate patriots—they were also always aware of a miasma of anti-Jewish sentiment that hung like a pall over all Central Europe. In the famous Prater in Vienna in the 1860's there was a Punch and Judy show: "Hanswurst," Johnny Baloney, flourishes a club over the head of a frightened Jew and asks the mob "shall I or shall I not kill him?" and the *Gemuetlich* crowd roars a universal "yes" as the club descends. In the 1880's and 1890's ritual murder accusations were made against Jews in Hungary and Prussia. In 1900 at Konitz in West Prussia the military had to be called out to quell rioters who were convinced that their Jewish neighbors had murdered a Christian for his blood. Finally in 1867 Prussia and Austria-Hungary emancipated their Jews; by 1872 when Bavaria became part of the new German Empire it was compelled to accord equality to all its citizens, and by the 1890's Judaism was accepted as a legally recognized religion in the Austria-Hungary state.[7]

WHEN THEY CAME

The significant stream of German Jewish migration dates from the mid-1830's although there has never been a decade since the seventeenth century in which central Europeans did not set sail for America. Some came with the "Hessians" as sutlers during the Revolution but the European wars made travel difficult. The French Revolution and the Napoleonic liberation kept many at home, but the fall of the French in 1815 increased the flow of immigrants to the United States. In 1818 when Shearith Israel was rebuilt Mordecai Noah said that more room was now needed to provide for the newcomers. The following year the Hep Hep riots in Germany induced a number of Jews to leave. This may be deemed the first "wave," a trickle if you will. Yet the trickle made it possible by 1830 to create a new German congregation in New York City, Anshe Chesed, the Men of Loving Kindness. The second wave came after the failure of the European July uprising of 1830; by 1836 hundreds were pouring in, and the collapse of the liberal revolutions of 1848 brought numerous recruits to increase the size of the ever-growing American Jewish settlements. It took the Germans a few years after the failure of the revolution to realize that the hope for an American-type republican regime was abortive. Though conditions were improving in Europe many Germans were too impatient to wait. By the 1850's numerous liberals, farmers, and artisans —and Jews among all these classes—had decided it was time to turn their backs on the Fatherland. By that time the voyage to American was no real hazard. Speedy steamships had begun to displace the large three-masted sailing ships, and sometimes even kosher arrangements were available.[8]

THE GERMAN JEWISH MASSES REMAIN AT HOME

It is self-evident that the vast majority of Central and European Jews did not leave their homelands to come to the United States. In the decade in which German Jewish immigration reached its height, in the 1850's, there were about 250,000 Jews in Prussia alone, to say nothing of those in the other German states and the Austrian Empire. The hazards of the transatlantic crossing still frightened many and in the minds of some the Indians were still a menace. It should not be forgotten that Colonel George A. Custer's command, over 200 men strong, was annihilated by the Sioux as late as 1876, long after the Jews had decided that they had a future in the German lands. For many, America too was a land of wars, financial recessions, and whiskey-drinking, tobacco-chewing grobians. It was a "rendezvous of European scamps and vagabonds." It was no place for a cultured person. In spite of the cumulative depressive effect of petty laws and even pettier bureaucrats there was no question that Europe was becoming freer. The German customs union was expanding, industry was flourishing, and towns were growing—the opportunities were there. Jews began moving into the cities and prospered in business, in the professions, in the sciences and arts. The children and grandchildren of these middle nineteenth-century Jewish urbanites were to become the Nobel Prize winners in literature and science. By 1931 fourteen German and Austrian Jews were crowned as Nobel laureates. About 30 percent of all

German prize winners were Jews; 50 percent of the Austrian Nobel awards went to Jews, although they were less than 5 percent of the Austria-Hungary population and less than 1 percent in Germany. Even in the dark, unhappy days of 1848 there were some rabbis who urged their people to stay at home and doggedly fight for human rights: it is cowardly to run; don't let them drive us out. Within a decade and less the faith of these men was justified. Germany became the greatest Jewish cultural center in the world. Its hospitals, social welfare institutions, printing presses, libraries, schools, colleges, and literary societies were exemplary. It was the home and the hearth of the Science of Judaism, Jewish culture; as late as the 1920's American Jews who hoped for a career in the field of Jewish scholarship spent their apprentice years in the German and Austrian lands.[9]

OPTING FOR THE UNITED STATES

In some respects 1819 was the watershed year for many German Jews. The riots of that summer led many to doubt whether they had a future in the German lands. By 1822 the leaders of a Young Jewish Germany began to correspond with Mordecai Noah and by 1830, one of them, Immanuel Wohlwill, urged his students in Hamburg to think of the United States as a land of refuge. In that decade of the 1830's, after the failure of the July Revolution, Jewish societies were created to read about foreign lands with emigration in mind. The refusal of Czechs and Magyars in 1848 to accept the Jews as fellow nationals was traumatic for many. Even Louis Kossuth in Hungary believed that if Jews were to become part of the Magyar people they would have to surrender some of their traditional religious practices. Committees were formed in the Austria-Hungary lands to finance the emigration of those of limited means. The prime target for the emigrants was the United States and the year 1848 saw the rise of an "Up and On to America" propaganda barrage.[10]

A number of émigrés went to France and the British Isles but even some of those who landed in England treated it as a *Nachtasyl*, a halfway house. The Goldwaters of Arizona are a good example. For them and for most German wanderers America was the final goal. Why America, the United States? They knew they were welcome there; the people, the presidents, the press, urged them to come. As early as 1777 in a note to a nephew, Benjamin Franklin had expressed the hope that America might yet become "the Asylum of all the Oppress'd in Europe," and a number of presidents beginning with Washington had echoed that invitation. "The Hebrew persecuted and down trodden in other regions takes up his abode among us with none to make him afraid," said President John Tyler in 1843.[11]

New York's *Commercial Advertiser* of 1822 felt America would be glad to welcome rich and enterprising Jews. Did the editors have the Rothschilds in mind? By the 1820's the German Rothschild name was already a magic one in this country; the Rothschild myth got an early start. Even the Jews here—and this is indeed unusual—were quick to invite their co-religionists everywhere to establish their homes in this hospitable republic. After the 1819 riots Penina Moïse penned this verse:

> If thou art one of that oppressed race,
> Whose pilgrimage from Palestine we trace,
> Brave the Atlantic—Hope's broad anchor weigh,
> A Western Sun will gild your future day.[12]

And in the days of the Damascus blood accusation Abraham Hart, the Philadelphia publisher, urged the Syrian victims to sail for this "free and happy land where all religions are alike tolerated." However, it was not the need for religious liberty that prompted the Central Europeans to bend their course to America, despite the fact that they labored under religious disabilities and constantly had to cope with the censure of the established churches. On the whole, by the middle of the century European Jewry enjoyed religious freedom.

The United States had a good press in the European Jewish towns. Jews were among America's best propagandists. Ottensosser in his Judeo-German *History of the Jews* deliberately or inadvertently promoted a South Carolina state representative to the gubernatorial chair. The letters sent back to Europe glowed with pride in America's freedoms and the sons and daughters who preceded their families skimped and saved to bring over brothers and sisters one by one. The American correspondents of the *Allgemeine Zeitung des Judenthums*, Rabbis Lilienthal and Wise, gave a good account of this country, and Jewry here dispatched 8,000 florins to the Academic Legion of Vienna in the glorious days of the 1848 Revolution. A few years later the editor of the *Asmonean* was urging the unfree Swiss Jews to make America their new home. How many ambitious young Bavarians read that issue of *Das Fuellhorn* in 1835? It described the triumphant homecoming of Samuel Hermann who had left Roedelsheim in 1804, made a great fortune in New Orleans, and returned in 1836 to his old home where he made liberal gifts to the synagog and relatives. The newspaper account reported that he was a millionaire. He was in truth one of the most successful financiers in the New Orleans of his day, but what the newspaper could not have foreseen was that Hermann was to crash with thousands of others in the panic of 1837.[13]

In 1826 Isaac Harby wrote that Jews came to America to enjoy political liberty and economic opportunity. It is a question to what degree Jews were prompted to opt for this country solely in order to secure civil and

political privileges. True, Jacksonian America was the freest country in
the world: equality, democracy, separation of church and state, widespread suffrage, the apparent lack of class distinctions—these were en-
trancing concepts but it is doubtful whether they played the decisive part
in inducing emigration. Europeans talked a great deal about the virtues of
America. There was a tendency after 1830 to idealize American liberties,
particularly as contrasted with German and European disabilities. America
became a symbol of a utopian state. Liberty became an obsessive word;
Europe is slavery. This embittered evaluation was justified in the miserable months of 1849 when the Austrian oppressors and the Russian invaders marched into Hungary and the other revolutions collapsed as well.
Some of the Jewish Forty-Eighters were obviously political refugees from
the Europe of Metternich, yet, on the whole, physical persecution—riots
and attacks—were relatively light. There was a postemigration tendency
on the part of many American Jewish immigrants to romanticize the
cause of their leaving Europe: they came here because they were
"persecuted." Actually the economic pull of this country was the prime
motivation that moved most of them.[14]

As far back as 1722 Robert Beverley of Virginia had written that
America was the "best poor man's country in the world." This was still
true in the early decades of the nineteenth century when conditions were
bad in Europe: hundreds of thousands of Europeans, Jews among them,
hoped to improve their lot by coming here where land, food, clothes,
jobs, were in plentiful supply. There was every prospect of success for the
thrifty man who was willing to work hard. The American economy was
still predominantly agrarian; both farmers and city laborers were needed,
hence displaced workers in the German economy of the 1840's and 50's
fitted in well, especially in the expanding West. America needed willing
hands, quick minds, experienced entrepreneurs. Back in Hesse and in
other parts of Central Europe the states were legislating against Jewish
peddlers and petty traders. Here there were no restrictions against them.
As artisans or businessmen Jews could make their way both in the cities
and in the hinterland, and their knowledge of German was certainly no
hindrance in the German settlements of the Middle West. Like others the
Jews of that generation came to America because of the opportunities in
store for them.[15]

How Many Came

Jews were pushed out of the Central European lands by persisting disabilities, widespread prejudices, and a changing economy. Some, if not most
of the lands did not discourage their departure and did not regret their
leaving. In a debate in the Bavarian Diet one exuberant deputy yelled out:

"Banish the Jews to America," and there is a story that may or may not be true that when King Ludwig I of Bavaria was gently reminded that in the flight of his Jews he was losing some of his best subjects, his laconic answer was "I am no Pharaoh to go chasing after them." By the early 1840's so many of Ludwig's Jews were leaving it was found profitable to print special miniature Hebrew prayer books for travelers to the United States. At least four editions were produced at Fuerth in Bavaria between 1842 and 1860. As late as 1869 a Bohemian Jewish almanac published in Prague carried a special Guide to New York. It included a description of the different synagogs and their rituals and mentioned, briefly to be sure, the availability of schools, hospitals, orphanages, and other eleemosynary institutions. The emigrant was not exiling himself to a waste-howling wilderness. The *Hebrew Leader* carried an ad inviting the Bohemians to subscribe and learn all about American Jewry.

The migration of Central European Jewry was part of a larger migration of European peoples, and their passage in turn was only a part of a mass movement that saw 50,000,000 wanderers trek to new lands in the nineteenth and early twentieth centuries. Before this *Voelkerwanderung* would come to a halt in the 1920's, over 4,000,000 Jews would have pulled up stakes and pushed on to new homes. In relation to their limited numbers the Jewish exodus was the largest. How many "Germans," Central European Jews, came to the United States from 1820 to 1870? No one knows. Jews were not listed as such in the immigration records. One can only guess. Contemporaries report that there were 3,000 Jews in the United States in 1818, 6,000 in 1826, 15,000 in 1840, 50,000 in 1848 and 150,000 in 1860. Many if not most of these Jews were immigrants or the children of immigrants from Germany, Austria-Hungary, and the Polish lands. Some say that during this period only about 50,000 Jewish immigrants came to this country. Jacob Lestchinsky, the statistician, believed that 100,000 Jews came here between 1840 and 1870, but that 25 percent of them were East Europeans. Thus 75,000 "Germans" entered. Choosing a different range of time—1830 to 1870—Kenneth Roseman also believes that about 75,000 "Germans" came here thus pointing up the uncertainty of the figures. It has been established that between the years 1820 and 1870 the total number of Germans alone who were registered as they debarked in the United States was about 2,334,000. It is quite probable that as many as 100,000 Jewish Central Europeans reached here by the latter year. This seems to be a reasonable estimate.[16]

CHAPTER TWO

DAWN IN THE WEST: THE EXPANSION OF

AMERICAN JEWRY, 1654–1880

THE TIDEWATER MOVES WEST

NEW YORK JEWRY

For the Jew the West began at the New Amsterdam Battery. There, in the summer of 1654, the first émigrés landed after a long hazardous voyage from Brazil. New Amsterdam-New York City is the womb that gave birth to the American Jewish community, a community that moved north, south, and west until it penetrated every corner of this broad land. New York City was the most important dispersal center of American Jewry and it is still the most important center of Jewish life in this country. Starting at New Amsterdam-New York City in the middle 1600's individual Jewish traders moved into New England, or into the wilderness area later to become Pennsylvania and Delaware, or still farther on into the new Province of Maryland. In the next century the settlers took on flesh and blood and became settlements. New Yorkers were doing business in South Carolina in the early 1700's, where, even before they came, Sephardic refugees were already established. Some of them may have followed the Huguenots from France in the 1690's. In the middle of the eighteenth century New Yorkers accompanied the English troops to Montreal as sutlers; the first Canadian Jewish religious society ultimately adopted the name of America's mother synagog, the Remnant of Israel (Shearith Israel). By the time of the Revolution there were Jews in most of the New England states but only Newport supported a congregation. A Philadelphia community was established about 1740 by a scion of the New York Levys. This in brief is the reach of the larger New York Diaspora.

But there is a smaller New York Diaspora, that of both the city and the state. By the mid-eighteenth century Jews had moved out into Long Island as far east as the Hamptons. Somehow a quorum of ten Jewish

In 1841 there were about sixteen organized Jewish
communities in the United States. Total population about
15–20,000.

males was gathered together for worship in 1765 in the village jail of Jamaica where young Daniel Moses was circumcised. Papa was in the debtor's prison. At the same time enterprising shopkeepers were moving north from the Lower East Side into the Bronx and still farther northward into Westchester. The same circumciser who ventured into Long Island had gone north to Philipse Manor a decade earlier to initiate another infant into the Abrahamitic covenant. The dour Sampson Simson inherited an estate in Yonkers where he spent most of his seventy-six years before he passed away in 1857. His contemporaries relate that he was interested in farming and agricultural machinery, founded Jews' Hospital in New York, concerned himself with prison reform, and was always considerate of blacks. He was a rigidly observant Jew.

By 1825 New York City was the largest and busiest town in the United States. It connoted people, money, and opportunity. This was the place where most Jewish emigrants from Europe debarked; anywhere from one-fourth to one-third of all who landed here remained permanently. It was during the same year of 1825 that the monolithic Spanish and Portuguese Jewish community began to break up: the Ashkenazim in Shearith Israel seceded. They wanted their own rite, their own religious way of life, and they broke with the Sephardim who would accept no compromise. In the long span from 1654 to 1825 only seven congregations had been established in North America. In the short period from 1825 to 1852 at least sixteen new sanctuaries, all Ashkenazic, were opened in New York City alone. New York City Jewry now began to atomize, but this was good Jewish tradition. As the newcomers slowly found themselves they grouped religiously along ethnic lines establishing American, English, Dutch, Bohemian, German, Polish, and Russian synagogs.

Ever mindful of the Isaianic injunction to break forth on the right hand and on the left (Isa. 54:3) the Jews moved up the Hudson in the late 1830's and went west on the Erie Canal documenting their presence in the conventicles which they established. By the 1840's they were holding services in Brooklyn even if they had to ferry a tenth man over from Manhattan to achieve the necessary quorum. A decade later there were fully established congregations in Brooklyn and in the Bronx. In the generation between 1840 and 1870 there were Jews resident in every town of size in the state. Dozens of towns had communities that had started out modestly with a cemetery, an occasional religious service, or a mutual-aid society. By 1876 about one-third of all American Jews lived in New York State; about one-fourth huddled together comfortably on the southern half of Manhattan Isle. It has been estimated that in 1825 the New York City Jewish community numbered about 500 souls. In 1876 there were at least 60,000 Jews in Manhattan alone. This tremendous increase in such a relatively short period explains why American Jewry worked furiously to assimilate the newcomers. The difficulties were compounded in the 1880's when the East European refugees began pouring in by the tens of thousands.[1]

NEW JERSEY JEWRY

By the 1840's busy New Yorkers had crossed over into New Jersey. They were in no sense Jewish pioneers for some New Yorkers had been living in the North Jersey towns ever since the middle of the preceding century. Some of those early isolated shopkeepers had intermarried and reared Christian families. Those who were loyal to their tradition deemed it no great chore to celebrate the Holy Days with their friends in New York's Shearith Israel. The New Yorkers who settled in the Jerseys in the nineteenth century clustered together in the Newark and Paterson area and by the late 1840's were conducting services and organizing congregations. Ultimately Essex County would house one of the largest Jewish communities in the United States. In the 1850's Newark had a Frauenverein Naechstenliebe, a Woman's Society of Love Your Neighbor. By the 1870's the German and Bohemian Jews had organized conventicles in New Brunswick, Trenton, Orange, Hoboken, and Jersey City, and, after a while, these synagogs themselves began throwing off satellite congregations. David Naar, a Sephardi immigrant from St. Thomas, stood out as one of the best known politicians of the state in the first half of the century, and in 1849 he was elected mayor of Elizabeth.[2]

THE JEWS OF PENNSYLVANIA AND DELAWARE

Northern New Jersey was a "suburb" of New York City; southern and western Jersey leaned heavily on Pennsylvania. The New Amsterdam Jews who traded on the Delaware in the 1650's created no communities there. It was almost 200 years before the Pennsylvania Jews who moved up the Delaware began to hold services in Trenton. Philadelphia Jews began to move north in the 1700's. One of the founding fathers of Easton in 1752 was the shopkeeper Myer Hart. By 1780, five of the seven stores in town were owned by Jews. Joseph Simon and his companions bought a cemetery in the western town of Lancaster in 1747 and were conducting services there no later than the 1760's. Lancaster served as a center for the scattered sons of Israel in the surrounding villages where they did business with the German farmers. That same decade Philadelphia shot forth as the largest city in the country and the second largest in the British Empire. In 1790, as the capital of the new republic it attracted settlers, and five years later a group of German Jewish newcomers created a small religious association of their own. It is by no means improbable that it was some of these same congregators who organized a burial and sick-care conventicle in 1801. They called themselves the Hebrew German Society, Rodeph Shalom (Sholem), Pursuers of Peace, and by 1819 they could brag—but they did not—that they had a hazzan of their own, Jacob Lippman, Rabbi Jackey.[3]

By 1825 Pennsylvania had lost out to New York commercially, and in order to compete with its northern neighbor—eager to populate the state and to capture some of the western trade—it began building a canal and portage railroad system across the Alleghenies. This helped. Even before that, as early as 1808, Simon Gratz had laid out the town of Gratz in Dauphin County not far from Harrisburg. Jewish immigrants were constantly arriving, and by the 1830's they were to be found in almost all the important towns of the state. In 1839 the colonial Easton community which had long since died was born again, the first congregation in the state outside of Philadelphia to achieve permanence. During the following decade new congregations were organized throughout Pennsylvania. Because of the relatively poor roads and slow transportation in the backcountry each community was self-contained and served as a focal point for Jews of the immediate neighborhood. Between 1840 and 1870 pious associations and congregations were established in Lancaster, Reading, Allentown, Danville, Williamsport, Pottsville, Hazleton, Scranton, Wilkes-Barre, York, Harrisburg, Meadville, Altoona, Erie on the Lake, and even in little Honesdale tucked away in the northeast corner of the state close to the New York border. Many if not all of these towns grew up on rivers, lakes, pikes, canals, and railroads. Honesdale owes its existence to its location on a canal and a railroad that tied the Delaware River with the Hudson and with New York City. Looking forward to a great future it built a compact little synagog to house forty some people. The building was adorned with a wooden spire crowned by a Star of David.[4]

Although Pittsburgh dominated western Pennsylvania and was a gateway to the West and South, to the Ohio and to the Mississippi, it got off to a relatively slow start as a Jewish center. Cincinnati had an organized Jewry almost a generation before the squabbling Pittsburgh Jews could even set up a temporary society. The early nineteenth-century Cumberland Pike, the National Road, bypassed Pittsburgh despite the fact that it was a strategically located trading post at the Monongahela-Allegheny River Point. The blossoming of the iron and glass industries, the coming of the railroads, and the economic stimulus of the Mexican War helped the city and invited Jewish entrepreneurs. By 1847 there was a cemetery and a burial association, a House of Eternity society. But it was not until the 1860's, just about a century after the first Jewish businessman had first visited Pittsburgh, that the city could boast of two permanent synagog communities. As late as 1870 there were only 1,000 Jews in the Pittsburgh district, while there were at least 6,000 in the Cincinnati area. For Jews, Porkopolis, Cincinnati, was still the Queen City of the West. The dozens of new Jewish synagog communities in Pennsylvania and New York all adhered to the Ashkenazic, the Germanic rite. By the late 1870's New York and Pennsylvania together could account for almost one-half of the Jews in the country. Even then it was obvious that the Middle Atlantic area would shelter and dominate American Jewry for generations to come.[5]

Like South and West Jersey, Delaware was a cultural and spiritual satellite of Philadelphia. As a matter of fact the Three Lower Counties did not completely emancipate themselves politically from Pennsylvania until 1776. The 600 Jews of Delaware were part of the Philadelphia community as late as 1880. The first Jewish organization in the state, established about 1881, was a typical burial and charity congeries called the Moses Montefiore Beneficial Society. Some of its members may well have been East Europeans, Russians and Poles, for this was the decade in which the East European Jews began to arrive in significant numbers.[6]

MARYLAND JEWRY

The first Jew to settle in Maryland permanently was the litigious and picaresque Dr. Jacob (John) Lumbrozo who flourished in the 1650's and 1660's. By the middle of the next century, from the 1740's into the 1770's, Jewish colonists had started moving south from Pennsylvania. Here and there the newcomers found fellow Jews, among them three or four transports, criminals, dispatched by England to serve out their terms in Maryland as indentured servants. In the early 1770's one of the aristocratic Levys of New York and Philadelphia established himself in Baltimore permanently. In 1786 an inchoate Jewish group in that town already had a cemetery, and sporadic religious services were certainly held there in the early 1800's. Frederick seems to have been the core town for Jews in the middle 1700's, but by the end of the Revolution Baltimore had taken its place. In the 1820's Baltimore was an active port, the third largest town in the country, the most important city of the South and a chief source of supplies—and immigrants too—for Virginia and the Carolinas. Among those who landed at Baltimore in those early days were Jews from Western and Eastern Germany. The latter were labeled Polanders; this was no compliment. The newcomers to Baltimore found a growing community of native Jews, mostly Pennsylvanians, and a few Ashkenazic Europeans who had come to the city by way of the West Indies. Compelled to compete with canal-conscious New York and Pennsylvania, Baltimore helped father the National Pike and the early Baltimore and Ohio Railroad in order to capture its share of the western trade.[7]

By 1829 there were enough Jews in town to establish a formal religious organization, the Scattered Ones of Israel, Nidhe Israel. At first the General Assembly refused to incorporate the new group; some of the legislators were still furious that they had been forced by public opinion in 1825 to emancipate the Jews. By 1830 wiser counsels had prevailed and the charter of incorporation was granted. The elite native-born Jewish families, the Cohens and the Ettings—the Jewish "Cabots" and "Lodges" of Baltimore—did not participate, certainly not actively, in the new German Jewish synagog. They found it difficult to maintain close social relations with petty immigrant shopkeepers, butchers, and umbrella menders, although the Cohens and Ettings themselves were but one generation removed from the humblest and pettiest of occupations. It took only that one generation to make aristocrats of them; their snobbery was not ethnic for both natives and immigrants were of German origin.

These two families held services on occasion for themselves, had their own family cemeteries, and went their own "Sephardic" way. Yet they were proud conscious Jews, men who had spearheaded the Jewish Thirty Years War that finally brought the passage of Maryland's emancipatory Jew Bill. Most were religiously observant though intermarriage had already begun to take its toll: two of the Etting sisters had intermarried. Of the nine Cohen children three married Jews. The others died young or remained unmarried. They would not marry Christians; they could not marry Jews whom they deemed culturally inferior. The Cohens and Ettings belonged to the Baltimore elite. The Cohens, bankers and stockbrokers, were in the lottery and exchange business as well. An exception was made in their favor when the stock board was established; they were not compelled to appear on the exchange on the Sabbath Day. Jacob I. Cohen, Jr., was on the city council, helped found the Baltimore Public School system, was president of a fire insurance company, and a director of the Baltimore and Ohio Railroad. His brother, Dr. Joshua I. Cohen, was an aurologist, a geologist, and a mineralogist, a president of the Maryland Medical Society, and an intelligent collector of historical manuscripts. The family as a whole was interested in the arts and sciences. The Ettings were prominent merchant-shippers and for years had been engaged in the China trade. They too entered politics, served on the city council, helped found the Baltimore and Ohio Railroad, and served as officers in the state militia. One Etting carried on a correspondence with Robert Fulton in 1814 with the hope that the latter would turn his talents to the building of a steam vessel of war. There were very few important enterprises undertaken in Baltimore without the concurrence of these two distinguished families.[8]

They were an exceptionally able group but they were not blessed with the gift of prophecy. They could not foresee the future. How could they know that the butcher's son, young Leon Dyer, would one day serve honorably as a militia staff officer in the Florida Indian Wars, in the struggle for Texas independence, in the conflict with Mexico, and become a founding father of San Francisco Jewry in 1849. Leon's nephew, Isadore, was to stand out as a brilliant dermatologist and as one of the country's greatest leprologists. Nor could the Cohens and Ettings foresee that the children and descendants of Jonas Friedenwald, the erstwhile umbrella mender, would found a family of physicians who for three generations would be distinguished for their scientific work in the field of ophthalmology. Even had the foresight been given the Cohens and Ettings to pierce the future it would still have made no difference to them. In American Jewish social life Jews born on the wrong side of town, or sometimes the wrong side of the ocean, are untouchables.

In the decade of the 1850's and 1860's three other Jewish communities, small ones, came into being: Frederick and Hagerstown facing south and west and Cumberland facing west to Pennsylvania, Ohio, Indiana, and Illinois. The Jewish census of 1876 shows that practically all of Maryland's Jews lived in Baltimore; the Jewries of New York, California, Pennsylvania, Ohio, and Illinois were more numerous. The West was coming into its own.[9]

VIRGINIA JEWRY

Many people in Maryland had strong Southern sympathies and when the Civil War exploded one of the Baltimore Cohens, Edward, crossed the Potomac and cast his lot with the Confederates. That was in 1861, a little over 200 years after Moses Nehemiah had arrived from New Amsterdam or the Islands to do business in York County. In the 1740's Dr. John de Sequeyra was practicing medicine in Williamsburg, and some two decades later Isaiah Isaacs was securely ensconced as a businessman in the village of Richmond. Despite the fact that Virginia was the largest and most populous state of the Union around the turn of the eighteenth century Jews avoided it because there was so few towns of size where a shopkeeper could make a living. Nevertheless, by 1789, Richmond, where about 17 percent of all the whites in town were Jews, had a busy little congregation. Though the synagogal ritual was Spanish-Portuguese, the members were, for the most part, Germanic in provenance. Richmond after the Revolution offered opportunities; it was the state capital, important for its land office activity, and as a market for the farmers of the western valleys. In the 1790's Petersburg's rough Jewish pioneers had already organized a quasi-community but it soon died only to be reborn two generations later. Beginning with the early 1800's individual Jews found their way into the new towns that dotted the landscape. By 1818-1820 a man named Cohen—was he a Jew?—owned an estate on the Virginia side of the Ohio River not far from Marietta.[10]

One of the Richmond merchants after the Revolution was Benjamin Wolfe. He attained high rank as a militia officer, served as a member of the Common Hall, and through his political influence with the town fathers secured a burial plot for the local Sephardic congregation, Beth Shalome, House of Peace. His body was the first to be interred in it. When this successful businessman died in 1818 at the age of fifty he left seven sons and one daughter. In later years the daughter's son taught medicine in one of New York's medical schools. One of the sons, James M., was probably the first Jewish lawyer to qualify in Virginia. Two of the boys studied in Charlottesville where one of them, as a captain of the local cadets, sat down to dinner with General Lafayette when he was entertained in the city in 1824. Seated at the same table were Thomas Jefferson, James Madison, and James Monroe. Another son married a Miss Garland of Virginia, a Gentile. Their three daughters married three Confederate officers, two generals and a colonel. One of the generals was James Longstreet, the corps commander. Two other sons of the Richmond merchant, doing business as Wolfe & Co., conducted one of the largest liquor businesses in the United States with extensive bottling works in Holland and in Germany. By the time of the Civil War they were shipping their products, primarily gin, to Australia, South America, and China. Udolpho Wolfe, the head of this firm, was one of the largest advertisers in New York City and probably one of the largest in antebellum America. Three, if not four, of the seven male Wolfes married out of the faith and their descendants are probably all Gentile. The other sons may never have married; it may well be that some of the daughter's descendants are still Jews.

Virginia grew commercially and industrially in the period before the War and the Jews prospered with the state. Like the "Germans" in Shearith Israel in New York, the Germans of Richmond were unhappy in "Spanish-Portuguese" Beth Shalome. In 1839 they set up a confraternity of their own, the Love of Israel, Ahabat Israel, which became a congregation two years later. Norfolk, a busy port, also established a short-lived congregation in the 1840's; a permanent synagogal organization emerged two decades later. Between the 1850's and the 1870's services were held or congregations established in Lynchburg, Petersburg, Danville, Charlottesville, and in Harrisonburg and Staunton in the Shenandoah Valley. The synagogs in the latter two towns were peopled by immigrants from the Austrian lands. The Staunton community owes much to Major Alexander Hart, a Confederate officer, who was commander of a battalion at the age of twenty-one. Alexandria, a port town on the Potomac carrying on trade with both America and Europe, established a congregation in the late 1850's, but it owes its growth and prosperity to the Civil War and the fact that it bordered on the national capital, Washington. In 1876 there were about 3,000 Jews in the Old Dominion, over half of whom resided in the towns of Richmond and Norfolk. Jews nearly always prefer the cities.[11]

At one time Congregation Beth Ahabah of Richmond had members living as far away as North Carolina where there was no organized Jewish community until the second half of the nineteenth century. There was little to induce Jews to settle there. The state had always been poor and Jews were never unconscious of the fact that they were forbidden to hold office. This disability was not removed until the adoption of the new constitution after the Civil War. Someone has written, and it has an element of truth, that North Carolina was a valley of humility between two mountains of conceit, Virginia and South Carolina. North Carolina was hardly ever without Jews. Joachim Gaunse, a metallurgist, was sent over by Sir Walter Raleigh and his associates in 1585 and worked on Roanoke Island. This was some thirty years before the Pilgrims landed at Plymouth in 1620. Gaunse returned with Sir Francis Drake in 1586. There was a permanent settler in the province in 1760 but it was not until the first half of the nineteenth century that a few families drifted in. Wilmington, in the southern part of the state, lay within the spiritual if not commercial ambit of South Carolina and its Jewry. Judah P. Benjamin's parents lived in Wilmington for a time. By 1852 it had a cemetery and burial society and, finally, a synagog in the 1870's. By 1880 Jewish life began to stir in Tarboro, Charlotte, Goldsboro, Newbern, and Statesville. All these towns had some type of communal or institutional organization if only a cemetery to tie their Jews together. There were quite a number of Jewish families in at least ten other towns, and some of these certainly held services, at least on the High Holy Days. As late as 1876 there were fewer than 1,000 Jews in the entire state scattered in about twenty towns. North Carolina was still a backward state.[12]

What North Carolina Jewry lacked in numbers it made up in interesting personalities. Jacob Henry, a tidewater planter, fought a courageous and successful battle to remain in the House of Commons, even though legally no Jew was allowed to hold an office or place of trust under the constitution of 1776. It is a tribute to Henry that his colleagues sustained him when one of his fellow legislators moved that his seat be declared vacant because he was a Jew. The cultured Mordecais ran a most successful girls academy in Warrenton in the first quarter of the nineteenth century. Their clientele was largely if not entirely Christian. In the 1850's Lazarus Fels moved into Yanceyville and peddled in the neighborhood. His son, Joseph, grew up to become one of the world's greatest soap manufacturers; Fels-Naphtha was sold everywhere. Early in his career Joseph became convinced of the validity of Henry George's Single-

Tax idea and spent large sums of money here and abroad furthering the concept that a tax on land could equitably supply sufficient revenue to support the state. He encouraged the back-to-the-land movement, arranged for the translation of George's *Progress and Poverty* into a number of languages, including Chinese, and fought valiantly for women's suffrage. This humanitarian was also interested in settling Jews as a people on a land of their own.

In the 1850's, when the Felses were settling in Yanceyville, the Wallace brothers, Isaac and David, opened a general merchandise store in Statesville. Before long they branched out, collecting crude drugs, roots, and herbs. Ultimately they built up the largest business of its type in the world. In their heyday their warehouses contained over 2,000 varieties and they shipped out over a million and a half tons a year of the products they gathered. Single orders at times amounted to one-half million tons. One of their best customers was the Chinese to whom they sent large quantities of ginseng, the magic herb.[13]

SOUTH CAROLINA JEWRY

In some respects nineteenth-century South Carolina was not much different than North Carolina. The people in both states were confronted with problems of transportation, education, and economic opportunity. But South Carolina had Charleston and Charleston was unique. It was a cosmopolitan town with its English, Barbadians, Huguenots, Santo Domingans, and various Europeans. Jews had come along with the others from all corners of the world. The not inconsiderable second and third generations of Jewish Charlestonians were the most cultured Jewish group in all North America. When cotton replaced rice and indigo as the chief product of the flourishing state Jewish businessmen who ministered to the planters and the economy grew in affluence, some becoming quite wealthy. Charleston was America's largest Jewish community in the first two decades of the nineteenth century. Several years before the Philadelphia Ashkenazim established their German Jewish conventicle, a group of South Carolina Jews from Central Europe had already organized an Ashkenazic prayer association of their own, even though it was not destined to endure (1785). In 1784 the local Jewish community established a Hebrew Benevolent Society—it was a burial association—and in 1801 a Society for Relief of Orphans and Indigent Children, Abi Yethomin Ubne Ebyonim. These two Jewish congeries, still extant, are the oldest of their types in the United States. Charleston Jews of the first half of the nineteenth century had the right to boast. They were daring economic pioneers in banking, railroads, and shipping; they were to be found among the civic leaders of the city; they were distinguished in politics and in the professions, and there were intellectuals on a high niveau. The educated elite persisted in the city long after the 1820's when economic hegemony in the South shifted westward toward New Orleans and when the Jews of New York, Philadelphia, and Baltimore began to assert themselves commercially and culturally.

Although completely dwarfed by Charleston there were other Jewish settlements in the state, in Georgetown, Beaufort, Columbia, and Sumter. Jewish businessmen had wandered up the coast from Charleston to Georgetown as early as the 1760's, and from then on there were always Jews in town. It is hard to believe that they did not organize themselves at least temporarily and conduct High Holy Day services at various periods of the next century. The numbers were adequate. Still the Georgetown Jews may have preferred to sail to Charleston for the Holy Days and other religious occasions. Beaufort on the coast near Georgia, married, buried, and did business with Savannah. Columbia, the capital, had a confraternity as early as 1822 and a congregation in the 1840's. Jews began to move to Sumter in the 1820's and by 1877 that town had the second largest Jewish group in the state. That was the year when Judge Franklin J. Moses who lived there for many years, died. The judge, a native Charlestonian, was born Israel Franklin Moses (b.1804) but preferred to be known as Franklin J. Moses. Moses was a distinguished attorney highly respected for his knowledge of the law and for his integrity in its practice. During Reconstruction, in the period of social and economic distress after 1865, he became Chief Justice of the state's highest court. As a candidate of the Negroes and carpetbaggers, he was deemed a "scalawag," a man who had betrayed his Southern heritage. He in turn was deserted by his old friends though no one ever questioned his honesty. His father, Myer Moses, had been a state legislator, a banker, and an officer of the militia before he moved to New York City where he was active in Democratic politics. He was the Myer Moses who published an account of New York's celebration of the 1830 French Revolution. Myer's father, who bore the same name, had come to Charleston in the 1760's; he was highly regarded for the humanitarian services he had rendered his fellow citizens during the American Revolution.

Both Myer Moseses, father and son, were active in the Jewish community. Franklin J. Moses, the third generation of this notable family, married out of the faith and evinced no interest in Judaism. Franklin, in turn, had a son of the same name who was born and reared as a Christian, an Episcopalian. He served in the Civil War in an administrative capacity with the title of colonel. There is no question that he was an able man, a charming person, and in the Reconstruction period he emerged as one of the most important political figures in South Carolina. This Moses was governor from 1872 to 1874 but his public and private life was deplorable and scandalous in the extreme. After the Democrats seized power in 1876 there was no future for him in South Carolina. When he died in 1906 he was completely impoverished, a drug addict, a truly unfortunate man who had been in and out of jails for theft and fraud.[14]

There was a South Carolina Jewish entrepreneur who was always reaching out for larger opportunities. He pioneered in steamboating and in Florida land speculation after the United States acquired it from the Spanish in 1819. This man was Michael Lazarus (1786-1862), a grandson of one of the founders of Charleston's Beth Elohim and a son of Sergeant Major Marks Lazarus, a Revolutionary War hero. Michael was vice president of the Reformed Society of Israelites in 1825. In the early 1820's he bought 156,000 acres of Florida land; about 90,000 acres were not far north of what was later to become the city of Miami. He paid about a dollar an acre. The Spaniards, America's pioneer colonists, had come to this region in 1513. It is not improbable that among them there may have been some Marranos—secret Jews—but there is as yet no evidence to sustain this suggestion. In 1763 the English took possession of Florida and held onto it for two decades. It was during this period that Jewish merchants moved into what was then known as West Florida, primarily into Pensacola and Mobile. When the Spanish recovered the Floridas in 1783 they inherited a number of Jewish subjects. They left them alone: the Inquisition was no longer a power.

After the Americans took possession Jewish businessmen began drifting in; among them was Moses Elias Levy (ca. 1782-1854), a native Moroccan who had made his way to Europe and the Caribbean. By 1815 he was in Havana, a purveyor of goods and services to the Spanish authorities. It was then in the second decade of the new century that he bought thousands of acres in Spanish Florida, in its northern reaches. Assuming the role of an impresario he set out, in the 1810's and 1820's, to bring in Europeans to settle on his lands. He sought Jewish settlers too, but all in vain. No Jews came to Florida; all told there were only about 3,000 Jews in the United States, possibly a hundred in all Florida; this was the end of the world! This second decade of the century witnessed several attempts to induce Europe's oppressed Jews to settle on American soil. Levy failed as an impresario but busied himself on his plantations where he grew sugar cane. He built roads and invested heavily in improving his holdings, but continued to experience all the difficulties of a pioneer in a new country. Levy was in many respects a very unusual if not a remarkable man. Though an autodidact he was something of an intellectual, corresponded with Rebecca Gratz, lectured in London, constantly preaching the gospel of education for Jew and Gentile. One of his sons, Elias, was sent to Harvard. The other son, David, helped manage his father's plantations and then went into politics. When Florida became a territory David went to Congress, to the House, 1841; when it became a state, 1845, he was elected to the Senate. He was the first Jew to grace the halls of Congress. Like his father Levy was an innovative businessman; he helped develop Florida as a railroad entrepreneur. There is a Levy County in the state and a town named after him. The town is called Yulee. The Senator adopted an additional name calling himself David Levy Yulee. He was an assimilationist; he married out, and became a pious Christian; there is no question of his sincerity. The father, an ardent Jew, succeeded in alienating both sons; Elias, for a time, was a Swedenborgian missionary. Florida Jewry did not grow rapidly. For decades the state was frontier. The Seminoles were a threat; they harassed the Levys on their holdings. Seeking glory, Jews from South Carolina and other states rushed to join the forces that set out to crush the Indians.

Among the handful of Jews who wandered south into Florida in the early nineteenth century was the South Carolinian, Raphael J. Moses (1812-1893). During the 1830's and 1840's this fifth-generation American sought to carve out a future for himself in this new territory. First settling in Tallahassee he moved onto the boom towns of St. Joseph and Apalachicola on the Florida Gulf Coast. Moses was brilliant; he was a businessman, a bookkeeper, a railroad executive, a banker, and a lawyer. He passed the bar exam—such as it was—after six weeks of study. When the town of Apalachicola died he moved up its river to Columbus, Georgia, where he was to become one of the state's distinguished citizens. He was certainly its most distinguished Jew. He was a lawyer, a planter, a Confederate officer, a politician, an orator in the grand style.

Individual Jewish businessmen found their way into the state in antebellum days. Samuel Fleischman settled in Marianna, near Georgia, in the 1840's; a generation later in Reconstruction days, the Ku Klux Klan drove him out; he was friendly to blacks. He persisted in returning to Marianna only to be murdered, possibly by the Klan. In 1880 a census could find but 772 Jews in Florida; there were only about 20 Jewish communities in the state; practically all sheltered fewer than 80 members. Jacksonville with its 130 souls was the only exception. Jews here had a cemetery since 1857; occasional religious services were held in the next decade; a Hebrew Benevolent Society was founded in 1874, a permanent congregation in 1882. Its president was Morris A. Dzialynski, a German immigrant; he was also mayor of the city. As late as 1919 there were only 8 organized Jewish communities in Florida. In large part the state was still a wilderness.

The most interesting town in the state was—still is—Miami. When the railroads reached the village in 1896, the Jews, as always, were present at end-of-track. Religious services were soon held; denominational congregations were established, but the town did not really begin to blossom till after World War II. New York garment workers were among those who discovered this paradise. Retiring as blue-collar operators with their modest pensions and social security checks, they flocked to this city, particularly to the Beach. Ponce de Leon had told them that here was the fountain of youth. Ultimately Miami Beach became America's most Jewish town; about 80 percent of all the people there were of Jewish birth. The whole South Florida region began then to grow rapidly; tourism, real estate speculation, light industry, petty retailing were to bring in hundreds of thousands. By the mid-1980's there were over a half-million Jews here; this was then the third largest Jewish congeries after New York and Los Angeles. With numbers came skilled professionals, politicians, state and national legislators, and two "Jewish" governors. Both governors professed Christianity.[15]

GEORGIA JEWRY

The Jewries of Florida, South Carolina, and Georgia were closely linked; Beaufort in southwestern South Carolina looked to Georgia but, in reality, all of Georgia was in its early days an appendage of its northern Carolina neighbor. The relations between Charleston and Savannah Jewry were always close; the older city had served as a spiritual, cultural, and commercial base for Savannah Jewry ever since the eighteenth century. Some of the Charleston Jews, moving westward in the nineteenth century, made their homes in the Georgia metropolis; something of the glamor, the pride, the brilliant Carolina lustre and learning, was reflected in the leadership of the Jewish community to the south. When the census of Georgia Jewry was taken in 1876 Savannah boasted that it had a Youth's Historical Society with a library of 400 volumes. The congregation in Savannah dates from Colonel Oglethorpe's time. The Jewish community was born the day the Jews landed, July 11, 1733, for they came as a group prepared to establish a congregation immediately. Thus, in a way, Savannah is the second oldest Jewish congregation in the United States. In spite of several long breaks as the tide of Jewish population ebbed and flowed in the eighteenth century, Mikveh Israel, the Hope of Israel, has continued to this day. Despite Savannah's dominance Jews were found elsewhere in the state. Adventurous Jewish Indian traders moved up the Savannah River as far as Augusta in 1756. Immigrants began arriving in the 1820's during the days when Georgia was for a time the greatest inland cotton market in the country. Jews came in from Charleston on the Charleston-Hamburg Railroad, one of the longest in the United States. Hamburg was across the river from Augusta; the Hamburgers belonged to the Augusta congregation. There was also a direct steamboat connection between Charleston and Augusta established by that remarkable Charleston businessman, Michael Lazarus. By the 1840's the Augustans owned a cemetery, met together for worship, and conducted a Sunday School in the best tidewater tradition. In the summer of 1847 three Jewish lads between the ages of nine and thirteen were circumcised in town. All had Christian fathers who had passed away. One of the boys, under the influence of his Sunday School training, had convinced the other two to undergo the act of circumcision along with him.[16]

As in most tidewater states, Georgia Jewry, reenforced by European immigrants, began to establish backcountry societies and congregations. By 1870 there were at least thirty towns with Jewish settlers. Six, in addition to Savannah, had congregations: Atlanta, Macon, Columbus, Augusta, Athens, and Albany. Bainbridge, on the Florida border, had a Harmonie Verein, a club that was proud to announce that it had 100 volumes in its library. Atlanta began to emerge Jewishly in 1847 when it participated in a Union Sabbath School with Christians. The students met in a log cabin. The Jews held religious services and opened their own school in the next decade, established a mutual-aid pious association in the 1860's, and it, in turn, speedily flowered as the Hebrew Benevolent Congregation in 1867. The Scrolls of the Law it used were borrowed from Savannah and Augusta, but the congregants soon received their own as a gift from a member who lived in Newnan forty miles to the south. In the 1860's the first permanent "rabbi" warned the congregation "that the white race will not have supremacy forever." Just over a century later Atlanta, in the 1970's, had a liberal Jewish mayor who was put in office by a coalition which assured the blacks that they would not be denied equality. Talbotton in West Georgia apparently had no Jews by 1876. There had been at least one Jewish family there in 1853. This Jew was Lazarus Straus, a peddler and storekeeper. When in 1863, in the midst of war and scarcity, the local grand jury attacked Jewish merchants as a group for buying up merchandise and raising prices, Lazarus Straus left the city and moved to Columbus, Georgia. The apologetic grand jury insisted that it had other Jews in mind, certainly not the Strauses, but Lazarus refused to accept this ingenuous explanation. Years later his children bought and developed R. H. Macy & Co. into one of the great American department stores. In 1940 Ralph Straus, a member of the family, established a communal center for all the citizens of Talbotton. It was called the Straus-Levert Memorial Hall. Here was one Jew who turned the other cheek.[17]

DOWN THE OHIO TO THE ARKANSAS BORDER

By 1876 about 65 percent of all the Jews in the United States lived in the areas drained by the rivers flowing into the Atlantic. Apparently the immigrants among them had no desire to wander farther westward having already traveled thousands of miles as they made the miserable Atlantic crossing; they wanted to settle down. A few, not many, were romantics who were ready to go farther inland where only recently there was heard "the howling of wild beasts and the more hideous cry of savage man." This phase was coined by Joseph Jonas, a young Englishman who landed in New York in 1816. His goal was the Ohio Valley, but he was warned by his friends to stay on their side of the mountains: "In the wilds of America and entirely among Gentiles you will forget your religion and your God." Nevertheless he kept on moving; he spent the winter in Pittsburgh—the Ohio was frozen—and landed in Cincinnati in March of 1817.

Jonas was a personage. In later years he wrote an autobiographical fragment, recorded his views on biblical themes, busied himself in Democratic politics, and even served a term in the Ohio State legislature. One gets the impression that he thought himself the Jewish Christopher Columbus of the West. That he was not. Dr. Jonas Horwitz had been in Cincinnati as early as 1816 peddling vaccine to save the community—so he advertised—against a threatened epidemic of smallpox. His scare tactics were anything but effective, for he left town speedily. In addition, Cincinnati in 1817 was no longer on the frontier. Joseph Jonas arrived in Ohio at the tail end of the Great Migration. Settlers had been pouring over the mountains since the 1760's and in ever increasing numbers since the American Revolution. By the time this watchmaker had rooted himself in the community most of the tidewater states, the Ohio River Valley, and Kentucky, were filled with people. To the west of Ohio, Indiana and Illinois had already been admitted to the Union. Within a decade after Jonas's arrival, Cincinnati, a great river port, would be distinguished for its schools, its colleges, its theater, its wealth, and its culture. Jewishly, the town was still a frontier: for Gentiles the Jew was a curiosity and some would travel as much as a hundred miles to take a peek at him. Shortly after he came to town a Quakeress, so we are told, asked him: "Art thou a Jew? Thou art one of God's chosen people. Wilt thou let me examine thee?" She turned him around and at last said to him disappointedly, "Well thou art no different to other people."[18]

In 1818 a fellow Englishman, David Israel, passed through town on his way to Indiana to be with his brother Phineas, an Indian trader. The following year David Israel came back to Cincinnati to join in an informal service for the Holy Days. By that time this Jewish Hoosier had begun to call himself Johnson because brother Phineas had added that name to his own. The clan members have remained Johnsons to this day. Even before Jonas debarked at the wharf, a Russian Jew named Myers had stopped off in town, made a talk, and, it would seem, gave a vocal concert in a Presbyterian church. He was a double attraction, a convert and a singer who included Russian songs in his repertoire. During the next four years events moved rapidly. In 1821 the town's Jews were called to the bedside of a "Christian" by the name of Benjamin Lape. The dying man whose name was originally Loeb or Leib admitted that he was a Jew, and, despite the fact that he had reared his children as Christians, he was anxious to have a Jewish burial. His wish was granted when the group bought a plot from Nicholas Longworth. This burial ground, still in existence, is the oldest Jewish cemetery west of the mountains. When they were assured of a religious quorum in late 1823 or early 1824, the town's Israelites organized the first Jewish congregation in the Ohio Valley. Its nearest neighbor was Beth Shalome of Richmond, Virginia, hundreds of miles away. Determined to build at once, these aggressive Cincinnatians sent out a plea for help to England, the Islands, and the American communities. With Jews coming to town constantly, friends and relatives from England and an assortment of Dutch, Germans, and Poles from the Continent, the ritual adopted was a mishmash of German and Polish traditions. When the Germans seceded in 1841 to form B'nai Yeshurun and adopt a Germanic rite, the older congregation, B'nai Israel, returned to the Polish tradition. In 1836 B'nai Israel erected its first synagog, proudly displaying five large brass chandeliers sent it by Shearith Israel of New York. They had been salvaged from the old dismantled Mill Street Synagogue and may well have harked back to the eighteenth century. They symbolized the light of the Torah moving ever westward to the distant Pacific. Thirteen years after this modest building was consecrated in Cincinnati two assemblies of worshipping Jews were ushering in the High Holy Days in the jerry-built town of San Francisco.[19]

In fixing on Cincinnati as the town of the future, Jonas and his friends had chosen better than they knew. By the 1850's it was one of the great commercial cities of the country on its way to becoming the third or fourth largest industrial center in America, connected by river, steamboat, canal, and railroads with almost every state in the Union. Great cities tend to give nurture if not birth to great men. Two eminent rabbis and leaders graced Cincinnati in that generation. They were Max Lilienthal and Isaac M. Wise. Dr. Lilienthal (1815-1882), a university graduate, arrived in 1845 in New York where he served for years as a rabbi and a director of Jewish schools. In 1855 he came to the Queen City of the West and there spent the rest of his life as the rabbi of its pioneer congregation. He was a charming cultivated person, a good businessman, who served his people well and enjoyed the confidence of the larger community which put him on the Board of Education and on the board of the local university. Lilienthal was a clever man too, for through the long years of his ministry this urbane gentleman succeeded in maintaining good relations with his fellow townsman, Isaac M. Wise, the most distinguished rabbinic leader in postbellum America.[20]

Eager, ambitious young Jewish men had opened their shops and stores in a number of Ohio towns as early as the 1830's, but by 1850 there were only four large communities—Cincinnati, Cleveland, less than half the size of the Jewish metropolis on the Ohio, Dayton, and Columbus. By 1876 organized Jewish communities, congregational or societal, flourished also in Akron, Piqua, Hamilton, Portsmouth, Zanesville, Youngstown, Sandusky, Alliance, and Springfield. There were Jews in at least sixty towns and villages at that time. They were scattered in all parts of the state although, obviously, many had come in on the National Road or had settled on the Upper Ohio, or had moved up its tributaries, up the Muskingum, the Hocking, the Scioto, and the Miami. As in other states they had planted themselves in the villages in no particular sequential order. They took up residence in accordance with the dictates of an inscrutable fate, a fortunate accident, a bossy relative, or a canny wholesaler. There were even fourteen Jews in Wapakoneta, a town born to blush unseen till 1969 when one of its natives, Neil A. Armstrong, went to the moon.[21]

KENTUCKY JEWRY

Early settlers like Joseph Jonas followed the main highway, nature's road, the river. Jews had probably preceded Jonas on the Ohio River to present-day Louisville. Joseph Simon, the Lancaster fur entrepreneur, owned part of the original town site and had a mortgage on the rest of it, though he never traveled in that part of what was then western Virginia. There were Jews in Louisville in the early 1800's but they married Gentiles or faded away. By 1834 there was a Jewish benevolent society, a core burial and self-aid association, but it too disappeared and some if not all of its members assimilated. In that respect Louisville was not exceptional; many Jewish congregations are built on the ruins of earlier attempts to establish a permanent synagogal community.

Rebecca Gratz's younger brother Benjamin went west on family land business in 1818 and, the following year, settled down in Lexington where he married the granddaughter of Christopher Gist, the Ohio River explorer who twice had saved Major George Washington's life at the time of his mission to the French at Fort Duquesne. Years later when Gratz's first wife died he married out of the faith again although he himself was always a confessing and even an observant Jew. Gratz was one of the leading businessmen of central Kentucky, a hemp manufacturer, a patron of Transylvania and Kentucky Universities and of the Lexington Library, a builder of one of the first macadamized roads in the state, president of a railroad, active on the city council, a bank officer, and a founder of the Fayette Historical Society. The hamlet of Gratz in Owen County was named after him or one of his family. Henry Clay and this Lexington businessman were close friends and when the Senator ran into debt Gratz bailed him out. Anna, Benjamin's daughter, married Clay's grandson, Thomas Hart Clay, but long before that Clay's son James B. had married Susan Jacob, daughter of John J. Jacob of Louisville. Lewis Dembitz, Brandeis's uncle, said that the Jacob family was originally Jewish and that the descendants down to the fourth generation were typically Jewish in appearance—whatever that means. One of Martin Van Buren's political correspondents solemnly assured the ex-president in 1844 that Henry Clay would never become president because of his closeness to Jews—a groveling, avaricious people—possessing none of "the exalted characteristics of our nature." Ben Gratz lived to be ninety-two years of age and when he passed away the family asked the Cincinnati rabbi Isaac M. Wise to officiate at the funeral. After his return to Cincinnati, Wise told his students at the Hebrew Union College that it was the most remarkable funeral of his entire career. "What," asked the students, "was so remarkable about that funeral?" To which Wise responded, "There were only two Jews at the funeral, the corpse and myself."[22]

Louisville finally established a permanent Jewish community in the late 1830's. The state was prosperous; religiously observant German Jewish immigrants began to make their appearance, and they were fortified by some Polish Jews who had come all the way from Charleston, South Carolina, around the Gulf and up the river by steamboat. Louisville sheltered the first of a series of Kentucky Jewish settlements on the Ohio. Owensboro and Paducah followed with congregations in the middle fifties and sixties and Henderson in the 1870's. Lexington in the interior organized a Jewish burial association in 1872, and there is every reason to believe that it also conducted services during the Holy Days. The would-be intelligentsia who helped organize it called it the Spinoza Society. Poor Spinoza, what sins are committed in thy name! Of the 3,800 or 4,000 Jews in the state in the late 1870's over half lived in Louisville; less than a thousand were in the other large Ohio River towns and there were small clusters of petty businessmen in at least thirty-five other villages where most of them managed to make a comfortable living catering to their immediate neighbors and the surrounding farmers.[23]

MISSOURI JEWRY

Down in its southwest corner Kentucky borders on Missouri. Hickman, Kentucky, on the Mississippi River looking across at Missouri, had five Jews at the time of the 1876 Jewish census. Up the river, about 100 miles, was the old French town of St. Louis named after the pious French king who had instructed his generation in his own fashion that the only way a Christian layman could win a religious argument with a Jew was by plunging a sword into his midriff as far as it would go. Blissfully unaware of Louis IX's quaint dictum, St. Louis became an important river town just about the same time that Cincinnati and Louisville gave birth to viable Jewish communities. Several members of Benjamin Gratz's menage settled in St. Louis in antebellum days. Back in Lexington he reared and influenced a stepson and a number of able youngsters. His stepson Joseph O. Shelby became a Confederate general; the two Blair boys, early protégés, made great careers: Francis Preston Blair, Jr, went to the United States Senate; Montgomery Blair was in Lincoln's cabinet. Benjamin Gratz Brown, a cousin of the Blairs, became a governor of Missouri, and Rebecca Gratz Bruce, the daughter of a Gratz business partner, married General John H. Morgan, the Confederate raider. All these who lived and prospered in the magic Gratz circle were non-Jews by birth and Christian by avowal.[24]

The very year that Gratz came to Lexington and married his sweetheart Maria Gist, Phineas Israel Johnson settled in St. Louis (1819). He had come down the Ohio from Indiana to Louisville and kept on following the rivers to St. Louis where he made his home. He married Clarissa Clark, the granddaughter of a signer of the Declaration of Independence. Their daughter Matilda married Sol Levi, an observant Jew who helped found the first permanent Jewish community in town. But Phineas Johnson was in no way Missouri's first Jew. The Blocks (Blochs) were there before him. This Bohemian family had been drifting westward for almost a generation. Blocks had arrived in Baltimore in the 1790's and had branched out to Virginia, Ohio, and even Arkansas. By the second and third decades of the 1800's various Blocks were doing business in the Mississippi River towns of Troy, Perryville, Louisiana, Cape Girardeau, and St. Louis. One of the Blocks was a part owner of the Northern Mississippi Steamship Line.[25]

Several years before the Blocks began to dot the Mississippi River landscape, Joseph and Jacob Philipson came west to make their fortune in St. Louis. That was in 1807. They were originally Polish Jews who had gone into the fur, skin, and lead business in Philadelphia no later than 1803. To be closer to their sources of supply two of the brothers, Joseph and Jacob, established themselves in St. Louis; the third, Simon, remained in the East until 1821 when he joined the others. Joseph, the pioneer of the family, opened one of the first stores in town. He was also a brewer, a distiller, saw mill owner, and banker; he went broke in the depression that hung on after the War of 1812. Jacob and Simon were no more successful than Joseph; the former after fifty years in St. Louis may not have left enough money to pay for his funeral. Even in his Philadelphia days, Simon had made no stir in the world of business. In writing to Aaron Levy, Simon Snyder, a Gentile, later governor of Pennsylvania, had referred to Simon Philipson as a lazy jackass, using the Hebrew-Yiddish term *hamor*. But if he was a *hamor* he was an educated one.

All three brothers were men of superior culture and had something to give a town where many, if not most, of the French natives were still illiterate. After he was forced out of business Joseph made a living teaching music and was known for his fine library of English, Italian, and German works. Jacob supported himself by teaching English, German, and French. Simon owned several hundred fine paintings and prints which he unsuccessfully tried to sell to the city fathers for an art collection. It was undoubtedly the finest in the state for it included originals of Rembrandt, Da Vinci, Raphael, Rubens, Murillo, Holbein, and Titian. The Titian in those antebellum days was valued at $100. Intermarriage in the family was rife; those art and music loving cosmopolitans had little in common with the uncouth Germans of the pre-1848 period. None of the Philipsons joined the Jewish newcomers in their humble religious services, but neither did they join any Christian religious society. When Joseph passed away in 1844 the press pointed out that he was not a member of any church, but that he was "distinguished by his many virtues, by the constant practice of the precepts of Christianity." In other words he was an honorable man.[26]

Long before the first of the Philipsons had settled in St. Louis in 1807, Meyer Michaels had wandered in and out of the growing village. Born in South Haven, Long Island, in 1760, Michaels grew up in Montreal and made his living as a fur trader. St. Louis was one of his ports of call. There he did business with the Chouteaus and others around the turn of the century, shipping his furs down the Mississippi and up the Atlantic Coast to the St. Lawrence and to Montreal. One of his contemporaries was Solomon, a Jew, to judge by his name and pursuits, but really an ardent Catholic. He may have been a convert. He was an Indian trader, a shopkeeper, and a militia officer, intelligent, literate, active, knowledgeable in Indian dialects and, probably, in French and Spanish too, for he seems to have come to town in pre-Louisiana purchase days. In 1808 he was one of those who petitioned that the town be incorporated; J. Philipson, Jacob or Joseph, opposed incorporation.

Few of the pioneers did anything to build a lasting St. Louis Jewry though by the 1830's the city was about to emerge as the greatest commercial emporium in the transmississippi West. Steamboats jammed the wharves bringing in ever-increasing numbers of immigrants and larger stocks of goods. In 1837 a group of Central European newcomers gathered together on the second floor of a grocery and restaurant for what was in all probability the first Jewish religious service in town. This was just a year after Cincinnati Jewry consecrated its synagog, and just about the time that Louisville Jews established a permanent community. Jews were setting up outposts in the valleys of the Ohio and the Mississippi. It was not easy to round up a quorum of ten. One old-timer loved to recall with a chuckle that once an Irishman with a biblical name was coopted as the indispensable tenth man; willy-nilly he became a Jew and he was so flattered at his selection that ever after he attended services on all Jewish Holy Days. The congregation that finally emerged between 1839 and 1841 was called the United Hebrew Congregation, Achduth Israel; about the same time a cemetery was purchased, 1840, and two years later the Hebrew Benefit Society began its philanthropic work after a local physician sued a Jewish firm for the unpaid bill of a vanished peddler.[27]

The year 1848 brought in a new type of Jew: German, sophisticated, educated, ambitious, indifferent often to traditional beliefs and practices. A notable exception, religiously at least, was Isidor Bush (Busch) who landed in town in 1849. Here was an unusual man, scion of a well-established ennobled Bohemian family. Young Bush was not only trained in the arts and sciences but was also given a relatively good Jewish education. After the family moved to Vienna this teenager began his career editing Jewish serials. It was inevitable that he become involved in the anti-Hapsburg revolution of 1848 and when the republican hope was succeeded by military tyranny he fled to New York. He was already a devotee of the On-to-America Movement. Bush remained in the metropolis only long enough to publish the first German American Jewish magazine, *Israel's Herold*, and when that venture failed he left for Missouri. The move to St. Louis in 1849 was not strange. Germans and Jews too were pouring into the new boom town that faced the South and the West. Young Bush, now twenty-seven, was to become no captain of industry. He tried everything, for in turn he was a grocer, a hardware dealer, a real estate salesman, a banker, an actuary, a railroad executive, and finally a grower of grapes, a viticulturist. In this last endeavor he achieved a degree of success. He developed a vineyard at Bushberg and published the standard work on American grapevines, a manual that was translated into French and German. Bushberg was probably the largest grape nursery of its day in the United States.

Released finally from the onerous task of keeping his nose to the grindstone he plunged into the morass of Missouri slave and anti-slave politics of the Civil War period. He was an anti-slavery Union man in a slave state, fighting vigorously to protect the integrity of Negro families and to bring an end to slavery. In his demand, in 1863, for the complete emancipation of the slaves in Missouri, he was unsuccessful. His impassioned plea fell on deaf ears: "I pray you have pity for yourselves, not for the Negroes. Slavery demoralizes, slavery fanaticism blinds you. It has arrayed brother against brother, son against father. It has destroyed God's noblest work, a free and happy people." Bush was successful, however, in helping to keep the state in the Union but failed to prevent the radical Reconstruction Republicans from disabling erstwhile Confederates.

Despite the fact that Bush's wife and son did not share his fervent loyalties he was always a good Jew, for he was active in congregational life and was recognized as a leader in the Independent Order of B'nai B'-rith. By the 1870's, when Bush became president of the far-flung western District No. 2, St. Louis had already become a well-established city and mother in Israel. It was almost 7,000 strong and, next to San Francisco, the largest Jewish town in the West. It had three congregations and five charitative associations, four of which were led by women. Variety and choice had made for a viable community. Over 1,000 Jewish settlers had found homes in about thirty-five other towns in the state. Missouri was filling out.[28]

THE ERIE CANAL, THE HIGHWAY TO CLEVELAND

In the summer of 1826 Jacob S. Solis attempted unsuccessfully to establish an American Jewish Asylum in New York's Westchester County. This was to be an institution to shelter orphaned American Jewish boys and girls and refugee children fleeing from oppression abroad. Here on the banks of the Hudson they were to be given a good elementary education and taught to work at a trade or to plough a furrow. This proposed self-contained little Jewish colony is in a way related to a movement by Jews to penetrate the West in the decade of the 1820's. The defeat of Napoleon in 1815 is one of the great watersheds in the history of American Jewry, for it ushered in a political reaction which impelled thousands of Jewish Europeans to immigrate ultimately to the United States. The year after Waterloo, 1816, that ardent Jew, Moses E. Levy, was already flirting with the hope of settling Jews in this country. By 1818 his plans were fixed. Somewhere in America's interior prairies he hoped to establish agricultural colonies where young Jews, boys and girls, would be trained in the arts and sciences and tillage of the fields, and at the same time be given a good English and Hebrew education which would indoctrinate them ethically. The rise of utopian communistic communities such as the Shakers, the Harmonists, and the Zoarites certainly influenced Levy and his circle. The big year was 1819, for then a number of schemes began to emerge. A handful of European Jewish converts to Christianity, encouraged by pious Christians, thought of establishing a settlement here for Christianized Jews. By the following year the American Society for Meliorating the Condition of Jews had begun formulating plans to colonize Christian-Jews. Working closely with M. E. Levy, Samuel Myers of Norfolk hoped to set up Jewish urban cells to raise large sums of money in order to put Jews on the soil.[29]

The anti-Jewish Hep Hep riots in Central Europe in the late summer and fall of 1819 stimulated the drive to bring Jews to North America. W.

D. Robinson, an American businessman and adventurer, published a pamphlet in London urging the establishment in the Mississippi Valley of colonies as havens for the oppressed Israelites of Europe. His brochure was widely read in Europe and in the states. Fully cognizant of the program of action of Levy, Myers, Robinson, and the Christian missionaries, Mordecai Noah also began agitating in 1819 to bring large masses of Jews to this country. By 1820 he was negotiating with the New York state authorities for possession of Grand Island in the Niagara River, opposite the little town of Buffalo. It was to be the site of a Jewish colony. The riots in Germany and the reemergence of the German and Austrian police states was a blow to Jews in Europe. Equal rights for them were certainly not in the offing; disillusioned Jewish intellectuals began to preach the gospel of emigration and settlement in distant America. By the spring of 1825 the American Christian missionaries had already leased a farm in Westchester to serve as a refuge for Christian-Jewish converts, and there can be little doubt that Solis's blueprint for an asylum in the same county, published the following year, was a Jewish answer to the "colony" of the Christian conversionists.

By the summer of 1825, at least six years after he had begun to play with the idea of a colony for Jews, Noah was finally ready to move forward. It was only a matter of weeks before the Erie Canal would be open all the way to Buffalo, to Lake Erie, and to the great American West. A highly intelligent man like Noah realized the tremendous economic significance of this new highway into the American interior. Buffalo, the western terminus, was destined to become a great city; the water power of Niagara guaranteed the industrial future of the region. Accordingly, in September, 1825, he issued a proclamation urging the Jews of the world to come to Grand Island and to help establish a Jewish colony. Because his name was Noah, he called the new settlement Ararat, for that was where the ark of the biblical Noah found its resting place after the great deluge. No preparations were made, nothing was accomplished; no Jews came although there was a magnificent dedicatory ceremony. Noah himself probably never set foot on Grand Island. European Jewish leaders looked with disdain if not with contempt upon an American Jewry that all told did not number much more than 6,000 souls. They were shocked by the impudence of a Noah who had appropriated to himself the title of Governor and Judge of Israel and had dared to order them about in his grandiloquent proclamation. Some of Noah's friends had purchased acreage on the island; they—if not he—hoped to make money. The Major certainly received a tremendous amount of publicity both here and abroad, and as a politician he knew the value of such recognition. He did want to help European Jewry; his utter devotion to his people at this stage was beyond question. It may well have been naive on his part but he did hope to establish, temporarily at least, a "city of refuge," as he called it, where Jews of the world could find rest till the final restoration to the Land of Their Fathers. It was a bizarre failure in its day, yet a century later American Jewry spent millions, hundreds of millions, to help Russian Jews survive by colonizing them on the Ukrainian steppes and on the Crimean flatlands. Those colonies, too, had no future.[30]

Unless Noah was a fantasist and a charlatan—and that he was not— he had misjudged the nature of the Jewish émigrés who were arriving in New York City in ever larger numbers. That very year, 1825, the new- comers were numerous enough to secede from Shearith Israel and start their own congregation, Bnai Jeshurun. They had no intention to rush out to Grand Island, to head for the tall timber. In all the United States there was in that year only one organized community west of the moun- tains, Cincinnati. Because they were cautious and conservative, the slow- moving newcomers waited thirteen years wandering up the Hudson to es- tablish the first conventicle outside of New York City. That was in 1838, in Albany, just about 180 years after Asser Levy visited the village on a business trip. By the time the Bohemian rabbi, Isaac M. Wise, arrived in town in 1846 there were already two synagogal groups in Albany. Using the canal as the northeastern gateway to the continent, New York ped- dlers, sometime between the years 1839 and 1841, had inched their way west to Syracuse and had met for services in the notion supply house of Bernheim & Block. The peddlers stuck to the canal; they could not afford to be reckless. It took almost another decade before communities were founded in Utica to the east and in Rochester to the west. By 1848 the good people of Rochester had a Jewish congregation and a Jewish ceme- tery to say nothing of seven baseball teams. In 1858 Dr. Nathan Mayer, a physician and surgeon, visited the city and wrote to the Cincinnati *Israel- ite* describing how fat and stately bankers, dressed like children in colorful striped uniforms, chased one another around in a field and struck one an- other with a soft ball. It was so utterly childish, he confessed to his read- ers, although it was also true that the exercise was beneficial and an excel- lent device to develop the muscles.[31]

In 1847 a community had risen in Buffalo, the scene of Noah's Ar- arat. This was the House of Zion, Beth Zion. Individual Jews had been percolating into the city, as in most canal towns, ever since the 1830's, but it took time to establish permanent synagogs. The terminal towns were now fixed, New York, Albany, Buffalo. Filling in the interstitial spaces was the task of the next generation. Moving north out of New York City on the Hudson, Jews settled down in Newburgh, Poughkeep- sie, Kingston, and Hudson, though not in any set order. Kingston soon had a large Jewish community for it was the eastern terminus of the Dela- ware and Hudson River Canal. It had been a town under the Dutch; Jacob Lucena, who was known to have a roving eye for women, had traded there as early as the 1670's. The Jews of Troy, above Albany at the head of navigation, probably began to hold services in the late 1840's and by the 1850's had organized themselves into a burial Society of Brotherly Love whose members proceeded to drag one another into the courts in a most unbrotherly fashion. Having met the squabbling peddlers and petty shopkeepers of Troy it is understandable why Major Alfred Mordecai, commandant of the arsenal in West Troy, Watervliet, would not identify with them. That was asking too much of a third-generation American aristocrat who was the country's outstanding ordnance expert. Still farther north lay the younger Jewish communities of Plattsburg on Lake Champlain and Ogdensburg on the St. Lawrence. At the other side of the state, on the far western end of Lake Ontario, the Jews had organized a congregation at the Falls, in the town of Suspension Bridge. Patterning themselves after their Buffalo neighbors the congregants at the Falls also called themselves Beth Zion.[32]

Moving east and west along the canal in complete chronological and geographical disorder, the Jews united to form a congregation in Schenectady just after Mordecai Myers became mayor there in the early 1850's. There is no reason to believe that this scion of a humble observant colonial family, like Major Mordecai, had much to do with the local immigrant Jews. By 1851 Jews had wandered down Lake Seneca or up the Pennsylvania State Canal to Elmira where, in 1862, a Jewish community was permanently established. The Elmira federal stockade for Confederate soldiers once held over 12,000 captives. Almost 3,000 of these unfortunates died; among them were over 20 Confederate Jewish veterans who found their last resting place in the prison cemetery. By 1880, thanks to the canals and railroads, there were at least 70 towns in New York sheltering Jews; only 2 of them, New York City and Brooklyn, were large. Brooklyn was the third largest Jewish city in the country with a population of at least 13,000 Jews. It grew rapidly after the first bridge to Manhattan was opened in 1883 becoming one of the largest Jewish communities in the world.[33]

NORTHERN OHIO JEWRY

The stream of traffic that moved along the canal to Buffalo continued westward to Cleveland and Toledo until it finally reached Chicago and Milwaukee. In 1835, even before the Jewish Germans began coming in large numbers to America, two New Yorkers of good family found their way to the neighborhood of Cleveland. Joshua Seixas, a son of the Revolutionary War hazzan, was teaching Hebrew at Oberlin, and Daniel Levy Maduro Peixotto had become Professor of Theory and Practice of Physic, Obstetrics, and Diseases of Women and Children, at Willoughby. After studying under Dr. David Hosack, Peixotto struck out for himself professionally at the age of nineteen. He patterned himself on his teacher; like Hosack he did not limit himself to the practice of medicine. Unlike Hosack he was not a physician of any distinction. Peixotto was president of the New York Medical Society in 1830 and, following in the footsteps of his father, found time to busy himself in the Jewish community. His job at Willoughby was not an onerous one; a teaching term lasted about two months and he taught for only two years, from 1835 to 1837.[34]

The year Peixotto returned home to New York was the year Simson Thorman landed in Cleveland to become the founding father of the Jewish community. He had arrived in New York in 1835 or in 1836, remained there for about a year, and then moved west on the Erie Canal and on to Cleveland. He wrote back to his friends and family in Unsleben, Bavaria, and a number of them decided to join him. This was a migration "en masse." About eighteen persons, including Thorman's fiancée, sailed steerage from Hamburg on the "Howard" and arrived in New York City in 1839. They went on directly to Cleveland and organized an Israelitish Society that very year. It was an all-purpose organization that conducted services, looked after the sick and the poor, and buried the dead. By 1840 they had a cemetery of their own. Thorman started out at first in the grocery and dry goods business but later made his living in wool, hides, and furs. By the end of the Civil War he had become a councilman and was remembered gratefully in later years for his efforts to bring gas, water, lighting, and a police force to the growing city.

Cleveland was speedily connected by canal with important cities in the state as far south as Portsmouth on the Ohio River. Both Akron and Youngstown, Cleveland's neighbors, had well-developed Jewish communities in the late 1860's. Youngstown, joined by canal to both Cleveland and Pittsburgh, apparently leaned toward the latter community for the Youngstown Jews called their synagog, Rodef Sholom, Pursuer of Peace; that was the name of the leading congregation in Pittsburgh. Sandusky to the west of Cleveland had to wait till the late 1870's before its first permanent Jewish society came into being. This was the typical Hebrew Benevolent Association. Toledo Jewry exercised influence in northwestern Ohio and in eastern Indiana; the city on the western end of Lake Erie was the northern terminus of canals that ran south to Cincinnati and west across Indiana to the Illinois border. In the 1860's Toledo's Jews were already conducting public services but the creation of a formal permanent Jewish association was, as always, a slow painful process. It was not until 1863 that a community emerged. The first Jews came to that city in the 1830's and 1840's. Among those early settlers was William Kraus who arrived about the year 1845. He was a clothier, a distiller, a banker, and a real estate speculator. Because the local Germans loved and respected their banker they elected him mayor, but when the national economy collapsed in the panic of 1875 Kraus went down with a host of others. He was indicted for loose business practices and fled to Canada where he lived for years until he returned home to die, a broken man. He was no swindler; he was an irresponsible, incompetent banker. It would be interesting to determine, if it could be done, how many Jewish businessmen of that postbellum generation managed to attain—and keep—a degree of affluence. The expensive county histories popular at that time list only the successes, the men who could afford to have their "mugs" reproduced.[35]

CHAPTER THREE

JEWS OF NEW ENGLAND, THE OLD SOUTHWEST,

AND THE BORDER STATES

THE JEWS OF CONNECTICUT

Seeking opportunity with a minimum of competition, many of the German immigrants of the late 1830's moved out of New York City. Less than ten years after Albany had established the first congregation outside of the metropolis—in fact in only five years, 1840 to 1845—Jews succeeded in organizing themselves permanently in Connecticut, Rhode Island, and Massachusetts. Jews were not newcomers in New England. New Amsterdam Jewish peddlers were knocking on doors in Hartford in the 1650's. On at least one occasion a large Jewish family, passing through Connecticut in 1771, succeeded in collecting ten males for a service. Jacob Pinto was one of the petitioners in 1783 who sought the incorporation of the town of New Haven. The new Germans started coming into this city by the 1830's but were, it would seem, not welcome. About the year 1840 there was a congregation in New Haven and a few years later in Hartford also. A New Haven newspaper of the 1840's declared that "Yale College divinity deserves a court-martial for bad generalship" because it had not kept the Jews out of town. But not all New Havenites were hostile and when a synagog was dedicated in the next decade generous Christians helped it financially. In 1850, Dr. Joseph Goldmark, Louis Brandeis's father-in-law to be, stopped off in New Haven to see Professor Agassiz, but was appalled by the blue laws of the pious Puritans: Sunday in New Haven was a death sentence. Not all Jews shared his prejudices; by 1881 one of the Germans was president of the Board of Education.

New Haven and Hartford were the only two Jewish communities of any size in the state before the coming of the East European Jews in the 1880's. The total Jewish population in the state at that time may then have been less than 2,000. There were about fifteen towns in Connecticut which housed Jews; not one of these had as many as 100 Jewish inhabitants. Norwich was probably typical of these smaller settlements. The pioneer Jew arrived there in 1851 but the first organization was not established till 1878. It almost foundered before it came into being because of a bitter fight over the name of the proposed community. Was it to be a congregation, a lodge, or a society? Quite properly, Noah Webster's *Dictionary* was consulted and the new group called itself the First Hebrew Society. It was a charity, worship, and burial association.[1]

RHODE ISLAND JEWRY

The New England states of Connecticut, Rhode Island, and Massachusetts have this in common: All three fashioned Jewish communities of a sort during the first five years of the 1840's, yet all had sheltered Jewish settlers since the second half of the 1600's. Rhode Island, however, was unique; it could boast of two earlier communities, neither of which had survived. Due to the influence of Roger Williams and his tolerant successors it was not difficult for the Jews of those early days to organize themselves and to worship publicly. Newport had an informal congregation in the period 1678 to 1685 and a well-organized synagogal group from about 1750 to the end of the century. The Salvation of Israel congregation met in the beautiful Peter Harrison sanctuary which was dedicated in 1763. Nineteenth-century Newport citizens never forgot the halcyon past when their town was one of the great American ports and when Aaron Lopez was Newport's most distinguished merchant-shipper, "for honor and extent of commerce probably surpassed by no merchant in America." Generations later the Newporters believed that prosperity would be restored to their deserted wharves with the return of the Jews. Thus when a Jewish peddler once came to town they licensed him, but when he desecrated the Sabbath by making his usual rounds they indignantly withdrew his right to peddle. Aaron Lopez had kept his warehouse closed from Friday sundown to Monday morning. The old Newport synagog was reconsecrated in 1883 with the coming of the East Europeans.

Westerly, the Rhode Island-Connecticut bordertown on the Pawcatuck River, attracted a sprinkling of Jews by the 1870's who settled there because of its textile industry and shipping. There is no evidence that they even attempted to conduct services. The only organized Jewish settlement in the state was in Providence which had a community of about 1,000 men, women, and children. There were two congregations in town but all told they sheltered but 105 members (ca. 1877). Practically all the Jews of Rhode Island had crowded into that one town, a very important manufacturing center. Providence's Jewish Pilgrim Father, the Holland-born Sephardi, Solomon Pareira, arrived there in 1838 when Providence was a city of over 20,000. By the early 1840's the Jews were numerous enough to meet in his home for services; in 1849 they had a cemetery; a few years later they had a congregation which proceeded to hire a man to serve as cantor, shohet, and teacher. This factotum was Joseph Spiro, a German-born talmudist who was paid $5.50 a week, a modest sum even in those days. A year later he had gone back to New York. Pareira was the president of the congregation; the secretary-treasurer was the Mexican War veteran, Jacob R. Hirschorn (Hershorn). Hirschorn, a Bavarian, had arrived in New York City in 1846 at the age of sixteen and soon enlisted in a regiment of New York Volunteers. Because of his knowledge of French and German he was put in the quartermaster corps and did an excellent job as a forager in Mexico. On the way home he was stricken with yellow fever in New Orleans and was carried to La Charité where the good sisters nursed him tenderly and tried to save his immortal but infidel soul by reading him edificatory Catholic tracts. He survived unconverted to return to New York and later to Providence where he married one of Pareira's daughters who bore him ten children. In Providence he made his way at first by retailing hosiery; later he and a partner were in the embroidery business.

When in need Jews in town could always turn to the congregation but by 1877 the first social-welfare society was set up as the charity arm of the community. The Montefiore Lodge Ladies Hebrew Benevolent Association was a mutual-aid, religious, sick, and burial association which enjoyed the ministrations of two coeval presidents, a "gentlemen" and a "lady."[2]

MASSACHUSETTS JEWRY

Providence was the second largest city of New England; Boston was the largest and for centuries had been one of America's leading ports. Jewish merchants had been in and out of it ever since the day when Solomon Franco landed in 1649, yet it had no formal Jewish community until about the year 1843. In 1733 the handful of Jews had even bought ground for a cemetery but it disappeared after a couple of decades. Although there is no evidence, private religious services were probably held in town in the 1830's. It is not easy to understand why native and immigrant Jews avoided this metropolis which already had a hundred thousand inhabitants in the 1840's before the Jews began to settle there. It is true Massachusetts was a conservative state; the constitution was not liberalized as far as Jews were concerned till 1833. There were economic reasons as well: few European packets and steamers selected Boston as a terminus; the capital-poor Jews could not hope to engage in shipping or merchandising, and the Erie Canal after 1825 made New York a more desirable haven for migrants. Jews held their first service in Boston in 1842; the following year this group of humble artisans and shopkeepers—Germans for the most part—organized the Lovers of Peace, Congregation

Ohabei Shalom. By 1844 the Jews had purchased a burial ground after which there came a ritual bathhouse (mikveh) for the women and later an all-day school where Hebrew and the basic secular subjects were taught, probably in German.

Within a decade the Jewish newcomers had begun to settle in a number of other places in the state and by the 1870's they were well ensconced in New Bedford, Fall River, Worcester, Springfield, and elsewhere. They were careful to pick the ports, the rivertowns, and manufacturing centers that were also served by railroads. Leopold Morse, an eighteen-year-old Bavarian, opened a clothing store in New Bedford about the year 1850. Shortly thereafter he moved to Boston where he became one of the largest clothiers in town. In 1870 he entered politics, and although he lived in a rock-ribbed Republican district he was sent to Congress in 1877 as a Democrat and served for five terms. Although he was not affiliated with any synagogal group, the first Jewish old-folks home and orphanage in New England was established through his generosity. After his death it was called the Leopold Morse Home for Infirm Hebrews and Orphanage. His younger brother Godfrey followed him from the Bavarian Palatinate, went to Harvard where he edited the *Harvard Advocate*, and served as manager of the first crew that rowed against Oxford; by 1883 he was president of the Boston Common Council.

The census of Massachusetts Jewry taken in 1876 showed 8,500 Jews in Massachusetts, 7,000 of whom were in Boston. This was a tremendous growth in a period of less than thirty years. There were at least ten congregations in Boston, two literary associations, a Y.M.H.A., a musical congeries, a city-wide United Hebrew Benevolent Association, and a Hebrew Ladies Sewing Society. There were also several Jewish literary and musical organizations. The fact that mid-century Boston was the cultural "hub" of this country may have been of some influence in furthering Jewish groups of this type in Boston, but it is well to bear in mind that there was no Jewish community of size anywhere in the United States that did not set up formal literary or musical associations. In this characteristic effort the Germanic influence was probably determining.[3]

MAINE JEWRY

Congregation Ohabei Shalom of Boston, the mother synagog of Massachusetts and of northern New England, had its beginnings in a Jewish New Year service in 1842 at the home of Peter Spitz. Haiman Philip Spitz, his brother, was also one of the charter members of this congregation. Seven years later a group of Jews assembled in Haiman's home, then in Bangor, Maine, and established the first synagog in that state. When Haiman came to Maine he was of course not its first Jew. Individuals had been drifting into a number of cities and villages ever since the Revolution. The earliest Jewish settler of whom there is any known record was Susman Abrams, a German from Hamburg who lived in Waldoborough, Thomaston, and Union near the coast where he owned and ran a tannery yard. Like other small town Jewish pioneers he married a Christian and attended Christian services. Haiman Spitz was a Prussian Pole who had come to New York via England and had turned to the manufacture of clothing, selling many of his products in the South. When he was about twenty-four years of age he moved to New Orleans; later at the time of the Mexican War he enlisted in the army serving under General Zachary Taylor. After the Mexicans were defeated he went back North and made his home in Bangor where he was joined by his brothers Peter and Julius. Bangor, a good-sized town in the 1840's, was the lumber center of the world, connected by water to the principal east coast ports and by railroad, via Waterville, to all the cities of New England and the Atlantic tidewater.

Bangor's Ahavat Ahim, Brotherly Love, was a typical all-purpose pioneer organization providing religious services, eleemosynary aid, care of the sick, and burial. The functionary hired for $175 a year was expected to chaunt the liturgy, provide ritually-slaughtered beef and fowl, teach the children, circumcise the infants, sit with the sick, and be the "servant" of the community. Influenced possibly by their Puritan neighbors the congregants expelled a member of the synagog who was living with a woman who was not his wife. Such surveillance of personal morals was untypical in immigrant conventicles. The congregation did not continue uninterrupted. Either competition from the new timberlands of Michigan and Wisconsin or the early onset of the panic of 1857 shattered the Maine lumber trade and drove the handful of Jewish peddlers, dry goods merchants, and clothiers out of business. The congregation closed its doors in 1856 or 1857 and shipped its Scroll of the Law and ritual silver to Ohabei Shalom in Boston for safekeeping. Some time in the 1870's an entirely new set of worshippers reorganized Ahavat Ahim and retrieved the Sefer Torah from its Boston caretakers.

By 1876 there were about 500 to 600 Jews in Maine, most of them in the four larger towns of Portland, Bangor, Lewiston, and Waterville. They had begun to make their appearance in the 1860's in order to take advantage of the opportunities in those ports and towns where shipping, fishing, and the manufacture of textiles and machinery had begun to flourish. By 1874 there was a formal community in Portland. The Jews here had clustered around the B'nai B'rith lodge which also conducted religious services and looked after the needy. Lewiston and Waterville had sufficient numbers to pray with a formal quorum but there is no evidence that congregations were forged. In the southern and western part of the state, in Bucksport near Bangor and in Sanford near Portland, there was a handful of Jews and far over to the east, on the other side of the state, German Jewish immigrants had settled in Houlton, Pembroke, and in the important commercial city of Eastport. In all probability these business-men opened shops there with an eye to the trade in the neighboring Canadian province of New Brunswick.[4]

NEW HAMPSHIRE JEWRY

When the eighteen-year-old Leopold Morse arrived in the United States from Wachenheim in Bavaria someone shipped him out to Sandwich, New Hampshire, an upcountry town many miles from nowhere. There must have been opportunities there in 1849 or his wholesaler would not have dispatched him to that spot. At least he learned English, for there was probably not another Jew or German in the place. In general Jews were few and far between in the Granite State; they avoided it, unhappy with the fact that Jews as non-Christians were disabled politically. When the last restrictions against their holding office were finally abolished in 1877 there were fewer than 200 Jews in all New Hampshire.

The first Jews came to Portsmouth during the Revolution but they did not remain there. They were birds of passage, West Indians, or French, who owned or captained privateers which preyed upon British shipping. After the war, a Prussian Jewish couple opened a shop and pros-pered. Despite the fact that Abraham Isaac and his wife kept their store closed on Saturdays, or mayhap because they kept it closed on their Sab-bath, people respected them and patronized them. On Isaac's death in 1803 this Jew, the only one of his tribe in town, was buried in the Chris-tian cemetery. His fellow townsman, the poet Jonathan Mitchell Sewall wrote the epitaph which closed with these words:

> Through various toils his active spirit ran,
> A faithful steward and an honest man.
> His soul, we trust, now freed from mortal woes
> Finds in the patriarch's bosom sweet respose.

Sergeant-Major Abraham Cohn of the 6th New Hampshire Volunteers was awarded the Congressional Medal of Honor "for conspicuous gal-lantry displayed in the battle of the Wilderness, Virginia, in rallying and forming under heavy fire, disorganized troops; also for bravery and cool-ness in carrying orders to the advance lines under murderous fire." This immigrant who began his military career as a common soldier rose through the ranks ultimately to become the regimental adjutant, the colo-nel's right-hand man, because of his linguistic skills and his ability to command the respect of his associates. He may well have been an obscure businessman, a clerk or a peddler in New Hampshire, when he enlisted in 1864 under Colonel, later General, S. G. Griffin.

In the decade of the 1870's there were two or three families in Northumberland and Groveton, far to the north on or near the Connecticut River; in the capital city of Concord on the Merrimack there were but two Jews; and even in Portsmouth on the Atlantic Coast there were only twenty-nine men, women, and children in 1876. In this, the second largest city in the state, there were probably ten Jews above the age of thirteen but no community was shaped. Two smaller towns, Rochester and Great Falls, up the Salmon River from Portsmouth, could together muster fifty-three Jews, twenty of whom were gainfully employed. It may be assumed that a substantial number were young peddlers who used Rochester and Great Falls as their home base while scouring the countryside for business. Now that the Yankee peddlers had gone west, a German-accented Jew could hope to survive. In 1857 the Great Falls contingent with the aid of the Rochestrians, established a burial society—the only formal Jewish organization in all New Hampshire. But why active in these two particular mill towns? Was there no economic balm in the other villages of New Hampshire? No one but the peddler himself knew why he singled out a special spot. He had his reasons, probably, and unless he wrote his memoirs—and told the truth—there is no way to determine his motivations. Post-eventum reflections may be entirely wrong. Why were there at that time no Jews in Manchester, New Hampshire's largest city?[5]

VERMONT JEWRY

There were very few Jews in New Hampshire; there were even fewer in Vermont. The Jewish census of 1876 put the total number of Jews in the Green Mountain State at 119. Obviously the Central Europeans who were coming down the gangplank at Castle Garden felt that there were better opportunities elsewhere. The first permanent Jewish settler of whom anything is known is Joshua Montefiore, and if he was not the first Jew in Vermont, he was certainly the most distinguished one. Joshua was the uncle of Sir Moses Montefiore, the world's most respected Jew in the nineteenth century. Uncle Joshua was a little bit of everything—lawyer, soldier, author, editor, farmer, and above all, adventurer. After he became a solicitor and notary public in London of the 1780's he left for Jamaica where he sought to practice his profession. He was not permitted to hang out his shield for his fellow-attorneys barred the way, pointing to an Island law of 1711 which forbade Jews, mulattos, Indians, and Negroes to assume any civil or political office. Disappointed Joshua returned to England and satisfied his martial spirit by becoming a soldier in an expedition that set out in the early 1790's to colonize an African island off the coast of Sierra Leone without the use of slave labor. When that expedition failed he returned home and began to write commercial manuals and legal compendia. In this he was quite successful; his books were popular, useful, and widely read. Obviously he was an able and competent man. No later than 1811, he came to this country after wandering about in many Southern European lands and fighting in the West Indies during the Napoleonic wars. When he landed in Philadelphia he was already a man of forty-nine. Here in the United States he continued to publish his works and, for a time, edited a weekly which was subsidized by the British government.

He drifted about going as far west as Indiana before he decided to settle down as a farmer in St. Albans, Vermont, near the Canadian border. Moses Montefiore, his nephew, sent him money regularly. The elderly Joshua was to end his life as a "remittance man." At seventy-three years of age this widower, still stouthearted, married a young woman, a Christian, and before he died in 1843 he had fathered eight children. His youngest was born when he was about eighty years of age. The children were reared as Christians but he was buried on his own farm as a Jew in a ritual ceremony which he had prepared.

St. Albans was to have its day in the sun in 1864 when a group of Confederate soldiers coming in from Canada raided the city, looted the banks, and fled back toward the border. It was during the 1860's that Jews began to enter Vermont and to create their first community. Among those who made their appearance at this time was Herman Seligson who enlisted in Middlebury, in 1862, in the 9th Regiment of Vermont Volunteers, infantrymen. He was a diminutive, black-haired Prussian who gave his occupation as a "salesman." (Peddlers were also salesmen.) A month after he enlisted he was elected as first lieutenant, and before the year was over he was detached from his command and put in charge of a mountain howitzer battery. By the first of January, 1863, he was made captain, and before he was separated from the service in 1865 he had served as a division provost marshal and, finally, as regimental commander of the 9th Vermont with the rank of lieutenant colonel. For an immigrant youth to rise from private to regimental commander while still in his early twenties was quite an achievement even in those days when George Armstrong Custer became a major general at the age of twenty-five.

It is not improbable that some Jews may have crossed over into Vermont from Canada, for by the late 1870's there was a handful in Charleston, not too far from the Province of Quebec. In Burke, somewhat farther south, there were almost enough for a religious quorum, but this group may have wandered up from the south, up the Connecticut River, through Connecticut and Massachusetts, into Vermont, and then northward by way of the Passumpsic River. Charleston and Burke were remote towns with populations of about 1,000 each. It is worthy of note that in Vermont, as in New Hampshire, these early peddlers and modest shopkeepers bypassed the large cities. In 1876 no Jews were reported in Burlington, the largest town in the state. Actually Nathan Lamport, a Polish immigrant, was already there in 1874; before he died in 1928 he was to become a distinguished New York City businessman and a generous giver to Orthodox institutions. Montpelier, the capital city, reported but two Jews. Obviously the humble immigrants who came in the 1860's and on believed that they would fare better in the villages. Many of the Central Europeans who did enter the state ended up in one county in western Vermont, near the New York border, in the two towns of Rutland and Poultney. Some may have come most of the way from New York on the Hudson; others may have used the train connections with Albany, Boston, and New York City. By 1876 at least half of the Jews in Vermont were in this one county. Most were in Poultney, the smaller of the towns, and it was here that Congregation Benai Israel was established in 1867. Why settle down in Poultney, a town of some 3,000 or less? A few Jews planted their residences there and later newcomers agglomerated around them; Jews are lonely people. The place became a peddlers' center and Jews from Fair Haven and even Bristol, forty miles away, came in for the Holy Days. When they arrived they found not only Rutland County Jews but some from the neighboring New York towns of Granville and Hartford. The congregation was thus a regional one as was the cemetery that was purchased in 1873.

It is doubtful whether there were ever more than twenty householders who participated in the services. They met in a private home over the second floor of a Jewish-owned store and conducted services on the New Moon and the Holy Days. Not all was peace and harmony. On one occasion a group of Jews who came to town to worship refused to pay the one dollar fee and raised such a disturbance that the police had to be called in. By the time the troublemakers got out of court the fines they paid were five times as large as the modest admission charge of the synagogal fathers. In 1872 the members allowed themselves the luxury of secession and for a year there were two separate conventicles in the county. The congregants were mostly Germans, probably Bavarians, in view of their indiscriminate interchange of "b's" and "p's." Judging from the extant minutes they were rather literate in German; their Hebrew and their Yiddish transliterations of Hebraic terms left something to be desired, but they were a pious lot and devoted to their ancestral traditions. In conducting synagogal business they hewed to the American line and, following parliamentary rules, took care that every motion should be properly "gemovved." The names of those who were born and who died were recorded for most of the years from 1874 to 1891. The list of "Birds" beginning in 1866 turned out to be a list of "Births."[6]

JEWS IN THE OLD SOUTHWEST

ALABAMA JEWRY

The 1840's may not have been a fabulous decade for American Jews but it is clear that those years were important, very important. By that time the entire eastern half of the country was settled, with the exception of Michigan and Wisconsin in the North and Florida in the South. As the cotton culture shifted westward with the planters and slaves, farmers and shopkeepers, the native and immigrant Jews, moved too. A generation later, by the 1870's, there were more Jews in the Gulf states of Alabama, Mississippi, Louisiana, and Texas than in all of New England, and this despite a devastating Civil War and the uncertainty of the Reconstruction years. The lure of new opportunities drew able men from the Atlantic tidewater to the new cotton lands of the Old Southwest. The move west began in the 1820's extending all the way from Georgia to Texas. Philip Phillips, Solomon Heydenfeldt, and Aaron Lopez, all three Charlestonians, settled in Mobile in the short period from 1834 to 1841. Not yet thirty years of age, Phillips soon became one of the leading citizens of the state and was sent to Congress in 1853. He remained in Washington after he refused to run again for office and was speedily recognized as one of the great lawyers of his day. By the time he passed away in 1884 he had pleaded about 400 cases before the United States Supreme Court. Heydenfeldt served as a judge in Talapoosa County before he pushed on to California where he was the first man to be elected to the state Supreme Court by the vote of the people; Aaron Lopez, a descendant of the well-known Newport family, practiced medicine in Mobile, pioneered in the field of mental health, and became a vice president of the American Medical Association.[7]

Mobile on the Gulf was the chief Jewish settlement in Alabama during antebellum days. Jewish traders had lived in the town under the English in the 1760's but no community was organized till 1841, in the decade that Mobile was to become the second largest cotton market in the world. The group called itself Congregation Gates of Heaven and He That Considereth the Poor, Shaarai Shomayim u-Maskil el Dol (Ps.41:2). Among the founders were the two Jones brothers from London. It was they, probably, who suggested that cumbrous names which reflect Anglo-Jewish religious and philanthropic institutions and traditions. The Joneses started out modestly as cleaners of clothes (second-hand clothes?) and became merchants, politicians, communal workers, and business entrepreneurs. Israel L. Jones, once acting-mayor, brought the streetcars to Mobile, and Solomon I., his brother, was treasurer of Alabama's Grand Lodge of Odd Fellows, a leader in the fire department, an alderman, a port warden, and a lieutenant colonel in the militia. Both brothers were very interested in the new congregation. Israel was president and Solomon was a trustee despite the fact that his wife was a member of a local Episcopal church where she was inscribed in the rolls as a "Jewess." Either she was of Jewish birth or she was born Christian but dubbed Jewish by virtue of her marriage. Israel was also president of the Mobile Musical Association. Joseph Bloch and Sigmund Schlesinger, Germans, were well-known local musicians. Bloch ran a music store, published sheet music, and taught music in a local Catholic college; Schlesinger wrote Civil War songs and a series of services for the Reform synagog. He was one of the country's first composers of modern settings for the Jewish liturgy. In his compositions he followed the German Protestant tradition and did not hesitate to borrow frequently from Italian operatic writers such as Verdi. A whole generation of American Jews was thrilled by his vibrant, dramatic, occidental melodies.[8]

Montgomery was the only other Alabama Jewish settlement of any importance in the mid-nineteenth century. Jewish beginnings in the Montgomery area go back to the 1780's when the Pennsylvanian Abram or Abraham Mordecai settled there. That was a generation before Alabama was admitted to the Union, when it was still part of Georgia, then one of the largest states in the Union. Mordecai was a son of a Jewish father and a German Christian mother. He fought in the Revolution, drifted south, and became a trader among the Indians in what is today Alabama. He worked with the Indian agents around the turn of the century, ransomed whites taken captive by the Creeks in the Kentucky forays, fought in the War of 1812, married an Indian African woman, and raised a brood of children. He bought his supplies at Augusta, Pensacola, New Orleans, and Mobile, trading furs, roots, and cotton cultivated by the sedentary Indians; he built the first cotton gin in his part of the country. Though not without some education he was a rough and earthy frontiersman, feuding with the Indians who once clubbed him unconscious, left him for dead, and cut off one of his ears. The United States agent in the Creek Nation rated him as a "bad character."

Mordecai was not uninterested in Jews. Like his older contemporary, James Adair, who also traded with the southern Indians, he believed that the Indians were descendants of the Lost Ten Tribes and still preserved Jewish religious traditions. Frontiersmen like Mordecai paved the way for the first squatters but they built no synagogs. It remained for the German émigrés who came to Montgomery from the 1830's and on to establish the first congregation in 1846. This was the Society for Visiting the Sick, Chevra Mevacher Cholim, a religious organization that provided worship facilities as well as sick-care and burial. Christians came from long distances to watch Jews as they prayed; they were a curiosity. By 1849 after the Jewish community had more than doubled it called itself Kahl Montgomery, Montgomery Congregation. Among the members were the Lehmans, founders of the family that in a later generation would stand out in the financial and political life of New York.

Kahl Montgomery had a number of notable rabbis, including James K. Gutheim, a fiery Confederate patriot who refused to take the oath of loyalty to the federal government in New Orleans, and Adolph Moses who had fought as a Red Shirt under Garibaldi in the Italian liberation war. Moses left Montgomery to serve Mobile Jewry after the resignation of "Rabbi" Abraham Jaeger who, during his second year in the pulpit of Mobile, had become a Christian, joining the Southern Baptists. In 1873 Jaeger published an account in Chicago of his acceptance of Christianity, describing the psychological process that had impelled him to change his religion. He called it *Mind and Heart in Religion, or, Judaism and Christianity*. Kaufman Kohler, then the rabbi of Sinai in that city, examined the book and wrote to Jaeger: "I knew when you became a Christian that you had lost your heart, but now after reading this book I am convinced that you have also lost your mind." In 1853 Claiborne on the Alabama River between Mobile and Selma had a congregation of fifteen members and a hired officiant. But when the railroads supplanted the steamboats and took over cotton transport, the congregation and the whole town died. Nothing was left; it was not even a ghost town. In the 1870's there were over thirty villages and hamlets in the state with a handful of Jews. By that time Montgomery had passed Mobile; only four other places had congregations or societies: Selma, Uniontown, and Eufaula in the south, and Huntsville in the north. Birmingham, the future Pittsburgh of the South, had only twenty Jews.[9]

MISSISSIPPI JEWRY

In the 1830's and 1840's adventurous Jews could steam north from Mobile up the Tombigbee River into eastern Mississippi into Columbus, go still farther west into Mississippi proper, up the Pascagoula to Meridian, or hug the Gulf Coast at Biloxi. A cemetery was laid out in that city in the early 1840's. Meridian, a substantial community, had a congregation in the 1860's; Columbus was organized much earlier, by the 1840's, for Germans and Alsatians had already been drifting in for a decade. It was during the 1830's that Colonel Chapman Levy, one of the South Carolina argonauts, moved into the Columbus area with his mother's slaves and started planting cotton. As a nineteen-year-old, Levy had been admitted to the bar in Columbia, S.C. In 1812 he had been elected to the Carolina state legislature and had served in the War of 1812 as a captain of militia. During the Nullification Controversy of the 1830's he had returned to the state House of Representatives as a strong Union man. On his way west to the rich cotton lands of Mississippi he had stopped long enough in Georgia to become a state senator. By then he was already

Colonel Chapman Levy, an influential Democratic politician high in the counsels of the party leaders in Washington. By the time he died in 1850 he had moved still farther west to the village of Camden. There is no evidence that he was concerned with the developing Jewish communities of Mississippi.[10]

The rich counties in the state were not in the eastern but in the western section—the river counties. The largest number of Jewish settlements was on the Mississippi and up its tributaries. By the 1850's Woodville, near the Louisiana border, had a congregation of sorts; Natchez in the adjoining county was the state's largest town in the 1830's when the Jews started arriving in larger numbers. Almost eighty years before these Germans, Alsatians, and Polanders arrived, the Monsantos of Louisiana were already doing business there; one of them had settled in Natchez in the 1790's, farming and trading under the Spanish. Some time around the year 1840 the Central European newcomers established a burial society; by 1843 they had an organized community. During the Civil War the Yankees shelled the town but the only casualty was little Rosalie Beekman, age seven. When Vicksburg fell in July, 1863, Union soldiers occupied Natchez. The Jewish soldiers from the North were welcomed by the local foreign-born Jewish shopkeepers; their daughters, more ardent in their patriotism, rejected the advances of the Jewish Yankees although ultimately some of them married into local families and stayed in Mississippi. Acculturation had done its job well in Natchez as all through the South. Jacob Mayer of Natchez changed his first name to John; one of his older daughters had a good European name, Theresa, but a son born in 1864, in the heat of the War, went through life with the mouth-filling militant name, Joseph Eggleston Johnston Mayer. The Natchez Jewish maidens smuggled contraband goods through the Union lines in their hoopskirts. The Jewish quartermasters from the North who secured passes through the lines for the girls never realized that the billowy, bulging skirts covered socks, shirts, and trousers, to say nothing of shoes and boots for the brave boys in gray.[11]

A sick-care and burial confraternity was founded in Port Gibson in the 1850's. Eugene H. Levy, a son of Jack (Jacob) Levy, was born in Grand Gulf in 1840 and together with two brothers enlisted in Louisiana batteries and companies during the War. After the surrender at Appomattox Courthouse, Eugene entered his father's banking business in New Orleans, turned later to planting, and then went north to New York City where he lost his fortune during the depression of the 1880's. But his education and skill as a writer made it possible for him to become a financial reporter and, finally, the owner of the Dixie Book Shop. He was a cultured gentleman highly esteemed by New York's intelligentsia. Over 100 miles farther north up the Mississippi lay Greenville destined in the postbellum period to shelter the second largest Jewish settlement in the state. Like other towns Greenville testifies to the rise of the merchant class after the War and to the fall of the planter aristocracy. And as the bourgeois rose to power financially and politically the Jews rose with them. Greenville Jews were worshipping together, meeting at the local B'nai B'rith Lodge in the 1870's. Below Greenville lies Mayersville, the county seat of Issaquena County, named after the businessman David Mayer. The big town in the next county to the south was Vicksburg which housed the largest synagog in the state. By the 1870's there were over 500 Jews, many of them shopkeepers, in town; Greenville had over 300; Natchez over 200. Meridian, Canton, Port Gibson, and Columbus were still smaller, and there were at least twenty to thirty other villages where Jewish groups had established themselves. Many of the settlers had come up the river by way of New Orleans; they peddled, opened stores, and then moved on as the river traffic gave way to the railroads. Vicksburg was an important steamboat, railroad, and cotton-shipping point in the mid-nineteenth century. A burial society was established there in 1841, but it was not until 1870, a generation later, that a synagog was dedicated.[12]

Vicksburg, like Montgomery and Mobile, attracted a number of interesting rabbis during its heyday. The Rev. Bernhard Henry Gotthelf, who had served the Union Army as a hospital chaplain in the Louisville area, received a call from the Vicksburg congregation after the Civil War. He officiated with distinction until carried off by the yellow-fever epidemic of 1878. One of his successors—this was in 1883—was Herman Milton Bien who was born in Germany and had received a good Jewish education in the Cassel teachers' seminary. After he came to the United States in 1854, a young man of twenty-three, he went into business but soon wound up in San Francisco with a private school of his own. When the school closed because of the accidental death of one of his charges, he accepted a rabbinical position. His headgear in the synagog attracted attention; following the prescription in Leviticus for the high priest he, too, wore a tall linen mitre on which he had inscribed in Hebrew, Sacred to the Lord (Lev. 16:4). Before he left San Francisco he published Jewish periodicals and when that venture also failed he crossed the border to Virginia City, Nevada, where he opened a private school and sat in the territorial legislature and later in the state assembly. He then returned east to New York City where he edited German and Jewish weeklies. His next shop was at Port Henry, on the shores of Lake Champlain. There he finally engaged in business successfully and settled down to married life. But yearning for the world of books he took rabbinic positions in Chicago and Dallas before accepting the pulpit in Vicksburg where he spent the last years of his life. Bien was a prolific writer. He fancied himself an intellectual and indeed he was a man of education and culture. Maybe he was competing with his brother Julius, an eminent lithographer, map engraver, and international president of the B'nai B'rith. Herman wrote and published sermons, poetry, dramas, plays for Purim and Hanukkah, and a novel *Ben Beor* to counter the lurid tales of the Wandering Jew written by Eugene Sue and other Christian writers. The title *Ben Beor* was chosen with Lew Wallace's *Ben-Hur* in mind. *Ben-Hur* sold close to 2,000,000 copies; Ben Beor probably never sold as many as 2,000 copies. The career of Bien is important historically because it is typical of the educated German Jewish immigrant who wandered everywhere, tried his hand at everything, and frequently succeeded at nothing. Bien was a litterateur, a violinist, a pianist, a poet, and a frustrated unhappy man; he committed suicide.[13]

ARKANSAS JEWRY

For a stretch of almost 200 miles in Mississippi one can look across the Father of Waters and see Arkansas. Jews had begun settling in Arkansas Territory ever since 1823 when it was true frontier sheltering fewer than two people per square mile. It is eloquent testimony to the enterprise of Jews that at least nine Arkansas villages have been named after them despite the fact that as late as 1880 they numbered less than one-fourth of 1 percent of the total population. Abeles, Altheimer, Berger, Bertig, Felsenthal, Goldman, Levy, and Wiener is not the roster of a German turnverein but a list of Arkansas place-names. Arkansas Jewish settlers of the antebellum generation were not usually American born but were Central European emigrants. After their arrival in America some traveled down the Ohio and Mississippi from the North; most, however, started out from New Orleans and, it would seem, ascended the Mississippi, turned off to the left in Louisiana, and climbed the Ouachita and Red Rivers into Arkansas. Still others continued up the Mississippi into the state and then veered to the left working their way up the Arkansas and White Rivers. In the days before the railroad supplanted the steamboat, rivers and canals were the most frequented highways in America.

   One of the first Arkansas Jewish pioneers was one of the numerous Blocks who had moved from Maryland, Virginia, and Ohio to Missouri; this one, Abraham Bloch, kept on going down until he came to the mouth of the Red River. He pushed toward the Upper Red River country and finally around 1823 he settled in Washington, Hempstead County. By then Bloch was already forty-three years old and had been in this country for more than two decades. Throughout his years in the Arkansas back counties till his death in 1857, he kept in touch with the Jewish world by reading Leeser's *Occident*. The Mitchells of Little Rock, Galicians by birth, were also territorial pioneers. They may have come as early as 1830. There were three brothers; one of them, Dr. Jacob Mitchell, was an Indian herb doctor who practiced for a time in Nashville, Tennessee, where he helped found the young community in 1848. The Mitchells were merchants who dabbled in anything that spelled profit; they ran a stagecoach line to Hot Springs where they had hotel interests. A branch of the Mitchell business was established at Fort Smith, on the border of Indian Territory.[14]

Just six miles away from Fort Smith lies the town of Van Buren. Like Fort Smith it traded with the Indians in the neighboring territory and served as an outfitting point in the 1850's for settlers taking the southern route to California. The Baers and Adlers were in business in this small place selling merchandise although they did some farming also. One of the Adlers, Samuel, went east to marry a Sulzberger in Philadelphia; his pious father-in-law insisted that the young man learn ritual slaughtering so that his daughter might eat kosher food on the Indian frontier. Samuel Adler and Sarah Sulzberger's son Cyrus grew up to become America's most influential communal worker in the first third of the twentieth century. The Adlers lived on the western edge of the state; the Hirsches lived on the White River in northeastern Arkansas. Eighteen-year-old Aaron Hirsch arrived in New Orleans in 1847 and joined his brother who lived in a village near Natchez. Aaron peddled for several years; his ability to speak French earned him a welcome at some of the plantations. That made him a compatriot of Lafayette and Rochambeau! He crossed the Mississippi River and moved up into the interior to Batesville where in the course of about ten years he built up the largest merchandising establishment in northern Arkansas. "We had for sale everything from a needle to a farmer's wagon, horses and mules, and occasionally bought and sold a few slaves." The Hirsches also ran a four-horse stage to a neighboring town. In the postwar period when Batesville was bypassed by the railroad, Aaron moved down the White River to Newport and gave the Episcopalians the ground for their first church.

It was not until the late 1860's, after the War, that the German Jews started coming in numbers to Arkansas. Little Rock certainly had a religious quorum before the War, for a burial society was put together in 1860, the very year that Jonas Levy was elected mayor of the town. The congregation was formed in 1866. A year later, Pine Bluff, down the Arkansas below Little Rock, set up its congregation, and by 1869 Louis Altheimer had settled there. Altheimer was only thirteen years of age when he and his sixteen-year-old cousin Simon Bamberger landed in New York City in 1863. Simon was one day to become governor of Utah; Louis was destined to become a wealthy merchant and planter. After Altheimer had learned English on an Indiana farm, he went to Mississippi and opened a grocery store. He was then a mature youngster of fifteen years. But business was bad and he went west to Nebraska following the tracklayers of the Union Pacific. He built a portable store and shifted it ever westward till the tracks reached Cheyenne. By that time he was tired of wandering; he missed the trees and he dreaded the hard winters. Before leaving Germany he had read Friedrich Gerstaecker's book on America and Arkansas. That was the state! He went back to Europe, married a girl there, and then returned to settle down in Pine Bluff. By the turn of the century he was a wealthy businessman and planter owning thousands of acres of farm land. When the Arkansas overflowed its banks and the heavy rains ruined his crop he was in trouble, but, with the help of a son, he recouped his losses through the Altheimer Dry Goods Company in Little Rock which soon boasted of its seventy employees. He had branch stores in other towns, including Altheimer which he and his brother had founded in 1885.[15]

In the late 1870's when Louis Altheimer was making his mark, there were at the most 2,000 fellow Jews in the state scattered in about thirty towns. Most of the villages had fewer than twenty Jews, almost half of Arkansas Jewry lived in Little Rock. Six towns had established communities: Little Rock, Pine Bluff, Helena on the Mississippi, Camden on the Ouachita, Fort Smith, and Texarkana sitting astride the borders of Arkansas and Texas. In 1876 the Jewish businessmen in Texarkana turned to their fellow citizen Charles Goldberg and asked him to conduct services for them. He agreed to do so. Goldberg, a Pole, came to the United States in the 1840's and peddled in the Missouri River Valley till he fell sick. Nursed back to health by a Christian family and importuned by a clergyman he became a convert and prepared himself for the Presbyterian ministry. When the Civil War erupted he left his charge in Texas to become a chaplain in the Confederate Army, the only "Jewish" chaplain to serve the South. After the War he officiated in towns in Texas and Arkansas including Washington, Abraham Block's village. Then when the railroads built Texarkana in 1873, Goldberg soon became the city's Presbyterian minister and one of its first school teachers. Thus it was that the Rev. Charles Goldberg of the Pine Street Presbyterian Church was available to preach to the Jewish congregation during the High Holy Days; when one of the local boys wanted to become bar mitzvah Goldberg prepared him. He never sought to convert his former coreligionists. Jewish tradition would have it that on his death bed he called the Jews to his home, read the Shema, and asked them to bury him in their cemetery. The Christians in town vigorously deny this, yet it is interesting to note that he lies at rest today not in the Pine Street Presbyterian Church burial ground but in a nondenominational cemetery.[16]

LOUISIANA JEWRY

In his appeal in 1825 for funds for Cincinnati, Joseph Jonas wrote that if it had a synagog hundreds of Jews would come up from New Orleans for Holy Day services. If there were hundreds of Jews at that time in New Orleans, why then did they not create a congregation of their own? Jews had been in and out of the city for a long time. Six years after Bienville founded the town in 1718 he promulgated a Black Code which contained an article expelling Jews. But this is in no sense proof that there were any Jews in town. All that the governor had done was to republish a 1685 Black Code which was originally issued to regulate slavery in the French West Indies and to expel the Jews who were then living there. The governor had not bothered to remove the anti-Jewish clause which was not relevant in the New Orleans of 1724. It was not until the French and Indian War that Jews began to find their way into the Spanish city. Dutch-born Isaac Rodrigues Monsanto arrived in 1775 and was soon followed by his family. As merchant-shippers the Monsantos carried on trade south along the Gulf Coast, into the Caribbean to the Islands, east to Europe and, closer to home, north up the Mississippi to the Illinois Country. A year or two after the coming of the first Monsanto some English Jews from the British West Indies sailed up the river under the specious pretext of exchanging prisoners. Actually they were traders seeking to do business with beleaguered New Orleans, desperately in need of goods and provisions. By 1759 or 1760 there may have been enough Jews to conduct a service; there is no evidence that they did.

After 1803 when New Orleans became American the town began an economic expansion that within a generation was to make it the second largest port in the South. Hundreds and thousands moved into the city to take advantage of its worldwide trade. Jews from the States, from Europe, the Islands, and even from Mexico bent their steps to the new El Dorado. By the 1820's there were more than enough Jews in town for a good-sized community but many were indifferent and others were intermarried, hampered in their Jewish affiliation by a Christian wife and Christian children. The catalyst arrived in the person of Jacob S. Solis, an English-born Jew who in 1827 or 1828 founded the first Jewish congregation in town, the Gates of Mercy, Shanarai-Chasset. The synagogal constitution published in 1828 is interesting for it reflects a "frontier" community. The first president Manis Jacobs, though devoted to his task, was himself intermarried. Provision was made for interment in the newly purchased cemetery of Christian wives and children, suicides, and even the occasional adulteress. Those who joined the congregation constituted but a fraction of the potential membership and were outnumbered by donors who refused to become members in a formal sense. Among those who gave but kept their distance was the pioneer merchant Judah Touro, now an old-timer who had been in the city for about twenty-seven years. Why were so many Jews unconcerned about their people and their faith? No one answer is adequate. No one will ever really know why an individual refuses to identify with his tradition and his group. Words such as "alienation," "rebellion," "assimilation" explain nothing. For many Judaism—its obligations and practices—had always been a burden. In a wide-open town like New Orleans, with its freedoms and opportunities, there was but one goal, wealth, power, recognition, and the drive to that end moved the humblest Jewish shopkeeper as it did the brilliant Judah P. Benjamin.

Among those who neither joined nor contributed was Samuel Hart. His will is eloquent testimony to a form of Americanization that was not unique. He was a Galician Jew who had come to the United States, probably by way of England, where he had picked up the typical Anglo-Jewish name of Hart. Two of his brothers back in Poland bore the good English name of Robinson. By 1823 Hart was already a man of substance; he owned one-half of the steamboat "United States," four Negro slaves, $20,000 in bank stock, and two lots in Louisville. Had he once lived in that town and then moved down the river to lusher pastures? Apparently he had a slave mistress and a mulatto child for he made ample provision for them. In 1832, on the eve of death, when he rewrote his will nothing was said of Polly and her son; he was now anxious to endow the four children of Cecilia Beni, a woman of color. One of the boys bore his name, Samuel. Hart had traveled a long way, spiritually and culturally, from the little Orthodox Jewish village of Stry in Galicia.[17]

New Orleans was the staging area for European immigrants who settled in the lower Mississippi Valley in the states of Mississippi, Arkansas, Louisiana, and East Texas. It was the most important town in the Old Southwest, an ever-expanding commercial center until the 1850's when the railroads began diverting its river traffic. The Crescent City benefited from the fanning out of brilliant Charleston Jews. Some went to Georgia and even to northwest Florida, others pressed on to Alabama, Mississippi, and to Louisiana, to New Orleans. Three friends, all remarkable men, were part of this Push to the West. They were Judah P. Benjamin, his cousin Henry Michael Hyams, and Dr. Edwin Warren Moïse. In the 1850's these three were among the most powerful leaders in the state. Benjamin was in the Senate; Hyams, banker, landowner, able lawyer, was lieutenant-governor; Moïse, physician-turned-lawyer, was Speaker of the Louisiana House.

Had these three men remained in Charleston would they have achieved the success which distinguished them in their new Louisiana homes? All three intermarried and were accepted in the best social circles. Was this assimilation a precondition for acceptance? In a state where the

Jewish vote was inconsequential these three achieved a dominant position, not because they assimilated but because of their superb talents. The Parisian visitor Baron Solomon de Rothschild referred to Benjamin as "perhaps the greatest mind on this continent." He also wrote that all these men had Jewish sympathies. It is true that none of them converted, but it is equally true that none affiliated with a synagog. Hyams was the only one of the three who was something of a "Jew." In the 1820's, before leaving Charleston, he had served as a secretary of the Reformed Society of Israelites, and there is evidence that throughout his life he never forgot his inherited Jewish faith. These three men were part of an elite group of Jews, both native and foreign born, professional men and brilliant entrepreneurs, who acquired wealth and power, intermarried, and played leading roles in the life of a great city. In contradistinction to Europe, the genius of America permitted these Jews to rise without submitting to baptism. The banker Michael Heine married a Creole but always remained a Jew; his Catholic-reared daughter Marie married the Duc de Richelieu and, after his death, the Prince of Monaco.[18]

Jews like Heine, Benjamin, Hyams, and Moïse did nothing for the Louisiana Jewish community as such. The humble European Jewish immigrants, the men and women ignored by them, built the Jewries of New Orleans and the backcountry. The start made in 1828 with the founding of Congregation Shanarai-Chasset was something to use as a base. Incoming Alsatians, Rhinelanders, Poseners, and East Europeans founded the present-day Jewish community of New Orleans. In the relatively short space of about fifty years New Orleans Jewry grew from about around two hundred unorganized Jews to a thriving community of about ten congregations and pious associations. The synagogs followed the German or the Polish rite and even the new Reform or American tradition. The New Orleans of the 1870's might well brag of its 5,000 Jews, its sick-care and burial society, its men's and its women's charity associations, its hospital and old-folks home, its society for orphans and widows, its education and literary societies. There was a special organization to aid the poor of Jerusalem and only New Orleans had a Hebrew Foreign Mission Society dedicated to the furtherance of the unhappy Jews of China. Let the Christians send their missionaries to Africa; Rabbi Julius Eckman was ready to sail for China.[19]

In the decade of the 1870's there were about 2,000 to 3,000 Jews in the upcountry. The pattern of settlement there created by the shotgun of accident and opportunity is not easy to trace. As in the rest of antebellum America, townsites on the river were inevitable and popular. The larger places were already settled by the 1850's followed by a lull of activity because of the Civil War and its aftermath, but in the 1870's there was a renewed push up the rivers and bayous. Newcomers leaving New Orleans

went up the western bank of the Mississippi to Donaldsonville and Pla-
quemine and then veered to the eastern side at Baton Rouge. When the
Jews established a congregation there in the 1850's they numbered about
a dozen families more or less. The town itself had a population of about
5,000 and was known for the beauty of its location and its surrounding
sugar plantations. In those days Louisiana Jews would occasionally buy
land and plant cotton but only a few, like the Lemanns of Donaldsonville,
turned to sugar.[20]

Sugar was big business; it required a large capital expenditure for
slaves, overseers, technicians, and machinery. Traditionally Jews preferred to remain in the buying and selling of soft goods, in urban commerce and industry. Back in the 1840's Judah P. Benjamin had sunk huge
sums in Bellechasse, a sugar plantation near New Orleans. He had practically given up the law, determined to become a planter, an aristocrat, and
a gentleman. He was and remained a gentleman, but fate and ambition
had decreed that he was not to remain a planter in spite of the brilliant
effort he exerted to make Bellechasse a success and a showplace. Just
about the time that Benjamin turned to planting, Antonio Mendez, one of
the founders of the Louisiana sugar industry, passed away. He was born in
1750 in Havana but went north to Spanish New Orleans about the year
1784. One of the first things that he did there was to secure a "blood
purity" or *limpieza* certificate to document that he was free from the taint
of all "impure races" such as Jews, Moors, mulattoes and Indians. These
statements were essential for those who wished to be socially acceptable
and eligible for ecclesiastical offices; anyone having a drop of Jewish
blood in his veins was prone to heresy. Mendez experimented with the
manufacture of sugar which he began to produce in the 1790's although
not in commercial quantities. When the Americans took over Louisiana,
the first governor, William C. C. Clairborne, appointed him in 1804 as a
civil commandant of a district, but the Spaniards there hesitated to acknowledge his authority because of his "Jewish extraction." In order to
keep the peace, Clairborne thereupon revoked the appointment. There is,
however, no known evidence that Mendez was really a descendant of
those Jews who had been forcibly baptized by the Spanish and Portuguese
300 years earlier.[21]

Continuing northward and eastward Jews settled in Bayou Sara and
Clinton where they could trade with the neighboring Mississippians.
Those Jews who kept going up the river beyond Baton Rouge preferred
the Mississippi towns of Natchez and Vicksburg, establishing no substan-
tial communities on the Louisiana side. Although Opelousas and New
Iberia in south Louisiana had thriving communities during this period,
more of the immigrants turned up the Ouachita to Monroe, Bastrop, and
Farmersville near the Arkansas border; still larger groups moved up the

Red River through Avoyelles Parish to Alexandria, Natchitoches, and Shreveport in the direction of Texas and Arkansas. There were at least ten other clusters of Jews in other villages and hamlets of the state.

Shreveport Jewry was only about a fifth as large as that of New Orleans, yet it was the second largest Jewish community in the state. Pioneers had moved into that part of Louisiana in the 1820's when cotton was beginning to come into its own and cattle driven from Texas brought profits to venturesome merchants. Fourteen-year-old Jacob Bodenheimer arrived in New Orleans from Speyer on the Rhine in 1822. After spending a few years in the big city he took passage up the Red River to the northwestern border at a time when the country was still wild. He traded with the Indians, peddled among the whites, ran a ferry, opened a tavern, and built one of the first stores in that remote corner. Strangely enough he and his family remained religiously loyal and observant; that was most difficult and altogether atypical.

South of Shreveport on the Red River lies Alexandria where Jews created a full complement of Jewish institutions in the 1850's and 1860's. It was the third largest Jewish town in Louisiana. Still farther south in Avoyelles Parish there were practically no Jews, but there were two "Jewish" towns: Marksville and Bunkie. The former was named after a Jewish businessman by the name of Marc Eliche who had emigrated from Alsace before the Civil War. The latter was built by the family of Colonel A. M. Haas and was given that name as a compliment to the Colonel's daughter who pronounced "monkey" as "bunkie." Thus local tradition. Marksville is the county seat.[22]

JEWS IN EAST TEXAS

With their eyes fixed on the beckoning West, men left New Orleans to travel up the Mississippi to the Red River and on to Natchitoches. Then they cut over to Nacogdoches, the most important town in East Texas in those days. This is the route that young Adolphus Sterne took in the 1820's although he had already wandered as far north as Tennessee. This native of Cologne was something of an adventurer for by 1826–1827 he was involved in the abortive revolution that created the ephemeral Republic of Fredonia. He managed to come out of the episode with a whole skin. Though arrested he was either included in the amnesty that followed or his Masonic friends intervened for him. He made his peace with the Mexican government and was appointed an alcalde in the city. He was one of the town's outstanding citizens. When the Texans revolted in 1835 and sought independence Sterne supported them enthusiastically; he acted as their agent in New Orleans, recruiting, outfitting, and transporting American supporters up the Red River to Texas. His friend Sam Houston was baptized as a Catholic in the home of this Nacogdoches

Jew; Sterne's Catholic wife served as Houston's sponsor. Sterne intervened in a brawl between Houston and a Colonel Jordan, late of the Federal Army, just in time to stop the irate Colonel from hacking Houston to
death with an axe. After the Republic was proclaimed Sterne led a company of men in battle against invading Cherokees and in later years served
his fellow citizens in the state legislature.

Even before the war for Texas independence in 1835-1836 brought
in daring men from all parts of the United States, Lieutenant Samuel
Noah, a West Point graduate, had fought in one of the Mexican revolts as
early as 1812. During the fateful March-April days of 1836 when Fanning's men were massacred at Goliad and Houston defeated Santa Anna at
San Jacinto, Jewish volunteers played their part. There is no evidence that
the Wolf who died in the Alamo with Bowie and Crockett was a Jew;
Lieutenant Edward J. Johnson, a nineteen-year-old artillery officer who
was executed at Goliad, was one of the Cincinnati Johnsons; Moses Albert Levy of Virginia served as a surgeon in the Volunteer Army; Levi
Charles (Myers) Harby, a brother of Isaac Harby, resigned from the navy
to help the Texans gain their freedom. All through the 1830's before and
after the battle for independence, Jews in small but increasing numbers
settled in Nacogdoches, along the Gulf Coast at places like Velasco and
Galveston, or steamed up the rivers into the interior. They were soldiers,
adventurers, businessmen, empresarios, and land promoters; some were
United States citizens; some were immigrants. The Galician youngster,
Simon Wiess (Weiss) had left home at the age of sixteen and had wandered all over Europe and the West Indies before deciding to make his
home in the United States. By the middle 1830's he had left New Orleans behind him and had established himself in the new Republic of
Texas where he was appointed a deputy collector of customs at Sabine-
town, near the Louisiana border. He married a Christian girl in Natchitoches and then planted himself permanently in a place of his own in Jas-
per County on the Sabine River. He called it Wiess Bluff. This
enterprising storekeeper shipped cotton down the Sabine in those early
days thus helping to develop the river traffic. Some time before he died in
1868 he wrote an ethical letter to his sons as they were about to enter the
business world: Never hesitate to say no; be meticulous in fulfilling a contract; allow no loafing or drinking in the store; maintain a one-price policy; sell for cash; read good literature, and associate with the best people.
This was good advice in postbellum Texas; it is still good advice anywhere.[23]

Texas had no dearth of adventuring Jews in that thrilling decade of
the 1830's. After having suffered reverses in Alabama, Simon Mussina, a
Philadelphian, edited English newspapers in Matagorda and Matamoras,
Mexico, across the Rio Grande from Brownsville which he helped to lay

out. In later life this businessman, druggist, newspaper editor, and land promoter became so involved in land litigation that he finally turned to law as a profession. His investigation of titles brought him to the capital, Austin, where he became an officer of the local Episcopal church though he never became a Christian. The last rites over his body were performed in Galveston where he was buried from the First Presbyterian Church. Early Texas is an excellent laboratory for a most fascinating study of the assimilative process as it affected Jews in a pioneering area. Logic and tradition fade, tolerance prevails, and the commonweal is the highest law.[24]

It is not too much of an exaggeration to maintain that almost everyone in Texas in the 1840's was in the land business: Texas had nearly 270,000 square miles and a population of less than 200,000. That would allow at least a square mile to every inhabitant. In its eagerness to secure immigrants the Republic signed contracts with colonizers, empresarios. One of them, a Frenchman, Henry Castro, was very probably of Jewish descent though he, too, like many other Texas notables of that generation, was married to a Gentile. Castro had come to this country in 1826 and became a citizen. He did not concern himself with Texas colonization until 1842. In the course of the next four years he sent over some 2,000 emigrants in twenty-seven boats. Four towns, scattered over sixty miles, were founded by him, including one named Castroville. These villages were the first permanent white settlements between San Antonio and the Rio Grande. Despite skillful propaganda in Germany and in France and the expenditure of large sums of money he was certainly not successful, at least financially. Involved in colonizing Algiers, the French had no desire to send people out to the dreary Texas plains; fear of a war with Mexico frightened others off, and Castro departed this world in the 1860's a poor man. Castroville and Castro County in the Texan panhandle are monuments to the memory of a Marrano-like figure who loved to boast: "I descend in line direct from Jean de Castro, Viceroy of the Portuguese Indes and Goa."[25]

Castro's contemporary, Jacob de Cordova, a member of a distinguished West Indian rabbinical family, was equally unsuccessful in his attempt to profit from his huge holdings. Some time before 1820 this Jamaican had come with his parents to Philadelphia where they joined one of the synagogs. They were observant Jews and Jacob was given a good Hebrew education though this did not deter him from marrying a Christian in 1826 in a Presbyterian ceremony. A decade later he was in New Orleans in business. The following year, in 1837, he was in Galveston selling tobacco, liquor, and stationery. Before his life ran its course he was to be a merchant, a newspaper publisher, founder of the Texas Odd Fellows Lodge, legislator, map maker, land promoter, and town builder. He was one of the original proprietors of the Waco townsite. By 1845 he had opened a land agency anticipating admission to the Union and the thousands of settlers who would pour into the country. He bought up soldiers' land scrip and by 1855 he either owned or controlled over 1,000,000 acres. But he discovered too late that he had over-extended himself; interest on borrowed money ran anywhere from 8 to 10 percent; by 1859 his empire had collapsed. In pursuit of his policy of peddling his lands to prospective settlers Jacob became a propagandist publishing newspapers, maps, and books—*The Texas Emigrants' and Travelers' Guide Book* and *Texas, Her Resources and Her Public Men.* He became an avid booster for his adopted state, lecturing on its potentialities in New York, Philadelphia, and even in Manchester, England. However it is very much to be doubted whether his proslavery attitude sat well with some of his English audience. He was an entrepreneur with vision; in 1865 he proposed the establishment of mills in Bosque County for the manufacture of cloth. De Cordova died in 1868 and was buried under a large stone cross erected by his pious Christian admirers.[26]

In the 1840's before he became an important land agent and locator, Cordova had established himself as a wholesale and retail merchant in Houston. Jews had come to town as early as 1835 and strangely, since originally it was certainly not the largest nor the most important Jewish settlement in the state, Houston led all other Texas Jewries in laying the foundations for a Jewish community. In relatively rapid succession the town's Jews established a cemetery in 1844, held services in the late 1850's, hammered out a permanent Ladies' Hebrew Benevolent Society in the 1870's, and in the next decade fashioned a Hebrew and German English School which Christians also patronized. The surest index to the stability of the Houston Jewish community is that two reverend gentlemen from Jerusalem spent five days in town in 1868 collecting money for the schools of the Holy Land. Two years later the Houston Jews began to build a synagog of their own and received large sums in contributions from local Christians. By 1880 there were almost 500 Jews in town.

In 1858 the twenty-one-year-old Harris (Hirschel) Kempner had a brush with the law in Houston. Houston was then a growing town of about 7,000 and insisted that its ordinances be obeyed. This malefactor was arrested and fined for riding through the streets at about five miles per hour. That was forbidden. Young Kempner at the age of sixteen had landed in New York City where he worked as a bricklayer for some time, and then in 1858 had moved on to Cold Springs, Texas. When the War came along he joined the cavalry as a private and came out as an officer. After the South surrendered he settled down in Galveston where he and his associates and his children after him built a very imposing commercial empire. A century later the Kempners of Galveston were still a great power in banking, real estate, sugar, and a host of other activities. Part of

Harris Kempner's success must be attributed to his wife, a Seinsheimer from Cincinnati. He saw her for the first time in New York City where he had gone to buy tobacco, snuff, and canned goods in carload lots. He and his partner were wholesale grocers and liquor dealers. He stayed in a boarding house, probably one run by Jews, where food was dished out in family style. Kempner was attracted very much and impressed by a sturdy young lady who was shoveling in the food at a good rate. She was vivacious and attractive. That girl, he said to himself, is vigorous and healthy and would make a man a good wife. On his next trip north he went to Cincinnati to buy whiskey—by the carlot—proposed to her and married her. The marriage was a great success; their eight children rallied around their mother when Harris Kempner was snatched away at a relatively early age.[27]

Up until the turn of the nineteenth century Galveston was the largest and most cultured city in the state. In the late 1870's almost one-third of the 3,300 Jews in Texas lived in this Gulf Coast town. There were twice as many Jews in Galveston as in Houston. The early settlers, aside from those Europeans who arrived by boat via New Orleans, had come in from the Atlantic tidewater, from declining Charleston, from Baltimore, and from Philadelphia. The most notable families of Jewish immigrants to the Lone Star Republic were the Ostermans, the Dyers, and the Seeligsons; all of them started out in the dry goods business. It took years before the Galveston Jews pulled themselves together and purchased ground for a cemetery. That was in 1852, just a year before Michael Seeligson became mayor; he took the job, he wrote Isaac Leeser, to confound those Christians who were crusading against Jews. By 1870 there was a congregation in town, a social club—the Harmony—a charity and burial group, and a ladies welfare organization.

It is quite probable that Galveston was slow in putting a Jewish community together because there were so many disparate elements. In this it resembled New Orleans which waited a whole generation after the Americans took over before the first congregation shaped itself; also as in New Orleans many Jews were probably indifferent. When Rabbi M. N. Nathan was called in from New Orleans to consecrate the cemetery in 1852 he chided his listeners because they concealed their origins, intermarried, held no services, and did not circumcise their children. The "frontier" took its toll. Isadore Dyer was reputed to have encouraged the Jews to hold the first service in his home. He was one of the Dyers of Baltimore, an observant family that had helped found the first Baltimore congregation in 1829. Dyer left half of his residual estate to the Protestants Orphans Home, the other half to the local synagog. This man had married out, actively supported the Episcopal church, and permitted his wife to rear their children as Christians, but when one of them died he insisted on a Jewish burial.

Isadore had a sister, Rosanna, who had come to Galveston in the late 1830's with her husband Joseph Osterman. She kept a kosher home; even when the port was blockaded during the Civil War she refused to compromise by eating forbidden food. She won the love and respect of the sick and wounded in the Confederate States Hospital by her devoted ministrations. In 1866 coming down the Mississippi her boat burnt to the water's edge and she died of exposure in the cold February waters. When her will was opened it was found that she had left the bulk of her estate to numerous Jewish and Christian institutions. Undoubtedly patterning herself on Judah Touro, she made provision for Jewish societies in Philadelphia, New York, Cincinnati, Galveston, and Houston. The New Orleans Hebrew Foreign Mission Society—the Chinese!—was given a legacy and the Jews of Palestine were also remembered. In Galveston she left money for the care of sailors, for prison reform, and for a nondenominational widows and orphans home "for are not all men brothers before God?"

Rosanna's Amsterdam-born husband had predeceased her by five years. In certain respects the Ostermans were a tragic family: they had no children; she died in a steamboat accident; he was accidently shot to death in a gunsmith's shop. Osterman had been in business first in Philadelphia and then in Baltimore where he had been defrauded; he moved on to Galveston, probably at the suggestion of his brother-in-law Major Leon Dyer who had served the Republic of Texas. Osterman arrived on a schooner with a load of goods from New Orleans about the year 1839. He opened for business in a tent and in the course of a very short time became the largest retailer in town, for he was a brilliant innovative entrepreneur. Osterman imported wines from Holland and, in turn, shipped the Dutch cotton. In a more modern variation of the triangular trade his schooner brought in ice from New England, rum, molasses, and lime juice from the West Indies and, undoubtedly shipped the New Englanders and the West Indians products which were in short supply. This resourceful businessman sold the first sheet-metal stoves in town, manufactured soap and candles, sent out loaded mule trains to the hinterland to trade with the settlers and Indians, built roads and a ferry, advanced the planters money on their crops, paid interest on time deposits, sold the Texas army some of the new percussion caps and revolvers, and helped finance Gail Borden, Jr, as he began manufacturing condensed milk. Osterman is an interesting combination of merchant-shipper and merchant-banker. His contributions to the pioneer economy are evident.[28]

At an early stage in the history of the Republic and State of Texas Jews began to move into the towns of the backcountry in the eastern, northern, central, and southern areas and to settle in the Gulf Coast towns all the way from Sabine Pass near Louisiana to Brownsville on the Mexican border. Isaac Jalonick may well have been Belton's only Jew, but he saw a copy of *The Occident* and hastened to write to Leeser whom he praised to the skies as a "poblick advocate" of the Jews. By 1880 there were about forty towns with Jews, at least twelve of which had organized communities. Most of these settlements began to flourish in the 1870's with the expansion of the railroad systems.

Early Jewish Dallas is an interesting community which developed rather rapidly. In the one year, 1872, it bought a cemetery, held services, and established the usual all-purpose benevolent society. Two Sanger brothers were presidents of the congregation. Services were often held on the second floor of the Sanger Brothers store, and in 1874, Philip, another brother, was vice president of the budding congregation. The five Sanger brothers reflect the influence of the Rothschild myth on American Jews. The successes of the Rothschild brothers in Europe profoundly influenced many large American Jewish families. If brothers would only work together in harmony there is nothing they could not accomplish; there must be a common effort and a common treasury. These hopes and these goals are reflected to a greater or lesser degree in the efforts of the Seligmans, the Guggenheims, the family of Max Lilienthal, and the Kempners and Sangers of Texas.

Isaac Sanger, the oldest of the five brothers, came over from Bavaria in 1851 and learned the rudiments of business the hard way, as a salesman in New Haven and then as a bookkeeper for a clothing manufacturer in New York City. Six years later he struck out for Texas and, together with a partner, established a store in McKinney in the northern section of the state. His goods came by oxcart from Shreveport or from Millican, the railroad terminal. In 1855 with the aid of two other brothers the main store was shifted to Weatherford and branches were maintained at McKinney and Decatur. Then came the Civil War; at least two of the brothers enlisted in the Confederate Army. After the War they started over again, this time at the Millican railhead, and they moved north, town by town with the advancing end-of-track until in 1871 they reached Corsicana. By that time all the brothers and the rest of the family had come over from Bavaria, even papa and mama, and Isaac had moved to New York to become the resident buyer and financier.

Alex, one of the brothers who had come from Germany in 1865, served his apprenticeship in Cincinnati and became a partner in the family business in Corsicana in 1872. That year the others sent him on to Dallas, the new railroad terminus, to open a store. With the help of Sam and Lehman, two other brothers, the Waco store was opened. Later branches were established in Fort Worth and Wichita, Kansas. Ultimately the family opened a wholesale department in Dallas and also manufactured their own overalls and jumpers. The Dallas retail store became one of the great institutions of Texas and by 1910 could brag of having installed the first

escalator in the South. It had nine acres of floor space and at its peak employed about 1,800 people. The store sold merchandise—that was its
main job—but it sponsored art exhibits, gave book reviews, conducted a
theatre for adults and teen-agers, offered hospitality to the Girl Scouts and
the Parent-Teachers Associations, sponsored lectures, staged style shows,
presented choral singers, and opened a branch post office. The employees
were offered sick and death benefits, insurance, and the convenience of a
building and loan association. Quite early brother Philip built a beautiful
home "far out in the country" with three drawing rooms and a third-floor
ballroom. The problem of transportation was solved by asking one of the
brothers who controlled the local mule-drawn streetcar to extend the line
to his residence. To make sure that the conductor would not drive off
without him before breakfast was finished, Philip would toot on a little
silver whistle and the driver would wait patiently. Philip then sauntered
out to the car and to the day's work.

On November 30, 1901, Eli Sanger, one of the brothers, bought one
of the first automobiles in Dallas. It was a Locomobile and cost $850.[29]

JEWS IN THE BORDER STATES

THE DISTRICT OF COLUMBIA

By 1828 when New Orleans' Gates of Mercy were opened to receive
those Jews who were determined to be Jews, the initial penetration of the
interior of the Continent was complete. At one end was Cincinnati, at the
other New Orleans. In the decade of the 1830's the Jewries of Louisville
and St. Louis would come into being; during the 1840's the wandering
Arameans would move up and down the Ohio and the Mississippi Rivers
and their tributaries, ranging east to the Appalachians and west to the
Great Plains. It was during this same decade, the 1840's, when the Jews
were settling in all parts of the Old Southwest, laying the groundwork
for future Jewish communities, that for the first time in its almost fifty
years of existence the national capital began to shelter Jews in numbers.
The District of Columbia, Washington and Georgetown, attracted few
Jews in the early national period because there were few in the United
States. When the Central Europeans started coming to these shores the
District soon received its share. Like almost all towns and areas settled by
Jews at this time, Washington and Georgetown had pioneers who preceded the "masses" by a generation or two. The first known Jew was already ensconced in the District in the 1790's before the capital was
officially transferred from Philadelphia to Washington in 1800. Isaac Polock was a third-generation American, grandson of a prominent Newport
merchant-shipper. In 1792 Isaac was in Savannah where he was hauled

before the congregation on the charge of having desecrated the Sabbath by keeping his store open on a Saturday. When he explained that some wares which he had ordered had arrived on the Sabbath and had to be stored at once, he was exonerated. Three years later he was in Washington building houses which were ultimately to serve as offices and residences for cabinet members. Like his grandfather he was a merchant-shipper, busying himself for the most part in the coastal trade. In those days Washington, Georgetown, and Alexandria were ports. The Polocks were observant; despite the fact that they were apparently a lone family they had their own "priest" who acted as shohet and Hebrew teacher.[30]

During the early 1830's there was a bare sprinkling of Jews in town, including a directory publisher and an army officer; even as late as the early 1840's when Captain Alfred Mordecai wanted a minyan to help bury a child, ten male Jews could not be found. Religiously speaking, the Jewish congressmen were almost a total loss. They kept to themselves. By the late 1840's and 1850's immigrants started coming. It was they who succeeded in fashioning a congregation in 1852. They called it the Washington Hebrew Congregation; the name may have been a variation of the Baltimore Hebrew Congregation. The congregants were fortunate in securing the help of Captain Jonas P. Levy, a brother of the wealthy, assertive Uriah P. Levy, then a high officer in the United States Navy. Jonas Levy, a maritime officer, had been an active participant in the Mexican War and had been put in charge of the port of Vera Cruz by General Zachary Taylor. Like his brother Uriah he was a good businessman and was the head of a company that sought to bring gas light to Washington. Levy called his enterprise the Washington Benzole Gas Light Company. His most ambitious project—which at $100 a share never got off the ground—was the proposal to build a road from New York to New Orleans, to Tampico, Vera Cruz, and the Mexican West Coast, near Acapulco, from where steamships would carry the travelers on to the California El Dorado. It was a brilliant but not unusual idea in those days before the Union and Central Pacific Railroads spanned the continent. Levy served as president of the new congregation after it was chartered by Congress in 1856.[31]

Like their fellow Jews in Baltimore a generation earlier the Washingtonians ran into a roadblock when they set out to incorporate their new religious association. Up to that time only Christian churches in the District were recognized and when Jonas Levy's petition for a charter reached Congress a gentleman from Mississippi, Hendley Stone Bennett, objected to the "Hebrews." The Kentuckian Humphrey Marshall who was pushing the bill responded laconically that Mr. Bennett "objected to the bill in regard to the Hebrews. My bill is in regard to the Americans." The House laughed and approved the charter. This brief passage between

Bennett and Marshall is interesting and confusing: Bennett was a Democrat; Marshall was a member of the nativist American Party which was then agitating against Catholics and immigrants. Even Jews were not untouched by this xenophobia: the congregational constitution of 1857 declared that only citizens could be officers—this at a time when the majority of the stalwarts of Washington Hebrew Congregation spoke with a foreign accent.

Jews in the national capital began to spread their wings in the 1860's. The census of that year discloses that of the fifty-one gainfully employed Jews in the District at least forty-one were in some form of retail merchandising. On February 1, 1860, Rabbi Morris J. Raphall of New York City opened the House of Representatives with prayer, the first Jew to do so. Fully caparisoned with praying shawl and velvet skull cap he prayed before a crowded gallery. He was "listened to with marked attention." The Jews swelled with pride although some Christians were nonplussed: "going to pray for ten percent a month"; "a Jew praying for the American House of Representatives! The next thing we shall have will be a shaking Quaker dancing a reel" or "Brigham Young, surrounded by his harem, threatening to send the administration to hell."[32]

Numerous Jews settled in the capital to take advantage of the business opportunities offered by the War. The young Bavarian Simon Wolf had left Ulrichsville, Ohio, as a clerk; he read law for two years and hung out his shingle in Washington in 1862. For the next sixty years Wolf was to glory in his position as the appointed—and self-appointed—lobbyist for an American Jewry that was to grow from 150,000 to 4,000,000. In 1863 the Washington Hebrews dedicated their first synagog building and asked their friends throughout the country to help finance the bold undertaking. Their appeal was supported by Mayor Richard Wallach, a Unitarian, son of a Roumanian father who, it is not too audacious to venture the guess, was born a Jew. After the War, veterans and others moved to town to fill civil service positions. By 1871 there were three congregations in the District and two ladies philanthropic societies. Before the decade ended it was to shelter at least 1,500 Jews.[33]

There is today in the National Archives, in Washington, a document of particular interest to Jews of the capital and all of America. The cinema entrepreneur Barney Balaban gave it to the government in 1945. Shortly before that time a professor of the Hebrew Union College of Cincinnati working in the field of American Jewish history visited Dr. A.S.W. Rosenbach in his office in New York and asked the distinguished bibliophile if he had any old papers of significance for Jews. In answer to his query Dr. Rosenbach took him into the vault and pointed to an old document lying on the floor. "That is the most important Jewish document I own," he said. The professor picked it up; it was an original copy of the Bill of Rights. This is the document which now graces the National Archives.[34]

WEST VIRGINIA JEWRY

The District, as it is known, was created out of land originally ceded to the national government by the states of Maryland and Virginia. About six weeks before the Washington Jews dedicated their first synagog building, formerly the Methodist Episcopal Church South, President Abraham Lincoln signed the bill admitting the western part of Virginia to the Union as a state. The non-slavery counties of northwestern Virginia were loyal to the Union. There were of course Jews in that part of the state even as there were some almost anywhere where towns of size grew up. Jews had certainly been passing through Wheeling at least since 1820 for the city lay on the Cumberland Road and on the Ohio, the main southern and western artery for trade and travel. The Baltimore & Ohio Railroad reached the city by 1853. Jews planted themselves in Wheeling because it was a very active commercial, manufacturing, and port city. There were about 11,000 people there in 1850, but long before that in the 1840's the Jews had begun to hold services; by 1849 they had a congregation and a cemetery. Jews set up a charity association in the 1850's and their efforts were reenforced in the 1860's by the Ladies Hebrew Benevolent Society. The ladies provided sick-care, shrouds, a funeral carriage, relief for all in distress, and, as a matter of course, financial aid to a congregation that was always in need of cash.

Farther down the Ohio was Parkersburg where Jews had stopped to settle in the 1850's. By the end of the 1860's, in 1869, the first society around which the community was to gather, was a Young Men's Hebrew Association. It offered not only fellowship but also religious services and aid for itinerants. Still farther down the river close to the mouth of the Kanawaha lay the village of Point Pleasant. No Jews were to stop there till the middle of the twentieth century but some did go up the river to Charleston in the mid-nineteenth century; others undoubtedly came from the East on an old road that ran across the mountains from Richmond to the Ohio. The Parkersburg community began as a Y.M.H.A.; Charleston Jewry began in 1873 as a Hebrew Educational Society that taught children, held services, lent money to its members, and started a German Club. When the sanctuary was built by the Society in 1875 no man could join the Club who had not contributed to the synagog. This was a well-integrated group. In 1885 Charleston members got rid of their rabbi with whom they were unhappy and advertised for a teacher who was to lead in services and teach the children Hebrew, German, and religion. They said specifically they wanted no rabbi. Charleston, Wheeling, and Parkersburg were the three leading Jewish towns in the 1870's. Wheeling had about 300 Jews; Charleston and Parkersburg, fewer than 100. There were about a half-dozen other Jewish settlements either on the Potomac or its tributaries, oriented to Virginia, or on the Monongahela, satellites of Pittsburgh.[35]

TENNESSEE JEWRY

Immigrants coming up the Mississippi from New Orleans or western pilgrims floating down the Ohio past Wheeling, Parkersburg, Louisville, Owensboro, Henderson, and Paducah, might well decide to remain in Memphis. Because of its superb location it was one day to become the biggest city on the Mississippi between St. Louis and New Orleans. There was no Memphis in 1795 when Benjamin Myers settled in Nashville. This Myers was the son of a Newport religious factotum of the 1770's and a brother of Major Mordecai Myers, the veteran of the War of 1812. Nashville in the 1790's was still on the edge of settlement. Here, too, it took a half - century before a community was established by humble emigrants from Central Europe. Services were held in 1848, and a burial association was established and a cemetery purchased in 1851. The new group called itself the Hebrew Benevolent Burial Association, Shield of David. The founders, consisting of "five families and eight young men," may have chosen the name Shield of David because they lived in Davidson County. Nashville was by then a prosperous town of about 20,000 just about to complete railroad connections south to the Atlantic at Charleston. After that there was no question of its future.

Ultimately Memphis was to become the most important city in the state. The first Jewish pioneer was Joseph I. Andrews, a grandson of Haym Salomon, Robert Morris's bill broker in 1781; Andrews's wife Miriam was a granddaughter of "Major" Benjamin Nones, a veteran of the Revolution. Andrews bought a cemetery for local Jewry in 1847/1848 after a brother died and by 1853 there was a burial society and a permanent religious community. Memphis was a great cotton center and grew rapidly. By 1876 the population had more than tripled since the 1850's and the Jews had grown from a handful to over 2,000, despite the recurring yellow-fever epidemics which took a terrible toll. The butcher, Henry Seesel, who was in charge of the Jewish cemetery, buried 100 men, women, and children in 1873 alone. Seesel, of Speyer on the Rhine, had established himself permanently in the town in 1857 after about ten years of stopping in about a half-dozen towns engaged in at least seven different occupations. His experience as a stockkeeper and clothing salesman in Cincinnati lasted but two days. When his boss told him to stand outside the store and pull in customers his first prospect turned out to be a country bumpkin who knocked him down and called him a "damned Jew dog." Seesel quit immediately.[36]

Chattanooga, Brownsville, and Knoxville were much smaller than Memphis. In the 1870's Chattanooga had fewer than 200 Jews and the other two towns fewer than 100 each. All three Jewish communities were organized in the postbellum period. The Knoxville Jews came together when they bought a cemetery plot in 1865 to bury a Confederate soldier.

This goad to organize is reminiscent of the creation of the Hebrew Benevolent Society in New York City in 1822. Money was collected there in 1820 to provide for a dying Revolutionary War veteran and the unspent surplus was used to create a new social-welfare society. The Knoxvillians held services from 1866 on in the basement of a wholesale vinegar establishment; the humble worshippers used the barrels as seats until they emerged from the depths in the early 1870's to enjoy the hospitality of the First Presbyterian Church.

Almost from the very first day, Squire Julius Ochs was the "rabbi" of the Knoxville Benevolent Society Congregation. Ochs was a Bavarian, born in Fuerth in 1826. His father saw to it that he received a fine education in the classics and in modern languages; at his bar mitzvah Julius read some of his own poetry in German and spoke briefly in English, French, and Italian. Reverses at home and the severe Bavarian laws impelled him to join members of his family in America in 1845. In order to take the ship in Bremen he walked 250 miles. His life in America was a series of almost bewildering ups and downs. He was a peddler, a teacher of languages in a Kentucky girls seminary, a part-time rabbi in Louisville, a Mexican War soldier, and even an owner of a chain of stores in the South. He was welcomed everywhere for his culture and his ability to play the guitar. One begins to suspect that he was not a "practical" person. He spent his last dollar in New York City to listen to an opera and sold a successful business he owned to finance a brother; then he went to work for the new owners. Ochs helped manage a cotton factory in Louisiana, led a Masonic lodge, wrote an operetta for a drama and music club, traveled in the transmississippi West and in the South for a wholesale jeweler, and opened a business for himself; he made money, he lost money. All this before the War of 1861, during which he was a Union militia officer. Unlike many others, Jews included, he refused to participate in the smuggling so common then, particularly in the Memphis area. He managed to keep the peace beautifully with his wife, an ardent "rebel"; in later years she was active in the Daughters of the Confederacy and he was a chaplain in the Grand Army of the Republic. Toward the end of the War he settled in Knoxville; once more he was in and out of the army and then by the spring of 1865 back in business for himself. This time he became wealthy but when Lee surrendered, prices collapsed and Ochs, left with a huge inventory bought at inflated war prices, had to liquidate his business. There were days when he was literally down to his last loaf of bread.

His friends rallied around him and elected him squire, justice of the peace. Now at least he and his numerous family had enough to eat. The boys went to work delivering newpapers; the eldest son Adolph, with two younger brothers, arose at 3:00 in the morning, took care of the paper route, finished at seven, and then went on to school. Adolph decided to learn the printer's trade, moved to Chattanooga and at the age of twenty bought the *Chattanooga Times*. Then he brought the squire and the entire family to Chattanooga and put them to work in his new enterprise before he finally moved on in 1896 to rebuild *The New York Times*. The last ten years of the squire's life, to his death in 1888, were good years. He never became wealthy but "I never betrayed a friend, never received a favor which I did not return, nor borrowed a dollar which in the end was not paid back." Ochs's life in America is not typical. He was cultured, generous, idealistic, yet in his ups and downs he is more typical of the German immigrant than the Seligmans, the Guggenheims, and an August Belmont.

When Ochs moved to Chattanooga to join Adolph in 1878 there were fewer than 4,000 Jews in Tennessee. The state then sheltered the eleventh largest Jewish group in this country.[37]

CHAPTER FOUR

JEWS IN THE MIDDLE WEST, PRAIRIE STATES, AND

FAR WEST

INDIANA

In his futile search for security Squire Ochs had worked his way up and down the Ohio and the Mississippi as far north and west as Burlington and Des Moines where he had almost frozen to death in the winter of 1860. By that year the line of Jewish settlements had steadily advanced into the Middle West up to the Great Plains. Long before that, as early as the 1770's, the firm of B. & M. Gratz of Philadelphia was speculating in land in Indiana and Illinois, and by 1807 Michael Gratz's sons were shipping provisions up the Wabash to Governor William Henry Harrison in Vincennes. Some time about the year 1816 or 1817 Phineas Israel Johnson was trading in the Brookville and Connersville area near the Ohio frontier; his brother David joined him in 1818. Still another Jew came to Indiana in 1818, Samuel Judah, a young lawyer. This grandson of Aaron Hart, the first permanent Jewish settler in Canada, had gone to Rutgers, studied law, passed the bar examination, and had journeyed west to Vincennes. Although he was then but twenty years of age it was not long before this brilliant and highly educated man became one of the most distinguished citizens of the state. By 1827 he was a member of the state legislature; four years later he was an unsuccessful candidate for the United States Senate, and in 1840 he was the speaker of the Indiana House. His law practice carried him on occasion to Washington where he represented clients before the Supreme Court. Like most Jewish "pioneer" settlers he had married out and his children were reared as Christians. A whole generation was yet to pass before a congregation would be established in Vincennes, in 1867.

Adam Gimbel, a peddler for years, settled in the town in 1842 and opened a small store. He was successful over the next forty years but it remained for his more fortunate sons to establish the Gimbel Brothers department store empire that ultimately embraced numerous branches in the cities and suburbs of America, all the way from New York to California. (By the 1980's the empire had disappeared.) In this town of fewer than 2,000 in the 1840's, the two men, Judah and Gimbel, could not have failed to know one another. What did they have in common? Both men had certainly been bar mitzvah; Gimbel, a typical German Jew, had at best an elementary education; Judah had a fine library and was at home in the Latin and Greek classics. And the townspeople? They made no distinction between the two; both were Jews.[1]

The German Jewish immigrants, the men and women who were to build the American Jewish communities of the transmontane country, moved slowly and cautiously into the new states. When they arrived in Indiana in the 1840's it already numbered a population of about 750,000. By the next decade the Wabash & Erie Canal would connect the Great Lakes and the Ohio, New Orleans, and New York City. Indiana was no frontier. In 1848 the first Jewish community in the state was established when the Jews of Fort Wayne banded together into the Society for Visiting the Sick and Burying the Dead. Years later when they adopted a more formal structure they called themselves the Congregation of Unity and Peace, Achduth Vesholom. Twenty-eight years before the first religious service was held in the home of Frederic Nirdlinger in 1848, a Jew had moved into the stockade at Fort Wayne as the Indian agent. This was John Hays of the New York and Canadian family of that name. Hays, an honest, conscientious man, despised the whiskey-peddling traders who degraded the Indians; he distrusted the Miami chieftain who cheated the very men he was called upon to protect. Hays made a determined effort, not without success, to make farmers out of the Indians. He was proud of their achievements in growing grain and raising milch cows and chickens, and he bragged about the butter which they churned. But after three years of hard labor he resigned in 1823 to go back to his farm in the Illinois Country. He missed his family and the annual visit back home took two solid weeks of travel.

The preamble—in German—of the constitution of the Society for Visiting the Sick and Burying the Dead begins with these solemn words: "We who like so many other immigrants from Europe have come to these fortunate shores in order to find a refuge against European oppression; we who have gone away from our native homes, kinfolk, and everything that was precious and sacred to our youth . . . have bound ourselves hereby to stand by each other in every trouble of life." Frederic Nirdlinger was the first president and the first to sign the new constitution. His daughter Ella married an Alsatian, Charles Naret Nathan; their son was George Jean Nathan, one of America's most sophisticated, clever critics of the drama, editor of the *Smart Set*, and a founder, together with H. L. Mencken, of the *American Mercury*. Two of the Nirdlinger brothers changed their names to Nixon and became theatre magnates. "The Nixon" in bright lights on the marquee certainly looked better, sounded more American, and required fewer electric bulbs than "The Nirdlinger."

Lafayette, like Fort Wayne, on the Wabash & Erie Canal, fashioned its Jewish community in the 1840's. One of the early members was Abraham Kuhn who later joined with his brother-in-law Solomon Loeb and a man named Netter to form a clothing company in Cincinnati. Still later in 1867 Kuhn & Loeb established a banking business in New York City; when Loeb's son-in-law, Jacob H. Schiff, was taken into the firm it soon became a power on Wall Street.

In the 1870's, Jews in Indiana numbered almost 4,000; there were at least 60 towns with Jews, about 15 had a Jewish society or a congregation or even a synagog. The lines of settlement were obvious. Newcomers floated down the Ohio from Cincinnati to Evansville and Mt. Vernon, dropping off or going back to find a home in Lawrenceburg, Madison, Jeffersonville, and New Albany. New Albany, at that time the largest city in the state, had no organized Jewish community; the Jews there were serviced by Louisville across the river. There was another group of Jewish towns in the northwest near Chicago: La Porte, South Bend, and Plymouth. In the northeast, in addition to Fort Wayne, there were Columbia City, Ligonier, Auburn, Goshen, and Elkhart. La Porte in a county bordering on Lake Michigan organized a regional congregation in 1854 drawing members from Michigan City, South Bend, Valparaiso, and even from Plymouth thirty miles distant. One of the founders of the congregation and its volunteer rabbi for many years was the German, Jacob Wile, who had arrived in town in the early 1850's. He opened a bank which helped finance Studebaker Brothers in South Bend and a large company in La Porte which later became part of Allis Chalmers. It was his bank, too, that handled the financial affairs of the University of Notre Dame. Wile's brother Simon was a partner with several other Jews in establishing La Porte's largest industry, the woolen mills. In 1869 Simon Wile sponsored one of the first child labor laws in the country, establishing thereby a legislative pattern that was adopted in other states. Many of the newcomers journeyed up the Wabash, its big canal, and the river's state-encompassing tributaries to Terre Haute, Attica, Lafayette, Delphi, Peru, Washington, Indianapolis the capital, Columbus, and Anderson.[2]

The Gerhard Foremans had settled in Delphi on the Wabash about 1850 and were soon joined by members of the family who then moved on to nearby Frankfort. The two towns were joined by a plank road. Writing back to dear friends in Germany, Foreman compared Frankfort in Indiana with its 500 to 600 inhabitants, with the metropolis Frankfort on the Main, in Europe. The rulers of Frankfort in Germany, he wrote, are a gang of "bloodsuckers . . . counselling with each other how to oppress the poor downtrodden people more and more in order to make dogs and slaves of them." Our Frankfort, in Clinton County, is a "city where one does not have to wait a brief eternity for the right to style oneself a citizen, and where no one enquired: 'Are you a Jew, a Catholic, a Protestant?'"[3]

When John Hays, a sick and tired man of about fifty-three bade an unreluctant farewell to Fort Wayne in 1823 he left for Cahokia on the east bank of the Mississippi, just about five miles south of St. Louis. Cahokia had been his home since 1790, if not earlier. He had come to that part of the country as a Canadian fur trader when the French villages there were the only white settlements in all of present-day Illinois, and he remained there until he died in 1836. Pioneer though he was, Hays was not the first of his tribe in that French enclave. "Dr." Isaac Levy had lived and prospered there as a businessman in the 1770's and 1780's, selling goods to the townfolk, provisioning the Virginia troops, and physicking the inhabitants. He might well be that "worthy little French Jew" who had made his appearance in the Illinois Country in the 1760's although the Monsantos, too, were then trading up the Mississippi. Hays soon became a man of importance in the district for he was literate, sensible, and an English-speaking American even though he was also fluent in French. He continued to barter for furs, sold merchandise, ran a farm and a ranch with the help of black and white indentured servants, served as a militia officer, justice of the peace, and sheriff of Saint Clair County. How Jewish was he? In spite of his Christian wife and family he never affiliated with any church and his descendants still possess the Jewish calendar and the Hebrew prayer book found among his possessions. Uncle Andrew was a pillar of the Montreal synagog.[4]

On his infrequent trips from home to Fort Wayne, Hays could have gone up the Illinois River to the Chicago portage near Lake Michigan before cutting east to his Indian agency on the Maumee. The Chicago area was destined to shelter the fourth largest Jewish settlement in the United States. A few Jews had wandered into the town in the late 1830's, many more in the next decade, for Chicago on Lake Michigan, connected by river and canal with the Mississippi, could tap all the resources of America from the Rockies to the Atlantic Coast. And when the railroads came in the 1850's the city grew from 30,000 in 1850 to a metropolis of over 300,000 when it was swept by the disastrous fire of 1871. Like others the Jews sensed that Chicago had a great future and they started moving there. One man even bought a quarter-section of land near the city and farmed; he may have hummed as he worked:

> Our lands they are broad enough, don't be alarmed
> For Uncle Sam is rich enough to give us all a farm.

Most of his fellow Jews, with their eyes on the city and not on the soil, would have preferred to sing:

> Then move your family westward,
> Good health you will enjoy;
> And rise to wealth and honor
> In the state of El-A-Noy.

In 1845 Chicago Jews held services, created a burial society, and purchased a cemetery. Realizing their "frontier" role the newcomers established a congregation the next year proudly calling themselves the Men of the West, Anshe Maarav, and promptly and improperly pronounced the name Anshe Maariv which meant something entirely different: Men of the Evening Prayer. But then they had never enjoyed formal courses in Hebrew grammar and in English transliteration back home in their Bavarian villages. The organization meeting of the Men of the West took place in Rosenfeld's and Rosenberg's wholesale dry goods establishment. Both men, Levi Rosenfeld and Jacob Rosenberg, married sisters of Michael Reese; when the will of this California adventurer was probated it was found that he had left $200,000 for Jewish charities. The trustees Mr. Rosenberg and Mrs. Rosenfeld used the money to establish the Michael Reese Hospital in Chicago.

Included among the early Jews were Henry Horner, Leopold Mayer, and Henry Greenebaum. Horner, a successful wholesale grocer, was the grandfather of Judge Henry Horner who was twice elected governor of the state in the days of the New Deal. Leopold Mayer, a Hessian who had graduated from a teacher's seminary in Germany, became a Hebrew and German teacher in Chicago before he made his way in real estate and banking. In his memoirs he recalled that there were about 200 Jews in town in 1850, mostly dealing in dry goods, clothing, and tobacco, but he lists also some wagon-peddlers and even a plumber and two carpenters. Mr. Benedict Shubart, a merchant-tailor, had one of the few brick houses in town and lived on the second floor. Most homes were made of wood and had but one or at the most two floors. Nearly everybody kept kosher; people were religiously observant, and if a hazzan added or omitted a prayer during the services there was bound to be a row. In the winter people went sleigh riding; in the summer they hired a carriage and drove around. There were parties and balls, happy days; the dread cholera epidemic of 1848-1849 brought sorrow and tragedy.[5]

When they hit their stride the Chicago Jews became apparel retailers and wholesalers, bankers and politicians. In a way Henry Greenebaum was the classical example of an outstanding Chicago Jew of the mid-nineteenth century. This fifteen-year-old German immigrant had received an excellent education at home including some training in Greek and Latin. After his arrival in Chicago he started out as a hardware clerk and shifted to banking; before he was twenty-one he opened a bank with his brother Elias. Ultimately the Greenebaums opened two banks with millions on deposit, but like thousands of others they went down in the depression of the 1870's. Henry then surrendered his personal fortune to protect the depositors and creditors and turned to life insurance. There was little in the cultural, political, and philanthropic life of Chicago that did not concern him. He helped found Jewish charities and congregations, aided in the rise of B'nai B'rith lodges, organized the Beethoven Society, entertained Adeline Patti in his home, sat as an alderman, and stumped for Stephen Douglas. And let it not be forgotten, he was captain of Engine Company No. 6.[6]

In its growth the Jewish community kept pace with the city of Chicago. By 1876 there were about 10,000 Jews in town. This tremendous increase brought with it new congregations as well as new societies for education, relief, and sociability. Most Jews arriving in the state gravitated to the metropolis on Lake Michigan, but in the quarter of a century to 1876 communities were also founded in Quincy, Peoria, Rock Island, Springfield, and Ottawa. The cement that held the Ottawa Jews together was not a burial association but a Young Men's Hebrew Literary and Educational Society. At least ten smaller cities enjoyed some type of formal organization; among these Quincy had the largest number of settlers, about 500. All told about sixty smaller towns had Jewish populations that ranged anywhere from one to about sixty Jewish inhabitants.

Practically all Jewish towns were in the Illinois River Valley or on the Mississippi. The state capital, Springfield, near the Sangamon, had about 150 Jews, several of whom like the Hammersloughs, clothing merchants, had come to town in the 1850's. Samuel Rosenwald, one of the clerks, married Augusta Hammerslough; their son born in 1862 was Julius Rosenwald, the mail-order magnate of a later generation. That same decade Julius Hammerslough, one of the brothers, moved to New York, the manufacturing and financial Mecca of Jewish merchants, and there founded and served as the first president of the New York Clothiers' Association. A generation earlier, when the Jews still clung to the tidewater, the irrepressible Heinrich Heine had prophesied that a time would come when Jews would chew unleavened bread on the banks of the Mississippi. This was certainly true of the Jews of Quincy who were already settled there in the 1830's. One of the earliest Jewish arrivals was Joseph Jonas's brother Abraham. In the 1820's Abraham crossed the Ohio into Kentucky, opened a store, ran for office,and became a state legislator. An ardent Masonic worker he became a Most Worshipful Grand Master of the state's Masons. By 1838 he had crossed the Ohio once more this time into Illinois, to Quincy, where he repeated the pattern, selling, politicking, and Masoning. He became the first Grand Master of the Illinois Masons and sat in the state legislature where he worked with Abraham Lincoln becoming his closest Jewish friend. Five of Jonas's boys were in the Civil War; four served with the Confederate Army, one, with the Union forces. When Abraham Jonas was dying in 1864, Mrs. Jonas telegraphed Lincoln asking that her son Charles, a Confederate prisoner, be permitted to return home to bid his father farewell. Lincoln immediately sent the following telegram to the War Department:

Allow Charles H. Jonas, now a prisoner of war at Johnson's Island, a parole of three weeks to visit his dying father Abraham Jonas at Quincy.[7]

MICHIGAN JEWRY

When Chicago became the great business center of the Upper Mississippi Valley and of the Great Lakes after 1850, it dashed any hopes that Detroit may have had to outdistance Cleveland to the east and Chicago to the west in the race for commercial supremacy. Detroit was certainly an older Jewish town. In the 1760's Chapman Abrams, a fur trader, had settled down at this important British military post after undergoing a traumatic experience during the French and Indian War. He was captured by the Indians and according to one contemporary account was to be burnt at the stake but escaped by feigning madness. He survived the captivity to become a successful businessman. After his death his young widow married the merchant-shipper, Moses Myers, the first Jewish settler in Norfolk, Virginia. During the Revolution the Gratzes of Pennsylvania helped finance George Rogers Clark in a proposed expedition to capture Detroit, then the most important British post in the West. Nothing happened and the Gratzes never completely recovered the advances they had made to Virginia and to Clark. In the 1790's, an Isaac Moses—there are at least three contemporaries with that name—was a member of a local Masonic lodge.[8]

From the 1760's and on, there was never a time that Detroit was entirely without Jews. But here too, as elsewhere, Jewish immigrants started arriving in appreciable numbers only in the 1840's. These newcomers moved along a line that extended from Bremen and Le Havre to New York City, the Erie Canal and Buffalo to the western end of Lake Erie. By 1850 there were two parallel railroads in Michigan carrying settlers across the state toward Chicago. Moving westward from Monroe, the Michigan Southern passed through Adrian and Coldwater. As this line was being built, Jews followed the tracks, opening little stores wherever opportunity offered. This was a process that continued into the 1870's. North of the Michigan Southern, the Michigan Central, starting at Detroit, passed through Ann Arbor, Ypsilanti, Jackson, Kalamazoo,

and Dowagiac. Although there were Jewish businessmen on the main
streets of all these towns, only Detroit, Jackson, Kalamazoo, and Bay City
survived as organized communities by the eighth decade of the century.
The Monroe, Adrian, Ann Arbor and Ypsilanti Jews, bunched together in
the southeastern corner of the state were attracted to neighboring Detroit.
In the 1850's practically all Jewish settlers lived in the southern half of
Michigan; the northern areas were still wilderness.

The family Freedman opened a shop in Adrian, relocated in Detroit
in 1844 and by the 1860's owned the largest dry goods business in the
state. By that time they were rich. The Jews of Monroe and Adrian were
probably too few to hold services. The Ann Arbor-Ypsilanti sector in the
1840's housed a group of Bohemians, Hungarians, Silesians, and Bavarian
Jews who rallied around the Weil family. The humble Jewish immigrants
of this area were peddlers and shopkeepers, trading with the farmers,
many of whom were Germans. A few of these immigrant village Jews
even tried their hand at farming but usually not for long. The first minyan in Ann Arbor, and indeed the first one known in Michigan, was in
1845; there was a cemetery a few years later but by 1850 many of the
Jews had moved on to Detroit. By 1850 and 1851 Detroit Jewry had a
congregation, a sick-care society, and a burial plot. If Jews deserted the
smaller towns in the southeastern corner of the state and moved into Detroit it was because they saw that the future lay with that city. Its good
harbor, steamboat connections with the lakes, Buffalo, and the Erie
Canal, a Territorial Road, and railroad ties west toward Chicago and
north toward Canada promised much. By 1850 it had far outdistanced all
the other towns in Michigan. Jewish growth picked up speed after the
Civil War: in 1850 there were only a few families there; in 1861 about
150 souls; by the middle 1870's, at least 2,000.[9]

One of the earliest Jewish arrivals in Detroit was Edward Kanter
(1824-1896), a native of Breslau in Silesia. Kanter came from an upper
middle-class family; his father was not a poor man, and his mother was a
Lasker, a member of the family that included Edward Lasker, the distinguished German politician, and the Texas Laskers, one of whom was ultimately to become the head of one of the largest advertising firms in the
United States. Young Kanter wanted to see the world. He went to France,
stowed away on a boat to New Orleans, was stricken with yellow fever,
peddled cigars, clerked on a Red River steamboat, went north to St. Louis,
and finally in 1844 arrived in Detroit, a mature twenty. Once more he
clerked on a steamboat, got a job with the American Fur Company serving it sometimes as an interpreter, for he spoke French and several Indian
dialects. In 1846 he went to work for the Leopold and Austrian clan in
Mackinac and was such a hustler that the Indians called him Bosh-bish-
gay-bish-gensen which meant Fire Cracker. He opened a store of his own

on the island, married a state senator's daughter, moved to Detroit, established a bank, was elected to the state legislature, and became a member of the Democratic National Committee. Yet in spite of his intermarriage he was active in the local synagog. This man was indeed a real firecracker.

In 1846 Kanter had gone to work for the Leopold and Austrian firm. Lewis and Samuel P. Leopold and Julius Austrian had settled in Mackinac in the 1840's. They sold goods to the islanders, traded with the Indians, and packed and shipped large quantities of fish to Cleveland on their own sloop. By the next decade they had a chain of at least five stores in Michigan. On their arrival in the states these two families had Americanized their names: the Austrians had once been Oesterreicher; the Leopolds had once called themselves Freudenthaler. Today Austrian and Leopold are very good Jewish names. In the middle 1840's Mannes Israel settled in Kalamazoo, but there was no organized congregation in town till the 1860's. Mannes Israel's son, Edward, born there in 1859, went to the University at Ann Arbor and at the age of twenty-two joined the Lady Franklin Bay Arctic Expedition under Lieutenant A. W. Greely as astronomer. He rendered important scientific service before he, like others, died of starvation. At the burial, Greely, conscious of the fact that Israel was a Jew omitted the Christological portions of the religious service.[10]

Grand Rapids Jews succeeded in forming an all-purpose society in 1857. Among those who helped establish it was Julius Houseman who had arrived five years earlier in this little town of over 5,000. This young Bavarian was destined to make a name for himself. Arriving in the United States at the age of sixteen he worked as a clerk in various towns of Ohio before he and a partner set up their own clothing business in Battle Creek and Grand Rapids. By then he was twenty. Houseman's success as a clothier and apparel manufacturer in the 1860's and 1870's brought him wealth and recognition; by 1876 he had disposed of his mercantile holdings and turned to lumber, banking, land speculation, furniture, fire insurance, and streetcar transportation. Like many other successful postbellum businessmen he went into politics, becoming in turn an alderman, mayor, state legislator, and finally, in 1883, a United States Congressman.

The Jackson, Michigan, Jews banded together as a congregation in 1859; Bay City and Alpena established communities in the 1870's, by which time there were more than thirty towns in the state sheltering Jews. As the Jews crawled up the shores of Lake Huron and Lake Michigan they planted themselves in the coastal towns and occasionally moved into the interior. A few had reached Saginaw not later than the 1870's. Among them was Jacob Seligman. This native of Frankfort on the Main opened a clothing store in Pontiac in the middle 1860's and then sold out and shifted to Saginaw. Only five feet tall, he exploited his diminutive appearance in an age of bizarre advertising by extolling the bargains to be had from "Little Jake." Seligman prospered as a clothier and a banker but suffered heavily in the crash of the 1890's. He was no shrinking violet that was born to blush unseen. When he erected a large building in Saginaw he adorned it with a life-sized metal statue of himself. As central and northern Michigan began to fill out in the period after the Civil War, Jews moved in along with the others. In remote Hancock, in the Lake Superior country, where the Leopolds and Austrians had once operated a branch, there was a sizeable nucleus of thirty-six people but no formal organization. Of the 3,000 Jews in the state in 1876 about 60 percent lived in Detroit; no other town had more than 217 Jewish inhabitants; most of them had less than twenty-five.[11]

WISCONSIN JEWRY

By the 1850's the Leopolds, Samuel, Henry, and Aaron, and their brother-in-law Julius Austrian had moved westward from Mackinac into Lake Superior and had settled in the Wisconsin island town of La Pointe, not too far from present-day Duluth. They helped also to found the nearby mainland town of Bayfield. Nevertheless the Leopolds and Austrians were not Wisconsin's Jewish pioneers; Jacob Franks of Montreal had bought peltries and traded with the Indians since the early 1790's using Green Bay as his base. The town, the oldest in that part of the country, was strategically located on the water highways linking the Mississippi to the Great Lakes and the eastern tidewater. At first Franks was an agent for a Canadian firm; by 1797 he was on his own. He enjoyed several years of prosperity before the game, the furs, and the Indians began to fade away and before he had to cope with the competition of John Jacob Astor's formidable American Fur Company. Franks was an innovative entrepreneur. Around the turn of the century he built a blacksmith shop, a dam for water power, a saw and grist mill, ran a farm and began a family of Indian children, before he finally went back to Mackinac and then to Montreal where he rejoined his Jewish wife.

Sometime after 1813 when Franks went back east he turned his properties over to his sister's son, John Lawe. His nephew John had come out to Wisconsin as a teenager to help Uncle Jacob when the latter set up his own business and the two men worked closely together. From the vantage points of Mackinac and Montreal, Franks purchased supplies and sold the furs which Lawe gathered together from the agents and the Indians. Franks was a practicing Jew; he was one of the earliest members of the Montreal congregation; Lawe, son of a Christian father, evinced no interest in Judaism though he was known as a Jew. He elected to remain in Wisconsin, married a woman of Indian descent, joined the church, entered politics, became a judge and territorial legislator, and was widely known and respected for his ability. But he made little money in the fur business. In 1846, the very year that Lawe died, Nicholas I of Russia issued a ukase forbidding Jews to wear certain types of furs. That sumptuary prohibition was felt in the distant American forests and trading posts.[12]

As America's immunities and resources brought thousands of Germans to Wisconsin, German-speaking Jews also began arriving in substantial numbers. As late as 1850 most settlers in Wisconsin remained south of a line that ran from Green Bay and the Fox River to the Wisconsin River portage and on to the Mississippi. And it was in this southern Wisconsin zone that Jews, too, planted themselves, though most of them preferred the urban advantages of Milwaukee. Jacob Franks had an agent there in 1804 but there were to be no services, no cemetery or congregation in town until the years 1847-1848.

No two Jewish newcomers were exactly alike, except that most of them worked hard to make a living and to get ahead. When the Heller family came to Milwaukee from Bohemia there were still Indians in town living behind the two-room cabin into which this family of seven had crowded. The Hellers labored hard and gradually prospered and even bought a farm that later found itself within the city limits. Sophia Heller had plenty of friends including the three Pereles boys: Franklin, Madison, and Jefferson. Her parents pulled her out of school at thirteen for she had to help in the family. Married at sixteen, she moved to Chicago, managed to keep her house on three dollars a week and when she was lonely amused herself by playing in the kitchen with the mama cat and the five little kittens. Henry Stern was of a different breed. This Bavarian who came to Milwaukee about the year 1850 had been well educated and arrived in New York City with $800 in his pockets. He had no trouble getting a good job in Boston but left town because his boss housed him in a dirty room. Though there was no financial need to do so he peddled among New York and New Jersey farmers in order to learn English. Stern was eager to start his own import business and to go to California but papa back home forbade it. After a short stay in New Orleans he moved north to Milwaukee, found a partner, and began selling dry goods, mirrors, and clocks. When business was slow he loaded a wagon and peddled in the backcountry. Papa helped finance him at 12 percent a year—the usual rate—and when he married made him a gift of the loan. By 1852 Stern had a capital of $2,600; ten years later, before the War had gotten into full swing he was worth $70,000. He had purchased a huge inventory and it had soared in price. "Who is wise? He who foresees the future."[13]

Madison had a Jewish congregation in 1866 and its own cemetery in 1859; La Crosse, the only Wisconsin Jewish community on the banks of the Mississippi was organized in 1857. The Jews of La Crosse established a social welfare and burial society which conducted services and purchased a cemetery. The mayor and another distinguished citizen of this city were prepared to make a very substantial gift if the Jews would also build a synagog but the Jews were hesitant; ten years later they did erect a house of worship. Why would Mayor E. D. Campbell and Colonel C. A. Stevens offer $500 if the Jews would erect a house of worship? A synagog would attract other Jews to La Crosse and Jews bring business. John Meyer Levy was one of the founders of La Crosse and of its Jewish community. His father was a London hazzan who seems to have given him something of a Jewish education. After living in Amsterdam and Paris he came to St. Louis in 1837 and married a German Christian girl. They moved north to Prairie du Chien in 1845 and then cut their way through the woods to La Crosse. The Levys were the fifth white family in town. He became an Indian trader but here too, as with Frank and Lawe a generation earlier, when the Indians left or were driven out, the fur trader was through. Levy worked hard trying unsuccessfully to keep the Indians in Wisconsin; the chiefs powwowed in his home upsetting his German wife who wanted to kill them because they spat on her immaculate floor. Levy nibbled at everything: he was a merchant, hotelkeeper, an unsuccessful banker. His first trading shack was on the river's edge; supplies in summer came up on the steamer; in winter by sleigh. He built a dock, a wharf boat, served as alderman and mayor of the town, helped conduct Jewish services, joined the B'nai B'rith, taught in the Jewish Sunday School, and died impoverished—buried by a Universalist minister probably because there was no Jew in town who could do the job.[14]

Appleton, a lively manufacturing town on the Fox River, had a cemetery, congregation, B'nai B'rith lodge, and a ladies aid society in the 1870's. The acting rabbi was the Hungarian Mayer Samuel Weiss. His son Ehrich, born in Appleton, became America's most famous "escape artist," calling himself Harry Houdini. He ran away from home at the age of twelve and studied magic, worked in sideshows, circuses, and vaudeville theatres, and gradually emerged as a master magician. There were no locks, no chains, no safes, no containers that could hold him. In Moscow, Russia, he escaped from a prison van; in Detroit, Michigan, he leaped from a bridge, handcuffed, into the icy waters of the river and emerged unshackled. After his death, his excellent library on magic and spiritualism was given to the Library of Congress.

As late as the middle 1870's there were only four organized Jewish communities in all of Wisconsin. North Wisconsin was still forest, scrubland, and aftergrowth. About the year 1870 Mr. L. S. Cohen took his friend Joseph I. Levy for a ride behind a beautiful matched pair of roans. Cohen was a logger, lumberman, drover, rancher who used to drive his cattle hundreds of miles north to Lake Superior whence they were shipped to the stockyards. As they drove by some of Cohen's cutover lands he offered Levy a thousand acres if he would only pay for the recording of the deed. Cohen was accustomed to let the denuded acres revert to the county for unpaid taxes. Levy refused the offer; it was not worth the fee for the trouble. Years later that particular parcel was occupied by the city of Rhinelander. In 1876 about 80 percent of Wisconsin Jewry—then numbering about 2,600—lived in Milwaukee; the total number in all the other towns was about 500; most places had fewer than 25 Jewish settlers.[15]

IOWA JEWRY

Part of Wisconsin Territory in 1836 was the present state of Iowa. When "Rabbis" Jacques J. Lyons and Abraham De Sola published their *Jewish Calendar for Fifty Years* in 1854 there was no mention of an Iowa Jewish community. Much of the transmississippi West was still frontier in that decade and only the eastern section of Iowa along the Mississippi and for about 100 miles inland had a population of more than six people per square mile. Individual Jews had crossed into Iowa as early as the 1830's and 1840's; most of them had probably come up the river from St. Louis. By the 1850's a number of Jews had settled down and begun to do business in the Mississippi River towns of Keokuk, Fort Madison, Burlington, Muscatine, Davenport, Clinton, Dubuque, and McGregor hoping to remain there permanently.[16]

The first Jew to fix his residence in the Iowa area was a young Frenchman by the name of Alexander Levi who came directly from France in 1833 and settled in Dubuque. He started out selling groceries and provisions, then went into dry goods, and finally turned to lead mining. Levi, a pioneer and successful merchant, became one of the leading businessmen in the city. When in 1837 he went down to St. Louis to become a citizen it would seem that he was the first foreigner in the territory to be naturalized. He was elected to serve as a justice of the peace and contributed to the support of a local Presbyterian and a Catholic church. Two ministers complained to Levi about "tricky" Jews when a local Jewish businessman, who had become a Christian, was arrested as a fraudulent bankrupt. Levi pointed out very quietly that as long as this man had remained a Jew he was highly respected; he had been accepted into the finest social circles and had married into one of the best Christian families. The evil he committed occurred only after he had become a church member. No longer a Jew he was no longer responsible for his actions as a Jew. Respect the Jews who remain Jewish! In the early 1850's Levi gave a cemetery to the Jews who had followed him into the city; by 1854 services were held, and four years later there was a congregation in town.[17]

Keokuk is the first town of any size on the Mississippi north of Missouri. It also lay at the head of navigation because of the Lower Rapids and is at the mouth of the Des Moines River which leads to one of the fertile valleys of the state. By 1855 when the Jews began to gather in Keokuk in large numbers it was already a city of at least 5,000 people. It is said that there were dozens of Jewish families there and for a very brief period this Jewish community may even have outnumbered that of Chicago. The town was a jumping-off spot for the West; Jewish peddlers in large numbers made it their bridgehead. Local Jewish jobbers, in daily touch with St. Louis downstream, outfitted the peddlers and sent them trudging all over the state. By the spring of 1855 Keokuk Jewry had a burial mutual-aid society, the Benevolent Children of Jerusalem, and later, a congregation, the Children of Israel, B'nai Israel, but the panic of 1857 and the War of 1861 dealt the town severe blows. The initial depression caused by the War was overcome in 1863; the moribund congregation was revived and a Ladies Benevolent Society made its appearance. It, too, was a mutual-aid burial association, primarily for the women, and although a contemporary described it as only a kaffeeklatsch it gave an annual ball and raised money to help build the synagog in 1877. The ball was an important social event; the local Christians looked forward to it and attended it in numbers. The synagog dedication was also quite an affair. The Reverend Dr. Max Lilienthal of Cincinnati, a notability, was imported for the consecration address and did full justice to the occasion. Judaism, he assured the Jews and the Gentiles present, is in full accord with truth, justice, and liberty and in harmony with the spirit of Christianity. The fundamental principles of Judaism are: belief in one God, immortality of the soul, a future life in which all good men and women will participate, and a wholehearted acceptance of the biblical command: "Love thy fellowman as thyself" (Lev.19:18). To judge from this ecumenical discourse Lilienthal was not only a Jew but a latter-day Deist.[18]

In the 1850's and 1860's Dubuque, Burlington, and Davenport Jews held services sporadically and began organizing communities. Davenport had a cemetery and a Young Men's Hebrew Literary Association in the 1850's, and a congregation in the 1860's. One of the first Jews in this town was a Viennese by the name of Samuel Hirschl, apparently an 1848 émigré who left Austria for political reasons. He went into the grocery and provisions business, wholesale and retail, made a fortune, and by the 1870's had returned permanently to Vienna. Some of his sons were left behind to look after his interests; one of them went to Harvard. Henry Deutsch, a Hungarian came to Davenport after the Civil War, sold notions and clothing, and established one of the first coat and suit factories west of Chicago. Wherever there is commerce and trade there is also litigation and not infrequently fraud and chicanery. The Davenport newspaper for the year 1866 reported the arrest of a crooked Jewish horse trader and the story of two Jews who were accused of cheating a German countryman out of $350. The following year the congregation employed a very attractive young man as its rabbi. His name was Cohen. In spite of his youth—he was in his early twenties—he had traveled all over the world and spoke nine languages—or so he said. The children in the religious school loved him. On the Jewish New Year he made a collection for the synagog and the school and then took the next eastbound train, decamping with the collection and a beautiful broadcloth suit for which he had never paid.[19]

Although Burlington Jewry owned a cemetery in the 1850's it was not fated to found a congregation until the early 1870's. By that decade the Jewish businessmen were moving up the Mississippi River tributaries into the interior, to Des Moines, Oskaloosa, Webster City, Iowa City, Cedar Rapids, Waterloo, and Mason City. Des Moines already had a well established congregation in 1873 for that was the year it sent a gift to help relieve the yellow fever victims in Memphis. By that time Jews had been living in town for decades. William Kraus had located himself there in 1846 when it was a hamlet known as Raccoon Forks; two years later he opened the first store in the village. Other Jews followed him. In 1857, J. and I. Kuhn, selling dry goods and clothing, were soliciting patronage from peddlers and country merchants. Like most city retailers they were always ready to do a little wholesaling. A census of the Des Moines Jews for 1866-1867 enumerated three married couples and about fifteen single men. Most of the latter were either clerks or peddlers, eager to traffic with the farmers, homesteaders, and adventurers headed for the mines in Colorado and Idaho. The first wedding in the Des Moines synagog took place in 1874. The groom was dressed in black and wore a white vest and gloves. The bride glowed under an immense bridal veil that reached from crown to sole. A number of Christian friends were invited, and inasmuch as Mr. Frank Maloney catered the meal, the food could hardly have been kosher. The presents, some from distant Pennsylvania and New York, were listed in a detailed newspaper account and included a pair of spittoons and a china chamber pot set.[20]

The nationwide Jewish census for the 1870's listed more than forty Jewish settlements in Iowa; two had over 200 people; two had over 100; almost all the others had fewer than 50 Jews; most, less than 20. Altogether Iowa sheltered some 1,200 Jews. Two of the Jewish towns were on the western border, on the Missouri River: Council Bluffs and Sioux City. The Jews of Council Bluffs were in no hurry to establish a community of their own; they could always cross the river to Omaha and join the Nebraskans for the High Holy Days. The first Jew to remain in Sioux City arrived about the year 1857/1858. This was a Hessian from Darmstadt by the name of Godfrey Hattenbach. In the 1840's other Jews found their way into the town, among them E. R. Kirk who announced to the world that "old Kirk has just returned from Jerusalem with the largest stock of clothes and dry goods ever imported from the country." He ran this ad in 1869 the very year that Hattenbach gave the budding community a burial plot. The cemetery association that came into being that year seems to have been the only Jewish organization in town till 1884 when a Jewish Ladies Aid Society was founded to help the necessitous and to raise money for a synagog. There were about fifty Jews, men, women, and children in town in 1876, but they did very little, apparently, to create a religious community.

In the 1890's Unitarians established a church in Sioux City which many Jews joined either as enrolled or contributing members. Sigmund Schulein accepted an appointment on the Board of Trustees of the church. The Unitarian clergyman married and buried the Sioux City Jews, and some of the women joined the church's sisterhood. In the middle 1890's the Jewish Ladies Aid set out vigorously to raise money for a temple, holding a fair and serving oysters, a favorite delicacy in that generation. In all likelihood the Jewish old-timers were prompted to leave the church by the arrival of Orthodox East Europeans who shamed them into taking action. A Reform Jewish congregation was finally established in 1898 with the aid of those erstwhile Unitarians who had never given up their Judaism. The new organization called itself Mount Sinai Congregation (Temple). Patterned in name and philosophy after the radical Chicago Sinai of the left-wing Emil G. Hirsch, it held services on Sunday and did not read the weekly pentateuchal portion from the Sefer Torah. There is no evidence that it even owned a Scroll. One of the founders of the new temple was the son-in-law of Godfrey Hattenbach, D. A. Magee. He had fallen in love with Hattenbach's only daughter Ada and in order to win her made his way to Cincinnati where he was instructed and converted. In the 1880's Magee, a pillar of the meat-packing industry, was elected mayor of the city.[21]

MINNESOTA JEWRY

Before Minnesota became a territory in 1849 it was for a time part of Wisconsin and Iowa territories. In Minnesota as in most states there was a wave of Jewish pioneers who came early, often a decade or more before some form of Jewish institutional life made its appearance. Jewish fur traders roamed in the territory from the 1840's on, bartering with the Indians on the rivers and on the reservations. They were among the first white settlers in Minnesota. Julius Austrian had a trading post in Minnesota in the 1840's and he may once have owned the land on which Duluth now stands. In 1851 in the dead of winter he drove a dog sled team loaded with hundreds of pounds of supplies into St. Paul; his arrival created a sensation. Isaac Marks, John Levi's partner at La Crosse, was another early Jew in Minnesota. He had moved westward across the Mississippi with the Winnebago Indians in 1848 when they were driven out of Wisconsin and continued as an Indian trader in central and southern Minnesota until he finally settled down in 1856 in Mankato where he remained till his death. When Marks married a German girl in 1862 every man at the wedding appeared heavily armed: it was not a "shotgun marriage" but it was the year of the Sioux Uprising.[22]

By 1856 Mount Zion Hebrew Association was organized in Saint Paul to hold services, provide for the needy, and bury the dead. A rival congregation was speedily set up; there were disagreements over rituals; Bavarians and West Germans were pitted against Polish East Germans, and intermarriage with Christians speedily became an issue, but by 1871 communal peace was restored and Mt. Zion survived as the only congregation in town. One of the pillars of the early Jewish community in St. Paul was Joseph Ullmann, a well educated young man who landed in the United States in 1852 and worked his way north by way of New Orleans, Louisville, New Albany, and St. Louis. His business in the Missouri metropolis was the sale of liquor. By 1854 he was at St. Paul at the head of Mississippi River navigation prepared to take advantage of the western and Canadian fur trade, the increasing production of wheat, and the heavy steamboat traffic down the river to the Gulf. Minnesota was booming; the population grew from 6,000 settlers in 1850 to 35,000 in 1854, and 150,000 in 1857. There were bad times too: the panic of 1857 was a major disaster, and the Indians went on the war path during the Civil War. But in spite of everything the city and the state prospered and the Jews prospered with them. Ullmann switched from liquor and groceries to furs and within two years was doing a business in the hundreds of thousands of dollars. By 1900 with headquarters in Germany and offices all the way from Chicago to Shanghai he was one of the world's largest fur and hide dealers. Both Ullmann and Austrian, too, were active members and supporters of the St. Paul congregation.

One of Ullmann's clerks, for a time at least, was a man named Isidor Rose, and when Ullmann moved on to Chicago in the middle 1860's Rose was appointed as his resident manager. Earlier, during the 1850's and 1860's when Rose was on his own, he was a liquor and cigar merchant; he moved into the fur business only when he found it necessary to accept skins in payment for goods sold. Specie was scarce. Rose was a clever merchant: when the snows were high he kept the road between his store and the saloon most heavily patronized by the fur traders clear. His children and their descendants carried on the fur trade in St. Paul well into the twentieth century. Neighboring Minneapolis developed much later than St. Paul as a Jewish community. The German and Bohemian Jews who came to that town of less than 10,000 after the Civil War serviced the lumbermen and the flour mill workers. It was not until 1876, twenty years after St. Paul's Hebrew Association had come into being that the Montefiore Burial Association and another welfare society were fashioned. By then Minneapolis was already a very large city. When the Minneapolis Burial Association was set up there were about 225 Jews in St. Paul, about 175 in Minneapolis, and fewer than 500 in the entire state.

Jews, both native-born and immigrant, were very slow to cross the Mississippi into the territories and states. They remained east where there were numbers, culture, and institutions, where there was an opportunity to lead a full Jewish life. The Austrian family who had ridden the western wave from Mackinac to St. Paul in the course of twenty-five years was not typical of the Jewish masses. If we except eastern Missouri, Louisiana, Texas, and Pacific Coast Jewry, the total Jewish population of all the other states and territories from the Mississippi to the Sierras added up to 6,000 out of a gross total of 230,000 Jews. Adventurous Jewish individuals were among the earliest pioneers of the transmississippi West, but the Jewish masses clung to the East and the metropolitan centers in other areas. By 1870 the German Jewish emigration had run out of steam; the East European mass emigration was just beginning.[23]

THE PRAIRIE STATES: THE MISSOURI RIVER SPRINGBOARD STRIP

KANSAS JEWRY

Jewish traders and entrepreneurs had moved into the second tier of transmississippi territories no later than the 1840's. By the 1850's many more of these pioneers, mostly Europeans, had gone up the Missouri River and had begun to lay the foundations for future Jewish communities in west Iowa, west Missouri, and in the Kansas and Nebraska territories. These men came west to do business with the settlers and with those emigrants who stopped in the Missouri River towns to outfit themselves before crossing the Great American Desert. The caravans of traders and home-seekers which had started to move across the Great Plains toward Santa Fe, Oregon, and California in the 1840's became an almost endless stream after gold was discovered in California in 1848. During the next three decades thousands were drawn to take advantage of the gold and silver strikes in Oregon, Colorado, Montana, Idaho, and the Black Hills of South Dakota. Though most of the trekkers started their western odyssey from the Missouri River towns which stretched from Omaha to Westport Landing (Kansas City), others moved west and south from the Fort

Smith-Van Buren sector in Arkansas. By the early 1870's men headed for the Black Hills could buy what they needed in Sioux City.

It was the Kansas and Nebraska Act of 1854 that brought large numbers of settlers into the new territories. Based on the principle of popular sovereignty the Act had declared that the people, the voters, would determine whether the new territories were to be slave or free. Proslavery and antislavery men, sobersides and ruffians, idealists, corrupt politicians, and speculators streamed in by the thousands, prepared if necessary to fight to attain their ends. Among those who came to fight, vote, settle, and to get ahead was a twenty-two-year-old Viennese by the name of August Bondi. He crossed into Kansas from Westport on May 2, 1855, traveling light; two four-inch Colts constituted his baggage.

At the age of fourteen Bondi had fought in the Academic Legion in Vienna hoping to establish a German republic. The family left Austria in 1848 for St. Louis during the counterrevolutionary reaction. Young Bondi was not an abolitionist but he speedily became antislavery. Primarily he was a boy seeking adventure; he just missed going on the Lopez-Crittenden filibustering expedition to Cuba. He was lucky for fifty of those "pirates" were caught and executed. He failed to go with Admiral Perry to Japan but did the next best thing: he became a Kansas Free-Soiler. In his seventy-four years he was to play many roles—barkeeper, grocery clerk, farmer, police judge, printer, tanner, storekeeper, Civil War cavalry top-sergeant, schoolteacher, lawyer, politician, postmaster, real estate and insurance salesman, and Kansas guerrilla. He was a guerrilla but he was also an idealist, a man of integrity, an opponent of bigotry and tyranny. He was interested in Jews and Judaism, though probably unaware of the fact that he was descended from a long line of Bondis who were talmudic scholars and that one of his ancestors was Jonathan Eybeschuetz, one of the most notable rabbis of the eighteenth century.

Bondi settled in eastern Kansas where he and a group of Jews hoped to farm on a large scale and to establish a trading company to take advantage of the commercial opportunities of the growing territory. Leaving a partner behind in St. Louis as a resident buyer, he and two others, Jacob Benjamin and Theodor Wiener (Weiner) established a store at a crossroads then called Weinersville. It was here in 1856 that Bondi and his partners joined up with John Brown in the Bleeding Kansas prelude to the Civil War. Wiener, a tough 250-pound Pole who had come up from Texas and Louisiana, had been with John Brown in May when Brown and his family murdered the proslavery men in the Pottawatomie Creek country in retaliation for the sack of Lawrence. Bondi and Benjamin fought at Osawatomie when the Jayhawkers under Brown battled against an overwhelming number of "Border Ruffians." That was on August 30, about two months after Bondi and Wiener had crawled up the side of a hill during the successful attack at Black Jack, carrying on a whispered conversation in Hebrew and Yiddish until fear of Old Man Brown silenced them. In 1884 Bondi wrote his memoirs; many years later he showed them to the Reform rabbi of Kansas City. Because of their Rabelaisian asides the rabbi asked him to clean up the text. What a pity.[24]

After the Civil War Bondi settled in Salina and later ran unsuccessfully for the lieutenant governorship. At that time, the middle 1870's, there were twenty some towns and villages in the state with Jews. Only two, apparently, had congregations; others had cemeteries. Almost all the Jews in Kansas lived in the eastern part of the state on the Missouri and in other river towns. More than half of the 800 Jews in the state lived in Leavenworth, the most important city in Kansas for a generation. It was a base for military expeditions into the southwest, a very important military and civilian supply and freighting center for the plains area, and a jumping-off point for the entire western territory. With the coming of the railroads in the 1860's Leavenworth continued to prosper. Services in town were held in the 1850's, and by 1859 the local Jews had purchased a burial ground and established Congregation B'nai Jeshurun. Despite the fact that the congregation numbered only forty-seven members, there were two feuding liturgical groups which compromised by holding separate services on the Sabbath. The Orthodox worshipped early in the morning and when they were finished the Reformers took over.

There were ninety Jews in Atchison; forty-five were members in a Civil War congregation which had adopted the same name as the neighboring Leavenworth community. Of the twenty other Jewish settlements, sixteen could not number twenty men, women, and children. Fort Scott, a Missouri River town like Atchison and Leavenworth, had eighty-six Jews but no communal organization; in 1863 Eudora advertised for a shohet and hazzan but insisted on a young candidate; it could not or would not support a married man. Kansas City, Kansas, was not even listed in the 1876 census; obviously its Jews worshipped with the Kansas City, Missouri, congregation just across the state line. In 1859 Lipman Meyer of Kansas City, Kansas, had a four-story building—albeit incomplete—where the constitutional convention met two years before the state was admitted into the Union.

Wichita, on the Chisholm cattle trail from Texas, was the most important town in southern Kansas. Hundreds of thousands of heads of cattle were driven through the area in the late 1860's and early 1870's at a time when Maurice W. Levy was one of the pioneer builders of the city. Still a young man in his twenties, Levy, an Alsatian, arrived in Wichita after the Civil War when it was not much more than an Indian trading post. He came via San Francisco where he had received a good education and had studied law. Unlike most of his Jewish contemporaries who stuck to dry goods and men's clothing he managed to become a banker and rail-road enterpriser, allying himself with Jay Gould and helping to build the Wichita and Western Railroad. In 1893 he was elected as first president of the Kansas Bankers' Association. A clever and able politician, Levy served as the chairman of the Republican State Central Committee for fourteen years, and like many other bankers and railroad speculators, he moved on to New York where he lived to his death in 1932.[25]

WEST MISSOURI JEWRY

August Bondi set out for Kansas in 1855 from St. Louis which was al-ready a very important Jewish community. By the middle 1870's it in-cluded over 80 percent of all the Jews in Missouri. The Jewish census of 1876 lists about twenty-five small towns in eastern and central Missouri, few of which sheltered as many as fifty Jewish settlers. Some of those towns may have had Jewish cemeteries, although it is probable that most of them shipped their dead down the Missouri River to St. Louis. Chilli-cothe on the Hannibal & St. Joe Railroad which linked the Mississippi and the Missouri Rivers was an exception. All told there were only forty-eight Jews in this town but they had their own charity and burial society. Among the forty-eight was a twenty-three-year-old merchant, a member of the clothing firm of Walbrun & Alexander. Thirty-nine years later this German immigrant, Moses Alexander, was to become the first Jew to serve as a governor of an American state. Tucked away in the extreme southwestern corner of Missouri was Joplin bordering on Kansas and In-dian Territory. It was a brand new town, yet it had more Jews than Chil-licothe and was growing rapidly, for it was the center of the American lead and zinc industry. There is no evidence that its Jewish newcomers had begun to organize themselves by 1876.

Chillicothe was just about seventy miles east of St. Joseph, which in 1859 had become a terminus of the Hannibal & St. Joe Railroad and was the only Missouri River town in the state to have railroad connections with the East. It was the second largest Jewish community in Missouri. Jews had settled there in relatively large numbers in the 1850's, for it was the starting point for transcontinental emigrants moving on to Denver and the Pacific Coast. The glamorous Pony Express started across the plains from St. Joseph and it was served by the lively steamboat traffic up and down the Missouri. There must have been about 200 Jews in town in 1860; in 1876 there were at least 325. They had a cemetery in 1858 and a congregation about the year 1860 which called itself The Community of Joseph, Adath Joseph, named in this instance not after Saint Joseph the husband of the Virgin Mary, but after the biblical patriarch Joseph. By the middle of the 1860's there was a B'nai B'rith lodge in town, the only one between St. Louis and Virginia City, Nevada.[26]

Bunched together in the northwestern corner of Missouri and the northeastern corner of Kansas were seven towns all rivals in the transcontinental trade and all hoping to become the new Queen City of the West. By the 1860's St. Joseph was the largest of the seven. Down the river in Kansas lay Leavenworth, and across on the Missouri side twenty miles below St. Joseph lay Weston. Still farther south lay Liberty, Independence, Westport Landing, and Westport. Weston was one of the first of these towns to attract the attention of Jewish businessmen. Jews were there in the 1840's; they profited from the town's prosperity in the 1850's when the emigrants started streaming west. When a disastrous fire drove some of the Jews out, they moved across the river to Leavenworth. A Jewish merchant who had planted himself in nearby Liberty in 1852 became one of its wealthiest citizens, and the townspeople so admired and respected him that they elected and reelected him as their mayor. Independence, south of Liberty, was one of the most important western supply and outfitting towns and speedily attracted Jewish merchants. It would seem, however, that by the middle 1870's they had completely identified themselves with the neighboring Jewish community of Kansas City, for there is no record of any Jews living in the town. Abraham Watters was there in 1847. This Prussian-born Jew had emigrated to England, picked up a good Anglo-Saxon name, moved on to Georgia in 1837, and turned up a decade later in Independence. He had come up the Missouri River from St. Louis. Two years later this Argonaut was in San Francisco where in the fall of 1849 he met in a tent with nine others and helped create the first Jewish congregation on the Pacific Coast. A few miles southwest of Independence below the Missouri and Kansas Rivers, lay Westport which had high hopes during the 1840's and '50's of becoming the outstanding commercial community of this Missouri jumping-off strip. Those hopes were never realized. Two miles west of Westport, at the junction of the two rivers, lay the village of Kanza or as it was derisively called, Westport Landing. This was the Missouri River city of the future. It is the present-day Kansas City.

Cahn & Block set up a general store in Westport Landing in 1839-1840 at a time when the village was little more than a trading post. By the 1850's the town, Kansas City, had started to grow; there were about a thousand people there in 1853 and Jews from the neighboring villages began to move in to provision and clothe the emigrants who were passing through in increasing numbers. Land near the city had already skyrocketed to a price of $250 an acre. The typical basic "Benevolent" society was established in 1865 with membership dues of fifty cents a month. The cemetery was purchased a year later, a lodge was established in 1868, and a congregation, the Sons of Judah, B'nai Jehudah, was organized in 1870. At that time Kansas City was already a metropolis: by the end of the Civil

War the population had soared to 3,500; five years later it was 32,000. It had become a great commercial emporium because of its enterprise, its railroads, its meat-packing establishments; it was a very important supply center for all the states and territories west to the Rockies.

The first president of the congregation, Benjamin A. Feineman, owned the largest liquor business in town. He had come down from St. Joseph where he had been president of the synagog and the lodge. While in St. Joseph he had unsuccessfully courted an attractive young widow who had been left with four girls. He went back in 1870 and married her seventeen-year-old daughter and after the honeymoon the mother and the three other sisters moved in on him. In 1871 during Feineman's presidency, the Hebrew Ladies Relief Society gave a ball and raised a goodly sum for the congregation, but when the ladies heard of the fire in Chicago they sent the money there instead to help relieve the misery of the 100,000 inhabitants who had lost their homes. Feineman was succeeded as president by Louis Hammerslough. Feineman was a Bavarian; Hammerslough was a Hannoverian who had left for Baltimore in 1854 to join his three older brothers who were clothing manufacturers. After two years of apprenticeship with them he was sent to Springfield, Illinois, where he and brother Julius opened a retail outlet. In 1858 Louis moved on to Kansas City and opened still another branch during the Civil War supplying uniforms to the Illinois state militia. By the late 1860's Hammerslough stood out as the most successful clothier in Kansas City. If Kansas City was to grow it needed railroads and it was Hammerslough's financing which made it possible for the Missouri Pacific to lay its tracks into his city. The first locomotive to arrive was called the "Louis Hammerslough." The next quarter- century were years of ups and downs: he speculated heavily and unsuccessfully in railroads, turned to real estate, ran a large but unsuccessful daily newspaper, and once more went in and out of the clothing business; nevertheless this "King Clothier" always found time to engage in civic causes and to help the local Jewish community. It was he who in 1870 gave the congregation its rather unusual name, the Sons of Judah.[27]

NEBRASKA JEWRY

It is easy to romanticize, uncritically, German Jewish businessmen like Hammerslough, but there can be no doubt that many of them were entrepreneurs of exceptional energy, imagination, courage, and ability. A common characteristic of these pioneer Jewish westerners, one that they shared with the Gentiles, was their physical mobility. Many of them took seriously the divine promise: "Thou shalt spread abroad to the west and to the east, and to the north and to the south" (Gen.28:14). Jewish businessmen like Feineman and Hammerslough moved about not because they had an itch to travel but because they sought to improve their lot. Hammerslough who had pulled up stakes in Hannover and ended in Kansas City believed that the grass was greener on the other side of the fence. Lewis Wessel went up the Missouri from St. Louis to Nebraska City in May, 1855, and opened a small general store; it was to become the oldest department store in the state. When buying their yard goods the farmers' wives wanted Mrs. Sarah to wait on them; her husband Lewis was a good buyer, but apparently a poor salesman. In 1856 Dr. Carl Ernst Louis Goldring went north on the river from Leavenworth to Plattsmouth where he practiced medicine and traded with the Indians. That same year Aaron Cahn and Meyer Hellman opened a store in Omaha which clothed many an emigrant about to start the long trek cross the westerly wastes. As business improved they ordered a prefabricated building in Cincinnati and shipped it on to Omaha where it was put together. It was not long before their store was the largest in the territory.

Why did the Jews come to Nebraska? For the same reason that they settled in Kansas or in western Missouri. Ever since 1849 people were passing through by the thousands to take advantage of the mining strikes farther west; many remained. Others came to buy cheap lands or, after the passage of the Homestead Act of 1862, preempted homesteads in the territory. Wherever people settled the Jewish storekeepers were also present. These petty businessmen with their small stocks began trickling into the Nebraska backcountry in the 1860's and 1870's. Not too many came; as late as the 1880's the western half of Nebraska was without farmers or towns. The Indians were still an ever-present danger. Harris L. Levi arrived in Plattsmouth just about the same time as Dr. Goldring, married the daughter of a German Christian farmer, and started peddling among the Indians. In 1869 he homesteaded on Cedar Creek and, eager to make an extra dollar, joined a surveying party massacred by the Indians.[28]

The first Jewish merchants remained in the Missouri River towns of Nebraska City, Plattsmouth, and Omaha; some who came after followed the Platte or its tributaries into the interior. Though individuals did move west with the Union Pacific, practically all the Jewish settlements were in the east and southwest, in Norfolk and in West Point on the Elkhorn, in Fremont, Columbus, Grand Island, and Hastings on or near the Platte. This seems like an impressive penetration of the interior; these modest merchants did a good job of supplying the homesteaders with wares and provisions. Yet as late as 1876 there were not 300 Jews in all Nebraska; not one Jew is recorded in the state capital, Lincoln. Another town no longer on the map, had one: he was the postmaster and probably the town merchant. Crete, southwest of Lincoln, had eight Jews; Nebraska's largest Jewish community had sixty-six men, women, and children—it was easy to count them. This large Jewish community was Omaha, the only one with a burial society, a cemetery, and a religious factotum who taught the children and slaughtered the cattle. The first services were held about the year 1868; the society came into being in 1872 and was followed two years later by a formally organized congregation.

In 1876 this congregation, B'nai Israel, had twenty members; some of them were interesting personalities; one of them was outstanding: this was Edward Rosewater. His parents, Bohemian immigrants whose culture was Czech rather than German, brought him and a host of other children to Cleveland in 1854. Although only thirteen he was sent out to peddle, for the family was very poor. He studied telegraphy, became an accomplished technician, and early in the Civil War joined the United States Military Telegraph Corps, working with the army in the field, frequently under enemy fire. Sometime in 1862 he was transferred to the War Department office in Washington where in 1863, according to a common report, he tapped out the Emancipation Proclamation. That same year he left the corps to work for the Pacific Telegraph Company at its Omaha terminus. He supplemented his income by serving as telegraph correspondent for some eastern dailies and as an agent for the Associated Press.

In 1871 Rosewater was elected to the state legislature where he fought for a public school system. In order to reach the people—a necessity for a politician—he established a small tabloid newspaper of his own. This tiny giveaway, *Punchinello*, grew into the Omaha *Evening Bee*, one of the great newspapers of the country. The very year the *Bee* went to press Rosewater published also a Bohemian and a German newspaper, Nebraska's first two foreign language gazettes. Although a Republican, and a National Committeeman, Rosewater was a maverick, a man of independent mind and moral integrity who fought crooks and monopolists. He did not hesitate to break with the party when he deemed its choice unworthy or the Democrat a better man. As a fighter for the rights of the common people, for public education, libraries, and government ownership of the telegraph, Rosewater was in the best Populist tradition. Attacking the all-powerful railroads cost him the election to the United States Senate. His enemies hired thugs who almost beat him to death; he horsewhipped an editor who slandered his family, and when his opponents burnt his presses he built a multi-story million-dollar fireproof building to house one of the finest printing plants in the United States. In 1897 he presided at some of the sessions of the Universal Postal Congress in McKinley's Washington, for, apparently, he was the only American delegate who could speak French.[29]

Rosewater and his wife were interested in the young Jewish community and were among the founders of the local Jewish hospital. Together with Julius Meyer he brought Adeline Patti to Omaha for a concert which grossed $9,000, a huge sum in those days. Meyer was one of four brothers who came from Bromberg in Posen. Three of them landed in the United States shortly after Lee had surrendered at Appomattox Courthouse; Julius, the fourth, arrived in January, 1866. Rosewater and the Meyer brothers, Max and Julius in particular, were in the next two decades to become leaders in the civic and cultural life of early Omaha and builders of the Jewish community. It would seem that originally Max Meyer sold jewelry and music instruments. Under his leadership the company expanded into a wholesale concern that ultimately—as it was said— did a business of about $1,000,000 a year. Max was one of the founders of the Commercial Club, a predecessor of the Chamber of Commerce. He helped stage an exhibit of the Western Art Association and, together with another Jewish entrepreneur, opened the first opera house in town. Experiencing business reverses, Max left Omaha and turned to New York.

Julius was the most colorful of the four brothers. He started his career as an Indian peddler-trader bartering cheap jewelry, trinkets, and tobacco from the family store for furs, moccasins, and wampum pouches. Because he was clever, intelligent, honorable, and quick at picking up Indian dialects, the Indians accepted him as one of their own and called him "Curly-Haired-White Chief with One Tongue." Ever the showman, he exhibited a group of Indians at the Paris Centennial Exhibition of 1889 never realizing that in this enterprise he was no pioneer. In the mid-eighteenth century, after the French and Indian War, Hyam Myers of New York paraded a group of Mohawks in the taverns of London and Holland before Sir William Johnson put an end to his "Wild West" circus. Shortly after the Civil War Julius opened the Indian Wigwam, a curio shop, which was well patronized after the new Union Pacific Railroad brought hosts of tourists to the Great Plains. Meyer had his picture taken with some of the most notable Indian chiefs of that day—Sitting Bull, Red Cloud, Standing Bear, Spotted Tail, and Swift Bear. These photographs, still extant, are works of art.

Like Max, Julius too was very much interested in music. He was one of the organizers of an orchestra in which he was the flautist and Aaron Cahn of Cahn & Hellman played the violin. It was Julius, too, who established one of the first social clubs in Omaha for the Jewish and Christian elite. It was called the Standard. Later it became the Metropolitan but by then it accepted Jews only. Young and small communities make few social distinctions; social rivalries, discrimination, and polarization come with large numbers, wealth, culture, and pretensions to aristocracy. Imaginative, artistic Julius once staged a chess game in which all the pieces were live men and women, appropriately dressed, and because he loved children he gave 125 of them, the sons and daughters of his friends, a huge party on his fiftieth birthday. A happy, exuberant, creative, sensitive man? He was found dead in a park shot through the heart.[30]

JEWS IN THE FAR WEST

CALIFORNIA JEWRY

It is no exaggeration to state that at least 20,000 emigrants crossed the Missouri River in the summer of 1849 on their way across the plains to California. They were in search of gold, in one form or another. People came from all over the world; many went around the Horn; others crossed the continent at Panama or Nicaragua. Thousands of Jews joined this endless stream. Among them was Dr. Samuel Sussman Snow, a Pomeranian German who after arriving in the States in 1837 studied at a New York medical school. In 1843, he went out to La Crosse, Wisconsin, as an Indian trader and two years later took John M. Levy as his partner. When in the late 1840's the Winnebagoes were driven across the Mississippi into Minnesota, Snow moved farther westward. He settled in Council Bluffs but his pregnant wife found the Iowa winter too severe. In 1840 he set his course for California. Snow was made the head of the wagon train for he was a physician and had years of experience with the Indians. Emanuel, his oldest son, was born just as the pioneers were about to start across the plains. Snow got his party through without mishap and he and his family settled down at Dogtown, near Placerville. He opened a tent store for the miners; by the time that he died in 1892 he had owned and operated a hotel, a mine, a bowling alley; he had farmed, kept store, traded for furs, and practiced medicine. When it was reported in the digging that he had brought his wife with him a miner walked thirty-two miles just to look at a "white woman."[31]

As far as Jews were concerned Snow was anything but an old-timer in California for Lewis H. Polock of Philadelphia had arrived there as early as 1837, eleven years before gold was discovered. Young Polock was an adventurer who had left a good home to see the world; he settled in California after deserting the whaling ship on which he had signed up for a voyage in the Pacific. Two years later he was the proprietor of a small general store at Yerba Buena, a village of about 100 people. In addition to some horses and cows which he had probably received by way of barter, his inventory included saddles, bridles, dry goods, and 200 pair of pantaloons. He might well have been denominated the Pants King of the Peninsula. In 1840 he was seized in a raid by the Mexicans and was imprisoned for a short time with about forty American malcontents suspected of plotting revolution. California became part of the United States in 1846 and Yerba Buena became the town of San Francisco in 1848. By that time war had been declared against Mexico and Polock had served as a top sergeant. In 1849 when he heard that gold was discovered in California, Polock, then in Panama, went back to his old haunts as a professional gambler. On June 22, 1851, a huge fire broke out in the city and two

Jews were burnt to death trying to salvage some of their stock. That same
day Polock was shot to death in a house of ill fame by Samuel Gallagher
in a dispute over one of the girls. He was all of thirty-two years of age.
Gallagher was arrested by the Vigilantes, turned over to the courts, found
guilty of murder, fined $500 and sentenced to prison for three years. He
was pardoned after serving less than three weeks; his lawyer was Solomon
Heydenfeldt. In 1855 a Mr. Levy found guilty of smuggling cigars was
fined $30,000 and sent to the state prison for a year; he should have em-
ployed a good Jewish lawyer like Judge Heydenfeldt. Polock and Levy
were not solid citizens; most Jews were. Lewis Polock's brother Moses
was the first American collector of rare Americana; their nephew, Dr. A.
S. W. Rosenbach was to become a fine bibliographer and one of the
world's great bookdealers.[32]

Most California Jews of that generation settled in San Francisco, the
commercial center of the state; some preferred Sacramento, the gateway
to the northern mines; others chose Stockton, a starting point for the
southern diggings. In the earliest days many newcomers flocked to the
mines in the Sierra Nevadas, in the Mother Lode country, and that of
course is where the Jews also went. A few of them were miners, but most
of them were shopkeepers selling food, clothing, and tools. They settled
in Downieville, Nevada City, Grass Valley, Hangtown or Placerville,
Coloma, Diamond Springs, Fiddletown, Volcano, Jackson, Mokelumne
Hills, Jesu Maria, Columbia, Sonora, and other camps, as well as in the
fringe towns of Marysville and Folsom. Many of these Jewish settlements
speedily acquired cemeteries and societies to provide for burials; a few of
the mountain towns like Placerville and Jackson even built synagogs. Because so many Jews came to California in the space of a year or two there
was no time lag before institutions were created. In the smaller places like
the towns in the Sierras where numbers were limited the blending process
was rapid and the Jews organized themselves speedily. In the larger cities
of San Francisco and Sacramento where Jews were in good supply, polarization took place almost immediately; separate groups with different rituals established themselves creating their own services, congregations, and
charities. Whether Jews came together more quickly than Christians is
difficult to determine. Yet though the Jews did join together almost at
once for religious purposes, services in the mining towns, even in some of
the places where there were synagog buildings, were usually held only
during the High Holy Days. In Jackson, Jews, it would seem, had but one
criterion for the good Jew: someone who kept the store closed on Holy
Days.

By the 1860's, as the gold began to peter out, the shopkeepers started
the trek down the mountains and back to the cities. Some remained to ca-
ter to the townspeople but by 1900 even these shopkeepers had left in or-

der to enjoy the security of larger Jewish communities where they had
the advantages of a Jewish environment and the possibility of marriage
within the fold. Sonora in Tuolomne County in the southern diggings
was an exception; faithful Jews kept the services going till 1907. In 1860
this community, identifying with World Jewry, had sent a generous gift
east for the oppressed Jews of Gibraltar and Morocco. A study of that year
shows that the Jews in the county, about 1/2 of 1 percent of the population, paid over 8 percent of the taxes. One of Sonora's merchants was
quite an entrepreneur. Emanuel Linoberg bought and sold gold mines,
ran a mule freighting train, and set up Russian steambaths that were guaranteed to help those afflicted with rheumatism, pulmonic diseases, and
chronic nervous distress.[33]

It is very difficult to determine how many Jews lived in the Sierra
Nevada diggings. Miners and storekeepers were constantly coming and
going but a rude guess that there were about 1,000 permanent Jewish inhabitants in the Mother Lode towns in the 1850's may not miss the mark
by too much. In those pre-railroad days the Californians, like the East
Coast settlers, preferred ocean and river towns where transportation and
freight problems were reduced to a minimum. Starting in the south and
moving north along the coast there were Jews in San Diego, Los Angeles,
San Luis Obispo, Santa Cruz, San Francisco, Oakland across the Bay, and
Petaluma. In the interior, moving from north to south, Jews had settled
in Shasta, Marysville, Sacramento, Stockton, Bakersfield, and San Bernardino. By the middle 1870's none of these towns sheltered more than 300
Jews; most of them had considerably fewer. There were at least ninety
towns and villages in California with Jewish inhabitants; eight had formal congregations; many of the others had cemeteries and supporting societies. Most of the smaller settlements had fewer than fifty men, women,
and children; some fewer than ten. San Francisco was the exception. Of
the approximately 19,000 Jews in the state, well over 80 percent lived in
that city.

In 1853 Marcus (Mordecai) Katz drove the hundred or so miles from
San Bernardino to San Diego to be married. Although the Jewish census
of the 1870's does not even list San Diego, services were held there in the
1850's. Louis Rose, a Hannoverian, came to San Diego in 1850 and sold
dry goods and groceries, operated a tannery and a brickyard, worked copper and silver mines, and owned a hotel and wharf. He laid out a suburb
which he called Roseville. Rose tried to manufacture mattresses using dry
seaweed; it may have been a good idea, but the buyers did not think so.
On different occasions he served the town as postmaster and treasurer,
and like other businessmen overtaken by hard times he went broke more
than once. Other merchants, like the partners and brothers-in-law, J. S.
Mannasse and Marcus Schiller, who also arrived in town in the 1850's,

were more successful although they too suffered heavy losses in the late 1880's when the land boom collapsed. They were ranchers, financiers, real estate promoters, and merchants who imported wares from San Francisco on their own brig and sold adobe houses on the installment plan. In 1859 M. Manasse, a cousin of J. S., traveled fifty miles to worship in San Diego. While the tiny group of ten adults was conducting services for the Day of Atonement, he was summoned to testify before a grand jury, and because he refused to go on this the holiest day of the year a sheriff's posse forced him to go along with it. He still refused to testify because of the sanctity of the day and the judge committed him to jail from which the sheriff finally released him. San Diego Jewry and Jews throughout the United States were outraged at this lack of consideration on the part of the San Diego authorities.

Two years after this unfortunate episode and again in the early 1870's local Jewry attempted to fashion a permanent religious organization but it was not until 1888 that a congregation was firmly established. Marcus Schiller was active in all these efforts to create a viable Jewish community. The most successful Jewish businessman in town was Abraham Klauber. In the 1850's Klauber lived in the Mother Lode town of Volcano where he was the proprietor of a general store and the owner of a mule freight train that ran between Sacramento and the mines. The next decade found him in Nevada; arriving in San Diego in 1869, Klauber began shipping wool, wheat, and gold dust to San Francisco and when the firm turned to wholesaling he moved to that metropolis as a resident buyer. Always reaching out in new enterprises he bought a ranch in Mendocino County north of San Francisco where he raised cattle and cut timber.

When Marcus Katz traveled to San Diego in 1853 to be married he had already been living in the Mormon stockade of San Bernardino for three years. The Mormons wanted him to become one of them but he refused; as he pointed out in later years, if he had six wives he would also have six mothers-in-law. Most of the merchants in San Bernardino at that time were Jews, although Katz was the only one in the book and stationery business. For many years he was the town's Wells Fargo agent and like many others dabbled in politics. He was of a literary turn of mind and once wrote an essay on the *Merchant of Venice*. Jews are businessmen and they have always resented Shakespeare's revengeful moneylender; even today "Shylock" is an accepted English word for an extortionate creditor.[34]

By 1870 there were about 150 Jewish men, women, and children in this little town. When they needed goods they went to Los Angeles where the largest grocery and merchandise supply houses in southern California were owned by Jews. They shipped goods not only to San Bernardino but as far north and east as Utah. Unlike the Jews of northern California the Los Angelenos were too few to indulge in the luxury of divisiveness. They were united by 1854 in a Hebrew Benevolent Society led by Joseph Newmark, an ardent religionist who had helped St. Louis Jewry organize a congregation in the 1840's. Wherever Joseph Newmark went he worked to strengthen or to create religious institutions. Because there were no Jewish schools in town in these early days the parents sent their boys to the Catholic school where they carried off many of the prizes.

The big man in the city was Isaias W. Hellman, a Bavarian. By the 1870's he was the most important citizen of Los Angeles. He had come to town as a teen-aged immigrant and in a very few years had opened a dry goods and clothing store. His next move was to haul a safe into a corner of his shop and start an illustrious career as a banker. He helped bring the railroad into the city and worked to establish schools, and to give Los Angeles gas, water, and street railways. In 1879-1880 together with a Protestant, and a Catholic, he donated the land for the University of Southern California and helped provide the means also to endow this institution. This was good business; it was also good citizenship. When the cornerstone of a beautiful synagog, "the finest church edifice" in Los Angeles, was laid in 1872, Hellman was the president.[35]

Unlike the Jews of Los Angeles, the Jews of Sacramento were numerous enough to divide along ritual lines. South Germans versus North and East Germans (Poles!). Nevertheless the men's and women's philanthropic societies, the young men's social club, and the lodge were institutions making for unity in spite of the two rival congregations. On a Friday night in December, 1863, when the religionists, at least, should have been in the synagog, the Jewish actress Adah Menken gave a benefit performance for a local congregation. The dilemma of whether to go to the synagog or to the theatre was very probably resolved in favor of La Menken or through the device of an early service. Late twentieth-century rabbis have been plagued with similar problems. What happens to the religious service when New Year's Eve with the attendant parties and country club festivities falls on a Friday night?[36]

Two of the most creative and innovative merchants in all California appeared in Sacramento in the decade of the 1870's. They were the half-brothers, David Lubin and Harris Weinstock, ardent Jews and even more fervent political liberals concerned with the welfare of the masses. The Mechanics' Store that they opened was a one-price store selling good merchandise marked in plain figures. They did not operate a "cheap John" type of business. They insisted on morality in trade in a day when the philosophy of many businessmen was summed up in the phrase: "Let the buyer beware." Seeking to win the country trade they published a catalogue and soon enjoyed a very large mail-order business.

Both men were highly intelligent and well-read. Harris Weinstock was a religious radical; Lubin, a reader of Spencer, Mill, and Huxley, was both a capitalist and a populist, an agrarian rebel. This concern of rich Jews for the welfare of the people as a whole is not altogether unusual. The department store Filenes of Boston and the soap Felses of Philadelphia were a similar breed. Lubin was interested in his employees, in workingmen, in labor practices such as strikes, lockouts, and arbitration, in farmers, cheap parcel post, and fair freight rates. He was opposed to the discriminatory practices of the railroads and aided farmers to establish selling cooperatives. It was his firm conviction that farmers were entitled to equal treatment with the industrialists: the latter had their tariffs; let the former enjoy export bounties so that they may receive a decent price for their crops. Lubin, an almost obsessed apostle of social justice, was wise enough to realize that there was no local or even national solution to the problem of the farmer and the consumer. When he pursued his ideas to their logical conclusion he began working toward an equitable economic world state. He thought in terms of a United States of the World. Because he was sincerely concerned with the welfare of the masses, this Polish-born Jew shared many goals with New York socialistic sweatshop workers. Lubin sought international control and distribution of food supplies for the benefit of all, buyer and seller. At the least there should be worldwide information about crops so that neither the grower nor the consumer should be disadvantaged. To accomplish his purposes he finally succeeded in inducing Italy to sponsor an international Institute of Agriculture that would provide data making it possible for nations to regulate the production and distribution of the world's foods, particularly grain. The work of this Institute was later taken over by the Food and Agricultural Organization of the United Nations.[37]

One cannot help but wonder what impression, if any, the views of Lubin and Weinstock made upon another "Jew" who lived for a brief period in Sacramento. This man was Washington Bartlett, one-time mayor of San Francisco, who as governor of the state in 1887, made his home in the capital. This scion of an old New Hampshire family, one of whose members had signed the Declaration of Independence, was technically, halakically, a Jew, for his mother was a Jew. Thus he was the first "Jewish" governor in the United States, but as far as it is now known he evinced no particular interest in Judaism.

In 1862, after a bad flood, the wholesale grocer Lewis Gerstle of Sacramento, decided to return to San Francisco whence he had come. After living for a time in Louisville this Bavarian immigrant had journeyed west to San Francisco where he sold fruit and worked in the mines before joining with two others to establish a general store at the state's capital. In San Francisco he and his brother-in-law Louis Sloss opened a brokerage office and after they were firmly established founded the Alaska Commercial Company, the first large Alaskan American trading firm. By the decade of the '60's San Francisco was the most important trade and financial center west of St. Louis. The city grew more rapidly in 1869 when the Central Pacific Railroad linked up with the Union Pacific in Utah. As the gold mines in the mountains began to give out, Jews who had made money, or not made money, fixed their residence in San Francisco. Merchants from many of the small towns of the state moved there not only because it was a supply and banking base but because it was a place where one could raise a Jewish family. Jewishly speaking California was in one respect similar to all the other states; it was a one-town state: indeed for a short time in the 1870's San Francisco was the second largest Jewish city in the United States. In the 1880's the Atlantic tidewater towns would once more take the lead as they mushroomed in population with the coming of the East European multitudes.[38]

As in Sacramento, the San Francisco Jewish argonauts of 1849 were sufficiently numerous to set up religious institutions with little delay. That Fall two rival conventicles with different rites held separate High Holy Day services. One of the groups met in a tent; the highly respected soldier from Baltimore, Leon Dyer, was volunteer precentor. Many of the forty-niners were men of learning, culture, competence, and achievement who had been attracted to California by the lure of gold and the hope of making their way quickly. By 1850 at the latest there was a cemetery in town, and a year later the hundreds of Jews who were pouring in were given the choice of membership in two benevolent societies as well as the two congregations. In 1855 avid joiners from the East could become members of B'nai B'rith Ophir Lodge, a most appropriate name, for Ophir was the biblical California, the land of gold. That same year a Jewish newspaper made its appearance, the first one west of Cincinnati. During the Civil War, in 1863, Philo Jacoby published a weekly he called *The Hebrew*. Jacoby was a "strong man" who could twist horseshoes out of shape with his bare hands and he was the Champion Rifle Shot of the World. Some of his Jewish journalist brethren in the East snickered at the mention of his name. They could not understand how a man could do what he did and still be sufficiently intelligent to edit a Jewish newspaper.[39]

With all the wealth of talent that flowed into San Francisco it is not surprising that Jews were active politically from the first. Extralegally some of the best Jews in town served on the Vigilance Committees of the 1850's. More properly, during the first two years of the 1850's a Jew served as an alderman, another was the county treasurer, and still others were sent to the state assembly at Sacramento. Henry A. Lyons sat on the state's first supreme court (1850) where he was later joined by Judge Solomon Heydenfeldt of Alabama. Within less than a year after his arrival in 1850 Heydenfeldt was running for the United States Senate. The legislators at the capital turned thumbs down on him because he was a states' rights man, but in 1851 he was elected by popular vote to the Supreme Court. He served for several years before resigning to devote himself to a very lucrative law practice. Like his Alabama contemporary, Philip Phillips, he was a great lawyer and possibly the foremost legal mind in the state. Encouraged by Felix Adler of New York, Heydenfeldt helped establish the first free kindergarten in San Francisco. Heydenfeldt belonged to a generation in which it was not uncommon for notable Jewish politicians to marry out. Despite his marriage, he evinced ethnic loyalties and the Jewish community turned to him when it needed a "representative" Jew. The German-born Dr. Abraham Jacobi, the country's most distinguished pediatrician, was his brother-in-law.[40]

Unlike the Irish in the East, the Jews of San Francisco made no profession of politics; their métier was business. By far the majority of them were retailers, petty for the most part, surviving because they were sober, industrious, and willing to sell cheap. If they were successful, storekeepers turned to jobbing, establishing branches in the mines or subsidizing others with liberal credits. California Jews, with startling similarity to their fellow Jews in all America's big cities, were in clothing, dry goods, tobacco, and jewelry. Some who turned early to the manufacture of clothes used immigrant Chinese labor; a few freighted supplies to the mines; the successful elite turned to banking. As the nineteenth century moved on San Francisco Jews were outstanding in the wine and liquor, wool, leather, hides, tanning, fruit, and coffee trades.

This brief survey of their economic activity is accurate but in no sense reflects the struggle and heartaches of individual tradesmen most of whom were immigrants facing what at times seemed to be almost insuperable odds. Morris Sloss was a one-eyed, dark-skinned Pole, five feet tall, hardly a prepossessing figure. This forty-niner worked at first in a gambling house where he played a musical instrument for his ounce of dust and his "grab" of silver from the monte table. He was burnt out twice. Once when he hurried out to a new strike on the coast, only to find it was a false alarm, he kept himself alive eating beans, crackers, and clams. While up north he befriended the bandit Joaquin Murrieta and on the strength of this friendship Sloss was hired by the Adams Express Company to bring a shipment of gold dust down from Shasta to San Francisco. He carried out this mission successfully. In San Francisco he joined the Vigilantes, attended the hanging of James P. Casey and Charles Cora, and finally ended up in the coal business.

Fires which burnt out the wooden shacks of the uninsured shopkeepers were one of the greatest hazards of the 1850's. When Alex Meyer was burnt out, he wrote his friend Ed Bomeisler in Philadelphia, "I wish to God California would went before I heard something about this country." But he changed his mind after Samuel Whittaker and Robert Mc-Kenzie were hanged by the Vigilantes in 1851: "I tell you, Ed, that it [is] a great country." Isaac Friedla[e]nder, a native Oldenburger, would probably have agreed with both these statements. At the age of thirty Friedlander controlled the wheat crop of California if not of the entire Pacific Coast. This organizing genius firmly established the international grain trade of the Pacific with Australia and England and bought hundreds of thousands of acres in the San Joaquin Valley with the intent to irrigate them; he went bankrupt more than once. He was a cultured gentleman, enjoying vast credits for his far-flung enterprises, an honest man who attempted to meet all his obligations.

Friedlander, the Grain King, attempted to corner the wheat market; Joshua A. Norton, a native of the British Isles, tried to corner the rice market. Not only did he lose the fortune he had brought with him from South Africa in 1849, but he also lost his mind. Prior to his mental breakdown he had been an eminently successful businessman, real estate speculator, and import commission agent. When he reappeared on the San Francisco scene in 1857 he was dressed in military uniform, epaulettes, sword, and military cap, accompanied by his two dogs, Bummer and Lazarus. It was his belief that he was the emperor of the United States and he was so listed in a local directory. He issued grandiose rescripts and printed promissory notes with a face value of fifty cents under the imperial signature of Norton I. The town humored him, honored his paper money as legal tender, and treated this once widely respected businessman with courtesy and consideration. Ten thousand people turned out for his funeral in 1880 when he was buried in a Masonic cemetery. The sermon was preached by a well-known Christian minister, although Norton was always known as a Jew. A poet of that day wrote these lines:

> For death alone did he abdicate.
> What Emperor, Prince, or potentate
> Can long avoid a similar fate
> Or win a better end![41]

Friedlander and Norton are brilliant examples of success and unsuccess. Many others were fortunate. The recorded gold shipments out of San Francisco harbor and the tax lists of Civil War days show that a number of Jewish firms were very prosperous. Four Jews were among the founders of the San Francisco Stock and Exchange Board. Mr. A. A. Cohen turned to steamships in 1876 after selling his extensive local railroad holdings to the Central Pacific. Successful clothing firms, moving east with their profits, opened banking houses with branches in New York,

London, Paris, and Frankfort. Among the successful clothing jobbers who turned to banking in the East were the Seligman brothers. They had been very fortunate in the disastrous fire of 1851 for their stocks of goods were housed in a brick building that survived the holocaust. Another clothing jobber who did well for himself was a Bavarian by the name of Levi Strauss. Strauss had gone into dry goods and clothing in 1853; his two brothers back in New York were his buyers. He specialized in work clothing that would resist wear and tear; Lubin and Weinstock also strove to produce durable overalls, but in this area Levi Strauss was more successful. He used very heavy cloths, canvas, duck, and sturdy denims, and at the suggestion of a Nevada Jewish tailor reinforced the pockets of his bibless overalls with copper rivets. The Strauss overall with its pockets which could hold quartz rocks and small tools without ripping was perfected in the 1870's and helped make the firm famous and rich. An excellent product helped by brilliant advertising, the Strauss overalls were widely acclaimed and in the mid-twentieth century gave the American language a new word "Levi's." As Strauss prospered he invested in insurance, woolen mills, ranches; he sat on bank boards. A century after his copper-riveted Levis went on the market the firm, still controlled by members of his family, owned more than thirty plants and was one of the world's largest manufacturers of pants. Levi Strauss & Company with its assets of over $150,000,000 is listed on the New York Stock Exchange. This is an untypical California success story.[42]

NEVADA JEWRY

If it is any distinction, let it be noted that Virginia City, Nevada, was the birthplace of Levi Strauss's copper-riveted overall pockets. Like other mining towns, Virginia City attracted Jews as long as the mines were productive. The Nevada diggings, contiguous to the Mother Lode, are located in the mountains on the California-Nevada border a few miles northeast of Lake Tahoe. Many of them are part of Mount Davidson and the Comstock Lode where silver was discovered in 1859. Mount Davidson, it is said, was named after Ben Davidson, a Jewish argonaut who was one of the Rothschilds' agents in San Francisco in the 1850's. California —the Pacific Coast—was the terminus of the "West"; farther land expansion dictated that newcomers reach out north to Oregon or east to the Great Plains. The Nevada Jewish community owes its rise to the "western" expansion eastward. After the 1859 strike Jewish businessmen crossed the Sierras to Virginia City, the most important town in the new mining area. Writing for *Harper's Weekly* in 1860, J. Ross Browne, a journalist, who made the trip on foot, describes a Jewish peddler he met on the road who stole his dirty stockings and later decamped with his boots. But there was no viciousness in Browne's reports to *Harper's*. It was all good clean fun for Browne was a frontier humorist embroidering or inventing his stories for the edification of the American reading public, telling them what they expected to hear. These German Jewish peddlers and clothiers sold "worthless garments at ruinous prices." It would take at least two more generations before this standard cockeyed view of the Jewish businessman would begin to disappear.[43]

Clustered around Virginia City were Gold Hill, Silver City, and Dayton; south of it lay Carson City and Genoa; all had Jews. During its prosperous two decades, from 1859 to about 1879, Virginia City at times sheltered over 20,000 inhabitants; after San Francisco, it was the largest city west of the Rockies. Services were held in town in the early 1860's on the High Holy Days and in the course of the next few years there was also a burial society, a cemetery, a lodge, and some form of a congregation. At the same time the smaller Carson City was also in the process of establishing such institutions. When the Jewish world traveler I. J. Benjamin II visited there in 1861 he found twenty Jews, but only one married couple.[44]

When in 1874 the Virginia City Jews heard that Adah Isaacs Menken, the actress, was coming to town, they were probably very pleased; inveterate theatregoers they were sure to come to her performance. The show was a howling success; the miners literally showered her with silver bullion. She was a sensation as Mazeppa, in pink tights, tied to the back of a horse dashing around on the slopes of an improvised open-air theatre. Menken was then about twenty-nine or thirty years of age and had already dispensed with at least two husbands and some lovers. Her first husband Alexander I. Menken came from a good Jewish family; she herself was a devoted fervent Jew, of this there can be no doubt. She wrote poetry for Isaac M. Wise's *American Israelite* and prayed out of his *Minhag America*, his Americanistic prayer book. (Her prayer book is in the Harvard Library.) In 1857, just about the year she began her career as an actress in New Orleans, she wrote an article for the local *Sunday Delta* defending Shylock, the merchant of Venice. Adah Menken was an imaginative, intelligent, sensitive poet, superior to Penina Moïse who enjoyed a better reputation as a litterateur among Jews. In 1868, the year Menken died, her collected poems were published as *Infelicia*, the unhappy one, and they were to be reprinted at least four more times in this country in the next twenty years. During the four years between her appearance in Virginia City and her death in Paris she was to have a sensational career in America, England, and France. She numbered among her friends Walt Whitman, Bret Harte, Joaquin Miller and Mark Twain in this country, Dickens and Swinburne in England, Dumas père in France. The latter two were her close friends. She was an unconventional American Bohemian, a poet, an indifferent actor, a linguist, and all in all a woman of considerable culture.[45]

The year that Menken died Samuel Michelson, a Jewish immigrant, opened a dry goods store in Virginia City. Earlier he had been in business in Calaveras County in the Mother Lode, the home of Mark Twain's celebrated Jumping Frog. Michelson came down the east slope of the Sierras to try his luck in the fast growing metropolis of Nevada. There were the closest of ties between California and Nevada. Michelson ordered fresh patterns and wares from the wholesalers at Sacramento and San Francisco; in turn, much of the wealth accumulated in the Silver State returned westward to the Golden State whence not only its goods but also its settlers had come. About a year after Michelson landed in Virginia City, his wife Rosalie gave birth to their son Charles, who grew up to become a brilliant influential newspaperman. Charles was an editorial writer and a managing editor for Hearst papers, a Washington correspondent, and a shrewd effective writer of publicity for the Democratic National Committee during the days of the New Deal. His father Samuel must have gone back to Calaveras County, or left his wife there, for Miriam, a daughter, was born there in 1870. She, too, was of a literary turn of mind and was widely known as a writer of stories and numerous novels. The oldest child in the family, Albert Abraham Michelson (1852–1931), had been born in Posen, not too far from Russian Poland, before the Michelsons migrated to the United States. Albert grew up to be a physicist, the first American scholar to receive a Nobel Prize in the sciences. The Michelsons were a gifted family.[46]

During the 1860's another German Jewish immigrant in Nevada was a man named Adolph Heinrich Joseph Sutro (1830-1898). Some time after the death of his father in Germany the mother and children had moved to Baltimore; Adolph struck out speedily for the West, for California. Although only twenty-one he was already a seasoned businessman with a great deal of experience behind him. His financial progress was slow, very slow, but by 1860 he had established a small quartz reducing mill in the Comstock Lode area and had begun to think in terms of limitless scope. Many of the mines in the Lode could not be worked because of problems of heat, flooding, and lack of fresh air. Sutro was convinced he could overcome these difficulties by building a tunnel through the mountain, a tunnel that would draw off the water and gases, provide fresh air, and expedite the transportation of the ore. He had the basic engineering skills for he had studied at a good German high school; he was ambitious, clever, and possessed of an indomitable will that recognized no failures. In the early 1860's this brilliant entrepreneur began to preach the gospel of the Sutro Tunnel to save the Comstock Lode; by 1879 he emerged victorious, a rich man. In between he had fought corrupt officials and sabotaging bankers but had also won the support of the miners, the state legislature, the United States Congress, and some venturesome British businessmen. The battle of this stubborn tough German to build the tunnel against almost unbelievable odds is one of the great sagas of the West.

Sutro's venture was so successful that when he sold his holdings in 1879, he realized a very large sum of money. He then moved to San Francisco where he invested heavily in land and soon became a large property owner. He loved books and collected—rather unintelligently to be sure—a huge library of rare works and manuscripts. Because of his bitter experiences with crooked politicians and unscrupulous bankers, he was only too willing to head a Populist ticket, the People's Party, in 1894, and the masses, impressed by his integrity, elected him mayor. Less than a decade later these same masses rallied around the Union Labor Party which turned out to be but the tool and instrument of Abe Ruef. This brilliant Jewish lawyer built up one of the most powerful and crooked political machines in the history of a city that was noted for its corrupt past. Although Ruef's crimes finally caught up with him and he was sent to San Quentin prison, the many utility and railroad magnates who benefited from their association with him escaped punishment. Hiram Johnson who helped prosecute him became governor of California, a United States Senator, and a candidate for the presidency. This interesting concatenation of circumstances may well account for the fact that Abe Ruef's career received wide coverage in the standard histories of the state; ironically, the notable Jewish builders of California are almost all passed by.[47]

Sutro thought of capturing one of Nevada's seats in the United States Senate but his plans miscarried. In much the same fashion as the California pioneers, early Nevada Jews turned to politics. In the relatively short period from settlement till the 1880's at least nine sat in the state's Assembly and Senate. One Jew became Carson City's chief of police and others owned and edited newspapers in the mining camps. A few individual Jewish businessmen deserted traditional paths; Louis Lobel drove cattle over the Sierras from Placerville and ran a truck farm near one of the mining settlements. As a rule though Jews were storekeepers in some form or another of the retail apparel trade. Some of them were quite successful. There were at least five Jewish merchants in Reno in 1879 when they were burnt out by a disastrous fire. One firm, Barnett Brothers, lost stock and fixtures worth $60,000. Doing business in the Nevada of that day was not without its hazards of violence and death; the turbulence of the camps could affect everyone. A Jewish merchant in distant Nye County had to kill a man in self defense; two Jewish peddlers were axed to death; an unoffending Jew in Virginia City was shot down by a trigger-happy policeman, and an Elko County Jew was murdered in a quarrel over a woman.

By the 1870's there were still 300 Jews in Virginia City and about 500 in eleven other towns. Virginia City, Eureka, and Reno had communities and Carson City may have had at least one Jewish organization. A total state population of 800 Jews does not seem very impressive, but there were more Jews in Nevada than in Maine or New Hampshire or Vermont. There was little outside of the mines to induce people to take root in Nevada. As late as 1880 the state was still a sparsely settled desert with but 62,000 people rattling around in its 110,000 square miles. After 1880, when the silver gave out, many people, Jews and non-Jews, left, and it was not until the 1950's that there were as many Jews in Nevada as there had been in 1880. The Nevada Jewish community took on new life with the modern "gold rush," legalized gambling.[48]

OREGON JEWRY

There can be no doubt that Nevada Jewry was a California colony. This is true too of Oregon, though individual Jews had begun to find their way there even before Oregon was organized as a territory, years before gold was discovered in California. In the late 1840's and early 1850's Dr. Israel Moses, an army surgeon who was to make a name for himself in the Mexican and the Civil wars, served under General William W. Loring then commander of the military department of Oregon. Some of Oregon's Jews of the 1850's crossed the plains like Louis Fleishner who was to become the state treasurer, but most of them moved north from California during the gold rush to trade with the farmers who were supplying the mines with cattle and produce. As early as 1850 San Francisco Jewish businessmen were shipping large stocks of goods to the Oregon market. Among those moving north were two Jews who came from the Mother Lode; Philip Selling had once lived in Sonora; Aaron Meier had worked in Downieville. Philip's son Ben was one day to become speaker of the Oregon House; Meier's son Julius became governor of Oregon in the 1930's.[49]

The first Jewish community in the state was not destined to survive. This was Jacksonville across the border from California, oriented towards its source of supply at San Francisco. Jews moved into this town after a gold strike in the early 1850's and began to hold services no later than 1856. When the gold gave out the Jews stayed on to share in the agricultural prosperity. One of the Jewish merchants had a brick building with iron doors which the townspeople used as a fort during the Rogue River Indian War of 1855-1856. As late as 1880 there were still some Jews in town, but when the railroad bypassed it Jacksonville was doomed as an important mercantile center and the Jews began to leave. As the Jews drifted into the territory and the state in the 1850's and 1860's most of them settled to the west of the Cascade Mountains, in the Willamette Valley, a fertile section which was of course a prime area of settlement for almost all who entered Oregon. Jews opened shops and stores in Eugene,

Corvallis, Albany, Salem, and Oregon City, but the only town in the state that developed a substantial Jewish community and institutions before 1880 was Portland. It had two congregations, a German and a "Polish" one, and two benevolent societies, one for men and one for women. The only town in the state, besides Portland and Jacksonville, that had a cemetery and a burial association was Albany. It might have been tempted to brag that it was Oregon's second largest Jewish town—and it was—but all told it could muster but sixty-two men, women, and children in the late 1870's.

Portland was the big Jewish town. Of the 900 or less Jews in the state at that time over 600 lived there. Among the Jewish pioneers was Bernard Goldsmith, a German emigrant who had come in the late 1840's. He had served in a cavalry troop in the Oregon Indian wars and had been commissioned a lieutenant. He became a successful merchant, shipped wheat to Europe, and raised Durham cows and merino sheep. In 1869 he was elected mayor, the first of several Jews to serve as Portland's chief executive. By 1858 there was a congregation in Portland which soon had a hazzan who not only chaunted the service but also taught the children Hebrew and some secular disciplines. He was paid $1,000, a rather substantial salary. Benjamin II, who visited the city in 1861, wrote that the congregants were not very generous. "Perhaps the cold and damp climate has affected their hearts and killed every warm feeling." Obviously they had given him little or nothing when he approached them with outstretched palm.[50]

Benjamin II also reported that all of the Jews in the state were well-to-do. If this was literally true then there would have been no need for the benevolent societies of Portland. But, on the whole, he was right. As in many other western states the Jews were shopkeepers and merchants selling clothes, provisions, and miners' supplies, too, if they were close to the diggings. Specialization in goods handled was not to come for a generation. Stocks of merchandise were readily accessible, for there were good steamboat connections with San Francisco, and boats plied both the Willamette and Columbia Rivers. Jews owned ships on these rivers and worked to build locks on the Willamette so as to open new towns to river traffic. Enterprising individuals grew fruit, built local railroads and telegraph lines, and, as early as 1859, ran an intercounty stagecoach express west of the Cascades. Portland, the state's central commercial depot, also stocked shops in Washington, Idaho, and Montana territories. In turn the Oregon merchants and wholesalers were dependent on the San Francisco suppliers. San Francisco Jewish businessmen like A. Cohen & Company financed or supplied or controlled branches in Portland and The Dalles in Oregon, Walla Walla and Colville in Washington Territory, and Boise in Idaho Territory. Using river steamboats and pack trains Jewish businessmen reached almost every obscure town in the outback in those pioneer pre-railroad days.[51]

In 1851 Aaron Rose, a butcher and innkeeper, crossed the plains and settled in the Umpqua River Valley in southern Oregon. Roseburg, the present seat of Douglas County, grew up around him; the local citizenry sent him, the town's founder, to the territorial legislature in 1856-1857. When President Rutherford B. Hayes made his Grand Western Tour in 1880 he stopped in Aaron Rose's town on his way north to Portland. In Portland the President was welcomed to the city and state by Solomon Hirsch, one of the most successful merchants in the Northwest and at that time president of the state senate. In 1899 Hirsch was to serve as President Harrison's Minister to Turkey. On the morning of Oct. 1, 1880, the President and his family may or may not have been disturbed by a shooting affray in the shadow of the hotel where they had spent the night. Mr. A. Waldman, a businessman, met his rabbi, Mr. M. May, and proceeded to thrash him soundly. There had been bad blood between the two. Personal differences may have been exacerbated by the fact that the Rev. May leaned toward liturgical reform. When the rabbi recovered from his initial shock he reached into his hip pocket, pulled out a pistol, and fired twice point blank at Mr. Waldman, missing him both times. It is deplorable how unskilled some Jews are in the use of firearms.

Although most Jews lived west of the Cascades there was probably not a town of any size in the state in the 1860's and 1870's which could not count at least one Jewish settler or family. Thus they were to be found on the other side of the mountains in Klamath Falls in South Oregon and in Burns in the southcentral area. Tucked away in the northeast, in the mountains and around the tributaries of the Columbia and the Snake, they made homes for themselves in Baker, La Grande, Pendleton, and Heppner. S. A. Heilner as a young man in his twenties was in business in Crescent in southern Oregon and was probably not as miserable and lonely as his diary seems to indicate. In this little Klamath County village of the 1860's he found time to read, sketch, play chess and billiards, hike, pick blueberries, take guitar lessons, ride horseback, attend the races, and even visit the services at a Christian church. Posen-born Henry Heppner, who had come up the Columbia in the 1860's to do business on both sides of the river, in Washington and in Oregon, ran a mule pack train to the eastern Oregon mountains and to the Idaho mines across the border. He finally settled down in Morrow County and the town that grew around his place of business was called Heppner; it is the county seat. Like Nevada, and indeed like most of the trans-Missouri country, Oregon, except for the Willamette Valley, was sparsely settled. Of the twenty or so towns into which the children of the Chosen People had wandered only two had more than fifty souls.[52]

ILLUSTRATIONS

Abraham Rice (d. 1862) of Baltimore was probably the first
diplomate rabbi to serve a congregation in the United States
(1840). His traditionalism did not find a welcoming response
in acculturating America. Courtesy, Jewish Historical
Society of Maryland.

Beth Elohim, The House of God, of Charleston, South
Carolina, is the oldest Reform synagog in the United States
(1841). Photo by Furchgott Studios, Charleston.

David Levi Yulee (1810–1886), Florida pioneer, was the first
Jew to sit in the House and Senate in Washington, D.C.
(1841 and 1845). Courtesy, American Jewish Archives.

Penina Moïse (b. 1797) of Charleston was the best known
Jewish poet of antebellum America. Courtesy, National
Federation of Temple Sisterhoods.

Israel Baer Kursheedt (d. 1852) of Richmond and New York, was an eminent Hebraist, a congregational reader, and merchant. Portrait by Cephas Giovanni Thompson.

Jacob De Cordova (1808–1868) was a Texas pioneer land agent, journalist, and booster.
Courtesy, American Jewish Archives.

Mordecai M. Noah married Rebecca Jackson in 1826/
1827. Rebecca, then age sixteen, bore him seven children.
He was twenty-five years older. Courtesy, Stella F. Simon.

Henry Jones (Heinrich Jonas), a German immigrant, was one of the organizers of the B'nai B'rith fraternal order in 1843. Courtesy, American Jewish Archives.

Henry Russell (b. 1812) in England was one of America's most popular ballad singers in the mid-nineteenth century. He composed and sang over 800 songs, many of which were published. Courtesy, American Jewish Archives.

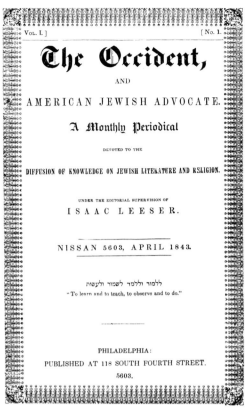

VOL. I.]   [No. 1.

The Occident,

AND

AMERICAN JEWISH ADVOCATE.

A Monthly Periodical

DEVOTED TO THE

DIFFUSION OF KNOWLEDGE ON JEWISH LITERATURE AND RELIGION.

UNDER THE EDITORIAL SUPERVISION OF

ISAAC LEESER.

NISSAN 5603, APRIL 1843.

ללמוד וללמד לשמור ולעשות

"To learn and to teach, to observe and to do."

PHILADELPHIA:
PUBLISHED AT 118 SOUTH FOURTH STREET.
5603.

Title page of Volume One, Number One, of *The Occident*,
the first permanent American Jewish periodical, 1843.

Temple Ohabei Shalom of Boston is the oldest active
congregation in New England, it was organized about 1842.
Courtesy, American Jewish Archives.

Dr. Isaac Hays (1796–1871) was the first American Jewish
medical scientist. His field was ophthalmology.
Courtesy, American Jewish Archives.

Dr. Abraham Jacobi (1830–1919), a German political
refugee, was one of the founders of the modern science of
pediatrics. Courtesy, American Jewish Archives.

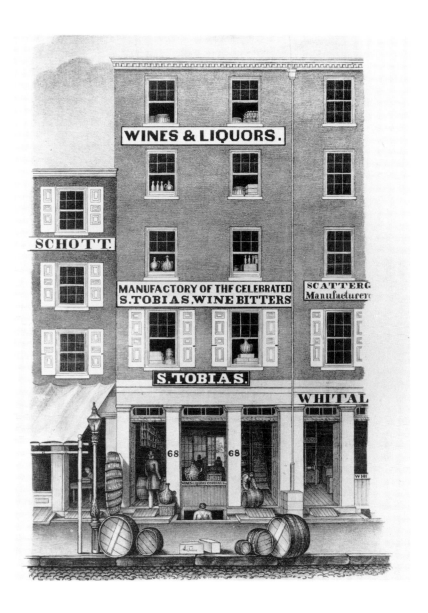

Store and factory of a Philadelphia wine merchant, 1845.
Courtesy, Library Company of Philadelphia.

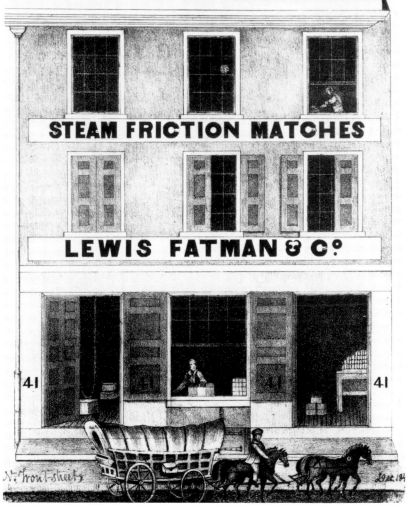

Factory of a Philadelphia Jewish industrialist, 1847.
Courtesy, Library Company of Philadelphia.

This ship of Judah Touro was sent with a cargo of goods
around Cape Horn to California in 1849. Courtesy, Pcabody
Museum of Salem.

Judah Touro (b. 1775), a New Orleans merchant, was
America's greatest antebellum Jewish philanthropist.
Courtesy, American Jewish Archives.

PARTICULARS

OF THE

MURDER OF NATHAN ADLER,

ON THE

NIGHT OF NOVEMBER SIXTH, 1849,

IN

VENICE, CAYUGA COUNTY, N. Y.,

INCLUDING THE

WHOLE TESTIMONY TAKEN BY THE CORONER,

AND THE

INQUISITION AND ARREST

OF THE

THREE BAHAMS.

PUBLISHED BY FINN & ROCKWELL.

AUBURN, N. Y.
FINN & ROCKWELL, PRINTERS, STEAM POWER PRESS.
1850.

Not infrequently peddlers were murdered as they traversed the backcountry. Their tragic fate was retailed in chapbooks, such as this one, 1850.

Home of Abraham Tobias (d. 1856). This Charlestonian,
scion of a pioneer South Carolina family, was active in the
general community of his city. He was a merchant and
banker. Photo by Louis Schwartz.

Abraham Hart (1810–1885), a large-scale book publisher,
was a leader in the Jewish community of Philadelphia.
Courtesy, American Jewish Archives.

Solomon Heydenfeldt (b. 1816) of South Carolina,
Alabama, and California was a brilliant jurist and served
on the California Supreme Court.
Courtesy, American Jewish Archives.

Morris J. Raphall (b. 1798), one of America's most
distinguished, cultured, and articulate ministers, was the first
Jew invited to bless Congress (1860). Courtesy, American
Jewish Historical Society.

David Einhorn (b. 1809), a learned religious radical, came to
the United States, 1855, and served congregations in
Baltimore, Philadelphia, and New York. Courtesy,
American Jewish Archives.

Samuel Adler (b. 1809), a leader of Reform Judaism in
Germany, served Temple Emanu-El, New York, 1857–
1874. Courtesy Temple Emanu-El.

This is the young Rabbi Isaac Mayer Wise just about the
time he left Albany for Cincinnati (1854). He was soon to
become the outstanding spiritual leader of the Reform
movement. Courtesy, American Jewish Archives.

Polish-born Ernestine Rose (b. 1810), feminist and
social reformer, may well have been America's most
distinguished woman of Jewish origin.
Courtesy, American Jewish Archives.

Congressman Philip Phillips (b. 1807), a representative from
Alabama, was one of America's great lawyers. Courtesy,
American Jewish Archives.

Major Alfred Mordecai (b. 1804 in North Carolina) was one of America's notable ordnance officers and arsenal administrators. Pencil sketch by Kates of portrait by Thomas Sully.

Solomon Nunes Carvalho (b. 1815) of Charleston, South Carolina, was an artist, photographer, and transmississippi explorer. Courtesy, American Jewish Archives.

August Bondi (b. 1833) fought with John Brown to make
Kansas a free state. During the Civil War he was a soldier in
the Fifth Kansas Cavalry. Courtesy, Kansas State
Historical Soceity.

This home was dedicated in 1856. The address then was
made by Benjamin F. Jonas, later United States Senator.
Courtesy, Tulane University Library.

Accompanied by Judge John A. Campbell, Gustavus
Adolphus Myers, a notable Virginia lawyer, met with
President Lincoln and discussed the South's surrender. This
was April 5, 1865. Portrait by Thomas Sully.

This is the home of Edwin Warren Moïse of Sumter, South Carolina, a heroic Confederate officer. In later years he practiced law successfully. Courtesy, American Jewish Archives.

This is a picture of the interior of L. J. Levy's "palace of trade" in Philadelphia. It was opened in 1857. The artist and printer of this picture were Jews. Courtesy, Historical Society of Pennsylvania.

The Morris Mensor store, Jacksonville, Oregon, 1858.
Courtesy, Jacksonville Museum.

Passover was a very popular holiday. The baking of matzos,
unleavened bread, was supervised by a religious official; no
leaven was tolerated. This is a scene from an antebellum
bakery. Courtesy, American Jewish Archives.

PROCEEDINGS

IN RELATION TO THE

MORTARA ABDUCTION

———

Mass Meeting at Musical Hall,

San Francisco, California, January, 1859.

———

ADDRESSES

By the Hon. SOLOMON HEYDENFELDT; Rev. Drs. ECKMAN, SCOTT, PECK and HENRY; Col. E. D. BAKER; Messrs. F. P. TRACY, M. M. NOAH, and others.

Preamble and Resolutions, unanimously adopted; Letter from Rev. Dr. CUTLER; Remarks of the Press, etc., etc.

———

SERMON

On "RELIGIOUS INTOLERANCE" (delivered at the "Unitarian Church.")

———

SAN FRANCISCO:

TOWNE & BACON, PRINTERS, EXCELSIOR BOOK AND JOB OFFICE,
No. 125 Clay Street, corner of Sansome.

1859.

In 1858 the papal authorities in Bologna, Italy, removed Edgardo Mortara, a Jewish child, age six, from his home and raised him as a Christian. Protest meetings were held in Europe and the United States, including San Francisco.

Samuel N. Pike (b. 1822), a Cincinnati businessman, built
Pike's Opera House in 1859. Courtesy, Cincinnati
Historical Society.

Samuel Myer Isaacs (d. 1878), a native of Holland, was
reared in England but came to New York City in 1839 to
serve the first Ashkenazic congregation in that city. This
minister, the founder of the *Jewish Messenger*, was one of
the leaders of the New York Jewish community.
Courtesy, American Jewish Archives.

J. Ross Browne, a reporter and artist, visited the Nevada
silver diggings in 1860. In the above drawing he depicts a
Jewish peddler-prospector. From *A Peep at Washoe*.
Courtesy, American Jewish Archives.

The St. Louis Cathedral, Third and Walnut, with the
ineffable Name of God in Hebrew. Courtesy, Alexander
Piaget, Missouri Historical Society, St. Louis.

The Minis House in Savannah. The Minis family were
Georgia pioneers. Courtesy, David A. Byck, Savannah.

Isidor Bush (1822–1898), litterateur, publicist, and
viticulturist, edited the first American Jewish paper. He was
a leader in the general and Jewish community of St. Louis.
Couresty, American Jewish Archives.

CHAPTER FIVE

BUSINESS SURVIVAL IN THE TRANSMISSISSIPPI

STATES AND TERRITORIES

THE JEWISH ROLE

Almost half of the lands in the United States lie between the Cascades and the Sierras on the west and the 100th meridian on the east. This vast mountain, desert and plateau country first attracted numerous settlers when gold and silver were discovered. Interest in mining was nothing new for the Jews. Joachim Gaunse, the first known Jew in what is now the United States, was a mining expert (1585). In the sixteenth and seventeenth centuries Marranos, crypto-Jews, were listed among the mine owners of Mexico, and as early as the 1660's a "gold-finding Jew" failed at his task in Barbados. The only precious metal he found was a gold chain which Charles II gave him and which he had to return. In the mid-eighteenth century, Isaac Levy was interested in exploiting Canadian coal mines and the Franks-Gratz consortium of the 1770's looked forward to the discovery and exploitation of mines in the Mississippi Valley. At the time of the American Revolution the Simsons and Myer Myers were hoping to mine lead in Connecticut for Continental rifles and muskets.[1]

The decade following the California gold rush of 1849 brought Jews to the mining country by the thousands. A peevish Christian minister of the day told his audience that Jews would not work in the mines, that they would not labor manually, and that in pursuit of gain they observed neither the Jewish Sabbath nor the Christian Sunday. He was right when he said that they neglected the Sabbath, wrong when he intimated that there were no Jewish pick and shovel miners. Individual Jews were found in all the diggings of the Mother Lode but by the end of the 1850's most of them were no longer attempting to pan gold. When they found that nuggets could not be shoveled off the ground they turned to trade, treating mines as a commodity: they worked and leased them, bought and sold claims, and grubstaked diggers and prospectors. Without the credit that the Jews gave, many miners would not have survived. This was the pattern not only in California but in all the "strikes" up to the turn of the century. As late as the 1890's Jakie Cohen at the Monte Christo camp in the Cascades of northern Washington grubstaked miners at his hotel. When shaft and machine mining came in, the Jews, except for a few capitalists, went out. If they remained in the camps, it was as clothiers and general merchants.[2]

As new discoveries were made the California Jews moved north and east following the gold-seeking throngs. They crossed the border northward to Oregon and moved east to Nevada. Traveling still further, Jewish adventurers and businessmen moved into Idaho to profit from the strikes in the valleys of the Snake, the Salmon, and the Clearwater. In the 1890's Joseph Kline was in the Coeur d'Alene country as a shopkeeper if not as a miner. Crossing the plains from Leavenworth in the 1860's he had made almost every "excitement" since the Pike's Peak or Bust boom in Colorado. He had wandered into Colorado and Montana sometime in the 1860's, into New Mexico and the Black Hills in the 1870's, and was back at Leadville, Colorado, in the 1880's heading north once again for Idaho. He was not exceptional. What prompted men like Kline to wander: profit, adventure, escape from the humdrum bore of family life?[3]

When Joseph Kline pushed north into Montana in 1863 he had been traveling seventy-two days with a mule or ox train. Like many others he was moving toward Alder Gulch or Virginia City; a year later the throngs swarmed into Last Chance Gulch or Helena and by the late 1860's miners were trying their luck along the Sweetwater River in central Wyoming. Not many Jews owned claims in Wyoming. It was not mining country, but among those who mined there for a brief time was the Pole, Isidore Morris. Shortly after this youngster landed in California the Civil War erupted and he joined the Union Army rising to the rank of lieutenant. After the War he drifted to Utah where he opened a general store and spread out into mining in Idaho and Wyoming. Morris, an Orthodox Jew, married a Mormon girl and converted her to Judaism. He was very close to the leaders of the Latter Day Saints and interceded successfully with President Cleveland after one of them, a bishop, was imprisoned on a charge of polygamy. When, in the same decade of the 1890's, he sponsored Montefiore Congregation, an Orthodox synagog in Salt Lake, the Mormons mindful of his friendship in their hour of need, rallied to help him financially. In the small community of Salt Lake City Morris must have known the Bamberger brothers intimately. Of the four brothers, Herman, Simon, Jacob, and Louis, Simon was the most capable and helped to make the others rich. All four of them were in mining, in gold, silver, copper, and coal. Jacob was tied up with the Guggenheim interests. Simon made a fortune out of his gold mine, the "Centennial Eureka," but lost most of it building a rail line to the coal fields of southern Utah and another between Salt Lake and Ogden.[4]

Though the mining industry was of no significance in bringing Jews to Wyoming, the opposite was true in Colorado where the Jewish community was built by the men who came to Denver in the Rush to the Rockies in 1859, and later to Central City, Canon City, Boulder, and California Gulch, or as it was later known, Leadville. Among those in California Gulch when it was a boom town of over 10,000 was the young East European, Wolfe Londoner. He had come out with a wagon train, but was compelled by the wagon master to walk most of the way; when his hobnail boots tortured him he walked barefoot. A St. Louis wholesaler named Hanauer put him in charge of a branch store in California Gulch; his place of business, a commodious room, served also as the office of the county clerk, the recorder, the clerks, and the postmaster. As the recorder of the county, Londoner made $10,000 in fees in one year alone. But by 1865 the Gulch was almost deserted only to rise again in the late 1870's as the bustling city of Leadville when silver and lead were mined.

It bears repetition: wherever there was a strike, there Jews were to be found. In the 1880's there was even a Jewish cemetery tucked away in the obscure town of Tincup in Gunnison County, Colorado. The Cripple Creek gold stampede of the 1890's brought in a young adventurer from the East by the name of Bernard Baruch. He invested in one of the mines hoping to become wealthy, but until his ship came in he went to work as a mucker shoveling ore until he was promoted to the blasting crew. When one of the diggers tried to bully him, Baruch, a skillful boxer, knocked him out. Frequently he spent his evenings in a gambling house and did very well until the owner invited him not to return. It did not take Baruch very long before he learned an important lesson: "People who try to get rich from mining often put more into the ground than they take out." He went back to New York, to Wall Street, and to a great career as an eminent American.[5]

There is a pattern in the lives of those Jewish businessmen of the Great Plains who were in the mining industry. Their bread and butter money came from their stores. They always had to have something solid on which they could fall back when they engaged in a speculative enterprise. Isidore Morris of Salt Lake had a general store; Luis (Louis) Lessing of Beaver County, Utah, had a hotel in Minersville as early as 1859 and later had an interest in a smelter; Moses Hirschman of Salt Lake was a freighter and owner of a shoe store; Samuel Schwab of Provo was a clothier; his sons attended the Mormon Sunday School although they remained Jewish. All these men owned and operated mines in different parts of the Mormon state; Lessing and Hirschman had mined in other states before settling down in Utah; the lure of quick money was hard to resist. The element of adventure was never absent; this was certainly true of those Jews who settled finally in Arizona. As early as the 1860's, the

California Pole, David Lubin, had wandered through the Arizona mountains as a prospector just about the time that Michael and Joseph Goldwater followed the same eastward path after fortune had evaded them in the Mother Lode mines and in a Los Angeles shop. Two other Polish Jews who had come from California, the Goldberg brothers, Hyman and Joseph, owned mines in Tombstone and the Dragoon Mountains. But like most of their Jewish compatriots in that line of business they lacked the golden touch; the precious metal lay only in their names.[6]

Among the most important miners were members of the Freudenthal-Lesinsky clan who had started out as large-scale retail and wholesale merchants in Las Cruces, New Mexico. Julius Freudenthal, an East German, had coopted the services of a sister's son, Henry Lesinsky, and two sons of his brother Louis. In 1865 Lesinsky had gone down into Mexico to look at an old Mexico mine, and in the 1870's the firm bought into the Longfellow, a copper mine. Later it bought out the original owner. The Longfellow was over 200 miles from Las Cruces and many hundreds of miles from the nearest railroad; the firm was compelled to freight all supplies along bad roads through Apache country. The Freudenthal-Lesinsky men were in no sense miners or engineers yet they built a narrow-gauge railroad to a rude experimental smelter which they had contrived. As employers of six hundred men they were the first large-scale mining operators in Arizona Territory. Until the Santa Fe Railroad came west the smeltered copper was hauled by an ox cart over the trail to Independence, Missouri. The trip took five months. The isolated miners were paid in scrip which was exchangeable for goods and provisions in the company's store operated by Ben Michelson, one of the Nevada clan. The Freudenthal-Lesinsky group sold the Longfellow to a foreign syndicate in 1882 and the mine was ultimately taken over by Phelps Dodge & Company. Lesinsky, the guiding spirit of the Arizona end of the business, was a self-educated highly intelligent sensitive freethinker, a cultured man. Though he had in his youth received a good Jewish education he had no interest whatsoever in Judaism.[7]

Just about the time that Henry Lesinsky and his associates sold the Longfellow, Leopold Ephraim, another immigrant, moved south in Arizona to the Mexican border and settled in Nogales, originally the Jewish crossroad hamlet of Isaacson. Ephraim owned a mine in nearby Sonora which he operated in the 1890's with 300 workers, mostly Chinese. John B. Newman of Globe was another mining entrepreneur of that generation. Blackjack Newman, as he was known, arrived in the United States in 1876, married out of the faith, joined Roosevelt as a Rough Rider in the Spanish-American War and made a fortune as a copper miner despite being illiterate. The only time in his life that he got drunk was when his son Sam was born and Blackjack stood for free drinks for everybody in

Globe. The copper enterprises of the Arizona Jews, beginning in the 1870's, were in no sense "stampedes." They were big business involving large expenditures of capital. One of the last stampedes was in 1875 and 1876 when thousands joined in the gold rush to Deadwood Gulch in the Black Hills of Dakota, a rush in which the Jews participated. Yet with a few notable exceptions Jewish interest in mining was, as has already been noted, peripheral. There were, however, a number of eastern Jewish capitalists who turned to mining and helped build it into one of the great corporate industries of this country.[8]

In the middle 1850's placer mining began to give way to shaft mining; the manual processes were superseded by mechanical ones. As the ores were dug up by the hundreds of thousands and millions of tons, mining came under the control of creative capitalists. In New York City the three Lewisohn brothers from Hamburg, Leonard, Julius, and Adolph, turned from the feather, bristle, and wool business to the metal trade in the 1860's. By the late 1870's they had become copper mine owners and refiners helping to develop one of the most important copper sales agencies in the United States.[9]

The Guggenheims were probably America's most powerful mining family at the turn of the century. The father, Meyer, had come up the hard way. At nineteen this Swiss-born immigrant had accompanied his parents to the United States escaping with them from the petty disabilities to which they were exposed in the Canton of Aargau. Meyer became a city peddler, moved on to the manufacture and sale of shoe polish and lye, sold groceries, and after twenty-five years of grinding labor turned to the Swiss embroidery business. His seven sons worked closely with him. In the early 1880's Meyer drifted into the metal trade through purchase of mines in Colorado but soon turned to smelting and refining. In 1899 the family created the successful Guggenheim Exploration Company becoming prospectors, engineers, promoters, and financiers. By 1901 it had taken over the "trust," the American Smelting and Refining Company, which through the genius of Daniel Guggenheim, the oldest of the seven sons, became an international firm with far-flung interests. It controlled tin mines in Bolivia, nitrates in Chile, gold mines in the Yukon, diamond fields and rubber plantations in the Congo, and copper mines in Alaska, Utah, and Chile. In the late 1870's when Meyer Guggenheim, already a rich embroidery importer, bought his first mines in Colorado, the Jews of Aargau were finally accorded the rights of citizenship. For the Guggenheims America had spelled freedom, opportunity, and fabulous wealth.[10]

The Jewish communities west of the Missouri owe their existence to the mining strikes. Were it not for the hope of speedy wealth Jews and most others would have remained at ease in Zion. Most of the old mining towns in the High Plains that still sheltered Jews survived for fortuitous reasons: new economic opportunities in trade and in commerce, tourism and industry. Denver has long outgrown the gold rush of the 1850's.

JEWS AND THE CATTLE INDUSTRY

The miners opened up the Great Plains; the cattlemen continued the conquest and occupied the territory. Ranchers of course are typical of a pioneer economy; they spring up on the edge of settlements—the cutting edge of the frontier. The earliest Americans grazed their herds in the forests and meadows on the fringes of their tidewater farms. The Minises and Sheftalls of eighteenth-century Georgia, innkeepers, shopkeepers, and merchants, ran their AM, 5S, and L Diamond S brand in the Georgia hinterland, and as the frontier moved west, the ranchers moved with it. Thus before 1870 when North Wisconsin was still unsettled, a Jewish cattleman drove his herds north to the Great Lakes for transshipment to Chicago or to the East. The cattle industry found its classical locale and its home on the semi-arid plateaus of the Great Plains and in the intermountain region as far west as California. California has been an important cattle, sheep, and wool country since the Spanish days. The Jewish businessman of the 1850's became involved in the cattle and sheep industry because cattle and sheep were a medium of payment used as barter or to settle debts. Cattle and sheep were basic commodities and Jews trafficked in them as they did in mines, and, in the eighteenth-century East, in furs. They had no choice. In 1859 B. Bachman of Los Angeles drove 500 head of cattle from Salt Lake to Los Angeles. He was apparently bringing coals to Newcastle, but there can be no doubt that this wholesale grocery, hardware, and clothing firm was collecting as best it could payment for shipments to the Mormon country. From the 1850's into the twentieth century Jewish merchants even became ranchers, opening ranches in various parts of California, in the Sierras, and particularly in the Southwest. A mountain peak in the Sequoia National Forest area was named Mt. Goldstein in honor of Isaac Goldstein, a one-time Idaho miner who owned a large ranch in Tulare County.[11]

All through the second half of the nineteenth century Jewish merchants found themselves dealing in sheep and wool in southern California, Texas, New Mexico, Arizona, and even Montana. Nathan Bibo of Bernalillo, New Mexico, lost his large herd in a snowstorm in 1876; the Navajos took some and a bandit made off with others and when Bibo caught up with him the Jewish merchant could not bring himself to kill him although urged by a companion to do so. Murder is not a Jewish business. The Bibos of Bernalillo were relatively small traders but their interest in sheep was typical of the New Mexico Jewish businessman who would turn to any regional industry that promised a profit. As early as the

1870's, Lehman Spiegelberg and an associate were financing Navajos on the reservation to raise sheep and goats for them. By the next decade the Rosenwalds and the Ilfelds of Las Vegas, New Mexico, were also active in the sheep and wool industry adapting and developing a complex partnership system with the Indians whereby they, the capitalists, supplied the money, the administration, and the marketing of the products. It was a variation of the merchant-shipping put-out system. The Ilfelds and their associates persisted in this industry well into the twentieth century despite the hazards of drought which on occasion made devastating inroads into the huge flocks. Like the cattle business it frequently failed to show a profit.[12]

The Solomons of Solomonville in southeastern Arizona introduced sheep into their part of the territory but their herders were killed by the Indians. Isaac Gronsky of Texas and New Mexico was once acclaimed the Sheep King of the United States, a title, generously conferred by a newspaper, which need not be taken too seriously. There were probably numerous sheep and cattle entrepreneurs of the late nineteenth century who owned herds that ran into the many thousands. Gronsky was a Russian Jew who landed in Montreal in 1852 and contracted to supply the horses to pull the street cars; when cholera killed off his stable he turned to ox power. From Canada he moved south to Fort Worth where he secured a grading contract from the Texas & Pacific Railroad which was building a line from Fort Worth to El Paso. After that he opened a country-town hardware store and when he was burned out moved on again, started anew with a peanut stand. In the course of time he opened a grocery store, an ice factory, and an electric light plant. His fourth Texas remove found him in Big Springs where he bought a herd of two thousand sheep at $1.25 a head. He was now in the sheep business and before his flocks were wiped out by cholera and other misfortunes he owned herds of 50,000 to 65,000 head which grazed in Mexico, Texas, and New Mexico. He died in 1911, a poor man.[13]

Other early Texas Jews also found themselves in the cattle business. In a way the Halff brothers, Adolphe, Mayer, and Solomon, were typical. After working out of Galveston in the 1840's as a pack peddler, Adolphe settled in Liberty, East Texas, and was soon driving cattle on the old Spanish Trail to New Orleans. The cattle he drove east had been received in barter. In the 1860's the Halff brothers, now a wholesale dry goods house, moved west to San Antonio where they soon spread into ranching. Their Circle Dot ranch with its 50,000 acres of grazing lands was situated in Brewster County near the Mexican border. Very few Jews were actually cowboys; Samuel L. Lazarus was one of the exceptions. Unlike most of his coreligionists he was a native American. After running away from home at the age of thirteen he moved on from New Orleans to

Texas where he clerked, bought hides, punched cows, and traded in cattle. This was in the 1870's. By 1883, a man of twenty-seven, he was vice president of a cattle company. From then on he moved up rapidly. In turn he became the receiver of a railroad, president of a railroad, a cement manufacturer, a banker, a real estate entrepreneur, and one of the most influential politicians in St. Louis and Missouri where he finally settled. As president of the city council he was on occasion acting mayor of the city. When Rabbi Leon Harrison buried him in 1926 he said that Lazarus's life was "a great prose poem" written "across the face of our American southwest." "He helped to extend the frontier of American civilization into the wilderness."[14]

In the pre-railroad days some of the Jewish cattlemen undoubtedly participated in the drives north to the railheads in Missouri, Kansas, Nebraska, and Wyoming. The great drives of the post-Civil War period to the 1880's made it possible for the West Texans to tap the markets of Kansas City, Chicago, and the factory metropolises of the East. The Jewish traildriver, like the Jewish cowboy, was an exception. Among the traildrivers north to Dodge City, Kansas, was the Mexican war veteran, L. M. Kokernot, a member of a Dutch Jewish family and a successful businessman. When paid off, the cowboys and trail bosses who stayed sober and did not gamble away their hard earned wages could buy new outfits in the Jewish stores of the cow towns. In Abilene they could replenish their wardrobes in Jacob Karatofsky's Great Western Store, M. Goldsoll's Texas Store, or at the emporium run by Reuben and Ringolsky.[15]

In the late 1880's and early 1890's as the railroads expanded, the Texans made an effort to set up their own slaughter and refrigeration plants for the processing of cattle and the shipping of beef to the East and to Europe. Isaac Dahlman, a Brooklyn clothier who had settled in Fort Worth, had a contract with English businessmen to ship 60,000 head of slaughtered cattle to England, but his gallant attempt to establish a packing industry in Fort Worth failed. As the Texas cattlemen drove their herds north they discovered the advantages of the open range with its free grass. By the 1870's Texas cattle grazed the northern plains from the Mississippi River west to the Sierra Nevada. With the buffalo and the Indians gone the cattle industry boomed. Expenses were minimal, profits great; individual Jews now tried their hand at ranching. In the 1860's Simon Nathan went into farming and ranching in Colorado's Arkansas Valley after a stint at mining in California Gulch. While he was ranching in the valley, Indians kidnapped his baby but he was successful in ransoming the child. Ranching, however, was not his métier and he soon turned to storekeeping in nearby Pueblo where he edified his neighbors by bringing the first tin bathtub into town. Later he delighted his daughter Rebecca by hauling in a piano for her. It came by ox cart. Nathan was very active in the local Jewish community and most generous in his gifts to it.[16]

Some Jews came into the cattle industry as investors; Charles Popper, a wholesale butcher, branched out into ranching to provide for the army posts where he had meat contracts. After living in San Francisco and in Virginia City, Nevada, he had settled in Salt Lake in 1864 where he opened a slaughterhouse. As an observant Jew he kept his plant closed on Rosh Hashanah and Yom Kippur, and his Christian colleagues out of deference for him also closed their places of business on those days. Popper, in turn, closed his slaughterhouse on Pioneer Day out of respect for his Mormon friends. He established large ranches in northeastern Utah, in the Duchesne region, and when the roundup was over he drove his cattle to the railroad in western Colorado whence they were shipped eastward.[17]

After peddling along the line of the Union Pacific Railroad Henry Altman turned to the liquor business and then, together with both Jewish and Christian partners, developed the finest cattle-breeding farm in Wyoming. The 35,000-acre ranch on the outskirts of Cheyenne bred registered Herefords which were fed with hay grown on 700 acres of irrigated land. There were cattlemen in the Wyoming Stock Growers' Association with "German Jewish" names such as Hecht and Goldschmidt, but names alone prove nothing. By the turn of the century, some of New Mexico Jews were active in the cattle trade; like most Jewish cattlemen they, too, were primarily urban businessmen. The Floersheims of Springer, New Mexico, are typical of this involvement. For the last two generations they have been primarily cattlemen. Las Jaritas—the Willows—their 60,000-acre holding, is one of the most beautiful ranches in all the West. Its completely fenced pastures are patrolled in jeeps and the entire huge operation is administered by fewer than a dozen permanent employees.[18]

During the hard winter of late 1886 Louis S. Kaufman of Helena, Montana, wrote to one of his cowboys inquiring as to the condition of the herd. Kaufman, a Jew, and his Christian partner, Louis Stadler, were owners of the OH ranch. The cowboy responded by sending a card on which he sketched a gaunt dying cow with his rump to the blizzard flanked by hungry waiting coyotes. He signed it CHR. This was the sketch "The Last of Five Thousand" which marks the beginning of the career of Charles H. Russell, one of the most distinguished painters of the American West. His first sketches were only worth a drink at a bar; "When the land belonged to God," a 1914 oil painting of his was recently valued by its owners at $250,000.

In the Dakotas, in the Black Hills in 1882, there was a small ranch holding, the "RMK" brand of Rosenbaum and Mankin. Rosenbaum may have been one of the Rosenbaum brothers of Chicago. These two Bavarians, Morris and Joseph Rosenbaum, had come to Iowa in 1850 to join their father. During the Civil War the undersized Joseph joined the 31st Iowa Infantry and rose from private to lieutenant and regimental adjutant.

It was his boast that "he never missed a roll call or a meal—when he could get one—while in the service." The brothers went out on their own as storekeepers, made money, and then opened country banks. By the 1870's the wealthy Rosenbaum Brothers had started a livestock commission house in Chicago; in a good year it would gross $10,000,000 in sales. In later years the firm became interested in the grain trade and may have become the largest grain house in the country. When Montana ranchers lost their cattle in the terrible blizzard of 1887 they turned to the Rosenbaums who advanced them over a million dollars. Twenty years later in the panic of 1907 when the Rosenbaums themselves were about to go bankrupt their Montana friends rallied to their aid and saved them. Even in the realistic world of business fairy tales sometimes come true. This is fortunate, for it restores our faith in fairies.[19]

JEWS IN THE FENCED CATTLE INDUSTRY

By the time the Floersheims of Springer applied themselves seriously to the cattle industry and deserted the counter for the stockpen and the corral, the cattle business had undergone a revolution. Lands were now owned outright or leased, live stock was fenced with barbed ("bob") wire, wells were driven, winter feed was grown, and improved breeds were carefully developed. Unlike the twentieth-century ranch-owning Floersheims, few Jewish businessmen limited themselves solely to raising cattle. Like Jews involved in the mining industry, most Jews in the speculative cattle trade retained their interests in other—safer—enterprises. Simon Newman of Newman, Stanislaus County, California, had turned to ranching in the San Joaquin Valley in the 1870's but the passing of decades found him and his dynasty involved in storekeeping, in agriculture, dairies, grain storage, and banking. Like Charles Popper of Utah, August Heilbron of Sacramento and San Francisco began his career as a butcher. By the 1850's he was packing pork and by the 1870's he was raising his own beef on ranch lands. Ultimately, in the 1880's, he owned a huge ranch; all 60,000 acres of his holdings were fenced and during a busy season he might employ anywhere from 200 to 400 men. Farther south in Kern County, German-born Henry A. Jastro turned from California-Arizona freighting to farming and ranching. In 1870 he married a daughter of Thomas Baker, the founder of the city of Bakersfield. Jastro was primarily an agriculture and ranching administrator and at an early period identified himself with the interests that became the Kern County Land Company. At one time the company controlled over a million acres of farm and ranching land in California, New Mexico, and Arizona. One of the holdings of this agriculture and cattle empire included "the greatest irrigated farm in the world." Jastro, the general manager of the empire, was once president of the American Live Stock Association, a regent of the University of California, the head of a local bank, and the president of the County Board of Supervisors. A critic once wrote sarcastically that he controlled the money, the land, and the taxpayers of Kern County.[20]

As president of the Los Angeles Farming and Milling Company, Levi Strauss, the clothing manufacturer, found himself the head of a ranch that owned thousands of head of cattle and sheep. Newman, Heilbron, Levi Strauss, and Jastro were Californians; Nelson Morris whose success far exceeded theirs was a Chicagoan. Morris, a native of Germany's Black Forest area, started his career in the Chicago stockyards where he soon became a large-scale trader shipping cattle to the East and Europe. By the 1870's, already a millionaire, he established his own countrywide packing business ultimately known as Morris & Company. The corporation which owned large cattle ranches in Indiana, Nebraska, and the Dakotas, also had a 300,000-acre holding in Texas. Morris imported stock from Europe to improve breeds and at one time was deemed the largest cattle feeder in the world.[21]

In spite of the notable success of individuals, cattle was not a Jewish business, certainly not in the United States. It would seem that most Jews in the industry drifted into it to salvage loans and to protect credit advanced. It was a peripheral business for them and most of them got out of it or were forced out by bad times. Very few Jewish ranchers made money.

THE URBAN FRONTIER

For the Jews in the High Plains commerce was most important. When numerous sedentary merchants came into the Southwest in the 1850's, they were not the first Jewish arrivals; they were preceded by traveling merchants—itinerants, but certainly not peddlers—who had followed the Santa Fe Trail into New Mexico and northern Old Mexico. The Santa Fe Trail and the Mexican province of New Mexico had been opened up to American trade in 1821 after the Spanish rulers were driven out. Jewish merchant-traders began to make their presence felt in the 1840's as they carried in large quantities of consumer goods and carried out gold and silver. As they continued to move south they penetrated Mexico for 1,000 miles, and found themselves about 1,800 miles distant from their secondary source of supplies, the towns on the Missouri River. This Santa Fe trade persisted to 1880 when the railroads finally reached the New Mexico capital.[22]

The most notable of these large-scale itinerant Jewish merchants was the Prussian Albert Speyer (Speyers, Spears, Spiers) who may have been related to the Frankfort banking family of the same name. Speyer was in

California in the pre-gold rush days and may then have carried on large-scale trade with the Mexicans. At all events by the early 1840's he was moving along the Trail with a large caravan of his own. The men of that day who carried on the commerce of the prairies knew him well and respected him as a highly cultured, intelligent gentleman. After noting that Speyer had purchased a painting that turned out to be an old master one writer pointed out that Speyer was a Jew who knew a good thing when he saw it. He remained in the Santa Fe traffic until the end of the decade exhibiting courage and competence as he battled with Comanches, Apaches, and Navajos, with blizzards, sutlers, and the exorbitant demands of corrupt Mexican officialdom.

In 1846, shortly before the declaration of war against Mexico by the United States, Speyer was already on the road with his wagons and a small consignment of munitions. The first American troops sent west had orders to seize his ammunition to prevent it falling into the hands of the Mexicans. Speyer, a Prussian citizen who also carried an English passport, was determined to sell his supplies, including his gunpowder and arms, before he was held up by the advancing American troops and the accompanying competing traders. He beat them to Santa Fe. Among the troops were the men of Col. Alexander William Doniphan's First Regiment of Missouri Mounted Infantry. Benjamin J. Latz of St. Louis, a private in Company A, fought in all its engagements in Mexico till he was mustered out in New Orleans in 1847. He liked New Mexico well enough to return there in the 1850's and to fight in its Indian wars, yet when the Jecarilla and Mescalero Apaches sued for peace he was one of their representatives. During the Civil War, after the Confederates invaded the territory, he joined the Union forces at the battle of Valverde. Just two years later, in 1864, he was laid to rest by the Masons and Odd Fellows. After leaving the Santa Fe Trail, probably in the late 1840's, Speyer next appeared, about 1861 as a Broad Street broker in New York City, married into a prominent New York Christian family. When Jay Gould and James Fisk, Jr., and their cohorts set out to corner the gold supply Speyer was one of their purchasing agents, but when the government finally intervened and broke the corner on Black Friday, September 24, 1869, Speyer's principals disavowed him and ruined him. Apparently he made some sort of a comeback after that fateful day as he turned to real estate and to the production and sale of fertilizer. When he died in 1880 he was given a Christian burial.[23]

FURS AND HIDES

Even Albert Speyer of the 1840's was no Jewish Pilgrim Father of the plains; Jewish fur buyers, traders, and outfitters had preceded him. Young

Philip Philipson of St. Louis had gone west with the mountain men in the early nineteenth century (1830), and David Solomon, who may have been a Jew, was doing business with the Sioux Outfit in the 1830's. In that same decade Martin W. Oppenheim, a German Jew, had come to New York from London where he had represented the family fur business. In the United States he competed with Ramsay Cook's American Fur Company and even reached out to control the market in furs and deerskins. Oppenheim, who commuted between London, New York, and the American Middle West, was an aggressive businessman who was willing to work on a small margin of profit.[24]

The traders and fur enterprisers were rarely settlers; the Jewish hide men, however, were established businessmen who specialized in hides and robes during the days when the buffalo were being exterminated. Killing of the bison was big business; the thousands of hunters and skinners were joined by the hide buyers. In the late 1870's the outstanding hide firm west of the Rockies was Bissinger & Co. whose headquarters was in San Francisco; east of the Rockies some of the largest hide and robe buyers were Jews, like J. & A. Boskowitz whose purchases over a few years amounted to almost a million dollars. The W. C. Lobenstein (Lowenstein) company of Leavenworth, which had been in the leather business since the 1860's, advertised in the 1876 *Fort Worth Directory* that it was the largest dealer in the world in hides, peltries, and furs.[25]

The hide people did their own freighting and hauling in large eight-horse team wagons. Jews participated actively in the freighting business in pre-railroad days. Some St. Louis Jewish firms freighted their goods into Colorado and New Mexico; it was more common for the important sedentary merchants of the plains to haul their own goods from the Missouri River to their central depots in Denver, Salt Lake, or in Las Vegas and Albuquerque, New Mexico. Once a merchant had a base he shipped his goods out to a neighboring satellite territory whence they were carried on to still smaller towns. Freighting and merchandising were closely related and most freighters were themselves merchants. The Jews who had contracts to supply the army posts with grain, hay, and provisions were heavily involved in various types of freighting operations. There was a constant shipping and transshipping, not only between the Missouri jumping-off strip and the Southwest but between Denver, Salt Lake City, and the mining and cattle towns of Wyoming, Montana, and Idaho.[26]

VIOLENCE

The merchants of the western plateaus faced many commercial hazards; they were also exposed to physical violence in the days when the plains were opened up to settlement. The tradition of the West—as a scene of uninterrupted violence, of robbing and killing, and deeds of derring-do by peace officers—has been kept alive by the paperback and movie accounts of stagecoach and railroad holdups, by tales told of marshals like Wild Bill Hickok, Bat Masterson, and Wyatt Earp, by countless chronicles of the heroic Texas Rangers. Was there, in fact, more danger and more un-natural death in this pioneer country than in other places? Wherever there is no firm organized government there is violence and killing. The first English settlers in North Carolina in the 1580's were probably killed off; the New Englanders in the early 1600's had to fight Indians to survive. And in 1867 when Henry Siegel took out a $10,000 life insurance policy with the Equitable Life Assurance Society of New York he was told that he could go west as a merchant but not as a miner.

Actually the brutality of the West has not only been glamorized but also exaggerated, the insurance companies notwithstanding. They are never hesitant in imposing restrictions to their own advantage. The Indians to be sure were always a potential threat, particularly in Arizona. Michael Goldwater and Michael Wormser, both businessmen, were wounded in Indian attacks. Goldwater carried a rifle on the road but no pistol in the city. Wormser was wounded by Apaches when one of his pack trains was attacked and he had to abandon an irrigated farm because of the forays of Indians who harassed and killed his workmen. This was in the post-Civil War period. In the southeastern part of the Territory the Apaches were troublesome as late as the 1880's. Apaches from the San Carlos Reservation killed a number of Isidor Solomon's herdsmen and ran off with his mules; the Jewish owners of the copper mine at Clifton were apprehensive as Geronimo raided nearby settlements, killing miners and engineers.[27]

Hard-boiled customers could at times be as dangerous as Apaches on the rampage. Wolf Cohen, a young Jewish merchant in San Bernardino in the 1860's, brawled with a man named Dick Cole. After calling the storekeeper a "damned Jew, son of a bitch," Cole reached for his pistol and murdered him. Isaac Cohen, a brother who had come in from Los Angeles, then ran for a gun and killed Cole. One of the newspapers hinted at a lynching but the grand jury took no action, refusing to indict. Young Cohen, only twenty-four years of age, was buried in the San Bernardino cemetery, and tradition with distortions of its own, soon maintained that he had been killed by Indians as he was driving a prairie schooner.[28]

Samuel Dittenhoefer, a member of a notable New York family, ran a store on one of the Navajo reservations in western New Mexico. Familiarly known as Navajo Sam because of his knowledge of the New Mexico and Arizona country, he had served as a scout and had fought the Apaches under Victorio and Geronimo. One day in November, 1891, a horse and cattle rustler by the name of Tom Collins came into Sam's store and started to quarrel with him. Sam, a tough frontiersman with a bad temper, punched Collins who then shot and killed Sam and rode off. No effort apparently was made to apprehend the killer. In 1883 Aaron Morris of Hailey, Idaho, was murdered on the road at night by a highwayman who knew that the storekeeper was carrying a large sum of money. In 1892 a Jewish peddler, Sam Bernstein, was found murdered in the mountains of northwestern Colorado. His partner Israel Engel, who was accused of killing him, maintained his innocence and turned to his fellow Jews in Colorado for help. The B'nai B'rith Order sent out an appeal to the lodges of the South and Southwest asking them to provide the funds for Engel's defense; it is not known whether Engel was exonerated or not.[29]

Of this there can be no question: in a region where law and order were in a state of becoming and where resort to force was deemed a respected aspect of manliness, some Jews also adopted the mores of their peers. A tombstone in a Jewish cemetery in San Antonio, Texas, has a very interesting bas-relief showing two frock-coated men with drawn pistols confronting one another. Tradition has it, and this is apparently authentic, that two Jews, Siegmund Moses Feinberg and Benedict Schwartz, a pawnshop owner, quarreled and on the night of December 10, 1857, Schwartz killed Feinberg. Tradition further adds the detail that they dueled and the fight was over a dog. Regina Feinberg, then pregnant, gave birth to a girl after the death of her young husband. The infant soon died and was buried alongside her father. The bereaved and distraught wife had the tombstone made in Philadelphia whence it was shipped to a Gulf port and then hauled overland by oxcart to San Antonio. Strangely enough, no accounts of the killing were found in the local newspapers. Were shootings too common to be reported? Schwartz too died of violence; he was stabbed to death in his pawnshop. Both Feinberg and Schwartz were native Russians.[30]

Nathan Bibo, a brilliant and able businessman, was the post trader at Camp Apache, Arizona, in the 1870's. He and his family built one of the first roads—if not the first road—for commercial purposes between New Mexico and eastern Arizona. At the fort, Bibo also had a bar and when he once refused to serve a soldier who was already drunk the latter took a shot at him but fortunately missed. One of Nathan's cooks attempted to assassinate him but a watchful dog alerted the storekeeper who escaped injury; the cook in turn was later killed by Solomon Barth, a well-known Arizona Jewish pioneer. The Bibos had a branch known as the Block & Bibo store at Grants in Valencia County in the 1880's. Like other western emporia it sold beer and when on June 20, 1889, three cowboys became drunk and unruly they were ordered out at the point of a gun by Sol Block. The cowboys took the gun away from Block and started to beat him; Simon Bibo, a deputy sheriff, rushed in with a Winchester, but they disarmed him too. By this time Sol had picked up his gun and started shooting and when the smoke cleared, one cowboy was dead, a second wounded, and the third had fled. The court exonerated Block, declaring that he had fired in self-defense.[31]

By the very nature of their business Jewish saloonkeepers were bound to get into trouble. Moses Adler, a Denver barkeeper, who stabbed and killed a soldier in 1861, was jailed, and a man named Faraber, who ran an inn and bar in the Sange de Cristo pass in Colorado, was accused of murder (1874). Though Faraber had a bad reputation, he stoutly insisted on his innocence and the Denver B'nai B'rith Lodge helped him secure counsel. He ended up in the penitentiary to which he was sentenced for a period of five years. In Montana in the 1890's, Jew Jake ran a saloon in the mining town of Landusky near the Fort Belknap Indian Reservation. Jake had only one leg using a rifle as a crutch to replace the leg he had lost in a fight with a deputy sheriff in Great Falls.[32]

In general Jews on the western frontier were very rarely involved in homicide. Abe Rothschild was one of the exceptions. In 1877 he was arrested for the murder of Diamond Bess, a fast woman, and found guilty. The case dragged on for years: the venue was changed; his family, a Cincinnati pioneer in the installment furniture trade, spent large sums on him, and the Jews of Jefferson, Texas, one of the state's large Jewish communities, exerted considerable pressure to save him. They were aghast lest he be convicted of murder and reflect on their status as law-abiding citizens. Rothschild finally escaped prison or the gallows on a legal technicality. The appeal record in 1880 ran to 800 pages. Though Jewish killers were rare, Jewish gamblers were common. Even a solid businessman like Nathan Bibo was said to have lost $5,000 in a single night at cards, but he was no professional gambler. Jim Levy who was interested in a milling enterprise in Virginia City, Nevada, was a gambler. He had been in Deadwood in the Black Hills and came over to Cheyenne where, on February 9, 1877, he got into a game with Charles H. Harrison, partner in a faro bank in Omaha. Drunk, the two men quarreled, returned to their rooms for their guns, and then started shooting at one another. Harrison was fatally wounded; Levy was not touched. The cause of the brawl? Harrison maligned the Irish; Levy was an Irishman. In spite of his name he was not Jewish but Catholic.[33]

Jim Levy shot it out with Charles Harrison to defend the good name of the Irish. A Jew named Fridenberg soundly thrashed an Irishman who called him a vile name. The burly Irishman had come into Fridenberg's store in Sonora, California, and wanted to try on a pair of kid gloves. When Fridenberg refused to permit this the customer went outside, cursed the Jew, and invited him to step out and take a beating. When the

Jew accepted the invitation, the Irishman shot at him and missed; before he could take a second shot Fridenberg disarmed him and thrashed him. This was the third ruffian he had been compelled to disarm; the Sonora *American Flag* for October 8, 1863, headed the story, "Jerusalem on Top."[34]

George Morris of the same town, an assistant postmaster, was killed at the age of twenty-three "while defending the United States mail from robbers." Still other western Jews put their skills in fighting and their lives at the service of their country. Jacob Zacharias of the California 6th Infantry rode as a guard protecting the United States mail from Indians and holdup men. Otto Mears fought with the California Column against both Confederates and Indians in the Southwest, and Solomon Davidson, a California cavalryman, carried dispatches and orders "from one part of the command to another regardless of storms and dangers of Indian ambush." Davidson who never rose beyond the rank of private, was frequently on detached service in Arizona during the Civil War. It is a pity that he left no diary to tell us of his duties and experiences and the reason he was subject to a general court-martial! He was no stranger in the guard house. Service records have no emotions and only hint at exciting stories.[35]

Captain Ullman of the 7th cavalry, Company E, died with Custer at the Little Big Horn in June, 1876. Ullman, a Civil War veteran, was said to have been a Jew from Philadelphia. Confronting men like the Bibos, Fridenberg, Otto Mears, and Abe Rothschild, one is tempted to question whether there is a typical Jew, a High Plains Jewish stereotype. A study of Sigmund Shlesinger (Schlesinger) only serves to compound the confusion. Shlesinger was a Hungarian who came to the United States in 1864 at the age of sixteen and took a job in New York City as a conductor on a horse-drawn streetcar. Two years later, after clerking in Leavenworth, he moved to end-of-the-track on the Kansas Pacific. He tried his hand at everything he could think of and failed egregiously at all he attempted. With a combined capital of $5 he and a partner opened a cigar store at Hays City which enjoyed the patronage of Custer, Buffalo Bill, and Wild Bill Hickok. He was a barkeeper in a tent liquor store, cooked for teamsters, night-herded mules, waited on table, improvised a bakery, and brewed beer in a wash basin. After two years on the plains, broke, he enlisted in a company of volunteer scouts though he hardly knew how to mount and stay on a horse. As an undersized Jew with a piping squeaky voice he suffered as the butt of one of his comrades. While on the hunt for Indians who had been raiding the Kansas-Colorado border, his company of fifty was attacked by about 500 Sioux, Cheyenne, and Arapahoes on the 17th of September, 1868. For four days and nights the troops held off the Indians; before they were relieved on the 26th they had suffered casualties of five dead and eighteen wounded. It was here, at the Battle of

Beecher Island, that Shlesinger distinguished himself by his heroic conduct:

> When the foe charged on the breastworks
> With madness and despair,
> And the bravest souls were tested,
> The little Jew was there.

While lying entrenched in a sandpit of the Arickaree, the middle fork of
the Republican River, he kept a diary with the stub of a pencil: "scalpt 3
Indians"; "killt a coyote & ate him all up."

All told Shlesinger stayed five years on the Plains before he went back
east to New York and later to Cleveland where he opened a cigar store
and finally a wholesale tobacco house. He married and settled down in
1874, became a president of a B'nai B'rith lodge and a Knights of Pythias
lodge, a vice president of a synagog, an organizer of a Hebrew Free Loan
Association, of a Hungarian Benevolent and Social Union, of an Educational Alliance, and a president of the Hebrew Relief Association where
he served for twenty-one years. He died April 20, 1928, at the age of sev-
enty-nine. His numerous descendants are respected business and professional men scattered throughout the Midwest.[36]

In 1876 just about eight years after Shlesinger enlisted under Major
George A. Forsyth to fight Indians, Adolphus Gluck, another Hungarian
who had come to these shores at the age of sixteen, arrived in Dodge City
in Kansas and opened a jewelry store. He was then about thirty-three,
married, with a number of children. Two years later he became a member
of the city council which soon employed Wyatt Earp to keep the peace in
this "Bibulous Babylon of the Frontier," this wide open cow town of soldiers, buffalo hunters, cowboys, and dance hall girls. Gluck soon became
one of the leaders of Dodge City. He encouraged Bat Masterson, another
famous western marshal, to stand for sheriff, organized a hand-drawn
hose company, and served as mayor for five terms. Gluck became a cattle
man, bred Herefords, made and lost a fortune in bonanza wheat growing,
brought a railroad into town, helped arbitrate a railroad strike, aided in
setting up the city water works, and was successful in establishing a Car-
negie library. As a Civil War veteran he interested himself in the Grand
Army of the Republic and played an important role in the local Masonic
order. He died a rich man despite having lost more than one fortune in
the 1886-1887 blizzard and in the great panic of the mauve decade.
When his body was shipped to St. Louis for burial every store in Dodge
City was closed in respect.[37]

CHAPTER SIX

JEWS MOVE INTO THE GREAT PLAINS,
THE ROCKIES, AND THE NEW SOUTHWEST

Although Sig Shlesinger and Adolph Gluck lived on the West Kansas frontier in the 1860's and 1870's, most large-scale Jewish general merchants of that day operated out of East Kansas where they had easy access by water to their sources of supplies in the eastern metropolises. Theodore Weichselbaum was typical of those businessmen who carried on trade with the sparsely settled counties to the west in a day when the Indians roamed the plains and the farmers were just beginning to inch their way westward. Weichselbaum, a Bavarian, had arrived in Leavenworth in 1857, in territorial days, and slowly began to make a place for himself as a merchant, army contractor, freighter, and brewer. By the 1860's he had settled down in Ogden, Kansas, near Fort Riley, and the better to operate in the western regions had established a branch at Fort Larned, building a store of stone. His business was now big enough to take him to New York, Chicago, and to St. Louis; he shipped his wares to the forts in the western part of the state where he worked closely with the sutlers and with the army authorities for whom he freighted. For years he bought buffalo robes and antelope hides from the Indians and sold them at a fancy price to W. O. Lobenstein of Leavenworth who made a fortune from these transactions. Lobenstein spent his declining years in Milan, Italy. Many of the robes and peltries that Weichselbaum bought were acquired from the Indians with whom he traded directly. He was no gentle counterjumper. He was tough and aggressive. When pushed too far by Indians or robbed by them, he used his heavy freighter's whip to put them to flight; his intrepidity shocked even the soldiers. In 1862, his parents picked out a wife for him sending him a photo of the girl. His was a good marriage blessed by eight children. His wife was "the best woman who ever lived."

The Plains settlers in western Kansas got their goods from Leavenworth; those in western Nebraska from Omaha. When the gold rush hit
the Black Hills in 1876 Jews who wanted to outfit the miners freighted
their goods into the small Nebraska town of Chadron near the Dakota
border and to Sidney farther south. Sidney became a lively Jewish town
sheltering the fourth largest community in the state, all of twenty-seven
souls, merchants and saloonkeepers. One of those saloonkeepers was Moritz Urbach, a Hungarian cabinet maker who ran a bakery and a restaurant,
as well as a saloon. His baby girl was the first child in Sidney to be
wheeled about in a baby carriage—a cultural advance.[1]

COLORADO JEWRY

When mounted scout Sig Shlesinger rode into eastern Colorado with his
troop in September, 1868, he was hardly aware that Jews had been in the
Territory since the early 1850's. A man named Morris Bielschowsky ran a
general store in Costilla near Fort Garland in the San Luis Valley not far
from the Rio Grande and the New Mexico border. Solomon Nunes Carvalho, the artist, had crossed the Rockies with the explorer Col. John C.
Frémont in the winter of 1853. Despite the presence of these Jews the
Jewish community owes its origin to the Pike's Peak Gold Rush of 1858-
1859. By the Fall and Winter of 1859 religious services were being held
in the mining camp that was to become Denver and about a year later local Jewry had a cemetery and burial association. In 1860 the Stettauer
brothers were proud of their brick building which not only housed their
nostalgically named New York Store but also served for a time as the territorial capitol. Though the community was well on its way in the
1860's, the real growth came in the 1870's—the Civil War was over, the
Indians were gone, and the Plains had been spanned by the first transcontinental railroad. Denver grew from a city of 5,000 in 1870 to one of over
35,000 in 1880. In the first four years of the 1870's a male and female
Hebrew Benevolent Association, a B'nai B'rith lodge, and a permanent
congregation, Emanuel, were established. By 1876 when the Colorado
Territory became the Centennial State the Jews were securely ensconced.
They numbered about 500.[2]

Had the Jews wished to boast they could have bragged that they were
counted among the founding fathers of the territory. Abraham Jacobs
opened a liquor and grocery store in Denver in 1859 and the first meeting
of Masons was held that year in his place of business. Three Jews were
present, old-timers who had been members of the order in Santa Fe, Missouri, and in Nebraska Territory. By 1860 Jacobs was well-to-do and in
1867 organized the Denver and Santa Fe Stage and Express Line which
carried passengers, mail, and express to Trinidad where it joined the Bar-

low & Sanderson Stage which went on to Santa Fe. He was on the committee to draft the first constitution for the city of Denver and served on its first board of education. Rags to riches? Fires and hard times destroyed him and he spent his last days as a manual laborer.[3]

When the Masons first met in Denver in 1859 one of those other Jews who was present was Fred Z. Salomon. Salomon was one of three immigrant brothers from Posen. Fred Z. and Hyman Z. had first settled in New York, then in the South and Cincinnati before moving west to Dubuque and then on again to Las Vegas, New Mexico. When the stampede of 1859 carried thousands to Colorado the two brothers, in association with J. B. Doyle, a trader, brought several prairie schooners of supplies from Independence, Missouri, to Denver, where they opened a large grocery, hardware, and clothing store. Having no storeroom the company bought out a saloon and began selling dry rather than wet goods. The two brothers and their various partners opened stores in different territorial camps. At times a Doyle-Salomon train—thirty-five huge wagons—would bring in as much as one hundred tons of groceries, dry goods, and other staples from the Missouri River country.

Fred, the most energetic and successful member of the Salomon family, helped bring the railroad to Denver and start the first Colorado brewery which produced beer as a substitute for "strychnine whiskey and Taos lightning." He was a partner in an early water company, president of the Denver Board of Trade, a bank director, an organizer of a sugar beet company and the first mining exchange, founder of a town in Douglas County, and treasurer of the territory. Fred Salomon was also a member of an early chess club, a literary society, a social club, the State Historical Society, and of the Fifty-Niners which included only the original Colorado pioneers and their families. In their later years Fred and Hyman withdrew from Jewish life; they had few Jewish associates. Adolph Z., the third brother, had opened a huge general store in Greeley where he helped the potato farmers establish a "pool" to protect their interests. Defaulting debtors put him in the farm and ranch business though he lost heavily in the panic of 1893. Unlike his brothers, Adolph identified with the Jewish community. Why did Fred and Hyman drift away from their people? Successful Jews seeking status, new worlds to conquer, tend to abandon their fellow Jews and strive for recognition in Christian social circles.[4]

In 1859 Hyman Z. Salomon and a partner opened a company branch at South Park near the Continental Divide in the Tarryall diggings. During that winter when it was difficult to work the claims Salomon invited a group of miners to the store and formed a debating society, the Tarryall Lyceum. Culture was not lacking among the early settlers of the mining camps; many of them came from good homes and were not untutored, immigrant peasants. In 1879 Frank Damrosch came to Denver and spent about six years there. He was the organist and choir director of a Congregational church and later served the synagog and a Unitarian church. In addition Damrosch became the director of music in the public schools, the organizer of a string quartet in which he played cello, and the founder of the Denver Chorus Club which performed among other works oratorios by Handel and Mendelssohn.[5]

Undoubtedly Damrosch must have worked closely with Dr. John Elsner, a local physician who was a patron of the arts and whose beautiful home may well have been the most fashionable salon in the city. Elsner was an elegant, courteous, and cultivated gentleman who entertained Oscar Wilde, Joseph Jefferson, and Isaac M. Wise. A son of an 1848 Hungarian Jewish revolutionary, Elsner was brought to this country as a child, trained as a physician, both here and abroad, served in the Civil War, and came west because of a mine investment. When he set out to cross the plains in 1846 the men in the wagon train elected him as their head—he was all of twenty-two; he justified their faith in him bringing them across safely in spite of a number of encounters with the Indians. Four years after his arrival he established a hospital in Denver and, later, called the first medical society in the territory into existence, organized Colorado's first medical college, and, as a humanitarian, concerned himself with the welfare of Chinese and Negroes. In spite of his distance from eastern academic influences and his very busy schedule he interested himself in geology, paleontology, and mineralogy. He traveled north to Cheyenne and south to Santa Fe performing operations and circumcising Jewish children who because of the long waits involved were sometimes advanced in age. In Santa Fe he operated on Abraham Staab, the well-known New Mexico merchant. On another occasion, riding to help a wounded man, he had to skirt the camps of Indian hostiles. When offered a fee of $1,000 for that job he undoubtedly thought that he was well paid but he may have modified his opinion when Dr. Jacob M. Da Costa of Philadelphia told him that he made about $50,000 every two-three months. Da Costa was of Jewish stock but not a practicing Jew; Elsner was; he was identified with many Jewish causes, served as president of a B'nai B'rith lodge, and was active in the leading congregation in town.[6]

When Colorado was admitted to the Union in 1876, over half the Jews in the state lived in Denver. The Jewish census of that year reported 260 Jews in Denver, 54 in Central City, 37 in Boulder, 24 in Black Hawk, and 30 in Del Norte. Except for Denver none of these towns had a permanent Jewish organization, though religious services were occasionally held in Central City. The Jews of Boulder succeeded in effecting some form of religious organization in 1898. Their leaders were East Europeans. Individual Jews settled in any town in the mountains or in the valleys on the east slope or on the west slope, wherever they could strike roots and make a living. Sam Cohen at Fairplay in Park County grub-staked prospectors, invested in mines, and sold wooden ties to the Denver and Rio Grande Western; David M. Hyman and his friends, mining en-terprisers, laid out Aspen in 1880, and sold lots for $10; later some of them brought $10,000. Morris Strouse (Strauss) opened a clothing store at Grand Junction in 1882, bought wool, and traded with the Utes, buy-ing their deer and bear skins. Jews came to Pueblo in the 1860's as farm-ers and shopkeepers but they did not build a synagog until 1899, the same year the Jews in Cripple Creek met in the Masonic Temple and set up Temple B'rith Abraham. Cripple Creek was a gold rush boom town in the 1890's and for a few years enjoyed the convenience of a synagog and a B'nai B'rith lodge, but when the gold gave out the Jewish community with its clothing and second-hand shops, its merchant tailor and shoe store, its cigar stand and saloon, its loan broker and auction house, disap-peared.

Leadville ultimately shared the same fate as Cripple Creek. Silver and gold created a city almost overnight but when the precious metal petered out the people left and the Jewish community ceased to be. The original mining town of California Gulch faded away in the late 1860's but when, in the late 1870's, lead, silver, and gold were again discovered the new city of Leadville rose. A vigorous Jewish community of at least 200 souls came into being and by 1884 there was a cemetery, a congregation, a Sab-bath school, and a social club. During those prosperous years the Jewish women in town fashioned cultural associations, gave strawberry festivals, and sponsored an annual Purim ball that was patronized both by Gentiles and by Jews. The Reform temple of 1884 and the later Orthodox syna-gog were given substantial aid by the local bonanza king, H. A. W. Ta-bor, but in the early twentieth century as the town declined the Jews faded away.[7]

TRINIDAD JEWRY

When Abraham Jacobs of the Denver and Santa Fe Stage and Express Line stopped off at his southern terminus in Trinidad in the late 1860's he probably took time out to meet Maurice Wise, a Bohemian Jew, who had just arrived in the adobe village. Wise, one of the first shopkeepers in town, prospered; he wore a plug hat and gave his friend the Catholic priest a lot on which the townspeople built the Trinidad church. Wise owned the butcher corral which may well have been used by David Gott-lieb, a butcher and cattle buyer who arrived in town in 1871. Gottlieb came from Abilene where he had operated a clothing store in a cornshed and had become friendly with Abilene's marshal Wild Bill Hickok. Hickok once bet $500 that Gottlieb could outguess any man in town in judging the weight of a bull. Gottlieb's closest opponent was off by 140 pounds; Gottlieb came within seventeen pounds of the scale's weight. He is said to have been the first man in Las Animas County to raise potatoes and his was the first store in town to have glass windows. David Gottlieb was not the only person drawn to Trinidad; others also began to arrive in order to take advantage of the growing trade of this coal, cattle, and farming town on the Santa Fe Trail. The city soon became a bustling commercial center for southern Colorado and northern New Mexico.

In Trinidad's heyday its Jews were primarily in the dry goods business; some owned clothing and shoe stores. In the early days the merchants accepted sheep and wool and grain in payment for goods sold on credit. By 1872 there were two Jewish physicians in town and when the local medical association refused to accept them the two Jews and a Frenchman created a society of their own. In 1875 the Jewish merchants working with others tried unsuccessfully to open an academy. The Biernbaums, who were protégés of the Spiegelberg clan of New Mexico, built a hall in town in the 1870's, and in 1885 the Jaffas erected the beautiful Opera House which is still standing.

No later than the early 1870's Trinidad Jewry began to hold services, at least for the Holy Days, and by 1878 there was a B'nai B'rith lodge which was patronized no doubt not only by Trinidad shopkeepers but by others from southern Colorado and northern New Mexico. The Jewish census of 1876 ignored Trinidad yet by that time it sheltered one of the largest Jewish communities in the state. In 1883 a congregation was founded and a cemetery was established; in 1889 a beautiful Moorish style synagog was built with the help of the Hebrew Ladies Aid society. It is now a Colorado historic site. The marriage fees prescribed in the 1889 constitution were on a sliding scale: marriages in the synagog cost $10; marriage by gas light, $15; with choir, $20; with choir and gas light, $25. In the nineties a young men's association, the Montefiore Literary Society, came into being, and even the children of the Sabbath school formed an association of their own. Trinidad is the second oldest Jewish community in Colorado. At one time it numbered several hundred Jews, but in the 1980's, a century after the Israelites first arrived, the community had dwindled to about seven households in town and in nearby Raton, New Mexico. Services however were still conducted regularly in the historic sanctuary largely through the devotion of Mrs. Gilbert Sanders who officiated as a "rabbi" and presided over the destinies of Congregation Aaron.[8]

OTTO MEARS OF COLORADO

Trinidad is on the east slope of the Rockies where most Colorado Jews have always lived. There is still no organized community on the other side of the Divide, yet one of the most distinguished Jewish Coloradans made his home and career on the western slope. This was Otto Mears, frequently referred to as the "Uncrowned King of the San Juans," and "the Pathfinder of the San Juans." Mears was a Colorado pioneer, road builder, railroader, and politician. In his part of the territory, in the San Juan country of southwestern Colorado, he built the first irrigation ditch, set up the first saw and grist mill, introduced the first threshing machine, and constructed hundreds of miles of toll roads. The roads he built brought in settlers, stockmen, foods, clothing, hardware, supplies for the mines, and carried out ore and grain. With and without the help of partners, Jews and Gentiles, Mears operated hardware, dry goods, and general stores. His pack trains and freighters shuttled back and forth on both sides of the Rockies, going as far east as Denver; he contracted with the government to haul the mail through the passes and when his dog sled teams were snowbound this frail wisp of a man shouldered the mailbag himself and carried it through two feet of wet snow and over ice cold streams.

Mears's name was closely associated with the Utes. He furnished provisions and supplies to the Indian agencies, redeemed the women captives seized by them after the Meeker Massacre, and was primarily responsible for the peaceful removal of the Indians from Colorado to Utah. Though he had intimate friends among them, spoke their language and represented them on occasion in Washington, some of the Utes, deeply resenting his maneuvering which brought about their exile, attempted to assassinate him. Though disdaining violence this shrewd, tough, businessman was anything but an enlightened protector of the Indians. Like many others he believed there was no place for semi-nomads in a growing agricultural economy. To speed up traffic and trade in western Colorado Mears built narrow-gauge railroads and flattered his friends by giving them beautiful passes made of buckskin, silver filigree, and gold. He developed two towns, Saguache and Lake City, and "promoted" them by publishing his own newspapers. Lake City did so well that before long there were enough Jews in town to hold religious services. In that same decade of the 1870's Mears turned to politics and soon became a force in the Republican party. Through his control of his district, the balance of power in the state lay in his hands.

But who was Otto Mears: a Yiddish-accented Russian Jewish immigrant who moved west to San Francisco as a child, worked as a tinsmith, and labored in the California and Nevada diggings before going east to New Mexico with the California volunteers to fight Confederates and Navajos. After the war he clerked and managed stores for New Mexico Jews, crossed the northern border into Colorado in 1865, and at the age of twenty-five began his remarkable career. His home base was Saguache on the west slope though he lived also in Denver, Washington, and California. In Denver he joined the Temple and the B'nai B'rith, served as trustee of a Jewish hospital, and contributed to the relief of stricken Russian Jews. His wife was a Christian and his children were reared in her faith. As with many others his empire almost fell apart in the collapse of the '90's but he built a railroad in the East and finally turned to the West, to California where he invested in ranch and hotel property. In the Colorado state capitol with its gold-covered dome there is a portrait in glass of Mears, the pioneer, who was memorialized while he was still alive. He came to Colorado in the 1860's when grain was still threshed by hand and he lived to become one of the officers and financiers of a great American automobile corporation, the Mack Truck Company. Even in his lifetime he was a myth. A governor of the state was once ordered off a Denver street car because he had left his purse at home and did not have the few pennies for his fare. "But I am the governor," he expostulated. To which the conductor responded: "I wouldn't let you ride this car without pay if you were Otto Mears himself." Mears began to make a living at the age of eleven selling newspapers in San Francisco; he had little formal education. His may not be a typical American story yet it is American to the core.[9]

DAKOTA TERRITORY, 1861-1889

Colorado Jewish businesmen were among those who freighted goods to the Black Hills of South Dakota at the time of the 1876 gold rush. People of all types, classes, and cultures poured into Deadwood Gulch from different parts of the country. Almost overnight it became a city of about 15,000 people among them Jews: miners, traders, freighters, businessmen, and even an occasional gambler. Jew Jake Kaufman was a well-known professional gambler in the Deadwood of the early days. Sometime in the 1870's or possibly later there were enough Jews in town to hold an occasional High Holy Day service.

There were a few Jews in the 1880's who homesteaded on the fertile prairies of the eastern sector of the territory, in the later North Dakota. Though some of them survived on the soil they were not destined as a group to become farming folk. The hazards were almost insuperable. One Jewish farmer who had left his wife and child for a brief moment in the midst of a blizzard found them later frozen to death. Venturous Jewish businessmen of the seventies and eighties settled in Minot near the Canadian border; others came up the Missouri to Bismarck from Iowa or settled in the Red River towns of Fargo and Grand Forks. They created no communities in those early days.[10]

Rather than wander further afield some of the newcomers who steamed up the Missouri dropped off at Yankton in South Dakota. This was then the territorial capital and an important outfitting center for those who were bent on moving west to the Black Hills. Long before the Sioux were driven out of the Black Hills, Jews had already settled in Yankton. The Katzes were there in 1862, and in the 1880's. Harry Katz, the proprietor of the "Popular Clothing and Furnishing House," advertised:

> Though short or tall,
> Or great or small,
> 'Though lank and lean,
> Or fat and mean,
> 'Though you come from any nation
> Or hail from any station,
> You can get FITS at
> Harry Katz's.

Yankton was the only town in the territory mentioned in the Jewish census of 1876. Deadwood which certainly had more Jews was ignored and no Jews were listed for North Dakota. If, despite the gold strike, Jews avoided the Dakotas the reason may well be that they were wary of the Indians. That June, Custer and his detachment were annihilated, and fourteen years later in 1890, when the men, women, and children of the Pine Ridge Indian Reservation were slaughtered, young Oscar Pollak, a Jewish cavalryman, was one of the army casualties. This was no place to raise a family.

Individual Jewish entrepreneurs made a place for themselves in the Black Hills economy. The Hattenbachs of Sioux City, Iowa, lived on the Dakota border and it was easy for them to go up the Missouri and west into the Black Hills. Three brothers, Jacob, Aaron, and Nathan, engaged in a variety of businesses: they mined, smelted ores, and sold groceries, but made very little money even in the booming Deadwood of the 1870's. The team of Harris Franklin and Ben Baer was more fortunate. Franklin was a Polish Jew who came to the States in 1867, still a teenager. As his anglicized name indicates he probably stopped over in England. In this country he moved west through Rochester, New York, and Burlington, Iowa, where he married and then continued on to Nebraska City and Cheyenne. He joined the gold rush of 1876 and finally located permanently in Deadwood as a wholesale liquor dealer, miner, cattle rancher, and banker. In the 1890's the American (First) National Bank was also known as the Franklin-Baer Bank. By that time Franklin, who had audaciously sunk large sums of the bank's money in the Golden Reward Company, a mining enterprise, was a millionaire, and Ben Baer, his partner, a man of substantial wealth.

Baer was a cultured musical Alsatian who spoke French and German. As a good citizen he served as captain of Deadwood's volunteer fire department, participating actively in its annual Fourth of July drill and race; as a good Jew he desired that his son Ira receive a religious education; he permitted him to attend a Christian Sunday school. Eventually like many other successful Jewish businessmen he moved his family to a large city where it could luxuriate in a Jewish milieu. About the turn of the century Baer settled in St. Paul where he opened a bank bearing the same name as the Deadwood institution with which he was affiliated, the American National Bank.[11]

MONTANA JEWRY

As in the Dakotas, Jews had first come into Montana in the 1860's to make their fortune in the mines. Among them were miners, traders, storekeepers, freighters, teamsters, wagon bosses, journalists, lawyers, cooks, peddlers, boardinghouse owners, dressmakers, cattlemen, saloon-keepers and the inevitable merchant who graduated into banking. Louis H. Hershfield drove into Virginia City, Montana, from distant Colorado with twenty-six oxcarts of goods and soon became a banker of substance who could afford to be the largest donor to a local Baptist church. Others reached out into steamboating, hotels, meat packing, and the lighting industry. All these pioneers had a history behind them akin to that of Isadore Strassburger. Like many others on their arrival in this country Strassburger had peddled, clerked, and run businesses in several states before he found himself in the 1860's the owner of a tent store in Virginia City. These Jewish adventurers dotted the streets and gullies of Bannack, Virginia City, Helena, Butte, Bozeman, Missoula, Fort Benton, and even of Miles City on the Yellowstone—all this before 1880.

The Bannack of 1862 did not last long; Alder Gulch or the Virginia City of 1863 was more fortunate; as late as 1876 there were still nineteen Jews in town. Last Chance Gulch or Helena was the Jewish metropolis of the territory; its 112 souls were over 80 percent of all Montana's Israelites. By the middle 1860's this Rocky Mountain conglomerate had a Jewish community of sorts with cemetery, charities, and services, all encapsulated in a Hebrew Benevolent Society which was prosperous enough to send a donation to aid the Jews of Europe. Butte, the largest Jewish town in the state in the late twentieth century, was not even mentioned in the 1876 Jewish census although by the early 1880's it too had a modest organized Jewish community. Adhering to the typical Jewish transmississippi pattern of participation in the life of the larger general community, Henry Jacobs, a clothier, became the first mayor of the city in 1879. Montana Jews were active in politics and in the fraternities; four of them served as Masonic Grand Masters.[12]

There was hardly a town in Montana's territorial heyday that did not shelter at least one Jewish entrepreneur. Moses Solomon, a Polish Jew, lived on the Marias River in the northwestern part of Montana, not far from Fort Benton. After a sojourn in California he had wandered north in the 1860's to the Montana mining towns. In 1868 he and seven others were attacked by 300 Sioux Indians. Solomon was wounded and four of his companions were killed; the Indians lost five dead and several wounded. Six years later Solomon was feuding with S. J. Perkins, a saloonkeeper, who shot him twice. By the early 1870's Solomon still surviving had opened a trading post where he sold the Indians whiskey and took advantage of them. In the next decade he devoted himself largely to his farm where he raised hogs, chickens, and turkeys; with the introduction of electricity, he played with the idea of stringing electric bulbs in his hencoop to fool the chickens into laying two eggs a day. When the railroad was being built in his part of north Montana, he was arrested for selling liquor along the line of track under construction but escaped punishment. At his death in 1906 the *Kendall Miner* said that he was a courteous gentleman. Maybe he was by the Montana standards of that generation.[13]

Another Jewish "Pole" was Julius Basinski who hailed from Posen. Four years after he landed in New York City in 1866 he was in Helena selling cigars, part of a consignment of 1,000 which he had purchased on credit. He settled in a village near Helena peddling candy, cigars, and fruits in the towns and mines, before moving on to Bozeman where he bought butter and eggs from the farmers. His next stop, in 1876, was in east Montana where he made a living selling goods to the troops on the Yellowstone. He liked that part of the country well enough to make his home in Miles City. As a businessman specializing in books and stationery, he catered to the soldiers at Fort Keough and branched out into sheep raising. In order to give his children the advantages of a large city he finally turned west and settled down in Tacoma, Washington. At times there had been a quorum of Jews in Miles City, sufficient to hold High Holy Day services; in Tacoma Basinski joined the synagog even though he had married out. It is probable that his children were reared as Christians. After the turn of the century, then a man in his sixties, Basinski became a successful fruit grower. He died in Albany, Oregon, in 1926, at the age of eighty-one.

Apparently Julius Basinski and Moses Solomon had little in common except they were East European Jewish pioneers in early Montana. Abraham Oettinger (1829-1911), another settler in the Treasure State of Gold and Silver, was of an altogether different breed. Oettinger came from the Orthodox Jewish city of Frankfort on the Main. As a boy he had wandered into Italy where he made a living copying music; in 1846, at the age of seventeen he began peddling notions in the United States. Years later—it was in 1886—he went west at the suggestion of Leonard Lewisohn, the mining magnate, and opened a cigar store in Butte. His children, musicians like himself, followed him to Montana where he soon established a Jewish Sunday school. He was very much interested in Jewish learning for he was a devoted Jew and a man of culture. He spoke German, French, and Italian and was at home in Hebrew. Every Friday night he gave a party for the children if they had faithfully attended the religious school; if they had not they were not invited: no attendance, no party! It worked! The Presbyterians lent him their church to hold High Holy Day services for the ten families in Butte and he officiated to the edification of the Christians who sat in the rear pews and also fasted on the Day of Atonement. As good Christians they were mindful that Jesus had once fasted for forty days and forty nights. Serving as the "rabbi," Oettinger bar mitzvahed the children, officiated at marriages, wrote the prescribed Aramaic marriage contracts. He was respected as a fine spirit who was especially considerate to Indians, Negroes, and Chinese. After 1900 he moved back east to Philadelphia living in an immigrant neighborhood where the Jews were religiously observant. As a decorous American, however, he cautioned his neighbors not to go out on the streets clad only in trousers and underwear.[14]

WASHINGTON JEWRY

Montana, the Dakotas, and Washington constituted the four omnibus states that were admitted to the Union in 1889. There were Jewish settlers in Washington Territory in the late 1850's. More came in the early 1860's. A few, very few, had wandered in overland; most had come down from British Columbia or up from Portland. Settlements, not communities, were established in four areas. The Colville gold rush in the northeast brought a few hardy souls; by the 1870's a number of Jews had moved into Spokane and they may even have met for services there in that decade. They were the pioneers in that part of the Inland Empire, the lands that lay between the Cascades and the Rockies. In the southeast, a sprinkling of Jews gathered together in Colfax and Walla Walla, orienting themselves toward Idaho in the days when gold was discovered on the Salmon River. For Jews, Vancouver was the only important town in the southwest. As a Columbia River town at the head of navigation for seagoing vessels it trafficked with San Francisco and transshipped goods up the river to Walla Walla and eastern Washington. It was close to the Oregon border and Portland. By 1861 there were already six Jewish families in Vancouver, all of them doing well. In general, though, most of the Children of Israel in Washington Territory settled in the northwest, in the towns on Puget Sound: Olympia, Steilacoom, Port Townsend, Seattle. By the late 1870's Seattle was the Jewish metropolis with all of fifty-six souls; the entire territory could muster about 145. That was the official count; there were probably a few more.

The "Jewish" town in the northeastern mountains, in Stevens County, was not Colville but Marcus. As early as 1859 L. Abrams had a store in Colville; Marcus Oppenheimer came to town about the year 1863 and started business in a log cabin. Not long after his arrival he homesteaded a site at White's Landing on the Upper Columbia. Years later the place was called Marcus after him, and it is still a town though it was shifted when its original site was covered over by the Grand Coulee Dam. Oppenheimer, a Badensian, had crossed the plains with a wagon train which included a number of Jews, men, women, and children. A Jewish party led by Alec Kaufman had joined a larger train at Omaha in 1862. After a crossing that took three and a half months and an attack by Indians and a white renegade, these pioneers reached The Dalles. Marcus Oppenheimer was joined at times by his two brothers, Joseph and Samuel; either alone or in association with them and Christian partners he established an important trading center. The goods they ordered came up the Columbia from Walla Walla. They grubstaked miners, built a grist mill, brought in the first thoroughbred pigs, supplied army posts, and hauled supplies across the border for the Canadian Pacific then preparing to lay its transcontinental tracks.[15]

When Marcus Oppenheimer crossed the plains he was accompanied by Ben Burgunder, and in later years the two worked together as partners in mining and freighting. By 1879 Burgunder was doing business in Colfax on the Snake south of Spokane but he was certainly not the Jewish pioneer in town for Julius Lippitt was already established there as a general merchant. Phillip Lippitt, the other half of Lippitt Brothers, was the firm's San Francisco buyer. Julius became a grain buyer and shipper when the railroads reached Washington in the 1880's and then branched out into banking and led the city as mayor. Lippitt Brothers carried the farmers over the bad years, and forty years after their arrival the Whitman County Pioneers Association passed a resolution thanking them for the help and credit they had extended to humble beginners.[16]

Burgunder and Schwabacher, merchants, were competitors of the Lippitts in Colfax. In the early 1860's the Schwabachers had been based at Walla Walla. Sigmund Schwabacher was then in the grocery business. Toward the end of the decade Schwabacher Brothers & Company, a wholesale grocery firm, established a branch in Seattle and turned its management over to a brother-in-law, Bailey Gatzert. This German immigrant had peddled in the South, clerked in the Mother Lode, and worked in Portland before he took over the Seattle branch of Schwabacher Brothers in 1869. Gatzert was a brilliant businessman whose name is still one to conjure with in the city. There is a Bailey Gatzert Elementary School in Seattle and a Gatzert Institute for Child Development at the state university. Before he died in 1893 he distinguished himself in banking, steamboating, and street railways. He was also mayor of the city in 1882. Several years before Gatzert came to Seattle Gustave Rosenthal had already settled down in Olympia at the southern end of the Sound. He had started out modestly in a dry goods store but over the years had become one of the state's most enterprising businessmen. He founded a large-scale oyster shipping industry, dispatched barrel staves to San Francisco, dominated the wool trade, and supplied Atlantic Coast shipyards with lumber. It was his coal mine that sent out the first trainload of coal on the Northern Pacific and it was he who built the first wagon road over Naches Pass. In his day there were only about five Jewish families in town yet Olympia with its thirty men, women, and children was the territory's second largest community. The Hebrew Benevolent Association with its cemetery service and philanthropies was the first Jewish organization in the territory.[17]

Bailey Gatzert and Gustave Rosenthal and the scattered Jews in the Puget Sound towns were probably very proud of the fact that President U. S. Grant had appointed General Edward Selig Salomon as the territorial governor in 1870. Salomon had a notable career. This German immigrant had come to Chicago in 1854 at the age of eighteen and moved up the social and political ladder rapidly. He clerked, kept books, studied law, and become a city alderman at the age of twenty-four. He was a stalwart Republican and when the Civil War broke out he volunteered and made a name for himself as a brilliant courageous officer. Major General Carl Schurz wrote that he "displayed the highest order of coolness and determination under very trying circumstances" at Gettysburg. After the War Lt. Col. Salomon, brevetted a brigade general, became clerk of Cook County, Chicago, Illinois. Five years later Grant, who knew and respected him as a comrade-in-arms, sent him out to Washington Territory, where he served for one two-year term before tendering his resignation. Like some other Grant appointees his political morality was not of the highest order; he was involved in some unsavory speculation and an attempt to bribe a treasury agent. After he left the territory he settled in San Francisco where he served in the state legislature and as district attorney.[18]

Seattle began to grow in the 1880's with the coming of the railroads; it boomed in the late 1890's when gold was discovered in Alaska. There was a B'nai B'rith lodge in the city in the 1880's but it was not until the end of that decade that a permanent congregation finally emerged. By that time there were about twenty families in town. There is evidence to support the belief that occasional religious services were held as early as the 1870's not only in Seattle but also in Olympia and Spokane.[19]

IDAHO JEWRY

Idaho was admitted to the Union as a state in 1890 just one year after the Omnibus States. Jews had rushed into the Idaho country as early as 1860 when gold was discovered near the Washington border, and as the strikes continued in the 1880's in different parts of the territory Jews made their way to the new settlements. The mountain-mining pattern of Jewish settlers was typical: some were at the mines, a few were sutlers at the forts, but most opened shops. By the 1860's they were in business in Boise and Idaho City; in the 1870's they were in Silver City and Malad, and in the next decade they were in Hailey and Lewiston. They were in other towns too, like Maquoketa and Washington, but these are towns that are hard to find in today's atlas.

In 1865 the Jews of Idaho City were numerous enough to hold services on the Day of Atonement. The local theatre owner, a Jew, let them use his building. A layman preached on repentance, prayer, and charity, the themes of the day. Idaho City was then a town of thousands; today it is a village of a few hundreds. In Malad, near the Utah border, the town's most important citizen may well have been the Prussian immigrant, Myers (Meyer, Meyers) Cohn. After establishing himself successfully as a merchant he turned to ranching and farming and organized the first irrigation company in southwest Idaho. His neighbors elected him county commissioner and his friends back east asked him to poll the Jews in town (1876). He reported that they were fourteen all told. At the same time there were fifteen Jews in Silver City near the Oregon border. A twenty-eight-year-old Jew, Henry Seligman, was the county treasurer; E. Lobenstein was one of the richest men in town; he was in quartz mining and stock raising. In 1876 there were fewer than 100 Jews in all the territory but by the 1880's services were held in the growing city of Boise, and by 1895 the Jews there had acquired a cemetery and had set up a formal religious organization. The meeting to establish a congregation took place in the home of a local merchant by the name of Moses Alexander.

In 1895 at the age of forty-two, Alexander was a successful clothier. He had come from Bavaria, a fifteen-year-old boy, and made his way to a cousin in Chillicothe, Missouri, where he clerked for $10 a month and board. He learned the business, ultimately became his own boss, married a convert to Judaism, entered politics, and was elected mayor about the year 1888. A few years later he moved to Boise for reasons of health and soon became the most successful clothing merchant in that part of the country. After he had opened several branch stores he reached out for new worlds to conquer. In 1897 a reform group elected him mayor of the city and in 1915 this liberal Democrat became governor of the state. Idaho was thus the first state in the Union to elevate a Jew to its chief executive position.

Alexander, a vigorous witty campaigner, once addressed a group of country folk from the roof of a manure shed; when his friends objected to the spot he told his chuckling audience: "This is the first time in my life I've ever spoken from a Republican platform." During his second term with a Democratic legislature to support him he helped put through legislation on workmen's compensation and built state highways, a dam, a canal, and a series of irrigation ditches. When he traveled to Boston the immigrant Jews there were so enraptured with this newcomer who had made good that they gave him an enthusiastic reception in Faneuil Hall. When in the late 1860's Alexander left his native Bavaria the Jews of that country still labored under disabilities.[20]

WYOMING JEWRY

An Idaho hamlet was named Alexander after the governor; it is in Caribou County which borders on the state of Wyoming. In the early days Wyoming sheltered even fewer Jews than Idaho. As late as 1876 there were said to be only forty of them in all the territory, none outside of Cheyenne. Jews had started coming in what was to be Wyoming no later than the 1860's. Some were soldiers, a number were freighters; others were merchants supplying the cattlemen and miners. Several of the Jewish pioneers had come into the southeastern part of the territory when the Union Pacific built track in 1867 into Cheyenne which in those days was a "hell-on-wheels" town, wide open. All the hazard and excitement was not limited to Cheyenne however; a Mr. A. Liberman on the way from Deadwood to Cheyenne by stagecoach in the late 1870's was held up by road agents and wounded.

Not many of the early Jewish adventurers elected to remain in the Equality State as it later chose to call itself. Mrs. William Meyers (Myers) established the Cheyenne Jewish Circle in the 1870's for those who stayed on. This seems to be the first Jewish organization in the territory. Just when the handful of Jews in town first conducted services is difficult to determine; there was no formal congregation in Cheyenne till the late nineties although there was a Sunday school. Among the storekeepers of the 1870's was B. Hellman who stocked buckskin undershirts and drawers and who helped clothe a delegation of Indians which had just returned from Washington. These Sioux had refused to leave their homes in the Black Hills where gold had just been discovered.

Max Idelman, a Russian Jew, came to Cheyenne in the 1870's and soon laid the foundations for a successful wholesale and retail wine, liquor, and tobacco concern that did business in Nebraska, Colorado, Utah, and Idaho. He branched out into real estate, made a great deal of money, built one of the finest homes in the city, and filled it with art treasures.

Like many of the magnificent homes back east, it had beautiful oak stairways, stained glass windows, and a large ballroom on the third floor. In later years it became the governor's mansion. In 1884 Max J. Meyer, a New York entrepreneur, arrived in Cheyenne and helped establish the town's Frontier Days, one of the most famous of western rodeos. He was said to be the man who originated the ten-gallon hat. In the early 1880's Harry Mandel, a Montana prospector, crossed the border into Sheridan County and opened a store at a likely spot not too far from the Big Horn Mountains. The place was first called Mandel but soon changed its name to Sheridan. It eventually became a railroad division point and a bustling manufacturing center.[21]

UTAH JEWRY

In 1865, after the Civil War, Simon Bamberger, a young Hessian Jew, arrived at a tie camp at the end of track in Piedmont, Wyoming. Simon had come to collect a bill from a railroad contractor who had bought clothing from the Bamberger brothers, Herman and Simon. Herman was then twenty-two; Simon was nineteen. The brothers owned a tiny clothing manufacturing business in St. Louis. When the St. Louis business closed, Simon remained in the West and started discounting paychecks for the railroaders and renting tents and shacks to miners. Indian attacks soon put an end to the rental business and Simon moved across the border to Utah where, forty-eight years later, in 1917, he was inaugurated as governor of the state. Bamberger was the first Democrat and the first non-Mormon to be elected to that high office in Utah. The Mormons rallied around him and helped elect him; they obviously preferred a Jewish "Gentile" to a Christian Gentile, for the Mormons looked upon themselves as the heirs of biblical Israel. Thus there was a bond with those who were Israelites after the flesh.

Joseph Smith published *The Book of Mormon* and founded the Church of Jesus Christ of Latter-Day Saints in 1830. He was then living in western New York not far from where Mordecai Noah had hoped to found his city of Ararat a few years earlier. Ararat was to be a Jewish refuge gathering Jews from all over the earth. Noah hoped also to bring the Indians together preparatory to their restoration to Jerusalem and Palestine for he was convinced—or so he said—that they were the descendants of the Lost Ten Tribes. Similar ideas are reflected in The Book of Mormon. Because the roots of the Latter-Day Saints lay in ancient Israel where Hebrew had been spoken, Smith and his followers studied that language after they moved to Kirtland, Ohio. There were some Jews among the early converts to Mormonism; one of them was Alexander Neibaur, an Alsatian who had first converted to Christianity and then in the 1830's became a Latter-Day Saint in London. He was at Nauvoo with Prophet Smith in 1841 and as a student of Hebrew may well have known that the name Nauvoo was taken from the Isaianic and Canticles Hebrew word "navu," beautiful. Neibaur emigrated with his new coreligionists to Salt Lake City where he practiced dentistry and manufactured sulphur friction matches which were just being introduced. He was very probably Utah's first Jew. One of his sons-in-law was a Posen Jewish peddler, Morris Rosenbaum, who was baptized as a Mormon several weeks before his marriage to Alice Neibaur.[22]

In 1850 Utah became a United States territory; seven years later the federal government, contending that the Mormons were in rebellion, dispatched troops from Fort Leavenworth to bring them to terms. After a fashion this "war" was started by a Mormon Jew, Levi Abrahams. Levi was a freighter and storekeeper at Fillmore, the territorial capital. He quarreled with federal judge W. W. Drummond in a card game. What happened next is not clear: the judge sent his servant Cato to beat or even kill the Jew; Abrahams, handy with a bowie knife, defended himself and in turn called on the judge and threatened him with a gun. Abrahams was no shrinking violet; a Mormon jury had just acquitted him of the charge of murdering an unoffending Indian. Drummond and others complained to Washington that the Mormons were troublemakers and in 1857 President Buchanan sent troops to occupy the territory and subdue the "rebels."

Although this was a war without casualties, the Utah country had its bloody battles. In September, 1857, about 137 California-bound immigrants were killed by Indians—the Mountain Meadows Massacre. A Mormon may have been involved in this affair. Among the immigrants who perished was a Jewish girl on her way to California to join a brother. Rebecca was affianced to a Jew named Isaac Goldstein who, believing her still alive, set out to find her among the Indians of the High Plains. Crazed by grief, he searched everywhere; he was finally killed by Indians on September 29, 1877, more than twenty years after the massacre. This is the Goldstein story as reported in an eastern newspaper. Is it true or is it the fabrication of an imaginative news reporter who had accompanied a punitive army expedition and was short of copy? Sneering at hypercritics, Professor Gotthard Deutsch of the Hebrew Union College once said: "the fact that a story may be true is no reason why it is not true."[23]

One of the first non-Mormon Jews in the Utah Territory arrived in February, 1854. This was the artist and daguerreotypist Solomon Nunes Carvalho, a son of an early American hazzan, who had served in New York, Charleston, and Philadelphia. Solomon was invited by John Charles Frémont to join his expedition to explore the Rockies. Frémont was looking for a good railroad route across the mountains to the Pacific

Coast; Carvalho served as a photographer. Frémont and his men set out from St. Louis in October, 1853, and finally reached southern Utah in the dead of winter in February, 1854, after a journey of incredible hardships. They had problems with Indians, suffered from the cold, and almost dead of hunger were compelled to eat their pack animals. After a stay of several months in Utah where he painted the portraits of Mormon notables, Carvalho moved on to California before returning to the East. He described the expedition in *Incidents of Travel and Adventure in the Far West* (1857). The photographs which he left behind were never recovered.[24]

Even Carvalho was certainly not the first Jew to cross Utah; from the days of the gold rush thousands of pioneers on the way to California had passed through. No later than 1854, Jewish businessmen from California and Nevada as well as from the East decided to try their luck in Utah. Salt Lake City attracted them for it had become a reoutfitting center for overland trekkers. More Jews came after the Civil War and when the Union Pacific was united with the Central Pacific in the spring of 1869. Business was brisk; Utah was far more prosperous than the northern tier of territories. Jews found jobs—mostly among their own group—as clerks, as bookkeepers, and as merchants selling clothing, dry goods, liquor, tobacco, and meat. Some of the businessmen who made their homes in the Mormon State were brilliant and successful. Their careers in Utah were not exceptional but rather typical of the solid merchants in all states and territories in the 1860's and 1870's.

Two cases in point are the careers of the Siegels and the Cohns. After landing in the United States, Henry, Joseph, and Solomon Siegel, Bavarians, lived in various eastern states, Maryland, and Virginia, before moving on to Nebraska; as the railroad construction crews sledge-hammered their way westward, the Siegels followed them in wagons that served as portable stores. In the 1860's and '70's they sold clothing in Montana, Salt Lake, and the Black Hills. They were mobile—quick, maybe too quick, to sense the opportunities of new places, to move in when a boom started and to move out in a hurry when it burst. When business was good they had the courage to import huge stocks from the East, shipping the goods in their own mule and ox trains across the prairies, plains, and mountains. Louis and Alexander Cohn, Polish Jews, were contemporaries of the Siegels in Salt Lake City. After first trying his luck in California, in 1865, Louis Cohn left the diggings at Poker Flats and drove a team with his stock of goods all the way to Salt Lake. It was a long hard six-week trip. Alexander joined him there in 1867 and together they engaged in the dry goods trade. In later years Louis turned to mining and the manufacture of bricks. A Mason of high degree, Louis was also civic-minded; he became a member of the city council and served also as a police and fire commissioner.

The successes of the Siegels and the Cohns may well be typical of many Jewish settlers in Utah; Simon Bamberger's career was anything but typical; Jewish governors are few and far between. On landing at Castle Garden in 1860 he set out for Cincinnati where he had two half-sisters but the teenage lad fell asleep on the train and found himself in Indianapolis. A cousin there gave him a job and after some time he moved to Wilmington, Ohio, where his brother Herman had a store. And while Herman watched bridges with the militia during the Civil War, Simon kept shop. It was good experience. When the brothers' Missouri gamble in clothing manufacturing failed Simon moved on to Ogden, Utah. His first ventures were in the hotel business there and in Salt Lake City, then he turned to mining, banking, and railroads. Later he entered politics, sitting on the school board and in the state senate before he was elevated to the governorship. He came to power in the liberal Wilsonian days when the Populist tradition was still very much alive in the West. As governor he favored prohibition; he himself did not drink or smoke. He believed in the regulation of public service corporations: the telegraph, telephone, gas, power, light, and transportation industries. The governor was concerned about the public health, fought for a workmen's compensation act, believed in the right of labor to form voluntary associations, and pleaded for non-partisan selection of judges. Like his contemporary Moses Alexander he was also a committed Jew and served the Salt Lake congregation as president.[25]

Disturbed by the increasing influx of Gentiles into the territory and determined not to be overwhelmed economically by "strangers," the Mormons in the late 1860's established Zion's Co-operative Mercantile Institution; this was tantamount to a boycott of all non-Mormons. Jews suffered grievously, for they were practically all in business. To salvage what they could many Jews and other non-Mormons moved into the recently founded Gentile city of Corinne, close to the new Union Pacific Railroad. Salt Lake firms used Corinne as a base for freighting into Idaho and Montana. The town did well at first; in the middle 1870's it possessed the second largest Jewry in the state, all of thirty-five souls. In 1873 Corinne had twenty-five saloons and three churches including the Presbyterian sanctuary which the Jews had helped build. It was full of "white men armed to the teeth"; there were Indians and Chinese contract laborers; one of the latter entered the home of Julius Bernstein at night and chopped him down with an ax. There were at least fifteen Jewish firms in town, among them the Auerbachs and the Ransohoffs, still names to conjure with in the Salt Lake City and San Francisco of the late twentieth century.

Two Kuhn brothers, Abraham and Adam, were here also. Papa Kuhn had come to Mobile from the Palatinate as a youngster in the 1830's but had returned to Germany where he remained to rear a family. Abraham and Adam came to the States in the 1850's. The former was fourteen, the latter was ten. Abraham arrived in Salt Lake in 1864 after living and working in New Orleans, Vincennes, Council Bluffs, and Denver. Then in 1866 he went on to Montana where he remained until 1868. When Adam reached the ripe age of eighteen he went into business in Colorado, freighting into Montana and Utah and opening branch stores in Bannack and Virginia City, Montana. In 1869 Abraham and Adam joined forces, establishing a business in Corinne with branches in Ogden and in nearby Evanston, Wyoming, not too far from Piedmont where Simon Bamberger had hustled for a living. Corinne began to decline in the middle and late seventies and the Greenwalds, local Jews, had to abandon their beautiful hotel. Even in those days it had cost them $50,000 to build this spacious hostelry; they sold it later for $300. In 1880 the Kuhns, too, moved out; they went to Ogden where they established a successful wholesale dry goods and clothing firm which was housed in the magnificent new Kuhn Block.[26]

Most of Utah's Jews had settled in the towns that were clustered around Great Salt Lake. The territory's entire Jewry in the seventies could hardly have numbered 300 souls, over half of whom were in Salt Lake City. As immigrants with strong religious and traditional ties most of them were willing if not eager to found a formal Jewish community. They met for services no later than 1864 and two years later established the Hebrew Benevolent Society. The Mormons provided the "use of an elegant hall" for purposes of prayer and donated a plot in which to bury the dead, some of whom were brought in from Idaho, Montana, and eastern Nevada. Grateful to Brigham Young for his courtesy, the Jewish community published a resolution of thanks in the local press and in the Jewish newspapers of Cincinnati and San Francisco. Apparently the community fixed its criterion for Jewishness: a Jew is he who observes Rosh Hashanah and Yom Kippur! At that time that was the best that could be hoped for; the frontier is permissive. If one year Jews worshipped in a room offered them by Brigham Young, in another year they held services in Independence Hall, a Christian sanctuary built by the Young Men's Literary Association to which Jews also belonged. "Colonel" Samuel Kahn (pronounced "cane") was a practicing Jew who was glad to help the local Protestant Congregational Church by serving as one of its trustees. In 1866 Salt Lake's Jewry made a national appeal for funds for the upkeep of its cemetery. Provision had to be made for those transmigrants on their way farther west who died in town and were called upon to make their last "long journey."[27]

If the initiative for fashioning a community came from the men— and this was not always true—the actual job of raising funds for social welfare and for all religious purposes was frequently taken on by the women. The Ladies Hebrew Benevolent Society, already giving "socials" in 1872, may well have helped finance the congregation established the following year. The women and their men, concerned about the children and their Jewish education, opened a Sunday school, it would seem, in the early 1870's. The benevolent and religious societies sponsored an annual carnival and ball in order to secure the money they needed to carry on their work. The ball was the social event of the season; the governor, the judiciary, the officers at Fort Douglas—distinguished Civil war heroes —were happy to serve on the invitation committee.[28]

WEST TEXAS JEWRY

The presence of the commanding officer of the fort and his staff at Jewish social affairs was by no means unusual. Affluent Jewish businessmen, an elite group on the High Plains where poverty was common, maintained good relations with the officers with whom they had close economic ties and whom they frequently entertained. Many towns in the West had grown up around forts. This was as true in the New Southwest as it was in the plains, mountains, and territories of the North. At least three of the five "Jewish" towns of West Texas were also army posts: El Paso, Brownsville, and San Antonio. Even Victoria on the Guadelupe was not distant from the military installations on Matagordas Bay and Island.

El Paso was the gateway to northern Mexico, on the Trail between Santa Fe and Chihuahua. Nevertheless Jews were slow to settle there; the summer heat was almost unbearable. This did not deter individuals from drifting in, among others the two Schutz brothers, Samuel and Joseph, in the 1850's. It is not surprising that the firm of S. Schutz & Brother brought over nephews; it is somewhat of a surprise however that the two groups fell out and became bitter and vindictive enemies. A trade war ensued. The nephews induced wholesalers from St. Louis and Santa Fe to come into El Paso in order to ruin the uncles and the uncles retaliated by selling goods in their retail stores at wholesale prices, hoping to put their nephews out of business. In a town of fewer than a thousand people— and, of course, many fewer Jews—the two clans would not speak to each other. Obviously under circumstances such as these no communal life could come into being; the Jewish census of 1876 does not even mention El Paso.

Conditions for El Paso Jewry improved in the 1880's. The railroads came in; more Jews arrived, and the general population increased rapidly. Commerce flourished. The town was wide open; a saloonkeeper posted a sign over his bar: "If drinking interferes with your business, quit business." The old-timers went into politics and three Jews were to be elected mayor before the turn of the century. One of them was disqualified when it was discovered that he had never even taken out citizenship papers. By the late 1880's there was a cemetery, a women's relief society, and certainly an occasional service. By 1890 there was a Sunday school. A Jewish community was in the making—in 1898, finally, there was a congregation.[29]

El Paso was several hundred miles up the Rio Grande; Brownsville, on the river near the Gulf, was the southern gateway to Mexico as well as a very important port of entry. It was the fourth largest Jewish settlement in West Texas. In 1876 there were thirty-three Jews most of whom traded with the Mexicans across the border. Between 1868 and 1880 the Jews in town were joined in all of their efforts by the Jews on the Mexican side of the river at Matamoras. Together they succeeded in fashioning an all-purpose relief organization, a burial society, and a Sunday school. Farther east on the Gulf lay Corpus Christi at the mouth of the Nueces. Jews had started coming to this town in the decade before the Civil War and by the 1870's they were packhorse and wagon peddlers, merchants with branch stores in the surrounding towns, and wholesale and retail grocers. Some of them were ranchers and bankers. One of the firms maintained an office in New York City. That same decade this Jewry of some forty souls established a typical benevolent society, laid out a cemetery, and met together for worship on special occasions, particularly when there was a circumcision feast.[30]

The pattern is clear for West Texas in the 1870's: the farther west one went the smaller the community; the more easterly the communities lay, the larger they were. Victoria, a hundred miles or so closer to civilization—that is, eastward—was no exception. The Jewry there was about twice as large as that of Corpus Christi at the time of the 1876 census. Like Brownsville and Corpus Christi, Victoria was on the rich coastal plains and on a river that penetrated the interior. The successful Jewish merchant in Victoria was in no sense different from his compatriot in Corpus Christi; he was a wholesale supplier who catered to the ranchers, carried them in hard times, and banked their savings and surplus capital in good times. All that a lucky Jewish trader needed to make the transition to banking was integrity, some experience, good judgment, an iron safe, a barrel of whiskey, and a tincup. A. Levi & Company of Victoria opened a private bank in 1875 and ran it successfully for the next thirty-five years. Every adult Jew in town was probably a member of the Hebrew Benevolent Society when it was founded in 1867. The women here, too, had a relief society of their own in the next decade and one may assume that the town's Jews met for services at least on the High Holy Days. When Mr. G. A. Levi of the Levi clan polled his coreligionists in 1876 he counted eighty-five men, women, and children.[31]

Victoria and San Antonio were both on rivers that flowed into San Antonio Bay. Though an interior city, San Antonio, on the edge of the Great Plains, was the most important town in West Texas. With its population of over 300 it was the third largest Jewish community in the entire state. This made it a big Jewish town in the West of the 1870's. Its businessmen resembled those in other parts of Texas, and, for that matter, throughout the West. The Oppenheimer brothers, Anton and Daniel, of San Antonio, could have found their counterparts in almost any Texas city of that generation; the careers are strikingly similar, only the specific incidents are different. These two German immigrants came to Texas before the War and served in the Confederate Army, although in later years one of them recalled that he was not in sympathy with slavery or secession. (These post-eventum reflections, however, are frequently of little historic value.) The Oppenheimers were peddlers, traders, and storekeepers. When the cattlemen drove their herds north to Wichita and Abilene many of them stopped at Oppenheimers for a Winchester rifle, a hand gun, a slicker, a blanket, and a pair of boots, all on credit to be paid for when the drive was over. Because the ranchers had to be carried financially the Oppenheimers found themselves in the ranching and banking business. Trading was not without its headaches. On being refused further credit one rancher jumped on Anton and began to gouge and bite him. Daniel, hearing the scuffle, rushed in and when he found Anton bleeding profusely he came to his rescue by cracking the skull of the irate attacker. Anton's wife, unhappy with frontier life, moved to New York City whither her husband commuted as the spirit moved him. All this in the 1870's.

San Antonio may well be the oldest Jewish community on the High Plains, for it had a cemetery, a society, services, and a religious school in the 1850's; a women's organization, a synagog, a benevolent association, a rabbi, and a B'nai B'rith lodge in the 1870's. The synagogal bill collector in that decade was not the beadle but the gun-toting town marshal. Not all Jews in San Antonio were interested in Judaism. Those who refused to affiliate were warned that they would be denied religious ministrations in the hour of their need. Patently this was a threat that they would not be buried by Jews. Others who permitted the attending physician to circumcise the newborn were obviously indifferent to the religious demands of the occasion. Anticipating a common practice of the late twentieth century, the congregation encouraged such indifferentists to invite the rabbi to participate in some form of a religious ceremony.[32]

NEW MEXICO JEWRY

Under the Spanish, the Southwest was part of the viceroyalty of New Spain which included among other transmississippi regions present-day Texas, New Mexico, and Arizona. It has already been noted that large-scale American Jewish itinerant merchants had moved along the Santa Fe Trail no later than the 1840's and when New Mexico fell to the Americans in 1846 Solomon Jacob Spiegelberg was among the businessmen who accompanied the invading troops. He was not, however, a "Jewish" pioneer; as early as the sixteenth and seventeenth centuries, governors of Jewish ancestry, Luis de Carvajal y de la Cueva and Bernardo Lopez de Mendizabal, ruled in that part of the Spanish Empire.

Spiegelberg, a German immigrant, had Americanized himself in New York, Philadelphia, Baltimore, and Independence, Missouri, before moving west with the troops to become one of the first sedentary merchants in Santa Fe. The city and territory offered many opportunities: Santa Fe soon became headquarters for an army department that extended from southern Colorado through New Mexico into Arizona and was for years the commercial center of the territory. Spiegelberg started out modestly as a regimental sutler, opened a retail shop, and gradually won the confidence of the Eastern suppliers, many of whom were Jews. Then he branched out as a wholesaler selling all types of merchandise; he advertised in the Spanish-language paper and extended liberal credits to his customers. By the 1870's his store had plank sidewalks and glass windows enlivened and enhanced by a female dummy which displayed the latest fashions in women's garments. He and his associates contracted to forward the mail and to supply the army and the Indians. They invested in mines, land, and irrigation projects and sold insurance.

Spiegelberg was successful not only because of enterprise and integrity but because of the help he received from a number of brothers whom he brought over and put to work. They, too, seem to have been able men. By the end of the century Solomon and his numerous brothers had gradually liquidated their business interests and had resettled in the East, in New York City. Their wives, some of whom were American born, were not happy in the West although brother Lehman's home with its billiard table, grand piano, and beautiful gardens was anything but primitive. Brother Levy had been mayor of Santa Fe and its probate judge. It was not only the wives who urged the Spiegelbergs to go back to the urban East, for the men, too, were glad to return to "civilization." The Jewish population of New York City was ten times as large as that of the entire population of Santa Fe. The Spiegelberg men enjoyed living in a great city like New York with its excitement and its Jewish clubs and synagogs, its investment opportunities, and its supply of suitable wives and husbands for their children. Brother Emanuel married the daughter of Joseph Seligman, one of the richest Jews in the United States.

As early as the 1870's the Spiegelberg clan had a national bank which they controlled not only because of the need for funds but the better to cope with rivals who had their own banking facilities. One of the Spiegelberg bank directors was a nephew of the Catholic bishop, John Baptist Lamy, and when the cathedral was built Solomon Spiegelberg distinguished himself as a liberal contributor. The facade of the cathedral was decorated with the Hebrew divine name the tetragrammaton enclosed in a triangle. This Hebrew word YHWH gave rise to the legend that Bishop Lamy had added the name as a compliment to his Jewish friend and benefactor. There is probably no truth whatsoever in this assertion. The St. Louis cathedral contains a similar decorative inscription. Catholic interest in Hebrew is as old as the Renaissance, if not older; a Hebrew grammar was published if not printed in Mexico City as early as the sixteenth century.[33]

Solomon Spiegelberg brought over his brothers but it was his example, at least, if not his financial help that made possible the immigration of numerous relatives and friends. Santa Fe, especially in the 1850's, became the dispersal center for most of these newcomers; many if not all of them were given a start by the Spiegelbergs as clerks and resident partners. Some ended up as competitors; others were to become as successful if not more so than the Spiegelbergs themselves. The Seligmans and the Zeckendorfs were cousins. The three Seligman brothers, Sigmund, Adolph, and Bernard, merchants and bankers, were a rich and successful clan which helped finance the Denver and Rio Grande Railroad in New Mexico. Bernard's son Arthur, an Episcopalian, became governor of New Mexico in the 1930's. Financed by the Spiegelbergs, the Zeckendorfs opened stores in Albuquerque and Santa Fe in the 1860's; after the Civil War they moved on to Tucson, Arizona. Henry Biernbaum was given his start in business by the Spiegelbergs in the 1850's and finally settled in Trinidad, Colorado, where he became one of its Jewish elite. Abraham Staab who arrived in the 1850's also went to work for the Spiegelbergs. Abraham and his brother Zadok (Zoldac) built a commercial empire that was to reach out north into Colorado and south into Mexico and was to rival that of the Spiegelbergs. Jacob Amberg and Gustave Elsberg of Santa Fe made their way it seems without the aid of the Spiegelbergs, although one or both were their kinsmen. After running a dry goods store at Westport, Missouri they settled in Santa Fe in 1856, and in the course of a decade became two of the most important merchants of New Mexico with interests also in lumber and mining. They carried a huge stock of merchandise both at Santa Fe and in their Chihuahua, Mexico, outlet. Like the Spiegelbergs, they, in turn, employed newly arrived German Jewish immigrants and trained them for successful business careers.[34]

The Bibos, another of the many multi-brother clans, were also originally clerks working for the Spiegelbergs. Simon, the first of the family in New Mexico, had come west across the plains with a Spiegelberg supply train. He married a Spanish American girl who generously gave him eighteen children, nine of whom survived; all of them were reared as Jews. Brother Solomon married an Indian girl whom he educated and she too reared a family of Jews. Nathan, the oldest of the seven brothers, was the most sophisticated of the lot. He, too, had clerked for the Spiegelbergs and as an agent for Willi Spiegelberg operated the post store at Fort Wingate. Sam Dittenhoefer served as his clerk and Navajo interpreter. Later, as the trader at Camp Apache in Arizona, Nathan built a road complete with bridges from Zuni, New Mexico, to the Arizona fort. In order to fulfill a hay contract at Camp Apache he enlisted a host of Apache women, armed them with butcher knives, and set them to cut the hay by hand. With packs of 60 to 100 pounds of hay on their backs, and their children on top of the bundles, they plodded back to the fort.

In the early 1870's Nathan and Simon moved to Bernalillo, a small town between Santa Fe and Albuquerque, where they opened a trading post. This was to become their economic bridgehead. Over the years the family, fortified by the coming of younger brothers, opened branches in several other New Mexican towns. Nathan built a beautiful home in Bernalillo where he cultivated grapes which he shipped as far east as Kansas. Among the notables he entertained were Governor Lew Wallace and General William T. Sherman. The Bibos were close to the Indians; Solomon was twice "governor" of the Acoma Indians. The family brought the Indians American foods, clothing, and a new life style. It encouraged them in agriculture, supplied them with wagons and harness, and, for better or worse, taught them the use of patent medicines. As merchants it was to their advantage to cultivate the Indian trade and they made the most of their opportunities. None of them however attained great wealth. The enterprising Nathan, after a brilliant career in San Francisco where he had moved, returned to his New Mexico haunts to die a broken impoverished man who vainly tried to make a stake by prospecting.[35]

The Santa Fe, Albuquerque, and Bernalillo merchants were in the cities and villages lying near the Upper Rio Grande. In the Rio Grande area of southern New Mexico, Las Cruces was the core town for Jewish businessmen. The important merchants here were members of the Freudenthal-Lesinsky clan, German Poles. Julius Freudenthal, who married a Latin American girl, was the first of his family in the territory, for he was there no later than the 1850's and may even have come earlier. He did not remain long; he left for New York City as a resident buyer although he continued to dominate the clan's expanding concerns. Henry Lesinsky, his nephew, head of the Las Cruces retail and wholesale firm of Henry

Lesinsky & Company, was the brains of the family. At the age of fourteen the orphaned Henry was sent to England to learn a trade. A church society sent him on to the Australian gold fields. (Was he for the time being a professing Christian?) The teenager sent money home to his widowed mother, moved on in 1858 to the California gold fields, and a year later joined Uncle Julius in New Mexico, probably in Las Cruces. Henry and the firm—his Freudenthal kinsmen—prospered. Like other New Mexico merchants they engaged in army supply, ground their own flour for the forts, worked closely with a stagecoach line that carried men and mail through hundreds of miles of Indian country, and conducted a very substantial business with branches or outlets in Juarez, Mexico, Isleta, Texas, and in at least two other New Mexico towns. One of them was Silver City where for a short time they opened a bank. In 1870 having made a fortune, Henry and the clan concentrated on their copper and merchandise interests in Arizona.[36]

The Jewish settlements in New Mexico were clustered around the territory's two important rivers, the Rio Grande in the west-central area and the Pecos in the east. In those days Las Vegas was the most important business town in the Pecos country, and it was here that the Rosenwald brothers, young Bavarians, finally settled down in the early 1860's. The two partners, Joseph and Emanuel, had worked in the East for a few years before leaving for Missouri, Kansas, and the western territories. Joseph and a partner, Henry Rosenfield, moved into Camp Floyd, Utah, where they did a thriving business selling liquor to the soldiers. They bottled their barrel whiskey at night and sold it the next day. Unfortunately Rosenfield, it would appear, drank up much of the profits. Joseph and Emanuel then moved on to Denver, carried on trade at Fort Wise on the Arkansas, and then shipped ten oxcarts of merchandise to California Gulch—Ore City (Leadville). There was very little that they did not attempt; their varied experiences were grist for their mill. They tried their luck at placer mining and opened two branch stores at Buckskin Joe and Canon City. By 1864 Joseph had moved on to Las Vegas where Emanuel was trading with the soldiers at Fort Union. Joseph, as head of J. Rosenwald & Company, was very successful, becoming one of the territory's most distinguished entrepreneurs, though he was faced with tough competition. There were at least four other aggressive Jewish merchants in town in 1870. The Jews had been coming to Las Vegas ever since the 1850's. Rooted finally in general supply and wares, Joseph also helped bring the railroad into town, engaged in subdivision promotion, and furthered gas lighting and a street railway. When he passed away the street cars were draped in black. It was always a source of regret to him that he had failed to foresee the growth of towns like Salt Lake City and Denver where he had traded in the 1850's.

When Joseph Rosenwald was buried in May, 1888, one of his pall-bearers—and erstwhile competitors—was Charles Ilfeld, a younger member of the Ilfeld clan. In 1867 Charles had come to New Mexico where one of his brothers was already hard at work building his fortune. After crossing the plains with an ox wagon train, he hired out in Taos. In 1867 he became a partner of Adolph Letcher and began to emerge as a merchant capitalist. The same year Charles moved to Las Vegas and by 1874 had established the Charles Ilfeld Company, a mercantile house. At the turn of the century it was in all probability the largest house in all New Mexico. Up until the late 1880's Ilfeld and his associates were merchants and petty bankers; after that time they expanded their operations opening company stores, jobbing, wholesaling, and intensifying their interests in sheep husbandry and the wool trade.[37]

One of the men who worked for Ilfeld in the 1880's was an immigrant by the name of Sol Floersheim. After arriving in New York in the late 1870's he found employment in a matzo factory where he was paid $5 a week. By 1879 he was in Trinidad where he had hired himself out to a Jewish firm, but when his bosses sent him a bill for the food he ate when he was sick he quit and went to work for a Spanish American businessman in Las Vegas. His job was to sell liquor to the saloons on the Santa Fe right of way. This hazardous job meant he had to carry a pistol. A cowboy held him up and robbed him but he searched out his assailant, held him up in turn, and recovered his money. What he saved on his job he lost when his boss became a fraudulent bankrupt and refused to disgorge the sum which Floersheim had left with him. Then Floersheim took a position with Ilfeld as a clerk and as an agent in the sheep and wool branch of the business. The Jew he married in 1884 had been one of the Ilfeld clerks. Toward the end of that decade he went out on his own and wound up in the late 1890's in Springer. Since he was an honest merchant, liberal with his credits, he soon had a large following among the ranchers, farmers, and homesteaders in the Texas Panhandle, southern Colorado, and northern New Mexico. They came to trade with him from a distance of 100 miles. He shipped large quantities of wool eastward, invested in ranching lands, and his son Ben, who married one of the Bibo girls, devoted all of his time to the cattle industry.

Sol was an amateur frontier doctor and apparently very capable. It was not unusual for a Jewish merchant in those days to give medical advice. Louis Smadbeck, who worked for kinsmen, the Arizona Lesinskys, had a large medical book out of which he physicked the Clifton miners and townsmen. Springer turned to Floersheim. One of the family stories about Floersheim's medical practice was that after discovering that no one was buying the maraschino cherries stocked in the store he solemnly prescribed "one maraschino cherry three times a day."[38]

Very few of the Jewish merchants had any substantial capital at their disposal when they came to the territory. They began their careers as clerks, drummers, bookkeepers, managers, and partners. Frequently they were assisted by the members of the family with whom they first found a job; it is true, too, that very many of the important Jewish men were related by blood and marriage. Good men were taken into the family; eligible Jews were scarce. Thus the following were all kinsmen: Spiegelbergs, Seligmens, Zeckendorfs, Elsbergs, Ambergs, Ilfelds, Staabs, Nordhauses, and the Gusdorfs of Taos. But the caveat is always in order that kinship, even of blood, was no guarantee of cooperation. The cousins, brothers, nephews, friends, and landsleit who branched out for themselves, were dispersed in practically every town and village of size in the territory; the economic influence of the Jews is documented by the fact that the following New Mexico hamlets were named after individual Jewish merchants: Ilfeld, Levy, Bibo. Seligman, Straus, and Newman.[39]

BUSINESS, POLITICS, AND RELIGION IN THE WORLD OF NEW MEXICO JEWRY

A competent scholar has estimated that in the period from 1850 to 1900 there were more than 500 businesses in New Mexico operated by Jews, some with Christian partners. The Jews then constituted about 1/2 of 1 percent of the territory's inhabitants. Bernard Seligman reported in 1876 that there were 108 Jews in Santa Fe. Either he ignored the 15 or 20 other places in New Mexico where Jews dwelt or the other towns, such as Las Vegas, Albuquerque, and Las Cruces, were not asked or declined to submit data. Though their numbers were small it is quite clear that these German immigrants played a very important role in the economy of the territory. These businessmen were the sedentary merchants who ushered in the economic and cultural "revolution" in these hitherto unsettled lands. They are the ones who imported goods for the settlers and exported native products. In this activity they played a role not unlike that of the Jewish merchant-shippers of the eighteenth-century American tidewater. In a land where frontier conditions were to persist into the twentieth century these Jewish shopkeepers, merchants, and wholesalers made living tolerable and prosperity possible by the credits they extended. They tied the adobe villages to the urban economy of Santa Fe, Las Vegas, Kansas City, New York, and other eastern centers.

They worked closely with the Indians, learned Spanish, employed Latin Americans, and even a Negro in an executive capacity. They nourished fewer ethnic prejudices than the Anglo-Americans, and even some of the Catholic indigenes realized that Jews "are the same people as our Savior, Jesus Christ." If there was any rapprochement between the Span-

ish Americans and the Anglos and the Indians it was in no small part due
to the Jewish businessmen. They were the catalyst, the liaison bringing
the various elements together, if only in a modest fashion. When in the
1930's the Catholic and Protestant clergy of Albuquerque met for lunch
at the Jewish Institute of Religion, where they were addressed by Rabbi
Jacob R. Marcus, that was the first time those ministers had broken bread
together in a formal gathering. They came because the Jews had invited
them.[40]

New Mexico's upper middle-class Jews achieved recognition in many
areas. These successful merchants were not only socially acceptable but
were frequently leaders because they were also pioneers, deemed to be
"Anglos" in a world of Latin Americans and Indians, and above all because they were a literate and cultured group in a frontier milieu where
the majority was illiterate. They supported the arts, were among the best
musicians and music lovers, and because of their wealth were elected to
important political offices. A number of them served in the territorial legislature. In 1880, Columbus Moïse, Jr., sat on the bench of the territorial
Supreme Court; his father, a litterateur, had fought in the Florida Indian
Wars. Henry N. Jaffa, who had come to Albuquerque in 1869, became
the first mayor of the city, and Nathan, another member of the family,
was the mayor first of Roswell and later of Santa Fe. A man of talent, he
managed a store for the family in Las Vegas, and later, with W. S. Prager
operated a substantial business in Roswell. Nathan devoted himself to
banking until 1907 when President Theodore Roosevelt appointed him
Secretary of the Territory. By 1922, after New Mexico had been admitted
to statehood, he had returned to Santa Fe, this time as president of a bank.
The following year he was appointed president of the Board of Regents
of the State University and before he died this 33-degree Mason had
served as the Grand Master of the state's lodges.

In 1874 a man named Sol Loewenstein, living in Mora County in a
hamlet called Ocate, wrote the Union of American Hebrew Congregations that there was no congregation in all the territory. That was true but
it is equally true that services were held sporadically in Las Vegas and Albuquerque in the early 1870's. The opening of a B'nai B'rith lodge in Albuquerque in 1882 was the first formal Jewish organization in the territory. A cemetery and some form of a congregation were also established
in the next few years. The Jews of Santa Fe may have met for worship on
the High Holy Days as early as the 1860's, and there was a Sunday school
of sorts in town in the 1880's, but there was to be no religious community till the next century. Santa Fe as a business town was outstripped in
the later decades of the nineteenth century by Albuquerque and Las Vegas. In 1884 the Jews of the latter city established the first congregation
in the territory naming it after Moses Montefiore, the grand old man of

World Jewry, who was then celebrating his hundredth birthday. In 1886 as the congregation prepared to build the first synagog structure in the territory the leaders circulated an appeal to all American Jews asking for financial aid. Among the signers of the plea were Charles Ilfeld, Joseph Rosenwald, and Louis Sulzbacher, a lawyer. Sulzbacher, was something of an anomaly. He was one of the few German immigrants on the High Plains who had turned to a profession. True he, too, began as a clerk for the Spiegelbergs, but he read law and practiced in Las Vegas and Kansas City until 1900 when he was appointed the chief justice of the Supreme Court in Porto Rico. Four years later he became the United States Judge for the Western District of Oklahoma and Indian Territories.[41]

ARIZONA JEWRY

Until 1863 Arizona was part of the Territory of New Mexico, and long after that time New Mexico Jewish merchants continued to turn to Arizona for new opportunities and challenges. In the 1860's the Zeckendorfs trekked west to Tucson; moving slowly through Apache country, they took months to transport their twelve wagonloads of goods. In the next decade, the Bibos, already experienced in pathfinding, pioneered the way from Camp Apache to northern Arizona, halfway across the territory. It was just about that time that the Freudenthal-Lesinsky combine of Las Cruces moved west into the wilderness about Clifton and began to work the Longfellow Mine. But the first Jewish settlers in Arizona did not come from the East, New Mexico, but from the West, California. After gold was discovered in the late 1850's and early 1860's they moved in from southern California, from San Bernardino, San Diego, and Los Angeles to do business with the miners who had flocked to the new diggings. A number of them settled at La Paz, a town on the Colorado River between California and Arizona; among them was the Polish-born Michel Goldwater (Goldwasser). This East European immigrant, a tailor and cap maker, had moved west from Poland to Paris, London, the States, and then on to California, the Mother Lode, and Los Angeles. Michel and brother Joseph ran a toy and stationery shop in Los Angeles before they moved on to La Paz in late 1862 and when that boom town began to die Michel helped establish nearby Ehrenberg, named in honor of a well-known German Christian adventurer and pioneer.

Beginning in the 1860's the Goldwaters, Michel, Joseph, and their children established a modest mercantile empire that stretched from Prescott in the north to Bisbee in the south. At different times, independently or in partnership, they opened a series of stores in at least half a dozen towns. They were dealers in general merchandise, prepared to sell almost anything needed by miners, farmers, and townspeople, but they were also government supply contractors, freighters, jobbers, and mine operators. Michel liked to do his buying in San Francisco during the High Holy Days; it gave him a chance to attend at the synagog. When he finally retired from business he settled there and became active in one of the congregations. Arizona in those days was not without its hazards; in 1883 a band of armed men robbed a Goldwater store in Bisbee. Three innocent bystanders were killed but five members of the gang were caught and executed, a sixth was lynched.[42]

Like a number of other western Jews the Goldwaters took time out to busy themselves in politics. In 1871 Dr. Herman Bendell, a New Yorker, was sent by President Grant to serve as Superintendent of Indian Affairs. Grant put him in because he was a Civil War surgeon with a fine record. Unlike some other Grant appointees, Bendell was a man of great integrity but a Board of Missions objected successfully to his reappointment because he was not a Christian. Emil Ganz, a Confederate War veteran, was elected mayor of Phoenix. Michel Goldwater and his son Morris each served as mayor of Prescott. Morris a 33-degree Mason, was also chairman of the Democratic Central Committee of Arizona. It was his nephew Barry, a Republican, who served the state in Washington as a United States senator.[43]

Several Jews sat in the territorial legislature, among them the pioneer Sol Barth who was also to serve for two years in a penitentiary as a perjurer. Barth was widely known and when he passed away in 1928 at the age of eighty-six the flags in the state were flown at half staff. Barth arrived in Arizona with a Mormon Jewish uncle; still a youngster, he lived in Utah and then in California whence in the early 1860's he began freighting to Tucson. In 1862 he worked for Mike Goldwater in La Paz, ran a store for the family in still another mining town, contracted to carry mail to New Mexico through Apache country, and traded with the Indians; in spite of brushes with them he managed to escape with a whole hide. In the 1870's he and some associates established the town of St. Johns in Apache County. Barth's brother was the first sheriff; Barth was, himself, county treasurer for a while, built a toll bridge across the Little Colorado, opened up northeastern Arizona for settlement, and claimed ownership of the Grand Canyon of the Colorado. This rugged individualist, a true frontiersman, was a trader, storekeeper, freighter, Indian fighter, sheep rancher, and legislator. He worked with Mormons and married a Latin American who saw to it that he was given a Catholic burial. Writing his eulogy a newspaper declared that he was "one of the most distinguished citizens and characters of pioneer days."[44]

The two Drachman brothers and the two Goldberg brothers—Poles, as were the Goldwaters—also came into Arizona by way of La Paz. Like most other Arizona Jewish businessmen of the 1860's and 1870's Philip and Samuel Drachman and Hyman and Isaac Goldberg were merchants, freighters, army suppliers, mine owners, and saloonkeepers. When Isaac Goldberg shipped goods in the early days from San Bernardino to La Paz he recovered some of his high freight cost by selling the wooden boxes in which the goods were packed. The buyers used them for coffins and for furniture. In that same decade of the 1860's Goldberg set up a bar in the new territorial capital of Prescott; his equipment consisted of two bottles, a cup, and a counter behind which he stored the barrels of whiskey which he had hauled in. The Drachmans and Goldbergs, kinsmen and at times partners in business, tried their hand at a host of jobs and challenges and like many of their contemporaries never became wealthy. Indian depredations, the high cost of goods, a small population, bad credit risks—all these factors militated against them as they did against others. Pioneering in the semiarid regions of the High Plains was always backbreaking and almost as frequently unrewarding.[45]

Philip and Samuel Drachman were both in the territorial legislature as was another Arizona businessman Adolf Solomon. A son of Hyman Goldberg married a niece of Adolf Solomon. The Solomon clan had planted itself in southeastern Arizona. Isidor Elkan Solomon, Adolf's brother, went into the livery stable business in Towanda, Pennsylvania; returning to his native Germany for a visit, he found himself a bride. Marrying Anna Freudenthal made him a member of the Freudenthal-Lesinsky family. Isidor and Anna moved west to Las Cruces, New Mexico, and then on to Clifton. Isidor went to work in the mine as a day laborer—the pay was good—but soon signed a contract with his kinfolk to supply their copper smelter with charcoal. Anna ran a little shop in a nearby village of four adobe huts. The couple bought out one of the hut-owners, took over his ranch of fifty acres, fed travelers, changed the name of the hamlet to Solomonville, and began a slow upward climb to prosperity and wealth. Their shop became a trading post; their town became the county seat of Graham County, and Isidor was appointed postmaster. Eventually the village shop became a wholesale grocery; they opened branch stores in other towns and by the turn of the century had established a family bank. As the children grew up they were sent to the East to be educated. The family remained staunchly Jewish. Like the Goldwaters, papa and mama Solomon spent their declining days in California. Solomonville has long since disappeared.[46]

Many of the early Arizona Jewish families were tied together. Mike Goldwater had come to the United States with Philip Drachman; the Goldbergs and Drachmans had intramarried, and both families were in turn related by marriage to a man named Sam Katzenstein. Katzenstein had settled in Charleston, Arizona, where he owned a store, ran a hotel, and served as postmaster and justice of the peace. Another storekeeper in

that South Arizona town was a Mr. Aaron who had a son Sam. Sam refused to be a "nice Jewish boy." Sam's career began in the early 1880's
when he was not yet twenty years of age. He worked as a miner, led a
strike at a smelter, clerked, ran a store, traveled as a clothing drummer,
operated a saloon, a gambling house, and a bucket shop, shepherded a theatrical troupe on the road, and ended his life rather ingloriously, but in an
odor of respectability, as a successful clothing retailer in San Jose, California. At the age of sixteen or seventeen he had even been sworn in as a
deputy United States marshal. Back in Charleston he had served as a faro
dealer in a gambling house where he was known as the Lucky Jew Kid.
When his father left him with almost $1,000 to pay bills, Sam gambled it
all away. He went to work in a stamp mill as a common laborer; in a very
short time he became one of the night bosses and he stuck to his job until
he had made good the loss.

Sam reached southern Arizona sometime after Marshal Wyatt Earp
and his cohorts had their shootout in Tombstone at the OK Corral in
October, 1881. Thus the young Jewish adventurer's knowledge of that
affair could only have been hearsay, nonetheless Sam considered Earp a
desperado no better than the men against whom he warred. His hostility
to Earp reflected a sentiment common to many Arizonians of that generation; they deeply resented ruthless, homicidal peace officers. In his memoirs Sam reported that when Earp was threatened with arrest after the
killings a Jewish banker in Tombstone by the name of Solomon offered to
go bail for him; a biographer of Earp wrote that this banker, H. Solomon,
helped arm the Earp contingent when it left the city. In later years Earp
married a California Jew, Josephine Sarah Marcus, and at his death in
1929 his widow saw to it that he was buried in a Jewish cemetery. Many
years later the Wyatt tombstone was stolen, carried off probably by some
avid but strong souvenir hunter; the granite marker weighed about 500
pounds. The marker was later recovered.[47]

The glamorous men, the guts-gore-gun men, were rarely builders.
More prosaic types are often of greater historical significance in a pioneer
economy. Such a one was Michael Wormser, a French and German-
speaking immigrant; the Latin Americans whose language he also learned
called him "El Judio Miguel," Michael the Jew. Like many of his Jewish
confreres, he made his entry into the territory in the 1860's through the
town of La Paz starting out, again like others, as a general merchant. He
then moved on to the new town of Prescott which in the next decade was
destined to contain the largest Jewish population in Arizona, thirty-six
men, women, and children. As early as 1870, Wormser's cousin Ben
Bloch and his partner Aaron Barnett had helped found Phoenix on the
Salt River. There they operated a large general store, grew grain on irrigated land, and brought in one of the first threshing machines. When the

ineptness of Bloch, a genial schlemiel, ruined the business, Wormser and his partner Aaron Wertheimer, bought them out in 1873; from then on Wormser devoted most of his time and energy to his Phoenix holdings.

Wormser was the solid citizen par excellence, the hardworking shrewd merchant who was busy vending goods, grubstaking miners, buying and selling town lots, and speculating in water rights. By the middle 1870's he had already turned from merchandizing to farming. He became a large-scale agricultural enterpriser producing grain on irrigated lands; the laborers were Mexican sharecroppers. Always alert to new possibilities and added profits he experimented with sugarcane and sugar beets. As an elected supervisor he husbanded the resources of the county, helped build roads, bridges, a courthouse, and a hospital. He and his associates appropriated funds to keep out diseased cattle and to raise posses to fight the Indians. This bachelor was thrifty to a fault and the *Arizona Miner* once reported facetiously that "had it not been for the high cost of freight our old friend M. Wormser would have brought a wife from the East." In spite of frequent reverses Wormser died a wealthy man.[48]

Apparently all the western territories have this in common: they had but few Jews but these few were scattered throughout the region. Jews could be found in almost every town of any size; often a village would shelter a lonely unmarried shopkeeper, occasionally a single isolated family. Statistical confusion is compounded by the fact that these petty sedentary merchants were very mobile—moving about constantly in search of the perfect town and an assured livelihood. Thus in Arizona Territory there was a Jew or Jews in Bisbee, Tombstone, Tucson, Solomonville, Clifton, Globe, St. Johns, Phoenix, Wickenberg, Prescott, La Paz, Ehrenberg, and Nogales. In the years from 1862 into the 1880's they were concentrated in the towns and villages in the central and southeastern regions of the territory. It bears repetition that as late as the 1880's Arizona, like all the territories in the Great American Desert, was truly frontier; demographically the spots on the map indicating settlements were but a few isolated freckles on the white-faced deserts and mountains, enormous unsettled areas. Tucson is not even listed in the Jewish census of 1876 which reported a total of only forty-eight souls in all Arizona, although an additional note in the original census manuscript discloses that a Mr. J. S. Mansfield of Tucson knew of 105 Jews in the territory.

The three Zeckendorf brothers from Hannover, Louis, Aaron, and William, had opened a store in Tucson as early as the 1860's; when their business was taken over in the 1870's by a nephew it became one of the largest retail and wholesale concerns in Arizona. In later years Albert Steinfeld, the nephew, was a mine owner and president of the local Chamber of Commerce. Just about the time that the Zeckendorfs decided to remain in Tucson, Mark Jacobs, a Californian, sent his two sons, Lionel and Barron, there to open a branch retail store. Their stock came from San Francisco by water around the Gulf of California to Yuma and then on by mule team. Sometimes a shipment was ninety days on the way. When the Jacobses became wholesalers they encouraged Sonora merchants to cross the border and trade Mexican flour, liquor, sugar, and dried fruits for American dry goods. When the firm prospered the Jacobses followed the typical western pattern of successful Jewish businessmen. By the 1870's they had branched out into money exchange and loans and then in 1879 they opened a bank which was probably the first in Tucson. In the following decade they invited other members of the family to settle in the territory and helped them open stores in a number of towns.[49]

Nogales was originally nothing but an adobe trading post established by a Russian Jew named Jacob Isaacson who had peddled his way south from Tucson in the early 1880's. When he first settled down near the border the place was known as Isaacson and he served as its first postmaster. After he left, the growing town changed its name to Nogales. Yuma on the other side of the territory had six Jews in the 1870's. Sam Drachman, Philip's younger brother, passing through the town then known as Arizona City (1867) was pressed into service at the courthouse to record a trial in progress. The defendant was found guilty, and fined $100; for lack of a jail he was then chained to a log. Taking pity on the prisoner, local citizens induced the judge to accept a payment of $10, cash money, on condition that the judge treat all hands, and no sooner said than done. Why pity the prisoner? Yuma was one of the hottest spots in the country. Writing to his parents back in Germany, Ernst Kohlberg of El Paso told them about the soldier who had served in Fort Yuma and had gone to Hell but almost immediately sent back to the fort for his blankets to keep from freezing to death. Abraham Frank was one of the Jews who decided to make Yuma his home. He, too, had first settled in La Paz and then in Ehrenberg, but instead of moving across the territory like most other Jews he went down the Colorado River to Yuma. Highly respected as a businessman he was sent to the territorial legislature, made a prison commissioner, elected mayor of the city, and finally was called upon to serve as probate judge.[50]

Most Jews have a sense of community, a desire to belong, to organize themselves in a formal fashion. The Jewish Arizonians certainly felt this way but it took them almost twenty years to transmute emotion into action. Despite the fact that there were probably enough Jews in Prescott in the middle 1870's to assemble a minyan, no services were held even for the High Holy Days. Intragroup hatreds? Possibly! As late as 1878 Isaac Goldberg had to travel all the way to San Francisco to have his five-month-old son circumcised. He drove half way across the state to Yuma

in order to board a train going north. By the early 1880's the desire for an
organized community began to put on flesh. Tombstone held High Holy
Day services in the Turnverein Hall in 1881 and the following year a B'-
nai B'rith lodge came into existence even though it was not destined to
last. Five years later the Ladies Hebrew Benevolent Society staged a ball
that was the social event of the season. It is hard to believe that at that
time there was no Jewish cemetery in town. As the century drew to a
close the Jews of Tucson, led by Sam Drachman, conducted services during the Days of Awe. In Phoenix too the growing Jewish community
gathered together for worship during the nineties; after Michael Wormser's death in 1895 his heirs generously gave the Jews a few acres for a
burial ground, but there was to be no congregation as such in all of Arizona till the early twentieth century. *The Jewish Encyclopedia* published in
1902 does not even have an entry under "Arizona."[51]

OKLAHOMA JEWRY

The Indian and Oklahoma Territories were one of the last if not the very
last of the areas to be settled by Jews. Though the western part of Oklahoma bordered on the semi-desert Great Plains the present state is on the
whole fertile country, far more productive than New Mexico and Arizona. Yet the Jews like all others were compelled to bypass this inviting
region because it was reserved by the government for numerous tribes of
displaced Indians. Jews who started moving west from Fort Smith and
Van Buren in western Arkansas were not permitted to go up the Arkansas
River and settle permanently among the Indians. Jewish traders, however,
penetrated this country trafficking with the tribes, supplying the forts,
and in later years outfitting the railroad gangs that built the lines linking
Texas, Kansas and Missouri. Typical of these pioneers was "Boggy" Johnson a Jew who came into the territory after the Civil War and married a
Chickasaw Indian.

Licensed Jewish traders began to drift into the area after the Civil
War. Proof of their presence is documented by the very Jewish names
born by some of the Indians, and it is hardly to be doubted that these
"Jewish" Indians were love tokens left behind by amorous itinerants. The
traders bought furs, hides, and roots; they cashed checks, serving in a
primitive fashion as petty bankers. Joseph Sondheimer, one of Oklahom-
a's first Jewish businessmen, was not a typical trader even though he married a Cherokee. He was a Bavarian who had Americanized himself by
clerking in Baltimore and managing a store in an obscure village in northwestern Pennsylvania. Continuing westward he finally made his home in
St. Louis as a fur, hide, and pecan dealer. Because his chief source of supply was in Indian Territory he moved his headquarters there, settling

down in Muskogee. With the expansion of his business he established branches in Texas. Ultimately as the railroads came in and trade improved he began shipping his wares directly to leather manufacturers in Europe.[52]

The first beginnings of Jewish life in Indian Territory were in Ardmore, a town in the south oriented toward Texas. By the late 1880's the Jewish merchants there began to meet occasionally for religious services and by 1898 they had even laid out a cemetery. But Ardmore was a fairly isolated case; the Oklahoma Jewish community of today owes little to the traders and occasional merchants of the early 1880's. Jewish life really began when Jews joined the thousands who made the "runs" as the government threw open the Indian lands after April 22, 1889. These Jews staked out lands and homesteads for themselves. Some of the newcomers were men of capacity, for two of them sat in the first territorial legislature in 1890. Like California's San Francisco, Oklahoma's Jewish towns are part of an "instant" Jewry; they sprang up overnight. There were 50,000 participants in the 1889 dash for lands; that same year there were 10,000 settlers in Oklahoma City and 8,000 in Guthrie, and it is not surprising therefore that as the High Holy Day season rolled around, there were enough Jews to hold services in Guthrie in 1889, in Oklahoma City in 1890. By the 1890's there were Jews in Enid also and a railroad station without Jews—on the Kansas City Southern—was dubbed Spiro in honor of an Arkansas Jewish merchant. After the turn of the century both Oklahoma City and Guthrie possessed cemeteries and conducted regular religious services. It was then estimated that there were about 1,000 Jews in Indian and in Oklahoma Territories.[53]

CHAPTER SEVEN

THE JEWS AND THE WEST, 1649–1880:

AN EVALUATION

DEFINING THE WEST

For the Jew the West began in October 1492 when the Sephardi Luis de Torres, Columbus's interpreter, climbed over the side of the ship to palaver with the native Americans. The Americas have been an area of Jewish immigration from that time on until the 1920's when the quota laws took effect. For the European Jew the westward movement became a reality in the second quarter of the nineteenth century, a period of nascent industrialism and urbanization. As far east as Poland village Jews began drifting into the cities; farther west the Central European Jews moved into Vienna, Berlin, Paris, London or continued across the Atlantic to New York or until they had reached the shores of the Pacific. Everybody's West, and that meant the Jewish West, too, extended from the Vistula to San Francisco Bay.

The American Jewish West that is evaluated and summarized here then is essentially the West of the Central Europeans, the German immigrants. Begun by them in the 1840's, it was fleshed out in 1881 when the East Europeans, the "Russians," began to percolate into the hinterland, to reenforce the old communities and to build new ones in their own image. The Far West at that time was still frontier, in no sense settled and occupied; as late as 1880 almost one half of the United States was still frontier country, literally. For the Jewish storekeeper in the villages of America the "West" came to an end only in the 1920's: good roads and the automobile either drove him out of business or pushed him into the next larger city whence he commuted back daily to his small-town clothing and gent's emporium. Once Jews and non-Jews started westward they moved fast; the occupation was rapid. The first congregation west of the Alleghenies was established in Cincinnati in 1824; by 1849 there were two congregations in San Francisco. In the brief span of about 45 years, from 1836 to 1881, Jews in substantial numbers moved out of the tidewater across the continent to California and then, doing an about face, penetrated the Rockies and the High Plains to the east. It is well to note that in the 1860's, Ohio and Illinois supplied Jewish contingents to the Union Army smaller only than New York's. Between 1851 and 1873 the B'nai B'rith Order set up district grand lodges all the way from New York City to the Pacific; four of the seven districts were west of the Cumberland Plateau.[1]

WHY AND HOW JEWS WENT WEST

A very substantial percentage of the mid-nineteenth-century European Jewish emigrants ultimately left the eastern seaboard where they landed. No all-inclusive formula will explain why the newcomers turned their faces to the setting sun: adventure, the lure of gold, less competition, more opportunity, the desire to start once more after depressions and bankruptcy? Were they attracted by the hope of fewer disabilities in the West? Hardly. In spite of the fact that political limitations were still imposed on Jews in some of the tidewater states, the majority of American Jews remained in the original thirteen provinces. The selection of a place to settle was often accidental. Many Jews crossed the Appalachians because a relative beckoned or a wholesaler dispatched them to a little town. If Jews congregated in Cincinnati, St. Louis, Chicago, and Milwaukee it was for the same reasons the German Christians also flocked to them—opportunity beckoned.

Because they landed in northern ports the immigrants tended to stay in the North. Though many went to the South by way of Baltimore and New Orleans most newcomers avoided that region. They feared the heat and the yellow fever; they sensed that the plantation system with its slave labor offered them little. The natural habitat of the Jew was the flourishing farmsteads, the towns, and the growing industrial society of the North with its numerous factory hands and potential customers. By the 1840's when the Jews began arriving in goodly numbers they moved west by the Erie Canal or across the mountains to the Ohio and then down the river to the Mississippi whence they penetrated inner America from the Great Lakes to the Gulf. Canals and railroads, shuttled the Jews east and west rather than north and south.

STAGES OF PHYSICAL EXPANSION

The Jews wandered westward by stages. The "Germans" of 1836 and 1840 did not discover America. When the first Jew of the seventeenth century ventured north from the Battery to the Bowery the first step had been taken. In just a few years Jews had moved north and east up the

Hudson, to Long Island, and to New England; the individuals who had turned south reached Maryland. By the first half of the next century Philadelphia, a satellite of New York City, and Charleston and Savannah, offshoots of London, had come into being; by the time of the Revolution Jewry had moved into the piedmont, to Richmond. The outlying villages of the North and the South began to shelter Jews; as early as the 1740's Pennsylvania's Lancaster had become a western outpost. The second stage of expansion extends from the early nineteenth century through the 1840's. Crossing the Appalachians by the middle 1830's the Central Europeans occupied the cismississippi West both in the North and in the South. Jews reached out from New York City and established themselves in Albany, Syracuse, and Cleveland; they traveled west from Philadelphia to Cincinnati, Louisville, and crossed the Mississippi at St. Louis. By that time, in 1828, advancing by land and sea they had founded a community in New Orleans.

And when in 1840 those terminal points were all fixed they backed and filled, occupying the Old Southwest of Alabama and Mississippi. But behind them still lay areas they had bypassed: Florida, North Carolina, Delaware, New Hampshire, and Vermont sheltered no "Jewish" towns.

In the 1850's the westward penetration gained momentum coevally in two widely separated areas: the Mississippi Valley and the Pacific Coast. Crossing the Mississippi in ever larger numbers the Jews began to settle in Minnesota, Iowa, Louisiana, and Texas, and, steaming up the Missouri, reached Leavenworth. Here on the jumping-off strip, from western Iowa south to Arkansas, they outfitted the gold rush caravans moving across the plains. Many Jews were also among the western argonauts although most of them crossed the Isthmus or rounded the Horn. Overnight, almost literally, a new Jewry was born in California and Oregon. In the years from 1860 into the 1880's—the fourth and final stage—Jews filled in everywhere, in all parts of the country. They fattened old Jewries or created new ones in New England, Delaware, Florida, Arkansas, and Texas. The only new penetration was in the intermountain regions and on the High Plains, the semi-arid Great American Desert. This, the last frontier, extended westward from the 100th meridian to the Great Valley of California and included parts or all of the states and territories of the Dakotas, Nebraska, Kansas, Oklahoma, West Texas, Montana, Wyoming, Colorado, New Mexico, Idaho, Utah, Arizona, Washington, Oregon, and Nevada.

Moving out of California and the Sierra Nevadas after the decline of the Mother Lode boom Jews found their way eastward onto the Great Plains; the mining strikes brought them to the diggings in at least half a dozen of the new territories. As they began to move eastward in the 1850's they met fellow Jews crossing the plains westward headed for California. Ultimately in the two decades between 1849 and 1869 thousands of Jews left the Missouri River jumping-off strip to take advantage of the new discoveries in the gold, silver, lead, and copper mines. Like others they came in oxcarts, mule teams, and stagecoach; some walked. With the exception of the Union Pacific, the transcontinental railroads were not to be built till the middle 1880's. On rare, very rare occasions, Jews trekked as a group: in the Spring of 1861 ten Jews, seven young men and a family of three, set out from St. Joseph, Missouri, for the Golden West.[2]

The plains and the mountains are America's romance. This is the world of the cowboy, the Indian, the buffalo, and the gunman—the American folk myth. It is romantic because it is so recent and yet so different. Custer and his troops were killed in the 1870's; thousands were still living in the late twentieth century who had seen Buffalo Bill in the flesh. There are few people today who have not read the "westerns," the paperbacks that sell in the millions, or viewed rodeos and western movies. There were individual Jews who were a real part of this romantic country, yet this storybook West was unreal for the vast majority of settlers and certainly for most Jews too. It is doubtful whether 1 percent of the men on the plains in the 1870's were cowboys; by that decade, in spite of the depredations of the Sioux and the Apaches, most Indians were already safely locked up on their barren reservations. There were desperados, courageous marshals, and a fullness of violence; there were drunken cowboys and hard-boiled Jewish saloonkeepers; there was sudden death, but there were probably fewer killings in a roaring mining camp than in an eastern metropolis.

ECONOMIC DIFFERENCES ON THE HIGH PLAINS

On the surface Jews on the plains and in the western mountains seemed to participate in an economy which differed from that which characterized Jews in the other sections of the United States. They played a part in mining, ranching, cattle, sheep, and freighting of army and civilian supplies, although they were only on the periphery of the mining and cattle business and very few were in ranching. It is true that eastern Jewish capitalists were active in large-scale shaft mining. A number of Jews were involved in the sheep industry but it was not until the end of this period that a handful of Jewish entrepreneurs engaged in the fenced-cattle industry as breeders, feeders, large-scale wholesale butchers, and as commission men. Thus, in a way, they were specialists. Jews were important in the hide and buffalo robe trade, and were busy as freighters and suppliers for the army, for the Indians on the reservation, and for their own wholesale supply houses. In reality the typical Jewish businessman in that part of the United States differed little, basically, from his confreres in other areas.

On the plains the Jew still remained the traditional retailer and whole-saler but rather than satisfying the needs of farmers, villagers, and city folk he dealt instead with miners, cattlemen, homesteaders, and towns-people. Because the country was semi-desert and there was relatively little traffic and profit few Jews settled there permanently. The plains played little part in American Jewish history. Only one town—Denver—was to persist into the twentieth century as a place of importance, and that is be-cause of its industries and its tourism. By 1880, less than 3 percent of American Jews made their homes on the high plateaus; the general popu-lation in the territories and states was equally sparse.[3]

PIONEERS

The westward advancing waves of Jewish settlement described here are predicated on the establishment of religiosocial communities, not on the coming of the first Jews. As early as 1823 when Richmond was the west-ernmost Jewish town, Heine in Germany prophesied that Jews would move toward the valley of the Mississippi. By the 1830's there was al-ready a Jewish community in St. Louis! Jewish pioneers, it has been noted, started moving out of New Amsterdam in the 1600's; in the 1700's hardy souls settled in Mackinac, Green Bay, and in the Illinois Country, and by the 1830's, years before the gold rush, there was already a Jew in a Mexican village situated on San Francisco Bay. Those Jewish adventurers who made their way across the continent in the early days were frequently enterprising creative men; they are not unimportant for the study of general American history. Their presence everywhere is doc-umented by the fact that there are probably about 100 villages and ham-lets founded by or named after them. These towns extend from Aarons-burg in Pennsylvania to Newman in California. Yet with exceptions, these men are not important for American Jewish history. They were not interested in building Jewries; they were interested in themselves, in their own careers. Communities are built by men, not by a man. In traveling westward the Jews came quite late, in the 1840's and '50's, after several waves of American immigrants had already crossed the Appalachians. As part of the Central European thrust that began in the late 1830's, the Jews settled only where there were towns, people, markets, and improved forms of transportation. By the time Horace Greeley got around to his pontifical "Go west young man and grow up with the country," the coun-try had already been settled and the Jews were selling goods almost every-where.[4]

Everywhere? What does that mean? They not only went up and down the rivers, they wandered up the tributaries, went down to the mouths of the streams and then started back, sometimes settling in towns they had once leapfrogged. Apparently there was no logic in picking the spots where they pitched their tents but the Jewish newcomers knew, or thought they knew what they were doing. Why were Boston and Pittsburgh so long bypassed? Why were Cincinnati and Louisville settled before Albany? Did the Jews think that the grass was greener in the distant towns toward which they trekked? Maybe. Often the settlement was a chance event; sometimes there is a story to explain it. Thus, it is said, three Jewish Mississippi River peddlers, two of whom became distinguished and successful businessmen, landed in Petersburg, Va. It was all a mistake; they thought they were headed for Pittsburgh.[5]

CORE TOWNS

Jewish businessmen were well aware that certain states were prime business centers. The whole country was already a satellite of New York City. In the eighteenth and early nineteenth centuries North Carolina and Georgia lay within the commercial ambit of South Carolina; in the 1850's and '60's Nevada and Oregon were economic vassals of California, and, in turn, Oregon dominated Montana, Washington, and Idaho; there are numerous other striking examples of nuclear states and cities. All the way from San Francisco to New York City every major town where Jewish retailers and wholesalers planted themselves was an economic bridgehead. Philadelphia was the chief market center for Pennsylvania, and Pittsburgh, itself a satellite town, forced dozens of smaller places to move in its orbit. The city at the forks of the Ohio was the chief market place for western Pennsylvania, eastern Ohio, and northern West Virginia. The dependence of these neighboring areas is reflected in synagog names. Philadelphia's first Ashkenazic conventicle was called Rodeph Shalom, The Pursuer of Peace. Pittsburgh's big synagog has the same name and so have the smaller congregations of Johnstown and Homestead, both in the Pittsburgh area. The Tree of Life Congregation of Pittsburgh gave its name to synagog societies in Clarksburg, Morgantown, and Moundsville —all in northern West Virginia.[6]

It was not only the major cities that stand out as supply depots for larger tributary regions. Hundreds of smaller towns throughout the United States served as distributing centers for still smaller towns and villages. Even modest shopkeepers speedily branched out as petty wholesalers spreading their nets in the surrounding villages. Out of dozens of examples of sub-entrepots one can mention Bangor, Maine, in the 1840's, Alexandria which served central Louisiana in the 1850's, and Trinidad, Colorado, which attracted custom from southern Colorado and northern New Mexico in the 1870's.

Once a base was established be it in a smaller or a larger spot, the Jewish founding father brought in or attracted relatives and friends from his native town in Europe. Thus a number of communities began to take on the appearance of a landsmanshaft. Villagers from Ingweiler in Alsace flocked to Cincinnati; Bohemian emigrants from Ckyn settled in Ann Arbor and those from Muttersdorf made their way to Madison, Wisconsin. After a Jewish nucleus was created others joined it for social reasons, expecting to enjoy (?) the use of a cemetery and eventually a congregation. This accretion of numbers served to further business expansion and thus it was that in the 1860's an obscure town like Poultney, Vermont, became a commercial depot, sheltering a regional congregation and a regional cemetery, attracting Jews from the surrounding areas and even from neighboring New York state.[7]

DEAD AND DECLINING TOWNS

Many of these bridgeheads are no longer of any significance. For a brief moment they had their day in the sun but having served their purpose they have been swept on to the dust heap of history. Shifts in transportation destroyed or injured them; the railroads displaced the steamboats and the prairie schooners. Even St. Louis was left behind by Chicago in the Civil War period: as a transportation hub, with river, canal, lake, and railroad connections, the Illinois metropolis was able to tie itself to New York in the East and to the prairies, plains, mountain states, and territories in the West. Lancaster and Easton of the eighteenth century died as Jewish communities but it was their good fortune to be reborn in the century that followed; Claiborne, Alabama, once a prosperous Jewish community, no longer exists as a town; Virginia City, Nevada, a metropolis that could once boast of more Jews than some New England states is now little more than a ghost town. At least seven Jewish towns on or near the Missouri River might have emerged as the metropolis of the jumping-off strip. Today only Kansas City, Missouri, is of importance.

THE URBAN WEST

The Jews who left the Atlantic seaboard in colonial days and moved westward remained town dwellers; they were seldom tillers of the soil or herders of sheep and cattle. They clung to the mining villages, did business at the tie camps, followed the end-of-track from the cismississippi East to Promontory Point in Utah. Indeed there was hardly a spot in the United States that had not at one time housed a Jewish "merchant." Very often they found themselves stuck in hamlets; sometimes they actually preferred these crossroad nooks for they offered them a real chance to survive. Jews were conscious that they were of alien birth and tongue and limited in capital; they were wary of competition. Certainly if they had a choice they would all have lived in the larger towns and cities. As a "community" people, in need of a social, cultural, and religious life of their own, it was imperative that they live together; a community, they knew full well, could exist only where there was a substantial number of Jews. From the eighteenth to the late nineteenth century the towns in which they found themselves were nearly always on the populous not the cutting edge of the frontier. These marketing centers dominated the frontier though they were not of the frontier. Jews favored them because as a rule they possessed transportation facilities adequate for the shipment of raw materials and the import of finished goods. Such as they were, these towns were the centers of culture. These were the places where political decisions were made and where the power structure resided. If a Jew lived in the Far West and if he had a choice he would move to San Francisco. In the 1870's it was the largest Jewish town in the United States, second only to New York City.

REGIONAL DIFFERENCES

Were there any differences that distinguished the Jews of the several sections of the country? Can one differentiate in that generation from 1840 to 1880 between the Jews of the various regions: the Tidewater, the South, the Midwest, the Pacific Coast, the Great Plains? There are variations but no real distinctions. The differences lie only or primarily in the commodities in which they dealt and these were determined by the ecology of the countryside. The assimilated professional Jewish politicians, particularly in the South and Old Southwest, took on the coloration of the people among whom they lived, but the Jews, as a group, the masses, if you will, were all of one piece. One cannot conjure up any dissimilarities between a Jew of Belton, Texas, and one from Honesdale, Pa. They both had one common concern that tied them closely together; they wanted to run their stores and to provide for their families.

Between San Francisco and New York City there was a constant drift to the larger centers, to Portland, Oregon, Santa Fe, Salt Lake, Denver, Leavenworth, Galveston, Chicago, Milwaukee, St. Louis, New Orleans, Detroit, Indianapolis, Louisville, Memphis, Cincinnati, Montgomery, Savannah, Charleston, Baltimore, Philadelphia, Newark, New Haven, and Boston. Though the High Plains denizens had close connections with the Pacific Coast the wealthier among them were oriented toward New York City. For Jews the resources that spelt opportunity were most accessible in the East. This is why the Jews remained there in such large numbers. This generation of American Jewry never emancipated itself from the eastern megalopolis. New York was a mother and city in Israel distinguished for its culture, its clubs, its congregations, its leaders, its national organizations. Before 1873, when the Union of American Hebrew Congregations rose in Cincinnati, there was no national institution west of the Hudson. Almost one-third of all the Jews in the United States lived in the twin cities of Brooklyn and New York.

SOME NOTES ON JEWS AND THE ECONOMY

Whether Jews did business in a small town or a growing metropolis one of the problems they faced was acquiring honest competent help. Naturally they preferred family and if there was a plethora of brothers they fancied themselves another Rothschild clan. The Rothschild myth of fraternal cooperation was constantly nourished by Jews. The Seligmans, the Spiegelbergs, and the Guggenheims were American Jewry's prime examples of what a family could accomplish if it worked together. And if brothers were in scarce supply there were always relatives or good friends from the old home town in Posen, Bavaria, Bohemia, or the Palatinate. Coopting family frequently worked out but families also fell out and ambitious clerks, family members or not, were always eager to go out on their own, and many did.

There were exceptions of course but in the pre-1880 days Jews were not farmers, homesteaders, ranchers, physicians, or lawyers. They were peddlers, clerks, drummers, managers, owners of stores, and wholesalers. With each new westward wave that carried people and the economy toward the plains and the mountains there were always some Jews present to provide the basic necessities, and as the towns grew the Jews and their shops multiplied. In exchange for the hard, wet, and dry goods they shipped in, they shipped out staple commodities. These they acquired by purchase or barter; invariably they were generous with their credits. In colonial times the tidewater merchant prince—that is the merchant-shipper—exported raw or semi-finished materials and imported manufactures. Large-scale merchants in pre-and post-revolutionary days dispatched pack trains west to the Ohio and as they reached farther out shipped goods down the river to the villages in the Illinois country. If currency was scarce they were always ready to accept payment in furs and skins. But these big businessmen of the seaboard and piedmont were but a handful. The petty merchants in their general stores were the rule. By the 1820's the Jews, discovering the sizeable towns of the Mississippi Basin, moved in with their wares for farmers and townsmen. Speedily they resorted also to jobbing and wholesaling and as they spread out into the plains bordering on the Gulf of Mexico they outfitted the ranchers.

During the very years they reached the far side of the Mississippi, they were also planting themselves in ever-increasing numbers on the Pacific Coast. Not many remained in the mines of the Sierras but even there in the Mother Lode they opened shops; it was not long before all the important towns, both coastal and interior, sheltered their quantum of Jewish retailers, wholesalers, and provisioners. The bolder spirits became land promoters and petty bankers. Despite the presence of Jews in almost all California towns, about 90 percent of the state's Israelites lived in San Francisco. The big San Francisco businessmen bought bullion, sold liquors, provisions, fruit, and speculated in grain and rice. In a much more traditional fashion they manufactured clothing, bought and sold wool and hides, and were widely known as jewelers, tobacco merchants, and stock brokers. Above all, here as elsewhere, they were retailers and wholesalers of merchandise. In many, in most of these economic activities, the Jews of San Francisco differed in no sense from those of New York City.[8]

In 1859, a decade after the stampede to the Sierras, new mining discoveries opened up the mountains and the Great Plains. But at least fifteen years before the rush to the Washoe, itinerant merchants like Albert Speyer had struck west following the Santa Fe trail deep into Mexico. Speyer's caravans were an echo of the pack horse trains of the eighteenth-century Frankses and Gratzes and they in turn were but a faint echo of those Jewish Radanites who in early medieval days had trekked from France to China. The Jewish newcomers into the High Plains supplied the miners, sold at retail and wholesale, financed sheepmen, and outfitted the far-flung western ranches.[9]

To whom did the Jewish purveyors turn for their inventories? Whether in the eighteenth-century tidewater or the Great Plains of the 1870's, the small merchant was dependent upon his nearest regional wholesaler. With increasing prosperity the retailer journeyed farther on to secure his goods from big city suppliers. In the postbellum period the Far Western merchants who had made good stocked up in San Francisco but many of the big men on the plains made their purchases in the large cities of the Middle West, or preferably in New York City. Whether they lived in the 1600's or in the 1800's the shopkeepers were all alike in that they were mobile. It was not unusual for some of them to travel thousands of miles before they found a spot where they could take root. The career of Jacob Pelton in the mid-nineteenth century, is in no sense atypical. He married and began to raise a family in Poland before he sailed with his wife and two children for the United States; three more children were born in Kansas, a son saw the light of day in Indiana, and his last three children were natives of Kentucky. When next heard from he was making a living in Colorado. Why did he move? Why did practically all Jews move about? Were they enamored of distant horizons? Their sole desire was to find a likely town where they could make a good living.[10]

Ultimately most of them found a spot which pleased them; they began to do well and then almost immediately they diversified. In the East, on the whole, they limited their activities to soft goods which is in a way a form of specialization. They began to open larger and larger retail establishments, continued as wholesalers, and often established branch stores in distant states. The westerners, those on the far side of the Mississippi, imported huge stocks from the East, freighted their own supplies, contracted to furnish the army with fodder and provisions, and took on jobs as sutlers. A chosen few became merchant bankers. They dabbled in mining and ranching, planted sugar beets, built irrigation ditches, ran stage coach lines, contracted to carry the mail, built steamboats and traction lines, introduced lighting and water into their towns, and even built hamlets of their own. Once firmly established—or to convince themselves that they were—they built a brick or stone "block." This was true both in the East and the West where their sturdy buildings stood out as symbols of success. A brick building was insurance against being wiped out in a fire and it always looked good on a credit rating sheet. The first or best stone or brick building in town was erected by Jews in Chicago, Omaha, Leavenworth, Salt Lake, Corpus Christi, Seattle, San Francisco, and in a number of other places.[11]

Though most Jews strove for upward mobility not all managed to climb to a higher rung on the ladder. There is a possibility of course—and this is only a guess—that it was easier to reach the top in the newer western areas. Wherever there were fewer people, where society was more fluid and opportunities not monopolized by entrenched groups, there the Jews found it easier to clamber to the top. But once at the top there was little assurance that they could remain there, for the hazards to success in mid-century America were numerous. Unwise purchases, bad credits, fires, floods, the high cost of transportation, Indian attacks, and above all the utterly devastating national panics and depressions—all these conspired to destroy many. Only a small number managed to stay rich. The beautifully bound nineteenth-century "mug" books with their excellent engravings can be misleading: the "mugs" in the books were rich but their successes were anything but typical.

POLITICS

Jewish merchants were often in politics if only to help bring a railroad into town with all that it meant in the way of new opportunities. The tidewater Jews were a little late in becoming political somebodies. Emancipation for them did not come until after the adoption of the Federal Constitution; indeed, some of the original thirteen states did not grant equality to infidels until after the Civil War. Still, by the early 1800's

Gentiles did begin to accept Jews and to elect them to office. In the new lands of western Georgia, Alabama, Mississippi, and in New Orleans a number of brilliant Charleston Jews rapidly rose to power. Society was not petrified; the race was to the swift. It is possible—and this, too, is a guess—that some Jews in cismississippi may have felt that they did not advance as fast politically as their merits justified. The reason for this may well be that these émigrés of the 1840's were latecomers and alien born. However there can be little question that the immigrant Jews had come into their own politically. In these underpopulated regions in transmississippi, especially on the High Plains and in the mountains, good men were at a premium. Jews were literate and hard working. Honest, intelligent, and able, they were respected businessmen, "wealthy." A Jewish shopkeeper in Nogales, Arizona, who had a $3,000 stock—even though bought on credit—was certainly one of the richest men in the village. Political and social power in the new frontier towns had not yet been crystallized. The community was happy to elect Jews to office, and the Jews were happy to serve for they craved status. Thus by 1880 transmississippi Jews were found frequently in municipal and state offices. They were mayors, legislators, judges, and attorney generals. In the late nineteenth century a professing Jew from Oregon was sent to Turkey as a minister; the first Jewish governors in the country were in Plains states.[12]

RELIGION AND THE COMMUNITY: THE RISE OF AMERICAN JEWISH COMMUNITIES, 1654–1880

As many Jews backed into the West they did not want to get too far away from a Jewish community. Ever since the 1650's when the first group of émigrés held services Jews found comfort in the organizations which they had established. By 1790 five core communities had already been set up in the tidewater and one in the piedmont: Newport, New York, Philadelphia, Charleston, Savannah, and Richmond. All followed the Sephardic rite. With the turn of the century the Ashkenazic immigrants, the Central and East Europeans, who already outnumbered the Sephardim, began to build conventicles of their own. From then on practically all new religious communities in the United States were Ashkenazic; by the 1840's these Europeans were so numerous in New York City that they could indulge themselves by herding together according to their national origins: there was a German, Polish, Bohemian, and a Dutch bethel. The first permanent Ashkenazic congregation was already established by 1801 in Philadelphia; by 1824 the Ashkenazim had crossed the mountains and had organized a community in Cincinnati, and by the 1840's they had set up congregations in all parts of the Mississippi Basin and on the Pacific Coast. This growth of Jewish associations across the face of the land is but one aspect, a very minor one, of the American expansion westward. Wherever Jews foregathered in numbers they congregated together and fashioned some form of communal life, thus the anomaly of religious societies in the Nevada and Montana mining camps before there was a single one in Delaware.[13]

By the 1850's America was studded with Jewish societies, one even on the High Plains. How rapid was the organizing process? In general a whole generation elapsed, possibly two, after the coming of the pioneers before the first communal society came into being. In some states, as in Florida and Connecticut, it would take decades before the Jews would establish a congregation. There are some striking exceptions. In 1855 a number of Jewish Indian traders met on an island in Lake Superior in the frontier village of La Pointe, Wisconsin. The Indians were assembled there to collect their annuities and the Jews were present to dun their debtors before they dispersed. There were enough Jews for a minyan and a service was held. That was the beginning and the end of La Pointe Jewry. Another historical accident is the "instant" community. The Jews of Savannah arrived from London in 1733 already organized as a congregation; San Francisco Jewry of the Gold Rush was able to establish two religious groups without delay and Oklahoma City and Guthrie were born overnight during the 1889 "run." All this is completely atypical.[14]

There are other interesting vagaries of American Jewish religious growth, the short-lived congregation, for example, those that sprung up in the Sierras and in the Rockies. They rose from the 1850's into the 1890's during the mining strikes and developed into flourishing communities, but when the gold and silver gave out they withered and disappeared. All that is left of many of those once bustling religious communities is a sadly neglected cemetery. And there is still another interesting characteristic of American Jewish religious history. A community is born, it dies, and another is built on its ruins, and even the second, too, may die before a viable organization is effected. New Amsterdam rose and fell; Newport rose and died at least twice; Louisville had a false start, and Pittsburgh was immersed in a welter of societies before a permanent congregation began to emerge. Thus it is exceedingly difficult in many towns, impossible in fact, to determine when the "first" congregation saw the light of day.[15]

When Jews set out to create a community it would rarely have occurred to them to set down a formal statement of their motivation. In their minds none was needed. As European immigrants, committed religious Jews, they took it for granted that a born Jew had to be a Jew; that is, it was incumbent upon him to assemble together with other Jews, hold services, and be mutually helpful. When in 1848 the Fort Wayne Jews created their first society—it was a sick-care and burial organization—

they took the very unusual step of formulating their motivations. It is interesting to note that even here there was no overt commitment to religion. If confronted they would have responded that Jews make no distinction between the religious and the secular. Such sharp distinctions are Protestant, foreign to Jews. All facets of life and experience are embraced in the process of living as a Jew. This explains, too, why the first association established in many towns of the West was not overtly religious. The Fort Wayne Jews solemnly declared that as refugees from European oppression it was their duty to unite and to stand by each other. Their society's name was later changed to "Unity and Peace," Achduth Vesholom. The insistent emphasis upon unity and peace among American Jews of that generation reflects the fears of those émigrés. They believed devoutly that uniting under a Jewish aegis would bring them the feeling of security for which they so desperately yearned. In an age when Jews were riven by many differences, peace was one of the most commonly used nouns in congregational names, for with peace came unity.[16]

A community was usually founded by an individual who rounded up a religious quorum or who created an institution around which the Jews agglomerated. It is interesting to note that the original institution varies from town to town following the predilections or prejudices of the local group. In a real sense the medium was not important; joining was. Frequently a town started with a cemetery but others initiated their communal existence with a B'nai B'rith Lodge, a Young Men's Hebrew Association, a social club, an educational society, a woman's charity, even a sewing circle. There is however one type of society that seems to predominate; from 1784 to 1880 dozens of new communities were partial to this primary form of communal organization. This was an all-purpose confraternity that provided mutual aid and charity, sick-care, burial, a cemetery, and a religious service. It was commonly called the Hebrew Benevolent Society, Hevrah Gemilut Hasadim. The emphasis on mutual aid reflects the poverty and the fears of an immigrant generation. When in the course of time charitable needs were relegated to special organizations, the Benevolent Society often evolved into a congregation; that was the Protestant "church" influence. Once the congregation came into being an omnibus factotum was employed to serve as slaughterer, circumciser, teacher, and precentor. The next step was to buy an old church building and convert it into a synagog.[17]

After a start had been made and some form of association had been adopted the evolving communities gradually created other societies and institutions. Before they were through they had a cemetery, a male and female benevolent society, a Jewish lodge, a congregation, a synagog building, and a literary-social group which might well be a YMHA. Most of these YMHAs were on the east side of the Mississippi. Prior to 1880 there were fewer than a dozen in transmississippi; the only one on the High Plains was in San Antonio. There was no pattern of sequence in the rise of these organizations although the Benevolent Society and its cemetery were often the first on the scene. If the smaller communities had but five or six associations it was because the Jews were limited in numbers and the multiformity which many so ardently desired was a luxury that they could ill afford. The larger towns—in the East for the most part— often had an orphan asylum, an old-folks home, a hospital, religious schools, and a Jewish newspaper. The only two towns on the west side of the Mississippi that could support a Jewish weekly were St. Louis and San Francisco. The latter town had more than one. In addition to these associations the larger Jewish communities also included numerous charities, several literary and social societies, and even an occasional club house. The more populated Jewish towns could even luxuriate in a number of similar or parallel associations because of the desire of the people for small more intimate social groups. Following a tradition that has been characteristic of European Jewry at least since the seventeenth century, Jews created multiple organizations in order to give play to the need for self-expression. Where Jews abounded variety, divisions, were possible.[18]

Numbers and wealth in the larger towns could also bring dissension, prejudices, and preferential loyalties. Men and women rallied around their favorite society to the exclusion at times of support of worthy institutions. The constantly growing numbers of newcomers in the cities made proliferation through secession a possibility if not the rule in congregational life. Divisiveness expressed itself in quarrels over the minutiae of tradition. Ritual differences were common because of the variations in the customary law and liturgy of the various German Jewish communities; the congregants were almost fanatically attached to their hometown rites. A new element that made for estrangement came in the mid-nineteenth century when Reform Judaism began to loom on the horizon. The breach between the Orthodox and the Reformers was often a serious one. The divisiveness between West Germans and East Germans (Polacks) was characterized by acerbity if not by hatred, and this polarization expressed itself not only in the rise of German and "Polish" congregations but even at times of separate institutions for the relief of the poor. Not infrequently these hostilities were exacerbated by the personal and business quarrels of unhappy men and women whose egos had to find expression in a narrow compass.[19]

RELIGIOSITY AND LOYALTIES

How religiously observant were the Jews, particularly those of the nineteenth-century frontier? When a few traditional Jews in New Orleans succeeded in 1828 in establishing a congregation in that assimilationist environment they made a number of concessions. Children of mixed marriages were tolerantly accepted as Jews. About fifteen years later, when reenforcements—newcomers reared in European traditions—poured in, the congregation tightened its rules and turned back to traditional particularism and punctiliousness. In defining Judaism and Jewish practice the Mother Lode town of Jackson apparently made but two important demands: Keep your business closed on the High Holy Days and do not intermarry; in the sizeable city of Sacramento there was one congregation that met only on the Jewish New Year and the Day of Atonement.[20]

What does all this signify? In the western milieu the younger a group the more apt it was to be permissive. The smaller and more isolated a community, the less the social control. Were these "Western" communities and congregations liberal because of their democratic "frontier" environment? No, they resorted to expediency because they had no choice. At no time did the immigrant Jews who were deeply attached to their European traditional way of life dream of rejecting Judaism as such. European émigrés were dominant in American Jewish religious life from the 1654's to about 1885 when the Americanistic elements began to take over. No matter how permissive an Orthodox group might be its abandonment of traditions and practices was but temporary, pragmatic; there was no concession in principle. Standards might be ignored but they were not forgotten. The typical immigrant was invariably loyal to his religious past and once a community began to take on flesh customary practices and taboos were reinstated, in part at least.

Jewish Indian fighters and stagecoach drivers built no communities. Older settlers, pioneers, the acculturated and the affluent, often kept aloof. The Jewish towns, societies, and synagogs of America, the communities, were built by lower-class or middle-class immigrants. They were the core. They identified themselves as Jews to Jews and non-Jews; they stressed Jewish practices knowing full well that practices, not beliefs, made men Jews. They insisted on Jewish burial knowing that in a very real sense it was often the cemetery that kept Judaism alive. They gathered at services—not too often of course—and they observed dietary laws when they could. The cities everywhere had kosher butchers and kosher boardinghouses. There was always a saving remnant like that German Jew who stopped the stagecoach in Indian country, stepped outside, put on his phylacteries, and calmly and devoutly recited his morning prayers.[21]

In spite of their strife and their frequent squabbles Jews hesitated to leave the magic circle. Ambivalence was omnipresent. Though centrifugality was the rule it was transcended by the higher law of unity. The fact that nearly all Jews were storekeepers in one form or another, all in the same line of business and with the same ambitions, made for cohesiveness.

They were drawn to one another by the accident of birth. That was an infrangible bond. They worked together because they had to. In some towns the non- polarized lodges, clubs, and societies served as an offset to rifts. Beer and cigars healed many a breach. In the final analysis Jews hesitated to break completely with other Jews. They were fearful of what they would find beyond the frontiers of Jewish life; it was cold on the outside. Poles and Germans might snipe at one another; Sephardim might disdain Ashkenazim, but quarrels or no quarrels Jews had to help one another. Ever since colonial days and all through the nineteenth century whenever and wherever a Jew built a synagog he turned to other Jews for a donation. That was the least one Jew owed another. They knew they were all one ethnos: without verbalizing it, Jews sensed that they had a common ethic, that they shared the same religious goals, practices, and prejudices, which they were determined to transmit to their children.

JEWISH-CHRISTIAN RELATIONS

ACCEPTANCE OF JEWS BY CHRISTIANS

As the Jews moved westward carrying their traditions and their own way of life they found that the Christians, too, shouldered their own impediments. Anti-Jewish Christians did not discard their prejudices when they breathed the fresh air of a new country but though Judeophobia was always present it does not appear to have inhibited Jewish development in the western lands. Many Christians and Mormons worked closely with Jews, lending them their sanctuaries and halls on the Holy Days and even remaining to attend services reverentially. It was quite common in many states and territories for Christians to contribute liberally to the building of a synagog. Why this toleration, encouragement, and support of Jewry and Judaism? The humanitarian aspect was certainly not absent; courtesy to Jews was not necessarily a positive aspect of liberalism so much as a reflex of the tidewater culture which was a pattern to be emulated. Gentile businessmen eagerly invited Jews into town because they enriched it, and some Christians, hewing to the religious line, were convinced that a synagog would improve Jewish morals in the same sense that a church made for better Christians.

Some Christians were gracious to Jews for the simple reason that they accepted individual Jews as their leaders. In numerous towns west of the tidewater and piedmont and particularly on the far side of the Mississippi outstanding Jewish businessmen were highly respected. In the rather fluid society of the mid-nineteenth century vertical mobility was common and Jews often made their way to the top. Frequently they were among the wealthiest men in town although "wealth" in this instance was relative. One needed little to impress the struggling farmer, homesteader, or village worker. But there were wealthy Jews with financial know-how, men who were invaluable in the conduct of municipal affairs. Because they were literate and cultured these Jewish leaders sponsored libraries, clubs, theatrical and musical productions. As adherents of a neutral religion they found it easy to serve as liaison between the Catholics and the Protestants, particularly in the New Southwest. Inasmuch as they had concern for the community in which they lived and because they were among the largest taxpayers, they sat on important boards in town. They were very definitely part of the power structure; they were of the socially elite. When in 1865 the Indian fighter General Patrick Edward Conner was feted at Camp Douglas the Jew Aaron Stein was asked to respond to the toast: the President of the United States. In many towns, particularly in the Far West, the annual ball given by the Jews was the social event of the season.[22]

GENERAL CULTURE AND THE JEWS

It has been pointed out that many of the Jewish leaders in the new towns were literate. In an age when the percentage of illiteracy in the entire country was high there were few Jews who did not know the three r's. Individuals among them were literate in a very special sense; they were men of classical culture. This was true of a number of American-born Jews who left the tidewater for the Middle West or for the new cotton lands of Alabama, Mississippi, and Louisiana. Quite a number of the German Jewish émigrés were linguists and musicians; many of the 1848 political refugees had studied at a university. The first English book published in California was printed in 1849 by the "Jew," Washington Bartlett. The Library of Congress copy had been presented to Bishop John H. D. Wingfield by I. N. Chomsky, a Polish Jew who owned the Antiquarian Book Store in San Francisco.[23]

JEWISH ACCEPTANCE OF CHRISTIANS

The social acceptance of Jews reflected in Christian support of Jewish religious institutions found its reciprocation in the courtesies Jews accorded Christians. Substantial gifts to churches were common; a Colorado Jewish pioneer on the Santa Fe trail gave Catholics a lot for a church, and a Galveston Jew helped the Lutherans in town raise money for a sanctuary. In that same state of Texas an unconverted Jew volunteered to serve as an officer of an Episcopalian church and a Salt Lake Jewish worthy was a board member of a Congregational house of worship. It is doubtful whether such manifestations of "public service" were paralleled on the eastern side of the Mississippi. This desire by Jews to aid Christian churches appears to be unique and its acceptance by Christians is characteristic of the permissive transmississippi West.

ACCULTURATION, JEWISH IDENTITY, JEWISH CULTURE, INTERMARRIAGE, AND ASSIMILATION

When European Jewish newcomers, children of an unbending Orthodoxy, concerned themselves with the welfare of Christian churches there can be no doubt that the American acculturative process had almost overpowered them. It would seem that the farther west the Jew went and the smaller the town he chose the quicker he Americanized himself. In reality he was deculturating himself, neglecting ceremonial and ritual practices, divorcing himself from rabbinic control. Prior to the 1880's there were many "ministers" but hardly any ordained rabbis west of the Mississippi. Anglicization moved apace. After a number of years all German congregations, wherever they were, stopped writing their minutes in their native tongue and turned to English. Practically all Jews who settled in the new world, making new lives for themselves, emerged as Americans culturally, with but one very important reservation. Desperately eager as they were to be of the general community they refused to sacrifice their identity as Jews even though their religious observance were most tenuous.

Conscious of the assimilatory character of the new environment did the Jews ever attempt defensively to preserve their heritage by furthering Jewish culture? There is very little evidence that they set out to limit the impact of acculturative forces in the new communities in which they found themselves. Outside of some of the larger eastern communities little was done to promote Jewish culture. Isaac Leeser and some of the other rabbis were exceptions. Recognizing the twin problems of acculturation and deculturation they attempted to cope with them; parents also, felt the need to educate their children Jewishly but religious schools in the smaller towns were either poor or nonexistent. Little, too, was done in a formal sense to educate adults Jewishly, although in the larger towns, especially in the cismississippi areas, the rabbis lectured in the synagog and thousands read the Jewish newspapers. These weeklies were important; they were not gossip sheets; most of them carried articles of serious import reflecting studies in Jewish history and literature copied or adapted most often from the excellent Central European papers. The lodges and the YMHA's were in theory concerned with adult Jewish education. Since there were over 600 male lodges to say nothing of female auxiliary branches in the 1870's, and there were dozens of Y's, the impact on Jewish culture was potentially enormous. Whether their Jewish programs were effective is difficult to determine.[24]

Was there then nothing to retard the assimilatory process especially in the smaller and more obscure towns and communities? Not necessarily. Deculturation was retarded to a certain degree by an osmotic process that kept Jews from becoming dejudaized. Jews went to services at times; there were always some ceremonies to which they adhered; they constantly used Yiddish and Hebrew phrases, and they associated intimately with their fellow Jews. There was a constant exposure to Jewish thinking and values; there was always some absorption and diffusion and interchange of Jewish concepts. These impacts should not be underrated. Was it the desire to become 100 percent American that impelled many Jews in well-organized towns to avoid formal affiliation? The fact that only nineteen families out of 140 Jews belonged to the synagog in St. Joseph and that only twenty-eight were members in a St. Paul community of 225 does not mean that the mavericks had rejected the faith of their fathers. Many of these Germans were exceedingly thrifty; they were merely trying to save the cost of membership. The acculturative and assimilatory process is often documented and confirmed by intermarriage. It is almost axiomatic in American Jewish history that Jews who settle and remain in small towns where there are no Jewish associations intermarry and with rare exceptions divorce themselves from their faith and their people. This was true of eighteenth-century colonial Connecticut, a "western" satellite of New York, and it was equally true of the first settlers in the villages west of the Appalachians.[25]

Intermarriage, indifference, drifting, and assimilation were common also in the new cities that rose in the West. The three great Jews of antebellum New Orleans all married out; none affiliated religiously with Jewry, yet none was baptized. Isadore Dyer of Galveston, who was active in the local synagog, married an Episcopalian, supported her church, reared his children as Christians but when one of them died insisted on a Jewish burial. Dyer certainly looked upon himself as a good Jew. One of the outstanding Jews and citizens of the Los Angeles of the 1870's was Bernard Cohn. He was president of the congregation and the Hebrew Benevolent Society and quite traditional in his practices. Yet he made no secret of the fact that he raised two families, a Jewish one and a Latin American Catholic one, and apparently his friends and associates did not look askance at him. The Gentiles referred to his Latin ménage as the Chile Pepper family, to the Jewish ménage as "the Jew family." On the whole intermarriage led to defections; the numbers lost in the tidewater and the advancing West since the eighteenth century must have been large but there is no way of estimating how many disappeared. Not indoctrinated as fervent traditionalists as were their Europe-born parents, the native-born American Jewish children were more prone to intermarriage; the pull of the non-Jewish environment was often too strong to resist. But let there be no doubt of this: most Jews were loyal according to their lights.[26]

THE WESTWARD-MOVING JEW: CHARACTERISTICS

What are the characteristics of the westward-moving Jews? Were they all able and successful men? Some, possibly many, were undoubtedly failures back home who had turned their faces to the West with the hope of starting a new life. Few had a background of success; if they had been men of means they would have remained in the East. Were there any differences between natives and immigrants? There are no ascertainable differences between the two in their western homes. It is probable that the European-born newcomer was more aggressive, patently more eager to make good; native Americans, more secure, did not have to prove themselves.

Wherever his "West" lay the typical westerner was a man of some courage. It takes moral stamina to strike out for a new country and to face new challenges. The western Jew was thrifty, disciplined, and an incredibly hard worker. He was quiet, peaceful, very ambitious, constantly seeking to improve his lot by engaging in new business ventures. He was energetic, optimistic, commercially enterprising, resourceful, and intelligent. His individualism expressed itself in his resentment against restraints on his business operations. On the whole these are the qualities of the middle-class Jewish merchant who lived west of the seaboard. But these very qualities were equally true of successful Jews wherever they were found. They were certainly characteristic of well-to-do Jewish businessmen who had never left the East. As far as the Jew is concerned all of the United States was "the West"—a land of opportunity. There are no essential differences between eastern and western Jews; in the broadest sense they are a homogeneous lot made so by their common commercial interests and their constant intercommunication.

What if anything did the West beyond the Atlantic Coast do for the individual? It gave him a larger geographical field in which to maneuver, one much more extensive and inviting than the new Pale of Settlement, Manhattan Island. It gave him a huge area in which to cultivate his native talents, but it is equally true that if he was a man of talents he could demonstrate them in Pittsburgh, Chicago, and New Orleans as well as he could in Tombstone, Arizona. The Jew certainly moved westward to improve himself but the West did not make him; he helped make the West and this was true of any area where he dug in. Once Jews had made good in the West it was often their desire to leave it, to become metropolitans, to settle in the big cities, particularly those of the East. Why this yearning to return to a principal center of activity? The religious motivation was probably not an impelling one; the financial one was more compelling.

They had capital and there were many fields in the metropolis where money could be put to work. Persuasive for many was the hope for wider Jewish social relationships; decisive for many was the wish to live and marry among Jews, to provide a better general if not a Jewish education for the children, and to open up for them the opportunities of a large city. The city offered them a wider choice of friends, the anonymity that was absent in the smaller towns where loneliness, pettiness, and intrigue were common.

Many moved to the larger towns because they had no choice. Smaller places suffered and declined as the improvement in transportation induced customers to shop in the larger centers. There was a constant flight from satellite towns to core centers, to the larger cities which everywhere dominated territories and states. Small-town Jews turned to Detroit, Chicago, Milwaukee, Dallas, Denver, Los Angeles, and to dozens of other cities with a future. It probably did not require much persuasion to influence a senior partner to settle permanently in San Francisco or New York as a resident buyer. One of the Goldwaters retired to San Francisco and even Wyatt Earp, the frontier marshal, turned his back on Arizona in order to enjoy the flesh pots of California. A number of the far western notables looked to distant New York City for it was the chief American mart for goods and finance. It was not uncommon for some of the successful, after they had prospered, to move even further east than New York—back to Germany. Mid-nineteenth-century Germany was a land of culture, good medicine, and a multitude of conveniences and comfort.

WHAT THE JEWS DID FOR THE TOWNS IN WHICH THEY SETTLED

When an Arizona Goldwater went on to San Francisco or a Texas Sanger made his home in New York City those two probably never asked themselves what they had done for the regions they left behind them. Yet the cities where they had labored for years bore their impress. Some Jews had left their cultural stamp on their western homes, for they had demonstrated an interest in music, literature, debating, the arts. The Jews who built the western opera houses were not grobians concerned only to cash in on their investment. Many of them, too, were active in municipal administration and finance. In the New Southwest the Jew was called upon to play a special role; he served as a catalyst to bring the Anglos, the Indians, and the Spanish-speaking natives closer together. Because ethnic and ancient prejudices were not pronounced among Jews, they found it easy to work with the native Americans even as the Jewish shopkeepers in the Deep South were more considerate of Negroes than their Gentile competitors.[27]

The obvious contribution of the Jew was in the area of commerce. The new settlements needed goods, for people poured in more rapidly than supplies. Wherever the Jew went whether it was Easton tucked away in a corner of Pennsylvania or Bisbee, Arizona, he stood out as the bringer of goods, necessities; he maintained, if he did not raise, the standard of living. To the delectation of the Latin American natives and the Protestant American newcomers he tied Mora, New Mexico, to New York City. The wholesaler had clients all over the West and even the retailer served loyal customers in an area of hundreds of square miles. As a progressive businessman with his reminiscences of the East the Jewish storekeeper brought in glass windows, manikins to display garments, stone buildings, new crops, and the latest in farm machinery. He was supplier, banker, and friend in the sad days of drought, fire, blizzards, and economic depression. He was the man who gave the farmer and the rancher credit in a day when their only security was personal integrity. This Jewish merchant was found everywhere performing these important services in a host of towns and villages. A traveler in 1869 made the simple statement about the German Jewish shopkeepers in Santa Fe: "Their stores are well filled with everything." This was eleven years before the railroad reached Santa Fe, a city then 800 miles by stagecoach or oxcart from Leavenworth or Kansas City.[28]

THE TYPICAL "WESTERNER"

If we survey the American Jew for the period 1654 to 1880, and more narrowly from 1836 to 1880, how shall we describe this man as he headed west from New York City, Philadelphia, and Baltimore? He was a Central or East European teenager with enough education to run a small business. If he did not stop over in England to anglicize himself he learned to become an American in the United States after he found a job in a coastal city or a midwestern town or village. At first he was either a peddler or a clerk, then a store manager comfortably entrenched in the apparel trade. Then he started looking about seriously for a place where he could remain permanently. Not always, but almost always, he drifted westward, that is, to a new area, opened a store with a partner, and soon joined a lodge, preferably the Masons. Once he made a living, he stopped roaming, went east or to Europe for a wife, began to branch out, became a wholesaler, and flirted with any venture that would show a profit. By this time he had joined a Hebrew Benevolent Society and engaged in Jewish and civic causes. Was he now a successful businessman? Only moderately so. Squire Julius Ochs who had been in and out of a half-dozen states and had more downs than ups was far more typical of his generation than a Meyer Guggenheim.

The normal, unexceptional shopkeeper was pro-American because this land afforded him a scope and encouragement in politics, commerce, and social acceptance which were still denied him in his native European home. As late as 1880 the more than 70 percent of European Jewry that lived in Poland, Russia, and the Balkans was still unemancipated. These unfortunates were second-class citizens. In 1881 the Russians would begin to attack and murder their Jews; in this the Rumanians had long anticipated them. But this European newcomer, this pro-American was also very much resolved to remain a Jew. His generation has been referred to as "society of individuals" in which social values and institutions were shaken and modified. The Jew qua Jew never took individualism too seriously if the fate of Jewry was at stake. There was never any doubt in his mind that he could not remain a Jew except in a setting wherein he could adhere to Jewish traditional institutions and communal values. In principle the Jew had to have a community in order to survive; this he knew and never forgot. Yet remaining a Jew was probably not his highest priority; that was allocated to the job of making a living. Next came the obligation to be a Jew, albeit a permissive one, and close on its heels was his fervent wish to become an American. The final priority for some Central European immigrant wanderers was to remain German.[29]

SOME STATISTICS

In 1840 American Jewry had about 15,000 Jews, twenty some congregations, one orphan asylum, no newspaper, no seminary, no national organization. Almost all of Jewry lived on the eastern side of the Father of Waters. And in 1880? By that time there were five hospitals, three in the tidewater, one in Cincinnati, and the other in New Orleans. There were eleven orphan asylums, all in cismississippi, except for one in San Francisco. There were four Jewish national secret orders with something less than 50,000 members, excluding those who belonged to the female auxiliaries. These orders spoke grandiloquently about their moral, social, and cultural goals but they were primarily insurance and mutual-benefit societies. By this time there were almost twenty Jewish weeklies in the country so that even he who ran might read. There were four in San Francisco and one in St. Louis; the others were published in the eastern half of the country. There may have been fifty YMHA's with widely disparate and assorted programs; about ten were to be found in the transmississippi regions. In 1880 the Hebrew Union College in Cincinnati, a rabbinic seminary, was already five years old; the Union of American Hebrew Congregations was already seven years old and had 120 affiliates, but that was less than half of the American congregations and synagogs. In all there were at least 280—to say nothing of numerous East European conventicles.

Closely associated with the Union was its Board of Delegates on Civil and Religious Rights, a civic defense political and philanthropic organization with both national and international goals. In this instance it is interesting to reflect that American Jewry reached out abroad long before the United States envisaged itself as an imperialist or world force. All told there were close to 300,000 Jews in this land at the beginning of the ninth decade; about 40 percent of all Jews lived in New York and Pennsylvania, but only 18 percent of the general population dwelt in those two states. The overwhelming mass of American Jews and all their institutions of importance were located east of the Mississippi. These figures are important if one is to keep the Jewish West of 1880 in proper perspective.[30]

CHAPTER EIGHT

ECONOMIC LIFE OF THE JEWS, 1840–1860

INTRODUCTION

The Far West was taking on flesh, but with the exception of California much of transmississippi was not significant numerically or financially, if all American Jewry is envisaged. The West was a field for growth; some Jews saw in it the reality or the illusion of opportunity. It may well be that even in those days some of them were already impressed by the myth of the romantic West. It has been noted that as the farmers moved west the Jewish storekeepers were close on their heels. Although Jews actually on the farm were few in number there were always some who tilled the soil, and there were always others who urged their Jewish fellows to return to the plough. In the 1840's, in the decade of the Brook Farm Institute of Agriculture and Education, the New England peddler Abraham Kohn was eager to colonize Jews but he, too, went on to become a successful businessman and politician in Chicago. Socially ambitious Jews with capital in South Carolina and the Old Southwest did become planters, for the plantation was the symbol and the arena of the gentleman, the aristocrat. One wonders if these Jews were ever completely accepted socially. In hours of stress Judah P. Benjamin's enemies would never cease to remind the world of his Jewish origin, an origin that he was willing to forget.[1]

When the young Bohemian rabbi Isaac Mayer Wise arrived in this land in 1846 he remained in the East. The growing cities with the many things they had to offer attracted many Americans both native and foreign born. New York City was certainly more exciting than Jebenhausen in Wuerttemberg or La Paz in Arizona. This was the age that witnessed the appearance of the telegraph, the reaper, the mowing and the sewing machine, photography, gaslit streets, elevators, running water in the houses, ether, Pullman sleeping cars, the transatlantic cable, and the Colt revolver. This was the generation when Goodyear vulcanized rubber and the Jewish itinerants who peddled stretchable suspenders gathered for worship in Chicago's India Rubber synagog. New York and Pennsylvania were great manufacturing centers; two-thirds of the Jewish New Yorkers were in commerce and industry; here was opportunity. By 1860 the United States was the second largest industrial country in the world. Between 1840 and 1860 the population in this land increased almost 100 percent; Jewry increased 1,000 percent.[2]

The German and Polish village Jews, traders, craftsmen, and shopkeepers did not change their economic pattern appreciably after they landed in New York's metropolis of 300,000 souls. Many of these "traders" continued as peddlers. Some probably dubbed themselves "merchants"; it was a noble word. Peddling was the line of least resistance for capital-shy immigrants without a trade. Herschel the Thief (a term of affection) would give almost any Jew a pack on credit. A few took to peddling to learn the language. Sink or swim! Some became city peddlers; even wives occasionally took a basket and peddled from house to house. Many were rural peddlers. Quite a few moved west, frequently as a group, and, basing themselves on a small town where a supplier was established, they began to scour the countryside. Often they were the pioneer business people. They carried a pack and after their initial success moved by wagon or skiff. Most of them sold clothing, dry goods, and notions; some specialized in cheap jewelry. They sold for cash; a few engaged in barter.[3]

SUFFERINGS OF THE PEDDLERS

Peddling was a miserable life at best. The pack peddler carried a huge bundle, waded through mud on rainy days, and battled the farmer's dogs. Many people were hostile to him for peddlers were deemed cheats. Depressions were recurrent leaving the peddlers without sales and hungry. Frequently they were emotionally distressed; loneliness and the pains of acculturation in a strange land were hard to bear. One despairing soul cried out, "here I am buried alive." Jewish associates were few; the Sabbath and the dietary laws were neglected; wives and children were left behind, and there were "strange women" to trap the hungry. License fees were heavy; peddling was forbidden in some areas, and avaricious constables lay in wait; in the South peddlers were accused of trading illegally with the slaves. Some successful peddlers in their latter-day memoirs spoke fondly of the good treatment accorded them. This may or may not have been true. The murder of peddlers was not uncommon, and chapbooks were issued by enterprising publishers describing in detail from court records the brutal killing of these pilgrims of the road.[4]

THE PEDDLER'S CONTRIBUTION

Did the peddler make a contribution? The rural peddler brought indispensable consumer's wares to the farmers and the villagers living in isolated areas remote from larger towns and stores. He helped them maintain some sort of standard of living. His services were of no cultural import; frequently he spoke little English. What could the immigrant peddlers teach a farmer who subscribed to at least one paper or a magazine? The Jew was a purveyor of goods, not ideas. Peddlers were superior to the poor whites and the slaves in the South but what did the Jewish peddlers have in common with them? Peddlers were birds of passage, moving on to better things, like the Seligmans and the Guggenheims. Only the failures remained in the business. But even the failures were frequently fine human beings. On occasion they were not without some influence. Soloman Dewald, an Alsatian peddler in the South in antebellum days, opened a store, served in the Confederate army, and later went blind temporarily. When he recovered his sight he went back to peddling in Georgia and occasionally preached on Sunday in the village churches. The people of Rutledge, Georgia, loved him and named a Masonic lodge after him.[5]

CRAFTS

Many of the Germans who landed in New York were craftsmen and pursued their vocations here for a time at least till they started to climb the commercial ladder. Many of the women became seamstresses, the men, tailors, but it was literally true that there was hardly a trade or a craft that did not number at least one Jewish artisan. Some of them were competent technicians, lithographers, instrument makers, workers in gems and precious metals. One was an "operator on corns." Many were self-employed.[6]

RETAIL

Self-employment was a tradition among the pre-industrial European Jews. Here in this country where there was no hampering legislation as in Central and Eastern Europe some of the artisans sold their productions in shops which they set up. Thus they became retailers as did many of the peddlers and clerks. Clerks especially—and they were numerous—were often sent out to the small towns to open a store for the wholesaler or large retailer. Some of these shops were destined to become department stores in postbellum days. A few Jewish retailers were pawnbrokers; others were dealers in second-hand clothing, especially in New York City. The typical Jewish retailer sold men's and women's clothing, or dry goods and accessories, or boots and shoes, or hats and caps. Others dealt in tobacco or liquors, groceries or jewelry, furniture, and even art. At least one-half of all Jewish businessmen were in some form of retail trade.[7]

WHOLESALERS AND IMPORTERS

It was the hope of many Jewish retailers to become wholesalers and in order to realize their ambitions they frequently though not always had to move into larger towns. Wholesalers and importers were one step higher in the economic hierarchy. Though profit margins were often smaller there was much larger volume. A few wholesalers were primarily auctioneers thus disposing of large quantities of goods. Like the retailers most Jewish wholesalers were in apparel. On occasion large firms in different cities would establish a consortium and would work closely together. Among the wholesalers there was considerable diversity. Some were in carpets, fancy soaps and perfumes, groceries, stationery, hardware, guns, wallpaper. So many Jews in New York City were in dry goods—about 25 percent—that prices fell during the Holy Days when Jewish buyers were absent. Many Jews were wholesalers or importers of tobacco. This, too, like jewelry was a "Jewish" business. Teen-aged Solomon Roth of Wuerttemberg was a peddler, bookkeeper, and rural storekeeper before he began to pack leaf tobacco in southern Wisconsin. He is reported to have been the first to send a shipment of tobacco to Wyoming via the new Union Pacific Railroad. A Detroit house imported tobacco from Sumatra and Cuba and had branch offices in Amsterdam and Havana.[8]

VARIETY IN COMMERCE

It has been frequently pointed out above that the Jews of this period were primarily in the business of clothing and adorning people. This was the job to which peddlers, clerks, salesmen, retailers, wholesalers, importers, and manufacturers devoted themselves. But it is also no exaggeration to maintain that there was hardly an economic field in which they were not found. There were literally dozens if not hundreds of different forms of commercial enterprise in which they engaged in the larger towns and cities. In general, however, participation in these nonapparel fields was limited to a handful. Individual Jews were junk dealers, cemetery watchers on the lookout for bodysnatchers, drovers, insurance salesmen, ship chandlers, and undertakers. Others were servants, innkeepers, brokers, nurses, and cartmen. One man owned a "mourning store."

To illustrate this diversity one need but turn to the printed word. Printers, publishers, and editors of general and Jewish newspapers and books were found in many of the major cities of the country. Some of the editors and publishers in the general field were men of some distinction like Mordecai M. Noah of New York City, Abraham Hart of the Philadelphia firm of Carey & Hart, David Naar, the New Jersey newspaperman, and Jacob Newton Cardozo, the well-known Southern economist. Henry Boernstein of St. Louis was the publisher of one of the first German newspapers west of the Mississippi; Samuel Hart, Sr., of Charleston brought out an anthology edited by William G. Simms; Moritz Pinner edited an abolitionist newspaper in Kansas City, and B. W. Cohen published directories in New Orleans. Lewis Charles Levin, the Philadelphia politician, issued *The Temperance Advocate* and later *The Sun*, a nativist organ.[9]

PROFESSIONALS

One is tempted to say that almost nothing in the world of commerce and vocations was alien to the Jews. This is true. They were farmers, mechanics, politicians—this was also a business for some—merchants, financiers, industrialists, and professionals. Individuals were not only civil engineers who built railroads, they were also superintendents, practical railroaders, and, more realistically, financiers who sat on the boards of directors. Yet though Jews were active in this new form of transportation their numbers were small. For the most part the few Jewish professionals were teachers, nurses, opticians, druggists, musicians, civil servants, architects, notary publics, artists, and an occasional naval officer like Captain Uriah P. Levy. The typical Jewish professional of this generation was a lawyer or physician and even here their numbers were limited. Professionals are frequently second-generation Americans; that first generation of immigrants was concerned primarily with bread and butter; a college or a professional school was for the children of thôse who achieved success.[10]

JEWS IN INDUSTRY

Jews of course were not absent in industry. During the 1840's and 1850's they began to turn slowly to manufacturing. But here, too, lack of capital was an impediment for the immigrants, and often for the native born as well. By this time manufacturing had become very important; the sales of iron, boots, shoes, and leather goods exceeded those for cotton. With rare, very rare, exceptions Jews played no significant part in iron, steel, leather goods, pottery, railroads, textiles, shipping, clocks, firearms, lumber, flour, wagons, metal products, and sewing machines. Isaac M. Singer, the man who perfected the sewing machine in the 1850's, was not a Jew despite his name. Individuals, especially in the West, owned mines and occasionally refineries; the Liebmans of New York City started their ca-

reer as beer brewers (Rheingold Beer); William Frank and his partner
Ephraim Wormser built a glass works in a Pittsburgh suburb, Frankstown.
In his memoirs Frank maintains that the district was named after him; he
was wrong; Frankstown was named after an eighteenth-century Indian
trader. A Milwaukee firm began to fabricate iron safes; in other towns
Jews were fish and meat packers, distillers, matzo bakers, and illuminating
gas entrepreneurs. Joseph Braunschweig (Brunswick-Balke) had already
begun to make billiard tables; Brandeis's father-in-law, Dr. Joseph Goldmark, chemist and dermatologist, manufactured ammunition; Moses Lazarus, the father of Emma and Josephine Lazarus, the writers, was a successful sugar refiner; Nesbet & Levy of Macon, Georgia, owned a gold-
medal award machine shop; by the 1860's New York Jews were already
in the business of cutting and polishing diamonds.[11]

APPAREL

In potentia at least the "Jewish" industry was "apparel." This word may
be defined to include almost anything to "wear," men's and women's
clothing, underwear, headgear, shirts, shoes, corsets, hosiery, ties, trim-
mings, and even pocketbooks. It is not altogether clear how Jews got into
the manufacture of clothing. It is possible—and this is only a guess—that
they came into retail ready-to-wear via the pawnbroking and second-hand
clothing business during pre-industrial days. For obvious reasons, the
Chatham Street second-hand dealers in New York City were expert in
cleaning and renovating garments. Some shipped substantial stocks to the
South; certainly some of these reconditioned clothes were destined for the
slaves on the plantations. Jews were already in *Confection*—clothing manufacturing—in the Germany of antebellum days, and they may well have
brought the industry with them. It is by no means improbable, however,
that the real source of this business was England where Jews were already
manufacturing "slops," cheap clothes, in the 1830's. By 1830 an Englishman named Hyam employed 6,000 people, domestic workers, of course.

As early as the 1830's individual Jewish "clothiers," retailers of new
ready-to-wear garments, began to move slowly into wholesaling and
manufacturing. Aaron Lopez had already done so in the pre-Revolutionary War period. The domestic, put-out system of the pre-factory days was
to continue into the Civil War period at least if not later. The industry as
such got a modest start in the 1840's. Clothing, hats, caps, and shirt manufacturers began to appear; among them were Jews though they were still
few in number. New York and Cincinnati were the important manufacturing centers. The two towns were able to forge ahead because they had
an ample labor force, good shipping facilities to the South and West, and
a substantial reservoir of purchasers at home. By the 1850's immigrant

Jews who by that time had been in the country long enough to accumulate capital and experience began to turn to apparel fabrication in substantial numbers. The New Yorkers established wholesale outlets as far south as New Orleans and as far west as San Francisco. Manufacturers also rose in Baltimore and Rochester; Jews in the latter town sold clothing to the immigrants moving west on the Erie Canal. By the 1860's Jews, though in no sense dominant in the apparel industry, were nevertheless ready to take advantage of the opportunities offered by the conflict of 1861. The supply of uniforms for the troops was to become a multi-million-dollar business.

A number of German immigrants who came in the 1830's and '40's then began careers which were to make them clothing manufacturers of national distinction. Practically all of them started as peddlers. Among them was the young Henry Sonneborn. Back home he went to work when fifteen years old, buying cattle, hides, and skins. At the age of twenty-three he landed in Philadelphia without money enough to move on to Baltimore his destination. His relatives there brought him on and sent him out to peddle among the "Pennsylvania Dutch," whose patois he of course understood. He made $1,200 the first year—no small sum—sent some of it home to feed his parents, opened a store in what is today West Virginia and almost immediately a series of branches in different parts of the country, manning them with his numerous brothers. He then sent for his sweetheart in Germany, moved back to Baltimore, opened a store, and turned also to the manufacture of clothes. This was the beginning of Henry Sonneborn & Company. When his branches could not dispose of his product he went out on the road himself as a peddler or drummer. By 1855 he was entirely out of the retail business, manufacturing for the wholesalers only, and with the coming of the twentieth century he was one of the largest clothing manufacturers in the world.[12]

Advertising

Exotic advertising is not an art first reflected in the glossy magazine of the late twentieth century. Nineteenth-century retailers were just as persistent, clever, hard-hitting advertisers as those of today. In 1855 during the Crimean War when Sevastopol in Russia was under siege, John Nathan, a Providence, Rhode Island clothier, advertised in the local journal with this startling heading: "Sevastopol is Taken"; but he went on, "The excitement at Sevastopol is not so great as is caused by the bargains offered in Ready Made Clothing at the Model Clothing Store." Get here in a hurry. "Look out for the Rush-Ons [Russians!]." Nathan's rival, Louis Lewisson, who was also a manufacturer, offered a good Thanksgiving dinner to every poor man in Providence. John Nathan responded in an ad that his bargains were so good, his customers would not have to turn to Lewisson for charity.[13]

WEALTH AND POVERTY, AND MOBILITY

Some of the estimated 150,000 Jews in the land in 1860 had achieved their share of riches and success. The new wealth is obliquely documented by the beautiful synagogs which big city Jews had begun to build. There is more than ample evidence that vertical financial mobility was in no sense exceptional. Individuals kept moving into the upper middle class; a few, very few, were in the wealthy upper segment of commercial leaders. By 1840 when New York had already succeeded Philadelphia as the financial capital of the country there were a number of Jewish banking houses in the city such as that of August Belmont and Speyer & Company. The former represented the Rothschilds of London although this English house had several fiscal agents in this country. All across the continent merchants served in a modest way as petty bankers for their customers. With the coming of thousands of Jewish immigrants and the growth of their communities, bankers and dealers in foreign exchange made their appearance to expedite remittances home. Jewish leaders in commercial banking appeared in almost every large city. Isaac Rosenfeld, Jr., a Bavarian, was cashier in the largest bank in St. Louis in the decade of the 1850's; there were days when it did more than a million dollars business. Rich Jews often embraced a variety of commercial and financial activities in the course of their careers. They were not specialists. Jews, natives as well as newcomers—a small number to be sure—also began to make their mark in insurance, railroads, cotton, steamboating, gas lighting, imports, canals, coal lands.[14]

The core money was still nearly always made in trade, apparel and dry goods. A few men were speedily successful. In 1850 Henry Stern, a German Jew, and his Christian partner started business in Milwaukee as peddlers and storekeepers with a joint capital of $1,600. By 1853 Henry had $4,000; in 1860 he was worth $31,000, and two years later during the War his estate had risen to $70,000. This was success with a vengeance, but most unusual. Moses Y. Beach, one-time owner of the *New York Sun*, published *The Wealth and Biography of the Wealthy Citizens of the City of New York*; the edition of 1855 included fewer than a dozen Jewish families. Captain Uriah P. Levy was credited with $250,000 which he had made in real estate. The only millionaires were the Hendricks copper clan but there were five families in this group. Harmon Hendricks was very probably the richest Jew in the United States.[15]

Wealthy Jews bought or built beautiful homes; most of these houses were in the $15,000 to $25,000 range which was a great deal of money in the mid-nineteenth century. A very rich Jew might be tempted to own a $50,000 home but even the very wealthy Israelites could not afford the palatial mansions erected by the non-Jewish tycoons. In general Jews of this generation were slow to invest in expensive homes, for they might need cash for their businesses. On their way up most Jews preferred living in multiple unit buildings. The young unmarried newcomers, peddlers and clerks, lived with relatives or in Jewish boardinghouses. Some of these hostels were large or at least pretentious such as the Hotel de Paris of Cincinnati. By 1860 many Jews, particularly in the smaller cities, began to live in one-family houses and the numbers in the Jewish boardinghouses declined. As in the twentieth century Jews then tended to cluster together in the same ward or wards. As their economic status improved they moved away from those core settlements and their homes were speedily occupied by a later wave of Jewish newcomers. The Jews left the waterfronts in the big cities seeking always to live in better quarters. In New York City Jewish areas of settlement reflected different strata of wealth. After 1840 when large numbers of Central Europeans and a sprinkling of East Europeans began to make their presence felt the Jews tended to herd together according to their regions of origin. In Jewish history there is a direct ratio between numbers and centrifugality. Or, putting it differently, in areas of residence as well as in religious organizations where Jews are numerous they start dividing up and bunch together according to national origins and liturgical predilection.[16]

POVERTY AND CRIME

The Jews of that generation were able to testify to the accuracy of the Deuteronomic prophecy: "The poor shall never cease out of the land." Poverty among Jews was almost traditional. In spite of their thrift, modesty of expenditure, hard work, and long hours, many never succeeded in rising financially. The Lower East Side ghetto, a slum at its worst, sheltered many Jews who would never start the trek north on Manhattan Island. In the 1850's only about one-half of the Jewish children of school and academy age was receiving an education in Charleston, Cincinnati, and Philadelphia; these children had to go to work. But by 1860 as their parents got on their feet they began sending their children to school and college. In the 1850's the number of Jewish children receiving an education was lower than that of their non-Jewish neighbors; the reverse was true in 1860; the generality of the Jews was on the way up. Poverty breeds crime and some Jews were arrested, usually for offences against property, not against person. The Jews of Richmond bragged in the 1840's that few Israelites in Virginia had "been subjected to arrest and trial for any crime," and in spite of the fact that Jews lived in the crime-ridden Lower East Side of New York City the *National Gazette* of that day said that they had the lowest crime rate in the city.[17]

ECONOMIC IMPORTANCE OF THE JEWS

By the end of this period, in 1860, there were many thousands of small Jewish businessmen in the United States. They were to be found in every state and territory; about half of them were foreign born. The social structure of the Jews ranged from upper to lower class, but most were actually encompassed in a very large "middle class." The upper class which included stock brokers, bankers, and a rare manufacturer of national status like Harmon Hendricks, was very small. However, the upper middle class was beginning to assume sizeable proportions; it included the successful professionals, wholesalers, importers, and a growing group of prosperous manufacturers. At the bottom was the lower middle and lower class of peddlers, street vendors, servants, and artisans. The middle-middle category, petty manufacturers employing a few hands, and, most numerous, retailers, embraced the majority of Jews in the United States. It is probable that outside of New York City the typical Jews fitted into this category. Although there were scores of occupations which afforded many Jews a livelihood the majority were in some form of the apparel industry. Even in an acculturated city like Charleston where the percentage of foreign born was relatively low, most Jews were in "clothing." Their occpation groups throughout the country were very often small; their goal was to be self-employed.

Jews in the United States were growing in economic importance. In the San Francisco of the late 1850's steamers did not leave on the Day of Atonement because the Jewish places of business were closed; across the country in New York City prices for dry goods fell on the Holy Days when the Jews were closeted in their houses of worship. In a twenty-year period when the country almost doubled in size and population the Jews took advantage of the new transportation, the telegraph, and the postal service to move everywhere offering their wares for sale. After a fashion they helped tie the whole country together with shoe laces. Because they offered almost everyone access to goods at competitive prices they helped raise the American standard of living.[18]

CHAPTER NINE

THE JEWISH RELIGION, 1840–1860

RISE OF THE ASHKENAZIM

If Jews helped raise the standard of living of antebellum America they did it only too often at a price—the sacrifice of many traditional practices. This was true in part in the larger cities; it was even more true in the smaller towns and villages where they could not keep kosher and were compelled to keep open on the Saturday-Sabbath in order to eke out an existence. Violating basic commandments was a wrench for these Jews, most of whom were new Americans, immigrants, bred to the punctilious observances of the Commandments. By 1840 these Ashkenazim of Central and Eastern Europe had taken over American Jewry; the socially prominent tidewater Sephardim and their Spanish-Portuguese rite no longer dominated the scene. The first German Jewish congregation had made its appearance in Charleston, South Carolina in 1786 but disappeared very speedily; by 1795 there was an Ashkenazic confraternity in the capital, Philadelphia. It was this same group, very likely, that bought a cemetery in 1801 and soon founded the Hebrew German Society, Rodeph Shalom. By 1810 the members constituted themselves a congregation that provided not only services but also sick-care, burial, and a degree of mutual aid.

Rodeph Shalom hired a hazzan in 1819, Jacob Lippman; the youngsters in the congregation called him Rabbi Jackey. The synagogal fathers started him out at $50 a year but they raised his salary later. He made a living not by intoning the services but through his eloquence in selling second-hand clothing, and he supplemented his income through ritual slaughter, circumcision, collecting dues, and, probably, by teaching the children their Hebrew abc's. The congregation held services in rented quarters; those occupied about the year 1830 were over a carpenter shop and displayed the Hebrew verse from Genesis 28:17: "How dreadful is this place. This is none other than the House of God." To help make ends

meet Rodeph Shalom once rented the cellar of a house it occupied to a
beer company but the noise and activity on the Sabbath and Holy Days
was more than the congregation could tolerate. German newcomers in
town were pressed to join; members were fined twenty-five cents for non-
attendance. The congregation kept itself busy legislating against intermarriage and concerning itself with uncircumcised children; it supervised
the baking of unleavened bread for the Passover, decorated the synagog
with flowers on Pentecost, and doused an occasional convert in the Delaware River. Rodeph Shalom's records were first kept in Yiddish, then in
English, but when the Central Europeans began arriving in numbers they
were switched to German.[1]

A young English Jew who landed in Philadelphia in 1816 set out for
the West, for Cincinnati, and by 1824 succeeded in establishing the second permanent Ashkenazic synagog—B'nai Israel—in the United States.
The following year a group of Ashkenazic Englishmen established Congregation Bnai Jeshurun in New York City, the first new Jewish synagogal organization in that city since the Sephardim met toqether in New
Amsterdam in the middle 1600's. These New York Englishmen and their
continental allies, members of Shearith Israel, had established a Hebrew
Benevolent Society in the congregation as early as 1822, but a few years
later, 1825, they began to push for autonomy. They created a separate educational pious association which called itself Hebra Hinuch Nearim, the
Society for the Education of Children. They were ready to remain in
Shearith Israel and were even willing to retain the Sephardic ritual, but
they wanted their own service; they were disturbed by the increasing laxity in observance and determined to educate the younger generation intel-
ligently and effectively. These English newcomers—sporting names like
Hart, Jackson, and Davies—were part of an Ashkenazic drive for ultimate
independence. They may not have realized it but they were fighting the
"establishment" in a generation of revolt that set Europe and the Americas aflame. On the Continent rebellion stretched from Spain to Greece
and on this side of the Atlantic Latin Americans all the way from Upper
California to the Argentine threw off the Spanish yoke.

The English, Germans, Dutch, and Poles certainly found the Sephardic nasal and gutteral pronunciation of Hebrew strange; far more important were the social, economic, and cultural differences between them
and the natives. Theologically there were no distinctions; both groups
adhered to the ancestral concepts, but even in these areas "acerbities are
keenest where differences are least." The rebels soon admitted that they
wanted their own ritual, that the Sephardic synagog was too far from
their homes, and that with the increasing arrival of immigrants another
congregation was needed, one of their own, where they could be themselves. For the most part the Sephardic natives would have liked to ignore

the new arrivals even as a few decades later, the Germans of the 1880's sought to ignore the East European immigrants. But the newcomers were too numerous to ignore in 1825. Anticipating a statement ascribed to David Einhorn in the next generation, the Shearith Israel elite, one suspects, wished to remain *"klein und rein,"* small and pure. This is substantiated by the fact that it began to exclude most of the newcomers from the congregational franchise, and when the rebels seceded to found the Children of Jeshurun, Bnai Jeshurun, they left with the blessing of Shearith Israel's junta.[2]

SYNAGOGS

Thus by 1825 there were three Ashkenazic congregations in the country; by 1860 there were almost thirty times that number dotting the landscape in almost every corner of the Union, from Boston to San Diego. Why did the newcomers establish religious communities? Why does a man breathe? For strangers in a strange land it was almost instinctive for them to join together, to identify as Jews, to maintain the practices of their fathers. They savored the thought that they were Jews meeting together; they loved the autonomous Judaic world in which they enveloped themselves, and they were comforted in the knowledge that they had a cemetery of their own. In every town there was at least one good man to start a congregation; he it was who rallied the Jews about him and once there was an assembly or society, Jewish social pressure and the aloofness of the Christians served to hold it together. No two congregations were ever alike, yet there was a sameness to their histories. Beginning most frequently as a pious confraternity, or a mutual-aid society, or a cemetery association, the pioneer Jews shared a common odyssey: they met in a member's home, or rented a room, then a whole house, and finally they bought a church and renovated it after appealing to American Jewry for subventions. Along the way they started a school for religious and secular studies, hired a functionary, and watched him to make sure that he at least was observant. He was their vicarious Jew. A St. Louis shohet was dismissed because he was seen in a barber shop on a Saturday. The women, who needed no urging, held fairs and raised money to help finance the congregation, and the Ladies Hebrew Benevolent Society did not hesitate to lend the synagog money as long as it was assured that the advances would be returned—with interest, of course.

Each community, whatever its size, was a world in itself. The Men of Loving Kindness, Anshe Chesed, the third oldest synagog in New York, destined soon to become the largest congregation in the country, liked to recall that in the early days every member brought a piece of firewood from home to keep the oven going during the cold Friday nights. In Cincinnati the congregants sat with the sick and guarded the new graves. Members were expected to arbitrate their quarrels in the congregation and not run to the courts. Surplus funds in the treasury were lent to responsible members; the poor were fed and the children of the indigent were educated without cost. In Montgomery, the Kahal fined all members who did not come to services; hunting was certainly no excuse! Every store had to be closed on the High Holy Days. Baltimore forbade its worshippers to chew tobacco in the synagog; it was not polite to spit in church.

Yet in administrative structure and in activities all synagogs had much in common; they all had executive officers, a board, and hired personnel. This was as true of the synagog back home in Europe as it was in this new country. There were practically no differences. In all lands the parnas or president was autocratic and overburdened. Here in the United States his was the prime responsibility in dispensing charity, in the control of marriages, burials, ritual slaughtering, matzo baking, the liturgy, the services, the school, and the bath too (mikveh). It was he who led the fight against intermarriage, who insisted on decorum, who forbade the women to gossip in their segregated galleries, and it was he who scattered fines with a lavish hand. He watched over the members, the finances, and chose the men who sat up with the sick, the dying, and the dead. In most congregations he handled the paper work and bossed the personnel. In the small towns there was but one hireling, an omnibus functionary; in the larger congregations there was a beadle, a shohet, a teacher, a hazzan, a rabbi, and occasionally even a paid secretary to take down the minutes. As master of the finances, aided by a treasurer, the parnas watched over seat sales and rentals, dues, fees, offerings, legacies, and the price of a ritual bath: ten cents in Cincinnati, twenty-five cents in Buffalo. Brides in Buffalo paid a dollar. He it was who saw to it that the services were in Hebrew, though in some towns the prayer for the welfare of the government was read in English or in German. All in all he was the busiest man in the congregation, exercising a benevolent despotism that was ameliorated only by the fear of rebellion, withdrawal, and secession.[3]

RELIGION IN PRACTICE

The parnas, the president, never forgot that he was the Defender of the Faith. It was an orthodox age for Jewry even as it was for most church-going Christians. Isaac M. Wise tells us of a Protestant pillar of the church who having discovered that a tuning fork had been introduced into the choir loft raised his voice and shouted: "I demand that this instrument of Hell be removed from the House of God!" The new congregations in this country, thoroughly European in their adherence to the old ways, used traditional prayer books most of which bore European imprints. The Jewish bookstores stocked phylacteries, mezuzot, and the Roedelheim service books of Wolf Heldenheim. Cemeteries were important in the economy of Jewish practice. They were sacred spots that were often visited. More than twenty Jewish children died of scarlet fever in Cincinnati in 1853. No matter how weak their Jewish identity, almost all Jews wanted to be buried in consecrated ground. Two zealous New Yorkers were dispatched to Freehold, New Jersey, to pick up the body of a fellow Jew who had passed away and were embarrassed to find the corpse alive and well.

Synagogs almost everywhere assumed responsibility for burials although in the larger towns an affiliated confraternity often did the work. In some places burial associations were established that were independent of the congregation, for in that age of growing secularism there was an increasing number of Jews who desired no synagog affiliation. These unaffiliated Jews were not unaware of the fact that it was much cheaper to belong to a cemetery association than to pay dues to a congregation. It was during this antebellum period, that burial plots were introduced; in earlier days all dead were buried in chronological sequence next to each other. The introduction of the family plot was due in all probability to Christian influence. Congregations and constitutions constantly concerned themselves with burial regulations. Though frequent exceptions were made, intermarried Jews, Christian wives, apostates, and uncircumcised children were denied admission to God's acre. From the vantage point of the late twentieth century it is difficult to understand the strong prejudices on the part of some individuals against circumcision. For them the act was a throwback to savagery. Still the typical Jew was eager that his son be circumcised and some mohalim traveled hundreds of miles to perform the rite. When a male heir was presented to a Galveston congregant he refused to await the delayed coming of a mohel and he himself, without previous experience, ushered the child into the Abrahamitic convenant. Fortunately the baby survived the amateur surgery.[4]

No matter where he was found the typical Jew wanted kosher meats and foods; when he was joined by his aged parents, brought over from a Bavarian or Posen village, his desire was reinforced. Kashrut, the honest preparation of kosher foods, had been a perennial headache for the Jewish community since the earliest days. Preparing kosher food was always a business, often big business; preserved meats and fishes, sausages, cheeses, and the like were shipped out of the North American tidewater to all parts of the Western Hemisphere in colonial days. The larger cities teemed with kosher boardinghouses, restaurants, and caterers. Mt. Sinai Hospital (Jews' Hospital) served only kosher food in the early days. And where there is big business there is bound to be cheating and fraud involving the shohatim and the butchers. By the time of the Civil War some of the butchers using their own ritual slaughterers had already emancipated themselves from effective communal control. At certain times of the year Jews were particularly eager to observe the dietary laws. Eating unleavened bread on Passover was de rigeur. It was then that the peddlers came in from the country, the boardinghouses were packed; the synagogal supervisors breathed down the necks of the bakers and excoriated price gougers; Jewish newspapers advertised Passover foods, delicacies, and service books (Haggadoth) and even Christian grocers offered their Jewish clientele matzos and other Passover foods.[5]

Millennial experience had taught Jewish leaders that if their followers observed kashrut and the Sabbath, Judaism would be secure; Jews wanted to remain Jews; practice not creed made Jews. Though most of them went to service on the High Holy Days only a few were regular attendants at Sabbath worship. There were notable exceptions: the House of Levy and Daniels of Stillwell, Minnesota Territory, advertised in the 1850's that it was closed on the Jewish Sabbath from sundown to sundown, and the Jews of Philadelphia appealed to the French Jewish tragedienne, Rachel, not to appear in a particular drama on a Friday night because they did not wish to miss that performance. A hundred years later small town synagogs were almost empty on Friday nights when the local high school scheduled basketball games. The president and vice president of Cincinnati's B'nai Yeshurun were required to keep their places of business closed on the Sabbath.

There were many Jews who wanted to keep the Law and when Lilienthal and his associates set up a beth din, a court, in New York City in the late 1840's they were bombarded with legal queries. May Jews hold services in a Unitarian Church? The cause célèbre of the early 1860's was the push to commission a statue in honor of the late philanthropist Judah Touro. Jews of course knew that they were forbidden by the Ten Commandments to "make a graven image or any likeness of anything that is in heavens above and that is in the earth beneath" (Exod.20:4) but many, even rabbis, chose to disregard that prohibition; only the coming of the Civil War put an end to this project and the controversy surrounding it. There were always pious and observant Jews who let nothing deter them from fulfilling the 613 commandments enjoined on them. Moses Goldsmith of Easton donned his phylacteries in his shop and went to the back room to pray even if a customer had to wait, and a Cleveland congregation of the late 1850's was kept alive only through the heavy financial sacrifices of a devoted few.[6]

LAXITY

If the rulers of the synagog were concerned about Sabbath observance, intermarriage, circumcision, and the dietary laws, it was because there were many Jews who paid only lip service to the basic commandments. The well-known rabbi Bernard Illowy, a bulwark of American orthodoxy, wrote extensively in the ultra-conservative *Jeschurun* in Germany decrying the lack of religiosity in this country, warning the observant to stay home. His orthodoxy however did not prevent his colleague in Philadelphia, Hazzan Jacob Frankel, from attacking him for lack of religious scrupulosity. In 1860 charges were also brought against Lilienthal in Cincinnati. He was accused of eating forbidden food. There was a great deal of laxity in all matters religious. Some of the larger congregations had no ritual baths; most people kept their stores open on the Jewish day of rest; Cincinnati and Cumberland, Maryland, ran Sabbath observance campaigns. The only times on which the Jews flocked to the synagog were Rosh Hashanah and Yom Kippur but even then many sought admission without assuming any financial obligation. People stopped donning the phylacteries at morning prayers, and, as it has already been pointed out, intermarriage was rife, circumcision was disregarded, and kashrut left much to be desired. Kosher butchers expostulated: "We live in a free land! No one can order us about."[7]

Laxity spread because there was little rabbinic or social control in permissive America. Most Christians were unchurched. The attempts by Lilienthal and others to introduce and maintain religious standards and religious courts failed; the younger generation touched by modern culture and the teachings of the Enlightenment drifted away steadily. In a letter to Isaac Leeser in 1860, the Rev. H. Lowenthal of Macon, Georgia, wrote that it was difficult to gather a religious quorum for a service, that some men refused to pay dues, that kashrut was neglected, that his school was closed for lack of patronage, his salary was in arrears, and no member of the congregation had called upon him in the last six months.[8]

If people were religiously indifferent and declined making sacrifices they might well have offered the excuse that they were harassed by the problems of survival. This was true; it was hard to make ends meet. These immigrants were confused and troubled by the English language, American manners, dress, forbidden foods, and the constant tug of the Jewish Old World and its taboos that burdened the émigrés here with a heavy load of guilt. The harassments of life led to pettiness. Mikveh Israel dispensed with the services of Isaac Leeser; Joseph Jonas of Cincinnati, the father of the Jewish community, wrote: "The more I do for my congregation, the more I am insulted and abused," and the humble Rabbi Rice exploded: "I do not want to have anything to do with Jews."

Life's vexations made for frustrations, dissension, and meanness. When dedicating its new sanctuary in 1860 Mikveh Israel invited all the world but not its neighbor congregation Keneseth Israel. It was a troubled unhappy generation. Some—many?—of the immigrants were crude, uncouth boors coming from the poorest strata of Central European Jewish society. They were quick to resent real or fancied insults and even quicker to vent their frustrations on one another. Squabbling was nothing new. It was not unknown in the colonial synagog. Moses Lazarus was once amerced for referring to Shearith Israel as a "bog house," a lunatic asylum. If there was a constant and recurring appeal for decorum there was good reason for it. The synagog was notorious for its disorder if one is to judge by western standards. The prayers were read aloud by the entire assembly; men sang, shouted, and even bellowed; children were under foot, worshippers walked in and out of the sanctuary and gathered in the streets, and those who remained in the pews took time between prayers to gossip with their neighbors. Every now and then—and this was indeed rare—one of the worshippers was drunk; a prayer leader might occasionally take time out to make a scene and the congregants in one synagog discovered that cooking on the synagog premises during a service was most disconcerting. It happened too that there was so much bickering during a meeting that no business could be transacted. This occurred in the Congregation Pursuing Peace, Rodeph Shalom. Unfortunately those who pursued peace did not always overtake it. In 1854 Mr. S. R. Biesenthal of Congregation B'nai Israel in Cincinnati brought charges against fellow congregant Mr. I. Marienthal; the latter had hired an Irishman to assassinate Mr. Biesenthal. Mr. Marienthal did not deny the charges.[9]

SECESSION

Secession was always the last, if not the first recourse of angry men. The dissension that split Jews was certainly due in part to the fact that American Jewry was a mixtum compositum of heterogeneous "national" elements that could not easily be amalgamated culturally and liturgically. Since time immemorial Jews have gone their separate ways. Individualism was the hallmark of the Israelite even in the days of the Judges in the second pre-Christian millennium, and individualism was certainly encouraged in antebellum America. One of the reasons that Jews fashioned new organizations was their desire for the status of office. Benjamin II, visiting Louisville in 1860, noticed that a new Polish synagog had been established because of the desire of its founders for honors. He recalled a story that he had heard in Poland. In blessing a friendly congregation the prophet Elijah said: "May there always be only one of you who wants to be head of the community." And in cursing an inhospitable congregation he said: "I wish that each of you should strive for the honor of being head of the community."

In Europe a Jew who wished to titillate his ego could always join one of the many confraternities in the ghetto and play a part in it. Here if he was frustrated or unhappy he poured out his resentment on a power structure that was wont to monopolize the offices and the honors; he often felt snubbed. It is difficult to determine whether Jacksonian democratic influences tended to encourage secession. Secessionist groups were probably no more democratic than the parent bodies whence they had sprung although there are intimations that a brawl in early nineteenth-century autocratic Charleston was a revolt of the masses against the classes.[10]

German and Polish political and geographical particularism was constantly reflected in American Jewry. If you are not our kind of a Jew, you are not welcome in our congregation! Certainly the early Ashkenazim were not happy with the Sephardic pronunciation of the Holy Tongue. Every national and provincial Jewish group that migrated to this country wanted to be itself; the synagog was also an ethnic social institution. The conventicles enjoyed their German and their Yiddish mother tongues and a hazzan who gave them what they wanted. In this respect they were better off than the immigrant Catholics who had to respect the priest which the hierarchy imposed upon them even if he was not a member of their own national group. When the Ashkenazim of New York City finally broke with Sephardic Shearith Israel in 1825 it was a mutual parting of the ways; each group was by that time sufficiently numerous to survive independently.

Lilienthal in 1847 implied that secession was the natural order of Jewish life in this country. The characteristic history of a synagog began, so he wrote, with the death of a Jew. His friends then purchased a burial plot, moved to organize, hired a cantor, rented a room for services, fought for honors, and finally split into two congregations. This casual generalization is basically correct. It is well to remember that the term "Ashkenazic" is a catch basin for disparate European cultures. Here in America, when Jews were few, Sephardim and Ashkenazim worked together; all Jews regardless of origin prayed together; they had little choice. In their turn the first Ashkenazim were too few to make distinctions among themselves. Cincinnati in 1820 began as a united Polish and German ritual group. Bnai Jeshurun of New York embraced English, Germans, Polish, and Dutch but when the Europeans began to arrive in larger numbers the various groups, reenforced, allowed themselves the luxury of secession. Bnai Jeshurun once locked its doors and nailed down its windows to prevent a group of insurgent members from using the synagog for worship. Proliferation and ethnic atomization became the order of the day in almost every major town in the country. If the Poles were very numerous and created the first congregation, then the Germans or Bohemians seceded, and vice versa. Even the Sephardim took on a new lease of life and established Sephardic bethels in Baltimore, New Orleans, and perhaps in Macon, Georgia. Ultimately these separate ethnic groups themselves began to subdivide. German Poles from Posen frowned upon Poles from the kingdom of Poland and both it would seem could not endure Poles who stemmed from Russia proper. Secession was also caused by quarrels over the innovations, desired or actual, of the Reformers. The secessionists were justified through their own righteousness. When Isaac M. Wise and Isaac Leeser established secessionist synagogs they made it clear to the world that the truth—the only truth—abided with them. Wise's new congregation called itself, The Men of Truth; Leeser's sanctuary was The True Bethel. As good Jews who paid no homage to the New Testament they found no need to ask with Pilate: "What is truth?" They knew the answer.[11]

RABBIS AND MINISTERS

Thoughtful Jews were very much disturbed by the lack of uniformity in the rituals and in the standards of different congregations in such matters as marriage and divorce. Lack of uniformity, many believed, would impair the unity that held Jews together and ultimately lead to religious disintegration. Without historic perspective these protestants failed to realize that ritual differences had always been characteristic of Jewry everywhere and that near liturgical chaos had been normal in the American synagog for a long time. Early American Jewry lacked trained leadership. Laymen could and did conduct services; those who had good voices occasionally became cantors, hazzanim, even though they had no real knowledge of Jewish law and custom; some who had assumed the title of minister or rabbi were not men of moral stature. Thus in many instances antebellum congregations suffered under inadequate religious leaders at a time when American Jewry needed competent, honorable, and learned men to hold it together.

If the conduct of some congregations left much to be desired the fault was often that of the boards of trustees. They were petty, harsh, and drove a hard bargain. It may be that these immigrants had to be parsimonious for they were indeed poor. The congregation wanted an omnibus factotum and it wanted him cheap. It wanted a man who was at one and the same time rabbi, preacher, hazzan, shohet, teacher, Torah reader, shofar blower, amulet writer, and dues collector. This minister, the luckless wight, was underpaid and enjoyed little or no security of tenure. A Buffalo hazzan started at $5 a month and was fired after three weeks; the Wilkes-Barre incumbent augmented his salary by teaching guitar in the basement of the synagog. Metropolitan Philadelphia treated Leeser, its rabbi, shabbily and impugned his observance of the dietary laws; New Orleans's "Sephardim" promised their preacher a very handsome salary and then neglected to pay it. They expected the rich Judah Touro alone to support the rabbi and he did for many months till the indignant minister resigned in disgust.[12]

If some boards were rough, some of their hazzanim were even rougher. A frontier country lacking regulatory agencies has the tendency to attract riffraff, people who have worn out their welcome in their home country. It was not uncommon for adventurers, apostates, former missionaries, to apply for jobs and even to be called to serve substantial communities in this country. Charleston received an application from a man who was reputed to have been a missionary; a Mr. E. Marcuson, a "rabbi" who flirted with Christianity and had deserted his wife, served in a half-dozen American posts. He was a gifted Hebraist. At one time in the late 1840's, three of the twelve "reverends" of New York City were incarcerated in the Tombs on a variety of charges; a Cincinnati hazzan was dismissed as an inveterate card player in the public cafes; a Chicago "doctor" was shipped out by pioneer Anshe Maarav Congregation. He was a person of questionable character known for his resplendent High Priest's headgear, his plagiarized sermons, and his Irish (Catholic?) wife.

When Manis Jacobs of New Orleans passed away, his Catholic wife had to be restrained from putting a crucifix in the coffin; it was this rabbi who had assured his flock that fasting on Yom Kippur was "damned nonsense." Jacobs's successor was "Rabbi" Albert J. Marks, "Roley," a man of good character. He was by profession an actor and undoubtedly took the rabbinical job to help make a living and support his (Christian?) wife, his numerous children, and a retinue of slaves. He was also a chief in the fire department, and it would seem that at times his duties as a fireman conflicted with his obligations to the congregation. Although he is said by one source to have been a circumciser another report states that his own sons were uncircumcised. And when a congregant remonstrated that Roley had no right to officiate, the rabbi mounted the pulpit on a Rosh Hashanah and shouted: "By Jesus Christ! I have a right to pray." It was clear that some reverends were not worthy of reverence; they had taken ministerial jobs as a last resort. Many of them, foreign born, had no real understanding of the ethos of America. They were largely Germans, often completely devoted to the German people and culture that had repulsed them and driven them into exile. There was one expostulator who believed that harlequins, comedians, tinkers, tailors, and butchers had no right to serve as ministers; cantors must not be chosen just because they could chaunt sweetly. Such men made a bad impression on the Christians, repelled the youth, and drove them into the arms of the Reformers. The solution to this problem, wrote another remonstrant, was to establish a college which would train moral young men, Americans, as hazzanim.[13]

GOOD RABBIS

What has just been described reflects the pathology of the "rabbinate" during the antebellum period. Judaism survived despite the presence of some incompetent spiritual leaders; it survived because there were also numerous dedicated laymen and ministers. In every town and city there were at least a few businessmen who were determined to keep Judaism alive. In New York there was the eccentric Sampson Simson, the bustling Mordecai M. Noah, and the learned Israel Baer Kursheedt; in Philadelphia there was the energetic successful publisher Abraham Hart and in neighboring Easton two obscure laymen built the community. Jacob S. Solis and Gershom Kursheedt labored against great odds to establish congregations in New Orleans, and the peripatetic Solomon N. Carvalho, Frémont's photographer, worked on behalf of a school, a synagog, and a benevolent society in towns as far apart as New York, Baltimore, and Los Angeles. Though the synagog fathers often had to make shift with what they could get, they knew what they wanted: pious hazzanim who were at home in the English language as well as the German. In all likelihood they were not interested in securing real rabbis, ordained scholars of the canon law, Talmudists, who had held pulpits in Europe. In any event these professionals did not care to come to Godless America. They were not soul-saving evangelical pioneers. They came only where there was observance, stability, established institutions, concern for rabbinical learning. They were the generals who brought up the rear.[14]

Yet if rabbis would not emigrate others did—good men: reverends, hazzanim, ministers, preachers, who helped lay the foundations of a lively antebellum religious community. Why did they come? They came because thousands of Jews were leaving Europe and they went along. They were eager to deliver themselves from a reactionary continent where Jews, even in England, were still denied equality; they knew they were coming to the most free country in the world. Here there were also economic opportunities; in the larger towns the salaries were in general much better than those at home. Leeser had come to Philadelphia as early as 1829 and was succeeded in 1851 by the equally devout, but more attractive Italian, Sabato Morais. New York had a series of distinguished leaders. When Jacques Judah Lyons of Surinam had been called from Richmond in 1839 to officiate in staid Shearith Israel, he began to gather together American Jewish historical documents, amassing an excellent collection which is still extant. The Holland-born Samuel Myer Isaacs was appointed hazzan of New York's Bnai Jeshurun that same year and soon became one of the pillars of a progressive Orthodoxy; Anshe Chesed, which had broken away from Bnai Jeshurun, let its liberal-minded minister Leo Merzbacher go because he saw no need for obser-vant women to document their modesty by covering their hair with a wig (sheitel). Merzbacher became the first minister of the leftist Emanu-El and he in turn was succeeded in 1857 by Dr. Samuel Adler, a scholarly Euro-pean rabbi of repute. His son Felix founded the Ethical Culture move-ment.

During the 1840's Dr. Max Lilienthal, a cultured, refined, and knowledgeable German gentleman, became chief rabbi of three tradition-oriented congregations in New York and in 1847, the year after he landed in America, the Rev. Isaac M. Wise (Weiss) accepted a post in Albany. In less than a decade Wise was to be known as one of American Jewry's most distinguished clergymen. In 1849, three years after Wise emigrated from Bohemia, Morris J. Raphall, a native of Sweden, arrived from Eng-land to become a preacher and rabbi at Bnai Jeshurun. This brilliant ora-tor traveled through the country lecturing to large audiences, and in 1860, wearing religious regalia, opened the House of Representatives with prayer. Three thousand miles across the continent Rabbi Julius Eck-man settled down in San Francisco to teach and to edit a Jewish news-paper. As rabbi of Richmond he had led the Virginia House of Delegates in prayer in 1849 and had later moved on to the Bay City on the first leg of a journey west to China. It was his hope, never realized, to bring To-rah to the lost Jews of the Celestial Empire.[15]

Between San Francisco and New York there were at least a dozen substantial Jewish communities all of which secured "rabbis" in the years from 1840 to 1860. Most of these officiants were worthy men. The first rabbinic diplomate rabbi to serve a congregation in this country—the only one since the first Jew arrived in Puritan Boston almost 200 years earlier—was Abraham Rice of Baltimore. He came over from Bavaria in 1840 seeking a future here; as a cripple it is unlikely that he had ever been called to a good religious post at home. Rice was very pious, learned, un-compromising, and crotchety. The Baltimore Scattered Ones of Israel, Nitgy Israel, paid him so little that he was compelled to open a small dry goods store to make both ends meet. The congregation let him go in 1849 but when it reappointed him during the Civil War he turned back half of his salary. Apparently this devotion to traditional practices influenced some of Baltimore's Jews; the community remained a bulwark of conservatism for generations. Henry Hochheimer who succeeded Rice in 1849 was an able learned man. Baltimore Jewry also sheltered David Einhorn, a militant radical, who came to Har Sinai in 1855. Both men, university trained, were political refugees who had suffered under reac-tionary German and Austrian regimes. Farther south, in the Carolinas,

Gustavus Poznanski graced the pulpit in Charleston. In the Middle West, Isidor Kalisch, a scholarly writer, poet, and Hebraist, ministered to Cleveland Jewry. Kalisch wrote a learned disquisition, quoting profusely from the Bible and medieval legal pundits, to prove that women were allowed to sing in the synagog. Antebellum America, and Jewry with it, was not receptive to religious innovations.[16]

If an Isaac M. Wise threatened to resign, if Abraham Rice did quit, and if a Kalisch changed jobs frequently, it was due not so much to their captiousness as to their newly acquired American spirit. Well aware of the respect which Americans accorded their clergy, Jewish ministers did not want to be treated as hired hands; they cherished professional ideals and fought with their boards for more freedom. The rabbis were conscious of the basic problem which was to confront Jewry here to this day: How can one remain a good Jew and be completely open to American culture? They attempted to meet this challenge by accommodating Orthodoxy to Americanism without sacrificing religious practice. Most of them were loyal to the sacrosanct teachings of their ancestors, yet they were very much concerned with decorum, pointing out to their congregants that good manners in the House of God was not an American innovation but a traditional Jewish concept. They were determined to continue the teaching of Hebrew and most eager to retain the loyalty of the boys and girls who were exposed to a permissive Americanism. They were positive that good education was the answer to this problem and they worked to that end. The youth had to be saved for Judaism. Congregational singing was emphasized and by 1860 regular weekly preaching in English and German was part of the services in all good-sized towns. This seems to have been an Americanistic novum. Cautious and lagging Shearith Israel employed a lay preacher to supplement the services with an English address and as early as 1841 gave a Hebrew sacred concert in the synagog, even printing a program for the occasion.

These conscientious religious leaders attacked their problems with vigor and may well have achieved some successes in enforcing decorum and in improving Jewish education. The more notable of them answered queries from all parts of the country about Jewish religious practices, and through their constant preaching became the educators of a generation. They traveled up and down the land speaking everywhere; they wrote books which were widely read, and they influenced thousands through the Jewish newspapers which they edited. By virtue of all this activity they created a sense of community which tied Jews together. They made solid advances in the effort to harmonize Judaism and American culture. Even right-wing Abraham Rice insisted that the youth must be taught in English and he looked forward to an American Jewish translation of the Hebrew Bible.[17]

SUMMARY

Because most of the Jewish leaders, both clerics and laymen, were foreign born they were prejudiced in favor of the continental gemeinde system of centralized communal control of all Jewish institutions buttressed by the official support of the state. But here in this country the authoritarian community was never established because the American tradition of synagogal autonomy prevailed. The unitary Sephardic synagog community persisted only into the early nineteenth century when it broke down with the coming of the Ashkenazim. As the new United States moved toward the separation of church and state, and as the Protestant sects proliferated, congregationalism became typical of American Jewry as it was of many Protestants. As early as the 1820's even before they broke with the Sephardim who had taken them in, the Ashkenazim of New York began to move toward autonomy. American Jewry saw the disappearance of the European type of an authoritarian city-wide monopolistic gemeinde and the emergence of completely independent synagog communities. Each synagog was a kchillah or a complete Jewry embracing in its sphere worship, social welfare, and education, both Jewish and general.

The people, the Jews, just released from kahal control, wanted no overall communal restraint in free America, yet in the midst of increasing congregational atomization they started to regroup themselves. They were ever mindful—even those Jews serving on the pettiest of boards—that all Jews were responsible one for the other, and the Christians never let them forget it. Jews were quite aware that all of them had a common religion and a common past and that they all shared hopes for political equality, prosperity, and social tolerance. In 1845 Lilienthal in New York City had succeeded in creating a little community of three congregations and 700 families and had set up, if only briefly, a rabbinical court (1846). In Baltimore, in Richmond, and in other towns and states, Jews and their institutions were trying to reach out to encompass others—to maintain some unity in their diversity.

The pervasive sense of intimacy that was so true of Jewry never left it. Jews across the continent rallied to public meetings to protect persecutions and injustices to fellow Jews in Damascus, Switzerland, Rome. They bared their fangs at the missionaries and they dispatched funds to the sick, poor, and oppressed of Poland, Gibraltar, Morocco, and Palestine. The English Jews of Bnai Jeshurun in New York City never hesitated for a moment to petition London, Liverpool, and West Indies Jewry for help as well as American congregations as they established their new synagog. Everywhere Jews turned to one another whether they were building sanctuaries or fighting epidemics. Their feeling of kinship, of "community," transcended all barriers.[18]

The emotions that moved Jews to help one another prompted them also to join together in worship. One dedicated man and nine others constituted a service or a congregation or a community. By 1860 there was a chain of bethels stretching from coast to coast. The ten or less native-born Sephardic-dominated synagogs were now hopelessly outnumbered by the immigrant Ashkenazic conventicles. A new Orthodox cycle was in the making. These Ashkenazic congregations grew and prospered. On April 6, 1845, Emanu-El in New York started its career with a collection of $18.14; it grew very quickly and by the late twentieth century had become one of the great synagogs of the world with a budget in the millions. B'nai Israel of Cincinnati was one of the largest synagogs in the West; when it started to draw plans for a spacious new building a synagog worthy objected strenuously: "What's the use of building so large a house, you will have to buy the sexton a horse to ride around and hunt the members up; half that size will do."[19]

A synagog of that day was not only a house of worship; often, too, it was a field of battle, yet it always remained a cherished home. When Jews stopped quarreling in their conventicles it was often an indication that interest in religious affairs—in religion itself—had abated. Despite constant squabbles, rabbinical incompetency, synagogal proliferation, indifference, intermarriage, assimilation, Judaism survived and flourished. Laymen and boards sought to anglicize the schools and the pulpits; for the old-type synagog with its boisterous exuberance, they substituted the new ideal of a House of God distinguished for its Protestant sepulchral silences. The new congregational communities were completely American in administrative structure but in content and program they were still essentially traditional. The goals of a midwestern congregation differed little from those of a German or Polish community. Whether in Europe or in the Mississippi Valley, Jews met, read—with exceptions—from the traditional prayer books, bar mitzvahed the children with the same old chaunt, and helped one another in need. Here in the vast stretches of America, the immigrants survived anarchically in a foreign milieu reenforced constantly by streams of observant newcomers who poured out of the bottomless reservoirs of Europe's ghettos.

As late as 1860, two states, shown in shaded areas, did not accord Jews full equality:
New Hampshire and North Carolina.

CHAPTER TEN

SOCIAL WELFARE, 1840–1860

SYNAGOGAL PHILANTHROPY

Helping fellow Jews is an integral part of Judaism; any distinction between religion and charity is artificial. As far back as the third pre-Christian century a High Priest had declared that the Jewish world was built on the three pillars of the Law, the worship services, and on acts of loving kindness. Most early-nineteenth century Jewish confraternities were denominated societies of "loving kindness." Charity in Judaism was zedakah, "righteousness," and as the Bible declares "zedakah delivereth from death." (Prov. 10:2). Helping one's neighbor, the poor, the stranger, the fatherless, and the widow was as old as the Mosaic Code. It was only natural therefore that the Jewish emigrant landing here would carry on the charitative activities of his Polish or German homeland. Back in Europe aid was dispensed to the poor Jew through the community, or the pious association, or through gifts of individuals, and it was much the same in America. Every Jew was expected to help his fellow Jews, and many did. Judah Touro of New Orleans emerged during antebellum days as the classical American Jewish philanthropist. Most of the estate of this childless eccentric went to Gentiles and non-Jewish causes, but very substantial sums were also bequeathed to Jews and to Jewish institutions. Prodded by his friend Gershom Kursheedt the old man gave New Orleans Jewry a school, a synagog, and a hospital; American Jewry received generous sums for its hospitals, schools, and confraternities. Twenty orthodox synagogs from Boston to St. Louis were left welcome legacies, although the largest gift to Jews was destined for Palestine.[1]

But one individual, no matter how generous or wealthy, cannot provide for all the poor and distressed; communal giving was also necessary. Jewish charities in Europe were administered by state approved "communities," working primarily through pious associations. Since there was no formal Jewish community in most cities of the United

States, welfare work was carried on almost entirely by the synagog; this was true of some cities even in the late twentieth century. The synagog was dedicated to deeds of loving kindness. When B'nai Israel of Cincinnati, the first congregation west of the Alleghenies, received its charter in 1830 it emphasized its intention to raise funds to relieve the unfortunate; the Richmond Ashkenazic conventicle of the 1840's was incorporated as a charitable association that would prevent Jews from becoming a burden to the city and county. Particularly in its early stages the American synagog everywhere made provision for members in distress, for the local poor, and for the ever-present itinerant. It lent money to its members, and out of its sparse reserves sent generous gifts to others about to build synagogs and orphanages. It aided distant Jewries plagued by fires and epidemics, commissioned visitors to comfort the imprisoned, and dispatched sums to Palestine.[2]

NEED

It was obvious as early as the turn of the eighteenth century that the synagog could not carry the charity load. The problem of making provision for the poor and unfortunate became acute by the mid-nineteenth century as the immigrants poured in: between 1840 and 1860 American Jewry increased *tenfold*. Numerous agencies had to be established to look after the newcomers even though they did create self-help agencies of their own. In establishing the new societies the old-timers, American citizens, and the incoming émigrés were not motivated to any perceptible degree by the Christian humanitarian reforming spirit of the age. They were not concerned with temperance, women's rights, prison reform, elevation of the masses, abolition. First things first. Jews had to be helped; many of them were poor; in hours of sickness and despair the immigrant peddlers, many mere boys, turned to their coreligionists; the constant recurring depressions destroyed hundreds; the yellow fever and cholera epidemics were horrible. Jews had to be rescued or they might fall into the clutches of the omnivorous missionaries. The most patent form of relief was the mutual-aid socioreligious society so common to both Jews and Christians in this country, and so traditional in all European Jewries whence the immigrants had come. When the first Jewish mutual-aid society was fashioned in Philadelphia in 1813 there were already twenty such Gentile fraternities in town. Jewish immigrants, and natives, too, helped themselves by organizing along sectarian and ethnic lines. The Catholics and Protestants have societies, said a president of a Cincinnati confraternity. Why then can Jews not have organizations of their own?

Practically all of the early eleemosynary associations were affiliated to some degree with specific congregations. In effect these early and mid-nineteenth-century organizations constituted the social-welfare arms of the synagog; some congregations sponsored several societies which concerned themselves with different philanthropic tasks. All were autonomous, enjoying an organic structure of their own with a constitution, officers, and bylaws.[3]

AFFILIATED AND INDEPENDENT SOCIETIES

Power—independence—feeds on itself; the affiliated societies having tasted freedom wanted more. They began to move out of the orbit of the synagog. Was this because their leaders were freethinkers, philosophic materialists, anti-supernaturalists, secularists? A few may have been. The majority were religionists, albeit pragmatic ones, who saw the need for additional institutions to supply the immediate wants of the immigrants. The newcomers could not afford to join a synagog and pay dues; it was imperative therefore that they belong to a mutual-benefit society which could and would protect them in their hour of distress. If such a society was to survive and be effective it would have to steer clear of intra-Jewish religious prejudices and geographic particularism. It certainly could not afford to be involved in the growing quarrel between Reform and Orthodoxy; it must be above the fray. This is why the Jewish fraternal lodges of the 1840's, the mutual-aid and benefit societies, tabooed all religious and political discussions. At an annual dinner of one of the Cincinnati organizations, a notable capitalist, Philip Heidelbach, put it rather crassly when he said that the charity associations tended to unite the Jews of a community; the congregations tended to divide them.

Large numbers of societies sprang up in the 1840's and the following decade. Ninety-three were incorporated in New York state between the years 1848 and 1860; there were certainly others that did not bother to employ a lawyer to incorporate them. Though Jews were less than 10 percent of the population they established about half of all the welfare organizations of those twelve years. In 1854, New York City had over 40 Jewish societies, mostly of a philanthropic nature; Philadelphia, 17; Cincinnati, at least 10. The typical American Jewish charity was directed primarily toward mutual aid though it rarely failed to respond to the appeals of non-members and to Jewish communities in distress both here and abroad. It was an immigrant self-help device providing cash, food, fuel, and fixed grants in times of sickness, disability, and death. It offered free burials, aid in purchasing tombstones, and supplied watchers to guard the graves against the desecrations of the bodysnatchers. Religious services were held for the dead and the anniversary of their passing was piously observed. Benefits varied as did rules for admission. Candidates over fifty were not accepted; wives had to be Jewish; those with venereal diseases were rejected; to avoid the scandal of going to the courts members were expected to arbitrate their differences within the confines of the hevrah. As the nativism of the American Party, the Know-Nothings, made deep inroads into the American psyche, some of the Jewish mutual-aid groups admitted only those who had been granted citizenship; aliens were rejected.[4]

As in Wilmington, North Carolina, a typical smaller community, the benevolent society was very often the only Jewish organization in town; it was then, in effect, a self-contained community catering to the charitative, social, and religious needs of its miniscule Jewry. Some benevolent societies were fashioned by the more successful to help those who had come upon hard times, but in the last analysis these organizations, too, were of a mutual-aid type for they were ready to help their own members should the occasion arise. No two societies were totally alike though all had charitative goals in mind. Even the groups and clubs dedicated specifically to the cultural and to the social raised money for philanthropic purposes. A few, a very few charities, like the Eureka of San Francisco, went out of their way, unsolicited, to help others. Members of the Eureka boarded incoming ships in the Bay seeking out the impoverished and the sick.[5]

As in the religious area divisiveness, the tendency to unite along "national" lines, manifested itself early in the philanthropic field. This was of course possible only in the very large communities where Jews were so numerous that disparate ethnic societies could enjoy the luxury of particularistic survival. In New York City there were not only Portuguese, German, and Polish charities by 1860 but even one for the Dutch and for the French. Seeking to express themselves, young men and young women, school youth too, fashioned eleemosynary societies of their own as did the "ladies." The Talmud Yelodim school children gave a dramatic performance in Cincinnati in 1855 in order to raise money for charitable purposes. The women's societies were numerous. At times they served as auxiliaries of the congregations; often they were independent, and because the men—and the law too—assumed that they were not competent to manage their own affairs, they were frequently officered by males. Just like the men the women also divided along ethnic lines in the larger cities and there was hardly an area of social welfare work which they did not explore; they held fairs and balls to raise the funds for the purposes to which they had dedicated themselves. Frequently the men called upon them to do the investigative work when clients appealed for help.

Though practically all societies were directed toward immigrant aid, they sought, in the larger population centers, to gear their charities to very limited goals. Thus men, women, and young folk picked the specific fields which appealed to them; they supplied fuel, or loans, or matzos, or clothes; they educated poor children, supported the ritual bathhouse (mikveh), helped the sick and the dying, made grants to hospitals, to widows, orphans, and to the poor of Palestine. They provided free burials, helped young clerks, and searched out jobs for the unemployed. The unique New Orleans Mashmie Yeshuah, Proclaim Salvation, or the Hebrew Foreign Mission Society, as it was known, was concerned with Chinese and foreign Jews and hoped among other tasks to educate their children on these shores.

The different names adopted by the clubs and societies were almost as numerous as the organizations themselves. They were English or German or Hebrew or combinations in two languages. Loving Kindness and Brotherly Love were recurrent onomastic phrases. The names of great worthies in Jewish history were also immortalized by the throngs: Maimonides, Mendelssohn, Jacobson, Touro, and the still living Montefiore of England. There was only one group that called itself The Society of American Jews. It was almost inevitable that there would be overlapping, duplication, jealousy, and inefficiency in the work of these multiple agencies. There were exceedingly few paid workers and a common tendency to reserve too large a balance in the treasury, one which might better have been expended on helping others. Some organizations barely stayed alive; others were successful but autocratic in the conduct of their affairs. Yet the antebellum immigrants succeeded in helping themselves; they found social and emotional comfort, release, and psychological security in the ambit of their societies, and whether religious or not the new organizations encouraged them, compelled them, to stay "Jewish."[6]

THE INDEPENDENT ORDER OF B'NAI B'RITH

The problem of staying Jewish was tackled by an institution that was entirely new in American Jewry and for that matter in World Jewry. This was the fraternal lodge. Originally the American Jewish lodges were in essence mutual-aid and benefit societies with the added elements of secrecy, pomp, ritual, and regalia. There have been fraternal groups in Jewish life since at least the first Christian century and in the eighteenth century there were attempts to fashion secret mystical brotherhoods in Italy and Palestine. Jews were attracted to the Masonic order in the eighteenth century because of its humanitarian acceptance of the Jew in a day when he was nowhere accorded equality. In the 1840's American Jews began to establish fraternal orders of their own: the B'nai B'rith in 1843, the Independent Order of Free Sons of Israel in 1849, and the United Order of True Sisters, a male-controlled auxiliary of Emanu-El in New York which considered itself a national Jewish women's organization (1846). In the next decades the B'rith Abraham, the Covenant of Abraham, and the Kesher Shel Barzel, Iron Knot, came on the scene. Of these fraternal orders the B'nai B'rith was the most important. In imitation of the better lodges such as the Independent Order of Odd Fellows and the Masons to which many simple untutored German Jews could aspire, and where, on occasion, they were not welcome, a group of highly intelligent exceptional men, lower middle-class Jews, established the Independent Order of B'nai B'rith (IOBB)—the Sons of the Covenant or in German, *Bundesbrueder*, Brothers of the Covenant. The ritual was in German. It was hoped that the new order would appeal to Jewish artisans and petty businessmen, affording them the opportunity to associate with their peers. It offered them economic security, social acceptance, and all the glamour of ritual, mystery, and spiritual outreach.[7]

At the onset B'nai B'rith was nothing more than a sick-benefit society. Yet almost immediately it envisaged much more, for its approach to the immigrants was didactic and apologetic. It wanted to elevate the newcomers spiritually, make them better men and better Jews so that they would respect themselves and command the respect of the Gentiles about them. The declared goal of the IOBB was to educate, indoctrinate, and to regenerate a people beaten down by centuries of oppression. All Jews in the United States were to be welded together, irrespective of geographical origin. As in other lodges political discussions were forbidden; this was necessary if harmony was to prevail. In the troubled years before a Civil War which epitomized disunion, a nationwide society was fashioned emphasizing union. Jews were to survive as American Jewry, a cultured, moral, and ethical group, not congeries of factions at war with one another. New horizons were opened up to the peddlers and craftsmen from Posen, the Rhineland, and Bavaria. By the 1850's, the lay and rabbinical intelligentsia in the B'nai B'rith, caught up in the cosmopolitan and universalistic euphoria of Europe's 1848, was talking of the sciences and arts, patriotism, philanthropy, and humanity. The Jews were to become a beacon light to the nations. The lodge's motto of benevolence, brotherly love, and harmony began to assume universal dimensions.

The founding fathers of B'nai B'rith were German immigrants of humble background but they were on the whole an exceptional group. The chief architect of the new association, Heinrich Jonas, a mechanic from Hamburg (1811-1866), was typical of this group in the high quality of his leadership. As an American, with the new name of Henry Jones, he devoted himself to the growing Jewish community of New York serving as a clerk in the very sizeable Anshe Chesed, as a teacher in its Hebrew school, and as a founder of left-wing Emanu-El. As president of this national order Jones helped write its ritual and incorporated the principles of social equality and democracy which he had learned from the Odd Fellows and the Masons; these were principles denied him in his native

Hamburg where the rights granted by Napoleon had been summarily ab-
rogated when the French went down to defeat. The Jewish Hamburg
that he knew before his emigration in 1829 was that of Hakam Isaac Bernays, a modern Orthodox rabbi, and of the liberal religious Templars,
Edward Kley and Gotthold Salomon. The new and better Germany was
thus transferred to the United States in the person of Jones and his associates.[8]

The Order grew relatively rapidly. By 1860 there were about fifty
lodges in the United States, some as far west as the Pacific Coast. Seven
years after the first group opened its session in a Masonic hall on the
Lower East Side there was an English-speaking branch in Cincinnati, and
that very same year, 1850, a faction of young radicals in Baltimore moved
to admit Christians. Others raised their voices against the regalia and the
elaborate ritual. In the 1850's as the immigrants became Americanized
and more sophisticated, more fully aware of the dynamism of American
geographical expansion, political power, and cultural development, the
B'nai B'rith leaders began to think in terms of a total American Jewry and
even of a World Jewry. This sixth decade of the nineteenth century was
to witness the laying of the first Atlantic cable, a symbol of world unity.
During these notable years, too, the order built Covenant Hall in New
York City, the first non-sacral Jewish public building in the United
States. It was there in that center that they established the Maimonides
Library and initiated a series of lectures. As the Sons of the Covenant
gathered strength and self-confidence they outlined a program to settle
Jews on the soil, began to talk of founding a college, an orphan asylum,
and a periodical. The Order wanted to improve Jews culturally but it
fought shy of setting up a college with religious commitments which
would impair its theological neutrality and invite dissension. When the
United States government ignored the rights of its Jewish citizens by negotiating a treaty with Switzerland which discriminated against Americans of the Jewish persuasion B'nai B'rith protested vigorously to the
Senate in Washington. This marked the entry of the Order into the field
of national politics.[9]

ORPHAN ASYLUMS

The group in the B'nai B'rith that wanted a national college was led by
Rabbi Isaac M. Wise of Cincinnati but he lost out because of his aggressive personality and his close association with the rising Reform group.
The proponents of an orphan asylum were more successful; in 1868 a B'-
nai B'rith sponsored asylum was established in Cleveland. The effort to
provide for Jewish orphans in the United States began in Charleston,
South Carolina, in 1801 when that city sheltered the most important

Jewish community in the country. Modeling itself on older European and Caribbean island organizations a society was founded called Abi Yetomin Ubne Ebyonim or Society for the Relief of Orphans and Children of Indigent Parents. The goal of the Abi Yetomin was to relieve widows and to educate, clothe, and maintain orphans and the children of the poor. The children were to be taught morality and industry; the bright ones were to be picked out and given an education in the arts and sciences. The society did not establish an asylum for those orphaned by the recurrent fevers; widows and the poor were subsidized to keep their children at home. The B'nai B'rith had a similar Widows and Orphans Fund almost from the very beginning. It was deemed very important. The Charleston orphan society did open an all-day school for its charges in which Isaac Harby was one of the teachers; only in 1860 and then only briefly, after a devastating epidemic, did it open a resident asylum.

It is difficult to determine why the large Jewish communities of the country decided to establish resident asylums in the 1850's. In this one decade orphanages were set up in New Orleans, Cincinnati, Charleston, Philadelphia, and New York. The epidemics? There were plagues before the 1850's and long after that time. Was it cheaper to house the children under one roof than to subsidize the parents? Did the establishment of such institutions become fashionable and induce imitation? At all events the Jews of New Orleans—where there were already five non-Jewish asylums for children—organized an Association for the Relief of Jewish Widows and Orphans in 1855 and opened a kosher home in 1856. The new building was dedicated by Benjamin Franklin Jonas, a young lawyer all of twenty-two. In 1879 this scion of the Cincinnati and Illinois Jonases was to become a United States Senator from Louisiana.[10]

This New Orleans society was chartered in March, 1855; a month earlier a group of Philadelphia women, encouraged by Rebecca Gratz, had organized the Jewish Foster Home. Rebecca, who had been active in the non-Jewish Philadelphia Orphan Asylum, had come out in the *Occident* for a Jewish home for children as early as 1850. She and others were disturbed that impoverished Jewish children were out on the streets peddling matches. They had to be rescued from "ignorance, vice and misery." Children were ensconced in the new asylum in May of 1855; one boy had come all the way from Georgia. The boys remained in the home till they were thirteen when they were indentured and were expected to be self-supporting. The supervisory council which kept a wary eye on the women who had founded the home was of course male; the superintendent was a woman who taught English, German, and Hebrew for which she received her board and $2 a week, but the Christian physician who attended the children did not charge for his services. The institution was apparently a communal one for the ladies who devoted themselves to it were recruited from the several synagogs in town. Actually prestigious Mikveh Israel ran it until the postwar period when the inroads of democracy and the rise of a new generation and new leaders made democratic and communal control inevitable.

Cincinnati Jewry had a home for orphans in the middle 1850's but very little is known about it; New York did not open its asylum till the first year of the seventh decade. Why did this huge community lag behind other communities? It delayed because it was huge; it was too big, too divided, to pull together. There had been talk of a refuge for orphans ever since 1826 when Jacob S. Solis of Mt. Pleasant, New York, sought unsuccessfully to establish a trade and farming school for European refugee children and for American Jewish youth and orphans. Efforts of orphan support societies in the 1830's and 1840's also failed to create an asylum although these associations may well have contributed to the maintenance of underprivileged children. Crisis situations were important: constant epidemics and children on the streets may well have induced New Orleans, Cincinnati, and Philadelphia Jewry to take action. New York was stampeded by Christian missionaries who began to shelter and teach Jewish children. At a Holy Day service Rabbi Samuel Adler of wealthy Emanu-El frightened his congregation with a tale of proselytism and subversion and his congregants responded immediately with a huge sum. This was in the fall of 1859 just a year after American Jewry had been shocked by the story of Edgar Mortara, the six-year-old Italian child who had been taken from the arms of its Jewish mother to be reared as a Christian. New York pulled itself together and in 1859 merged the Hebrew Benevolent Society and the German Hebrew Benevolent Society, two of its largest charities, for the purpose of establishing a home for orphans and widows, for the aged and the infirm. The new institution opened its doors in 1860.[11]

HOSPITALS

Five years before the asylum welcomed its first youngsters, New York Jews, numbering 30,000 to 40,000 opened the doors of their first hospital. Jewish hospitals in the United States were founded relatively late; in England the Portuguese Beth Holim (Hospital) of London was established in 1747, that of the Ashkenazim, Jews' Hospital and Orphan Asylum, in 1795. From American colonial days into the nineteenth century, stricken transients and the impoverished sick were, like the orphans, either subsidized or boarded out in private homes; a few were compelled to seek the shelter of public or Christian denominational hospitals. New York Jewry began to agitate for a hospice-hospital after the yellow fever epidemic of 1805. New York, it then said, is destined to shelter the largest Jewish congregation in America; a hospital is a necessity. In 1813 the Board of Trustees of Shearith Israel, the leaders of New York's synagog community, hoped to establish a poorhouse for indigent Jews, widows, and orphans by means of a state-approved lottery. Nothing was done for a long generation; the rival eleemosynary organizations refused to work together.

The 1850's was the decade of decision not only for orphan asylums but also for hospitals in Jewish America. Thousands of immigrants had already arrived, thousands more were pouring in steadily. In an age of denominational hospitals where Christian piety was very much in evidence, the Jews insisted on having institutions of their own where their sick could be nursed, given kosher food, administered the last rites, and spared the importunities of Protestant and Catholic soul-hunters. Jews at their morning prayers did not want to be scorned as they donned their phylacteries. Eighteen-year-old Jacob Hirschorn, a Mexican War veteran recuperating in the New Orleans La Charité in 1848, was annoyed when the good sister who nursed him persisted in reading tracts to him. As a St. Louis Jew lay dying in a Catholic hospital, he was baptized and after he passed away the Jews in town had to appeal to the mayor before they were able to recover the body. Jews in Christian hospitals were frightened at the thought that they might awaken after a severe illness to find that they had been baptized; they were not flattered at the thought that they might become instant Christians; pious Jews were determined to go to a Jewish heaven.[12]

The agitation for a Jewish hospital in New York City became more vigorous in the 1840's as the Jewish population mushroomed. Isaac Leeser agitated for one in the pages of his *Occident*. The German Hebrew Benevolent Society was chartered with the goal of assisting the poor and building a hospice-hospital. But before the New Yorkers could make up their minds and open their purses the Cincinnatians stole a march on them. Four thousand men, women, and children died in the Cincinnati cholera epidemic of 1849, Jews among them, even though their mortality was the lowest in the city. Rumor had it that some Jewish patients in the city hospitals had been threatened with conversion. B'nai Yeshurun appointed a special committee to help Jews stricken with the cholera and the following year Hyman Moses, a very pious Jew and collector for Palestine, succeeded, with the help of devoted associates, in opening a modest Jewish hospice and hospital, the first Jewish institution of this type in the United States. Subscriptions and the proceeds of concerts and theatrical performances sustained the hospital until it received $5,000 through a bequest of Judah Touro. It was then able, in 1854, to erect a very substantial two-story building.[13]

The Charlestonians talked of establishing a hospital because of the frequent yellow fever attacks and in 1858 actually used the Hebrew Benevolent Society building as a temporary infirmary. During the epidemic of 1858 the children of the impoverished sick were looked after by a generous and kindly Christian woman and the grateful Hebrew Benevolent Society gave her an English Bible as a gift. The destructive Civil War put an end to all plans in that city for building a Jewish hospital. Chicago Jewry started collecting funds for a hospice and hospital in the late 1850's, but by that time the Jews of New Orleans had already established the Touro Infirmary. In 1852 Touro bought a large estate which he may have intended as a general hospital; by the terms of his will it became a Jewish infirmary in 1854 for needy Israelites. Other Jews were admitted on a fee basis and sick slaves, too, were accepted at commercial rates. Thus both the Cincinnati and New Orleans sanitaria were made possible through Touro's generosity.[14]

Touro's generosity was even more important for Jews' Hospital in New York. Of the three pre-Civil War Jewish institutions to shelter the sick the New York one was the last to open its doors. In 1850 a broadside of the Hebrew Benevolent Society had assured the public that a hospital was about to be established; a conference the following year of four local charities was equally fruitless. Dr. Simeon Abrahams opened a free clinic for Jews in 1852 but it remained for Sampson Simson and his friends to effectuate all the talk by incorporating Jews' Hospital in the city of New York. Simson was by that time seventy-two years of age, a third-generation American, a native of Danbury, Connecticut, where his family had taken refuge during the Revolution. After graduating from Columbia in 1800 and delivering an oration in Hebrew—which he had not written— he studied law under Aaron Burr and was one of the first Jews in the state —if not the very first—to become an attorney. Since he had inherited money he retired very early to his estate at Yonkers. Simson was arbitrary, old-fashioned in his knee britches and buckles, a crotchety bachelor like Judah Touro, but much more of a personality than the New Orleans merchant. The New Yorker served as a captain of militia in his early days, revered Andrew Jackson, the aggressive democrat, and like the president was a man of very positive ideas. Unlike most of his contemporaries, he was sympathetic to Negroes. As a gentleman farmer he was very much interested in agriculture and farming machinery and was hopeful that Jews both in this country and in Palestine would ultimately turn to the soil. Simson was a Mason of high degree, a public-spirited citizen, a humanitarian concerned with prison reform, but above all a pious and philanthropic Jew eager to build a Jewish orphan asylum, a Jewish hospital, and a rabbinical college. He made generous gifts to Catholic and Protestant churches and helped the first Russian Jewish émigrés on the Lower East

Side establish a synagog of their own. This was the man who stepped in to spearhead the move for a Jewish hospital. He it was who gave the land on which it was built, secured funds from others, including a priest who made a very generous gift, and proceeded to erect a fine building when Touro's generous legacy of $20,000 assured the success of his project.

When Jews' Hospital was opened in 1856 it had forty-five beds occupied for the most part by impoverished peddlers and domestics. A few Gentiles were also admitted. As a Jewish public institution it had a kosher kitchen and a chapel with the traditional Ten Commandments over the ark. The large gift and memorial tablets alongside the ark completely overshadowed the two tables of the Law received by Moses on Sinai's heights. But the later governors of the hospital were not unmindful of Moses' contribution. When the hospital became more or less nonsectarian and state grants were sought the name "Jews" was dropped and "Mt. Sinai" was adopted. The first year's budget was $5,500; in 1972 the board set a goal of $152,000,000 for the hospital and its school of medicine; it already had $121,000,000 on hand.[15]

SUPPORT

Although Touro money built America's three Jewish hospitals, a constant major effort was required to keep the infirmaries open and to finance all the other charities. The literally hundreds of American Jewish societies, both permanent and ephemeral, had to be supported by subscriptions, gifts, legacies, concerts and theatricals, fees, fairs and sociables, strawberry festivals, raffles, and bazaars. The articles sold at fairs and the liquors dispensed at sociables were donated. Large sums of money were raised at dinners and balls: Purim masquerade balls were often grandiose glamorous affairs. Substantial sums had to be raised because expenditures were heavy. The Hebrew Benevolent Society of New York City received about 2,000 applications for help during the 1857-1858 panic and gave out about $3,500. Some organizations raised money in order to share it with other more necessitous groups. Clubs and literary societies, men's and women's associations, allocated funds to their favorite charities, the Jewish Hospital, a funeral society, an organization to educate the children of the indigent, and the like.[16]

By the early 1840's it had become evident that money-raising was a big business and required joint efforts. In some of the larger cities the disparate eleemosynary groups united in their appeals for contributions. If Jews bragged—and they did—that a Jewish beggar was a phenomenon on the streets of the city, they still had to keep the beggars happy. The Hebrew Charity Ball Association reflecting a joint effort of various elements in Philadelphia collected substantial sums through balls and dinners. For humanitarian, political, and business reasons prominent Christians and great corporations made liberal grants. Adams Express and Anthony Drexel sent in their checks; even the alienated Jew August Belmont made a donation. Ex Vice President Alexander Dallas graced one of these affairs and Benjamin H. Brewster, later an attorney general in Washington, after proclaiming with lofty eloquence that "We are mingled together as one brotherhood in a sacred common cause," stooped to conquer: "I am a Goy, believe me, gentleman, still I am cosher." All this was reported literally in the daily press of 1854. The Jews loved it.[17]

These formal balls were gargantuan affairs. In New York the revelers enjoyed assembling at Niblo's saloon, a fashionable eating place. The organizations vied with one another in the sumptuousness of their repasts and the amounts they raised as they assembled in the early evening and remained until the first rays of dawn. The food was indeed lavish; at one dinner nine different types of hot meats, five desserts exclusive of fruits and nuts, and six different kinds of wine to say nothing of gin were offered. The toasts were many: to the society, to charity, to religious liberty, to the governor of the state, to the Jewish martyrs of Damascus, and of course to women. "Woman! What can man say of her when God deemed Paradise unfinished until she smiled amidst the bowers." At a banquet during the Mexican War, the Charlestonians raised high their glasses to Southern chivalry, to our Palmetto banner, and to the president of the United States. In the next decade as the irrepressible conflict neared they omitted the toast to President Buchanan. At midnight, after a 11:00 o'clock dinner, the guests were harangued by distinguished orators and eloquent rabbis on the virtues of benevolence and generous giving. Gorged with food, anesthetized by drink, the Jewish merchants found the extractive process completely painless. If it failed the sponsors could always resort to the bludgeoning technique: Rabbi Raphall called out the names of the solid citizens and asked them pointblank for their donations.[18]

UNITY-COMMUNITY?

In one sense these elaborate joint balls and dinners represented a desire on the part of the Jews to "take care of their own." There was still another reason; they feared Gentile public opinion if they were remiss in making provision for disadvantaged Jews. Were Jews more charitable than their Gentile neighbors? Very probably. The new united action in fund-raising reflected a realization that conditions in the social welfare area were verging on the chaotic, at least from a business point of view. Overlapping, waste, inefficiency were common; there was an urgent need for a better administration of public monies. There was a pressing if not clamorous demand for community-wide systematic control of the philanthropies and their operations. If critical contributors had been conscious of the connotation of the adjective "scientific," they would have employed it.

As early as the 1820's the Philadelphians began to use the word "united" to express the need for *communal* beneficences, and by the 1830's the word and concept had been adopted in Baltimore and in New York. By 1832 the New Yorkers had brought three congregations together to make a joint appeal on behalf of Palestine. "Communal" organizations made progress in the decade of the 1840's as congregations and societies began to work together and as joint appeals for funds were heard in Philadelphia and in New York. There was even talk of mergers. The fifties was an important decade in this drive toward "community" in the area of Jewish social welfare. As early as 1849 Leeser had pointed out clearly and succinctly that the current system of distributing charity was wrong in principle and that a union of all fund-raising ought to be effected and put under the control of a central board. The trend was patent in New York, Philadelphia, Cincinnati, Chicago, and probably in other towns too. The Bachelor's Hebrew Benevolent Loan Association of New York hoped that the day would come when the adjectives Portuguese, German, and Polish would disappear and all Jews would live as one large family. Societies began to merge in the effort to create one central Jewish relief agency. Intelligent socially-minded Jews of that generation were, unwittingly at least, working toward a federation of all charities; it is even possible—but this is moot—that unconsciously at least they were headed toward a unified local Jewish "community."

The B'nai B'rith of the 1850's was in the van of the movement toward unity and community. Very early the Order began to think in communal rather than in particularistic and societal terms. Members wanted eleemosynary help of a sound nature; they spoke of uniting all Jews; they began to think nationally. Conceiving of American Jewry as a whole they were eager to protect Jews politically, to deemphasize European ethnic backgrounds, and to further Jewry culturally, morally, ethically, and even religiously. The lodges realized that action would have to be taken on many fronts to acculturate Jews, to tie them together, and to elevate them spiritually.[19]

CHAPTER ELEVEN

JEWISH EDUCATION, CULTURE, AND SOCIAL LIFE,

1840–1860

JEWISH EDUCATION

E ven as religion and social welfare were tied together, so too were religion, social welfare, and culture all of one piece. The B'nai B'-
rith, a mutual-aid lodge, established the Maimonides Library, and congregations and special welfare societies assumed responsibility for the
education of the children of the poor. Underprivileged children were educated till thirteen and then apprenticed; the bright ones were helped to a
good education. Among Jews education was the responsibility of the parents; the community assumed no obligations except for those children
without a parent or without means. Jewish communal education in Germany and England and America was largely motivated by the desire to
educate the children of the poor. The first American Jewish all-day
schools in the eighteenth and early nineteenth centuries, though congregationally sponsored, were tuition schools, free only to the impoverished.
Similarly many of the first tax-supported public schools in colonial and
early national America were "charity" schools. There were no free all-day
Hebrew and English schools in mid-nineteenth century Jewish America.[1]

Prior to the late 1830's there was in reality no Jewish communal education in either Judaism or the secular subjects for the generality of the
children. The children of Central European immigrants were taught Hebrew by private teachers, or they attended an afternoon Hebrew pay
school till they were bar mitzvah. For their secular education most of
them turned to the common schools, such as they were. Although most
immigrants were resigned to educating their children in the Christianized
public schools, many, though a minority, were not happy. The very religious wanted to indoctrinate their sons and daughters Jewishly, religiously, and prepare them to live traditional lives. Even the less religious
feared the assimilatory influence of the common schools which were in
effect Protestant nondenominational institutions. The Orthodox believed

that their children would survive as Jews only if they attended all-day schools under Jewish auspices. Therefore, following an emerging pattern of all-day schools in Western Europe and an old American Jewish tradition, the newcomers began to set up "parochial" schools. All-day schools as such were nothing new in this country; the various Christian denominations had parochial schools of their own since the earliest colonial times. About the year 1830 an early school of this type was established by Congregation Anshe Chesed in New York City.[2]

The Anshe Chesed Students of the Torah (Lomde Torah) School was a congregational not a communal institution, which was practically impossible to establish in pre-Civil War America. In 1835 Leeser tried to set up a Hebrew and English school for boys in Philadelphia. It was not free because someone had to pay the teachers. Yet in a truly Jacksonian democratic sense Leeser wanted an institution for rich and poor and even for Christians. It failed, as did an attempt in 1841 when Leeser and his associates sought to set up a national system of all-day schools for boys and girls. Leeser was also closely associated with those Philadelphians who founded the Hebrew Education Society in 1851. This was communally supported—one of the very few in that generation—but to a large extent it, too, was a metropolitan charity school. An attempt to unite the two all-day congregational schools in Cincinnati made little progress. In town after town efforts to bring all groups together to support city-wide Hebrew-English schools were continually hampered by internal conflict both ethnic and religious and by the growing split between the Orthodox and Reform. A San Francisco rabbi-educator waxed sarcastic as he inveighed against Orthodox Hebrew grammar and kosher geography.[3]

Without any real sense of communal responsibility in the field of education, congregations began to create their own all-day schools in the 1840's and 1850's to provide for the children of the new German immigrants. Anyone from any congregation was admitted who could pay the fees; only the poor were given special consideration. These new schools were patronized by immigrants who had already begun to mount the economic ladder and had some means at their disposal. Almost every Jewish town of size in the United States had at least one all-day school in the 1850's. The larger cities had several. Lilienthal as chief rabbi of three German congregations in New York City succeeded for a very brief period in the late 1840's in forging a Hebrew Union School supported by separate Hebrew Union School Societies. New York City in 1854 had at least seven Jewish denominational schools with a larger total enrollment than all the city's Protestant institutions. Even tiny Scranton had an all-day school. The Hebrew Education Society of Philadelphia with a secondary school in view hoped that Jews throughout the land would rally to its aid financially. Although there were Hebrew-English schools as late as the 1870's most of them died before the Civil War except in the South and West. When the Confederacy was crushed in 1865 and Jews moved in and up to fortify the middle class, schools were necessary. The South of Reconstruction days had few good educational institutions and when enterprising Jews provided them Christian children were glad to attend. Good Jewish places of instruction dotted the South, the New Southwest, and the Far West as late as the 1880's. Since the Jewish courses were not compulsory for the Christians they remained away on Saturday and Sunday when Jewish subjects were often taught. There were postbellum Jewish parochial schools in the following towns of the South and West: Memphis, Mobile, Shreveport, New Orleans, Pine Bluff, Dallas, Chicago, Portland, Oregon, and San Bernardino. More than half of the pupils in the Pine Bluff school of the late 1860's were Christians.[4]

With exceedingly few exceptions these schools were limited to the elementary grades and were directed by the rabbi or hazzan. Congregational financing was rarely adequate. Thus in effect the schools were semi-private institutions, frequently an enterprise of the local religious factotum in his effort to augment his meager salary. Supported by fees, subscriptions, congregational subsidies, and the sums raised at annual suppers or contributed by special Jewish charity organizations, these schools managed to stagger along for a few years. Touro's legacies helped some of them to survive and even to erect school buildings of their own instead of remaining underground in the vestry rooms.[5]

ROUTINE, CURRICULUM, TEXTBOOKS

For most pupils learning had to be acquired by the age of thirteen. The schools varied considerably. In a few schools the children met together in a daily assembly, listened to a Bible reading in English, took final exams, and were rewarded with an annual picnic and excursion. Some schools had their own banners. A serious effort was often made to conduct the educational institutions along modern lines: Pestalozzi was not an unfamiliar name to the rabbis. In principle corporal punishment was forbidden. As in the church parochial schools the Jewish children were taught the three "r's," often by Gentile teachers; the girls were given additional instruction in needlework and drawing. Efforts were made to teach the classical and modern languages, science, history, music, and bookkeeping. One of the instructors in the Hebrew Education Society school in Philadelphia was the English-born Michael Heilprin, later to distinguish himself as an editor of the *New American Cyclopaedia*.

Nearly all the Jewish schools taught German; it was as sacrosanct for the newcomers of this generation as Portuguese had been for the first Sephardim and as Yiddish was to be for the East Europeans. Apparently

some afternoon Hebrew schools also taught German and it is quite probable that a few of the congregational institutions made that language the
medium of instruction rather than English. For the immigrants themselves the mother tongue was all important. They held on to German ten-
aciously in the home, in their newspapers, their lodges, their clubs, and
their synagogs. Some of them never were to master English completely;
sermons in German were still heard in acculturated Reform temples as
late as the twentieth century. Central European Jews of the mid-nineteenth century were oriented to the Fatherland culturally as Anglo-Saxon
America was to England. Even Isaac M. Wise, no German cultural nationalist like many of his confreres, had a contempt for certain aspects of
American life:

It appears to some observers that the nation which chews tobacco, drinks whiskey
as a common beverage, swears most unenlightened, bets on elections, horses,
fighting-men, dogs and cocks, has so many and so wellfilled jails,penitentiaries,
gambling houses, brothels and other low dens, is none too enlightened.

JEWISH SUBJECTS, BAR MITZVAH, CONFIRMATION

In all probability less time was devoted to the Jewish subjects than to the
secular program. Biblical and postbiblical history to the rise of Christianity was taught in catechetical and narrative works; later Jewish history
was usually ignored. The rituals, ceremonies, laying of phylacteries—all
this was taught, and in the catechisms that were conned ethical monotheism was stressed and the Maimonides creed and the Decalogue were
memorized. The emphasis on doctrine and on the Decalogue reflected
Protestant influence since traditional Judaism had never laid great stress
on dogma or the Ten Commandments. Jews were concerned, however,
that the children learn Hebrew, be able to lead in services, understand the
prayerbook, and if possible translate portions of the Pentateuch. Grammar
was taught scientifically. A number of institutions boasted that they intended to teach Talmud, rabbinics, and the Shulhan Arukh, the standard
code. One teacher was reported to be conversing with his students in Hebrew, but this was probably American brag. If the typical student could
not translate Hebrew, he could at least read it mechanically and thus
crown his efforts by a public bar mitzvah ceremony. Most students who
read their Hebrew portions in the synagog at thirteen were prepared by
private tutors; they were not graduates of the all-day schools.[7]

Protestant influence as well as German Jewish Reform traditions
were reflected in the adoption of the confirmation ceremony. The
Charleston Reformed Israelites had introduced it in the 1820's in this
country; the Philadelphia Orthodox of 1841 had their own manual, and
Lilienthal in 1846 attempted to popularize this ceremony in the tradi-

tional New York German synagogs where he reigned as chief rabbi. A Cincinnati Jewish clothing manufacturer who had begun his career as a peddler bequeathed money to Wise's B'nai Yeshurun to buy confirmation suits for the children of the poor.[8]

TEXTBOOKS

Hebrew "readers" were prepared and published here; books of prayers and meditations made their appearance, and the Hebrew Bible and Leeser's English translation were welcomed in school and home. Despite the fact that most Jewish school superintendents were rooted in European and German culture many of them realized the need for English textbooks; it was during the period from 1840 to 1860 that a number of English elementary school books appeared on the market. Practically all of them, like those that were published in the 1830's, were borrowed from England or translated and excerpted from the German or the French. Yet though there was no originality here the American Jewish textbook was one of the most significant aspects of American Jewish education. There was a need for the thousands of children and the need was met. These works in catechism or dialogue form, for the most part, were practically all traditional in theology. One work, Dr. Samuel Adler's Reform guide, was exceptional; it omitted the Maimonidian credo and emphasized the Mission of Israel, affirming the place of the Jew in the Diaspora. Simha Peixotto's Bible history betrayed its dependence on a similar work of the Christian American Sunday School Union:

Who tempted Adam to sin? Eve!!

In one of the later editions of her book there were 175 pages of these questions and answers and the smarter or more diligent children probably memorized every page. This was typical antebellum American religious education at its best—or its worst. Samuel Hirsch and David Einhorn also published catechisms, in German, in Philadelphia. Because of untrained teachers and ponderous tedious textbooks that took little notice of the child's vocabulary, the instructions and accomplishments left much to be desired. A few writers, however, made every effort to reach the children; their works and their books are quite good. Discipline in the Jewish schools was always a problem. Isaac M. Wise once wrote the president of his Albany congregation that keeping order with a rod made him physically ill. Yet with all its drawbacks the Jewish parochial school instilled a sense of loyalty to Judaism in the pupils along with the capacity to dash off the Hebrew prayers. This satisfied most parents.[9]

Types of Schools

JEWS AND THE RISE OF THE PUBLIC SCHOOL

Although a number of the Hebrew-English schools of the 1840's were certainly better than the common schools of the time, the Jewish schools were doomed. The future lay with the 80,000 public schools. There were two schools of thought about public education among the Jews. Most of the rabbis, particularly those who were centrist or right of center religiously, worried that the children were exposed to prejudices in personal relations and in ideology in the common schools; Jewish instruction in the parochial schools was necessary for the survival of Judaism. Other Jews were protagonists of the public schools; led by the Forty-Eighter, Isidor Bush, they pointed out that there were Jews who were not interested in a religious education for the children, that the public schools were more republican, and that sectarian institutions made for separatism and prejudice. They insisted in the 1850's that the public schools were better equipped, more conveniently located, and cheaper. To ask people to support two school systems would not only be double taxation but would mean less money for each; consequently both types of schools would be bad. The parochial school was a pay school; the public school was a free school to which one went as of right. Religious instruction? Put your money on the afternoon and weekend schools and on a good seminary and Judaism will come out ahead.[10]

Actually the Jewish Hebrew-English school was a transitional phenomenon, an immigrant institution bridging the gap between Europe and America. By 1855 these schools began to disappear in New York City and other metropolitan centers because the improved public schools were well on the road to secularization. In order to stop the advance of the Catholic parochial school movement the Protestants were reluctantly compelled to make the common school nonsectarian. Most Jews went along with the Protestants. By 1860 the immigrants who had been here for almost a generation were "American." They wanted integration, not "separation." As thrifty Germans they chose the cheaper system and ignored the reproach that they were reconciled to Jewish "mental pauperism." As natives the Jewish youngsters preferred the common school whose diploma served as a passport to institutions of secondary instruction. Because the public schools were deemed typically "American" the Jews, fearful of the recriminations of the chauvinistic Know-Nothings, also began to look askance at the Catholic all-day schools. Proud of their American nationalism the Jews were ready to close their own separatist all-day schools. When the cards were down the Catholics decided that religion was of paramount importance to them; the Jews opted for secular education.[11]

PRIVATE SCHOOLS

The line of division between congregational and private all-day schools was at times almost invisible. Though some of the private schools lost their justification with the rise of better public school systems many of them survived and others were established during the pre-Civil War period. It would seem that in a few instances Jews were not welcomed into Gentile private schools. Whatever the motivation this prejudice was a harbinger of a trend that was to become very patent in the later years of the century. On the other hand some Gentile owners of educational establishments were so eager to attract Jewish custom that they offered courses in Hebrew taught by Jews. Some of the Jewish private schools survived for decades, one even into the twentieth century. With the passing of time a number of them tended to deemphasize or eliminate the Hebrew courses and their Jewish identification. On the whole these private enterprises were well-conducted and of high quality and were attractive to some wealthy Jews who insisted on excellent instruction and preferred Jewish surroundings. This was particularly true of the small-town merchants who wanted their children, boys and girls, to identify with Jews and ancestral traditions. Thus many of the private schools of the day were boarding as well as day schools.

Private schools which existed coevally with those sponsored by congregations were relatively numerous by the time of the Civil War. There were about ten in New York City alone, and neighboring Yonkers could even boast of a Jewish military establishment in 1860. There was a line of schools extending from Boston, New Haven, New York, and Baltimore west to Cincinnati, Louisville, Chicago, and San Francisco. Some of them were limited to boys only, others to girls, many were coeducational; the courses were either classical or commercial. The Jewish curriculum differed little from that offered in the congregational schools although there seems to have been less exposure to Jewish subjects. In secular studies more emphasis was laid on music, dancing, fine arts, chemistry, astronomy, and even Hebrew-German writing. Was this German in the Hebrew script? The Palache School for Girls began to emphasize German as the newcomers became affluent enough to afford these private institutions. Isaac Harby conducted a private school in New York City for a few brief months in 1828.[13]

SCHOOLS FOR WOMEN, CHILDREN, AND LITTLE ONES

The Palaches established the first girls school in 1840 appealing originally, so it would seem, to natives and other Americanized Jews. Women were beginning to come into their own not only in the larger world but among Jews, too. The Sephardim had set up a girls school in London as

early as 1730, and girls and boys were studying together in Shearith Israel
in New York City no later than the 1790's. From then on girls were always represented substantially in the all-day schools. Young James K.
Gutheim who had just come over from Germany insisted that women be
educated because it was they who determined the nature of the home.
Rabbi Wise put them into his choir in 1846 in Albany and when he
opened his Reformist synagog in 1850 he introduced the family pew. In
an age when women were first being permitted to attend college with
men, Leeser urged the establishment of an academy where they, too,
could be trained to become teachers in Jewish schools. Yet the educational status of the typical Jewish woman was not particularly high.
When she did go to school, she learned reading, writing, and ciphering;
in addition she was given some music, drawing, French, and taught to
read Hebrew, by rote of course. But it is well to bear in mind that most
Americans of the time showed little enthusiasm for the education of
women. I. J. Benjamin who traveled throughout the United States in
1860 found that the religious education of Jewish girls was generally neglected, and Rabbi Morris J. Raphall published *Ruhamah, Devotional Exercises for the Use of the Daughters of Israel*, most of whom, he wrote, had little
schooling.[14]

Raphall's *Ruhamah*, (The Compassionate One, Hosea 1:6-8), published in 1852, was based largely on similar Jewish works which had appeared in Central Europe. This book documents his interest in the spiritual welfare of women. Rabbi Julius Eckman of San Francisco was
concerned with the education of young children. About the year 1854 he
established a private school which he called Heftsi-Vah, My Delight is in
Her (Isa. 62:4). Tuition was free for those who could not pay. After a
number of years he was compelled to close his doors despite his self-
sacrificial efforts to keep the school alive. It was a child-centered school
with a junior congregation holding services of its own and reciting English prayers especially prepared for it. Heftsi-Vah which included a class
for three-to-five-year old children was not the only Jewish school in the
country that admitted children of pre-elementary age. At a public examination in 1843 of the "scholars" of Miss Palache's Academy, as it was
called, a four-year-old girl repeated the entire Decalogue by heart in Hebrew, though it is very much to be doubted whether she knew what she
was reciting. The Talmud Yelodim Institute in Cincinnati had a class for
"infants" in 1861, and Jews in England were already teaching two-to-
five-year-olds in 1841. All this happened long before the Jew, Mrs. Carl
Schurz, and her associates opened a German kindergarten in Watertown,
Wisconsin, in the 1850's.[15]

Max Lilienthal, who ran one of the best Jewish private schools in
New York City from 1849 to 1855, did not admit anyone much younger

than seven. He was an excellent educator fully aware of the value of visual aids, a Ph.D. from Munich, and a good administrator. He had acquired a great deal of educational experience as director of the Jewish school in Riga to which he had been invited by the Russian authorities. Having gained the good will and respect of S. Uvarov, the Russian minister of education, he was entrusted with the delicate task of establishing state-supported modern Jewish schools in the Pale of Settlement. The Russian masses fought his proposals bitterly, convinced that he was a tool of the Czarists whose ultimate goal was to assimilate the Jews and speed up their conversion to Christianity. Apparently Lilienthal, too, began to suspect the motives of the Russians for he left the country and immigrated to the United States where he arrived in 1845. In New York City he served the three Orthodox German congregations and conducted their schools, but finally despairing of their acceptance of his leadership, he opened his own educational institution in 1849.

Major Noah who had entrusted Lilienthal with a son of his was an ardent admirer of the rabbi and his school. At all events he wrote a most glowing account of Lilienthal's Hebrew, Commercial and Classical Boarding School which sheltered students from as far south as New Orleans and sought others from the West Indies and the Pacific Coast. Puff or no puff it was from all indications a fine institution where the ancient classics were taught, French and German were spoken, and the students acquired a modest facility in translating biblical Hebrew. In 1855 Lilienthal was called to Cincinnati and there continued his educational activity at Congregation B'nai Israel. His charm, culture, and competence brought him many honors. As a respected and influential civic leader he fought vigorously to keep sectarian religious teachings out of the public schools. Wise and Lilienthal were the two Jewish religious leaders of Cincinnati, and despite Wise's eminence, Lilienthal played an important role in the life of the community, still one of the largest Jewries in the country. He distinguished himself as an associate editor of the *Israelite* and as an editor of one of America's first Jewish child's magazine, *The Sabbath School Visitor*. Wise saw to it that Lilienthal became a member of the faculty of the Hebrew Union College where he taught history and Jewish literature. In the 1880's shortly before his death he founded the *Hebrew Review*, the organ of the Rabbinical Literary Association of America which he had also helped to establish. He published a history of the ancient Israelites and a volume of German poems. He died in 1882 at the age of sixty-seven. Lilienthal was typical of the German Jewish intellectual elite who exercised a profound influence on the new American Jewish community that had begun to emerge in the 1840's.[16]

AFTERNOON SCHOOLS

The total number of those who attended Hebrew-English schools, congregational or private, could not have numbered more than a few thousand at most. Coeval with these all-day schools were others which made provision for the many more thousands of Jewish children; these were the afternoon, the week-end, and the Sunday Schools. Afternoon or evening schools, as they were often called, were nothing new and had been tried in this country since colonial days. In spite of the opposition of Leeser and others, afternoon schools sprang up everywhere in the effort to provide a type of Jewish education that would not conflict with public school instruction. Many were sponsored jointly by the congregation and the rabbi; the latter usually had a financial stake in the enterprise. The curriculum was completely Jewish, of course, and was usually taught by one man. Did these schools accomplish anything? Accomplishment is a relative term. As a rule American Jewish children were not interested in Hebrew, but they learned to read the magic words for bar mitzvah and at the age of thirteen emerged as full-fledged Jews religiously. Whether successful or not these afternoon schools were here to stay.[17]

WEEKEND AND SUNDAY SCHOOLS

Even the afternoon school with its emphasis on Hebrew rote reading was too much for the America-oriented child and parent. The children preferred the weekend and the Sunday Schools. Although the weekend school on Saturday and Sunday was almost invariably congregationally controlled it frequently admitted the children of non-members. Since, as a rule, no fees were required it was in effect a free communal school, one of the first Jewish efforts of this type in the United States. The Jewish curriculum was abbreviated and as the influence of Reform Judaism spread, more and more stress was laid upon materials written in the vernacular. But some children did learn to read Hebrew; one of the Cincinnati schools reported considerable progress in Hebrew writing and translation.

The majority of the Jewish children who did acquire some Jewish education went to the one-session Sunday morning school. This became —this still is—*the* Jewish religious school. Starting in the 1840's and 1850's the Jewish Sunday Schools appeared in towns all over the country becoming truly free communal institutions where every Jewish child could obtain a religious education, modest though it might be. The Baltimore Jewish Sunday School of 1856 thus became the first free Jewish school in that town. Unlike the Christian schools the Jewish schools were not united into a national association until the latter part of the century. The Christian American Sunday School Union embracing large numbers of schools had been welded together as early as 1824. Even though the Sunday School idea caught on among Jews because it was easy to set up, inexpensive, and typically American, it did have opposition. Some wealthy Jews thought that a communal school was an implicatory reproach that parents could not guide their children religiously; the poor suspected that it was a propagandistic Christian-like charity school, and others resented it because it held sessions on the Christian sabbath. Einhorn disliked it because women were the teachers and they knew no Hebrew. Thus they could no more understand Judaism than a blind man could understand color; women's theology would cripple the children spiritually.

History does have a way of repeating itself: In the 1830's Rebecca Gratz had pasted over the names Jesus and Christ in Christian catechisms and decades later Mary Prag in San Francisco was compelled to do the same. Jewish textbooks were not always available in the Far West in the days before the transcontinental railroad. Despite the ignorance of many of the women and lay teachers who knew only what was in the book, the children did learn something about Jewish history, doctrine, and morals. More important, they knew they were Jews. Children flocked to these schools. In 1859 Baltimore could number seventeen teachers and 300 children in its Sunday Schools. Not only did the youngsters survive as Jews, they found that being a Jew could be a pleasant experience. They enjoyed the pageants and plays, the final examination where they could show off what they knew, sing the hymns, repeat the Creed, recite poetry, declaim, and read essays on biblical characters. The lay teachers were often competent public school pedagogues and the children loved them. To cap it all there were always gifts, colored religious cards with Moses and the Ten Commandments, and wonderful excursions.[18]

SECONDARY SCHOOLS AND COLLEGES

The mass of Jews participated, but only to a limited extent, in the great democratic push toward education. There were thousands of Christian Sunday Schools and thousands of academies. The children of the immigrant Jews did flock to the public schools and even the Sunday Schools but not to the academies for most of them had to go out and make a living or help their parents. Attempts were made to establish Hebrew-English academies but not a single one maintained itself for any length of time. There were about 100 colleges in the United States in 1860; by that time the one Jewish college had risen and disappeared. At a very early stage in American Jewish life, certainly no later than the second decade of the nineteenth century, concerned Jews began to think in terms of higher education. They wanted knowledgeable Jews, American-trained to serve as religious leaders. Europeans would not do for the American scene. A later Jewish editor pointed out that rabbis trained under European conservative monarchies could not fit into free republican America. From 1818 on into the 1850's Jews of substance and intelligence agitated for a Jewish academy: Moses Elias Levy of Florida, Samuel Myers of Norfolk, Jacob S. Solis of Westchester, Mordecai Noah, and Rabbi S. M. Isaacs of New York City. In 1841 Leeser and his colleague Rabbi Louis Salomon hoped that American Jewry would rally around them and establish a national academy to train precentors, lecturers, and teachers. By 1849 the Hebrew Education Society of Philadelphia was chartered to open a "superior seminary of learning," and three years later Sampson Simson incorporated the Jewish Theological and Scientific Institution to perpetuate the "Orthodox Jewish faith." The Hebrew title of this proposed school of the Hebrew Education Society was Hinukh Nearim, Educating Youth, a name first adopted by New York's dissident Ashkenazim in 1825. Education was imperative. All these efforts were well-intentioned but led nowhere. Many talked; in the 1850's Wise set out to do something.

As early as 1848, in an appeal to the country, young Isaac M. Wise, only two years in the United States, had asked for the establishment of schools to prepare Jewish ministers and, after some fumbling, called the Zion Collegiate Association into being in September, 1854. The Association through auxiliary supporting societies in the larger cities was to help establish a Jewish university with four undergraduate colleges. A theological faculty was to prepare men for the ministry and for teaching. As an American cultural nationalist Wise wanted ministers who could train their people for American citizenship. The school, he said, was to be a monument to Jewish learning and enlightenment. During the winter season the professors were to travel about and lecture after the fashion of the lyceum circuit riders. Zion College opened in November, 1855, with fourteen students, two of whom were Christians. It was closed by June, 1856, because the Association members began to withdraw their support. They resented the fact that the school was established in Cincinnati and it may well be that Wise had promised to establish a branch of the university in New York. Some of the Jews suspected Wise's Orthodoxy and it is worthy of note that Simson's Orthodox seminary made an appeal for financial help in 1854 only after Wise had announced his intention to open Zion College. Zion failed for lack of funds. Mayhap the 100,000 American Jews could not or would not support a college. There were even some who did not want a separatistic Jewish academic institution. Undeterred by Zion's failure, Wise kept talking of opening a new school but the Civil War intervened; it was not until 1875 that he established a college that was destined to survive.[19]

SIMON TUSKA

In 1858 Wise was talking of educating a young man here in the secular schools and in a Jewish preparatory academy and then dispatching him to Europe for rabbinical training. Partly under the influence of Wise, one young man, Simon Tuska, son of the Rochester rabbi, went to the Breslau Seminary to prepare for the American rabbinate. The idea of sending an American boy abroad to study was not a new one; the Charleston Reformers thought of it very seriously and even looked for a likely candidate. Dr. Daniel L. M. Peixotto pursued a similar idea in an address he made in 1838. Apparently Tuska was the first graduate of an American college to attend a rabbinical seminary abroad (1858). Though he did not complete his studies, he returned to the United States and became the rabbi of Memphis where he served until his death in the year 1871 when he was about thirty-six years of age. Even before he set out for Breslau, when only a youth of nineteen or twenty, he had already published a very interesting booklet describing Judaism, its rites, ceremonies, and creed. It was probably written to enlighten curious Christians for he called it *The Stranger in the Synagogue*.[20]

YOUTH AND THE YMHA

Because the Jewish youth of the 1840's and 1850's had to go to work, they built and filled no Jewish academies or colleges. Yet theirs was an age of cultural striving enlivened by thousands of lyceum associations. Eager to improve themselves culturally and morally Jews, like other Americans, joined the lyceums. On one occasion—there may have been others —Jews were rejected by a local cultural society, the Henry Clay Lyceum of Baltimore. That was in 1856. Nothing daunted a Jewish Henry Clay Literary Society made its appearance in Chicago three years later. Thus like other ethnic groups young Jews and adults also began to establish literary societies of their own. The Jewish youngsters spread their wings as early as 1818 when they tried unsuccessfully to secure permission from Shearith Israel to organize a boys and girls choir. The young folks of Bnai Jeshurun were more successful. By 1830 a Jewish Literary Society was fashioned in London, 1837 in Germany, and during the next decade, as the immigrants began to arrive here in numbers, societies of young Jews were established in all parts of this land. In 1841 there was one in New York and one in Philadelphia. As the younger generation found itself it went off on its own, philanthropically, by establishing fuel and loan associations offering aid in this case to adults, not youths. Junior societies embracing youngsters from thirteen to about eighteen also began to make their appearance. In one somewhat unusual instance a literary society—the Alexandria, Virginia, Literary Society—was the pioneer Jewish organization in the community. In the large towns where there were adequate reservoirs of young people they divided and organized themselves, on occasion, according to their geographical provenance, just like their parents in the synagogs and charities—as natives, Germans, Poles. Wise's Zion Collegiate Association was set up as a national union of literary societies although the astute rabbi had his mind on the money it could provide to maintain his projected college.[21]

Was the creation of these societies a youth movement? The answer is no and yes. No, in the sense that these young people were dedicated to the bourgeois ideals of papa and mama; yes, in the sense that these youngsters, mostly in their late teens or early twenties, were totally American in their outlook. Culturally there was a gap between them and their parents. The older folks loved German; the young ones, English. The nature of their involvement is difficult to determine. Were they sympathetic to the growing nationalism, republicanism, democratic idealism of the young Americans advocated by that brilliant Jewish assimilationist, Edwin De Leon of South Carolina? Some of them certainly were infected with the post-1848 European and American cosmopolitanism, skepticism, reformism, and primitivism. Ideology, literature—whatever the announced purpose—was not really the principal motivation for their coming together. They wanted to be by themselves. Caught between the world of their parents and the New World on the western shores of the Atlantic, they created a world of their very own.[22]

In some towns the local youth society was known as the Young Men's Hebrew Association (YMHA). Those who adopted this name may have borrowed it from the Young Men's Christian Association; the YMCA was organized in 1851 and the first YMHA made its appearance in Baltimore three years later. Actually as early as the 1840's, before the formal establishment of the national YMCA, Jews had already begun to use the individual words young, men's, Hebrew, and association in longer titles, as for instance, the Young Men's Hebrew Benevolent Fuel Association. The adoption of the name YMHA in the 1850's is a form of superficial acculturation; its use may have been truly fortuitous. The Augusta, Georgia, YMHA of 1857 was not a literary society but a social welfare group organized by young, probably unmarried, clerks to take care of their own sick and impoverished. It was the first Jewish organization in town. A YMHA or Young Men's Hebrew Literary Association might well be a multi-purpose group. The Davenport-Rock Island YMHA of 1857 also conducted religious services, but this was exceptional. There was really little similarity between the YMCA and the YMHA of the 1850's. The Christian organization was essentially religious in origin although it embraced the social; the Jewish groups were social, leisure, secular, literary, and moralistic but definitely not religious. The wide variety of names adopted by individual youth groups sometimes reflects different degrees of acculturation or assimilation. The Judaists, admiring intellectuals and philanthropists, borrowed the names of Mendelssohn, Montefiore, and Touro; the Americanists liked Henry Clay or Daniel Webster, both of whom had just died in 1852, and of course there was bound to be a Washington Literary Society. The neutralists took refuge in titles like the Young Men's Mercantile Library Association or the Union Debating Society.

Most of the Y's were small in membership. Thirty was about average although the Zion Collegiate Association base branch in Cincinnati boasted of 200 subscribers. A few societies had their own building, all had well-equipped reading rooms with books and newspapers and were open nights and weekends. Although it is not always easy to distinguish the older from the younger groups it would seem that many of these societies, if not the majority, were young men's, rather than adults' associations. Women were invited to the open meetings and to the dances and balls where funds were raised for the Jewish charities. Jewish organizations of those decades, whatever their stated goals, rarely lost an opportunity to dance or to eat.[23]

PROGRAMS AND ACHIEVEMENTS

Despite the balls and dances they gave, these young men's associations were ostensibly literary. They insisted that they wished to further the literary fame of the Jewish people, that they were devoted to literature and the fine arts, that they wished to encourage culture and intellectuality. Their Jewish programs were on the whole minimal; some societies taught Hebrew and listened to an occasional lecture on Judaism and the Old Testament. Stress was on a general secular program; there were talks often by experts on almost any conceivable topic from the credit system to the statues of Rome. Reflecting the generation's interest in reform there were often debates on questions like the status of women or the abolition of slavery. Were the associations effective? Did they reach the goals they had set? They spoke of themselves as Young Israel but they were in no sense cultural revolutionaries and achievers. Leeser had hoped that they would bring positive changes into an American Jewish cultural life but little worthwhile was accomplished in that area. To be sure the young folks were serious and discouraged cards and gambling in their reading rooms. One suspects, however, that the social aspects of their programs were very important to them. They produced nothing of any significance, but the discussions under Jewish auspices did constitute a learning experience; something cultural certainly rubbed off on the members. Unfortunately this "youth movement" died when the youths became adults and married, but the next generation would see new youth organizations, new goals, and cherished togetherness.[24]

ADULT JEWISH EDUCATION AND JEWISH LITERATURE

The YMHA's and cognate groups were part of a total approach to Jewish education that was always the concern of the perceptive Jews of the pre-War generation. The Jewish religious court that Lilienthal and Wise envisaged in the 1840's had in view the publication of a basic manual of Judaism to enlighten, mold, and unite the Jews of the country. Colonial Americans had always emphasized the importance of Hebrew; Jews had been teaching the Holy Tongue in Christian seminaries for a generation and classes in advanced Hebrew were advocated in the synagogs of antebellum America. Some New Yorkers and Philadelphians even nursed the hope that Hebrew might be taught in the public schools of the 1850's. The Central European immigrants of the 1830's on brought with them the Hebraic tradition of their homelands and reenforced the small band of Hebraists who had been present in this country ever since the seventeenth century. In the years from 1840 to 1860 competent Hebraists were far more numerous than is generally known. It would not be difficult to make a list of at least two dozen men who were Talmudists and rabbinic scholars. A few of them possessed excellent Hebrew libraries. While still in New York City Lilienthal taught a class in the Talmud and read a medieval ethical classic with his students; Abraham Joseph Ash of New York guided students in the Talmud and answered queries in rabbinic law; Joseph Levy was eager to open a traditional rabbinic college (yeshivah) in Cleveland; Jacob Mordecai Netter wrote Hebrew poetry; an obscure merchant in Columbia, Tennessee, President Polk's town, pursued advanced Hebrew studies, and Samuel Adler of prestigious Emanu-El volunteered to teach Talmud to those evincing an interest.

Despite the fact that there was a sprinkling of well-educated Hebraists in almost every part of the country, and even a Russo-Jewish bet hamidrash (house of learning) in distant San Francisco, only one Hebrew rabbinic work was published during this period. This was the *Avne Yehoshua* (The Stones of Joshua), a commentary on the mishnaic ethical tractate of the *Fathers* which appeared in print in New York City in 1860. The author Joshua Falk, a Pole, had come to the states in 1854 already a man of fifty-five. After serving for a time as rabbi in Newburgh and Poughkeepsie he started his wanderings as an itinerant preacher. On his death in 1864 in Keokuk, Iowa—a peddling center—he left behind some unpublished Hebrew manuscripts on legal and religiophilosophical themes. Because of the *Avne Yehoshua* he is sometimes referred to as The Father of American Hebrew Literature. Thus it took a little over 200 years after the first Jewish community was founded in New Amsterdam-New York before American Jewry produced a Hebrew book, one written by a professing Jew. The United States was still on the frontier of Jewish culture and it was to remain there for at least another thirty years. With one or two exceptions, no scholarly Jewish works even in the vernacular were written in antebellum America.[25]

VERNACULAR LITERATURE

The typical American Israelite was not particularly interested in learning to translate the Hebrew prayers or the original of the Old Testament. He was content that he could read the magic Hebrew words for he was busy, very busy, trying to keep his head above water. Determined to educate his children Jewishly, he did not disdain improving himself Jewishly as well through readings in the German and English vernacular. This desire for more Jewish knowledge was even more true of his children, many of whom had been born in this country. As a result of the emancipatory spirit that followed in the wake of the French Revolution a new Jewish literature in German and in English had sprung up in Europe. This was part of the initiation of the Jew into the modern cultural world, an aspect of his desire to know more, a yearning that was to continue on these shores. The many Jews who joined the Jewish literary societies, clubs, lodges, and synagogs could not escape the flood of sermons and lectures which poured down upon them. A new literature, mostly in English, began to appear in the middle of the century.

What is this new American Jewish literature? It was anything but world shaking; there were no Jewish Prescotts, Emersons, Poes, Melvilles, Longfellows, Lowells, Parkmans, Hawthornes, Thoreaus, or Whitmans. But by 1860 after they had grown 1,000 percent in size Jews did need "food for the road." On the whole they continued to produce literature much like that of the pre-1840 days, borrowing, reprinting, or translating what their European confreres had already written. Much of it, almost all of it, was religious in nature. The mass was substantial. Leeser alone wrote, sponsored, or published about 150 different items. On entering a Jewish library in any large city the curious reader would find textbooks for the schools, prayer books in English and German, sermons, volumes of hymns, devotional literature for men, women, and children, Hebrew readers and grammars, almanacs for the Jewish year, volumes of rabbinical folklore, a pocket edition of apothegms, a geography of Palestine, and histories which threatened to carry the story down to the present day but stopped with the fall of Jerusalem in Roman times. There were books on the Jewish ceremonies and the life-cycle rites, a Hebrew Bible, an American Jewish translation of the Holy Scriptures; there was a work on the Lost Ten Tribes, a translation of Mendelssohn's *Jerusalem*, a work on Islamic and Jewish folklore, volumes of apologetics, polemics, and pleas for political equality. The printing presses of Jews and non-Jews were busy turning out congregational and societal constitutions, appeals for funds, dedication programs, and proceedings of meetings called to protest the abduction of Edgar Mortara and other issues of Jewish concern.

By the 1850's there was a very modest beginning in the field of pure literature, belles lettres. Adah Isaacs Menken moored in Cincinnati by the depression began publishing her poems in the *Israelite*. Penina Moïse continued for still another generation to write poetry and she was joined by another Charlestonian, Octavia Harby Moses, a daughter of Isaac Harby. Octavia Harby found time to compose her verses between giving birth to seventeen children. During the Civil War she sent five sons into the army one of whom was only fourteen and one of whom was shot down after he had surrendered. She wrote beautiful sensitive poetry as did her northern contemporary Rebekah Hyneman, daughter of a Jewish father and a Gentile mother, but a devoted Jewish religionist. Rebekah's son, Elias Leon Hyneman, a brave soldier in the Union Army, was captured by the Confederates and died of starvation in Andersonville Prison. As the Jewish newspapers began to appear in the 1850's, the editors and their friends dashed off potboilers, comedies, novels, romances, tragedies, dramas, in English and German. Some of the works were republished in hard covers. Solomon N. Carvalho issued his very readable *Incidents of Travel* and Max Maretzek, the ebullient opera manager, published his first volume of memoirs in 1855. All in all the Jews of this country wrote or published many Jewish works. Most of them were useful for that generation; few if any of those writings were of any cultural distinction, but then antebellum United States was in no sense of the term a center of world culture.[26]

ADULT JEWISH EDUCATION AND JEWISH LITERATURE

Three of the best known rabbis of that generation wrote histories of the Jews. In addition to Lilienthal and Wise, Morris Jacob Raphall also published a history of the Jews in biblical and in postbiblical days to the destruction of the Second Temple in the year 70 C.E. It is very probable that these rabbinical writers concentrated on the biblical period because the Old Testament and its characters were venerated as much, if not more, by Christians as by Jews. By 1860 Raphall was as well-known in the United States as Wise and Leeser despite the fact that he had no newspaper of his own to publicize his personal views. He was a master of English although he was a native of Sweden where his father had been a banker. After moving to England Morris Raphall traveled, studied modern languages, and earned his Ph.D. at the University of Erlangen. In 1841 he became a rabbi and head of a Jewish school in Birmingham. As one of the editors of the *Hebrew Review*, the first Jewish periodical in England, he translated several Hebrew classics and helped edit a volume on the Mishnah before he accepted a call in 1849 from Bnai Jeshurun, one of New York's great congregations. Raphall was widely known and highly respected by Christian America as an orator of note and as a lecturer on the literature and poetry of the Old Testament.[27]

Like Raphall the Jewish religious and cultural leaders of that day were all foreign born. This is not to imply that there were no American-born Jews of superior education and intellect: there were even some devoted Jews with a better than average knowledge of the history of their people. Dr. Joshua I. Cohen of Baltimore, one of the Cohens of Virginia and Maryland, a great clan whose first member was an early Jewish settler of the Old Dominion and a Revolutionary War veteran, was typical of this small group. Cohen's library was an unusually fine one; it included works in Latin, Hebrew, French, German, and Spanish. If he could read all these languages and if he had mastered the content of his Jewish works then he was indeed a learned man. His Hebrew books—and they were often rare prints—included the Bible, medieval works, the standard and best Hebrew grammars, dictionaries, reference works of the Buxtorfs, a Hebrew concordance of the Old Testament, and some of the basic books on the New Testament and the Septuagint. It is something of a surprise to discover that he had on his shelf a number of the best reference works on Hebrew bibliography. He owned Munk's French translation of Maimonides's *Guide for the Perplexed*, a set of the Talmud, and a number of works in French and English on the history of the Jews. Some of these were written by Jews, others by Christians. Abbé Gregoire, Voltaire, and Priestley were represented in his library and, as was to be expected of a Jew who was interested in Deism and the rise of Christianity, he owned a copy of David Friedrich Strauss's *Life of Jesus* in the French. Cohen was particularly interested in apologetics and polemics and missionary writings insofar as they touched on Jews and Judaism. The German scientific works of Zunz and Steinschneider and Jost, the historian, were missing; he was not a "Jewish scholar" in the academic sense.[28]

As Joshua Cohen represented that which was finest in antebellum Jewry of the North, Jacob Clavius Levy represented the best in the South. He was part of Charleston's finest American Jewish tradition, a fervent loyal religionist who followed his father Moses Clavius Levy in his devotion to the faith of his ancestors. The elder Levy was a native of Galicia who had come to Charleston in the postrevolutionary period and had made a fortune as a merchant. As one of the pillars of the congregation, Moses Levy had officiated as a volunteer hazzan, and when almost ninety had rushed to the synagog to save the Torahs in the disastrous fire of 1838. During the War of 1812 young Jacob Levy was a secretary of the Charleston Rifleman. In politics he was a Unionist during the bitter days of the Nullification Controversy. While on a trip to England he met and married Fanny Yates of the Yates-Samuel clan of Liverpool, the family to which the later twentieth-century Viscount Herbert Samuel, the first High Commissioner of Mandate Palestine, also belonged. When he brought her for the first time to the Charleston Theatre the entire audience rose in tribute to her beauty. His fortune was tied up with the Josephs of New York and when those bankers went down in the post-Jacksonian depression Levy suffered heavy losses, retired from business, and devoted the rest of his long life to cultural pursuits. When many of the Charlestonians moved west into the new cotton lands, he followed them and made his home in Savannah where he became one of the elite of the city. He died there in 1875.

Like Isaac Harby and others of early Charleston, Levy had received an excellent education emphasizing the ancient classics. It was characteristic of the man and his age that he saw to it that his son Samuel Yates was initiated into the mysteries of Virgil at the tender age of seven. Jacob Levy was at home not only in Latin and Greek but also in some of the modern languages; his Hebrew, however, was weak. He wrote poetry and hymns and reviewed books in the *Southern Quarterly Review* but his magnum opus, still unpublished, is the "Vindiciae Judaeorum." The title of course was not original with him but was borrowed from Menasseh ben Israel's defence of the Jews against slanderers in the days of Cromwell. Levy knew the work through M. Samuels's London edition. "The Vindication of the Jews" written shortly before and during the American Civil War is an impassioned defence of the Jew and an attack on Christianity and the church which had so often and so cruelly persecuted the Israelites. Persecution, the author repeats, brings out the best in the Jewish people; they are superior and will certainly survive those who seek to destroy them. Judaism, too, is superior to other cults because of its unitarian monotheism; the Jew is an exemplary citizen, a pattern of industry. If Jews are hated it is because of economic envy. It is true the Jews are rich; they rule the world financially! Like all his Jewish contemporaries he feared and hated the missionaries, despised converts to Christianity and, following the Deists and all Jewish writers, denied that Jesus was either a God or the promised Messiah. As the prince of peace he had brought only death and destruction to his oppressed coreligionists. Jesus of Nazareth was a good man, a reformer who preached love, and if the Jews of antiquity had but possessed the elasticity of Paul they could have made Judaism a world religion distinguished for its monotheism and its universal morality.[29]

LIBRARIES

Intellectuals like Jacob C. Levy, Dr. Joshua I. Cohen, and the nationally-known Jewish ministers had good libraries, but the interest in books of learning in that generation was not limited to men of this calibre. It has already been pointed out that most of the young men's literary societies of the 1850's had what were then considered substantial libraries; none, it is true, had as many as a thousand volumes. All of these libraries were associated with clubs or societies that also sponsored lectures. They were in effect Jewish lyceums; B'nai B'rith's Maimonides Library Association was one of the largest. With about 12,000 libraries in the country in 1850 these Jewish collections of books are of no significance in the broader areas of American culture. Their importance lies in the fact that they served as an Americanization agency for aspiring immigrants and the new generation of youth.[30]

THE AMERICAN JEWISH PUBLICATION SOCIETY

The attempt to raise the cultural and intellectual niveau of Jewry through libraries, the reading of books with Jewish content, was but one aspect of the antebellum drive of the Jewish leaders to create a national Jewish community, one united by common beliefs and common religious practices. Leeser and his friends were always reaching out in different ways toward this goal. In 1841 a nation-wide community was to be organized, reenforced by a national school system; in 1845 Leeser agitated for a national Jewish publication society. He wanted to fight off the zealous Christians who always threatened to proselyte the young. Undoubtedly, too, the organizational accomplishments of the Protestants—the different sects had publication arms—influenced him strongly. He was only too aware and envious of the successes of the American Bible Society and the American Tract Society, decades old already. It was imperative that there be a literature in English for Jews, both children and adults, a readable literature that would tie them to the faith. He wanted to create a school of writers and, lifting his eyes for once to a farther horizon, he dreamed of effecting a cultural revolution both here and abroad. Thus the American Jewish Publication Society came into being in November, 1845. It was to be a subscription organization publishing books, diffusing knowledge, and, when possible, making free distributions to the poor. The missionaries gave books away free! Auxiliary societies were to be established—one was set up in Richmond—to help spread "the Kingdom of our Heavenly Father, Israel's King and Savior." Actually it thought of itself as a book-of-the-month club. Patterned in part also on an Anglo-Jewish "cheap library," the American Society was to issue twelve pocket-size booklets, one every thirty days.

In reality, great plans produced smaller fruits. Over a period of about six years the Society published but fourteen of the pamphlets. Nothing except a short essay by Leeser on American Jewry was original; everything was taken from the English and French; the authors were not even all Jews. Most of the material was of an edificatory, religious nature. There was a biography of Mendelssohn, fiction dealing with biblical heroes, an account of a Jewish boy saved from the conversionists, an abridgment of Scripture, stories from rabbinic lore, and a protest against intermarriage. In December, 1851, the Society perished when it lost its inventory in a warehouse fire. In 1851 there were only some 50,000 Jews in the land and even $1 a year was too much for that poor but thrifty generation. Leeser was angry at the rich who would not help; $1,500—1,500 members—would have salvaged the Society but there was no balm in Gilead. However—and this is very interesting—in the 1840's proportionately more Jews joined the Society than in the 1970's![31]

BOOKSELLERS, PRINTERS, AND PUBLISHERS

As a publisher of Jewish books the Jewish Publication Society was preceded by the aggressive Solomon Henry Jackson of the 1820's; the Jewish book entrepreneurs of late eighteenth-century New York published few books of Jewish content; the less than three thousand Jews offered no ready market. The literary needs of the Israelites in early national America were satisfied by importations from England. The 1840's brought numbers and thus a ready-made market; booksellers made their appearance; soon there was no Jewish community of size in the country without its bookstore stocking cult accessories and Hebrew prayer books. Some of the booksellers were printers and publishers, most of whom remained in New York City catering to the newly arrived Jewish masses. There were publishers also in Philadelphia and in Cincinnati where Wise and his brother-in-law Edward Bloch established the firm of Bloch & Co. which printed the rabbi's edition of the Hebrew prayer book and some of his plays and other writings.

When Isidor Bush migrated from Vienna in 1848 he brought along Hebrew and German fonts and a supply of Hebrew books. The books, some of them of rare distinction such as the *Pahad Yitshak*, an eighteenth-century encyclopedia of the Talmud, were sold to scholarly connoisseurs. Bush was not successful but Henry Frank, an experienced printer and publisher of Hebrew books in Bavaria, was more fortunate. After his arrival in the American metropolis he founded a book and printing business which was later carried on by his family; a branch, Frank & Company, was even established in the 1860's in San Francisco. This enterprising man became the country's largest publisher of Jewish books: liturgies, textbooks, histories, and devotional works. His *Daily Prayers* and *Festival Prayers* in Hebrew, German, and English became standard works and even Christians interested in Judaism turned to him as their supplier. Frank's Hebrew Book Store was always ready to import books from abroad; the value of such a literary service should not be underestimated. His Hebrew-English prayer books, used by thousands in the course of decades, were important educational instruments for the new generation of German American Jews.[32]

THE PRESS

In a way the largest publishers were the Jewish newspapermen. When the immigrants started coming in numbers in the late 1830's there was not one Jewish periodical in all America, but the improvement of the telegraph and the power rotary printing press made the cheap newspaper and magazine a reality. Jewish enterprisers in 1842 and 1843 talked of publishing an English and a German paper but it remained for the omnificent Leeser of Philadelphia to issue the first copy of his *Occident* in April of the latter year. This important monthly advocating modern enlightened Orthodoxy continued publication until 1869, a year after the death of the founder. The first number of *Israel's Herold*, Bush's liberal German, sophisticated weekly with its promise of contributions from Europe's most distinguished scholars, went to press in March, 1849, but lasted only about three months. That same year Robert Lyon, another layman, began to publish his newsy, interesting, commercially-oriented *Asmonean*. It was successful, for Lyon was a good newspaperman. But it,too, came to an end when he died in 1858. At least a half-dozen newspapers made their appearance in distant San Francisco in the years between 1855 and 1857, and another was published in 1860; most of them were short-lived.

The important periodicals were printed in the East. In 1854 Wise began to issue the *Israelite*, still in existence. The following year he added a companion paper, *Die Deborah*, dedicated by him to the Daughters of Israel and to those who preferred German to English. The tone of Wise's weeklies was moderate Reform. Einhorn's German monthly *Sinai*, scholarly, religiously radical, made its appearance in Baltimore in 1856. German newspapers in the United States were not novel; there were then about fifty of them. A year later Samuel M. Isaacs of New York brought out the first issue of the *Jewish Messenger*, a moderate Orthodox organ, and in 1859 Rabbi Jonas Bondi began to publish his conservative *Hebrew Leader*. Bondi was not enamored of Isaac M. Wise but his daughter Selma became Wise's second wife after the death of her father. The only Jewish paper south of Maryland was published for a short time in New Orleans in 1859; it was called *The Corner Stone*.

There is no question that the important Jewish newspapers of the 1850's were edited by men who were unique; each one was a striking personality determined to win adherents for his cause, for his point of view. That was an age of vigorous hard-hitting editors, an age that produced Greeley, Dana, and Bennett. As in Germany Jewish editors represented every point of view from radical Reform to unyielding Orthodoxy. Some of the editors attempted to steer between the extremes of the committed leaders. But this they all had in common: they wanted to further Jewry and Judaism and to defend both from Gentile attacks. Wise's *Israelite*, probably the most popular of the weeklies, had a large national circulation for it was geared to the man on the street. Leeser's *Occident* was the least palatable; it was heavy, often dull. It rarely stooped to conquer, shunned jokes, and segregated its ads. Leeser's friends besought him to incorporate anecdotes and to appeal to the youth, but he ignored their suggestions; he could only be himself; he was a good man, maybe even a great man, but he was egregiously stuffy.

Were these papers successful? This is difficult to determine. Obviously those that survived were not unsuccessful. Many Jews in many towns had no interest in reading a Jewish paper. L. Cohen of Dalton, Georgia, wrote Leeser: "Keep your books; they are no use to me," "I have no time to read." Myer Strouse of Pottsville did read the *Occident* in 1843; he later became a United States Congressman. E. Wolff of Eagle Pass, Texas—population 400, situated on the Rio Grande across from Mexico —was glad to read the *Occident*, "living in this wild Indian region." The cultural impact of the Jewish newspapers was strong. Many of them borrowed materials or ideas from the excellent Jewish periodicals published in Germany. The papers here were full of articles on history, theology, interpretations of the Bible, sermons, and necrologies; the editorial page was often a delight. There were serials, novels, and stories to satisfy any taste, talks of the German ghettos and heroic romances of the struggle against the Syrians and the Romans in the days of old. Wise wrote hundreds of poems, eleven novels in English, sixteen in German, many of them "fillers" to pad his two magazines. The newspapers were also forums for discussions on religious differences, on the problems of the synagog and the societies, on the Jewish schools and education, on the missionaries and anti-Jewish prejudice, on the struggle to build colleges, hospitals, asylums, on the constant effort to consolidate the charities. News from all parts of the country, from Europe, Asia, and Africa made the whole Jewish world kin.[33]

JEWISH EDUCATION AND CULTURE:
FAILURE AND SUCCESS

In 1840 it did not seem that American Jewry had much of a future. Immigrants of traditional leanings had begun to arrive but the majority in the land were the children of immigrants and were trying "to make it" as Americans. It would appear that they were not enthusiastic Jews. There were three or four all-day schools, some afternoon and Sunday schools, but no college or academy. The rabbinic leaders of the new decade of the 1840's had grandiose plans to unite all American Jews through an all-encompassing all-embracing Jewish religious culture. Their formal schemata accomplished nothing. The immigrant Bavarian or Posen shopkeepers and craftsmen, an untutored lot, had more modest, more realistic goals. They were content that their children be able to read Hebrew and beamed with joy when the boys were bar mitzvah and the white-clad girls joined the boys in the ceremony of confirmation. The catechetical answers to questions on basic beliefs, on the holiday cycle, and on ethics were deemed a great achievement. It was their hope, and in the main it was realized, that their children in the Jewish schools would emerge loyal if not knowledgeable, that they would look askance at Christianity and reject intermarriage. Jewish culture? Culture was really not important to them. They believed that close Jewish social relationships were more important than book knowledge and would keep the younger generation loyal to the prejudices and the ideals of the parents.

Not very many of the humble émigrés could afford to patronize the all-day schools. Those who acquired some means, who were deeply involved in "Jewishness," who feared the persistent Christian quality of public instruction, turned to the parochial school. It offered a Jewish environment reminiscent of a nostalgically remembered Europe. Actually it was a halfway house to the public school, for even the Jewish all-day school laid much stress on secular subjects. It was a transitional phenomenon. The only widespread Jewish educational institutions were those that held classes on the weekends and more specifically on Sunday. The Sunday School was "American," acceptable to the children who wanted to identify with the larger Protestant world in which they lived.

The typical American Jew of that day was culturally ambivalent standing as he did with one foot in Europe and one foot in America. In the struggle within him between European Jewishness and American mores he opted for the new world. These newcomers were strongly influenced by many aspects of American cultural life. They spoke English, opened libraries, listened to lectures, and established a national publication society. They created literary associations and exposed themselves to the full range of contemporary political and social problems, reforms, and aspirations. Some of Isaac M. Wise's potboilers dealt with the fight for freedom in the days of the Second Commonwealth. Was this a reflection of pre-1848 European egalitarianism or of the American ideal of life, liberty, and happiness? The pedagogy, the method, the discipline in the Jewish schools—they were all American. The Sunday School was a novum, and the textbooks which made religion a formal subject were new to most adults and their children. This approach was Christian, American. Superficially this was true. Actually the content of most textbooks on religion was borrowed almost completely from Europe, from English, French, and German Jewish works, although these in turn were influenced by European Christian texts, certainly in structure and emphases. America in this age was trying to emancipate itself culturally from England; the Jewish immigrants here, through their catechisms, were more closely tied to Europe. The textbooks were important in that the few, widely used, served to unite American Jewry by giving it a common religious orientation.

Time brings perspective. After the lapse of a long century the late twentieth-century Jewish historian is aware that important changes were taking place in antebellum American life. There were better rabbis, regular preaching—this was new—in German and in English, better schools, vernacular newspapers, more societies, a developing appreciation of culture and of Jewish books, and the very faint beginnings of scholarship brought here by those newcomers who had been exposed to European canons of historicocritical methodology. Jews were kept Jewish because they were blanketed by a world of their own, a world of home, synagog, school, press, and many-faceted organizations. They identified with and remained loyal to their own way of life, a loyalty that was heightened by America's coolness toward the immigrants who were doubly disdained as Jews and as "Dutch" in a Know-Nothing xenophobic age. This emerging American Jewish culture was primarily a phenomenon of the North. There was little Jewish learning in the South with its slave economy and its disinterest in education for the masses.[34]

JEWISH SOCIAL AND LEISURE ACTIVITY

Like others the Jews wanted the best of both worlds, their own, and the world of their fellow Americans. They were insistent on a separatistic religiocultural life, yet looked enviously at the social life of their well-born Christian neighbors. Only in matters of morals and sex were the Jews puritanical; as a friendly this-worldly people they wanted a full social life, and they found it. The first years after they landed were hard, very hard; busy as peddlers and artisans, their shops were open late for they believed in the gospel of labor. Occasionally they relaxed in a *Biergarten* or in the bosom of the family; there were Purim parties, circumcisions, bar mitz-vahs, and weddings. The weddings were in the home, in the vestry rooms of the sanctuary, or in the synagog itself.

By the 1850's many of the German newcomers had begun to move into the middle class, with money and time for leisure and sociability. Almost every public meeting, even funerals, involved some social activity. When Rabbi Merzbacher of Emanu-El died the funeral was so large it was supervised by a grand marshal; several congregations participated and there was a series of orations at the graveside. No occasion was too sacred to deny the participants the pleasure of food and drink, even when services were held in the sanctuary on the eve of Pentecost and during the festival of Tabernacles. It was a bubbling and sparkling decade. Every opportunity was seized to dress elegantly and to dine elaborately in the best restaurants of the large cities. The literary societies, the charities, the lodges, luxuriated in dinners, concerts, dances, and speeches, in theatre and opera benefits, in dramatic presentations of their own, and in week-long fairs. Practically all of these gatherings were enlivened by fund-raising. People flocked in large numbers to cornerstone layings, dedications of synagogs and of hospitals, installations of rabbis, graduations. At an annual meeting of the Hebrew Benevolent Association of New York its president was bedecked with a gold medallion. The bemedaling started with Major Noah who loved to be caparisoned like the papal donkey. In 1825, a generation earlier, when Ararat was dedicated, Noah, with a gold medal dangling from his neck, had walked in the solemn procession that led to nowhere. The balls were grand affairs and the young folks looked forward to them. Alex Mayer in San Francisco wrote this plaintive note to a kinsman in Philadelphia: "Edwin, you did not write me any think that you have been last winder on the Hebrew ball."[35]

After their arrival here the Central Europeans began moving into the German Gentile societies, clubs, and lodges where they were among *Landsleute* and experienced no annoying language barrier. It is true that some of the Germans rejected them, ever mindful of the lower status of the Jew on his native heath, but most Germans accepted them. In fact in a number of these organizations, Jews were the leaders. The few Israelites with sport proclivities went into the turnvereins; more of them were found in the choral and singing clubs; Rabbi Wise bragged that he had established the first singing association in Albany, and Cleveland boasted of its Zion Singing Society, a Jewish institution. Ever since colonial days Jews had been very prominent in Masonic circles and the arriving immigrants speedily joined the lodges. Here too the typical pattern of separatism tended to assert itself; Jews formed Masonic and Odd Fellow fraternities of their own. This same ethnic and social impulse induced them to fashion separate military companies. In this they were no different than the French, Scots, Italians, and other Germans of New York City. Jews, too, loved the colorful uniforms; there were several Jewish military companies and troops in the city including the Asmoneans who preempted that name not because they wanted to emulate the Maccabees of old but because they worked on the Asmonean newspaper. During the war with Mexico a Jewish company in Baltimore rallied around a Christian captain, and a decade later the Israelites of Norfolk flocked to a Jewish rifle company led by Captain J. Umstadter.[36]

After a decade or more in the United States many of the Central Europeans had achieved financial success and with money came manners, culture, American mores, and social ambitions. The Jews were eager to join the elite social clubs. The club, a purely social institution, was something new to the European Jew. Though strongly social in their essential nature, the European hevrot, confraternities, were dedicated to religiocharitative ends and were immune to the concept of leisure. Early American Jews, especially in the South, frequently joined sociocultural and philanthropic Gentile organizations; the Jews of pre-Revolutionary Newport had a club of their own, the only one known to have existed prior to the late 1840's.

The Gentile clubs which were experiencing a rebirth in modified form in the second quarter of the century were socially exclusive. They were developing an aristocracy built on money, family, breeding, Christian background, and pioneer stock. These new Christian groups had no desire to share power with the Jews who were summarily rejected; Jews were not clubbable, *Salonfaehig*. Those Jews who were eager for status and recognition, if only among their coreligionists, began to establish separate clubs which many preferred; they wanted to be by themselves in an environment where their children would not be exposed to the hazards of intermarriage. Above all they sought a German-language enclave where they could speak, write, and entertain in the *Muttersprache*. As late as the 1880's and 1890's the records of these Jewish clubs were still being kept in the mother tongue. Thus it was that the Jews of the late 1840's and early 1850's created their own gesellschaften, close on the heels of the Christians. Clubs opened their doors in New York, Philadelphia, Cincinnati, Baltimore, and probably in other towns too; before the Civil War there were at least four in Cincinnati, three in Philadelphia, one in Baltimore, and one in New York City. Like the Christians the Jews, too, were bent on social exclusivity; there was never a lack of intramural prejudice. The proud Portuguese of New York with their "mock religious aristocracy" led the way for they had no social relations even with the wealthy and cultured Germans, and the latter in turn severely delimited the number of Germans whom they admitted into their clubs.[37]

The names the Jews appropriated for their new social associations are very interesting. If, as in Philadelphia they called themselves the Mercantile Club, it was because "merchant" was an honorific title reflecting the highest rung of colonial and early American economic aristocracy. The commonest titles were Allemania, Phoenix, Concordia, and Harmonia, or Harmonie, titles borrowed from German Gentile societies, lodges, and musical organizations. The deeper connotation of these names and one of which they were constantly aware was the prime need for harmony and concord in all social relations, for Germans, Gentiles and Jews were particularistic, rent by sectional prejudices and hatreds. It is curious, too, that in none of these names do the Jews identify as Jews; the wealthier, the more cultured, were deemphasizing, publicly at least, their Jewish loyalties. Some Jews, marginal in their sympathies identified as Jews only in the area of recreation.[38]

It was not given to that generation to create an institution that was dedicated solely to sociability. Jews could not jump out at their skins and change overnight. Within a very few years after its establishment in 1853, the Mercantile Club modified its name but not its program and called itself the Mercantile Reading Association. Were the members ashamed of the implication that they were only a social fellowship, that they had no higher goals? The 1854 Lyons and De Sola catalogue of American Jewish societies docs not list a single one devoted solely to social intercourse though some were already in existence. The Mercantile Club's first president was the Bavarian Louis Bomeisler who was anything but an uncouth peddler or artisan. His father had been a successful army purveyor in the days of Napoleon, and young Louis, educated at Heidelberg, had fought with the French in the European wars. After the fall of Napoleon he had been decorated by Louis XVIII and had joined the Masons in Paris before sailing to Philadelphia with a cargo of goods. After his arrival in 1819, he decided to remain, and in time became one of the most distinguished leaders of the growing Jewish community. Bomeisler was in the forefront of those who protested against the Damascus outrages, and in the course of years furthered the Jewish Publication Society, worked for the charities, and assumed the presidency of Congregation Rodeph Shalom. In all this he was a prototype of the American Jewish communal leader of the middle twentieth century.[39]

The Mercantile Club which Bomeisler led was not the oldest in American Jewry. The Harmonie of New York was older and is said to have been the second oldest club in the city. It may have been in existence as early as 1847, although, if so, it was reorganized in 1852. In its earliest days its program, like that of the literary societies and the later social organizations, reflected an interest in music, debating, theatrical presentations, and the raising of funds for local Jewish philanthropies. The Harmonie's history is in many respects the history of other clubs. It began in the Lower East Side with rented rooms, with a small library, and even with a rented piano, and soon occupied a whole house. Always moving on to better residential districts, in later years it erected a pretentious building of its own. Billiards was popular, card games were the prevalent form of relaxation, yet gambling for high stakes was always forbidden.

Before the decade of the 1850's closed a sprinkling of America's Jews were summering at Newport; others were enjoying the breezes in a Jewish hotel at Long Branch or rusticating at David Hays's kosher establishment in Westchester County, in Pleasantville. In January, 1860, young Myer S. Isaacs thought it was time for the Jews to have a real fun organization although it was self-evident that it, too, would raise money for the charities. And because the biblical holiday of Purim was the season "for feasting and joy" (Esther 9:22), Isaacs proposed that a Purim Association be founded to give "a good fancy dress ball." The proposal took on flesh in 1862 and the Purim Association had a long and successful life. After a fashion it was a miniature, decorous, Jewish carnival or Mardi Gras.[40]

Thus American Jewry created the educational, cultural, and social institutions which every pioneer ethnic group has founded to effect a successful transoceanic crossing. Jews here in the United States, comfortable as Americans, were also determined to live a Jewish life, one that fortified them emotionally and offered them the security that was imperative for survival.

CHAPTER TWELVE

REJECTION OF JEWS, 1840–1860

TYPES OF REJECTION

THANKSGIVING AND OTHER PROCLAMATIONS

If Jews quarreled with one another and exhibited strong intra-Jewish antipathies it is not surprising that the Christians with 1,800 years of anti-Jewish hate and guilt had no special regard for the Chosen People. The typical white Protestant American, especially in the North, enjoyed his prejudices. He detested abolitionists, Negroes, and Catholics, and looked down upon aliens and Jews. The Protestant believed that this was a Christian country; infidels, even though citizens, were of a lesser order; of this there was no question in his mind. As late as 1840 at least four of the original thirteen states—New Hampshire, Rhode Island, New Jersey, and North Carolina—still lived under constitutions that disabled the Jew politically. State legislator Mr. Crumpler of mountainous Ashe County, North Carolina, saw no reason for allowing Jews to hold office; they were cheats.[1]

Since this is a Christian land—and 120 million copies of McGuffey's Readers made it even more so—most Protestants saw no reason to respect the sensitivities of Jews when issuing Thanksgiving and other governmental proclamations. Presidents, governors, and mayors did not go out of their way to annoy Jews; the authorities simply addressed themselves to the American people 99 percent of whom were at least nominal Christians. That this was a de facto Christian country religiously was obvious to all Jews but they insisted that juridically, constitutionally, Christianity was not the religion of the land. At law—Jews maintained—Christians had no preference over others; no matter their faith, all individuals are equal; there must be a sharp division between church and state; Jews are not second-class citizens. And when the authorities ignored the presence of the less than 1 percent Jews, they protested vigorously. When poor William Henry Harrison was physicked to death and President Tyler called on all Christians for a day of mourning and prayer, Jacob Ezekiel of

Richmond remonstrated; Tyler apologized. When President Buchanan, using the newly laid transatlantic cable in August, 1858, told Queen Victoria that the United States was a Christian nation, Rabbi Isidor Kalisch of Milwaukee challenged him. Buchanan answered that he had "the highest personal regard for many Jews."

In their Thanksgiving proclamations governors very frequently called on their constituents to supplicate God and his Son Jesus Christ, the Redeemer. Officialdom was not even conscious that some of the citizens were not Christians. When this was called to their attention most executives made amends and were careful to issue unobjectionable statements in the future. The editor of the *Asmonean* reminded the governor of New York that the numerous Jews of his state had votes. Governor William F. Johnston of Pennsylvania admitted in 1848 that his proclamation had been written by the secretary of state, and had the secretary of state been upbraided for asking Jews to supplicate the Christian Redeemer, he would have admitted that he himself did not believe in the divinity of the historical Jesus. The secretary of state was a Hicksite Quaker. Governor James H. Hammond of South Carolina was a notable exception to these placatory administrators. Though no Christian religionist himself, he told his Jewish critics in no uncertain terms that this was a Christian land and as the chief magistrate of the state he addressed his people in Christian terms. The Jews of Charleston held a public meeting of protest in Masonic Hall but apparently achieved little. The governor implied that he was being mistreated by the Jews as was Jesus himself.[2]

BIBLE READING AND SUNDAY CLOSING
ORDINANCES

If Jews insisted on an absolute separation of church and state it was because they had learned through bitter experience that they were always disabled when the two were united; this was true as late as the nineteenth century in England and most of the lands on the continent. Jews did not want any religious acts or exercises in the public schools and state colleges. They objected to New Testament readings and accompanying commentaries, to Christian hymns and to prayers to Jesus, to examinations on Saturday, and to compulsory courses in Christian theology. The Jews, and particularly the immigrants among them who were fanatically devoted to this country, wanted to be good citizens, good Americans, but they dreaded any encroachments on their religion. They did not want their children to be exposed to any form of Christian religious indoctrination. In this determination to evade direct Christian and Christological influences and pressures the Jews found allies in the numerous secularists, civil libertarians, and the Catholic Church. The Catholics were resolute in their opposition to the public school reading of the King James Bible, a version which was unacceptable to them. They believed, and they were probably right, that the Protestants were using the public school system as a cultural and religious instrument to fight the Roman Church and to establish a nondenominational Protestant Christianity in this country. Actually many Protestants wanted their own "parochial schools" at state expense as they carried on a crusade to save America and its civil and religious liberties from papal domination. In 1858 Jews, Catholics, and liberals in Dubuque, Iowa, united to oppose Bible readings in the local public schools and threatened to vote the school board out of office. How would you like it, they said, if we took over and prescribed prayers in the classroom to the saints and to the Virgin Mary? To maintain communal peace Bible readings were proscribed in many schools but these local ordinances were honored more often in the breach, as they still are today.[3]

Municipal, state, and national appeals of a public nature which addressed the Christians and ignored the Jews were obviously a source of annoyance to the Children of Israel; Bible readings and Christian practices in the school rooms were another constant irritation. Even more disturbing were Sunday closing ordinances. They were a serious economic threat: Sabbath-observing Jewish businessmen would have to lose two working days out of every week. The rationalization for Sunday closing laws was couched in social and humanitarian terms; labor needed a rest. The Jews, however, were convinced that these police laws were Christian religious laws which legislators imposed because they believed that Christianity was part of the common law. Many Protestants were sorely disturbed by the desecration of Sunday as a day of business and activity. They had at times tried to stop the mails and the freight trains on that day and they even made an effort to close the canals on Sunday. A judge who condemned a Jew for selling a pair of gloves on the Lord's Day implied that Jews made enough money the rest of the week and did not have to keep open on the Christian Sabbath. If God punished America by carrying off President William Henry Harrison a few weeks after he was inaugurated it was because there were so many Sabbath-breaking Christians. Sunday closing laws were not universal and enforcement often varied from place to place. In many communities provisions were made for Jews who kept closed on the Saturday-Sabbath; they were allowed to keep open on Sunday. In many other places Jews, and Christians too, were fined and even jailed for violating the Sunday police laws. Christian farmers and Sabbatarians working on Sunday were arrested. Somehow or other the German-Christian immigrants accustomed to a continental Sunday succeeded in keeping open their beer gardens and their variety shows.

In 1855 William W. Stow [Stowe], the Speaker of the California House, not only favored a Sunday closing law for some of the counties but took the opportunity to vent his opinions about Jews. They have come out west only to make money and will then return to Jerusalem; they don't invest their capital in solid improvements. Jews ought to be taxed out of business and driven out of the state. Stow wanted the Bible to be followed, forgetting apparently that the Jewish Bible which the Christians venerated demanded that Jews observe the Saturday-Sabbath and said nothing of Sunday, the first day of the week. The Christian merchants who were behind this California Sunday-closing law resented Jewish competition. A San Francisco Jewish leader implied that Stow was a Know-Nothing xenophobe; back in Cincinnati Isaac M. Wise denounced him as a cannibal, a Jew-eater. Three years later Judge Heydenfeldt defended a Sacramento Jewish clothier who kept open on Sunday. When the California Sunday closing statute was repealed in 1883 the ground for its abrogation had already been laid by Heydenfeldt's close reasoning.

PROTESTANT AND CATHOLIC ANTI-JEWISH PREJUDICE

Adhering to a prejudice that was as old as the Gospels, Protestants and their clergy were frequently insensitive to the rights of Jews as American citizens. Because Rabbi Wise was not considered a minister the Albany preachers saw no reason why he should lead the state legislature in prayer, and when a few years later the legislature accorded courtesies to Rabbi Raphall of New York City the state clergy was deeply resentful. Horace Greeley's *New York Tribune* quietly reminded its readers that August Belmont's name was originally Schoenberg—it was not—and a Cassville, Georgia, preacher attacked President Pierce for appointing Belmont, a note-shaving, rag-trading Jew, to office. Actually Belmont, a banker and an influential leader of the national Democratic Party, was never affiliated with any Jewish religious institution. His wife, a Christian, was the daughter of Commodore Matthew C. Perry.[5]

On the whole the Catholics of that generation, belligerent in defending themselves and their faith, were not vocal in attacking Jews. They had troubles of their own. Every now and then a Catholic dignitary might blast the Israelites. The priests of the Philomena Church in Cincinnati told the domestics who came to confession that they would not be absolved if they continued to work for Jews. The clergymen were merely honoring a medieval statute that had long been forgotten. Rabbi Lilienthal wrote Archbishop John Baptist Purcell, one of the country's distinguished clergymen, that the priests ought to preach love and not hatred. He warned Purcell that if this boycott were attempted he would ask the Jewish garment manufacturers to discharge their Catholic employees. Nothing further was heard of the matter; obviously Purcell spoke to the priests. But less than a decade later Purcell himself erupted assailing Jews for not believing in Jesus and accusing them of constantly attacking the

Savior as an imposter who deserved death. Wise, Lilienthal, and the local Unitarian minister jointly turned on Purcell and he apologized for his tirade. Like a good Christian, Rabbi Lilienthal turned the other cheek and later helped to raise money for the Catholic Good Samaritan Hospital. We all believe in the Fatherhood of God and the Brotherhood of Man, he said on that occasion.[6]

The three decades before the Civil War were bad years for American Catholics. This was the era of the anti-Catholic mob. A Protestant gang burned an Ursuline Convent in Charlestown, Massachusetts, in 1834; ten years later Philadelphia was the scene of a miniature Protestant-Catholic war in which two Catholic churches and a number of homes were burnt. Many were killed and dozens were wounded. This rioting was quelled only after the militia was called out and bluejackets had been rushed in from the navy yard. It was at this time, the early forties, that a nativist pro-labor party came into being. Variously known as the American Republican party or the Native American Party, its avowed purpose was to protect the country from foreigners and European political domination. Let it not be forgotten that this was an age of repression in Europe when absolutism ruled and when the Catholic Church frowned on most forms of liberalism. The American nativists sought to retain the Protestant Bible in the public schools and to allow naturalization to aliens only after a twenty-one year period of residence and probation; this would deny them the vote and, implicitly at least, the right to hold office even after they had become citizens. The nativists were anti-immigrant holding the newcomers responsible for slums, crime, corruption, and wage undercutting. Irreconcilably and implacably anti-Catholic, these extremists were numerous and strong in the industrial states of New York and Pennsylvania.

One of the nativist leaders and a power among the Protestant laboring class was the Charleston-born Jew, Lewis C. Levin (1808-1860), very probably himself the son of an immigrant. After having graduated from college this brilliant young man went west to Mississippi, taught school in Woodville, and, after having been wounded in a duel, studied law and practiced in a number of states before settling down in Philadelphia. That was in 1818 when he was but thirty years of age. Levin was a clever, able man, a brilliant orator, a temperance reformer, and the editor of an antiliquor paper. He helped found the American Party about the year 1843, edited the nativist Philadelphia daily, *The Sun*, and represented the party in Congress for the years 1845-1851. Levin had no relationship with Jews and married out of the faith twice. After his death his wife and child joined the Catholic Church.

The 1850's witnessed the rebirth of nativism in the American or Know-Nothing Party. The platform was the same as that of the earlier nativists: anti-immigration, anti-Irish, limitation of the political rights of the newcomers, and a rabid anti-Catholicism. Unlike the earlier nativists, the Know-Nothings became politically powerful; they were to control several states, send eight men to the Senate and over a hundred to the House during the years 1854-1856. The Know-Nothings were convinced that the Catholics, Irish, and Germans had been dispatched to America by the Pope with the sole purpose of gaining control of the American Republic. This conspiracy concept of history, characteristic of populist parties, was to crop up again in the 1920's after the arrival of over 2,000,000 East European Jewish immigrants. Though the Know-Nothings had all the stigmata of an anti-Jewish party the leaders left the Jews alone. They had other fish to fry. The paltry 100,000 Jews in the land were no threat politically or financially; the Catholics pouring in by the hundreds of thousands—all potential voters—were the enemy that threatened Protestant power.

Where did the Jews stand? Were they anti-nativist? By no means. Levin was no exception. Some joined the activist secret lodges and the new party. Individual Jews—like many Gentiles—may well have joined the party because of its equivocal stand on slavery, for the Democrats refused to take a stand against the South's characteristic institution. Some Jews, émigrés from the harsh political and clerical rule in Bavaria and Austria, were anti-Catholic and honestly feared that the anti-Jewish European disabilities might be transplanted to these shores. The abduction of a Jewish child by the papal authorities in Italy confirmed many Jews in their fear of the Roman hierarchy. On the other hand most Israelites were also disquieted by the rising power of the Protestant nativists and shocked by the constant recurring bloody riots of the 1850's in St. Louis, Louisville, and other towns. As early as 1844, after the Philadelphia burnings and killings, Rebecca Gratz had written her brother in Lexington that unless the government intervened to maintain the constitution and religious liberty this land would no longer remain "the happy asylum of the oppressed and the secure dwelling place of religion." The *Asmonean* of New York and the *Israelite* of Cincinnati were anti-Know-Nothing but their opposition was in part politically motivated; both editors were Democrats. Some Jews—Felsenthal of Chicago, Wise, and Einhorn—were anti-nativist as a matter of principle. At first Wise thought of ignoring the Know-Nothings but speedily realized that they were a danger, for if they ever came to power Jewish rights in America would be imperiled. Protestant domination of this country, others believed, was no better than the threatened Catholic control. There must be a sharp separation between church and state. Jews who have suffered for their beliefs must not fail to be sympathetic to Catholics when they are attacked for the sake of religion, wrote an intelligent Georgia Jew to Wise's *Israelite*.

The cautious Leeser was quite prepared to assume a neutral stance as long as Jews were not attacked; Einhorn, a European radical who had just landed after being driven out of reactionary Hungary, jumped into the fray with both feet. He lashed out at the nativists in his *Sinai* in 1856 despite the fact that this was the year that an election mob went through the streets of Baltimore beating and killing people. If men are evaluated by their land of birth, he wrote, it is only a prelude to evaluating and condemning them for their religious convictions. Jews must fight for equality; the Mosaic law, he insisted, made no distinction between native and stranger. The former congressmen, Representative Philip Phillips of Alabama and Senator Judah P. Benjamin of Louisiana, attacked the nativists vigorously. Benjamin opposed them because they denied equal rights to all and fostered religious prejudices; Phillips wrote that they were promoting a bastard Americanism. Fortunately for Catholics and Jews the nativists, like the Democrats, foundered on the rock of slavery and were overshadowed by the new Republican Party. Most Americans of the 1850's were not anti-immigrant.[7]

GENERAL PRACTICE

It is doubtful whether the Jews realized how fortunate they were in those unhappy prewar days as riots raged and Catholics and Protestants fought and bled. Scenes of violence against Jews were few and far between. Some German Christians in Brooklyn attacked a Jewish funeral cortege but even such traditional anti-Jewish manifestations were rare. A Philadelphia high school punished its Jewish students academically for absenting themselves on the High Holy Days, and a pious Presbyterian minister equated Masonry, paganism, and Judaism with the powers of darkness. When a Missouri state legislator sneered at the Jewish Christ-killers, a Jewish colleague defended his coreligionists with the proud assertion that Jewish banks were solid and that Jews were not beggars, gamblers, or owners of fast horses. Whether this type of defense was efficacious is difficult to determine. A Christian might well adhere to the puritan ethic and still despise and attack Jews who embodied the finest Calvinist virtues of thrift and work. A lawyer vilified Jews in a Louisville court and evoked no rebuke from the acquiescent judge. Advertisements "No Irish wanted" served as patterns for the similar imperative, "No Jews wanted here," and Philadelphia Jewish garment manufacturers were accused of exploiting their Christian laborers. In distant Iowa Mr. Hirschel (Herschel) did not despair of America when he discovered that some insurance companies would insure no Jews. Hirschel sent his son to Harvard where the boy Clemens graduated to become one of the great hydraulic engineers of his generation.

Over the decades, Jews were sometimes denied insurance because many Gentile businessmen were taught to think of Jews as crooks and arsonists. A Jew was a haggler, a bargainer, a cheat, a usurer, a sheeney, a new word of contempt imported from England; "jew" or "jew down" became a verb used by Washington Irving and millions of others down to the present day. Even Jews were ashamed of the word "Jew"; they wanted to be Israelites or Hebrews. Though this prejudice was constant and pervasive, Leeser thought he had the answer to it. Jews should get out of the garment industry, go into the crafts and always pay good or high wages. It was essential that the Jew be distinguished for his low visibility. Thus the simplistic panacea of the naive rabbi.

Social prejudice against Jews was always present in the larger wealthier communities. Jews had come to Charleston, South Carolina, in the 1690's but there were circles in that city where they were still excluded as late as the nineteenth century during the period of its decline. Snobbishness frequently flourishes in inverse ratio to economic decay; retrogressing aristocrats have to salvage what they can; all that they have left is their pride and their rotting family trees. When Boston Jews petitioned for the right to lay out a cemetery they were at first confronted with difficulties. This is reminiscent of the colonial Savannahians who denied the Jews a right to a cemetery on the Commons because Christians would not want to buy a house looking out onto a burial ground sheltering infidels who cherished opinions "repugnant to those of our most holy religion." When Charles and Rachel Kahn bought a good-sized lot in the village of Clifton, hard by Cincinnati, they were politely told by some "gentlemen" that they were not welcome. The Kahns thereupon sold the lot to the Jewish Society of Brotherly Love to be used as a cemetery. It is plain to be seen that the Kahns were considerate enough to substitute dead Jews for live Jews.

The social cause célèbre of the 1860's was the successful effort of Captain U. P. Levy to keep from being dropped by the Navy. He faced numerous court martials, two courts of inquiry, and virulent Judeophobia but the more he was beaten down the harder he fought. The Secretary of the Navy, the eminent historian George Bancroft, a Democrat in party and principle, was glad to see Levy commissioned a captain but saw no reason to give the Jew a ship: "Harmonious cooperation" was most essential for the "highest effectiveness." Housing accommodations were also denied Jews; America was certainly coming of age. When told she could not rent a home, Mrs. Levy, a Cleveland Jew, responded: "Now I know why the Virgin Mary had to be delivered of her child in a stable." This particular incident may well be apocryphal but the fact that it appeared in a Jewish newspaper in 1860 testified to the fact that certain neighborhoods were closed to God's Chosen Ones.[8]

POLITICAL REJECTION OF JEWS

Since traditional prejudices are useful to politicians it was quite common in this period to identify a candidate as a Jew and thus to "smear" him. It was not imperative that the identification be accurate; dubbing a Christian candidate for office a Jew was often sufficient to damn him, as in New York City where the Christian Know-Nothing candidate for mayor bore a German name frequently found among Jews. Attempts were made in New Orleans to discredit E. P. Moïse and Judah P. Benjamin because of their Jewish birth. Though both these men had married Christians and were religiously unaffiliated they could not escape anti-Jewish bias. For some Christians nothing could wipe out the Jewish stigma. But in Catholic New Orleans the appeal to bigotry was not very helpful. Both men were singularly successful in their campaigns. Moïse overwhelmed his opponent despite the fact that the latter advertised: "Make hay whilst the sun shines or you will swallow a Charleston Jew." Like Moïse and Benjamin, M. C. Mordecai was also a Charlestonian but he chose to remain in the city of his birth. He, too, ran for office and was elected to the South Carolina senate by a huge majority. Unlike the others, however, he made his Jewishness an issue. As a Jew he insisted on religious liberty, civic equality, and freedom for all men even as he sought it for himself.

Political figures continued to be smeared as Jews or as having Jewish connections or traits. Henry Clay was denounced as a man who consorted with Jews; President Tyler was an accursed Jew; apparently this damnable fellow had vetoed a bank bill. And when John C. Frémont ran for the presidency on the Republican ticket a Democratic paper said that he was a Jew and had been educated in the Mosaic faith, but worse was yet to come —another Democratic organ said that he was a Jesuit. That was indeed a serious indictment in those Know-Nothing days.[9]

These inculcated prejudices were very real for many Gentiles. Even though they displayed no outward signs of hostility they were convinced Jews were inferior human beings. No matter what their status was de jure Jews were not deemed first-class citizens. As late as 1847 a Negro could not testify in a Maryland court against a white Christian but he could against a Jew. When David Levy [Yulee] arrived in Congress as the representative for the territory of Florida, John Quincy Adams referred to him as an alien Jew delegate with a dash of African blood. The Adams's contempt for Jews was rooted in English literary and folk conceptions that had been transmitted through Chaucer, Marlowe, and Shakespeare. The more recent Americans, Irish and German outlanders, brought in anti-Jewish prepossessions of their own. Within an hour after Wise landed at Castle Garden in the 1840's a German hackman called him a confounded Jew. In that decade, Wise wrote, the concept of the Jew was a caricature employed to frighten children. It was in line with this time-honored

usage that an American writer described a New Orleans Jewish businessman as someone who hoped that the yellow fever would continue so that
he might profit from his large stock of coffins which he had purchased in
Cincinnati.[10]

THE PRESS AND THE JEW

Of the press, pulpit, and books, the first was undoubtedly the most important in maintaining and enlarging the traditional negative stereotype of
the Jew. In evaluating their Jewish neighbors the newspapers of that antebellum generation tended to go to extremes: Jews were exceptionally
good or very bad. Complimentary articles lauding the Jews for their virtues abounded although critical stories seem to have been more common.
The decades of the 1840's and 1850's saw the rise of a vigorous often un-
bridled press in which license, attack, and vituperation were by no means
uncommon. The new German-language press transported age-old hatreds
from Europe. The *Volksfreund* of Lancaster, Ohio, attacked the work-
shirking Jews as usurers and cheats who ought not to be allowed to marry
Christian girls; like manumitted Negroes Jews ought to be shipped back
to their ancestral homeland. Extremes meet: at one end of the spectrum
was the reactionary *Volksfreund*; 140 miles to the south in Cincinnati the
socialist, anti-clerical freethinker, Friedrich Hassaurek attacked both
Christianity and Judaism in his radical *Hochwaechter*. This exuberant journalist and politician quoted Heine to the effect that rabbi and priest both
stink.[11]

    In the plays, songs, stories, books, and papers of the day, the Jew con-
stantly made his appearance as an untrustworthy peddler, as a greasy and
filthy immigrant, as a dishonest, tax-avoiding businessman. The official
organ of the Presbyterian Synod of New York, the *Missionary Record*, denounced the Jews who had participated in the European republican upris-
ings of 1848 as destructive revolutionaries who had no real interest in the
lands where they lived and the less pious *National Police Gazette* titillated
the interest of its devotees by recording stories of Jews as thieves, swindlers, and shoplifters. In New York City on the eve of the Day of Atonement, 1850, a man took a prostitute to a house behind the synagog and
someone started a rumor that the Jews had murdered the woman ritually
as a human sacrifice. A raging mob of about 500, led by three Irish police-
men, broke down the doors, robbed and rioted in their search for the vic-
tim. James Gordon Bennett's *Herald* in its "Mysteries of the
Talmud–Terrible Murder in the East," promised its readers the true story
of how the Jews of Damascus had bled a Christian missionary to death,
ground up his bones, and mixed his blood with unleavened bread. The
reader was solemnly assured that the Rothschilds had tried to prevent the
publication of the transcript of the trial where these facts were disclosed.

The *Herald* was a profitable business, for Bennett was an enterprising newsman.

Stereotypes die hard: Walt Whitman referred to "dirty looking German Jews"; Frank Soulé, the California writer who numbered Jews among his intimates, wrote of "thick-lipped, hook-nosed, ox-eyed, cunning, oily Jews," and his San Francisco compatriot, the multivolume history industrialist, Hubert Howe Bancroft, reminded his readers that the Jews he knew never worked with spade and shovel. Julia Ward Howe, who wrote

"in the beauty of the lilies Christ was born across the sea"

accepted the stereotype. In one of her plays Christ's cousin, the Jew, was the traditional unscrupulous usurer, a pattern that appeared also in Harper's "Easy Chair" then occupied by the distinguished reformer George William Curtis. But this very Curtis was also to speak glowingly of the genius of the Jew.[12]

HOW SERIOUS WAS REJECTION?

If Jews were plagued by their Christian neighbors, if their fellow citizens looked at them with a jaundiced eye, it was because they were remiss in their religious conduct; God was punishing them. If they had obeyed His precepts God and their Christian neighbors would have respected them. This is Rabbi S. M. Isaacs's interpretation of the Christian rejection of the American Jew. The this-worldly nontheological historian cannot always establish the causes of Judeophobia; he can only document its presence. Certainly anti-Jewish prejudices increased in the 1840's with the rise of the penny press which exploited traditional interreligious animosities. More Jews and more visibility made for more discrimination. If pettiness and bigotry were seemingly more prevalent in the North it was because there were more Jews there and more inpouring of aliens. The fact that the South now sent two Jews to the Senate is not necessarily an evidence of Southern liberality. There were fewer whites and fewer brilliant men in the South of that day. Ability was at a premium and competent Jews came into their own. The anti-Jewish narrowness of those decades was not racist in tone though there were always some intimations of racism. A correspondent of ex-President Van Buren attacked Jews in racial phrases that could have come straight out of the pages of Houston Stewart Chamberlain and the twentieth-century American racialists. The concept of the racial inferiority of the "Semites" was just in the process of development in France and Germany; the foundations then being laid by Ernest Renan and Christian Lassen were soon to be exploited by anti-Semites who wanted to prevent the complete emancipation and rise of European

Jewry. But Jews were already citizens here and most Americans had no choice but to pay lip service to their juridical equality; many, however, never fully accepted these descendants of the ancient Hebrews.

In the drama of interreligious strife the American Jews played no role of any import. The central struggle was between Catholics and Protestants. The Jews stayed gladly on the sidelines hoping that neither would win the battle for the American soul. Any form of church control would be for Jews a danger if not a major setback. If Jews tended to side emotionally with any group in this conflict it would be with the Protestants whose record of persecution was briefer and less sanguinary. Though real and omnipresent the anti-Jewish prejudice in the America of that day fades into insignificance when compared to the Catholic-Protestant killings and the treatment of the Mormons. Jews were condemned but not feared, hence not hated virulently. Grim hate was reserved by the Protestants for the Catholics and, possibly, by the Catholics for the Protestants.[13]

THE SWISS AFFAIR

Many if not most Americans felt that Jews were different and thus looked askance at them. The United States government as a nonperson could entertain no prejudices against Jews. Hebrew citizens—less than one-half of 1 percent of the population—were an inconsequential minority. Since many of them were voters nevertheless when an issue arose as it did in the 1850's, and the federal authorities in Washington had to make a decision between the economic welfare of the land and the constitutional rights of the Jews, the government opted for business. William Howard Taft would make a similar decision during his presidency. With the rapid development of industry in this country in the mid-nineteenth century, the Americans following hard on the footsteps of the French and the English, were eager to negotiate commercial treaties in Europe and the Far East. A. Dudley Mann, an agent of the United States, who was assigned the task of preparing these treaties, was quite successful. In November, 1850, Mann and the Swiss government agreed on a commercial convention that assured both parties reciprocal rights, despite the explicit statement of the first clause that "Christians alone are entitled to the enjoyment of the privileges guaranteed by the present article in the Swiss cantons." When the Jews heard of the discriminatory clause they were indignant. Jacob Ezekiel of Richmond wrote to his congressman protesting the acceptance of a block of granite sent by the Swiss for the Washington Monument. That great structure then in process of erection was to owe its completion in no small part to the generosity of the Jewish merchant Touro who would not have been permitted to reside and do business in some towns or cities of the Helvetic Republic.[14]

The Jews realized only too well that their constitutional rights as American citizens had been blatantly ignored. It is true that only a handful of them did business with Switzerland and thus would have been disadvantaged, but it was the principle that was important. Jews in the United States, whether natives or immigrants, were very sensitive to possible impairment of their privileges as Americans. All immigrants had experienced disabilities in their native lands and even in this country some natives had only recently been "emancipated"; they wanted their immunities whole and undiminished. They were particularly shocked by the treaty's discriminatory article because conditions for Jews were at that time on the mend throughout Europe. Baltimore Jewry was elated when Great Britain finally permitted Jews to sit in Parliament and a local mass meeting dispatched congratulatory resolutions to the American press and to English Jewry.

American Jews hoped to use the leverage of the proposed treaty to force the Swiss to emancipate their own Jews. As long as any Jew anywhere is not free, American Jewry is threatened; this they believed devoutly. But the American government had turned the clock back. Jews protested vigorously; together with like-minded Gentiles they signed petitions, held public meetings, fulminated in the Jewish newspapers, and rejoiced in the almost universal support they received in the general press. "This is not the country nor the age in which ancient and unjust prejudices should receive any countenance," said Henry Clay. Webster, the Secretary of State, was in agreement with him, and President Fillmore refused to approve the treaty because of its discriminatory reservation.[15]

When the 1850 proposed pact was amended and resubmitted by the President to the Senate in February, 1853, the disabling word "Christian" was omitted. Nonetheless the new article was no better. It stated clearly that reciprocal rights would prevail when such admission and treatment of citizens "shall not conflict with the constitutional or legal provisions, as well Federal as State and Cantonal, of the contracting parties." The Jews apparently did not know the exact wording of the revised article although they were wary and apprehensive. Senator Case delivered a notable speech on religious freedom and presented a petition of New York Jewry early in 1854 although it is by no means improbable that he had already seen the text of the revised article. Pierce's Secretary of State, W. L. Marcy, wrote Wise in July, 1855, over a year after the objectionable revised treaty had been accepted by the Senate, that nothing unjust would be done. Neither Senator Benjamin or Senator Yulee ever protested against a treaty that would have disabled them as Jews, nor did either say anything when the Chinese and Japanese pacts made provisions for Christian worship only. By May, 1855, the English minister to Switzerland knew that the American State Department had waived its objections

to the discriminatory article even as the British had done with respect to
their own Jews. Unlike the Americans, however, the British were fully
aware that they were betraying their Jewish citizens, but they salved their
conscience by warning the Swiss that if a single British Jew was disadvantaged they would remonstrate most vigorously. The roar of the British
lion frightened the Swiss president who promised that English Jews
would not be disturbed in their commercial pursuits. The Persians in the
late 1850's were more consistent than either the English or the Americans. These Moslems refused to make any arrangement with the Swiss
when told that religious equality would not be accorded them. The disabling Swiss-American treaty was proclaimed by the Americans on November 9, 1855, after it had passed the Senate, May 29, 1854.[16]

During the years that the Senate and the White House were tinker-
ing with the Swiss pact a resolution was introduced into the upper house
by Protestant religionists to protect their missionaries abroad. This resolution was designed to guarantee religious rights to Americans in foreign
lands; not only were future treaties to bear this in mind, but existing
agreements disabling Americans religiously were to be amended. The resolution was not aimed at helping Jews in Switzerland, and by the time
that it was adopted the Senate had already accepted the revised anti-Jewish discriminatory Swiss convention. Captain Jonas P. Levy, Uriah P.
Levy's brother, was then engaged in business in Washington. Named after his grandfather, Jonas Phillips, a Revolutionary War militiaman, Levy
was a stormy petrel who had served in the merchant marine during the
conflict with Mexico and had adventured in Peru. It was his belief that
the Swiss convention had been smuggled through the Senate, and he was
probably right. Jewish objections to the revised treaty were twofold: under the Swiss Confederation Constitution only Christians could obtain
full rights and cantonal autonomy was guaranteed. Some cantons granted
no Jews equality; the few living in the country, primarily in the Aargau,
were second-class citizens. One town would not even allow the Jews to
buy a cemetery and they were compelled to transport their dead across the
border for burial. Thus American Jews had few if any rights in the Swiss
Republic of Wilhelm Tell.

Negotiator Mann knew at all stages that American Jews would be
disabled but glossed over the difficulties. The State Department could not
have been unaware of the fact that American Jewish citizens would have
trouble, for A. B. Gootman, an American Jew who had settled in the
Swiss watchmaking town of La Chaux-de-Fonds, was threatened with
expulsion because he was not a Christian. Nevertheless the United States
government, represented by Mann, was eager to sign a commercial convention. Mann, a Virginian and an ardent Southron, was very hopeful of
selling cotton to the Swiss mills. His hopes were fulfilled; by 1859 Switz-

erland was buying 150,000 bales of cotton and substantial quantities of rice and tobacco from the United States. The trade between the two countries ran into millions of francs. Mann, a states' rights advocate, could honestly sympathize with the particularistic cantons in their desire to legislate as they saw fit for prospective Jewish settlers. The Swiss argued later that even as the American states could legislate for Negroes, the cantons could enact laws for Jews. You restrict slaves; we restrict Jews who are swindlers and usurers. Don't ask us to emancipate our Jews till you emancipate your Negroes. We are not the only ones to enact exceptional legislation against these people; look at our neighbors, Baden, Wuerttemberg, and Bavaria. In all of these lands no Jews are accorded equality. In our 1827 commercial treaty with the French, said the Swiss, that government did not insist that we grant any rights to French nationals of Jewish origin. The argument that the United States had no right to interfere in the internal domestic affairs of a foreign land found a welcoming echo in some American newspapers, not many to be sure. There were even a few American Jews who accepted this convention. If only to annoy his rabbi who was anti-Swiss, a Charleston Jew sided with them in a letter to the *Courier*. And when Cardozo, the economist, attacked the pro-Swiss Jew the latter insisted indignantly that he had been insulted: only the intervention of the lieutenant governor prevented the two Jews from trying to kill one another on the field of honor.[17]

Whether the treaty was smuggled through or not, the fact is that the Jews did not know the nature of the revised Article I till July and August, 1857, more than three years after the Senate had accepted it. The Assistant Secretary of State under Cass, John Appleton, an eloquent exponent of democracy and a devoted constitutionalist, told enquiring Baltimore Jews in August that the convention did not discriminate against Americans in any mode whatsoever and in the same communication blandly informed them that the United States had no control over the legislation of a foreign state. An American Jewish optician seeking to settle in Basel was denied that right, and when Wise of Cincinnati dashed off a note of enquiry to Secretary Cass the latter sent him a copy of the treaty without comment. This was in July. Now Wise knew what had happened. Furiously he denounced the treaty as an outrage and as an evidence of "unprincipled diplomacy." Leeser in truly traditional fashion lamented: "We are in Galuth (exile)," "strangers," "bondsmen," even in the United States. God is chastening the American Jews because they had departed from His Law; "modern progress is all a delusion." The Jewish leaders were now convinced that the government had deceived them. Leeser and Wise called on American Jewry to mount a campaign to petition the President and the Congress to remedy the wrong; the treaty must be amended or denounced. Once again petitions poured into Washington signed by Christians as well as Jews; protest meetings were held in at least ten cities as far south as Charleston and as far west as St. Louis. Delegations met with the authorities; the Jewish press and sixty American newspapers condemned the pact as unconstitutional. The issue was now a political one, for the Republicans were only too happy to attack the Democrats; the New York City Jewish vote was increasingly important.[18]

THE HEBREW NATIONAL CONVENTION

As early as May, 1852, Wise, then in Albany, had suggested that a national assembly of Jewish delegates be convoked to protest the inequities of the Swiss treaty. Five years later the Baltimoreans called for an American Jewish assembly, and set up a committee of correspondence. Only a handful of delegates, mostly Westerners led by Wise, answered the call. The New Yorkers and Philadelphians and some of the original Baltimore advocates boycotted the meeting. The Easterners resented Wise's brashness in taking over. He was a foreigner—probably with an accent—and he had been but eleven years in the country. Einhorn in Baltimore and Leeser in Philadelphia would have nothing to do with this upstart. Though American Jewry deeply resented the treaty's violation of its rights, the masses were slow to take action; the panic of 1857 depressed them sorely. Wise, the activist, jumped into the breach and headed the "national" delegation that called on President Buchanan to voice its protest and to ask him for help. Colonel Philip Phillips, the former congressman, introduced the delegates to his Democratic confrere, Buchanan, and in beautiful prose pointed out that the treaty imposed an odious discrimination on the American Israelites. Responding, Buchanan attempted to exculpate his predecessor in the White House and said that he would do what he could, "not inconsistent with international faith." This was his hint that he would not denounce the pact although he realized full well its constitutional impropriety. There was no question that Buchanan was sincere in his protestation. As long as the treaty itself was not imperiled he was ready to fight for American Jewish rights abroad. The threatened split of the Democrats over slavery and the rise of the Republicans enhanced the value of the Jewish vote. Inordinately pleased with Buchanan's avowals and feeling that the problem was all but solved the Hebrew National Convention delegates returned to Baltimore to celebrate. At the banquet Solomon N. Carvalho responded to the toast on woman: "the last and sweetest thought of creation." Much more realistically Wise rose and raised his glass to "Union": If the Jews would not organize they would accomplish nothing.[19]

THE CAMPAIGN TO REMOVE THE
ANTI-JEWISH SWISS DISABILITIES, 1853–1879

Pushed by the President and Secretary Cass, the American minister to Switzerland, Theodore Fay, waged a brilliant and courageous campaign to secure equal rights for American Jews in the Alpine Republic. Earlier, in 1858 under Pierce, his protest on behalf of A. B. Gootman seemed to be somewhat perfunctory but later, urged on by the new administration in Washington, he carried on the battle with vigor, skill, and utter sincerity. He was fully convinced that the contention of the Swiss that they had to protect themselves against all Jews if only to forestall an invasion of the "usurious" Alsatians, was a pretext, specious and untrue. To accomplish his end Fay addressed a very long note to the Swiss President and Federal Council practically demanding to know why some of the cantons restricted the privileges of American Jewish citizens contrary to the usages of civilized nations. He analyzed the sources of the Swiss cantonal prejudices and implicitly reproached them for their unchristian conduct toward an American Jewry that was one-fifth as large as the entire Swiss populace. It was an eloquent plea for rights for the American Jew, a plea that could well be applied to all Jews everywhere including the few native Swiss Jews who were disabled in Helvetic cantons. The Swiss federal government, sympathetic to his demands, distributed the so-called Israelite Note in French and German translations.[20]

The immediate effects of the Israelite Note were not perceptible; as late as 1858 the Swiss Consul General in Washington had informed the State Department that no American Jews would be permitted to settle in his country. Yet by that time conditions were already improving for Jews in Switzerland. The cantons were moving to the left; liberalism was on the march throughout Europe, and even darkest Russia, under Alexander II, was inching forward toward the periphery of liberalism. American Jewry and the Washington authorities were constantly pushing the Swiss. In 1861 President Lincoln appointed Charles L. Bernays, a Republican stalwart, as consul to Zurich. This was his reward for working among the Germans of Missouri and Western Illinois when he served as editor of the St. Louis *Anzeiger des Westens*. Bernays was of Jewish descent, probably a son of a Jew. He himself maintained that he was born and baptized as a Christian. It is difficult to determine whether Lincoln accredited this "Jew" to a Judeophobic country with a glint in his eye. At all events the Swiss dragged their feet for several months before they reluctantly accepted this new American consul. That same year a Mr. Wolff was appointed consul to Basel and he, too, was denied the exequatur until the Swiss discovered that he was not a Jew; the "Jewish" name Wolff had misled them.[21]

In their effort to secure immunities and liberties for their Jewish citizens the Americans had the sympathy of the French, English, and Dutch who were faced with similar problems of anti-Jewish prejudice. The Swiss who were particularly eager to do business with the Dutch negotiated a treaty with them in 1863 but it failed of acceptance in the Dutch Second Chamber largely because of the protest of Michael H. Godefroi, a former Minister of Justice. Godefroi was a Jew, a civil libertarian, very much concerned about the Jewish disabilities then prevailing in Switzerland and Eastern Europe. He was a highly respected, beloved Netherlander. The Second Chamber deliberately rejected the proposed treaty because of the cantonal attitude toward Israelites. The following year was important. The Swiss were very desirous of a commercial pact with the French who were determined this time not to sacrifice their Jewish citizens. The French insisted successfully on equality of treatment. Two years later, after the cantons approved of the French demands in a nationwide referendum, all other foreign Jews were of necessity granted similar privileges. Once Israelitish subjects of the treaty lands were recognized the Swiss had no choice but to grant rights to their own Jews. It was the French who had forced the hands of the Swiss. The new Swiss constitution of 1874 divorced freedom of settlement and trade from religious confession. But, constitution or no constitution, the Argovians refused to stop struggling. It was not until 1879 that the Jews of that canton were fully emancipated; that was only two months after the Christian citizens of New Hampshire permitted their Jews to serve in the state legislature.[22]

SIGNIFICANCE OF THE SWISS AFFAIR

As it has been noted, when the American State Department had to make a choice between an advantageous commercial treaty or none if the rights of citizens of the Jewish persuasion were to be respected, the authorities opted for a treaty as did both the French and the English. The American government believed that the country's welfare—as it understood it—came first; Washington was determined to export American goods; the Jews were determined to export American liberties. Grievously distressed and disillusioned by the government's decision the Jews undertook a campaign of protest in all towns of size. "Those who wish to be free," said Leeser, "must themselves strike the blow." The shift of many Jews to the Republican Party away from their traditional allegiance to the Democrats may have been motivated in part by their anger at what they deemed to be a betrayal. Eager to keep the Jews in the party, Wise, a loyal Democrat, urged Stephen Douglas to introduce a resolution in the Senate attacking the Swiss for their discrimination and the Pope for condoning the abduction of a Jewish child. In the series of protests throughout the country the western Jews stood out, for the West was coming into its own;

Jackson, Harrison, Polk, and Lincoln were western presidents. It was these Jewish westerners who dominated the Hebrew National Convention. Yet it was not the vehemence of their remonstrance that was decisive. It was a complex of events that brought relief: American diplomacy, including the incisive Israelite Note of Fay, the growing liberalism of the Swiss, the sympathetic understanding of the Swiss Federal Council, support from the English and the Dutch, and finally, the resolute action of the French.

The real victory in the Swiss Affair was not that Mr. Gootman could buy watches undisturbed in La Chaux-de-Fonds or that Sigmund Muehlhaeuser could fit glasses in Basel, not even that the State Department had finally succeeded in securing rights for American Jews. The greatest benefit that accrued to American Jewry was the growth of a sense of Jewish homogeneity here in this land. A common threat created a common Jewry. If the rights of Jews are disregarded abroad they will be disregarded at home; national agitation made for national Jewish unity. There was still no national organization tying Jews together but there is no question that national Jewish unity was slowly but surely being forged here in these United States.[23]

THE MORTARA AFFAIR

While American Jewry was still troubled by the Swiss Affair its distress was exacerbated by an incident in 1858 which compelled Jews to fight on two European fronts at the same time. Here on this side of the Atlantic Basin the dramatis personae were the same: American Jewry, President Buchanan, and Secretary of State Cass. But this time the Jews were not battling for their rights as American citizens in foreign lands; they were fighting to maintain the sanctity and the integrity of a Jewish family in the Papal States and they expected the American republic, a moral institution, to come to their aid. At stake was the fate of a seven-year-old Jewish child, Edgardo (Edgar) Mortara. On a June night in 1858, the 23d or the 24th, the officers of the Inquisition in Papal Bologna entered the home of Momola Mortara and presented a warrant for the arrest of young Edgar. He was taken that night from the bosom of his family and never returned to that home again as a Jew. Why? During an infant illness the Christian maid in the house, fearing that he might die, had saved him for all eternity by having him secretly baptized. When after years the story finally came out the Church authorities, particularly Pope Pius IX, held that though the baptism was illicit it was nevertheless a sacramental act and thus irrevocable. The child was Christian and could under no circumstances be left in a Jewish home; his immortal soul was at stake; he had to be taken away.

Almost as much as the child, the Pope is the important figure in this sad story. Pius who had started out as a liberal ruler, was nonetheless caught up in the unrest of 1848. Compelled to leave Rome when a republic was established in the Papal States, he returned an embittered conservative when his throne was restored in 1850. The Jews of Rome were forced back into the ghetto and the old medieval disabilities were reimposed, for these Israelites, seeking emancipation, had joined the anti-clerical forces of the revolutionary Risorgimento. Pius was politically conservative for he realized full well that if the North Italian House of Savoy came to power and united Italy, papal secular rule would come to an end. Rome would be lost. The Pope was in the van of those who fought political and religious liberalism and democracy. In a generation when millions were reading Comte, Herbert Spencer, and Darwin he threw himself into the breach desperately determined to save traditional Christian orthodoxy. It was almost inevitable therefore that having lost the political battle against a united Italy that at the Vatican Council in 1870 he would insist on enunciating the principle that the Pope is infallible in defining faith and morals for Catholics. Papal intransigence in the case of Mortara is a phase of the Catholic counterrevolution. The future of one child was not the real issue; Catholicism was threatened.[24]

THE CHRISTIAN REACTION TO THE MORTARA CASE

That a child could be taken by force from the arms of its mother in the year of grace 1858 shocked the whole western world. This was medievalism and medievalism was supposedly dead. Actually abduction of Jewish children and their baptism by violence were by no means uncommon in the Italy of that generation. Yet the Christians of Europe were very much disturbed; protests poured in from several lands and even the Catholic rulers of France and Austria, Napoleon III and Francis Joseph, interceded with the Pope. Here in the United States some Catholics were embarrassed and unhappy with the decision of the Church to keep young Mortara; a few even attended the protest meetings. But the Catholic newspapers, practically without exception, staunchly supported their spiritual leader. At first they denied the facts; later they justified the decision of the Roman hierarchy. The baptismal act was sacramental, sacrosanct, and when all was said and done the child was better off as a Christian. The family? It deserved what it got because the father had violated the law by employing a Christian servant. This generation undergoing great social changes revived the old statutes prohibiting Jews from employing Christian servants and efforts were made to implement them all the way from Galicia to Cincinnati. At this juncture the Catholics, attacked by the Protestants, intimated sardonically that the Protestants might well consider the beams in their own eyes rather than the motes in the eyes of their

Catholic neighbors. Catholic children in Protestant asylums were frequently baptized. If abduction is a crime why not censure the abolitionists for abducting slaves? Why not join the crusade against slavery itself? What about the Protestants of North Carolina who refused to emancipate their Jews? Because most Protestants detested the Catholics they and their church press had a field day, for they disliked Catholics almost as much as they did Negroes. Even in colonial times Catholics had suffered discrimination in the British American colonies and in Maryland Irish Catholics were subject to special taxation.[25]

The Protestants feared the Church; some actually believed that Catholic nurses would baptize their Protestant infants. This dread of Catholic baptism would seem to imply that subconsciously at least the Protestants were convinced of the efficacy and sanctity of the Catholic sacrament of infant baptism. In all this agitation the Catholics were not slow to point out that the Protestants were more anti-Catholic than they were pro-Mortara. The Protestant press did not need the pretext of the Bologna incident to attack the Catholics; any pretext would serve. It is equally true that the Protestants were more eager than the Catholics to convert Jews; no Protestant religious organization raised its voice on behalf of the abducted child or interceded with Buchanan or Cass. Thoughtful editors of the Protestant press realized that the issue at stake was the separation of church and state; they emphasized religious liberty for all and some hoped that the authorities in Washington would intervene to secure the restoration of the child to its parents. Because the Protestants were the dominant religious group in antebellum United States, the secular press, too, was largely anti-Irish, anti-Catholic, and on occasion Know-Nothing. Because of its sensational quality the Mortara Affair was stressed and for months—from October, 1858, to February, 1859—readers were overwhelmed with the heartrending story of the bereaved family. *The American and Commercial Advertiser* of Baltimore ran thirty-one large articles about it during this period. There was to be no such large coverage of a Jewish cause célèbre till the Russian massacres of the 1880's and the Dreyfus trial of the 1890's. As the Republican press waded in to fight for Mortara much of its enthusiasm was certainly engendered by the desire to denigrate the Democrats as the party which supported slavery and worked hand in hand with Papal Rome and the Catholic priesthood. It was imperative that the Democrats be "smeared" if the Republicans were to gain votes. Like the Protestant papers the general press affected to believe that the Roman Church menaced American liberties if not its very independence; human rights and freedom were threatened.[26]

THE EUROPEAN JEWISH REACTION

Once alerted World Jewry set out to rescue the child. Edgar's father, Momola, had appealed to the North Italian congregations under the House of Savoy and in August received their enthusiastic support, for the Sardinian kingdom of Victor Emmanuel II and Cavour was anti-papal. These Israelites of the North then turned to Europe's Jews, especially to the French and the English. European Jewry as a whole responded vigorously; Central and East European Jews fighting constantly for equal political rights felt threatened by the persistence of anti-Jewish legislation in the Papal States. Strange as it may seem one outstanding Jewish notable did not protest. Ignatz Deutsch, a leader of Austrian Orthodoxy, asked his rabbinic friends to disassociate themselves from the Mortara rescue; the liberals and radicals of the world, he said, were behind this agitation in order to discredit the conservative political and religious establishments. Deutsch, a prominent Viennese banker, familiarly known as the Duke of Jerusalem, was an intimate of Catholic notables and a financial adviser to influential prelates. Even after his bankruptcy he maintained himself as the leader of the right-wing Jewish religious group.[27]

The leadership among Jews in this worldwide battle was assumed by the Grand Old Man of Jewry, Sir Moses Montefiore, himself a native of North Italy. Montefiore, head of the London Board of Deputies, had the support of the English government which looked with favor on a united Italy under Victor Emmanuel II; a strong Italy under the House of Savoy would delimit the influence of Napoleon III, the French imperial rival of the British. Montefiore had interceded for the Damascus victims in 1840, and in 1859 accompanied by the American Gershom Kursheedt, he made a fruitless trip to Rome; the Pope refused to see him. It was Montefiore and his Board of Deputies who worked closely with Europe's Jewish communities and with large numbers of England's most notable Christians. Sir Moses and his associates dispatched a circular letter to the important Jewish congregations in the United States asking them to urge their government to intercede with the Pope. This general epistle, issued in late October, 1858, reached American Jewry in November.[28]

American Jewry, as a European satellite, was flattered by Montefiore's appeal to it: it was very eager to work with Europe's Jews who were spearheading the battle. Montefiore himself was almost worshipped by the Jews on this side of the Atlantic and indeed was also venerated by most distinguished American Christians. The letter from the Board of Deputies sparked a vigorous campaign here on behalf of Mortara although this country's Jews had already begun to take action before the Anglo-Jewish appeal arrived. American Jewish readers knew of the abduction as early as August, and on October 22 Lilienthal of Cincinnati called for a city-wide Jewish protest; eight days later a meeting was held, the first in the United States. Wise gave it his complete support but for some reason, difficult to fathom, he was never in the forefront of those who fought for Mortara. Leadership was seized by the East. Was this in defiance of Wise who had grasped the reins during the Swiss protest? Was Wise quiescent because he realized he had accomplished little or nothing in his fight against the Swiss? Had this enthusiastic realist lost faith in Buchanan and Cass?[29]

THE AMERICAN PROTESTS

The Jews went into high gear in November, 1858, the month when most protest meetings were held. The techniques of remonstrance were the same as those employed in the Swiss Affair: petitions, letters to the press, mass meetings, delegations to Washington. The goal of all this agitation was to influence Congress, the President, and his Secretary of State to work with the European powers in order to induce the Pope to release the captive child. Some communities even appealed directly to Rome. Both Christian and Jewish speakers at the mass meetings made it clear that the Catholics here were not responsible for papal action in Rome, but it is patent that the Jewish and Christian speakers were anti-papal and often even anti-Church. Did these Christian and Jewish speakers believe their almost hysterical implications and statements that Catholic nurses would secretly baptize their infant charges? Did the speakers, carried away by their own oratory, really believe that the Catholics in this country were a threat to the integrity of the family? Apparently some did. Were the speakers aware that for a brief period in eighteenth-century Maryland a Catholic mother might lose her child on the death of her Protestant husband? At the New York protest assembly the wealthy clothing manufacturer Joseph Seligman declaimed that if something was not done Rome would be filled with Protestant children who had been forcibly baptized, and in San Francisco Solomon Heydenfeldt, California's former State Supreme Court Justice, solemnly assured his audience that the "persecution of one, today . . . may be the fate of another tomorrow." In these fears the Jews here in the United States were certainly infected by their Protestant neighbors, and the *Jewish Messenger* went so far as to warn Jewish mothers to keep their eyes on Bridget or Mary if there were children in the home. It bears repetition that the American Jewish immigrants from Catholic lands were always apprehensive.[30]

AMERICAN JEWISH "MORTARAS"

Did American Jews have any reason to be fearful of illicit baptisms and conversions? They certainly believed "it could happen here," and it did, not too infrequently. Very probably it had happened in earlier days also but the Jews began to take note of incidents and to record them during the period of the Mortara agitation. As a Jew lay dying in a St. Louis Catholic hospital he was baptized even though, as it was reported, the still conscious man protested. When he died he was interred as a "Christian" in a Catholic cemetery. A Jewish witness to this forced baptism reported it to local Jews who appealed in vain to the archbishop; the Jewish community persisted and finally recovered the body. Another St. Louisian, a Bohemian Jew, had married a Catholic woman by whom he had three boys but they were not circumcised because of the strong objection of the wife's parents. When the wife was on her deathbed she urged her husband to have the boys circumcised after her death. However before he could do anything his parents-in-law seized the children and secreted them in a Catholic institution. The father finally recovered them and, fearing violence, fled to New Orleans where the boys entered the Abrahamitic Covenant. The oldest, a lad of seven, was asked whether he wished to be circumcised. His answer was: "Certainly, because my pa is also a Jew." This was in 1858.

In September of that year a French Jew, a Mrs. Levy, died of the yellow fever in New Orleans. During her illness her children had been taken care of by a nurse and when Mrs. Levy passed away the baby, Alice, was turned over to a Catholic, Mrs. Capdeville. The nurse told her the orphan had been abandoned. The pious Mrs. Capdeville proceeded to baptize the waif. The managers of the Jewish orphan home where the child was to have been placed traced the infant and after some difficulty were able to recover her and bring Alice to their asylum. The French authorities in Paris fearing probably that this might prove to be another Mortara incident had also made every effort to locate the missing Alice and turn her over to her Jewish guardians. The grateful Jews thanked the French stressing how different was their attitude from that of Pius in Rome. As in St. Louis and New Orleans the Jews of New York were also occasionally plagued by this problem. A nurse in that city who had baptized a Jewish child was compelled by the courts to surrender her charge. In 1859 Rabbi S. M. Isaacs warned the Jews that as long as there was no Jewish orphan asylum in New York it was inevitable that Jewish infants without parents would end up in Christian institutions and be baptized. Nine years earlier in 1850 Rabbi Isaacs had appealed to New York and American Jewry to support a hospital in Detroit conducted by the Sisters of Charity of St. Vincent de Paul. Their conduct had been exemplary in selflessly nursing sick and dying Jews who were brought to the shelter of their institution. A Jew who knew their work well referred to them as "ministering angels." Obviously the baptism and conversion of sick and dying Jews in Christian eleemosynary institutions was not customary.[31]

PROTEST MEETINGS

The Jews and their supporters did gather together, in St. Louis, New Orleans, and in at least fourteen other cities, to raise their voices against the detention of young Edgardo. In addition to New Orleans, meetings were held in two other Southern towns, Charleston and Mobile. In all three cities there was no insistence on intervention by the national executive. The statements of protest were cautious, dignified. It is possible that, as in the case of Switzerland, these cities of the South, conscious always of states rights, did not want to question the authority of a foreign state over its own subjects. It is far more probable though that these Southern Jews and their Christian friends, practically all Democrats, did not want to embarrass Buchanan or alienate Catholic voters. Was the first loyalty of these Jews to their party rather than to their faith and to their people? When Buchanan shrugged his shoulders and politely informed a Jewish delegation, non possumus, because the right of no American citizen had been impaired, the Jews countered that Van Buren and Forsyth in 1840 had made an effort to help the persecuted Jews of Damascus. It was also pointed out by Wise in the *Israelite* that this country had been most sympathetic to the oppressed peoples of Greece and Spanish America and that by joint resolution of the Congress a ship had been dispatched in 1851 to bring Kossuth, the Hungarian revolutionary, to American shores. The Cincinnati editor was angry that the Jewish politicians—Senators Benjamin and Yulee—had done nothing for Mortara; Wise maintained that the losses of the Democrats in the New York, Cincinnati, and St. Louis elections were due to the defection of the Jews annoyed by the refusal of the President to help save the Italian child.

Speakers at the mass meetings variously emphasized the rights of natural law, of the family, of human sensibilities over canon law; they wanted a complete separation of church and state. As contributions for the Mortara family poured in from the mining camps of the Mother Lode, 3,000 protestants gathered together in the far western city of San Francisco. This was the largest assembly on behalf of Jewry that this country had yet witnessed. On the other side of the country, 2,000 people, it is said, met in New York. Because this was a protest for all Americans, not merely for Jews, no German speeches were allowed. Among those who spoke was the popular Jewish preacher and humorist Raphael J. de Cordova. With the compulsory baptism of Mortara in mind he asked his tittering audience: If the Pope was carried off by violence and circumcised would that make him a Jew?[32]

THE ATTITUDE OF THE AMERICAN AUTHORITIES

All the meetings and protests were of no avail. Resolutions introduced into the New York state legislature calling on the President to intervene at Rome were not reported out or were tabled. Even though these resolutions were politically motivated, anti-Democrat, and sponsored by Know-Nothings, they were bound to win some Jewish ballots. A nativist congressman in the capital was equally unsuccessful with the resolution he offered on behalf of Mortara; it was ruled out of order. In general the Americans of the 1850's wanted no European entanglements and the politicians Buchanan and Cass would do nothing to offend 4,000,000 Catholics: the Democratic Party was in trouble and needed votes; there were only 150,000 Jews. At first Cass spoke of an "alleged forcible abduction"; the United States would not interfere "within the territories of an independent power . . . as they expect other nations to abstain from all interference, in the internal concerns of this country." This was on November 21, 1858, and by January 4, 1859, Buchanan had completely identified himself with the policy of non-intervention. After hammering away at the President and his Secretary of State, the best the Jews could achieve was to evoke expressions of sympathy from both. Cass finally wrote that carrying off the child was "an inexcusable act of cruelty." In a firm incisive letter to New York Jewry the President refused to do anything although he admitted it was a case "well calculated to enlist our sympathies." He was adamant.[33]

SIGNIFICANCE OF THE MORTARA AFFAIR

The Mortara Affair had little significance in the context of American history. The Democratic regime in power certainly had no intention or inclination to go off starry-eyed to restore a Jewish child to its mama. There were too many votes at stake; the Catholics, abused by Protestants and nativists for decades, were fiercely loyal to their spiritual leader in Rome. For the political opposition the Mortara Affair offered a welcome chance to attack the administration and to gather votes. The anti-Catholic Protestants relished the opportunity to strike still another blow at the Church and the Pope. The average intelligent American who read his newspaper and went to one of the protest meetings was more than ever convinced of the soundness of the first amendment. Religion must be kept out of politics.

The Mortara case had a great deal of significance for American Jewry. Jews vented their anger in public protests; that was healthy. Unhappy with the hands-off policy of Buchanan and Cass many decided to vote for the new Republican Party in 1860, a party that was not tied up with Catholics in the North or the proslavery men of the South. Far more important, however, was the belief of practically all Jews that if they had been united in a strong national organization they would have been able to induce the President to intervene with Pius IX. (They were wrong, of course, for the President was counting noses.) The emotional unity forged in almost every Jewish community in the country was a euphoric experience; it was unique in the history of American Jews, and they were determined to retain this precious mood and moment; they were proud that they could stand together. The fact that thousands of Christians sympathized with them was flattering; it gave them a sense of self-respect. The experience of fighting to help a coreligionist in a foreign land strengthened their ties to World Jewry. Influenced by Leeser many Philadelphia Jews were convinced that a national organization was the answer to their problems. "United we can accomplish almost everything, otherwise nothing." Isaacs's *Jewish Messenger* preached the gospel of influence through unity. Twelve metropolitan congregations joined to set up an Executive Committee of Representatives of the United Congregations of Israelites of New York City. It was originally created to call a protest meeting. It symbolized the strongest form of unity yet achieved by this disparate multi-congregational community. Out of it in 1859 there was to come the first formal interstate Jewish organization.[34]

EPILOGUE

And the hero of this drama? What happened to him? In 1859 when Bologna became part of Victor Emmanuel's Italy the Inquisitional officer who was instrumental in seizing the child Edgardo was tried but acquitted. Several years later while addressing a group of young Catholics the Pope turned to Mortara who was present and addressed him: "I have bought thee, my son, for the Church at a very high price." In 1870 when Rome was incorporated into the new national state Mortara, then about nineteen, could have returned to his parents' home had he so desired. The Pope was no longer ruler of a secular state. But by this time Mortara was a fervent devoted Catholic, grateful to the historic accident that had brought him into the bosom of the Church. Ordained a priest in 1873 he took the name of his benefactor Pius—he who had, literally, saved his soul. Intelligent, competent, and learned Mortara advanced in the Catholic hierarchy. As an accomplished linguist he undertook missions to work among Catholics in many lands and in 1897 served in New York City. On rare occasions he met with his mother and siblings, maintaining good relations with them. When he visited his mother he accompanied her to a kosher restaurant. He died at Liège in 1940, in his eighty-eighth year, just about a month before the Nazis invaded Belgium. Had they come a little earlier and had they seized him as a Jew he might well have perished in a concentration camp.[35]

CHAPTER THIRTEEN

DEFENSE: THE BOARD OF DELEGATES OF

ALLIANCE ISRAÉLITES

INTRODUCTION

If no one else was convinced, the Jews at least were sure that had they been organized nationally they could have induced President Buchanan and his Secretary of State to ask the Pope to release the Mortara child. The Jews were very much under the illusion that they could influence American foreign policy. They thought that they had helped move Van Buren to do something about the Jews who were tortured in Damascus in 1840; they were now annoyed that Washington would not insist on equality in Switzerland for Jews who held American passports. If English Jews had so much influence in Whitehall it was because they had been organized ever since the late eighteenth century as a Board of Deputies, so American Jewry believed. The Catholics and Protestants here in the United States are unified; why can't we pattern ourselves after them? In union there is power, and, quoting Matthew 12:25, Rabbi Samuel M. Isaacs had pointed out that a "house divided against itself shall not stand."

This Jewish drive for unity and power may reflect the national American expansion. This was the era of the American drive to the coast, of Manifest Destiny. Jews watched the progress of the telegraph, the western march of the steel rails; they, too, were entranced by the emerging nationalism; those who were recent immigrants had experienced its impact and its whiplash in the new Germany. They shared the desire of other Americans to push into Mexico, Central America, and the Caribbean; they knew of the interest in Hawaii and Alaska, of the treaties with China and Japan. If American Jewry was eager to unite on a countrywide basis it may well have been because it was caught up in the nationalism of the day and, more patently, was dismayed by local anarchy, by congregational independency and particularism, and by intra-Jewish ethnic disdain. The so-called local community was a congeries of competing and disparate religious, educational, and charitable societies. If there could be no unity at the bottom then let there be unity at the top.[1]

KINSHIP

If Jews wanted to escape from the local impasse it was because they believed they could unite nationally and even internationally where, as individuals, they were not immediately concerned or threatened. This desire to act as a single body to try to help other Jews was a genuine one, a feeling of ineluctable compulsion, of deeply felt kinship. It is perhaps no exaggeration to say that it is unique among Jews. World Jewry has always responded to other Jews in distress, whether they are neighbors or in a distant land. Strange as it may seem, or may not seem, often the more distant the Jew the greater the devotion. Jews were certainly very much concerned about European Jewry; American Israelites believed they were part of that body, its westernmost arm. Even as they responded wholeheartedly to the call of the New Orleans Jewish community struck down by yellow fever, they rallied sympathetically to the appeal of Jews' College, London, for aid, sent money to the Polish Jews during the rebellion of the 1860's, and dispatched funds to stricken Strasbourg Jewry during the Franco-Prussian War of the 1870's. Jews on this side of the Atlantic preened themselves on the thought that though a frontier Jewry they were nevertheless important. As brash Americans they wanted to play a role on the world Jewish stage. This reaching out by Jewry here may in turn reflect the coeval tentatives of a primitive American cultural, spiritual, and commercial imperialism. American Jews were eager to help Jewries everywhere, philanthropically and politically. Conservative Shearith Israel did not hesitate to write to Washington recommending Noah as chargé d'affaires at Constantinople. It wanted to protect the Jews in Syria, Palestine, and the Turkish Balkans. In 1852 Congregation Shaaray Hashamayim of New York City wanted the Jews to assemble in a mass meeting to urge the United States to stop the persecution of Jews in Europe; the editor of the *Asmonean* wanted to bring Europe's Jews here.[2]

RUSSIAN AND CHINESE JEWS

The expulsion and ruin of hundreds if not thousands of Jews from the West Russian frontier in 1843 aroused their coreligionists the world over. Not only was money collected here but an effort was also made in the next few years to unite New York Jewry to raise its voice in protest. But nothing was accomplished. In 1869, Samuel Adler's Temple Emanu-El sent Abraham Geiger 2,000 gulden for the suffering Jews of West Russia. About the year 1850 the putative needs of the Jews of China seem to have aroused even more enthusiasm among America's Jews. The motivations here were manifold. Jews in America, and England, too, were excited at the prospect of seeing real Chinese coreligionists, fellow Israelites who were reported to need help. Jews on both sides of the Atlantic were determined to forestall the Protestant emissaries and missionaries who had set out for the Orient to visit and convert them. Many Jews thought that these Chinese were the remnants of the Lost Ten Tribes whose discovery and ingathering must precede the long hoped-for coming of the promised Messiah. In the 1780's and 1790's New York Jews had made inquiries about their Indian and Chinese coreligionists. Now, two generations later, Anglo-Protestantism's concern with the Chinese Jews set off a chain reaction in Jewish America. New Orleans Jewry in 1853 established a Foreign Missionary Society for the Amelioration of the Social and Political Conditions of the Jews in Foreign Lands; Touro left this new organization money in his will; Gutheim of New Orleans wanted to dispatch men to China and to distant lands to help and teach Jews in distress; Mobile and other cities talked of making collections for the suffering Jews of the Far East; Jacob Ezekiel of Richmond proposed a national fund-raising campaign on their behalf; Leeser and Wise expressed interest, and more than one rabbi volunteered to sail for the Celestial Empire. Here too nothing was done; it is doubtful whether there were many if any Chinese Jews still left. Yet years later, in 1869, the Board of Delegates of American Israelites was ready to send money to the Alliance Israélite Universelle to help send Joseph Halévy, the orientalist, to China. Halévy had already been in touch with the Falashas, the black Jews of Ethiopia.[3]

PALESTINE

The concept of a restored Jewry, one of the motives that impelled the Israelites on these shores to interest themselves in the Chinese Jews of Kai Feng Fu, was compelling in stimulating the devotion of World Jewry to the Jews of Palestine. God had promised to bring the Jews back, and "God is not a man that he should lie" (Num.23,19). The pious Jews already in Palestine were praying and holding the fort until the promised day arrived. They had to be helped. Money had been sent them from America ever since the 1700's and Jews everywhere in the United States from that time on had continued their generosity to the ubiquitous and unreliable Palestine solicitors. Prudent Jews sent their monies to the Holy Land through Dutch and English bankers or directly to Montefiore. Palestine could always be depended upon since colonial days to unite American Jewry. The earliest intercongregational society in the United States, established in New York City in 1832, was created to help the Jews in the Holy Land; Palestine relief societies were set up and funds were collected in towns and cities as far west as San Francisco in the 1850's. In an appeal in the general press, Jews of Wheeling called on their Christian friends to alleviate the distress of Palestine Jews suffering from famine and epidemics. When in the early 1850's Rabbi Samuel M. Isaacs called for help for the Jews of Palestine that may well have been one of the first American

Jewish national campaigns for overseas relief. Nevertheless many Jews had misgivings as they poured money into the bottomless Palestine hole; a few believed that charity began at home; others were convinced that indiscriminative giving (*halukkah*) to Jews who spent all of their time in prayer and study encouraged pauperism. Thoughtful Jews, among them Leeser, wanted to train the Palestinians in trade, farming, and the crafts. The Board of Delegates of American Israelites was later concerned with this type of constructive social welfare.[4]

INTIMATIONS OF A STRUCTURED COMMUNITY LOCALLY AND NATIONALLY

Kinship was never enough; the challenge to American Jewry was to transmute kinship into structured entities both locally and nationally. Informal attempts to tie Jews together were made in 1790 by Manuel Josephson and in the 1820's by, among others, M. E. Levy and Jacob S. Solis. The latter two pleaded for the establishment of a nationally supported academy for the youth. By 1836 Leeser was already pushing for a national union of congregations and in 1841, with the coming of the Germans, Leeser and Rabbi Louis Salomon of Rodeph Shalom published a well-developed plan for a tightly integrated national and local hierarchy. The 1840 Damascus Affair and its attendant mass meetings taught the Jews of the United States that they could act in concert. In addition, the rising tide of American nationalism may have touched American Jewry and moved it to react as a socioethnic group. The 1841 plan which had the support of several Philadelphia Jewish lay notables proposed the establishment of a national union of synagogs which was to meet biennially, a college to train cantors and teachers in Hebrew and classical studies, and an authoritative ecclesiastical board of three to license slaughterers and teachers and to supervise the local school system. Schools teaching Jewish and secular subjects were to be established in every town of size; the teachers, male and female, were to be paid by a local community council, but each congregation was to enjoy complete autonomy although traditional Orthodoxy was to be the norm. It was daily becoming more obvious that because of the independency of each synagog some form of uniformity was desirable. The Leeser-Salomon plan was designed to answer this need. Leeser who was seeking to restore the structured German over-all community, the gemeinde or kehillah, may have been influenced by the consistorial organizations which had enjoyed a brief existence under the French in the Kingdom of Westphalia.

The 1841 plan, the first large-scale proposal of its type in American Jewry, failed not only because the population was still too few in number, but also because the newcomers were burdened with the challenge of eking out a livelihood. In addition there was the ever-present factionalism; the minority of Reform Jews would not subject themselves to majority Orthodox control and even within the ranks of the traditionalists there was no harmony; the Orthodox natives feared the dominance of the unacculturated "German" Central European immigrants. Even in a physical sense union was difficult; rapid transportation and speedy communication still lay in the future. If only in a limited way the drive for an overall structure, if not for national "community," continued throughout the fifth decade. The B'nai B'rith lodge, which had first made its appearance in 1843, soon spread and began to reach out nationally through its Constitution Grand Lodge; in the *Occident* which appeared in the spring of that year Leeser continued his long campaign for union: one God, one Law, one people. A contributor wrote that only through union could American Jewry effactually aid the oppressed Jews of Russia, Italy, and Syria. That was in 1844. The following year Lilienthal of New York federated three German synagogs and he and his associates talked of citywide shehitah supervision, an ecclesiastical tribunal, the establishment of graded schools, good textbooks, and a book of common prayer to counter the spreading liturgical deviations. That same year the nationwide Jewish Publication Society was established.[5]

THE WISE APPEAL OF 1848

In 1845 Leeser reprinted the 1841 Leeser-Salomon union proposal with the hope that this time it would catch fire. Spurred on by Leeser and by A. A. Lindo, a Jamaican communal worker who had settled in this country, Wise of Albany made an urgent appeal to the congregations of America for unity and union in December, 1848. To a degree Wise was reacting to the European revolutionary upheavals of 1848. Not unlike Marx and Engel in their Communist Manifesto, Wise, carried away by the infectious euphoria of the day, wanted union, peace, and good relations between all peoples. He wanted American Jews to unite and further international liberalism and cosmopolitanism. The twenty-nine-year-old émigré was an impassioned enthusiast who wished not only to reform Jewry but the whole world. In a more limited sense he, the newspaper editors, and all those who shared his Jewish hopes, desired a formal congregational union, good schools, a strong press, a ministers' association, an authoritative rabbinic court, a seminary to train American Jewish clergymen, English sermons, a standard liturgy, uniformity in practice and worship, and a children's asylum to rescue the orphans from the clutches of the conversionists. There was even some talk of federating the charities. Through union and new institutions that generation hoped to stop the inroads of the missionaries and the prevailing apathy and assimilation. Released from their European moorings the immigrants were drifting away from Judaism. Rabbi Isaacs of Shaarey Tefillah also deplored the disunity of the day: American Jewry has no commonwealth; the fifty different congregations of 1849 constitute fifty distinct republics.[6]

The Wise plan and drive for union failed for the same reason that the Leeser-Salomon appeal of 1841 fell on deaf ears. Though Wise, admittedly a Reformer, protested that he would make no changes outside the ambit of canon law (halakah), saying he would never sanction Reform against established practice (*din*), few took him seriously. Fearful of hierarchy and hugging their own autocratic powers, individual congregations would hear nothing of union; leaders, resenting Wise's obvious drive for leadership, rejected his pleas for unity. The Albany rabbi found it impossible to bridge the gap between the Orthodox and the liberals. He could not and would not deny his sympathy for Reformers and the New York leftist Friends of Light. Enthralled by the 1848 Revolution, these latter believed that the Messianic Age was about to dawn; some of them even thought in terms of a universal religion. And if the universalistic Messiah was about to gallop into town at any moment, what need was there for a parochial union of Jews?[7]

If the 1840's was the decade for talk, the 1850's was a decade for action. Jewry was now more substantial; it had put on flesh. Leaders began to push hard for union on a national scale. Leeser kept hammering away in his *Occident* and in his addresses on the imperative need for a rabbinical court, better schools, a college, and courageous trained American ministers, not "menials" subservient to the congregational autocrats. He asked for circuit "missionaries" who would supervise the local ministers and he pleaded for Jewish hospitals and asylums. The primary need was for "a federal union of all the congregations on the continent and islands of America." This plea for union to include the congregations of the Caribbean was made just about a year after the Lopez filibustering expedition had failed to seize Cuba! Leeser insisted on well-trained native American spiritual leaders because "here we can prepare ourselves for our mission to become the teachers of mankind, the messengers of an enlightened civilization." Thus he proclaimed the Mission of Israel three years before its great protagonist David Einhorn set foot on American soil. America needed well-trained Jewish ministers because it was to serve as a haven for the oppressed Jews of Russia, Austria, and the Italian ghettos. Thus Leeser in the early 1850's. And while Leeser was pleading, the Jewish Theological Seminary and Scientific Institute was organized in New York City, if only on paper; Wise assembled the Cleveland Conference, opened Zion College, and moved on to Baltimore to chair a small but pretentious committee that called on Buchanan, protesting the inequities of the Swiss Treaty. But union in a formal sense was to come only in 1859 after the

Mortara Affair; American Jewry was finally aroused to act by a tragedy abroad that touched the heart strings of every Jewish parent.[8]

ESTABLISHMENT AND PROGRAM OF THE BOARD OF DELEGATES OF AMERICAN ISRAELITES (BDAI)

Though they should not have been annoyed, the Jews of this country were resentful at the refusal of the Washington authorities to intervene with the Pope on behalf of Edgar Mortara. American Jewry was well aware that though it was at least twice as numerous as English Jewry it had much less influence. Because in their minds a national organization was imperative the American Jews followed the pattern of the ad hoc city-wide committee that had led the Mortara protest and, after a preliminary meeting, established the Board of Delegates of American Israelites on November 27 and 29, 1859. About twenty-four congregations joined together; including New York City twelve towns were represented, and, with the exception of New Orleans, practically all were from the East. The Middle Westerners, many of whom were partisans of Isaac M. Wise, stayed out; relations between the Easterners and Wise, by then in Cincinnati, were strained. San Francisco was not represented for there was as yet no transcontinental railroad. Aristocratic Orthodox Shearith Israel and Mikveh Israel refused to join and at this juncture the Reformers, too, would have nothing to do with a board that was predominantly traditionalist. All told about one-third of the better known congregations of the country became members of the new national organization. The headquarters were in New York; Philadelphia could no longer hope to exercise hegemony.

For a number of reasons the American Board patterned itself on the Board of Deputies of British Jews. Rabbi Isaacs, one of the prime movers of the new combination, was an Englishman as were other board members. Montefiore, the uncrowned king of the Jews, headed the British Board, and in truth the Americans were quite willing to follow the lead of the often influential London Jewry. The British Empire was then the most powerful state in the world.

When it came to the formulation of a plan of action there were differences of opinion. Leeser and others who sympathized with him and set their hearts on a religious program—Jews were a religious people!—they wished to implement the entire corpus of suggestions which they had recommended for almost two decades: they hoped for a seminary, a national all-day school, an ecclesiastical court, circuit rabbis, locally federated charities, a rabbinical conference, and a standardized traditional form of worship. About one-fourth of the Board voted for this type of program. The majority which included religionists like Isaacs rejected it for they realized they could never unite all the synagogs of America on a purely religious platform. Although the Board did acknowledge the need for a seminary and the importance of religious education it declared quite categorically that it would not interfere with the internal administration of any congregation or synagog.

In a later declaration of policy it included the need for the collection of statistics and the determination to work with Jewish organizations abroad. This meant it would cooperate fully with the British Board. Later it was ready to work with the Anglo-Jewish Association, with German and Dutch groups, with the Austrian Allianz, and with the French Alliance Israélite Universelle. Wisely established on a noncongregational basis, the French society, created in 1860 in response to the Mortara incident, was the most important. Reflecting to some degree the imperial aims of Napoleon III, its cultural program embraced Jews in many parts of the world; the Anglo-Jewish Association and the Allianz were patterned after it. The French Alliance itself may have taken its name from the British Evangelical Alliance, a world-wide Protestant organization that sought to protect oppressed Protestant religious minorities. Basically the BDAI limited itself to the promotion of closer relations with all Israelites everywhere and with the furtherance of Jewish rights and interests both here and abroad. In essence it was a civil and religious defense group.[9]

DIFFICULTIES ENCOUNTERED BY THE BDAI

The BDAI found it difficult to secure the necessary broad-based support to unite American Jewry. Liturgical, social, cultural, and ethnic backgrounds kept natives and immigrants apart and set native against native and newcomer against newcomer. Apathy, individualism, and jealousy made it difficult to harness sympathies and resources. North, South, and East Germans looked askance at one another, and congregations in the same cities were rivals. Individualists like Jonas P. Levy of Washington, who went directly to the Secretary of State during the Syrian riots of 1860, bypassed the BDAI. Philadelphia was envious of New York; the East in turn was determined to snatch leadership from the West where Wise now reigned. The majority of Jews in this land did not accept the BDAI; even when it protested against the unconstitutional and discriminatory Chaplaincy Act during the Civil War a group of Reform rabbis did not hesitate to denounce it: the Board could do no right; it did not represent American Jewry.

Some opponents believed that a separate political organization, even though its sole aim was to secure political rights for Jews here and abroad, would expose Jews to the accusation of dual loyalties. This frightened them. The Reformers, especially Einhorn and Wise, were implacable in their hostility to the Board. Wise was bitter in his opposition: these anti-Reformers had bypassed him as a leader; Einhorn lashed out at the new national organization because of his immutable doctrinaire principles. Having suffered in Germany and Hungary at the hands of a hierarchy, Einhorn, God's angry man, was opposed to any Orthodox union. His prime objection to the BDAI was that it had "political" goals. We do not want a state within a state; we do not want an ecclesiastical board; we do not want to go back to Palestine. Because we are the bearers of God's word our field is the world; we have a universal mission. Einhorn was flogging a dead horse, for the Board had from the very beginning rejected the religious goals of Leeser. That ignoramus Leeser, thundered Einhorn, wants to be the Pope of the American Jews. The leaders of the BDAI are insane, said Wise, a pack of liars. But the Board survived the vituperation of Wise and Einhorn and grew. New congregations joined, even St. Louis on the other side of the Mississippi. A few Reformers finally made their peace with this national organization for they knew that it had deliberately negated all Jewish denominationalism. It concerned itself with statistics, philanthropic tasks, and the political emancipation of Jews in all lands where they were subject to disabilities.[10]

If the New York Orthodox who formed the core of the new association evinced admirable restraint in not pressing their Orthodoxy, credit is due very probably to Rabbi Isaacs. First things first: he envisaged a nationwide society that would help the Jews in the Holy Land and work for all members of his faith who were still oppressed. The model he always held before his eyes was the London Committee of Deputies of British Jews, for although Isaacs himself was a native Hollander his family had moved to London in 1814 when the father, a banker, had lost his fortune. Young Isaacs was then but ten years of age. He and his brothers were given a good Jewish education; four of the five youngsters became ministers. After serving for years as principal of an orphan asylum in London, Isaacs sailed for New York to become the rabbi of prestigious Bnai Jeshurun. There he preached regularly in English, the first of the New York Ashkenazic rabbis to employ this device to bring some life and instruction into the lethargic community. Several years later he was appointed minister of the secessionist Shaarey Tefilah. Isaacs, a good stylist and a competent journalist, began to write for the *Asmonean* and *Occident* and in 1857 finally established his own *Jewish Messenger*. It became his mouthpiece in which he defended his Orthodoxy against the rising Reformers and urged the establishment of Hebrew free schools, a hospital, an asylum, a rabbinic seminary, a federation of New York charities, and the organization which came to be known as the Board of Delegates. His son Myer, later a New York judge, was the secretary of the Board from its beginnings to 1876 when he became its president.[11]

THE ACCOMPLISHMENTS OF THE BDAI
THE UNITED STATES

Though the religiocultural area was most sensitive the BDAI made some efforts to influence that sphere; Leeser was constantly prodding and most of the Board members were committed to traditional educational ideals. The BDAI did recommend that ministers submit to an examination by competent men, that rabbinic and religious conferences be convoked, and that an ecclesiastical court be established. It did not—dared not—carry these suggestions into practice. It was undoubtedly due to Leeser, the vice president of the Board, that in 1867 it viewed with sympathy the opening of Maimonides College, a rabbinical seminary; after some debate in the 1860's a new American Jewish Publication Society was founded in 1872, and in the 1860's the Board looked with favor on the Hebrew Free Schools on the Lower East Side of New York. Because the impoverished parents there could not afford to educate their children they had been exposed to the enticements of Christian missionaries who had conversion as their goal. By 1878 there were over a thousand Jewish children enrolled in the new Jewish institutions of elementary learning.

Statistical studies were made in the 1860's and, in the late 1870's the Board, jointly with the Union of American Hebrew Congregations, undertook a large-scale national survey of American Jewry. This important and very valuable population study was published in 1880. Inasmuch as all Jews felt threatened by disabilities the Board was able to move aggressively in the field of civil and political rights. It protested successfully against the discriminatory laws which prevented Jewish clergymen from officiating as chaplains during the Civil War in New York state and in the federal armed services; it helped campaign against Grant's notorious General Orders No. 11 whereby Jews were expelled in 1862 from the territories occupied by the Army of the Tennessee. The BDAI remonstrated to Congress when the Presbyterians, meeting in Pittsburgh in 1864, urged the national legislature to recognize Christianity as the religion of the land; the Board vigorously attacked this proposed amendment which was never given serious consideration. Establishing or recognizing Christianity as the religion of this republic had been sought by zealots ever since the Constitution was debated and it is still an issue today. That only Protestants could hold office in New Hampshire, that only Christians could take the test oath in North Carolina and subscribe to the terms of the proposed Reconstruction Act in 1866, were problems to which the Board addressed itself, successfully on the whole. In campaigning against a proposed North Carolina constitution of 1866 which limited officeholding to those who believed in the divine authority of the New Testament, the Board wrote a memorial addressed "To The Friends of Religious Liberty in the State of North Carolina." This constitution was not accepted. When in 1872 President Alexander Stewart Webb of New York's City College refused to excuse his Jewish students from taking an examination on the holiday of Pentecost, the Board went over his head and appealed to the trustees who deferred to the protesting Jews.[12]

IMMIGRATION AND THE BDAI

This problem of making Jewish youth take examinations on the Sabbath and Holy Days was to plague Orthodox Jewry in the next generation. Orthodoxy began to receive recruits from Eastern Europe as early as 1870. As famine and epidemic broke out in Western Russia large sums were raised here to aid the sufferers and hundreds of poor Jews were indiscriminately shipped here by Russian and other European relief committees. American Jewry and the BDAI resented the shipment of unskilled paupers to these shores. The Americans preferred that only the hardworking young and able mechanics be sent. In 1873 after disastrous anti-Jewish riots in Rumania a number of Jews from that country were also shipped to New York City. The Board talked of financing the education of some of the young Russians and Rumanians and even contemplated settling them in colonies somewhere out West. This scheme for colonization was adopted later in the decade by the Union of American Hebrew Congregations.[13]

THE BDAI AND THE JEWS ABROAD

Any scheme to help refugee Jews here met with opposition in some quarters. American Jewry of the 1860's and 1870's was disorganized and insecure. Almost any type of cooperation was hampered by areas of friction. But most American Jews were in agreement that European, Asian, and North African Jews were entitled to life, liberty, and happiness. And as the BDAI set out to send relief monies abroad and to help Jews politically it had the support of practically all Jews on this side of the Atlantic. Even the pugnacious Einhorn was eager to send relief to his coreligionists in Morocco. In order to appreciate this preoccupation with Jewry abroad it must constantly be borne in mind that when the Board began its overseas work there were really only two fully emancipated Jewries in the world in addition to the American: the French and the Dutch.

In rallying to the aid of European Jewry the BDAI was fully aware of the American policy of isolation and nonintervention that had been inaugurated by Monroe: "Our policy in regard to Europe . . . is not to interfere in the internal concerns of any of its powers." But the Jews here may also have been cognizant of another phrase in the 1823 Monroe Doctrine message to Congress: "The citizens of the United States cherish sentiments the most friendly in favor of the liberty and happiness of their fellow-men on that side of the Atlantic." To this latter statement American Jewry could subscribe wholeheartedly. The United States was reaching out commercially to Europe and was interested on humanitarian grounds in helping the oppressed everywhere; it had manifested this interest in the Damascus Affair of 1840. For Jews and for many other Americans liberalism and compassion were articles for export; American Jewry was determined to help Jews everywhere. To this extent the foreign policy of both groups was confluent. Thus Washington frequently worked with the BDAI as the French with the Alliance Israélite Universelle and the English with Montefiore's Board of Deputies. And it is worthy of repetition: the Jewish vote was daily increasing in size; of this the government was fully cognizant.

Working closely with the Jewish political, philanthropic, and cultural associations in Europe and above all with the Alliance Israélite Universelle and with the Board of Deputies of British Jews, the BDAI sent relief funds in the 1860's to Morocco and Tunis, in the 1870's to Persia. Conditions for Jews in Morocco were particularly bad. A Jew there who raised his hand against a Moor could have it cut off; a Moor who killed a Jew would not be executed, merely fined; and as late as 1905 the Jews of that unhappy land were not permitted to testify in Moroccan courts and were compelled to go barefoot and bareheaded when they left their ghettos. These Israelites suffered during the Moroccan-Spanish wars which dragged on from 1859 into the 1870's, and as hundreds of Jewish refugees fled across the Straits to Gibraltar and the neighboring towns the Jews of the United States led by the BDAI sent thousands of dollars to relieve them. A Jewish mariner, Charles S. Moses, volunteered the use of his ship, the *Ann Elizabeth*, to carry food and supplies to the refugees. About a third of all the funds raised by World Jewry for the Moroccans came from the distant American land. People who raise funds achieve influence. In 1863 at the request of the BDAI, Secretary of State Seward instructed the United States consul at Tangiers to intervene, and as famine and atrocities repeated themselves in the next two decades the United States constantly authorized its representatives in Morocco and its ambassador in Spain to do what they could for the Jews in that Moslem state. William M. Evarts, Hayes's Secretary of State, wrote the American consul to disregard technicalities and "shield Hebrews from oppression"; in 1880 American Jewry appointed a coreligionist to serve as its agent in Tangiers and to report on conditions there. Evarts remained concerned: "In the interest of humanity . . .," he instructed the American consul, "continue your good offices in behalf of the Jewish race." And when James G. Blaine succeeded Evarts he carried on this liberal tradition: "Help this unhappy race," he wrote the American consul at Tangiers.

In 1880 Lucius Fairchild, the United States minister to Spain, made representations, together with other diplomats, to the Moroccans because of their oppression of the Jews, some of whom were imprisoned or whipped to death. Later in Garfield's administration, Fairchild voluntarily crossed the Straits to study the status of Moroccan Jewry and to report to Blaine. In Spain itself conditions for its Israelites had improved in 1869 under a somewhat liberal regime; the 1492 decree of expulsion was repealed and the BDAI prepared to help the Spanish Jews build a synagog in the capital city. When a reactionary regime of the 1870's abridged the right of Spanish Jewish subjects, the Board intervened although unsuccessfully. Curiously enough the Spanish in 1881 informed the American government that it was ready to help the Russian Jewish victims of the 1881 riots and murders. Blaine wrote Fairchild to express the thanks of the American government for this humanitarian gesture.[14]

The Jews whom the Spanish were willing to help in 1881 were not only émigrés fleeing from the Russian pogroms but in all probability others—Sephardim?—who had fled to Palestine to avoid being crushed by the Russian and Turkish armies during the War of 1877-1878. Relatively speaking Turkey was good to its Jews, certainly much better than the Christians of the Balkans. The Jewish problem in Turkey was localized in Palestine: provincial governmental mistreatment though oppressive was endurable; poverty was endemic. The BDAI, individual American congregations, and the Free Sons of Israel raised and dispatched large sums of money to aid the impoverished and diseased, working closely with Europe's Jewish relief agencies, although Leeser and the Board really would have preferred to reconstruct Palestine Jewry economically. In this sense they were proto-Brandeisians. Relief alone was never enough. The BDAI and American Jewry were concerned to raise the moral and cultural standards of the native Jewish Palestinians and the incoming refugees; the future of a Jewish Palestine lay in crafts, farming, and secular education for the youth. The BDAI was eager to build homes for artisans and to help establish and further hospices and hospitals. Generous grants were forwarded to the Alliance's agricultural training school at Jaffa. Working through the Department of State at Washington, the Constantinople legation, and the Jerusalem consul, the Board attempted wherever feasible to protect the Palestine newcomers. Some ministers and consuls were more sympathetic than others.

Together with the other European defense agencies the BDAI worked fruitlessly in the early days to secure the release of the child Mortara; in 1870 during a bad flood it came to the rescue of Roman Jewry and, until it was no longer necessary, it urged the United States to insist on equal rights for Americans in Switzerland. In spite of the rise of anti-Semitism the problems of American Jews in Bismarck's Germany were not acute; most of these difficulties dealt with the unfulfilled milltary duty of native German Jews who had become naturalized Americans and were arrested when they returned to the Fatherland. When a stubborn Alsatian Jew caught on a visit back home refused to pay his fine and was imprisoned, Bismarck would not set the young Israelite free even though Andrew D. White, the American minister in Berlin, interceded with the chancellor personally. Pretending to be angry, White started to leave Germany by slow stages; by the time he reached Paris Bismarck had had second thoughts. White found a telegram awaiting him in the French capital: "Your man in Alsace-Lorraine is free."[15]

AMERICAN JEWRY AND RUSSIA TO **1881**

As in Germany, Russian Jews, too, who had fled onerous military service experienced annoyances when they returned to the land of their nativity. Because they were American citizens the United States government was compelled to intervene—ever since 1864—to assist individuals who went back to Russia. Naturalized American Jews, Muscovite by birth, who had come to do business in their former homeland, often ran into disabilities, for in essence the 1832 Russian-American Treaty declared that Americans in Russia must submit to Russian law, a law that disfranchised and disabled Jews. The United States government intervened on behalf of its Russian-born citizens of the Jewish faith and generally succeeded in aiding them, de facto if not de jure, and on one occasion the House of Representatives passed a resolution asking the President to stretch forth a helping hand to two Russian American Jewish citizens who were experiencing difficulties. John Hay, Acting Secretary of State, told the American minister to Russia that he wanted "religious toleration for our citizens abroad." John W. Foster, the American envoy, spoke to the Russian Minister for Foreign Affairs, patiently explaining that: "The experience of the United States had amply shown the wisdom of removing all discriminations against them [the Jews] in the laws and of placing this race upon an equal footing with all other citizens." For political reasons the British lagged behind the Americans, failing to wage a vigorous struggle to protect their citizens of Jewish birth who sought to live in and do business in the Romanov Empire.

Beginning with the Hayes administration the American government adopted a sterner attitude toward Russia requiring full equality for American Jewish citizens sojourning in Russia. Prior to 1880 the American consuls and ministers in Russia seemed to have accepted the Russian interpretation of Article I of the 1832 treaty: Jews in Russia were to be treated as if they were Russian Jews. Secretary of State Evarts and Minister Foster now insisted on equality without any distinction because of creed or origin. Blaine, who succeeded Evarts, pursued this egalitarian policy even more vigorously declaring categorically that the United States would not accept any discrimination by any state against American citizens even if there was no treaty in force.[16]

A more pressing issue in American relations with the czarist state was the latter's mistreatment of its own Jewish population numbering about two million in 1870. As in Morocco the Jews of Russia were experiencing distressing disabilities and the BDAI in the 1860's besought the American authorities to succor these East Europeans on humanitarian grounds. Refurbishing a law of 1825 the Russians in 1869 had ordered the expulsion into the interior of thousands of Jews who lived in the borderlands, especially in the gubernia of Bessarabia. A delegation of three Jewish notables, Simon Wolf, Henry Adler, and Adolphus S. Solomons, representing the B'nai B'rith and the BDAI, waited on President Grant and asked him to befriend the Jews. It was apparent that the State Department officers and the American minister Andrew G. Curtin would do little. Reporting to Secretary of State Hamilton Fish, Curtin wrote a cautious reserved letter which seemed to justify the Russian decree of forcible removal: the Jews are sharp, an evil influence, smugglers, evaders of taxes, and major contributors to the ruin of the improvident nobility and peasants. The Russians were not anti-Jewish; they were merely protecting themselves against lawbreakers. Grant was most gracious to the visiting delegates and promised to discuss their request with his cabinet and to forward a B'nai B'rith petition on this matter to the Russian authorities. He deplored the persecution of Jews in this age of enlightenment. From this time on American Jews were to urge their government constantly to uphold the rights of American Jewish citizens in Russia and to volunteer its good offices to ameliorate the condition of oppressed Russian Jewry.[17]

AMERICAN JEWRY, SERBIA, AND THE DANUBIAN PRINCIPALITIES

SERBIA

In a letter to the American minister at London, James Russell Lowell, the worst thing that the blunt-spoken James G. Blaine could say of the Russians was that they ranked with the Rumanians and the Moroccans in their treatment of their native Hebrews. That was a harsh but accurate indictment of both the Russians and the Rumanians. Blaine said nothing of the Serbians for they had kept the promises which they had made to the European Powers in 1878 at the Congress of Berlin; they had emancipated their Jews. From the 1850's into the 1870's the Serbians—nominally subjects of the Ottoman Empire—abused the Jews so cruelly that many fled the country. At the request of the BDAI, Seward wrote to the American minister in Turkey, Edward J. Morris, but the latter was disinclined to do anything for the Jews of that land whom he described as usurers. In interceding for Serbian Jewry the American Board of Delegates was but following the lead of the British Jews who had asked their government to intervene in the Balkans. Like the European Jewish defense associations, the BDAI later sought equality for all Jews in Serbia as a precondition of her independence at the Congress of Berlin. The Serbians assented and emancipated their Israelites and by the 1880's the Jews of that country had little cause for complaint; they were as free as Jews could be free in a Christian Balkan state.[18]

RUMANIA

When the Concert of Powers met at Paris in 1856 to settle the Crimean War it took up the Jewish Question. The Jews in the Turko-Christian Balkans had for generations been very much in the limelight because of the abuses to which they had been subjected. Because mid-nineteenth-century Christendom thought of itself in terms of culture, civilization, and humanity it behooved it to solve the Jewish Question. By the Treaty of Paris in 1856 the Jews of autonomous Moldavia and Wallachia were promised religious and economic rights and liberties but no political privileges. Two years later (1858) the Convention of Paris decided that all Christians, including the Protestants of those Greek Orthodox areas, were to be granted political rights and the hope was held out that these privileges would be extended to the Jews in the future. Though civil liberties were guaranteed them by the Convention economic security and personal liberty were often distinguished by their absence. In the new Rumania, the United Principalities of Moldavia and Wallachia, severe disabilities, violence, and expulsions were still the lot of the Children of Israel. The constant mistreatment of the Rumanian Israelites focused the attention of World Jewry on the Principalities. As early as 1854 the French Jews had already sought to protect the interests of their coreligionists in the Turkish Balkans; in 1861 Montefiore and his Board of Deputies turned to the English government and asked it to intervene, and when six years later the Rumanians told the English in effect to mind their own business the later retorted: "The peculiar position of the Jews places them under the protection of the civilized world." Influenced probably by British Jewry, the BDAI in distant America addressed itself that same year to the fate of its Rumanian Jewish brethren. It wrote Seward in 1867 and asked him to do what he could to ameliorate the sufferings of the Rumanian Jews. Morris, the American minister to Turkey—under the prodding of Seward—told the Rumanian agent in Constantinople that America could have no confidence in a state that persecuted its Jews.[19]

Ironically enough conditions improved for Jewry in Rumania in 1870. Aroused by a world-wide report of killings, which turned out to be false, the House of Representatives passed a resolution of sympathy, and President Grant, at the request of the BDAI and Simon Wolf, the American Jewish go-between in Washington, appointed Benjamin Franklin Peixotto as this country's consul to Rumania. Enthusiastic, gifted, adventurous, and impracticable, Peixotto was eager to help his fellow Jews as the defender of the faith. The thirty-six-years-of-age Peixotto had already had an interesting career. Like his father Dr. Daniel L. M. Peixotto he was always scanning the horizon for new worlds and new prospects. He studied law, became a Democrat, and supported Douglas against Lincoln for the presidency; by the early 1860's he had become the president, the Grand Prince, of the B'nai B'rith fraternity. After his term of office expired in 1867 he moved to New York and then to San Francisco where he continued his practice of the law. It is hard to determine whether he was successful or not but he was a charming man, brilliant and articulate. The consulship paid no salary but friends and the B'nai B'rith raised a purse for him and he managed somehow or other to maintain himself at Bucharest. When Peixotto stopped off in Washington to receive his official instructions he conferred with President Grant who said to him: "The United States knowing no distinction between her citizens on account of religion or nativity naturally believes in a civilization the world over which will secure the same universal views." This was strange but welcome doctrine from a Civil War general who eight years before had expelled the Jews from the areas occupied by his troops. The consul remained in Rumania until 1876 and undoubtedly served as a restraining influence on the anti-Jewish riotous elements. On occasion Peixotto was able to secure the support of other consuls to reenforce his protests.[20]

This American knight-errant and the other consuls, however, were not able to anticipate or stave off the brutal riots of 1872 when the Jews of Ismail and neighboring towns were beaten and robbed by mobs of looters. Rumor had it that the Russians had instigated the attacks. Sympathetic to the plight of Rumanian Jewry, Hamilton Fish, Grant's Secretary of State, instructed his ministers in Europe to make their remonstrances to the signatories of the treaty and convention of 1856 and 1858; Rumania had received autonomy at the hands of the Great Powers on condition that she would at least protect all her subjects. The American minister at Paris was sympathetic; the minister at Constantinople, George H. Boker, belittled the incident, and the American representative at Rome implied that the Russians had fomented the whole affair. The Russians in turn denied that there had been any riots. It was this affair at Ismail that moved Peixotto among others to urge his fellow Jews to meet in order to discuss the state of the Jews in the Balkans. Thus the first international Jewish conference in which American Jews participated assembled in Brussels, October 29-30, 1872. Peixotto and Isaac Seligman, the banker, represented the BDAI. The Americans were welcomed, for their Jewry was a large one and, what was equally important, a generous one. The conference indulged itself in far-ranging plans and utopian vistas; its goal was to free all Jews wherever they were in bondage and to raise the cultural and moral plane of Rumanian Jewry. It established a committee, sitting in Vienna, to work with European governments but it is not easy to determine whether it did any good. More realistically the conference deplored the flight of Rumanian immigrants to the United States unless they were prepared to cope with the rigors of life in a foreign land. The BDAI, practical, if nothing else, continued to send relief funds.

Because conditions in the Balkan states did not improve, World Jewry called a second international conference. It met at Paris on December 16, 1876. Jewries from nine lands were represented and the BDAI again sent a delegation. Three Americans spoke for it, William Seligman and two others. Because it was expensive to dispatch delegates from the States Jewish notables, visiting on the continent, were coopted to attend the conferences. With membership dues of only $10 a year the BDAI was unable to build up a war chest. The second conference called for civil and political rights for non-Moslems in the European Turkish-Christian lands; of course it had the Jews particularly in mind. One of the reasons the Israelites met in December was that the Great Powers were about to assemble at Constantinople to try once again to stabilize and improve political conditions in the Balkans. The Paris Jewish conferees sent a memorial detailing their hopes to the representatives at Constantinople but little if anything was accomplished even though they enjoyed the sympathetic cooperation of the American minister there. In the meantime the Russo-Turkish conflict has flared up into a full-scale war in April, 1877; the Jews were maltreated and killed by the Rumanians and the fighting forces, and thousands of panic-stricken Jews, especially Bulgarians, fled to Turkey leaving everything behind. Some made their way to Palestine. Led once more by the BDAI, the Americans organized a relief committee that forwarded thousands of dollars to the Alliance Israélite for distribution to the Balkan Jewish émigrés. The treasurer of this 1878 refugee committee was the German Jewish immigrant and banker Jacob H. Schiff; in the next generation he was to become the country's most distinguished Jewish philanthropist and communal leader. Myer S. Isaacs, the chairman of the relief committee and president of the BDAI, asked Secretary Evarts to use the good offices of the American ministers at Vienna and Constantinople to protect the Jews. Even better why not use our powerful Mediterranean fleet? Evarts, ever willing to help as he had in Morocco and Russia, wrote to Maynard at Constantinople and the latter instructed the American consuls in the Balkans to do what they could.[21]

RUMANIA AND THE CONGRESS OF BERLIN, 1878

When the Russo-Turkish War came to an end in March, 1878, the Jews of the world and the BDAI with them were determined to guarantee the rights of the Jews in the Balkans. For almost a generation French and English Jewry had moved to aid the disabled Jews of those Turkish provinces. In 1877 the BDAI had proposed a third international Jewish congress and in February the following year, foreseeing the speedy end of the Russo-Turkish conflict and wishing to anticipate the prospective peace congress it wrote the Anglo-Jewish Association. Thus when the Powers met at the Congress of Berlin in June and July in 1878 to redraw the map of the Balkans, the British Board of Deputies and the Alliance were prepared. They asked the Congress to make the independence of the Balkan principalities conditional on the grant of civil and political rights to their Jews. Secretary Evarts in Washington, Minister Bayard Taylor in Berlin, and Minister John A. Kasson in Vienna were ready to further the cause of the Jews. Kasson, who was present in Berlin, wanted complete equality for all American Jews living in the Balkan states and extensive rights for the native Jews. The statesmen at the Congress gave freedom to Rumania, Serbia, and Montenegro, with the understanding that they would accord full rights to all their subjects; Turkey had already promised freedom to its non-Moslems, and Bulgaria, still under the Turks, also agreed to emancipate its Israelites. Article XLIV of the 1878 Congress of Berlin unequivocally guaranteed civil and political rights to all the Jews of Rumania. Even Russia assented.

Shortly after the Congress adjourned the Jews met again in Paris in a third international conference convoked by the Alliance Israélite Universelle. This was on August 15. In a proposed program which the BDAI had suggested as early as 1877 the Board called for liberty and learning for all submerged Jews in Europe, Asia, and North Africa. The Palestine Jewish youth were to be trained in industry; Hebrew education was to be pursued, and a synod was to be called into being to study the needs and problems of modern Judaism. Obviously the influence of Leeser and his friends, oriented to western culture but steadfastly loyal to tradition, wanting to work out a synthesis of Orthodoxy and modernism, still continued. Once again nothing was done in these religiocultural areas; they were too controversial. Three American representatives of the BDAI appeared at the Paris Conference and limited themselves to pleas for selected immigration to the United States and constructive economic policies for Palestinian Jewry. These things were not new; the Americans were nothing if not pragmatic. In July after the Berlin Congress of the powers was over, and even before the Jewish conferees assembled in Paris, the BDAI was quite elated with the thought of what it had helped to bring to pass. "The Hebrews of Rumania are free." The Americans envisaged their continued collaboration with the European Jewish defense agencies. There was a job to be done; Russian Jewry was not yet free.[22]

DEBACLE

All the states except Rumania carried out the provisions of the Congress of Berlin, certainly as far as the Jews were concerned. The Rumanians began to employ subterfuges even while negotiating with Washington for recognition. The Rumanian Jews, said the Rumanians, are aliens, foreigners, irresponsible and undesirable like the Chinese whom you Americans are trying to exclude. You Americans ought to understand our problem. Nevertheless the rulers of this new state solemnly promises the Americans that the Jews would be emancipated. The BDAI began to have its doubts but Kasson at Vienna assured the authorities in Washington that the new state would meet its obligations. He advocated recognition and the United States accepted his recommendation. This new Balkan government then declared laconically that Jews were aliens and as such they would have to be naturalized; naturalization required ten years residence, and each petition for citizenship would have to be approved by an individual act of Parliament. In most cases the petitions were denied. Rumania consistently violated its promises down into the middle of the twentieth century; there was no lessening of discrimination.[23]

THE UNION OF AMERICAN HEBREW CONGREGATIONS (UAHC) STEPS IN

Though not outstandingly successful the Board of Delegates was certainly not moribund. Yet in 1878, the very year it played a not unimportant part at the third international Jewish conference in Paris, the Board merged with the Union of American Hebrew Congregations. What happened? No later than 1866 the Board had begun to reach out in order to embrace other American societies and institutions. Was this the postbellum American passion for bigness, expansion, union? There was also talk of inviting some of the Young Men's Hebrew Associations and educational agencies to join the Board but nothing came of these early approaches. It may well be that the BDAI merged with the UAHC because it was essentially a limited eastern regional club and it needed hinterland grass roots support. The UAHC was vigorous and growing relatively fast. Through the western and southern support which the UAHC could now lend, the Board hoped to become an important national Jewish instrument in this country, to exert more power in Washington, and to play an ever-increasing role in European Jewish affairs. In turn the Union, primarily a religious consortium, needed the eastern congregations, their manpower, and their megalopolitan money. Each organization represented only a limited constituency; each needed the other. Wise was ambitious; he and his Cincinnati lay leaders wanted an overall American organization to reenforce their religious base and to fortify the UAHC in the area of civic defense, foreign relief, and political power. It looked like a good offer for both parties and the marriage was consummated. The BDAI was not completely swallowed up; it retained its autonomy and became a standing committee of the Union: the Board of Delegates on Civil and Religious Rights. Nevertheless the merger may be deemed a victory for the Wise Men of the West, the men who for another generation were to dominate American Jewish life. Now the Union could boast that it represented a majority of the important American Jewish synagogs. The merger was a real achievement, for it united the American natives and the immigrants from half a dozen European lands. National American union, unity, had moved a step forward.[24]

REJECTION, UNITY, COMMUNITY: AN EVALUATION

Most American Jews believed that if they were organizationally, structurally united they could protect and further themselves more effectively. This concept is important: unity in the face of an indifferent or presumptively hostile Gentile world is the theme of much of American Jewish history. As America reached out beyond its borders, the Jews here, like the French and the Alliance, also reached out abroad. Knowing the importance of their numbers, wealth, and generosity the Jews of the United States were moved by a strong desire to play a part in World Jewry. This was a proto-hegemonic impulse. There was as yet no central national organization here but a feeling of kinship tied them to Jews in all lands and impelled them to offer help to the impoverished and the oppressed. The attempts since the late eighteenth century to bring all American Jews together in some sort of formal association were not successful though countrywide unity was furthered by national fraternal orders, newspapers, and a publication society. The Mortara Affair, disregard for the American passport, and the oppression of underprivileged Diaspora Jews gave birth to the BDAI, the first American Jewish defense association and the second oldest in the Jewish world. This attempt to combine American Jews into a tighter whole was but one phase of an all-inclusive drive to supervise and federate the instrumentalities for kashrut, education, charity, and culture; it was but one facet of the hope for a uniform liturgy and a more integrated community. In none of these areas was Jewry successful. Though devoutly wished for by some no overall association to control and improve all aspects of American Jewish life was possible to mid-nineteenth-century United States. There could be no consensus on such sensitive controversial issues. Unity came hard; Jews could come together only for relief and political defense, and these primarily for Jews abroad.

The barriers to unity were many: internal conflicts, personal rivalries, religious differences, rampant individualism. This was an age of centrifugality, for the American Jewish immigrant was still reacting against European Jewish communal control and the governmental autocracy of conservative and reactionary transatlantic states. The creation of the BDAI in spite of all these difficulties was a feat of no mean order particularly in view of the fact that it had no competent vigorous leadership. The unity of effort it achieved abroad helped to further unity here, locally and nationally; it established a pattern that was adopted by the more powerful UAHC. By its very existence as a united group the Board impressed the State Department; Washington was conscious that American Jewry now had a watchdog organization; its respect for this Jewry mounted and it moved forward to help Jews abroad in line with the highest American humanitarian traditions and avouchments.[25]

CHAPTER FOURTEEN

AMERICAN JEWRY, 1840–1860: A SUMMARY

COMING OF THE "GERMANS"

The twenty years before the Civil War are very important for the history of the American Jew. In 1820 there were about 3,000 Jews in this country; in 1841 about 15,000, in 1861 about 150,000. To America with its more than 31,000,000 souls this tiny Jewish community was not of great significance; to World Jewry the existence of a vigorous community of 150,000 enfranchised, economically prosperous, and generous Jews was very significant—unique. Like Jonah's gourd it grew up, as it were, overnight, in a single generation. Joining the millions of others who were leaving the old homeland, hundreds and ultimately thousands of Central European Jews crossed the Atlantic to grasp the political and economic opportunities which beckoned. Here the Jew could be a complete human being—spiritually, emotionally. These "Germans," who began coming in the Napoleonic period were of course not America's Jewish pioneers, for they found already here a native tidewater "Sephardic" community which looked upon the newcomers as strangers if not as interlopers to be held at arm's length socially; these immigrants were alien in tongue, manner, and title. Overwhelmed in numbers the natives affected to ignore the newcomers, but as soon as the Ashkenazim were numerically strong enough they opened their own bethels. Thus there were soon two American Jewish communities, one Sephardic and one Ashkenazic; and then in turn, the disparate Ashkenazim, coming from different European lands and provinces, began to set up sub-communities. By the 1840's the American Jewish community was a mulligan stew. This communal disintegration was to continue for a century till the older more traditional synagog community was completely pulverized. Dozens of new congregations sprang up each a law unto itself; surrounding them was a host of self-help confraternities, philanthropic societies, leisure and cultural associations. Many of these noncongregational societies were sec-

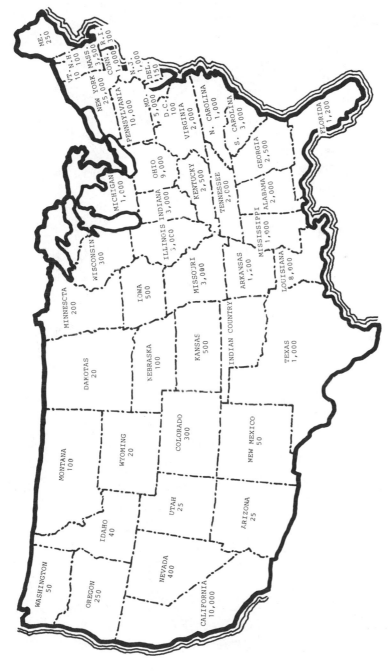

Total Jewish Population in 1860, 125,000–200,000. Shown in states and in areas that later became states. Note all numbers are contemporary estimates.

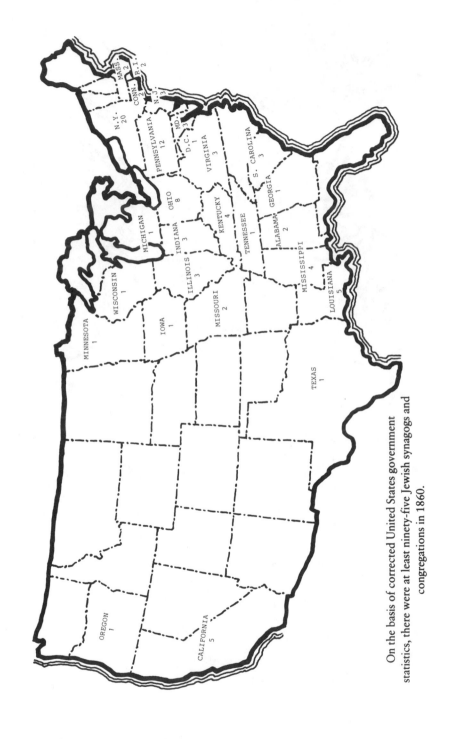

On the basis of corrected United States government statistics, there were at least ninety-five Jewish synagogs and congregations in 1860.

ularistic—not overtly religious, yet certainly not anti-religious. The synagog was not the center of Jewish life because there was no communal compulsion compelling affiliation, yet religion remained the substratum of all that was Jewish; it was the invisible, permanent, underlying continuum.

PROBLEMS THE NEW COMMUNITY FACED

Even as the Sephardic natives in the tidewater synagogs looked down upon the new arrivals, Gentiles looked down upon all Jews; at best they ignored them. As the Jews grew in number prejudice spread; the cheap penny press always found the Jew worthy of a column. Jews were very good, very rich, or very bad, but never uninteresting. Because the word "Jew" was nearly always a term of mild contempt, considerate Christians referred to their Jewish friends as Hebrews or Israelites. Prejudice, or better, disregard for the feelings of Jews expressed itself in exclusive social relations, Christological phrasing in public proclamations, Christian teachings in the schools, and punitive Sunday work laws. All this was annoying but in no sense calamitous, for the Jew was better off here than anywhere else in the world. In 1837 James Joseph Sylvester left Cambridge University because as a Jew he was denied a teaching position but he experienced no difficulty in securing an appointment at Jefferson's University of Virginia (1841). This is the man who was in time to become one of the great mathematicians of the nineteenth century. The brunt of antebellum prejudice was borne by Negroes and Catholics; for the time being the Jew was bypassed by the nativists. Yet rejection of the Jews may have spurred the new arrivals to hasten their acculturation. Desiring to be like their Gentile neighbors the Jew speeded up the assimilatory process; in a generation at most he became a suave, well-dressed, typical American businessman.

ECONOMIC PROBLEMS: THE TREK WESTWARD

Making a living was for many a real problem. It is wrong to understate the tribulations of these European immigrants as they struggled, often desperately, to keep their heads above water. There were numerous artisans, a limited few in the professions; most Jews were modest businessmen in some form of apparel sales. After years of trial and error these shopkeepers managed to find a likely town where they settled down and raised their families in comfort. The few individuals who acquired wealth in the newer towns of the transappalachian West frequently became part of the elite power structure. Though millions of European immigrants, farmers for the most part, crossed the mountains to the new lands of the boundless West most European Jews had their fill of travel when they landed; they preferred to remain in the northeastern sector of the country. Yet for reasons often known only to themselves hundreds and thousands of them crossed the Hudson and followed the endless stream of men and women moving westward. After reaching California they started trekking eastward in 1850 into the mountains and plains where they met their fellow Jews who had started westward from the Missouri. Some of these Jewish businessmen were pioneers, and dozens of Jewish towns named by or after them testify to their daring and their achievements. These transmontane argonauts fitted well into the new West, into this unsophisticated farming world, for this was the type of economic culture which had fostered them in Central and Eastern Europe. They were precapitalist village or small-town Jews thrilled at the thought that they were now part of a romantic world. In 1846 the first Jewish settlers in the booming town of Chicago called their synagog: The Men of the West, Anshe Maari[a]v. In villages and hamlets that stretched from the Blue Ridge Mountains to the Pacific Ocean Jews were nearly always present as retailers supplying the townsmen, farmers, ranchers, and forts with goods and provisions, helping them to maintain an eastern standard of living.

As a wholesaler the Jew made his warehouse the focal mart for the surrounding country; like a magnet he drew others, and in a sense became the core around which Jews and Jewish institutions agglomerated. The first Jewish organization was usually a Hebrew Benevolent Society, a religiosocial pious association built on a charitative base, but in the course of a few years the town would also have a cemetery, a hall for worship, a Sunday School of some sort, and a literary society or lodge. But any one of these different associations could and did serve as the town's pioneer Jewish institution out of which the community evolved. If the town developed into a city of importance it would in the course of years add an old-folks home, a card-playing and eating club, an orphan asylum, and even a Jewish newspaper.

Religion

The vast majority of synagog members were Orthodox, at least nominally. Through the "German" immigrants American Jewry experienced a resurgence of the European type of Orthodoxy. Most natives, too, were staunchly observant in principle although many of them, like their colonial forebears, honored the concept of salutary neglect. With exceptions of course Jews circumcised their youngsters, insisted upon the bar mitzvah rite, observed kashrut at home, remembered the Holy Days, and mourned in the traditional fashion by remaining at home for a week or less (shivah). The German emigrant brought certain religious principles and standards of conduct, ideals if you will, with him together with his prayer books, praying shawl, and phylacteries. When seventeen-year-old Solomon Roth landed in Philadelphia in 1854 he carried with him an ethical letter written by his apprehensive father: Help the poor; never say to them, "help your ownself," if they need you. Be thrifty and never exhibit money in public; don't trust strangers, avoid drunkards and gambling and learn to keep your mouth shut; don't lie; and shun the man who is loose with invectives. Don't count on the favor of important people and keep your conscience clear. Don't hate or envy anyone, be meek and patient; control your passion, stay away from women, and have nothing to do with prostitutes. Give a wide berth to missionaries, be loyal to your faith, and bear in mind constantly that man's true happiness lies in virtue and the fear of God.

Despite the fact that Orthodoxy was the dominant persuasion of the Jew in this land its authority was being chipped away on all sides. The Ashkenazim paid little heed to the Sephardic congregations; the multiple Ashkenazic voluntaristic synagogs weakened the concept of an unbending centralized authority; the adoption of the mores of the Christian majority made serious inroads into customary religious thought and practice. What the milieu undermined was further shattered by Reform. As the émigrés and natives moved into the orbit of Protestant influence, as they became more Americanized, they sought to create a westernized Protestant-like religion that would be acceptable to Jews and win Christian approval. Though Reform always remained a minority cult it rapidly became a national movement through the leftist German laymen and the secularly educated rabbis who migrated to America in the decades before the War.[1]

JEWISH CULTURE

One must never decry the influence of the synagog in that generation, yet it was but one, albeit the most important of the institutions that commanded the loyalty of Jews. Religiocultural Jewish associations and clubs abounded in antebellum America, mostly in the North. And in the South? Either there were too few Jews, or loyalties were less evident, or Jews sought closer integration into Gentile society.

Schools for Jewish and general studies are imperative in the economy of a "nation" of shopkeepers; a merchant dare not be illiterate. Because the public schools were inadequate and Christian in tone those Jews who had some means set up parochial schools which they promptly deserted in the days before the War as the public schools began to improve and as Christian religious indoctrination abated. But even during the heyday of the all-day religious schools most boys and girls received their Jewish training in Sunday Schools. Some adults who hoped to extend their cultural reach in the social and physical sciences joined lyceums but many of the younger Jews, both natives and newcomers who felt more at home among their kin, formed literary societies of their own. These are the Young Men's Hebrew Associations. Here in their own way the younger generation spread knowledge on topics of a Jewish and general nature. In this "youth movement," the young men, and women too, were not in open rebellion against what a later generation was to call the "Establishment," but they did desire to be by themselves and to address themselves to the world about them. Unlike their parents or their grand-parents they never looked backward to Germany or Germanic culture; they were completely America-oriented. They debated, read papers, established small libraries, and listened to lectures, more often than not on non-Jewish subjects.

Some of their alien-born fathers, though humble in their occupational pursuits, nursed far-reaching if not grandiose plans of inaugurating a cultural renascence as they drank their beer in their favorite saloon. A group of these Germans established an entirely new institution in world Jewish history, the lodge, the fraternity, which not only provided sick and death benefits but talked proudly of cultural, intellectual, and spiritual goals which every Israelite must set before him. Aspiring youth, far-visioned newcomers, and the established leaders of Jewry had much in common as they worked toward the creation of an American Jewish culture. They set up a national Jewish publication society which fell without having produced a single literary work of note. Newspapers had a better record: they persisted even though they adorned themselves with borrowed treasures from the better European Jewish periodicals. Excellent essays of German scholars, classics, were rendered into English. Leeser's English-Hebrew liturgies helped the religious understand what they voiced, and his translation of his edition of the Hebrew Bible encouraged the sensitive to emancipate themselves from the Christologies of the King James version. It was inevitable in that generation when Christian denominational colleges began to appear in large numbers, when rabbinical seminaries opened their doors in Paris, London, Breslau, and Padua, that Jews here, too, would also want a college of their own. With verbal fanfare and grandiloquent flights of oratory the enterprising Isaac M. Wise opened Zion College, a general academic institution which also envisaged the training of rabbis, but after a season it closed its doors. Wise's next attempt was more successful.[2]

SOCIAL LIFE

Though the Jews occupied themselves with cultural matters they were not stuffy or otherwordly. They were ever mindful of the injunction of the Gentle cynic: "A man hath no better thing under the sun than to eat, drink, and be merry" (Eccles. 8:15). Very social beings, the Jews enjoyed home parties, weddings, bar mitzvah feasts, theatre benefits, and synagog dedications. Most of the literary societies were social in nature; in fact the companionship element in all Jewish institutions, even those of a religious and charitative nature, was pronounced. The 1850's was a great social decade, for Jews joined non-Jewish lodges, German-Gentile clubs, and singing societies, founded choral groups of their own, and mustered in Jewish militia companies and troops who paraded in colorful and distinctive uniforms. Every occasion was looked upon as an opportunity to dine and the fund-raising balls and banquets were indeed grand affairs. In the years before the Civil War those fortunate ones who had made money established clubs where they addressed themselves seriously to the business of eating and card playing.[3]

THE CHARITIES

In their social activities the Jews were undoubtedly influenced by the Gentile masses who enveloped them, but it is very difficult to determine to what extent, if any, Jews patterned themselves after Christians in the giving of charity. Regardless of their stated aims practically all Jewish associations made grants at some juncture to help fellow Jews or Gentiles, particularly when calamities struck. The alms which Jews gave may not always have been adequate but in all probability they were more generous than their neighbors. The motivation for this giving was not merely kinship but the fear of what the Christians would say if Jews neglected to provide for their own. Of all areas the breakdown of the older identification of synagog with community is documented most clearly in the field of philanthropy. Alms giving in the earlier days was a prime obligation of the synagog; with the huge increase in the numbers of immigrant arrivals and the corresponding intensity of the need came the proliferation of social welfare organizations. Already by the turn of the eighteenth century auxiliary societies had been established to help the first trickle of Europeans who had fled here following the American Revolution.[4]

The new institutions were either part of the synagog or depended on it but some very quickly emancipated themselves from congregational control. In general two kinds of associations were set up: benevolent societies and mutual-aid groups. The benevolent society was prompted by the desire of those who had means to help others, the impoverished; the mutual-aid organization was concerned primarily with self-help, with sick and death benefits, that is, aid in times of unemployment and during the crucial funeral period. Because they were poor and thrifty, too, the newcomers who could not always afford the luxury of synagog membership gave their pittance to the self-help society rather than to the congregation. These charitative enterprises were established by and for adults, youths, and women; in the large centers of population societies were often founded along lines of geographical origin and other particularist prejudices. No two charities were exactly alike; each was unique. Not all had the same aims; some were viable, others ephemeral. Since there were so many societies, nearly all autonomous and without any centralized control, duplication in giving to the same client was unavoidable.

As autonomous institutions the societies were nearly always communal, accepting any Jew as a member, helping any Jew in need. Necessity compelled them to be neutral in determining the religious criteria for admission; emphasis on differences in faith made for ill-feeling. These societies often became "communes" for the members binding them together into a tight bond of loyalty. As early as the 1830's and 1840's the philanthropies began to issue joint appeals and to talk of federation on a local and even on a national level. In the 1850's there was a strong push for federation in order to improve administration, avoid waste, and secure adequate funds to build and support the hospitals and asylums which now began to make their appearance. Touro money built hospitals in New York, Cincinnati, and New Orleans. Fund-raising had become "big business"; dues alone could not support the new eleemosynary institutions and the Jews resorted to elaborate dinners and balls to which Christians were also invited. Substantial sums were raised. The Jewish public philanthropies were important not only for the aid they provided but for the sense of security which they lent to the givers. They were proud of their accomplishments. All this made for "community."

THE CHANGING OF THE GUARD

At first glance there seems to be nothing but chaos in this new Ashkenazic Jewry galloping off in all directions, certainly when compared to the earlier synagog community which controlled every aspect of communal activity. But what appears to be chaos may only be a process of change inevitable in a new world and a new environment. It was also a world of fresh opportunities, challenges, hopes, and possibly of a new and even a better kind of Judaism. Among the newcomers were men of education and culture, of capacity and leadership, congregational officiants with Ph.D. degrees, men who had played an important part in the Reform rabbinical conferences in Germany. It is not difficult to prepare a list of notables: Einhorn and Rice in Baltimore, Leeser and Morais in Philadelphia, Isaacs and Adler in New York City, Wise and Lilienthal in Cincinnati, Felsenthal in Chicago, Bush in St. Louis, Gutheim in New Orleans, Eckman in

San Francisco. Some of these rabbis as editors of influential newspapers had more than a local following; they were fast becoming national figures. In a way even more important than these celebrities were the hundreds of men who officiated as religious functionaries in the many small communities that stretched across the country. They are the unsung and unloved heroes who served and suffered but somehow or other held their people together; they are the unknown invisible immortals who helped make American Jewish history.

The Local and National Community

THE NEW SOCIAL ORDER: FAILURE AND SUCCESS

Wishing to survive as a large unified corpus the American Jews, particularly the immigrants, were of the opinion that only through integration could they hope to reach the local and national goals which they pictured in their mind's eye. Despite the difficulties involved in inducing Jews to work together the German Jewish masses here, encouraged by the B'nai B'rith, set out to create a new cultural social order which because of the numerical predominance of the Central European immigrants was bound to be a German Jewish community. Creating a formal local community was anything but easy; any Jewish structure would have to be self-imposed. Except in the smaller towns with their skeleton types of overall organization Jews refused to discipline themselves and to submit to a common authority. Communalization was almost impossible in the larger cities such as New York. On occasion segments of that metropolitan center would band together for a short time to bake and sell matzos, to supervise kashrut, and to bury paupers, but even these minor tasks speedily exhausted their mutual tolerance. Loyalties were essentially parochial; some congregations even forbade their members to hold a second membership in another synagog. For social, ritual, and cultural reasons the German aliens could not fit comfortably into a Sephardic commune but setting up a new gemeinde or kehillah was not a light thing. American voluntarism and Protestant fragmentation, a most attractive pattern for the German particularists, hindered them from integrating themselves into one large all-encompassing urban association. Ethnicity was not strong enough to counter differences; a structured local community was hardly possible.

The attempt to establish a national community, or at least a series of interlocking country-wide institutions and organizations, was also a failure. Leeser, Wise, the B'nai B'rith, and numerous highly intelligent men knew what they wanted: a publication society, a national school system, an ecclesiastical board, textbooks, a standard prayer book, a college, agricultural settlements, good newspapers, an all-inclusive congregational union, and a civic defense society that would impress the men in the national capital and help Jews politically and philanthropically here and abroad. Very little was accomplished to effectuate this overall national program in antebellum days.

Though helpful, an integrated community is not indispensable for the survival of a people. The numerous institutions which the immigrants hammered together satisfied their needs and served as bulwarks against assimilation. They established synagogs, schools, self-help societies, orphan homes, hospitals, and newspapers; they built families, businesses, conducted religious services, and enjoyed a full social life. They were not unhappy. After a fashion, all this is "community." On the surface American Jewry seemed to be moving toward national unity, for it had a semblance of success in the 1855 Cleveland Conference and the 1857 delegation that waited on Buchanan to protest Swiss discrimination. But it should be borne in mind constantly that the participants in these meetings were few and certainly not representative of the entire country. Yet national unity was developing on a different level. Like the Catholics Jews were held together by schools, charities, a press, social-literary societies, and lodges; on the other hand these unifying elements were countered by religious disunity. The Catholics had a common monolithic church; what united Catholics divided Jews—religion. Yet the Germans were coming together; the immigrants here were brewing a unity, the alchemy of a melting pot. As the older Europeans began slowly to die off, a united "German" Jewish type began to emerge, a type that was to dominate American Jewry in culture and mores till the 1920's.

A national community was beginning to evolve despite ethnic strains and institutional differences; the sense of being one and the need to cooperate was fired by an emotional identification that was present and real, especially in periods of crisis. Working together for common causes gave Jews a sense of homogeneity and a feeling of power, of influence, which they tended to exaggerate. By the late 1850's the Americanized newcomers who had been here for almost a generation were finally ready to act in concert. They had numbers, substance, and a desire to aid those here and abroad who needed their help. Their interest in one another, in all Jews, was heightened not only by the growing American Jewish press, but also by the steamship and cable that linked them ever more tightly to the Jews of the Diaspora. By 1860 as their fellow-Americans were baring their fangs at one another preparing to engage in a bloody Civil War Jews were seeking to unite. Curiously enough these Jews, too, wanted "states' rights," autonomy; they wanted to be left free and undisturbed but they were equally concerned to foster a national unity that would protect Jews everywhere, locally, nationally, and even internationally. It is significant that Touro's will and benefactions envisaged a Jewry that stretched from

St. Louis to Jerusalem. The Jews of this country like their fellow Americans were eager to export egalitarian concepts; Swiss intransigence and the Papal seizure of Edgar Mortara finally induced the Jews on this side of the Atlantic to build a national administrative institution.

THE BOARD OF DELEGATES OF AMERICAN ISRAELITES

Monetary relief and political intervention were the only areas in which there was almost complete agreement on the part of American Jews as they essayed to play a part on the world Jewish stage. Thus the Board of Delegates of American Israelites was created in 1859. Because the prime social unit in American Jewry was the synagog the new organization was a church federation; hence the almost weird anomaly of yoking religious organizations together for non-religious philanthropic and political purposes. Washington was probably under the impression that the Jews now spoke with a united voice. American Jewish unity began at the top and ultimately may have worked its way down stimulating local institutions to pull together. Did this new German Jewry save Sephardic Jewry and Judaism of the early nineteenth century? There is no proof that the Germans saved the Sephardim any more than the East Europeans saved the Germans or the Holocaust saved American Jewry of the mid-twentieth century. Jewries may fade but they rarely die. The pioneer Sephardim with their delusions of grandeur were dwarfed and bypassed but they survived in comfortable if not in smug isolation. What is true is that every infusion of Orthodox immigrants brings a resurgence of observance but with their acculturation this is succeeded by apathy. This was true of the Sephardim and the Germans as it is true of American Jewry of the twentieth century.

In the 1830's the arriving German Jews took over a small community and reinvigorated it by creating conventicles and societies in every town of size in the United States. Loyal if not always dedicated religiously this German Jewry survived sturdily.[6]

ABBREVIATIONS, SYMBOLS, AND SHORT TITLES

IN THE NOTES

This key may be considered a virtual bibliography for it includes all the unpublished records, documents, source collections, and works to which my notes refer with some frequency. Omitted here are works and manuscripts cited only once. All term papers unless otherwise marked are in the AJAr.

Adams, *History of the Jews*
> Hannah Adams, *The History of the Jews from the Destruction of Jerusalem to the Nineteenth Century* (2 vols., Boston, 1812).

Adler, *Kansas City*
> Frank J. Adler, *Roots in a Moving Stream, The Centennial History of Congregation B'nai Jehudah of Kansas City, 1870-1970* (Kansas City, Mo., 1972).

Adler & Connolly, *Buffalo*
> Selig Adler and Thomas E. Connolly, *From Ararat to Suburbia: The History of the Jewish Community of Buffalo* (Phila., 1960).

Agresti, *David Lubin*
> Olivia Rossetti Agresti, *David Lubin: A Study in Practical Idealism* (Boston, 1922).

AH
> *The American Hebrew.*

AI
> *The American Israelite* [until 1874: *The Israelite*].

AJA
> *American Jewish Archives* (publication).

AJAr
> American Jewish Archives (institution).

AJHQ
> *American Jewish Historical Quarterly.*

AJYB
> *American Jewish Year Book.*

American Jews' Annual
> *The American Jews' Annual* (Cincinnati, Chicago, and N.Y., 5645-57, A.M. [1884-1897]).

American State Papers (1949)
  American State Papers and Related Documents on Freedom in Religion (Washington, D.C., 1949).

Asmonean
  The Asmonean.

Auerbach, "Nebraska"
  Ella F. Auerbach, "Jewish Settlement in Nebraska, General Survey" (n.p., n.d.).

Auerback, "San Francisco Jewry"
  Norman Auerback, "A Study of San Francisco Jewry as Reflected in *The Weekly Gleaner,* 1857-1861" (HUC term paper, 1971).

AZJ
  Allgemeine Zeitung des Judenthums.

B. & B., *JOUS*
  Joseph L. Blau and Salo W. Baron (eds.), *The Jews of the United States, 1790-1840: A Documentary History* (3 vols., N.Y., 1963).

Bancroft, *Hist. of Calif.*
  Hubert Howe Bancroft, *History of California* (San Francisco, 1888, 1890).

BDEAJ
  Joseph R. Rosenbloom, *A Biographical Dictionary of Early American Jews: Colonial Times through 1800* (Lexington, Ky., 1960).

Beard, *Rise of Am. Civilization*
  Charles A. Beard and Mary R. Beard, *The Rise of American Civilization* (2 vols., N.Y., 1927).

Benjamin, *Three Years*
  I.J. Benjamin, *Three Years in America, 1859-1862* (2 vols., Phila., 1956).

Berg, *Kern County Land Company*
  Norman Berg, *A History of Kern County Land Company* (Bakersfield, Calif., 1971).

Berman, *Shehitah*
  Jeremiah J. Berman, *Shehitah: A Study in the Cultural and Social Life of the Jewish People* (N.Y., 1941).

Bibo, "Book of Remembrance"
  Arthur Bibo, "Book of Remembrance" (typescript memoir, n.p., n.d.), copy in Marcus Collections.

Bibo, *Reminiscences*
  Floyd S. Fierman, *Nathan Bibo's Reminiscences of Early New Mexico* (reprint from *El Palacio* (1961), vols. 68-69).

Billington, *Protestant Crusade*
  Ray Allen Billington, *The Protestant Crusade, 1800-1860: A Study of the Origins of American Nationalism* (Chicago, 1964).

Biographical Directory of the American Congress
  Biographical Directory of the American Congress, 1774-1971 (Washington, D.C., 1971).

Blum, *Baltimore*
  Isodor Blum, *The Jews of Baltimore, etc.* (Baltimore, 1910).

Breck, *Colorado*
  Allen duPont Breck, *The Centennial History of the Jews* (Denver, 1960).

Brickner, "Jew. Com. of Cin."
    Barrett R. Brickner. "Jewish Community of Cincinnati: Historical and Descriptive, 1817-1933" (Ph.D. diss., University of Cincinnati, 1933).
Brooks, Jews in Utah and Idaho
    Juanita Brooks, History of the Jews in Utah and Idaho (Salt Lake City, 1973).
Byars, B. and M. Gratz
    William Vincent Byars, B. and M. Gratz: Merchants in Philadelphia, etc., 1754-1798 (Jefferson City, Mo., 1916).

Carter, Jews in Early Utah
    Kate B. Carter, Jews in Early Utah (Daughters of Utah Pioneers, Lesson for April, 1952).
Carvalho, Incidents of Travel and Adventure in the Far West
    Solomon Nunes Carvalho, Incidents of Travel and Adventure in the Far West (Phila., 1954).
Caughey, California
    John Walton Caughey, California (N Y., 1953).
CCARYB
    Central Conference of American Rabbis Yearbook.
Chester, "New Orleans"
    Steven Chester, "The Economic Life of the Jews, New Orleans, 1850-1860" (HUC term paper, 1969).
CHISPA
    CHISPA: The Quarterly of the Tuolumne County Historical Society, Sonora, California.
Chyet, Lives and Voices
    Stanley F. Chyet, Lives and Voices (Phila., 1972).
Cleland & Dumke, California
    Robert Glass Cleland and Glenn S. Dumke, From Wilderness to Empire: A History of California (N.Y., 1959).
Cohen, "Rodeph Shalom"
    Irving B. Cohen, "The Religious Development and Transition of the Oldest Ashkenazic Congregation in America, etc." , (HUC term paper, n.d.).
Cole, Handbook
    Donald B. Cole, Handbook of American History (N.Y., 1968).
Cole, Irrepressible Conflict
    Arthur Charles Cole, The Irrepressible Conflict, 1850-1865 (N.Y., 1934).
Congress Weekly
    Congress Weekly: A Review of Jewish Interests.
Corning, Dictionary of Oregon Hist.
    Howard McKinley Corning, Dictionary of Oregon History, etc. (Portland, Or., 1956).
Cowan, Forgotten Characters
    Robert E. Cowan, Forgotten Characters of Old San Francisco (San Francisco, 1938).
Cubberley, Public Education
    Elwood P. Cubberley, Public Education in the United States, (rev. ed., Cambridge, Mass., 1947).
Curti, American Thought
    Merle Curti, The Growth of American Thought (N.Y., 1943).

DAB
  Dictionary of American Biography.
DAH (1942)
  Dictionary of American History (N.Y., 1942).
Davis, *Rodeph Shalom*
  Edward Davis, *The History of Rodeph Shalom Congregation, 1802-1926* (Phila., 1926).
Deborah
  Die Deborah.
Denver Round-up
  The Denver Westerners Monthly Round-up (Denver, Col.).
Dubnow, *Weltgeschichte*
  Simon Dubnow, *Weltgeschichte des juedischen Volkes* (10 vols., Berlin, 1925-1929).
Dushkin, *Jew. Ed. in NYC*
  Alexander M. Dushkin, *Jewish Education in New York City* (N.Y., 1918).

E. & L., *Richmond*
  Herbert T. Ezekiel and Gaston Lichtenstein, *The History of the Jews of Richmond from 1769 to 1917* (Richmond, Va., 1917).
EAH
  Richard B. Morris (ed.), *Encyclopedia of American History* (N.Y., 1953).
Edelstein, "Chevra Gemiloth of Boston"
  Jay Edelstein, "The Chevra Gemiloth Chesed of the City of Boston, December 25, 1853 to December 26, 1869" (HUC term paper, n.d.).
Edwards & Hopewell, *Edwards's Great West*
  Richard Edwards and M. Hopewell, *Edwards's Great West, etc.* (St. Louis, 1860).
Ehrenfried, *Boston*
  Albert Ehrenfried, *A Chronicle of Boston Jewry: From the Colonial Settlement to 1900* (Sherman Oaks, Ca., 1963).
EIAJH
  Essays in American Jewish History, etc. (Cincinnati, 1958).
Eichhorn, *Evangelizing*
  David Max Eichhorn, *Evangelizing the American Jew* (Middle Village, N.Y., 1978).
EJ
  Encyclopaedia Judaica.
Elbogen, *Cent. of Jewish Life*
  Ismar Elbogen, *A Century of Jewish Life* (Phila., 1944).
Eliassof, *German-American Jews*
  Herman Eliassof, *German-American Jews* (Chicago, 1915).
Ellis, *Am. Catholicism*
  John Tracy Ellis, *American Catholicism* (2d ed., revised, Chicago, 1969).
Elzas, *Jews of S. C.*
  Barnett A. Elzas, *The Jews of South Carolina* (Phila., 1905).
Elzas, *Leaves* (Second Series)
  Barnett A. Elzas, *Leaves from My Historical Scrap Book*, Second Series (Charleston, S.C., 1908).
Ernst, *Immigrant Life*
  Robert Ernst, *Immigrant Life in New York City, 1825-1863* (N.Y., 1949).

Essex Story
   The Essex Story: A History of the Jewish Community in Essex County, New Jersey (Newark, 1955).

Falk, "Oklahoma"
   Randall M. Falk, "A History of the Jews of Oklahoma with special emphasis on the Tulsa Jewish Community" (rabbinical thesis, HUC, 1946).

Fein, *Baltimore*
   Isaac M. Fein, *The Making of an American Jewish Community: The History of Baltimore Jewry from 1773 to 1920* (Phila., 1971).

Felsenthal & Eliassof, *History of K.A.M.*
   B. Felsenthal and Herman Eliassof, *History of Kehillath Anshe Maarabh, etc.* (Chicago, 1897).

Fierman, *Guts and Ruts*
   Floyd S. Fierman, *Guts and Ruts: The Jewish Pioneer on the Trail in the American Southwest* (N.Y., 1985).

Fierman. "Jewish Education"
   Floyd Sidney Fierman, "Efforts Toward Reform in American Jewish Education Prior to 1881" (Ph.D. diss., U. of Pittsburgh, 1949)

Fierman, *Some Early Jewish Settlers*
   Floyd S. Fierman, *Some Early Jewish Settlers on the Southwestern Frontier* (El Paso, 1960).

Fierman, "Some Higher Educational Efforts"
   Floyd Sidney Fierman, "Some Higher Educational Efforts among Jews in America prior to 1881" (Pittsburgh, 1949).

Fifty Years of the H.E.S.
   Fifty Years' Work of the Hebrew Education Society of Philadelphia, 1848-1898 (Phila., 1899).

Finkelstein, *The Jews* (1949)
   Louis Finkelstein (ed.), *The Jews: Their History, Culture, and Religion* (4 vols., Phila., 1949)

Finkelstein, *The Jews* (1960)
   Louis Finkelstein (ed.), *The Jews: Their History, Culture, and Religion* (3d ed., 2 vols., N.Y., 1960).

Fleishaker, "Illinois-Iowa Jewish Community"
   Oscar Fleishaker, "The Illinois-Iowa Jewish Community on the Banks of the Mississippi River" (Ph.D. diss., Yeshiva U., 1957).

Foster, "Milwaukee"
   Steven Foster, "A History of the Jews of Milwaukee as Reflected Through the City Directories, 1847-1860" (HUC term paper, 1968).

Frank, *Nashville*
   Fedora S. Frank, *Five Families and Eight Young Men (Nashville and her Jewry, 1850-1861)* (Nashville, 1962).

Frank, *Nashville Jewry, 1861-1901*
   Fedora Small Frank, *Beginnings on Market Street (Nashville and her Jewry, 1861-1901)* (Nashville, 1976).

Friedman, *Pilgrims*
   Lee M. Friedman, *Pilgrims in a New Land* (Phila., 1948).

Friedman, *Pioneers*
   Lee M. Friedman, *Jewish Pioneers and Patriots* (Phila., 1942).

Gartner, *Cleveland*
  Lloyd P. Gartner, *History of the Jews of Cleveland* (Cleveland, 1978).

Gartner, *Jew. Ed. in U.S.*
  Lloyd P. Gartner (ed.), *Jewish Education in the United States: A Documentary History* (N.Y., 1969).

GHQ
  Georgia Historical Quarterly.

Ginsberg, *Jews of Virginia*
  Louis Ginsberg, *Chapters on the Jews of Virginia, 1658-1900* (Petersburg, Va., 1969).

Glanz, *California*
  Rudolf Glanz, *The Jews of California: From the Discovery of Gold until 1880* (N.Y., 1960).

Glanz, *Jew and Mormon*
  Rudolf Glanz, *Jew and Mormon: Historic Group Relations and Religious Outlook* (N.Y., 1963).

Glanz, *Milieu*
  Rudolf Glanz, *Jews in Relation to the Cultural Milieu of the Germans in America up to the Eighteen Eighties* (N.Y., 1947).

Glanz, *Studies*
  Rudolf Glanz, *Studies in Judaica Americana* (N.Y., 1970).

Glanz, *The German Jew in America*
  Rudolf Glanz, *The German Jew in America; An Annotated Bibliography, etc.* (Cincinnati, 1969).

Glazer, *Jews of Iowa*
  Simon Glazer, *The Jews of Iowa, etc.* (Des Moines, 1904).

Goldberg, "Elem. Jew. Ed."
  Martin L. Goldberg, "Elementary Jewish Education in the United States from 1654-1860" (HUC term paper, n.d.).

Goldberg, "History of Am. Jew. Ed."
  Martin L. Goldberg, "History of American Jewish Education, 1840-1860" (M.A. thesis, HUC, 1953).

Goldberg, *Major Noah*
  Isaac Goldberg, *Major Noah: American-Jewish Pioneer* (Phila., 1936).

Goldstein, *Cent. of Jud. in NYC*
  Israel Goldstein, *A Century of Judaism in New York: B'nai Jeshurun, 1825-1925, etc.* (N.Y., 1930).

Goodkowitz, "Jew. Econ. Life, 1830-1860"
  Alex D. Goodkowitz, "A History of Jewish Economic Life from 1830 to 1860" (HUC term paper, 1933).

Goodman, *Documentary Story*
  Philip Goodman, *A Documentary Story of a Century of the Jewish Community Center, 1854-1954* (N.Y., 1953).

Graetz, *Geschichte der Juden*
  H. Graetz, *Geschichte der Juden von den aeltesten Zeiten bis auf die Gegenwart* (Leipzig, 1873).

Greenebaum, "Economic Activity of Cincinnati Jewry"
  William A. Greenebaum, 2d, "A Study of the Economic Activity of Cincinnati Jewry Prior to the Civil War" (rabbinical thesis, HUC, 1957).

Grinstein, *New York City*
> Hyman B. Grinstein, *The Rise of the Jewish Community of New York, 1654-1860* (Phila., 1945).

Grusd, *B'nai B'rith*
> Edward E. Grusd, *B'nai B'rith: The Story of a Covenant* (N.Y., 1966).

Haepke, *Wirtschaftsgeschichte*
> Rudolf Haepke, *Wirtschaftsgeschichte* (Leipzig, 1922).

Hansen, *Atlantic Migration*
> Marcus Lee Hansen, *The Atlantic Migration, 1607-1860. A History of the Continuing Settlement of the United States* (Cambridge, Mass., 1945).

Harris, *Merchant Princes*
> Leon Harris, *Merchant Princes: An Intimate History of Jewish Families Who Built Great Department Stores* (N.Y., 1979).

H.E., *Leiden*
> H.E., *Die Leiden und Verfolgungen der Juden, u.s.w.* (Budapest, 1882).

Heitman, *Historical Register*
> Francis B. Heitman, *Historical Register and Directory of the United States Army, etc.* (vol. 1, Washington, D.C., 1903).

Heller, *Isaac M. Wise*
> James G. Heller, *Isaac M. Wise, His Life, Work and Thought* (N.Y., 1965).

Heller, *Temple Sinai*
> Max Heller, *Jubilee Souvenir of Temple Sinai, 1872-1922* (New Orleans, 1922).

Henriques, *Jews and the English Law*
> H.S.Q. Henriques, *The Jews and the English Law* (Oxford, 1908).

Hirsch & Doherty, *Mount Sinai Hospital*
> Joseph Hirsch and Beka Doherty, *The First Hundred Years of the Mount Sinai Hospital of New York, 1852-1952* (N.Y., 1952).

Holbern, *Modern Germany*
> Hajo Holbern, *A History of Modern Germany, 1840-1945* (3 vols., N.Y., 1969).

HUC
> Hebrew Union College, Cincinnati.

HUCA
> *Hebrew Union College Annual.*

Huhner, *Judah Touro*
> Leon Huhner, *The Life of Judah Touro (1775-1854)* (Phila., 1946).

Hyman, *Romance of a Mining Venture*
> David M. Hyman, *The Romance of a Mining Venture* (Cincinnati, 1981).

I.L.
> Isaac Leeser (1806-1868), rabbi of Congregation Mikveh Israel, Phila., 1829-1851.

Jaye, "San Francisco"
> Harold Jaye, "The Jews in San Francisco: Their Economic Life, 1850-1860" (HUC term paper, 1969).

JE
> *The Jewish Encyclopedia.*

Jew. Ed.
  Jewish Education.
Jew. Rev.
  The Jewish Review.
Jewish Chronicle
  The Jewish Chronicle.
Jewish People
  The Jewish People: Past and Present (1946-1955).
Jewish Post and Opinion
  The Jewish Post and Opinion.
Jewish Times
  The Jewish Times (New York).
Jewish Tribune
  The Jewish Tribune (St. Louis).
Jewish Year Book
  The Jewish Year Book (London).
JM
  The Jewish Messenger.
JOAH
  The Journal of American History.
JQR n.s.
  The Jewish Quarterly Review, new series.
JRM
  Jacob Rader Marcus.
JSS
  Jewish Social Studies.

Kahl Montgomery, Constitution, 1852
  Constitution of Congregation Kahl Montgomery, Montgomery, Ala., 1852, copy in AJAr.
Karff, "Anti-Semitism"
  Sam Karff, "Anti-Semitism in the United States, 1844-1860" (prize essay, n.p., n.d.), copy in AJAr.
Kiev Festschrift
  Charles Berlin (ed.), *Studies in Jewish Bibliography, History and Literature, in honor of I. Edward Kiev* (N.Y., 1971).
Kirzner, "Detroit"
  Robert Kirzner, "A Statistical Analysis of Jewish Economics: Detroit, Michigan, 1850-1860" (HUC term paper, 1972).
Kisch, *Czechoslovakia*
  Guido Kisch, *In Search of Freedom: A History of the American Jews from Czechoslovakia* (London, 1949).
Kohut, *Geschichte der deutschen Juden*
  Adolph Kohut, *Geschichte der deutschen Juden* (Berlin, n.d.).
Korn, *Civil War*
  Bertram Wallace Korn, *American Jewry and the Civil War* (Phila., 1951).
Korn, *Eventful Years*
  Bertram Wallace Korn, *Eventful Years and Experiences* (Cincinnati, 1954).

Korn, *German-Jewish Intellectual Influences*
    Bertram Wallace Korn, *German-Jewish Intellectual Influences on American Jewish Life,
    1824-1972* (Syracuse, 1972).

Korn, *Mobile*
    Bertram Wallace Korn, *The Jews of Mobile, 1763-1841*. Reprint from *HUCA* (1970),
    vol.40-41.

Korn, *Mortara*
    Bertram Wallace Korn, *The American Reaction to the Mortara Case: 1858-1859* (Cincin-
    nati, 1957).

Korn, *New Orleans*
    Bertram Wallace Korn, *The Early Jews of New Orleans* (Waltham, Mass., 1969).

Krout and Fox, *Completion of Independence*
    John Allen Krout and Dixon Ryan Fox, *Completion of Independence, 1790-1830* (N.Y.,
    1944).

Lake, *Wyatt Earp*
    Stuart N. Lake, *Wyatt Earp: Frontier Marshal* (Boston, 1931).

Lamb, "Jewish Pioneers in Arizona"
    Blaine Peterson Lamb, "Jewish Pioneers in Arizona, 1850-1920" (Ph.D. diss., Arizona
    State University, 1982).

Lander, "Jewish Religious Education in Cincinnati"
    Yechiael Lander, "Jewish Religious Education in Cincinnati as Reflected in the Min-
    utes of Talmud Yelodim Institute, 1849-1885" (HUC term paper, 1964).

LC
    Library of Congress, Washington, D.C.

Lebeson, *JPA*
    Anita Libman Lebeson, *Jewish Pioneers in America, 1492-1848* (N.Y., 1939).

Lebeson, *Pilgrim People*
    Anita Libman Lebeson, *Pilgrim People* (N.Y., 1950).

Leeser, "Circular"
    Isaac Leeser, "Circular of the American Jewish Publication Society to the Friends of
    Jewish Literature, Dec. 10, 1845"), copy in Marcus Collections.

Leeser, *Discourses*
    Isaac Leeser, *Discourses on the Jewish Religion* (10 vols., Phila., 1867-1868).

[Lesinsky] *Letters*
    [Lesinsky] *Letters Written by Henry Lesinsky to His Son* (N.Y., 1924).

Levine, *Am. Jew. Bibliography*
    Allan E. Levine, *An American Jewish Bibliography . . . 1851 to 1875, etc.* (Cincinnati,
    1959).

Levine, "B'nai lsrael of Cin."
    Joseph Levine, "Some Aspects of the Life and Activities of the Oldest Jewish Congre-
    gation west of the Alleghenies, etc." (HUC term paper, 1977).

Levinson, *California Gold Rush*
    Robert E. Levinson, *The Jews in the California Gold Rush* (N.Y., 1978).

Lipman, *Soc. Hist. of Jews in England*
    V.D. Lipman, *Social History of the Jews in England, 1850-1950* (London, 1954).

Lipman, "Synagogal Philanthropy"
    Eugene J. Lipman, "A History of Organized Synagogal Philanthropy in the United
    States" (rabbinical thesis, HUC, 1943).

London *Jewish Chronicle*
 The Jewish Chronicle [London].
Louisiana Inventory
 Inventory of the Church and Synagogue Archives of Louisiana: Jewish Congregations and Organizations (New Orleans, 1941).
Lyons & De Sola, *Jewish Calendar*
 Jacques J. Lyons and Abraham De Sola, *A Jewish Calendar* (Montreal, 1854).

M. & M., *History*
 Max L. Margolis and Alexander Marx, *A History of the Jewish People* (Phila., 1956).
Makovsky, *The Philipsons*
 Donald I. Makovsky, *The Philipsons: The First Jewish Settlers in St. Louis, 1807-1858* (St. Louis, 1958).
Marans, *Jews in Greater Washington*
 Hillel Marans, *Jews in Greater Washington, etc.* (Washington, D.C., 1961).
Marcus, *AJD*
 Jacob Rader Marcus, *American Jewry: Documents, Eighteenth Century* (Cincinnati, 1959).
Marcus, *AJWD*
 Jacob R. Marcus, *The American Jewish Woman: A Documentary History* (N.Y. and Cincinnati, 1981).
Marcus, *CAJ*
 Jacob R. Marcus, *The Colonial American Jew, 1492-1776* (3 vols., Detroit, 1970).
Marcus Collections
 American Hebraica and Judaica in the possession of Jacob Rader Marcus, Cincinnati
Marcus, *Communal Sick-Care*
 Jacob R. Marcus, *Communal Sick-Care in the German Ghetto* (Cincinnati, 1947).
Marcus, *EAJ*
 Jacob Rader Marcus, *Early American Jewry* (2 vols., Phila., 1951-1955).
Marcus, *Jew in the Medieval World*
 Jacob R. Marcus, *The Jew in the Medieval World* (Cincinnati, 1938).
Marcus, *Jewish Americana*
 Jacob R. Marcus (ed.), *Jewish Americana, etc.* (Cincinnati, 1954).
Marcus, *Memoirs*
 Jacob Rader Marcus, *Memoirs of American Jews, 1775-1865* (3 vols., Phila., 1955-1956).
Marcus, *Rise and Destiny of the German Jew*
 Jacob R. Marcus, *The Rise and Destiny of the German Jew* (Cincinnati, 1934).
Marcus, *Studies*
 Jacob R. Marcus, *Studies in American Jewish History: Studies and Addresses* (Cincinnati, 1969).
Marcus, *United States Jewry*
 Jacob Rader Marcus, *United States Jewry, 1776-1985* (4 vols., 1989-1992).
Markens, *Hebrews*
 Isaac Markens, *The Hebrews in America* (N.Y., 1888).
May, *Isaac M. Wise*
 Max B. May, *Isaac Mayer Wise* (N.Y., 1916).
Md. Hist. Mag.
 Maryland Historical Magazine.

Meade, *Judah P. Benjamin*
    Robert Douthat Meade, *Judah P. Benjamin, Confederate Statesman* (N.Y., 1943).

Meites, *Chicago*
    Hyman L. Meites (ed.), *History of the Jews of Chicago* (Chicago, 1924).

Menorah
    The Menorah.

Meyer, *Western Jewry*
    Martin A. Meyer, *Western Jewry: An Account of the Achievements of the Jews and Judaism in California Including Eulogies and Biographies* (San Francisco, 1916).

MGWJ
    Monatsschrift fuer Geschichte und Wissenschaft des Judenthums.

Michael, "Cincinnati"
    Ann Deborah Michael, "The Origins of the Jewish Community of Cincinnati, 1817-1860" (M.A. thesis, University of Cincinnati, 1970).

Mikveh Israel, Phila., Trustees Minutes
    Minute Books of the Board of Trustees and Records of Congregation Mikveh Israel, Phila., 1781-1895, copy of MS in AJAr.

Morais, *Eminent Israelites*
    Henry Samuel Morais, *Eminent Israelites of the Nineteenth Century: A Series of Biographical Sketches* (Phila., 1880).

Morais, *Philadelphia*
    Henry Samuel Morais, *The Jews of Philadelphia* (Phila., 1894).

Morison, *History*
    Samuel Eliot Morison, *The Oxford History of the American People* (N.Y., 1965).

Myers, *Bigotry*
    Gustavus Myers, *History of Bigotry in the United States* (N.Y., 1943).

NA
    National Archives, Washington, D.C.

NAW
    Edward T. James, et al. (eds.), *Notable American Women, 1607-1950* (3 vols., Cambridge, Mass., 1971).

New Catholic Encyclopedia
    New Catholic Encyclopedia.

NMHR
    New Mexico Historical Review.

NMQ
    New Mexico Quarterly.

Noah, *Discourse* (1818)
    Mordecai Manuel Noah, *Discourse Delivered at the Consecration of the Synagogue K.K. Shearith Israel, etc.* (N.Y., 1818).

Nodel, *The Ties Between*
    Julius J. Nodel, *The Ties Between: A Century of Judaism on America's Last Frontier* (Portland, Or., 1959).

NYHS
    New York Historical Society, N.Y.

NYHSL
    New York Historical Society Library, N.Y.

Occ.
> The Occident and American Jewish Advocate.

Ochs, *Memoir*
> Julius Ochs, *A Memoir of Julius Ochs: An Autobiography* (n.p., n.d.).

P. & K., *Tourist's Guide*
> Bernard Postal and Lionel Koppman, *A Jewish Tourist's Guide to the U.S.* (Phila., 1954).

Padoll, "St. Louis"
> Burton L. Padoll, "The Culture, Practices and Ideals of the United Hebrew Congregation of St. Louis, Missouri, From 1841 to 1859" (HUC term paper, 1956).

PAJHS
> Publications of the American Jewish Historical Society.

Parish, *Charles Ilfeld Company*
> William J. Parish, *The Charles Ilfeld Company: A Study in the Rise and Decline of Mercantile Capitalism in New Mexico* (Cambridge, Mass., 1961).

Pelzer, *Cattlemen's Frontier*
> Louis Pelzer, *The Cattlemen's Frontier, etc.* (Glendale, Calif., 1936).

Philippsborn, *Vicksburg*
> Gertrude Philippsborn, *The History of the Jewish Community of Vicksburg, etc.* (Vicksburg, Miss., 1969).

Philipson, *Max Lilienthal*
> David Philipson, *Max Lilienthal, American Rabbi, Life and Writings* (N.Y., 1915).

Philipson, *Reform Movement*
> David Philipson, *The Reform Movement in Judaism* (rev ed.. N.Y., 1931).

Philipson & Grossman, *Selected Writings of I.M. Wise*
> David Philipson and Louis Grossman (eds.), *Selected Writings of I. M. Wise* (Cincinnati, 1900).

Pilch, *Hist. Jew. Ed.*
> Judah Pilch (ed.), *A History of Jewish Education in America* (N.Y., 1969).

Plaut, *Jews in Minnesota*
> W. Gunther Plaut, *The Jews of Minnesota: The First Seventy-five Years* (N.Y., 1959).

Plaut, *Mt. Zion*
> W. Gunther Plaut, *Mt. Zion, 1856-1956, The First Hundred Years* (St. Paul, Minn., 1956?).

Plaut, *Reform Judaism*
> W. Gunther Plaut, *The Growth of Reform Judaism: American and European Sources until 1948* (N.Y., 1965).

Pool, *Old Faith*
> David and Tamar de Sola Pool, *An Old Faith in the New World* (N.Y., 1955).

Quinn, *Roanoke*
> David Beers Quinn, *Set Fair for Roanoke: Voyages and Colonies, 1584-1606* (Chapel Hill, N.C., 1985).

R
> A.S.W. Rosenbach, "An American Jewish Bibliography, etc.," *PAJHS*, vol. 30.

R. & E., *Charleston*
> Charles Reznikoff and Uriah Z. Engelman, *The Jews of Charleston* (Phila., 1950).

RIJHN
   Rhode Island Jewish Historical Notes.
Rodeph Shalom, Phila., Constitution, 1849
   The Constitution of Congregation Rodeph Shalom, Phila., 1849, copy of MS in AJAr.
Rodeph Shalom, Phila., Minutes, 1811-1834
   Minutes of Congregation Rodeph Shalom, Phila., copy of MS in AJAr.
Rogson, "Leeser"
   Leon Rogson, "The Writings of Isaac Leeser" (HUC term paper, 1972).
Rose, "Mikve Israel"
   Emanuel Rose, "The Correspondence of Congregation Mikve Israel, Philadelphia, 1843-1857" (HUC term paper, 1955).
Roseman, "Charleston, 1850-1860"
   Kenneth D. Roseman, "The Jewish Population of Charleston, South Carolina, 1850-1860" (HUC term paper, 1969).
Roseman, "Cincinnati, 1850"
   Kenneth D. Roseman, "The National Census of 1850" (HUC term paper, 1966).
Roseman, "Cincinnati, 1860"
   Kenneth D. Roseman, "The National Census of 1860, Cincinnati, Ohio" (HUC term paper, 1967).
Roseman, "Jewish Population of America"
   Kenneth D. Roseman, "Jewish Community of America, 1850-1860: A Demographic Study of Four Cities" (Ph.D. diss., HUC, 1971).
Roseman, "New York CIty, 1860"
   Kenneth D. Roseman, "Jewish Community of New York City, 1860" (HUC term paper, 1967).
Roth, *Personalities*
   Cecil Roth, *Personalities and Events in Jewish History* (Phila., 1953).
Rothschild, *Atlanta*
   Janice O. Rothschild, *As But A Day: The First Hundred Years, 1867-1967* (Atlanta, Ga., 1967).
Russell, *Germanic Influence*
   John Andrew Russell, *The Germanic Influence in the Making of Michigan* (Detroit, 1927).
Rutman, "Swiss-American Treaty"
   Herbert Samuel Rutman, "The Swiss-American Treaty of 1850 and the American Jew. A Study Based upon Primary Sources" (rabbinical thesis, HUC, 1963).

Sachar, *Modern Jewish History*
   Howard M. Sachar, *The Course of Modern Jewish History* (Cleveland and N.Y., 1958).
Sajowitz, "San Antonio"
   William Sajowitz, "History of Reform Judaism in San Antonio Texas, 1874-1945" (rabbinical thesis, HUC, 1945).
Schaff, *Church and State*
   Philip Schaff, *Church and State in the United States, etc.* (N.Y., 1888, reprinted 1972).
Schappes, *DHJUS*
   Morris U. Schappes, *A Documentary History of the Jews in the United States, 1654-1875* (N.Y., 1950).
Schappes, *JIUS*
   Morris U. Schappes, *The Jews of the United States, A Pictorial History* (N.Y., 1958).

Schindler, *Israelites in Boston*
Solomon Schindler, *Israelites in Boston: A Tale Describing the Development of Judaism in Boston, etc.* (Boston, 1889?).

Schlesinger, *Rise of the City*
Arthur M. Schlesinger, *The Rise of the City, 1878-1898* (N.Y., 1933).

Selzer, *"Kike!"*
Michael Selzer (ed.), *"Kike!"* (N.Y., 1972).

Sharfman, *Jackson, California*
I. Harold Sharfman, *"Nothing Left to Commemorate": The Story of the Pioneer Jews of Jackson, Amador County, California* (Glendale, Calif., 1969).

Shinedling, *West Virginia Jewry*
Abraham I. Shinedling, *West Virginia Jewry: Origins and History, 1850-1958* (3 vols., Phila., 1963).

Shpall, *Louisiana*
Leo Shpall, *The Jews in Louisiana* (New Orleans, 1936).

Silverman, *Hartford Jews*
Morris Silverman, *Hartford Jews, 1659-1970* (Hartford, Conn., 1970).

Skirball, "Rodeph Shalom"
Henry Skirball, "The German Hebrew Congregation Rodeph Shalom, Philadelphia (1835-1847)" (HUC term paper, n.d.).

Somberg & Roffman, *Omaha*
Suzanne Richards Somberg and Silvia Greene Roffman, *Consider the Years, 1871-1971, Congregation of Temple Israel, Omaha, Nebraska* (n.p., n.d.).

Spring, *Cheyenne Stage*
Agnes Wright Spring, *The Cheyenne and Black Hills Stage and Express Routes* (Glendale, Calif., 1949).

Statistical History of U.S.
The Statistical History of the United States from Colonial Times to the Present, etc. (Stamford, Conn., n.d.).

Stern, *FAJF*
Malcom H. Stern (comp.), *American Jewish Families, 600 Genealogies, 1654-1977* (Cincinnati and Waltham, Mass., 1978).

Stern, *Temple Emanu-El*
Myer Stern, *The Rise and Progress of Reform Judaism Embracing a History Made from the Official Records of Temple Emanu-El of New York, etc.* (N.Y., 1895).

Stocker, *Jewish Roots in Arizona*
Joseph Stocker, *Jewish Roots in Arizona* (Phoenix, 1954).

Stokes, *Church & State*
Anson Phelps Stokes, *Church and State in the United States* (3 vols., N.Y., 1950).

Stokes & Pfeffer, *Church and State*
Anson Phelps Stokes and Leo Pfeffer, *Church and State in the United States* (N.Y., 1964).

Suwol, *Oregon*
Samuel N. Suwol, *Jewish History of Oregon* (Portland, Or., 1958).

Swarsensky, *Madison*
Manfred Swarsensky, *From Generation to Generation* (Madison, Wis., 1955?).

Sweet, *Story of Religion in America*
William Warren Sweet, *The Story of Religion in America* (N.Y., 1939).

Swichkow & Gartner, *Milwaukee*
    Louis J. Swichkow and Lloyd P. Gartner, *The History of the Jews of Milwaukee* (Phila.,
    1963).
Syme, "Bene Israel"
    Daniel Syme, "The History of Congregation Bene Israel, Cincinnati, etc." (HUC term
    paper, 1971).

Tarshish, "American Judaism"
    Allan Tarshish, "The Rise of American Judaism" (Ph.D. diss., HUC, 1939).
Temkin, "Isaac Mayer Wise"
    S.D. Temkin, "Isaac Mayer Wise, 1819-1875" (Ph.D. diss., HUC, 1963).
Temple Beth El
    *Temple Beth El: Twenty-fifth Anniversary Issue: History of the Jewish Community, Corpus
    Christi, Texas* (Corpus Christi, 1957?).
Tennessee Inventory
    Inventory of the Church and Synagogue Archives of Tennessee: Jewish Congregations (Tennes-
    see, 1941).
TJHSE
    Transactions of the Jewish Historical Society of England.
Tobias, *Hebrew Benevolent Society*
    Thomas J. Tobias, *The Hebrew Benevolent Society of Charleston, S.C., Founded 1784, etc.*
    (Charleston, S.C., 1965).
Tobias, *Hebrew Orphan Society*
    Thomas J. Tobias, *The Hebrew Orphan Society of Charleston, S.C., Founded 1801*
    (Charleston, S.C., 1957).
Todes, "Jewish Education in Philadelphia"
    David Uriah Todes, "The History of Jewish Education in Philadelphia, 1782-1873"
    (Ph.D. diss., Dropsie College, Phila., 1952).
Towne and Wentworth, *Cattle and Men*
    Charles Wayland Towne and Edward Norris Wentworth, *Cattle and Men* (Norman,
    Okla., 1955).
Towne and Wentworth, *Shepherd's Empire*
    Charles Wayland Towne and Edward Norris Wentworth, *Shepherd's Empire* (Norman,
    Okla., 1945).
Trachtenberg, *Easton*
    Joshua Trachtenberg, *Consider the Years: The Story of the Jewish Community of Easton,
    1752-1942* (Easton, Pa., 1944).
Tradition
    Tradition: A Journal of Orthodox Thought.

U.A.H.C. Statistics
    Statistics of the Jews of the United States, etc. (Cincinnati, 1880).
Uchill, *Pioneers*
    Ida Libert Uchill, *Pioneers, Peddlers and Tsadikim* (Denver, 1957).
UJE
    The Universal Jewish Encyclopedia.

Voorsanger, *Emanu-El*
    Jacob Voorsanger, *The Chronicles of Emanu-El, etc.* (San Francisco, 1900).

Vorspan & Gartner, *Los Angeles*
    Max Vorspan and Lloyd P. Gartner, *History of the Jews of Los Angeles* (Phila., 1970).

W. & W., *Philadelphia*
    Edwin Wolf, 2d, and Maxwell Whiteman, *The History of the Jews of Philadelphia from Colonial Times to the Age of Jackson* (Phila., 1957).

Walker, *Germany and the Emigration*
    Mack Walker, *Germany and the Emigration, 1816-1885* (Cambridge, Mass., 1964).

Wallach, *"Sinai"*
    Benno M. Wallach, "Dr. David Einhorn's *Sinai*, 1856-1862" (rabbinical thesis, HUC, 1950).

Wash. H.Q.
    Washington Historical Quarterly.

Watters, *Utah*
    Leon L. Watters, *The Pioneer Jews of Utah* (N.Y., 1952).

Wechsler, *Die Auswanderer*
    B. Wechsler, *Die Auswanderer* (Oldenburg, 1846).

Weiss, "Rodeph Sholom"
    Raymond Weiss, "The Culture, Religious Practice, and Ideals of Rodeph Sholom Congregation, Philadelphia, As Reflected in its Minute Book" (HUC term paper, 1956).

Weldler-Steinberg, *Geschichte der Juden*
    Augusta Weldler-Steinberg, *Geschichte der Juden in der Schweiz, u.s.w.* (2 vols., n.p., 1970).

Williams & Barker, *Writings of Sam Houston*
    Amelia W. Williams and Eugene C. Barker, *The Writings of Sam Houston, 1813-1863* (8 vols., Austin, Texas, 1938-1943).

Wischnitzer, *To Dwell in Safety*
    Mark Wischnitzer, *To Dwell in Safety: The Story of Jewish Migration Since 1800* (Phila., 1948).

Wise, *Reminiscences*
    Isaac M. Wise, *Reminiscences* (Cincinnati, 1901).

Wish, *Society and Thought*
    Harvey Wish, *Society and Thought in America* (2 vols., N.Y., 1950-1952).

Wolf, *American Jew*
    Simon Wolf, *The American Jew as Patriot, Soldier and Citizen* (Phila., 1895).

Wolf, *Sir Moses Montefiore*
    Lucien Wolf, *Sir Moses Montefiore. A Centennial Biography, etc.* (London, 1884).

Wolf, *The Jewish Question*
    Lucien Wolf, *Notes on the Diplomatic History of the Jewish Question, etc.* (London, 1919).

Wolf, *Yates & Samuel Families*
    Lucien Wolf (ed.), *The History and Genealogy of the Jewish Families of Yates and Samuel, etc.* (London, 1901).

WPA
    Work Projects Administration.

WSJHQ
    Western States Jewish Historical Quarterly.

WWW
    Who Was Who in America: A Companion Volume to Who's Who in America (6 vols., Chicago, 1943-1977).

WWW, 1607-1896
> *Who Was Who in America, Historical Volume, 1607-1896* (Chicago, 1967).

YA
> *Yivo Annual of Jewish Social Science.*

Yearbook of the Leo Baeck Institute
> *Yearbook of the Leo Baeck Institute* (London, 1965).

Zarchin, *San Francisco*
> Michael M. Zarchin, *Glimpses of Jewish Life in San Francisco* (Berkeley, 1952).

NOTES

CHAPTER ONE
THE COMING OF THE "GERMANS"

1. *PAJHS*, 27:475-79; Levi & Bergman, *Australian Genesis: Jewish Convicts and Settlers 1788-1850* (Rigby, 1974), 122 ff. The Isaac Garritson (Garretson) Case: Beth Elohim, Charleston, Minutes; *AJA*, June 3, 1839, 46-47; Frank, *Nashville*, 18, et passim; Frank, *Nashville Jewry, 1861-1901*, 2, et passim.

2. Gartner, *Cleveland*, 6 ff.; Eugene M. Kulischer, *Jewish Migrations: Past Experience and Post-War Prospects* (N.Y., 1943), 22; Hansen, *Atlantic Migration*, 256; Adler & Connolly, *Buffalo*, 26; *AJA*, 6:6 ff., 15:17 ff.; B. & B., *JOUS*, 7:778, 786-90; Elzas, *Jews of S.C.*, 97-99; *PAJHS*, 9:87 ff., 27:475-79, 38:185 ff., 41:225 ff.; Elzas, *Leaves*, Second Series, no. 5, p. 4; Morais, *Philadelphia*, 252 ff.; *EIAJH*, 247 ff.; *YA*, 6:82, 112-13, 9:332 ff., 12:131 ff.; *Yearbook of the Leo Baeck Institute*, 2:188-89, 191; Markens, *Hebrews*, 282-83; Abe J. Nebel, Cleveland, to JRM, July 1, 1966, Marcus Collections; Kisch, *Czechoslovakia*, 21 ff., 215 ff.; Grinstein, *New York City*, 530, n.18; W. & W., *Philadelphia*, 374.

3. "Austria," *JE*, 2:333; Henriques, *Jews and the English Law*, 261-63, 310 ff.; H. E., *Leiden*, 119; Philipson, *Reform Movement*, 77; *Journal of Economic History*, 30:248 ff.

4. Adler & Connolly, *Buffalo*, 25; Beard, *Rise of Am. Civilization*, 642; Wish, *Society and Thought*, 1:312-13; *PAJHS*, 41:243; Haepke, *Wirtschaftsgeschichte*, 94 ff.; Kisch, *Czechoslovakia*, 26 ff., 42-43; Elbogen, *Cent. of Jewish Life*, 10; *EIAJH*, 251-52; Holborn, *Modern Germany*, 3:34.

5. *Proceedings of the Massachusetts Historical Society* (Boston, 1926), 59:372-73; *PAJHS*, 23:106; Graetz, *Geschichte der Juden*, 11:338-39; Kohut, *Geschichte der deutschen Juden*, 776; "Prussia," *JE*, 10:238; Elbogen, *Cent. of Jewish Life*, 23; Philipson, *Reform Movement*, 23 ff.

6. B. & B., *JOUS*, 3:803; Marcus, *Jews in the Medieval World*, 49 ff.; Kohut, *Geschichte der deutschen Juden*, 784; *JSS*, 28:43 ff.; Elbogen, *Cent. of Jewish Life*, 11; *PAJHS*, 17:204-5, 38:185 ff., 201-2, 41:199, 231-36; Philipson & Grossman, *Isaac M. Wise*, 12-13; *Yearbook of the Leo Baeck Institute*, 2:191; "Austria," "Familianten Gesetz," "Oath More Judaico," "Saxon Duchies," "Saxony," *JE*; "Hungary," *JE*, *UJE*; London *Jewish Chronicle*, Mar. 23, 1860, p.3, c.l; H. E., *Leiden*, 117-121, 123-24; Holborn, *Modern Germany*, 3:22 ff., 104; Kisch, *Czechoslovakia*, 29 ff., 40-43; "Migrations," *EJ*; Wischnitzer, *To Dwell in Safety*, 18 ff.

7. London *Jewish Chronicle*, Aug. 12, 1864, p.8, c.1; "Konitz Affair," "Tizza-Eslar Affair," "Xanten," *JE*; H.E., *Leiden*, 129; *AJA*, 22:49 ff.; *EIAJH*, 35-36; Sachar, *Modern Jewish History*, 66, 102-3, 113-14, 165-66; Walker, *Germany and the Emigration*, 153-54; Elbogen, *Cent. of Jewish Life*, 170-77; Mailert Correspondence for Conditions in Germany in the 1830's, AJAr; Kisch, *Czechoslovakia*, 26 ff.; Edith Abbott, *Historical Aspects of the Immigration Problem* (Chicago, 1926), 271-75; M. Brann, *Geschichte der Juden und ihrer Litteratur* (3 vols., Breslau, 1896-1913), 3:130 ff. Disabilities: "Familianten Gesetz," *JE; YA*, 23-81 ff., 6:73 ff.; Graetz, *Geschichte der Juden*, 10:364; J.M. Jost, *Neuere Geschichte der Israeliten von 1815 bis 1845, u.s.w.* (Berlin, 1846), 1:23 ff.; *Israelitsche Annalen*, Aug. 16, 1839, p.260, c.2; Finkelstein, *The Jews* (1949), 4:1223; *PAJHS*, 9:87 ff.; Bruce Ehrman, "The Struggle for Civil and Religious Emancipation in Bavaria, etc." (rabbinical thesis, HUC, 1948), chap. 3; Wechsler, *Die Auswanderer*, 30; the legal status and disabilities of Prussian Jews in the early nineteenth century are reflected in Ludwig von Roenne & Heinrich Simon, *Die frueheren und gegenwaertigen Verhaeltnisse der Juden in den saemmtlichen Landestheilen der Preussischen Staates, u.s.w.* (Breslau, 1843). Very helpful too is Alfred Michaelis, *Die Rechtsverhaeltnisse der Juden in Preussen seit dem Beginne des 19 Jahrhunderts, u.s.w.* (Berlin, 1910); Schappes, *DHJUS*, 196-97; Dubnow, *Weltgeschichte*, 9:66-67; Haepke, *Wirtschaftsgeschichte*, 94 ff.; see "Austria," "Baden, Grand Duchy of," "Bavaria," "Hungary," Hesse," "Prussia," "Saxon Duchies," "Germany," *JE* and in other standard Jewish encyclopedias.

8. *JSS*, 18:121; Noah, *Discourse* (1818), 30; B. & B., *JOUS*, 3:778; *PAJHS*, 9:98-99; *MGWJ*, 12:365; Schappes, *DHJUS*, 195 ff., 198 ff.; Grinstein, *New York City*, 116 ff.; Sigmund Kaznelson (ed.), *Juden im deutschen Kulturbereich* (Berlin, 1959), 964 ff.; *YA*, 2-3:90, 9:361; Wischnitzer, *To Dwell in Safety*, 3 ff.; *Statistical History of U.S.*, 57.

9. Heinrich Silbergleit, *Die Bevoelkerungs- und Berufsverhaeltnisse der Juden im Deutschen Reich, u.s.w* (Berlin, 1930), 14; *American Quarterly*, 1(1949):60-61; Israel Cohen, *Jewish Life in Modern Times* (N.Y., 1929), 245-46; Marcus, *Rise and Destiny of the German Jew*, 189; *Jewish People*, 1:407 ff.; Sachar, *Modern Jewish History*, 116-18; *PAJHS*, 38:216 ff.; Kisch, *Czechoslovakia*, 50 ff.; *YA*, 9:348-49; Wechsler, *Die Auswanderer*, 30.

10. *PAJHS*, 17:204-5, 20:147-49, 23:187-89, 38:187 ff., 201-2, 41:235-36; B. & B., *JOUS*, 3:891-93; *AJA*, 14:31; *AZJ*, Dec. 5, 1837, p.424, Dec. 23, 1837, pp.453-54; Hansen, *Atlantic Migration*, 150; *Israelitische Annalen*, July 5, 1839, p.213, c.2, p.214, c.1; Finkelstein, *The Jews* (1949), 4:1223; Kisch, *Czechoslovakia*, chaps.1-3; *CCARYB*, 59:273 ff.

11. *Memorable Documents in American Jewish History* (N.Y., 1946), 10; *PAJHS*, 11:159; *"Whom We Shall Welcome": A Short Summary of the Report of the President's Commission on Immigration and Naturalization* (N.Y., 1953), 4; *NAR*, 126:299; Schappes, *JIUS*, 36.

12. Schappes, *DHJUS*, 157 ff.; Glanz, *Studies*, 360; Penina Moïse, *Fancy's Sketch Book* (Charleston, S.C., 1833), 131-32; Marcus, *AJWD*, 125.

13. Morais, *Philadelphia*, 52; Philipson, *Max Lilienthal*, 49; *PAJHS*, 17:204-5; Korn, *New Orleans*, 116 ff., 216 and Index sub "Hermann, Samuel, Sr."; Schappes, *DHJUS*, 651, n.13; B. & B., *JOUS*, 3:791-824; *Israelitische Annalen*, Feb. 21, 1840, p.73; *AJA*, 22:49 ff.; *YA*, 2-3:81 ff., 6:149, 9:333.

14. B. & B., *JOUS*, 1:86; W. & W., *Philadelphia*, 280; Davis, *Rodeph Shalom*, 44; Korn, *Eventful Years*, 1 ff.

15. Hiner Carey Hockett, *The Critical Method in Historical Research and Writing* (New York, 1955), 195; "Hesse," *JE*; Walker, *Germany and the Emigration*, 153-54; Maldwyn Allen Jones, *American Immigration* (Chicago, 1960), 110-11.

16. *AZJ*, Sept. 16, 1892, p.450; *PAJHS*, 6:141 ff., 35:207 ff.; *Luah le-shenat tr'l lp'k* [1869-1870] (Prague, 1869); Finkelstein, *The Jews* (1960), 2:1560, 1697; *Jewish People*, 1:407 ff., 4:62; Ernst, *Immigrant Life*, 249, n.28; Communication re German immigration to JRM by Dr. Kenneth D. Roseman, Dallas, Texas, copy in Marcus Collections; *Statistical History of U.S.*, 57; *YA*, 2-3:85.

CHAPTER TWO

DAWN IN THE WEST: THE EXPANSION OF AMERICAN JEWRY, 1654–1880

1. *PAJHS*, 10:109 ff.; Grinstein, *New York City*, 469, 472-74; *U.A.H.C Statistics*, 9 ff., 55; "New York City," *EJ*, 12:1075-75.

2. *Essex Story*, 40; "Naar, David," "Newark," *UJE*; "Essex County," "New Jersey," *EJ*.

3. Trachtenberg, *Easton*, 228; Davis, *Rodeph Shalom*, 31-33.

4. P. & K., *Tourist's Guide*, 533; Byars, *B. and M. Gratz*, 257.

5. Brickner, "Jew. Com. of Cin.," Table 2; Jacob S. Feldman, *The Early Migration and Settlement of Jews in Pittsburgh*, 1754-1894 (Pittsburgh, 1959), 12 ff., 30.

6. *U.A.H.C. Statistics*, 55; Bernard Postal, et al., *Jewish Delaware, etc.* (Wilmington?, 1976), 10; "Pennsylvania," *EJ*; "Delaware," *EJ, JE, UJE*.

7. Marcus, *CAJ*, 2:797-98; Fein, *Baltimore*, 7 ff., 19.

8. Fein, *Baltimore*, 17, 23, 43-44; B. & B., *JOUS*, 1:141, 202-3; Stern, *FAJF*, 32.

9. "Friedenwald," *UJE*; "Dyer, Isadore," *DAB*; Adolph Guttmacher, *A History of the Baltimore Hebrew Congregation, etc.* (Baltimore, 1905), 29 ff.; Stern, *FAJF*, 62; Frank H. Waldorf, "A Study of Maryland Jewry as Reflected in the *Occident*, 1850-1861" (HUC term paper, 1962), 25; "Maryland," *EJ*.

10. Marcus, *CAJ*, 1:340-41; *AJA*, 23:198 ff.; Reuben Gold Thwaites, *Early Western Travels, 1748-1846, etc.* (Cleveland, 1905), 13:53.

11. Walter Barrett, *Old Merchants of New York City* (3 vols., N.Y., 1863-70), 3(part 1):135, 152 ff.; Myron Berman, *Richmond's Jewry, 1769-1976: Shabbat in Shockoe* (Charlottesville, Va., 1979), 44, 139, et passim; E. & L., *Richmond*, 122, 258; Lawrence R. Loewner, Harrisburg, Va., to JRM, May 29, 1945, Marcus Collections; "Virginia," *EJ, UJE, JE*; *U.A.H.C. Statistics*, 20, 55.

12. *World Over*, May 16, 1952, p.8; Quinn, *Roanoke*, 92, 117; *The Roanoke Voyages*, Hakluyt Society, (London, 1955), 1:196, 274, 2:907, 909; Karen Ordahl Kupperman, *Roanoke: The Abandoned Colony* (Totowa, N.J., 1984), 40; *TJHSE*, 4:83-101; Marcus, *CAJ*, 1:347, 3:1193, 1325; *U.A.H.C. Statistics*, 21, 55; "North Carolina," *JE, UJE, EJ*; "Wilmington," *UJE*; Rabbi I.L. Freund and Lionel Weil, "Brief History of the Jews of North Carolina," typescript, copy in Marcus Collections.

13. *AJA*, 10:49; *PAJHS*, 16:46 ff.; "Fels, Samuel," "Mordecai, Jacob," *UJE*; "Fels, Joseph," *UJE, DAB*; Harry L. Golden, *Jewish Roots in the Carolinas: A Pattern of American Philo-Semitism* (Charlotte, N.C., 1955), 38; "North Carolina," *EJ*; Wallace Family Papers, Statesville, N.C., AJAr.

14. Elzas, *Jews of S.C.*, 45, 241, 245, 278, 285; *U.A.H.C. Statistics*, 23; for F. J. Moses, Senior and Junior, see Elzas, *Jews of S.C.*, Index; "Moses, Myer(1)," *BDEAJ*; *R*, no. 323, 334; "Moses, Franklin J.," *DAB*; "South Carolina," *EJ*.

15. *Proceedings of the Conference on the Writing of Regional History in the South, etc.* (Miami Beach, 1956); *PAJHS*, 10:172, 25:132-34; P. & K., *Tourist's Guide*, 114 ff.; Harry Simonhoff, *Under Strange Skies* (N.Y., 1953), 274 ff.; Malvina W. & Seymour B. Liebman, *Jewish Frontiersmen: Historical Highlights of Early South Florida Jewish Communities* (Miami Beach, n.d.); Elzas, *Jews of S.C.*, 98, 206-7; Lebeson, *Pilgrim People*, 182; "Levy, Moses Elias," *EJ*; "Jacksonville," "Miami," *UJE, EJ*; *U.A.H.C. Statistics*, 23, 55; Markens, *Hebrews*, 184; "United States," *JE*, 12:372; *AJYB*, 1(1899-1900):121, 21:355-56; Irving Lehrman & Joseph Rappaport, *The Jewish Community of Miami Beach* (n.p., n.d.); "Florida," *JE, UJE, EJ*; "Tampa," *UJE*; AJA release on Michael Lazarus (Cincinnati, n.d.); Marcus, *Memoirs*, 3:146 ff.; Polly Redford, *Billion-Dollar Sandbar: A Biography of Miami Beach* (N.Y., 1970), 211 ff.; *Michael*, 3:23.

16. Elzas, *Jews of S.C.*, 189-90, 192; *U.A.H.C. Statistics*, 24; Marcus, *CAJ*, 1:354, 369; "An Act of Faith at Augusta, Georgia," communication by Thomas J. Moïse, Aug. 17, 1847, to *Occident*, copy in Marcus Collections.

17. Rothschild, *Atlanta*, 1 ff.; "Atlanta," "Georgia," *EJ*; Hertzberg, *Atlanta*, 217; Marcus, *Memoirs*, 2:298, 303-4; P. & K., *Tourist's Guide*, 132.
18. *PAJHS*, 8:45, 10:18; Marcus, *Memoirs*, 1:207-8.
19. *PAJHS*, 8:44, 46, 54-55, 27:251, 259; "Cincinnati," *JE*; *Bulletin: Historical and Philosophical Society of Ohio*, 5:12.
20. "Lilienthal, Max," *JE*.
21. "Ohio," *JE, UJE, EJ*; "Cincinnati," *EJ*; *U.A.H.C. Statistics*, 30-32.
22. *PAJHS*, 1:99 ff., 17:81 ff., 22:96-97, 33:5; "Gist, Christopher," *DAB*; "Gratz," *UJE*; Robert Peter, *History of Fayette County*, edited by William Henry Perrin (Chicago, 1882), 612 ff., 830; Obituary of Benjamin Gratz, St. Louis *Republican*, Aug. 24, 1884, reprinted in an undocumented clipping, Marcus Collections. B. Gratz funeral: David Philipson, one of the students, to JRM; Byars, *B. and M. Gratz*, 262 ff.
23. *PAJHS*, 1:100; "Kentucky," *JE*; *U.A.H.C. Statistics*, 38.
24. *U.A.H.C. Statistics*, 38; Marcus, *Jew in the Medieval World*, 41-42; Byars, *B. and M. Gratz*, 264; "Blair, Francis Preston (Jr.)," "Brown, Benjamin Gratz," *DAB*.
25. Markens, *Hebrews*, 107-8; Stern, *FAJF*, 25; "Missouri," *EJ*.
26. Makovsky, *The Philipsons*; Sidney M. Fish, *Aaron Levy, Founder of Aaronsburg* (N.Y., 1951), 38.
27. St. Louis *Daily Globe-Democrat*, Jan. 1, 1940, p.4C; *Jewish Tribune*, Nov. 23, 1883, p.451; "Missouri," *EJ*; "Saint Louis," *JE*.
28. "Bush (Busch), Isidor," *JE, EJ*; *Historia Judaica*, 5:183-203.
29. Korn, *New Orleans*, 193; Korn, *Eventful Years*, 199-200.
30. *PAJHS*, 8:106 ff.; Schappes, *DHJUS*, 141 ff.; Jonathan D. Sarna, *Jacksonian Jew, The Two Worlds of Mordecai Noah* (N.Y., 1981), 61 ff., 127; Goldberg, *Major Noah*, 146 ff.
31. "Albany," "Syracuse," "Mayer, Nathan," *UJE*; *AI*, Nov. 26, 1858, p.165, cs.2-4.
32. "Buffalo," *UJE*; Marcus, *EAJ*, 1:35 ff.; Marcus, *CAJ*, 1:402; Samuel Rezneck, *A Century of Temple Berith Sholom: Troy, New York, 1866-1966* (Cohoes, N.Y., n.d.), 5 ff.; *U.A.H.C. Statistics*, 11-13.
33. "Elmira," "Schenectady," *UJE*.
34. Frederick C. Waite, Dover, New Hampshire, to JRM, June 20, 1947, Marcus Collections; *PAJHS*, 26:219-30.
35. Ship's passenger list, Abe Nebel Collection, Lazarus Cohen file, AJAr; Cleveland *Plain Dealer*, May 17, 1938; "Cleveland," "Toledo," *UJE, EJ*; Gartner, *Cleveland*, 8, 17; *U.A.H.C. Statistics*, 30-31; "Ohio," *JE, UJE, EJ*; Toledo *Commercial Telegram*, Dec. 10, 1883.

CHAPTER THREE

JEWS OF NEW ENGLAND, THE OLD SOUTHWEST, AND THE BORDER STATES

1. Marcus, *Studies*, 54, 81; Silverman, *Hartford Jews*, 5, 9; "Connecticut," *UJE, EJ*; Franklin Bowditch Dexter (ed.), *The Literary Diary of Ezra Stiles* (3 vols., N.Y., 1901), 1:283; Rollin G. Osterweis, *Three Centuries of New Haven, 1638-1938* (New Haven, 1953), 217-18; Schappes, *DHJUS*, 302; "New Haven," *UJE*; *U.A.H.C. Statistics*, 8; Arthur Goldberg, *The Jew in Norwich: Century of Jewish Life* (Norwich, 1956), 1, 3, 21-22.
2. George Alexander Kohut, *Ezra Stiles and the Jews* (N.Y., 1902), 138; "Newport," *UJE, EJ*; *U.A.H.C. Statistics*, 7; Marcus, *Memoirs*, 2:88 ff.; *RIJHN*, 3:148 ff., 4:50 ff.; *Dedication of Temple Beth El, etc.* (Providence, R.I., April, 1954), copy in Marcus Collections; Providence *Sunday Journal*, Dec.30, 1951; *Hamwasser*, 4(1864):31-32; "Rhode Island," "Providence," *EJ*.

3. "Morse, Leopold," *UJE, Biographical Directory of the American Congress*; Schindler, *Israelites in Boston*, chaps.1, 5; "Boston," *JE, UJE, EJ*; Marcus, *CAJ*, 1:304; *AJA*, 10:48; Ehrenfried, *Boston*, 336 ff.; *PAJHS*, 12:101 ff., 22:228-30; Lyons & De Sola, *Jewish Calendar*, 149-50; "Massachusetts," *UJE, EJ*; *Commentary*, 15:490 ff.

4. Schindler, *Israelites in Boston*, chap.1; "Boston," *UJE*; Marcus, *Memoirs*, 1:289 ff., 296-97; *PAJHS*, 11:96; Ehrenfried, *Boston*, 341; "Record of the Congregation Ahavat Ahim, Brotherly Love, Bangor, State of Maine, Penobscot County," copy in Marcus Collections; "Maine," *UJE, EJ*; Benjamin Band, *Portland Jewry: Its Growth and Development* (Portland, Me., 1955), 6 ff.

5. Wolf, *American Jew*, 224-26; *PAJHS*, 11:98-99, 23:171; "New Hampshire," *EJ*.

6. "Montefiore, Joshua," *DAB*; P. & K., *Tourist's Guide*, 616-19; *PAJHS*, 40:119 ff.; "Lamport, Nathan," *UJE*; "Vermont," *EJ, UJE*.

7. Marcus, *Memoirs*, 3:133; "Heydenfeldt, Solomon," *UJE*; Korn, *Mobile*, 52-53.

8. Korn, *Mobile*, 38 ff., 54 ff.; *PAJHS*, 12:113 ff.; "Alabama," *JE*; "Alabama," original typescript by B. W. Korn, for *EJ*, copy in Marcus Collections; "Mobile," "Schlesinger, Sigmund," *UJE*; *PAJHS*, 12:21; A.Z. Idelsohn, *Jewish Music* (N.Y., 1929), 325-26.

9. Korn, *Mobile*, 15-16; "Mordecai, Abram," *BDEAJ*; *PAJHS*, 12:124, 13:71 ff.; *Florida Historical Quarterly*, 31:3; "Alabama," *JE, UJE, EJ*; "Montgomery," *UJE*; *Kahl Montgomery*, 1 ff.; Eichhorn, *Evangelizing*, 110-11. Jaeger: Statement of Kohler to JRM; Lyons & De Sola, *Jewish Calendar*, 152; J.(?) Wolff, Clairborne, Ala., to I.L., Phila., May 1, 1853, copy in Marcus Collections; *U.A.H.C. Statistics*, 25-26.

10. "Georgia," *UJE*, 4:538; "Mississippi," *UJE, EJ, JE*; "Monsanto, Benjamin," "Monsanto, Mrs. Clara," "Monsanto, Jacob," "Monsanto, Manuel Jacob," *BDEAJ*; P. & K., *Tourist's Guide*, 260 ff., 263; Elzas, *Jews of S.C.*, 140, 141, 144, 193, 205-6, 245; Lyons & De Sola, *Jewish Calendar*, 153; U.S. Senate, Report on Sarah Levy, 27th Cong., 2d sess., Jan. 11, 1842, Sen. Report 44; *U.A.H.C. Statistics*, 26-27.

11. P. & K., *Tourist's Guide*, 267; Marcus, *Memoirs*, 1:264 ff., 270; Korn, *New Orleans*; B. & B., *JOUS*, 3:847 ff.

12. Marcus, *Memoirs*, 1:299 ff.; P. & K., *Tourist's Guide*, 265; "Mississippi," *EJ*; Leo E. Turitz & Evelyn Turitz, *Jews in Early Mississippi* (Jackson, 1983?); Philippsborn, *Vicksburg*.

13. "Bien, Herman," *UJE*; *PAJHS*, 5:207 ff.; P. & K., *Tourist's Guide*, 295; Nodel, *The Ties Between*, 20-21; Korn, *Civil War*, 82-83; Levine, *Am. Jew. Bibliography*, nos. 133, 203, 685-86; Philippsborn, *Vicksburg*, 15 ff.

14. "Arkansas," *EJ*; P. & K., *Tourist's Guide*, 19-20, 22 ff.; *AJA*, 8:67-68; Stern, *FAJF*, 25; Malcolm Stern, Norfolk, Va., to JRM, Feb. 27, 1952, Marcus Collections; *American Jews' Annual for 5650 A.M.* (1889-90), 95-96; Frank, *Nashville*, 22, 76, et passim.

15. P. & K., *Tourist's Guide*, 19, 21, 26, 511; Cyrus Adler, *I Have Considered the Days* (Phila., 1941), 4-5; Marcus, *Memoirs*, 2:135 ff.; "Arkansas," "Little Rock," *UJE*; Little Rock *Arkansas Gazette*, Nov. 20, 1919; Congregation House of Israel, *Scroll of Honor: Eightieth Anniversary Celebration* (Sunday, July 22, 1956, Park Hotel, Hot Springs National Park, Arkansas).

16. *Jewish Digest*, 1(no.10):23 ff.; Eichhorn, *Evangelizing*, 117-18.

17. *PAJHS*, 10:99, 53:3 ff.; Korn, *New Orleans*, 6-9, 265 ff., 268; Abraham P. Nasatir and James R. Mills, *Commerce and Contraband in New Orleans During the French and Indian War, etc.* (Cincinnati, 1968); David Max Eichhorn, "Christianizing America's Jews" (2 vols., 1938), copy in Marcus Collections, 1:28 ff.; Marcus, *CAJ*, 1:89, 373-74, 3:1446, nn.6-7; Wills of Samuel Hart, 1823, 1832, New Orleans Probate Court, copies in AJAr; "Louisiana," *EJ*.

18. Korn, *New Orleans*, 123 and index sub Benjamin, Hyams, and Moïse; Elzas, *Jews of S.C.*, 163; Marcus, *Memoirs*, 3:104.

19. *U.A.H.C. Statistics*, 25-26; Max Heller, *Jubilee Souvenir of Temple Sinai, 1872-1922* (New Orleans, 1922), 8-10; Julian B. Feibelman, *A Social and Economic Study of the New Orleans Jewish Community* (Phila., 1941), 79-80.

20. *U.A.H.C. Statistics*, 27; Bernard Lemann, *The Lemann Family of Louisiana* (Donaldsonville, 1965), 46 ff., 71.
21. Marcus, *CAJ*, 1:52, 3:1397, n. 11; Korn, *New Orleans*, 67 ff., 287-88.
22. *Louisiana Inventory*, 1 ff.; "Shreveport," *UJE*; P. & K., *Tourist's Guide*, 200-1; J. Fair Hardin, "Memorandum on the First Jewish Migration into North Louisiana," La. State Univ., Baton Rouge, La., copy in AJAr.
23. P. & K., *Tourist's Guide*, 596-97; *PAJHS*, 2:139 ff., 4:90-92; *Southwestern Historical Quarterly*, 30:139-40, 31:80; *Quarterly of the Texas State Historical Association*, 12:211 ff.; "Sterne, Adolphus," *Handbook of Texas*; Williams & Barker, *Writings of Sam Houston*, 1:478, n.3; Wolf, *American Jew*, 73, 75, 83; "Harby, Levi Myers," *UJE*, "Texas," *JE, UJE, EJ*; Beaumont *Enterprise*, Jan. 13, 1946.
24. Williams & Barker, *Writings of Sam Houston*, 7:371-72.
25. Julia Nott Waugh, *Castroville and Henry Castro, Empresario* (San Antonio, 1934), 1 ff., 67 ff., 73; P. & K., *Tourist's Guide*, 601-2; "Castro, Henry," *UJE*; *AJA*, 8:72-73.
26. *PAJHS*, 4:9 ff.; W. & W., *Philadelphia*, 356; P. & K., *Tourist's Guide*, 599, 608; Frances R. Kallison, San Antonio, to JRM, Apr. 13, 1964, Marcus Collections; James M. Day, *Jacob De Cordova, Land Merchant of Texas* (Waco, 1962).
27. "Houston," *JE, UJE, EJ*; Anne Nathan Cohen, *The Centenary History: Congregation Beth Israel of Houston, Texas, 1854-1954* (Houston?, 1954?); *U.A.H.C. Statistics*, 29; *AJA*, 8:75 ff.; I.H. Kempner, *Recalled Recollections* (Galveston, 1961), 13, et passim, and family traditions told to JRM.
28. *AJA*, 8:74, 76-78; *Occ.*, 10:379 ff., 24:511 ff.; *PAJHS*, 2:147 ff., 152 ff., 4:15-16; W. & W., *Philadelphia*, 356-57, 495; "Dyer, Isadore," *JE*; A. Stanley Dreyfus, "Hebrew Cemetery, No. 1 of Galveston" (typescript, Galveston, 1965), copy in Marcus Collections, 3; Henry Cohen, et al., *One Hundred Years of Jewry in Texas* (Dallas, 1936), 9-10; Galveston *Daily News*, Dec. 18, 1921, Apr. 2, 1922, Apr. 9, 1922; Statement of Dr. J.O. Osterman about Rosanna Osterman, Rosenberg Library of Galveston, copy in Marcus Collections.
29. *AJA*, 8:74-75; "Dallas," *UJE*; David Lefkowitz, *History of Temple Emanu-El, Dallas, Texas, 1873-1933* (Dallas, 1933); P. & K., *Tourist's Guide*, 603-607; *Woman's Wear* (New York?, Jan. 30, 1914), 6 ff.; Dallas *Times Herald*, Apr. 14, 1939, First Section, p.9, advertisement; "History of the Sangers, 1836 - Texas Centennial - 1936," typescript, copy in Marcus Collections; "A Picture of Jewish Life in Dallas From 1872 to 1955" (Dallas, 1955), typescript, copy in Marcus Collections; Harris, *Merchant Princes*, 157 ff.; Receipt in papers of Dallas Historical Society.
30. Marcus, *CAJ*, 3:1205, 1290-91; *PAJHS*, 48:1 ff.; Minutes of Mickva [Mickve] Israel Congregation of Savannah, Georgia, Mar. 11, 13, 1792, copy in AJAr; Marans, *Jews in Greater Washington*, 10 ff.
31. *Senate Journal*, 34th Congress, 1st and 2nd Session, July 10, 16, 1856; *PAJHS*, 11:17 ff., 26:213 ff., 27:507; "Levy, Jonas Phillips," *UJE, EJ*; P. & K., *Tourist's Guide*, 93-94; Bernard I. Nordlinger, *A History of the Washington Hebrew Congregation: One Hundred Years of Reform Judaism in the District of Columbia* (n.p., 1956), 4-11.
32. "Bennett," "Marshall," *Biographical Directory of the American Congress*; *PAJHS*, 26:211 ff., 48:185, 56:319 ff.; Korn, *Eventful Years*, 98 ff.
33. "Wolf, Simon," *DAB*; Marans, *Jews of Greater Washington*, 14; *PAJHS*, 56:319; *U.A.H.C. Statistics*, 18.
34. P. & K., *Tourist's Guide*, 103 ff.; "Washington, D.C.," *EJ*; the professor was Jacob R. Marcus.
35. "West Virginia," *EJ, UJE, EJ*; *U.A.H.C. Statistics*, 21; *Reform Advocate*, Oct. 7, 1916, p.9; Shinedling, *West Virginia Jewry*, 1:576 ff., 2:1119 ff., 3:1316, a monumental history because of its detail; *Congregation B'nai Israel Virginia Street Temple, Charleston, W.V., 1873-1948* (Charleston, W.V., 1948), 11.

36. "Myers, Benjamin," *BDEAJ*; "Tennessee," *JE, UJE, EJ*; Frank, *Nashville*. 15 ff.; Marcus, *Memoirs*, 1:353 ff.

37. "Knoxville," *UJE*; Grinstein, *New York City*, 145-46; *Tennessee Inventory*, 3, et passim; Ochs, *Memoir*, 3 ff., 51; "Ochs," *EJ*; "Ochs, Julius," *UJE*; *U.A.H.C. Statistics*, 55.

CHAPTER FOUR

JEWS IN THE MIDDLE WEST, PRAIRIE STATES, AND FAR WEST

1. Marcus, *CAJ*, 2:759 ff.; Ochs, *Memoir*, 31; Byars, *B. & M. Gratz*, 272; "Judah, Samuel," *DAB*; Marcus, *United States Jewry*, 1:chap.3 and index sub John Hays and Samuel Judah; "Gimbel," *UJE, New Columbia Encyclopedia*; Harris, *Merchant Princes*, 70 ff.; *Journal of the Rutgers University Libraries*, 47:77 ff.

2. Gideon M. Goldenholz, "The Emergence of a Jewish Community in Fort Wayne" (Ph.D. diss., H.T.C., Chicago, n.d.), 17-19; B. & B., *JOUS*, 1:125 ff., 271, n.111; Fort Wayne *Old Fort News*, 8:3 ff.; Indiana *Jewish Chronicle*, Apr. 23, 1948, pp.12 ff.; Brickner, "Jew. Com. of Cin.," 2:272; Kuhn, Loeb & Co., *A Century of Investment Banking* (N.Y., 1967?); "Notes on the History of the Jewish Congregation and Cemetery B'nai Zion of La Porte, Indiana," typescript, copy in Marcus Collections.

3. Gerhard Foreman, Delphi, Carroll County, Indiana, to Mr. & Mrs. F. Heyman and children, Germany, Mar., 1852, copy in Marcus Collections; *U.A.H.C. Statistics*, 33-34; P. & K., *Tourist's Guide*, 161 ff.

4. Marcus, *CAJ*, 1:375-76; "Levy, Isaac(8)," *BDEAJ*; *PAJHS*, 16:28 ff., 45:55; *Indiana Magazine of History*, 39:221 ff.; Marcus, *United States Jewry*, 1:index sub Hays; Hays data in the Perrin Collection, Saint Clair County Records, on deposit in the Illinois State Archives, copy in Marcus Collections.

5. Chicago *Daily Tribune*, June 10, 1947, p.C-27; "Chicago," "Horner, Henry," *EJ*; *PAJHS*, 2:24; Eliassof, *German-American Jews*, 46-47, 64; Meites, *Chicago*, 37-38, 137; Marcus, *Memoirs*, 2:281 ff.

6. Eliassof, *German-American Jews*, 55 ff.; Marcus, *Memoirs*, 2:284.

7. "Illinois," "Jonas, Abraham," "Rosenwald, Julius," "Springfield," *UJE*; *U.A.H.C. Statistics*, 36-37; *PAJHS*, 19:96-97; Wolf, *American Jew*, 109.

8. Marcus, *CAJ*, 3:1325; *PAJHS*, 13:56.

9. "Michigan," *UJE*; "Detroit," *UJE, EJ*; *PAJHS*, 13:66; Benjamin, *Three Years*, 2:276; Ely Grad, "Congregation Shaarey Zedek, Detroit, Michigan, Centennial History, 1861-1961," 1 ff., typescript in Marcus Collections.

10. *PAJHS*, 13:58 ff., 69, n.36; *Bulletin, Detroit Historical Society* 6(no.5):7-8; "Israel, Edward," *JE*.

11. "Grand Rapids," *UJE*; "Houseman, Julius," *UJE, Biographical Directory of the American Congress*; Detroit *Jewish News*, Oct. 4, 1968, p.10; *U.A.H.C. Statistics*, 40-41; John Cumming, *Little Jake of Saginaw* (Mount Pleasant, Mich., 1978), 1 ff.

12. Lebeson, *JPA*, 261; *PAJHS*, 9:151-52; *Wisconsin Magazine of History*, 64:11; Ramsey Crooks to Abbott, Dec. 22, 1846, Papers of American Fur Company, NYHSL; Marcus, *United States Jewry*, 1:chap.4.

13. Swichkow & Gartner, *Milwaukee*, 4, 11, 33, et passim; Marcus, *Memoirs*, 2:154 ff., 268 ff.

14. Schappes, *DHJUS*, 281 ff., 640; *La Crosse County Historical Sketches* (La Crosse, Wis., 1935), Series 2:78-82; *U.A.H.C. Statistics*, 41; Swarsensky, *Madison*, 37, 94.

15. "Houdini, Harry," "Wisconsin," *UJE*; P. & K., *Tourist's Guide*, 650; Joseph I. Levy, Ashland, Wis., to Wisconsin Historical Society, Madison, Wis., Apr. 24, 1923, copy in Marcus Collections.

16. Fleishaker, "Illinois-Iowa Jewish Community," 8 ff., 14-15, 161 ff., 176 ff.

17. Glazer, *Jews of Iowa*, 167 ff.; Fleishaker, "Illinois-Iowa Jewish Community," 8 ff., 23, 44 ff., 58; "Iowa," *UJE*; Jack Wolfe, *A Century with Iowa Jewry, 1833-1940, etc.* (Des Moines, 1941), 239.

18. Glazer, *Jews of Iowa*, 189-90; Fleishaker, "Illinois-Iowa Jewish Community," 163 ff.; "History of Keokuk," typescript, Keokuk Public Library, copy in Marcus Collections; *U.A.H.C. Statistics*, 42-43.

19. Glazer, *Jews of Iowa*, 201, 202, 209 ff.; *U.A.H.C. Statistics*, 42; Fleishaker, "Illinois-Iowa Jewish Community," 12-13, 18-24, 28, 53, 79-81, 84, 89-90, 98; P. & K., *Tourist's Guide*, 173.

20. Glazer, *Jews of Iowa*, 179 ff., 231 ff., 243 ff.; Frank Rosenthal, *Jews of Des Moines, The First Century* (Des Moines, 1957), 1 ff., 14 ff., 30, 54 ff., 58-60; "Des Moines," *UJE*; "Iowa," *JE, UJE, EJ*.

21. Bernard Shuman, *A History of the Sioux City Jewish Community, 1869 to 1969* (Sioux City, 1969), 4, 9-10, 19 ff.; *U.A.H.C. Statistics*, 42-43; Glazer, *Jews of Iowa*, 289 ff.; Martin I. Hinchin, "A History of the Jews of Sioux City, Iowa (1857-1846)" (rabbinical thesis, HUC, Cincinnati, 1946); "Centennial Historic Sketches [about Sioux City] Published in the *Jewish Federation Newsletter*," typescript, copy in Marcus Collections.

22. *PAJHS*, 13:58-59; P. & K., *Tourist's Guide*, 243, 644 ff.; Plaut, *Jews in Minnesota*, 12-15, 30 ff., 35, 51-52, 62-63; Plaut, *Mt. Zion*, 28.

23. Plaut, *Mt. Zion*, 3 ff., 13 ff., 26 ff.; Plaut, *Jews in Minnesota*, 31 ff., 34, 40, 43 ff.; *U.A.H.C. Statistics*, 42; P. & K., *Tourist's Guide*, 254 ff.; Statement of Harold Rose to JRM, St. Paul, Mar. 31, 1948, Marcus Collections; Marcus, *Memoirs*, 2:351 ff.; *AJA*, 8:102-3.

24. "Bondi, August," *UJE, EJ*; Schappes, *DHJUS*, 352 ff., 666 ff.; *PAJHS*, 23:51 ff.; P. & K., *Tourist's Guide*, 177 ff.; *AJA*, 8:92; Marcus, *Memoirs*, 2:165 ff.

25. P. & K., *Tourist's Guide*, 177 ff., 181, 183-84, 188; *AI*, Sept. 11, 1863, p.87, c.2; *AJYB*, 35:126; *AH*, July 22, 1932, p.204; "Kansas," *UJE*.

26. "Alexander, Moses," "St. Joseph," *UJE*; Adler, *Kansas City*, 19.

27. Watters, *Utah*, 142 ff.; Adler, *Kansas City*, 3-17, 22.

28. Omaha *Sunday World-Herald*, May 20, 1945, p.12-A; Somberg & Roffman, *Omaha*, 11 ff.; "Nebraska," *JE, UJE*; Auerbach, "Nebraska," 2, 10-11.

29. "Omaha," *UJE*; Auerbach, "Nebraska," 12 ff.; "Rosewater, Edward," *DAB, WWW, 1607-1896*; P. & K., *Tourist's Guide*, 290-91; "The Rosewaters: Western Pioneers," *AJAr* News Release, Aug. 22, 1955.

30. *AH*, Sept. 10, 1926, p.587; Marcus, *CAJ*, 2:814; *AJA*, 8:120; Auerbach, "Nebraska," 20 ff.; Somberg & Roffman, *Omaha*, 11-12; P. & K., *Tourist's Guide*, 290.

31. P. & K., *Tourist's Guide*, 645; "John Levy, Fur Trader," MS Biography, Wisconsin Historical Society; *WSJHQ*, 3:3 ff.

32. P. & K., *Tourist's Guide*, 28; *PAJHS*, 31:149, 159; Stern, *FAJF*, 252; Bancroft, *Hist. of Calif.*, 7:219, n.29; for Polock see Record Group 59, General Records of the Dept. of State Diplomatic Despatches, Mexico, vol.9; biographical data and letter supplied by Edwin Wolf the 2nd; "Polock, Moses," *UJE*.

33. "California," *JE, UJE, EJ*; Levinson, *California Gold Rush*; Sonora, Calif., *CHISPA*, 9:305-6.

34. P. & K., *Tourist's Guide*, 53; notes on Louis Rose, compiled by Dr. Norton B. Stern, copy in Marcus Collections; *WSJHQ*, 1:20 ff., 2:67 ff., 3:26 ff., 33-36; The City and County of San Diego, *Prominent Men and Pioneers* (San Diego, 1888), 93 ff., 112 ff., 150 ff.; "San Diego," *EJ*; *Occ.*, 17:222, 229-30.

35. Vorspan & Gartner, *Los Angeles*, 9, 19, 32, 37, 58-62, et passim; *Jewish Tribune*, Dec. 7, 1883, p.483, cs.2-3, p.484, c.1; P. & K., *Tourist's Guide*, 38; *U.A.H.C. Statistics*, 48; *El Clamor Publico*, Los Angeles, Sabado, Julio 30, 1859, p.l, c.3. I owe this reference to Dr. Norton B. Stern.

36. *The Far-Westerner* 2(no.2):11 ff.; Benjamin, *Three Years*, 2:9-10.

37. Agresti, *David Lubin*; "Lubin, David," *DAB*.

38. Bancroft, *Hist. of Calif.*, 7:433-34; "Gerstle, Lewis," *UJE, EJ*; Gerstle Mack, *Lewis and Hannah Gerstle* (N.Y., 1953), 24 ff.; Zarchin, *San Francisco*, 56-57; *U.A.H.C. Statistics*, 48.

39. *PAJHS*, 2:148-49; Voorsanger, *Emanu-El*, 16 ff., 138; Cowan, *Forgotten Characters*, 33-34; "San Francisco," *EJ*; Glanz, *California*, 38-39; Zarchin, *San Francisco*, 77, 81 ff., 169.

40. *PAJHS*, 10:129 ff.; "California," *UJE*; P. & K., *Tourist's Guide*, 55.

41. *PAJHS*, 31:162; Marcus, *Memoirs*, 2:264; *Der Deutsche Pionier*, 10:238 ff.; [Albert Dressler], *Emperor Norton: Life and Experiences of a Notable Character in San Francisco, 1849-1880* (San Francisco, 1927), 1 ff.; Cowan, *Forgotten Characters*, 41 ff.

42. *AI*, June 9, 1876, p.4, cs.3-5; P. & K., *Tourist's Guide*, 30; Zarchin, *San Francisco*, 60 ff. Detailed studies of Jews in early California may be found in *WSJHQ*.

43. Levi Strauss and Company, *Everyone knows his FIRST name* (San Francisco, 1942), advertising pamphlet; P. & K., *Tourist's Guide*, 298; J. Ross Browne, *A Peep at Washoe and Washoe Revisited* (Balboa Island, Calif., 1959), Introduction, 36, 89 ff., 110 ff., 184 ff.

44. P. & K., *Tourist's Guide*, 292 ff.; Benjamin, *Three Years*, 2:203 ff.

45. Marcus, *Memoirs*, 3:40; AI, Oct. 2, 1857, p.101, c.4, p.102, c.1; Bernard Falk, *The Naked Lady: A Biography of Adah Isaacs Menken* (London, rev. ed., 1952); Allen Lesser, *Weave a Wreath of Laurel* (N.Y., 1938), 21 ff.; Paul Lewis, *Queen of the Plaza: A Biography of Adah Isaacs Menken* (N.Y., 1964); Wolf Mankowitz, *Mazeppa: The Lives, Loves and Legends of Adah Isaacs Menken* (N.Y., 1982), 114 ff.; Adah Isaacs Menken, *Infelicia* (Phila., 1868); "Menken, Adah Isaacs," *DAB, NAW*; *PAJHS*, 34:143-47; P. & K., *Tourist's Guide*, 292 ff.

46. "Michelson, Charles," *UJE, WWW*, 1607-1896.

47. "Sutro, Adolph Heinrich Joseph," *JE, UJE, EJ, DAB*; Eugenia Kellogg Holmes, *Adolph Sutro* (San Francisco, 1895); Robert E. Stewart, Jr., and Mary Francis Stewart, *Adolph Sutro, A Biography* (Berkeley, 1972); Cleland & Dumke, *California*, 190, 226 ff., 307; Caughey, *California*, 455 ff.; "Johnson, Hiram Warren," *DAB*, Supplement 3; P. & K., *Tourist's Guide*, 294.

48. "Nevada," *UJE, EJ*; *WSJHQ*, 2:3 ff.; *AJYB*, 57:128.

49. For early Oregon Jews see the letter concerning Priest in H. Bancroft, *California Pioneer Register and Index*, 1541-1848 (Berkeley, 1964), 292; Military Record of Dr. Israel Moses, Oct. 11, 1870, Surgeon General's Office, Washington, D.C., copy in AJHS; *Journal of Mt. Sinai Hospital*; 10:512-21: "Loring, William Wing," *DAB*; Morais, *Philadelphia*, 463; P. & K., *Tourist's Guide*, 517 ff.; "Meier, Julius," *EJ*; "Fleishner, Louis," "Selling, Benjamin," *UJE*; Suwol, *Oregon*, 2-3; Corning, *Dictionary of Oregon History*, 85; Levinson, *California Gold Rush*, 129, 136.

50. P. & K., *Tourist's Guide*, 519-21; *Jewish Digest* 8:59 ff.; Corning, *Dictionary of Oregon History*, 111; "Oregon," "Portland," *JE, UJE, EJ*; Suwol, *Oregon*, 1 ff.; Nodel, *The Ties Between*, 71-73; Benjamin, *Three Years*, 2:158.

51. Benjamin, *Three Years*, 2:158 ff.; Glanz, *California*, 160-61; P. & K., *Tourist's Guide*, 518; Oregon *Daily Journal*, Feb. 22, 1924.

52. Nodel, *The Ties Between*, 24 ff., 60-62; Suwol, *Oregon*, 1 ff.; "Hirsch, Solomon," *UJE*; *AJA*, 10:121 ff.; *Ohio History*, 80:65; *Morning Oregonian*, Dec. 16, 1902; Corning, *Dictionary of Oregon History*, 112; P. & K., *Tourist's Guide*, 521.

CHAPTER FIVE

BUSINESS SURVIVAL IN THE TRANSMISSISSIPPI
STATES AND TERRITORIES

1. Quinn, *Roanoke*, 117; *TJHSE*, 4:83 ff.; *PAJHS*, 5:57 ff., 69; Marcus, *CAJ*, 1:46, 2:539-40, 670, 761, 765, 3:1322, 1497, n.11; Ray Billington, *Westward Expansion: A History of the American Frontier* (N.Y., 1949), chap.30; Makovsky, *The Philipsons*.
2. Manfred R. Wolfenstine, Seattle, to AJAr, Jan. 27, 1971; Levinson, *California Gold Rush*, 13 ff.; Benjamin, *Three Years*, 2:28; Scharfman, *Jackson, California*, 68-72; *PAJHS*, 44:12 ff.
3. Marcus, *Memoirs*, 3:40-43; Breck, *Colorado*, 20.
4. Carter, *Jews in Early Utah*, 343-45, 362; P. & K., *Tourist's Guide*, 613; Watters, *Utah*, 136-37, 163 ff.; Brooks, *Jews in Utah and Idaho*, 43, et passim.
5. Breck, *Colorado*, 15, 43-44, 124-25; Uchill, *Colorado*, 26-31; Bernard M. Baruch, *My Own Story* (N.Y., 1957), 79-81; Denver *Post*, Apr. 26, 1970, pp.38, 40; P. & K., *Tourist's Guide*, 72-73, 76.
6. Carter, *Jews in Early Utah*, 364-66; Watters, *Utah*, 161; Hirschman Papers, AJAr; Agresti, *David Lubin*, 28 ff.; *Memorial Book Konin* (Yiddish, Tel Aviv, 1968), 15-17: a letter in English about the Goldwaters of Arizona; *AJHQ*, 57:356 ff.; Stocker, *Jewish Roots in Arizona*, 7 ff.; *Southwestern Studies*, 1(no.4):27; *AJA*, 10:95 ff., 104, 18:3 ff., 25:161 ff.; *WSJHQ*, 2:172 ff.
7. [Lesinsky] *Letters*; Fierman, *Some Early Jewish Settlers*, 17 ff., 29 ff.; *AJHQ*, 57:356 ff., 384 ff., 427 ff.; Stocker, *Jewish Roots in Arizona*, 16 ff.
8. *WSJHQ*, 1:76 ff.; "Report of an Interview with Mr. Sam Newman . . . July 31, 1969, by Dr. Norton B. Stern," copy in Marcus Collections.
9. P. & K., *Tourist's Guide*, 15, 440-41; "Lewisohn," *EJ*; "Lewisohn, Adolph," "Lewisohn, Leonard," *UJE*; "Lewisohn, Leonard," *JE*; Stephen Birmingham, *"Our Crowd": The Great Jewish Families of New York* (N.Y., 1966), 213.
10. "Guggenheim," *UJE, EJ*; "Guggenheim, Daniel," "Guggenheim, Meyer," *DAB*; Edwin P. Hoyt, Jr., *The Guggenheims and the American Dream* (N.Y., 1967); Milton Lomask, *Seed Money: The Guggenheim Story* (N.Y., 1964); Hyman, *Romance of a Mining Venture*.
11. Marcus, *EAJ*, 2:342 ff.; Jos. I. Levy, Ashland, Wis., to Wisconsin Historical Society, Madison, Apr. 24, 1923, Wisc. Hist. Society; Cleland & Dumke, *California*, 149-57, 185; Caughey, *California*, 261, 394, 493-94; *AJHQ*,54:160 ff.; P. & K., *Tourist's Guide*, 38; Benjamin, *Three Years*, 2:100, 110; Levinson, *California Gold Rush*, 129-30.
12. *AJHQ*, 59:460 ff.; Bibo, *Reminiscences*; *NMQ*, 29:321 ff.; Towne and Wentworth, *Shepherd's Empire*, 252-54, 314-17; Edward Norris Wentworth, *America's Sheep Trails: History, Personalities* (Ames, Iowa, 1948), 239-40, 436-39; Berg, *Kern County Land Company*, 22 ff.; Parish, *Charles Ilfeld Company*, 42, et passim.
13. Stocker, *Jewish Roots in Arizona*, 16 ff.; Towne and Wentworth, *Shepherd's Empire*, 252-54, 318; *YA*, 14:223; P. & K., *Tourist's Guide*,17-18; for Ilfeld investment in sheep, see Parish, *Charles Ilfeld Company*; Elizabeth L. Ramenofsky, *From Charcoal to Banking: The I.E. Solomons of Arizona* (Tucson, 1984), 63 ff., 94 ff.; for Gronsky see unidentified Fort Worth newspaper clippings, probably 1911, copies in Marcus Collections.
14. John H. Waite, "The Activities of M. Halff and Brother," typescript, copy in AJAr. For Lazarus see unidentified St. Louis newspaper clippings for Mar. 6, 17, 1926, copies in Marcus Collections. For a Colorado Jewish cowboy, see Breck, *Colorado*, 47.
15. *PAJHS*, 2:151; Pelzer, *Cattlemen's Frontier*, 65; Joseph G. McCoy, *Historic Sketches of the Cattle Trade of the West and Southwest* (Glendale, Calif., 1940), 60.

16. Fort Worth, Historical Survey of Local Newspapers, Fort Worth WPA, 5:1778-79; Uchill, *Pioneers*, 288-89; Breck, *Colorado*, 23, 44, 53, 125.

17. Breck, *Colorado*, 156; Watters, *Utah*, 134, 172.

18. *Wyoming Industrial Journal*, 1(1898-1900): vii, Wyoming *Tribune*, Jan. 23, 1931, courtesy of Wyoming State Archives; P. & K., *Tourist's Guide*, 334, 656-58; *Commentary*, 40:63 ff.; *AJA*, 8:125; Pelzer, *Cattlemen's Frontier*, 9, 49, 62, Appendix.

19. *Montana*, 21:40 ff., 50, and both sides of the cover page; Norman Winestine, Helena, to JRM, Mar. 24, 1972, Marcus Collections; P. & K., *Tourist's Guide*, 287; Joseph Rosenbaum, Military Service record, copy in AJAr; "In Memoriam to Comrade Joseph Rosenbaum, Grand Army Hall and the Memorial Association of Illinois" (Chicago, 1919), copy in Chicago Historical Society; Albert N. Marquis (ed.), *A Book of Chicagoans* (Chicago, 1917), 583; A.T. Andreas (ed.), *History of Chicago* (Chicago, 1886), 3:297; Pasadena newspaper clippings, n.p., n.d., copies in Marcus Collections; Pelzer, *Cattlemen's Frontier*, 198-99; Towne & Wentworth, *Cattle and Men*, 268-69; Meites, *Chicago*, 182.

20. *WSJHQ*, 2:11 ff.; Statement of August Heilbron of Sacramento, typescript in Bancroft Library, Berkeley, copy in Marcus Collections; Berg, *Kern County Land Company*, 22 ff.

21. Meyer, *Western Jewry*, 156; "Morris, Nelson," *DAB*.

22. *NMQ*, 29:309; Julius Froebel, *Aus Amerika* (Leipzig, 1858), 2:3-4.

23. P. & K., *Tourist's Guide*, 270; *Jewish Tribune*, Dec. 21, 1883, p.514, c.3, p.515, c.1; W.E. Bergin, Adjutant-General, Washington, D.C., to JRM, Feb. 26, 1953, copy in AJAr; "Black Friday," *DAH*; *NMQ*, 29:309 ff.; James Josiah Webb, *Adventures in the Santa Fe Trade*, edited by Ralph P. Bieber (Glendale, Calif., 1931), 29-30, 41, 54, n.67, 107-8, 181, 186 ff., 189, 217, 248, 264; George Rutledge Gibson, *Journal of a Soldier under Kearney and Doniphan, 1846-47*, edited by Ralph P. Bieber (Glendale, Calif., 1935), 41-44, 65, 148, 268; Adler, *Kansas City*, 5; Director of NYHS, N.Y.C., to JRM, Sept.16, 1971, Marcus Collections; *Washington University Studies*, 11:262-78; R W. McAlpine, *The Life and Time of Col. James Fisk, Jr. etc.* (N.Y., 1872), 264 ff.; Dean Earl Wood, *The Old Santa Fe Trail from the Missouri River* (Kansas City, 1951), 137; *New York Times*, Dec. 24, 26, 1880; San Francisco *Alta California*, Jan. 1, 1881, p.4, c.4; Stella M. Drumm (ed.), *Down the Santa Fe Trail and into Mexico: The Diary of Susan Shelby Magoffin, 1846-47* (New Haven, 1926), 10, 96-97, 246-47; George F. Ruxton, *Adventures in Mexico and the Rocky Mountains* (London, 1847), 110; Max L. Moorhead, *New Mexico's Royal Road: Trade and Travel on the Chihuahua Trail* (Norman, Okla., 1958), 84-85, 89-91, 149-50, 153-55, 165, 173-76; Abraham Robinson Johnston, et al., *Marching with the Army of the West, 1846-48*, edited by Ralph P. Bieber (Glendale, Calif., 1936), 84, 88, 114, 122, 311; Philip St. George Cooke, et al., *Exploring Southwestern Trails, 1846-54*, edited by Ralph P. Bieber (Glendale, Calif., 1938), 75.

24. Marcus, *CAJ*, 2:719 ff.; Makovsky, *The Philipsons; Fur Trade Journal*, 10:413, in Missouri Historical Society; *Calendar of the American Fur Company Papers: Annual Report of the American Historical Association* (Washington, D.C., 1944), 1: nos.1052, 1483, 1488, 1508, 1572, 1810, 2995, 4150, 4388, 4468, 7756.

25. Meyer, *Western Jewry*, 166-67; Lloyd Hahn interview by JRM, May 17, 1938, Marcus Collections; Edward Everett Dale, *The Range Cattle Industry* (Norman, Okla., 1930), 44; *Ft. Worth Directory for 1876* (1877), sub Lobenstein; Fort Worth, Historical Survey of Local Newspapers, Fort Worth WPA, 6:2386; *Leavenworth Directory for 1861*, sub Lobenstein.

26. Watters, *Utah*, 160; Bibo, *Reminiscences*, 3, et passim; P. & K., *Tourist's Guide*, 611; Uchill, *Pioneers*, 30; Breck, *Colorado*, 19; Las Vegas, N.M. *Daily Optic*, May 22, 1888.

27. Watters, *Utah*, 4; *Journal of the West*, 7:445-49; *AJA*, 25:173 ff.; *AJHQ*, 57:379-80.

28. Vorspan & Gartner, *Los Angeles*, 51-52; Redlands, Calif., *Daily Facts*, May 6, 1967, column of Frank and Bill Moore.

29. Bibo, "Book of Remembrance"; Watters, *Utah*, 137; *AJA*, 8:88; Breck, *Colorado*, 136; Uchill, *Pioneers*, 136.
30. Frances Kallison, "Was it a Duel or a Murder?," typescript, copy in AJAr; P. & K., *Tourist's Guide*, 606.
31. Bibo, *Reminiscences*, 40 ff., 250-52; Bibo, "Book of Remembrance," sub Simon Bibo; Albuquerque *Tribune*, June, 1889, newspaper clipping in Marcus Collections.
32. Leroy R. Hafen and Ann W. Hafen (eds.), *Reports from Colorado: The Wildman Letters* (Glendale, Calif., 1961), 295, n.56; Uchill, *Pioneers*, 71; Breck, *Colorado*, 35-36; P. & K., *Tourist's Guide*, 286.
33. *Cases Argued and Adjudged in the Court of Appeals of the State of Texas* (1879-1880), Reported by Jackson & Jackson, 7:519 ff.; Theodore Mack interview by JRM, Dallas, April 10, 1939, Marcus Collections; *AJHQ*, 59:469; Cheyenne *Daily Leader*, Mar. 10, 1877; Lake, *Wyatt Earp*, 161-62.
34. Material supplied by Dr. Norton B. Stern.
35. *Congress Weekly*, Mar. 11, 1957, p.6; Wolf, *American Jew*, 125-26; Breck, *Colorado*, 40; Uchill, *Pioneers*, 51-52; "Mears, Otto," *DAB*; Solomon Davidson, Service Record, G.S.A., copy in AJAr.
36. Morais, *Philadelphia*, 498; Wolf, *American Jew*, 371; *AJA*, 20:16 ff.; *PAJHS*, 8:59 ff.
37. Schlesinger, *Rise of the City*, 37; P. & K., *Tourist's Guide*, 182; *AJA*, 8:93; Dodge City *Globe*, Oct. 4, 1917, p.4; *AH*, Aug. 10, 1934, pp.223, 236.

CHAPTER SIX

JEWS MOVE INTO THE GREAT PLAINS, ROCKIES, AND

THE NEW SOUTHWEST

1. Junction City *Union*, Feb. 17, 1962; Auerbach, "Nebraska," 5, 134-36; "Nebraska," *UJE*; *U.A.H.C. Statistics*, 52.
2. "Colorado," *JE, UJE, EJ*; "Denver," *EJ*; Breck, *Colorado*, 3 ff., 18, 27-30; Uchill, *Pioneers*, 10; Marcus, *Memoirs*, 3:38 ff.; *U.A.H.C. Statistics*, 53.
3. Breck, *Colorado*, 10, 14, 49, 52, 68; Uchill, *Pioneers*, 19-21, 118-119.
4. Breck, *Colorado*, 11 ff., 14, et passim; Uchill, *Pioneers*, 13 ff., 16, 36-40; P. & K., *Tourist's Guide*, 66.
5. Uchill, *Pioneers*, 15, 297-98; *The Lookout from the Denver Public Library* (Denver, 1927), 1:65-67.
6. Breck, *Colorado*, 25 ff., 123; Uchill, *Pioneers*, 42 ff.; *AJA*, 24:27 ff.
7. Breck, *Colorado*, 43-44, 46, 52-53, 132 ff., 138, 153 ff., 229; Uchill, *Pioneers*, 101-8; Hyman, *Romance of a Mining Venture*, 17 ff.
8. Uchill, *Pioneers*, 109 ff., 118; *NMQ*, 29:316, 320; *New Constitution and By-Laws of Congregation Aaron, Trinidad, Colorado, etc.* (Trinidad, 1899?); Morris F. Taylor, *Trinidad, Colorado Territory* (Pueblo, Colo., 1966), 42, 91, 132, 140-41, 156, 161, 163, 173 ff.; Breck, *Colorado*, 49 ff.; Trinidad *Chronicle-News*, Oct. 13, 1929, p.4; Denver *Jewish Outlook*, Nov. 24, 1905, p.46; *Temple Aaron Biblette: In Commemoration of Three Anniversaries, etc.* (Trinidad, Colo., 1949).
9. *WSJHQ*, 4:117 ff., 131; Uchill, *Pioneers*, 51 ff., 66; *Colorado Magazine*, 9:71-74; Helen M. Searcy, *Pioneers of the San Juan Country* (Durango, Colo., 1942?), 1:15 ff.; Breck, *Colorado*, 39 ff., 139-40; *Westways*, 40:18 ff.; "Mears, Otto," *DAB*; Pasadena *Star-News*, June 24, 1931, p.1 (obituary).
10. Lou H. Silberman, Omaha, to JRM, Sept. 13, 1948, copy in AJAr; P. & K., *Tourist's Guide*, 484 ff.; "North Dakota," *EJ*; *AJA*, 23:49 ff.
11. *AJA*, 8:104-5; Oscar Pollack, Service Record, copy in AJAr; Hattenbach typescript, copy in AJAr; P. & K., *Tourist's Guide*, 484 ff, 580 ff.; R.E. Driscoll, *Seventy Years of*

Banking in the Black Hills (Rapid City, 1948), 24-28, 74-75; Plaut, *Mt. Zion*, 75; Plaut, *Jews in Minnesota*, 158-59; Robert E. Driscoll, *The Black Hills of South Dakota: Its Pioneer Banking History* (N.Y., 1951), 10; Annie Tallent, *The Black Hills* (St. Louis, 1899), 501; Ira Baer, son of Ben, interview by JRM, St. Paul, Mar. 13, 1948, Marcus Collections.

12. *WSJHQ*, 3:113 ff., 170 ff., 227 ff., 4:35 ff.; P. & K., *Tourist's Guide*, 281 ff.; "Montana," *JE, UJE, EJ*; *AJA*, 8:109.

13. *AJA*, 8:110; Helena *Weekly Record*, Jan. 7, 1869, p.7, c.4; Benton *Record*, Mar. 1, 1875, May 1, 1875; Fort Benton *River Press*, Dec. 26, 1888, p.7, c.1; P. & K., *Tourist's Guide*, 282-83; Kendall *Miner*, Aug. 31, 1906, p.3, courtesy of Montana Historical Society. Data also received from John R. Foster, East Glacier Park, Montana; *WSJHQ*, 3:180 ff.; Paul F. Sharp, *Whoop-Up Country* (1960, rep. by Hist. Soc. of Montana), 61 ff.

14. *YA*, 14:219 ff.; *Montana* 22:60 ff.; biography of Abraham Oettinger, typescript in Marcus Collections.

15. Benjamin, *Three Years*, 2:163-65; *Wash. H.Q.*, 17:190 ff., 18:200; Lloyd Hahn, grandson of Joseph Oppenheimer, interview by JRM, Spokane, Wash., May 17, 1938, Marcus Collections; Edmund S. Meany, *Origin of Washington Geographic Names* (Seattle, 1923 [1968]), 159; Miscellaneous newspaper clippings on the Oppenheimer family from the Colville *Index* and the Spokane *Spokesman-Review*, 1888, 1901, Marcus Collections. See also *Spokesman-Review*, Dec. 11, 1938; Muriel Sibell Wolle, *The Bonanza Trail: Ghost Towns and Mining Camps of the West* (Bloomington, Ind., 1953), 265-66.

16. *Wash. H.O.*, 17:190 ff., 206; Whitman County Pioneer Association resolution, n.d., typescript, copy in Marcus Collections; Colfax *Gazette*, clipping, n.d., ca. 1928, copy in Marcus Collections.

17. "Washington," *UJE*; P. & K., *Tourist's Guide*, 633, 635, 637-38; *U.A.H.C. Statistics*, 54; *Jewish Tribune*, Oct. 18, 1918.

18. Wolf, *American Jew*, 164 ff.; Friedman, *Pioneers*, 353 ff., 360; Allan Nevins, *Hamilton Fish: The Inner History of the Grant Administration* (N.Y., 1937), 593; Heitman, *Historical Register*, 1:857; Charles M. Gates (ed.), *Messages of the Governors of the Territory of Washington to the Legislative Assembly, 1854-1889* (Seattle, 1940), 157.

19. "Washington," *JE, UJE, EJ*; "Seattle," *UJE, EJ*; P. & K., *Tourist's Guide*, 632 ff.; "Salomon, Edward S.," *JE, UJE*.

20. *JM*, Feb. 10, 1888, p.5, cs.3-4; Carter, *Jews in Early Utah*, 329 ff., 372; Brooks, *Jews in Utah and Idaho*, 127 ff., 136-37; *AI*, June 9, 1876, p.4, cs.3-5; P. & K., *Tourist's Guide*, 132 ff.; *AJA*, 8:128-30; *WSJHQ*, 2:61; "Idaho," "Alexander, Moses," *UJE, EJ*; "Bavaria," *EJ*; Arthur Weyne, "Great Journey: The Story of Moses Alexander," typescript, copy in Marcus Collections.

21. P. & K., *Tourist's Guide*, 137, 637, 655 ff., 658; *AJA*, 8:125; Breck, *Colorado*, 31; Spring, *Cheyenne Stage*, 49-50, 64; Cheyenne *Wyoming State Tribune, and Wyoming Eagle*, B,1O, July 23, 25, 1968; *AJA*, 8:127; "Wyoming," *UJE, EJ*; *AH*, Sept. 10, 1926.

22. Watters, *Utah*, 14, 16, 22 ff., 27, 163 ff.; Benjamin, *Three Years*, 2:224 ff.; Glanz, *Jew and Mormon*, 145 ff., 156 ff.; *Dialogue: A Journal of Mormon Thought*, 3(no.2):41 ff.; "Utah," *UJE*; Carter, *Jews in Early Utah*, 343.

23. *Der Zeitgeist*, Feb. 19, 1880, p.55; Watters, *Utah*, 25-26, 43-45; *Proceedings of the Utah Academy of Science, Arts, and Letters*, 44:535 ff.

24. Watters, *Utah*, 108 ff.; Carvalho, *Incidents of Travel and Adventure in the Far West*.

25. Watters, *Utah*, 138-40, 163 ff.

26. Carter, *Jews in Early Utah*, 341-42, 363; Watters, *Utah*, 55 ff., 60-64, 160; Glanz, *Jew and Mormon*, 208 ff.; Brooks, *Jews of Utah and Idaho*, 163 ff.; *AH*, Oct. 5, 1928, pp.689 ff.

27. Watters, *Utah*, 62, 66-93, 98, 129; *AI*, Nov. 24, 1865, p.165, c.2; Glanz, *Jew and Mormon*, 214, 216; *AJA*, 8:99-100; *JM*, June 25, 1869, p.5, c.1.

28. Watters, *Utah*, 72 ff., 75, 78, 81, 98-99, 101; Carter, *Jews of Early Utah*, 329; "Utah," *EJ.*

29. Floyd S. Fierman, *Insight and Hindsights of Some El Paso Jewish Families* (El Paso, 1983), vii; "El Paso," *The Americana, UJE; AJHQ*, 57:390, 393-94, 419 ff.; Fierman, *Some Early Jewish Settlers*, 12, 40, n. 22; Walter L. Kohlberg (tr.), *Letters of Ernst Kohlberg, 1875-1877* (El Paso, 1973), 35 ff.; Ernst Kohlberg, El Paso, to his family in Germany, June 28, 1876, copy in Marcus Collections; *1898-1928 Temple Mt. Sinai Year Book* (El Paso, 1928), 10 ff.

30. *AJA*, 8:77; *Temple Beth El.*

31. Booth Moony, *75 Years in Victoria* (Victoria, Texas, 1950), 8-9, 21, 27; *AJA*, 8:79; *U.A.H.C. Statistics*, 29-30.

32. Frances Kallison, San Antonio, to JRM, July 26, 1970, Oct. 22, 1971, June 6, 1972, copies in AJAr; Jesse D. Oppenheimer, *I Remember* (San Antonio, n.d.); *PAJHS*, 2:152; "Texas," *JE, UJE, EJ*; "San Antonio," *UJE, EJ*; William Sajowitz, "History of Reform Judaism in San Antonio, Texas, 1874-1945" (rabbinical thesis, HUC, 1945), 7, 43-44; *AJA*, 8:79; *Occ.*, 17:240.

33. Marcus, *CAJ*, 3:Index sub Carvaljal and Mendizabal; Fierman, *Guts and Ruts*, 7 ff; P. & K., *Tourist's Guide*, 330 ff.; *AJHQ*, 56:371 ff., 395, 434; *NMQ*, 29:315 ff.; *AJA*, 8:84 ff.; *Southwestern Studies*, 1(no.4):3 ff.; *Jewish Chronicle* (Oklahoma Section), Dec., 1933, p.3; Floyd S. Fierman, *The Triangle and the Tetragrammaton: A Note on the Cathedral of Santa Fe* (El Paso?, 1961); *NMHR*, 37:310 ff.; Burton C. Bernard, St. Louis, to JRM, ca. Feb. 9, 1970, copy in AJAr.

34. *NMHR*, 37:318, n.8; *NMQ*, 29:307 ff., 315 ff.; Fierman, *Guts and Ruts*, 27 ff., 73, 89; Fierman, *Some Early Jewish Settlers*, 9; Parish, *Charles Ilfeld Company*, 7 ff., 346-47; Ken Wells, Corrales, N.M., to M. Stern, Norfolk, Va., Sept. 10, 1959, June 11, 1960, copies in Marcus Collections.

35. Bibo, "Book of Remembrance," 3, 6; Fierman, *Guts and Ruts*, 49 ff.; *NMHR*, 37:319, n.12; *NMQ*, 29:317; Bibo, *Reminiscences*; *AJHQ*, 59:460 ff., 521; Albuquerque *Tribune*, obituary of Nathan Bibo, undated clipping in Marcus Collections.

36. *AJHQ*, 57:353 ff.; P. & K., *Tourist's Guide*, 332; Fierman, *Some Early Jewish Settlers*, 14 ff.; *NMHR*, 36:86; [Lesinsky] *Letters.*

37. Las Vegas, N.M. *Daily Optic*, May 22, 23, 1888; *NMQ*, 29: 315-18; Denver *Round-up*, Sept.-Oct., 1970, 26(nos.9-10):26-30; *AJA*, 8:84, 86; E.L. Moulton, *Seventy Years of Progress, Founding and Developing of Charles Ilfeld Company 1860-1935*, address given on July 25, 1935 to Albuquerque Rotary Club (n.d., n.p.), 2 ff.; *Bulletin of the Business Historical Society*, 24:216-17; Parish, *Charles Ilfeld Company*, 3 ff., 56-57, 378, nn. 28, 31; P. & K., *Tourist's Guide*, 331-32; *AH*, June 22, 1923, p.17.

38. Biography of Sol Floersheim by a member of the family, Springer, Jan. 1, 1959, AJAr; Raton *Daily Range*, Apr. 27, 1968, pp.1, 6; Fierman, *Some Early Jewish Settlers*, 31-32; The maraschino cherry story was told to JRM by Sol's son Ben Floersheim in October, 1959; Parish, *Charles Ilfeld Company*, 89, et passim.

39. P. & K., *Tourist's Guide*, 331-39; *NMQ*, 29:317-20; Bibo, *Reminiscences*, 236.

40. Marcus, *CAJ*, 2:843 ff.; *Jewish Chronicle* (Oklahoma Section), Dec., 1933, p.3; *NMQ*, 29:307-332; *U.A.H.C. Statistics*, 53.

41. Elzas, *Jews of S.C.*, 206-7; P. & K., *Tourist's Guide*, 334-335, 338, 514; *AH*, June 22, 1923, pp.117, 120; Denver *Round-up*, Sept.-Oct., 1970, 26(nos.9-10): 25-26; "Jaffa, Henry N.," "Jaffa, Nathan," *UJE*; Solomon Loewenstein, Ocate, N.M., to Lipman Levy, Cincinnati, Ohio, Nov. 7, 1874, Union of American Hebrew Congregations Collections, AJAr; "New Mexico," *JE, UJE, EJ; AJA*, 8:85-86; *WWW, 1607-1869*, sub Sulzbacher, Louis.

42. Bibo, *Reminiscences*, 251-52; Fierman, *Some Early Jewish Settlers*, 16 ff. For Jews in early Arizona, see Lamb, "Jewish Pioneers in Arizona." For information about Californians

in early Arizona, I am indebted to Dr. Norton B. Stern. *Congress Weekly*, Mar. 11, 1957, pp. 6-8; *Jewish Digest*, 16:74 ff.; Stocker, *Jewish Roots in Arizona*, 7 ff.; *Journal of the West*, 7:445 ff.; "Arizona," *EJ*.

43. Simon Wolf, *The Presidents I Have Known from 1860-1918* (Wash., D.C., 1918), 80 ff.; *AJA*, 8:96; "Bendell, Herman," *UJE*; Stocker, *Jewish Roots in Arizona*, 7 ff., 30-31; Lamb, "Jewish Pioneers in Arizona," 65 ff.; J. M. Long, Phoenix to N.J. Stone, San Francisco, May 31, 1888, Bancroft Papers, Bancroft Library; Matthew J. Ritchie, Phoenix, to Columbus Giragi, Sept. 30, 1948, copy in Marcus Collections; *PAJHS*, 19:96; "Phoenix," *EJ*.

44. Bibo, *Reminiscences*, 249, n. 48; Stocker, *Jewish Roots in Arizona*, 13 ff.; *AJA*, 8:94-95; P. & K., *Tourist's Guide*, 14, 18; *AJHQ*, 59:464, n.9.

45. *AJA*, 8:95-96, 16:135 ff., 18:3 ff.; *Arizona Historical Review*, 2:88 ff.; *WSJHQ*, 2:172 ff.; Stocker, *Jewish Roots in Arizona*, 25 ff.

46. *AJHQ*, 57:376, 380; *AJA*, 8:97; Stocker, *Jewish Roots in Arizona*, 16 ff.; Fierman, *Some Early Jewish Settlers*, 22 ff.; Lamb, "Jewish Pioneers in Arizona," 182-83.

47. *AJA*, 10:95 ff., 104, 16:135, 142; Lake, *Wyatt Earp*, 277, 328; *National Jewish Post and Opinion*, July 19, 1957.

48. *U.A.H.C. Statistics*, 54; Prescott *Weekly Arizona Miner*, Mar. 15, 1873, p.3, c.2; *AJA*, 25:161 ff., 181, n.68; Stocker, *Jewish Roots in Arizona*, 29; Lamb, "Jewish Pioneers in Arizona," 188-89.

49. Stocker, *Jewish Roots in Arizona*, 26-27, Bibo, *Reminiscences*, 242-43, J. M. Long, Tucson, to N. J. Stone, San Francisco, Dec. 1, 1888, Bancroft Papers, Bancroft Library; Fierman, *Guts and Ruts*, 87 ff.; *AJA*, 23:86 ff.

50. Stocker, *Jewish Roots in Arizona*, 21, 23-24; P. & K., *Tourist's Guide*, 15, 21; *WSJHQ*, 1:75; *AJA*, 8:95.

51. *AJA*, 18:19; Stocker, *Jewish Roots in Arizona*, 31; "Arizona," *UJE, EJ; The Jewish Encyclopedia (JE)* published in 1902 does not even have an entry under "Arizona."

52. P. & K., *Tourist's Guide*, 511-512; *AJA*, 8:122; Falk, "Oklahoma," 66 ff.

53. *AJYB*, 2(1900-1901): 253, 3(1901-1902):134, 147, 418; P. & K., *Tourist's Guide*, 513, 517; "Oklahoma," *UJE*; Falk, "Oklahoma," 3 ff.

CHAPTER SEVEN

THE JEWS AND THE WEST, 1649-1880: AN EVALUATION

1. Elbogen, *Cent. of Jewish Life*, 82; "B'nai B'rith," *JE*.

2. *AI*, May 31, 1861, p.382, c.3; Marcus, *Memoirs*, 3:39 ff.

3. *Statistical History of U.S.*, 123-80; *U.A.H.C. Statistics*, 55.

4. Hugo Bieber (ed.), *Heinrich Heine, Confessio Judaica* (Berlin, 1925), 15. Names of towns reflecting Jewish presence may be found in P. & K., *Tourist's Guide*.

5. Ginsberg, *Jews of Virginia*, 16-17.

6. Nodel, *The Ties Between*, 74; "Pennsylvania," *UJE*, 8:430; Shinedling, *West Virginia Jewry*, Index sub "Tree of Life."

7. *PAJHS*, 13:67; Nathan Berman, "German-Jewish Congregation at Madison, Wisconsin, 1850-1930" (B.A. thesis, U. of Wisc., 1931), 23.

8. *U.A.H.C. Statistics*, 48, 55; Schappes, *DHJUS*, 441 ff.; Markens, *Hebrews*, 139 ff.

9. "Radaniya," *EJ*.

10. Breck, *Colorado*, 65-66.

11. Watters, *Utah*, 126; *PAJHS*, 11:118; "Washington," "Kansas," *UJE*; Barry L. Weinstein, "Myer Hellman and Daughter: One Hundred Years of Temple Israel, Omaha, Nebraska," (HUC term paper, 1971); *AJA*, 8:93; Schappes, *DHJUS*, 442; *Temple Beth El*, 10; *JSS*,23:152.

12. "Hirsch, Solomon," *UJE*.
13. Grinstein, *New York City*, 472 ff.
14. *Occ.*, 13:372.
15. "California," *JE*.
16. Gideon M. Goldenholz, "The Emergence of a Jewish Community in Fort Wayne" (Ph.D. diss., H.T.C., Chicago, n.d.).
17. "Peoria," "Rock Island," *UJE*; Davis, *Rodeph Shalom*, 13; Elzas, *Jews of S.C.*, 282-84; Tarshish, "American Judaism," xiii; *Tennessee Inventory*; Rothschild, *Atlanta*, 1; Lipman, "Synagogal Philanthropy"; *PAJHS*. 27:311.
18. *PAJHS*, 37:309 ff.; Breck, *Colorado*, 1-30; *MGWJ*, 13:367 ff.; "Chicago," *EJ*.
19. "Buffalo," "Louisville," "Philadelphia," *UJE*.
20. Sharfman, *Jackson, California*, 74-75; Benjamin, *Three Years*, 2:9-10; Korn, *New Orleans*, 248.
21. P. & K., *Tourist's Guide*, 335.
22. Watters, *Utah*, 100-101; LeRoy R. Hafen and Ann W. Hafen, *Powder River Campaign and Sawyer's Expedition of 1865, etc.* (Glendale, Calif., 1961), 379; Vorspan & Gartner, *Los Angeles*, 14.
23. *Quarterly Journal of the Library of Congress*, 28:227.
24. *U.A.H.C. Statistics*, 56.
25. *U.A.H.C. Statistics*, 38; Benjamin, *Three Years*, 2:268.
26. Vorspan & Gartner, *Los Angeles*, 95-96.
27. Denver *Round-up*, Sept.-Oct., 1970, 26(nos.9-10): 23-24; *NMQ*, 29:324 ff.
28. William A. Bell, *New Tracks in North America* (London, 1869), 1:151.
29. Arthur Ruppin, *Jewish Fate and Future* (London, 1940).
30. *PAJHS*, 37:309-11.

CHAPTER EIGHT
ECONOMIC LIFE OF THE JEWS, 1840–1860

1. Marcus, *Memoirs*, 2:7; Elzas, *Jews of S.C.*, 143; Meade, *Judah P. Benjamin*, 46 ff.; Schappes, *DHJUS*, 662, n.2.
2. Cole, *Handbook*, 104; Cole, *Irrepressible Conflict*, 3.
3. "New York" sub "Population," *Americana*; Schappes, *JIUS*, 66-67; *Jewish People*, 4:72; Grinstein, *New York City*, 549, n. 12; *PAJHS*, 39:238-40, 44:1ff.; Glazer, *Jews of Iowa*, 173 ff.; Meites, *Chicago*, 40; Sigmund Griff, Louisville, to parents in Germany, Sept. 1, 1849, same to same from Nashville, Apr. 14, 1850, copies in Marcus Collections; Wise, *Reminiscences*, 38; Ernst, *Immigrant Life*, 84-85, 217, 253, n.4; *JQR*, 53:306-21; *JSS*, 7:119 ff.; Russell, *Germanic Influence*, 334 ff.; Marcus, *Memoirs*, 2:155; *AJA*, 3:108; *AI*, Feb. 2, 1866, p.244, c.4, p.245, c.1.
4. Wise, *Reminiscences*, 38; *PAJHS*, 35:112-13, 38:22 ff., 44:1 ff.; *AJA*, 3:81; *Georgia Historical Quarterly*, 37:7; *JSS*, 7:127 ff.; Schappes, *DHJUS*, 222; *Occ.*, 13:513, 18:308; Marcus, *AJD*, 1-2; Adler & Connolly, *Buffalo*, 29 ff.; Levie M. Goldsmit, Richmond, to I.L., Phila., Mar. 13, 1849 (Yiddish), copy in Marcus Collections; S. Sutro, N.Y. to I.L., Phila., Jan. 5, 1851, copy in Marcus Collections; Lebeson, *Pilgrim People*, 333; *Particulars of the Murder of Nathan Adler* (Auburn, N.Y. 1850); *The Trial of Henry Kobler Musselman and Lewis Willman, for the Murder of the Unfortunate Lazarus Zellerbach . . . Reported by J. Franklin Reigart* (Lancaster, Pa., 1839); *JQR*, 53:319, n. 46; Marcus, *Memoirs*, 2:28, 3:122.
5. Marcus, *Memoirs*, 1:6-10; Rothschild, *Atlanta*, 28.
6. Schappes, *DHJUS*, 668, n.3; Schappes, *JIUS*, 67; Glanz, *California*, 21 ff.; E. & L., *Richmond*, 94 ff.; Ernst, *Immigrant Life*, 216 ff., sub "Poland"; Grinstein, *New York City*, 549,

n.12; Chester, "New Orleans," 2, 7 ff.; Kirzner, "Detroit," 13; Jaye, "San Francisco"; Roseman, "Jewish Population of America, 1850-1860," 142 ff.; Roseman, "Charleston, 1850-1860," 23-24; Roseman, "Cincinnati,1860," 20 ff.; Auerback, "San Francisco Jewry," 42 ff.

7. B. & B., *JOUS*, 2:655, n. 93; Goodkowitz, "Jew. Econ. Life, 1830-1860"; Roseman, "Jewish Population of America," 142 ff.; Markens, *Hebrews*, 24; Cole, *Irrepressible Conflict*, 127; "United States," *JE*, 12:375; *Historia Judaica*, 8:212; *RIJHN*, 5:301 ff.; Schappes, *DHJUS*, 227; Swichkow & Gartner, *Milwaukee*, 13; Adler & Connolly, *Buffalo*, 38; Greenebaum, "Economic Activity of Cincinnati Jewry"; E. & L., *Richmond*, 70, 94-5, 142 ff.; Ernst, *Immigrant Life*, 86, 214-17 sub "Poland" and "Russia"; Auerback, "San Francisco Jewry," 42 ff.; Heyman, "Memphis," 4 ff.; Foster, "Milwaukee," 8 ff.; Chester, "New Orleans," 7 ff.; Jaye, "San Francisco."

8. Greenebaum, "Economic Activity of Cincinnati Jewry," 93; Swichkow & Gartner, *Milwaukee*, 17; Marcus, *Memoirs*, 2:154 ff.; Russell, *Germanic Influence*, 328-29; Schappes, *DHJUS*, 277 ff., 441-44, 677, ns. 4 & 5; R. & E., *Charleston*, 167; *JSS*, 7:125-26; "Newark," *UJE*; *AI*, Mar. 23, 1859, pp.303-4, advertisements; Markens, *Hebrews*, 101.

9. "Cardozo, Jacob Newton," "Hart, Abraham," "Levin, Lewis Charles," "Naar, David," "Newark," "Noah, Mordecai Manuel," "Pinner, Moritz," *UJE*; "Bush, Isidor," *EJ*; R. & E., *Charleston*, 80; *Historia Judaica*, 5:183 ff.; "Brooklyn," *UJE*, 2:556-57; Grinstein, *New York City*, 313 ff., 323-24; Schappes, *JIUS*, 67-68; Ernst, *Immigrant Life*, 88, 245, n.49; *PAJIIS*, 5:152-53, 26:249-50; Schappes, *DHJUS*, 215, 624, n.9, 651-52, n.18; Kirzner, "Detroit," 11; B.W. Cohen, New Orleans to I.L., Phila., June 10, 1854, copy in Marcus Collections; Morais, *Philadelphia*, 395-96; "Levin, Lewis Charles," *DAB*; Edwards & Hopewell, *Edwards's Great West, etc.*, 556 ff.; Goodkowitz, "Jew. Econ. Life, 1830-1860," Appendix A; Swarsensky, *Madison*, 18-19; Auerback, "San Francisco Jewry," 42 ff.; Swichkow & Gartner, *Milwaukee*, 103-4, 362, ns.103-4; Chester, "New Orleans," 2 ff.

10. Goodkowitz, "Jew. Econ. Life, 1830-1860," Appendix C; "Cohen," *UJE*, 3:233 ff.; *Md. Hist. Mag.*, 18:357 ff.; "Moses Cohen Mordecai," typescript biography by Elzas in Elzas Papers, *NYHSL*; Markens, *Hebrews*, 143; Elzas, *Jews of S.C.*, 166 ff.; R. & E., *Charleston*, 71 ff.; Schappes, *JIUS*, 67; Schappes, *DHJUS*, 663, n.3; Roseman, "Jewish Population of America"; Kirzner, "Detroit," 11-13; *AJA*, 15:21 ff.; Chester, "New Orleans," 7 ff.; Ernst, *Immigrant Life*, 214-17, sub "Poland" and "Russia"; E. & L., *Richmond*, 94 ff., 142 ff.

11. Marcus, *EAJ*, 2:22; Marcus, *Memoirs*, 1:302 ff., 308; *JM*, Nov. 2, 1860, p.133, c.3; Swichkow & Gartner, *Milwaukee*, 16, 18, 361, n.78; Fein, *Baltimore*, 47-48; *Occ.*, 18:180; P. & K., *Tourist's Guide*, 94; E. & L., *Richmond*, 140; Schappes, *DHJUS*, 646, n.19; Goldmark, *Pilgrims of '48*, 259-60; George White, *Historical Collections of Georgia* (N.Y., 1854), 269 ff.; W. & W., *Philadelphia*, 256; Grinstein, *New York City*, 306 ff.; "Brooklyn," *UJE*, 2:556-7, "Cincinnati," 3:209-10; "Lazarus, Moses," *JE*; Roseman, "Jewish Population of America"; *New York Times*, Feb. 4, 1972, p.34; Beard, *Rise of Am. Civilization*, 1:635.

12. *AJA*, 12:4-7, 8 ff.; Lipman, *Soc. Hist. of Jews in England*, 28; Marcus, *CAJ*, 2:677 ff.; *YA*, 2-3:180; *JQR*, 53:311; Blum, *Baltimore*, 165.

13. *RIJHN*, 1:121 ff. 5:304-5.

14. Benjamin, *Three Years*, 1:74 ff.; Schappes, *JIUS*, 104-5; "Belmont, August," *DAB*; Swichkow & Gartner, *Milwaukee*, 16; *PAJHS*, 27:402-3, 44:3, n.4; Morais, *Philadelphia*, 309-10; Edwards & Hopewell, *Edwards's Great West, etc.*, 440 ff.; Schappes, *DHJUS*, 652, n. 21; Morais, *Philadelphia* and W. & W., *Philadelphia*, see Index sub Gratz; Glanz, *The German Jew in America*, no.252; "Gratz," *JE*, 6:81 ff.; *JQR*, 53:306-21; Markens, *Hebrews*, 143-45; "Jacob Elsas," typescript biography in AJAr; Elzas, *Jews of S.C.* and R. & E., *Charleston*, see Index under Lazarus, Joshua and Michael, David C. Levy, and

M.C. Mordecai; For Mordecai, see "Mordecai, Moses Cohen," *DAB*; "Gatherings by the Wayside," by "A Charleston Worthy," Charleston newspaper clipping, n.d., n.p., copy in Marcus Collections, and biography in Elzas Papers, NYHSL.

15. Swichkow & Gartner, *Milwaukee*, 15; Marcus, *Memoirs*, 2:162; Moses S. Beach, *The Wealth . . . of New York City* (13th ed., N.Y., 1855), 38, 47-48; *The Rich Men of Massachusetts* (2nd ed., Boston, 1852), sub Isaac Samuels, 59; *PAJHS*, 27:400; Whiteman, *Hendricks*, 172; *JOAH*, 58:415 ff.

16. Roseman, "Jewish Population of America, 1850-1860", "New York City, 1860, "Cincinnati, 1860," "*Philadelphia*, 1860"; Foster, "Milwaukee," 6-9.

17. E. & L., *Richmond*, 103 ff.; Roseman, "Jewish Population of America"; Hirsh & Doherty, *Mount Sinai Hospital*, 3-5; *Deborah*, Sept. 7, 1860, p.38, cs.1-2; *YA*, 6:95; Schappes, *DHJUS*, 403; Ernst, *Immigrant Life*, 58, 240, n.79; *Occ.*, 12:575.

18. Roseman, "Jewish Population of America," "Cincinnati, 1850," "Cincinnati, 1860," "Charleston, 1850-1860"; Roseman, "The Jews of the South, 1840-1865" (HUC term paper, 1968); Lipman, *Soc. Hist. of Jews in England*, 27-29, 161-2; Benjamin, *Three Years*, 1:232; *RIJHN*, 5:291; Schappes, *DHJUS*, 277; Swichkow & Gartner, *Milwaukee*, 13 ff.

CHAPTER NINE
THE JEWISH RELIGION, 1840–1860

1. Elzas, *Jews of S.C.*, 116; Davis, *Rodeph Shalom*, 11 ff., 17 ff., 31 ff., 37 ff., 59 ff., 62-63; Adams, *History of the Jews*, 463 ff.; Friedman, *Pilgrims*, 391, n.10; Morais, *Philadelphia*, 70 ff., 71, n.77; W. & W., *Philadelphia*,225-26, 231, 233, 249-52, 266, et passim; *PAJHS*, 9:123 ff., 41:83 ff.; Cohen, "Rodeph Shalom," 25-27; Skirball, "Rodeph Shalom," 9, 15, 18, 23, 26, et passim; Weiss, "Rodeph Sholom," 6 ff., 14 ff., et passim; Rodeph Shalom Constitution, Apr. 11, 1849, Art.14; Tarshish, "American Judaism," xxxii, n.240.

2. Grinstein, *New York City*, 40 ff., 47, 145; Goldstein, *Cent. of Jud. in NYC*, 52-53, 57-59, et passim; *PAJHS*, 10:97 ff.; Benjamin, *Three Years*, 1:76; B. & B., *JOUS*, 2:540 ff.

3. Padoll, "St. Louis," 19; Ernst, *Immigrant Life*, 137; Grinstein, *New York City*, 51, 297-98, et passim; *AJA*, 12:120; "New York," *JE*, 9:270 ff., ca.1828; "Chicago," *JE*; Blum, *Baltimore*, 11; Fein, *Baltimore*, 50; B'nai Yeshurun, Cincinnati, Minutes, Sept. 18, 1842; *Kahl Montgomery*, Art. 4; Kraut & Fox, *Completion of Independence*, 32; Skirball, "Rodeph Shalom"; E. & L., *Richmond*, 258 ff.; Marcus, *Jew in the Medieval World*, 212 ff.; Tarshish, "American Judaism," 100; Adler & Connolly, *Buffalo*, 63; Syme, "Bene Israel," 31; Benjamin, *Three Years*, 1:80; Stanley Yedwab, "An Analysis of the Minutes of the Board of Trustees of Congregation Anshe Chesed, 1835-39" (HUC term paper, n.d.); Goldstein, *Cent. of Jud. in NYC*, vii; Swichkow & Gartner, *Milwaukee*, 469 ff.; "New York," *UJE*, 8:178-80; Auerback, "San Francisco Jewry," 10. The Lloyd Street Synagog in Baltimore, Anshe Chesed in Cleveland, and B'nai Israel, Cincinnati, had mikvehs, among many others.

4. Wise, *Reminiscences*, 113-14. Advertisements in Jewish newspapers: *Asmonean* Mar. 9, 1855, p.165, cs.1-2, Mar. 16, 1855, p.175, c.3; Plaut, *Reform Judaism*, 341-42; Grinstein, *New York City*, 313 ff., 321, 333 ff.; Adler & Connolly, *Buffalo*, 51; *AI*, July 18, 1856, p.13, cs.3-4; *AJA*, 8:69; M. Seligson, Galveston, to I.L., Phila., Nov. 1851, copy in Marcus Collections; Marcus, *Memoirs*, 1:30-31; Syme, "Bene Israel," 52 ff.; *AZJ*, Sept. 27, 1847, p.596.

5. Benjamin, *Three Years*, 1:80; Tarshish, "American Judaism," 110, nn.264-65; Grinstein, *New York City*, 298 ff., 309, 576, n.56; Fein, *Baltimore*, 52; Adler & Connolly, *Buffalo*, 45, 49 ff.; Berman, *Shehitah*, 287 ff.; *Asmonean*, Mar. 14, 1851, p.167, c.1, Mar. 9, 1855, p.161, c.2, Mar. 16, 1855, p.169, cs.1-2.

6. *JM*, July 17, 1857, p.13, c.2; *AI*, Sept. 1, 1855, p.86, c.1; *Rachel and the the World*, tr. by Leon Beauvallet (N.Y., 1856), 284; "Touro, Judah," *JE*; Benjamin, *Three Years*, 1:320 ff.; Trachtenberg, *Easton*, 115; B.F. Peixotto, Cleveland, to I.L., Phila., May 6, 1857, copy in Marcus Collections.

7. *Jeschurun*, 4:392-98, 437, 594-601, 658; "Illowy, Bernard," *UJE*; Tarshish, "American Judaism," 116-17; *Occ.*, 6:307, 11:235, 15:587; *Jewish Post and Opinion*, Oct. 6, 1972, p.11; *AI*, Nov. 17, 1854, p.148, cs.2-3; Plaut, *Reform Judaism*, 341-42; Grinstein, *New York City*, 304-6, 309; Berman, *Shehitah*, 287 ff; Syme, "Bene Israel," 73.

8. *AJHQ*, 53:344 ff.; Grinstein, *New York City*, 297 ff.; H. Lowenthal, Macon, Ga., to I.L., Phila., Aug. 17, 1860; for a similar letter see B.H. Gotthelf, Louisville, to I.L., Phila., Sept. 3, 1851, copies in Marcus Collections; B. & B., *JOUS*, 2:546 ff.; *Tradition*, 7:102 ff.; A.I.H. Bernal, Louisville, to I.L., Phila., Mar. 8, 1859, copy in Marcus Collections; Fein, *Baltimore*, 52.

9. *R*, nos. 681-82; Joseph Jonas, Cincinnati, to I.L., Phila., May 5, 1852; Abraham Rice, *Baltimore*, to I.L., Phila., 24 Ab, 1851, copies in Marcus Collections; Fein, *Baltimore*, 57; Tarshish, "American Judaism," 37; *PAJHS*, 35:198, 41:86, 48:207; *AZJ*, July 27, 1846, pp.448-49, Jan. 1, 1847, p.25; Marcus, *CAJ*, 2:1010; Lipman, *Soc. Hist. of Jews in England*, 45; Trachtenberg, *Easton*, 264 ff.; Baltimore Constitution (1830), Art. XXIV; Bene Israel Vestry Minutes. Oct. 10, 1839; Levine, "B'nai Israel of Cin.," 4; Rodeph Shalom, Phila., Minutes, Oct. 14, 21, 1827, Apr. 2, 1853; *AJA*, 11:201-3.

10. Benjamin, *Three Years*, 1:334; W. & W., *Philadelphia*, 249; *AZJ*, July 27, 1846, p.449. Synagogue minutes with their recurring names as officers provide evidence of cliques in office: Rodeph Shalom Minutes, 1811-1834.

11. Ellis, *Am. Catholicism*, 45; *AZJ*, Sept. 27, 1847, pp.595-97; *Occ.*, 3:210-11, 255-60; "Baltimore," *JE*, 2:480; Huhner, *Judah Touro*, 90 ff.; Benjamin, *Three Years*, 1:76-77, 317-18, 334, 2:275, 281 ff. For ethnic atomization see articles on the following cities in the standard Jewish encyclopedias or city histories: New York, Albany, Buffalo, Richmond, *Philadelphia*, Cleveland, Chicago, Cincinnati, Pittsburgh, Milwaukee, and Charleston. For congregations using "Truth" in their titles see: "Albany," *JE*; Morais, *Philadelphia*, 105-6; Swichkow & Gartner, *Milwaukee*, 35; Finkelstein, *The Jews* (1949), 4:1221; Grinstein, *New York City*, 49 ff., 412, 472 ff.; *Jewish Tribune*, Dec. 21, 1883, p.514, c.3, p.515, c.1; B. & B., *JOUS*, 2:540 ff., 3:865 ff.; B.H. Gotthelf, Louisville, to I.L., Phila., Oct. 11, 1850, copy in Marcus Collections; Adler & Connolly, *Buffalo*, 67-68; Goldstein, *Cent. of Jud. in NYC*, 51 ff.; Schappes, *JIUS*, 70; Leeser, *Discourses*, 9:239; R. & E., *Charleston*, 141; *Occ.*, 1:204 ff., 9:167-68, 14:454; Henry Kuttner, St. Louis to I.L., Phila., Feb. 8, 1860, copy in Marcus Collections; *AZJ*, Sept. 27, 1847, pp.595-97.

12. *PAJHS*, 27:185-90; Wise, *Reminiscences*, 45; Grinstein, *New York City*, 95-97; Adler & Connolly, *Buffalo*, 49, 67, 73; Tarshish, "American Judaism," 136, n.303; Rose, "Mikve Israel," 1; I.L., Phila., to Parnas and Members Cong. Mikveh Israel, Phila., May 15, 1840, and M.N. Nathan, New Orleans, to I.L., Phila., Jan. 9, 1853, Emily Solis Cohen Papers, copies in Marcus Collections; *A Century with Wilkes-Barre, etc.* (Mar., 1945).

13. Joshua Lazarus, *Charleston*, to S. Morais, Phila., Dec. 25, 1859, and undated answer of Morais, Morais Papers, Dropsie College, Phila.; Marcuson file in Leeser papers at Dropsie, copies in Marcus Collections; Plaut, *Mt. Zion*, 22-23, 25; Plaut, *Jews in Minnesota*, 37-8; Frank, *Nashville*, 43-44; Glanz, *The German Jew in America*, no.1730; *Asmonean*, Nov. 10, 1854, p.30, c.4; Syme, "Bene Israel," 61; Meites, *Chicago*, 65-66, 73; Felsenthal & Eliassof, *History of K.A.M.*, 32; Korn, *New Orleans*, 202, 237-45, 248, 337 n.12; *Occ.*, 5:25-27, 87-90.

14. For Simson, Noah, & Kursheedt see the various Jewish encyclopedias; Korn, *New Orleans*, 192 ff., 247 ff.; Trachtenberg, *Easton*, 235; Carvalho, *Incidents of Travel and Adventure in the Far West*, 13 ff.; *AJHQ*, 53:341 ff.; Jacob De La Motta, Savannah, to I.L., Phila., July 16, 1843, ad for a hazzan, copy in Marcus Collections; Grinstein, *New York City*, 93.

15. Pool, *Old Faith*, 178 ff.; Morais, *Eminent Israelites*, 153 ff.; Stern, *Temple Emanu-El*, 18 ff.; "Adler, Samuel," *JE*; Chyet, *Lives and Voices*, 3 ff. The scholarly Adler may have been a diplomat rabbi; it is difficult to determine whether rabbis had been certified in Europe. Lilienthal did have semikah. Grinstein, *New York City*, 90-91, 572, n.16; *Occ.*, 3:574-76; Philipson, *Max Lilienthal*, 46 ff.; *AZJ*, Mar. 1, 1847, pp.144-46; "Raphall, Morris," *JE, UJE, EJ*; *AJHQ*, 53:341; Korn, *Eventful Years*, 98 ff.; "Eckman, Julius," *EJ, UJE*; E. & L. *Richmond*, 244; Voorsanger, *Emanu-El*, 141 ff.

16. Blum, *Baltimore*, 11-13; *Tradition*, 7:1; Grinstein, *New York City*, 543, n.14; *Occ.*, 10:362-63; Fein, *Baltimore*, 56 ff.; *PAJHS*, 27:344; Elzas, *Jews of S.C. and R. & E, Charleston*, see Indexes for Gustavus Poznanski; *AI*, Nov. 9, 1855, p.148, c.4, p.149, c.1; Gartner, *Cleveland*, 33 ff.

17. *AZJ*, Jan. 1, 1847, p.26, Mar. 1, 1847, pp.144-46; Goldstein, *Cent. of Jud. in NYC*, 115 ff.; Schneiderman, *Two Generations*, 216; Grinstein, *New York City*, 91-93, 97-99; *Asmonean*, Nov. 10, 1854, p.30, c.3; Glanz, *The German Jew in America*, no.53; R, no.474; *AJHQ*, 53:341 ff.; Abraham Rice, *Baltimore*, to I.L., Phila., 24 Ab (Aug. 1851), copy in Marcus Collections.

18. Tarshish, "American Judaism," 211, 216, nn. 484-85; *AZJ*, Feb. 9, 1846, p.98; Fein, *Baltimore*, 60-61, 70; Ginsberg, *Jews of Virginia*, 31; *AJA*, 2:21 ff., 4:85-86; Ernst, *Immigrant Life*, 138, 272, n.24; Syme, "Bene Israel," 72; Grinstein, *New York City*, 440 ff.; John T. Hart, parnas, et al., Bnai Jeshurun, New York City, to Parnas, Rodeph Shalom, Phila., Jan. 1827, copy in Marcus Collections; Rose, "Mikve Israel," 9-10; Padoll, "St. Louis," 26; *PAJHS*, 36:3 et passim.

19. Stern, *Temple Emanu-El*, 17; *The American Jews' Annual for 5649 A.M.* (1888-89), 35.

CHAPTER TEN
SOCIAL WELFARE, 1840–1860

1. Huhner, *Judah Touro*, 129 ff.; Korn, *New Orleans*, 245 ff.

2. Marcus, *Communal Sick Care*, 55 ff.; E. & L. *Richmond*, 258, 262; Neveh Tsedek in Lyons & De Sola, *Jewish Calendar*, 164-65; *Centennial Volume, Congregation Gates of Prayer, Jan. 3-15, 1950* (New Orleans); Levine, "Sons of Israel, 1835-1858," 18 ff.; Adler & Connolly, *Buffalo*, 72; *Acts of a Local Nature . . . of the State of Ohio* (Columbus, 1847), 45:130-31; Michael, "Cincinnati," 65 ff.; Blum, *Baltimore*, 9, 48-49; Isaac Hart, New Orleans, to I.L., Phila., Oct. 15, 1858, Leeser Papers, Marcus Collections; Skirball, "Rodeph Shalom," 39; Davis, *Rodeph Shalom*, 43 ff.; Rose, "Mikveh Israel," 7 ff.; Lipman, "Synagogal Philanthropy".

3. Marcus, *Communal Sick Care*, 55 ff.; Michael, "Cincinnati," 55 ff.; W. & W., *Philadelphia*, 266 ff., et passim; Ellis, *Am. Catholicism*, 55 ff.; *AJYB*, 57:3 ff.; Schappes, *DHJUS*, 217 ff.; Grinstein, *New York City*, 131 ff., 161-62, 491 ff.; "Mutual Aid Societies," "Friendly Societies," "Fraternal Orders," *ESS*; Edelstein, "Chevra Gemiloth of Boston," 1 ff.; Lyons & De Sola, *Jewish Calendar*, 148 ff.; *Bulletin, Temple Beth El* (Detroit), Dec. 17, 1971; Benjamin, *Three Years*, 1:70 ff., 79 ff., 210 ff.; *JM*, Dec. 21, 1860, p.188; Joel Munsell, *The Annals of Albany* (2d ed., Albany, 1869), 1:179; "New York," *JE*, 9:272.

4. Brickner, "Jew. Com. of Cin.," 180 ff.; *AJHQ*, 56:27 ff.; Lyons & De Sola, *Jewish Calendar*, 151 ff.; Benjamin, *Three Years*, 1:70 ff., 210 ff., 302 ff., 2:49; Richard E. Singer, "Constitution of the Hebrew Beneficial Society of Richmond," (HUC term paper, 1942); William J. Leffler II, "Hebra Shel Bikur Holim Ugemilut Hasidim: The Hebra Kaddisha of Mikve Israel Congregation, Philadelphia, etc." (HUC term paper, 1956); Edelstein, "Chevra Gemiloth of Boston"; *AI*, Jan. 5, 1855, p.207, c.1; Adler & Connolly, *Buffalo*, 54-55; Markens, *Hebrews*, 321-22.

5. Lyons & De Sola, *Jewish Calendar*, 173; Tobias, *Hebrew Benevolent Society*, 1 ff.; *American Jews' Annual for 5649 A.M.* (1888-89), 57-58.

6. James Apple, "A Study of Pennsylvania Jewry as reflected in the *Occident*, 1850-1861, inclusive" (HUC term paper, n.d.), 28 ff.; "Chicago," *UJE*, 3:136; Michael, "Cincinnati," 55 ff., 73; *Bulletin, Temple Beth El* (Detroit), Dec. 17, 1971; Grinstein, *New York City*, 148-54, 161-62, 491-96; Benjamin, *Three Years*, 1:70-73, 303-4, 307, 311, 318, 355; *Occ.*, 5:461, 509. 6:619-20; *JM*, May 27, 1859, p.157, c.3. p.158, c.1; Lyons & De Sola, *Jewish Calendar*, 148 ff.; *AJHQ*, 66:27 ff.; Tarshish, "American Judaism," 264; Adler & Connolly, *Buffalo*, 54-56.

7. Carol H. Long, N.Y., to JRM, Mar. 26, 1972, Marcus Collections; "Fraternal Orders," *UJE*; "Fraternities," *JE*; Grinstein, *New York City*, 154; Schappes, *DHJUS*, 216.

8. Grusd, *B'nai B'rith*. 18-48; *Menorah*, 1:65-66, 165-66, 293-94; Tarshish, "American Judaism," 198 ff.; "Hamburg," *JE*.

9. "Free Sons of Israel, The," *UJE*; "B'nai B'rith," *UJE, JE*; Benjamin, *Three Years*, 1:72-73; Tarshish, "American Judaism," 198 ff.; Sachar, *Modern Jewish History*, 172 ff.; Stephen Spero Goldrich, "The Activities of the IOBB as reported in the First Two Years of the *Israelite*" (HUC term paper, 1956); Markens, *Hebrews*, 331 ff.; Maurice Bisgyer, *This is B'nai B'rith* (11th ed., Wash. D.C., n.d.), 6 ff.; Samuel S. Cohon (ed.), *B'nai B'rith Manual* (Cincinnati, 1926), 319 ff.; *National Jewish Monthly*, Sept. 1955, p.10; Sept. 1968, pp.14, 42, Oct. 1966, pp.6 ff.; *Menorah*, 1:12 ff.; Grusd, *B'nai B'rith*, 12 ff., 30, 44-5; Grinstein, *New York City*, 109 ff.

10. "Cleveland," *JE*; Marcus, *CAJ*, 1:129-30; Elzas, *Jews of S.C.*, 285; Albert M. Hyamson, *The Sephardim of England: A History of the Spanish and Portuguese Jewish Community, 1492-1951* (London, 1951), 85; Isaac S. Emmanuel, *Precious Stones of the Jews of Curaçao* (N.Y., 1957), 86; *Jewish Forum*, 38:114-15; "Jonas, Benjamin Franklin," *UJE*; *Louisiana Inventory*, 12-13, 92.

11. *Occ.*, 8:1 ff.; Markens, *Hebrews*, 310-11, 326; S.M. Fleischman, *The History of the Jewish Foster Home and Orphan Asylum of Philadelphia, 1855-1905* (Phila., 1906), 11 ff.; Grinstein, *New York City*, 148, 155, 160-61, 555, n.45; *AJHQ*, 52:313 ff.; Benjamin, *Three Years*, 1:71, 81-82.

12. Isidore Harris (ed.), *The Jewish Year Book: An Annual Review of Matters Jewish, 1675-76* (London, 1915), 254; *PAJHS*, 27:255-57; Schappes, *DHJUS*, 626, n.5; Trustees Minutes, Shearith Israel, N.Y., Dec. 19, 1813; Tarshish, "American Judaism," 324, n.773; Marcus, *Memoirs*, 2:98; Cole, *Irrepresible Conflict*, 186-87.

13. Michael, "Cincinnati," 55 ff.; Brickner, "Jew. Com. of Cin.," 182 ff.; *Occ.*, 8:259 ff.; *Jewish Hospital of Cincinnati*, 5; Tarshish, "American Judaism," lxxii, n.558.

14. Tobias, *Hebrew Benevolent Society*, 14-16; Meites, *Chicago*, 79 ff.; *Louisiana Inventory*, 87 ff.; Shpall, *Louisiana*, 25-26.

15. Hirsh & Doherty, *Mount Sinai Hospital*, 3 ff., 14 ff., 36 ff.; Grinstein, *New York City*, 156-59, 565, n.44; Markens, *Hebrews*, 312-13; Francis Moses, Cincinnati, to Harry Englander, Cincinnati, Apr. 11, 1926, copy in Marcus Collections; Huhner, *Judah Touro*, 72, 131; Irma M. Isaacson, "Jewish Philanthropy in New Orleans," (master's thesis, Tulane, 1937), chaps. 2 and 3; Broadside, New York Hebrew Benevolent Society, Oct. 15, 1850, copy in AJAr; Lyons & De Sola, *Jewish Calendar*, 167; *PAJHS*, 10:109 ff., 19:32, 37-38; *Asmonean*, June 8, 1855, p.62, c.2; "Simson, Sampson," *BDEAJ*; Schappes, *DHJUS*, 681, n.9; *New York Times*, Nov. 12, 1972, p.92, c.1.

16. *Asmonean*, Nov. 11, 1853, p.28, c.2; Swichkow & Gartner, *Milwaukee*, 54; Grinstein, *New York City*, 145 ff., 187-88; Brickner, "Jew. Com. of Cin.," 180 ff.; *Occ.*, 6:525-26.

17. *Asmonean*, Jan. 17, 1851, p. 313, c.3; Morais, *Philadelphia*, 137-38; "Philadelphia," *JE*, 9:676; *Occ.*, 2:59.

18. *RIJHN*, 5:297; *Occ*, 6:619; M. Mayer, Charleston, to I.L., Phila., 12 Elul, 5613, copy in Marcus Collections; Grinstein, *New York City*, 151, 184 ff.; "New York," *JE*, 9:273; Tobias, *Hebrew Benevolent Society*, 13 ff.; *JM*, Jan. 29, 1859, p.27, cs.1-2.

19. W. & W., *Philadelphia*, 278; Morais, *Philadelphia*, 143 ff.; *EIAJH*, 215, no. 99; Grinstein, *New York City*, 109 ff., 131 ff., 146 ff., 162, 443; Tobias, *Hebrew Orphan Society*, 118; Schappes, *DHJUS*, 217 ff.; *Asmonean*, Jan. 17, 1851, p.13; Meites, *Chicago*, 58-59, 77-80; Tarshish, "American Judaism," 268-69; Grusd, *B'nai B'rith*, 18 ff.

CHAPTER ELEVEN
JEWISH EDUCATION, CULTURE, AND SOCIAL LIFE, 1840–1860

1. Lyons & De Sola, *Jewish Calendar*, 165 ff.; Goldberg, "Hist. Am. Jew. Ed.," 41 ff., 93; Dushkin, *Jew. Ed. in NYC*, 53; B. & B., *JOUS*, 2:437-39; Fein, *Baltimore*, 68-70; Curti, *American Thought*, 421; *Jewish Year Book, 1915*, 254; Lipman, *Soc. Hist. of Jews in England*, 46, 49; *Sinai* 3:887-88; *AI*, Nov. 16, 1855, p.156, cs.1-3.
2. *Occ.*, 1:35 ff., 13:79 ff., 85-89, 18(The Advertiser):2; *AZJ*, July 27, 1846, pp.448-49, June 7, 1847, pp.364-66; Grinstein, *New York City*, 235-36, 246, 253 ff.; R. & E., *Charleston*, 149-50; *PAJHS*, 27:516-17, 42:54 ff.; "New York," *JE*, 9:273 ff.; Joseph Jonas, Cincinnati, to I.L., Phila., Sept. 16, 1845, copy in Marcus Collections; Rogson, "Leeser"; Ernst, *Immigrant Life*, 274, n.50; *AI*, Jan. 18, 1855, p.221, c.4, p.222, c.1.
3. See Auerback, "San Francisco Jewry," 12 ff., for the *Gleaner*, Sept. 16, 1859, p.5, Sept. 28, 1859, p.5, Nov. 11, 1859, p.5; *R*, no.391; *AJA*, 2:41-42; *Occ.*, 3:217 ff.; Morais, *Philadelphia*, 154 ff.; *Fifty Years Work of the H.E.S.*; Lander, "Jewish Religious Education," 20 ff.
4. *PAJHS*, 27:516-17; Fierman, "Jewish Education," see table "Principal Congregational Schools," 114 ff., 127, n.87; "Annual Report of the Commissioner of the Bureau of Education," in San Francisco *Hebrew*, Mar. 10, 1871, p.4; Grinstein, *New York City*, 225 ff., 233, 238, 545, n.34; *Occ.*, 5:316-17; *Jew. Ed.*, 13:23 ff.; Nodel, *The Ties Between*, 21-22, 35-36; Cole, *Irrepressible Conflict*, 50. No attempt is made here to document every known Jewish parochial school in the United States during this period. The following references, however, are helpful: Brickner, "Jew. Com. of Cin.," 134-42; Dushkin, *Jew Ed. in NYC*, 28 ff.; Pilch, *Hist. Jew. Ed.*, 25 ff.; *Fifty Years Work of the H.E.S.*, 1 ff.; Fierman, "Jewish Education," 39 ff.; *PAJHS*, 27:499-500, 29:129 ff.; Tarshish, "American Judaism," 23 ff., 282 ff.; *EIAJH*, 407-24; *AJA*, 7:84; Benjamin, *Three Years*, 1:78-79, 230-31, 2:274, 310; *HUCA*, 18:321 ff.; Lander, "Jewish Religious Education"; *Jew. Rev.*, 2:41 ff.; Goldberg, "Hist. Am. Jew. Ed"; *AI*, June 20, 1873, p.4, c.5, p.5, cs.1-2; E. & L., *Richmond*, 225 ff.; Todes, "Jewish Education in Philadelphia," 110 ff.; Lyons & De Sola, *Jewish Calendar*, 149 ff.; Michael, "Cincinnati," 75 ff.; Fein, *Baltimore*, 69; Blum, *Baltimore*, 16-17; *Essex Story*, 31; Marans, *Jews in Greater Washington*, 96. Southern and Western Schools: James A. Wax, *The Jews of Memphis, 1860-1865* (reprint from *The West Tennessee Historical Society Papers*, Memphis?, 1949), 7; Meites, *Chicago*, 54; *Louisiana Inventory*, 98-99; Shpall, *Louisiana*, 13; Markens, *Hebrews*, 112; Glanz, *California*, 103; Nodel, *The Ties Between*, 21-22, 35-36.
5. Blum, *Baltimore*, 16; B.H. Gotthelf, Louisville, to I.L., Phila., Sept. 3, 1851, copy in Marcus Collections; E. & L., *Richmond*, 228-29; Fein, *Baltimore*, 121-22; Lander, "Jewish Religious Education," 12-13; Michael, "Cincinnati," 75 ff.; *Fifty Years Work of the H.E.S.*, 27 ff.; Huhner, *Judah Touro* 135-36.
6. *Jew. Rev.*, 2:41 ff., 54; Goldberg, "Hist. Am. Jew. Ed.," 71, 80; Morais, *Philadelphia*, 159; Lander, "Jewish Religious Education," 6-7; Tarshish, "American Judaism," 282 ff., 298, lxxxi, n.654; Glanz, *Milieu*, 45-46; *Commentary*, 15:493; *Occ.*, 15:304-5; Glanz, *The German Jew in America*, no.1787; Grinstein, *New York City*, 207; *Jew. Ed*, 13:28-30.
7. Tarshish, "American Judaism," 286 ff., 292; *Occ.*, 10:158 ff.; *Jew. Rev.*, 2:54 ff., 193 ff.; *Jew. Ed.*, 13:23 ff.; Fein, *Baltimore*, 121-22; Grinstein, *New York City*, 247, 253 ff.; *AI*, Nov. 9, 1855, p.148, cs.1-4.

8. Lander, "Jewish Religious Education," 28; "Confirmation, the Rite of," *JE*; "New York," *JE*, 9:274.

9. *R*, nos. 190, 235, 321, 446. Among the more popular textbooks of those decades were the following: Simha Peixotto, *Elementary Introduction to the Scriptures, etc.* (13th ed., Phila., 1875); Louis Salomon, *The Mosaic System in its Fundamental Principles* (Phila., 5601 [1841]); Henri Loeb, *Derek Ha-emunah. The Road to Faith* (Kingston, Jamaica, 1841); M. Cahen, *Catechism of Religious and Moral Instruction* (Phila., 1845): R, no.526; Isaac M. Wise, *The Essence of Judaism, etc.* (2d ed., Cincinnati, 1868); S. Herxheimer, *Yesode Hatorah, Catechism of the Faith* (N.Y., 1850); Henry Abraham Henry, *Sefer Ha-Hinukh le Yalde vene Yisrael: A Class Book for Jewish Youth of Both Sexes* (Cincinnati, 1851); E. Pyke, *Scriptural Questions for the Use of Sunday Schools, etc.* (Phila., 1857); Emanuel Hecht, *Synopsis of the History of the Israelites, etc.* (Cincinnati, 1857); S. Adler, *A Guide to Instruction in the Israelitish Religion* (3d ed., N.Y., 1864), text in German and English. Grinstein, *New York City*, 257 ff.; Morais, *Philadelphia*, 151; Pool, *Old Faith*, 223-24; Marcus, *Memoirs*, 1:281-88; Korn, *Eventful Years*, 42-46; P. & K., *Tourist's Guide*, 29; *PAJHS*, 42:56 ff; *Jew. Rev.*, 2:196; Fein, *Baltimore*, 121-22; I.M. Wise, Albany, to President of the Congregation, Albany, Mar. 15, 1852, copy in AJAr.

10. Brickner, "Jew. Com. of Cin.," 142; Goldberg, "Hist. Am. Jew. Ed.," 102 ff.; Gartner, *Jewish Ed. in U.S.*, 83-86; *Occ.*, 13:81-89; *AI*, Dec. 8, 1854, p.174, cs.2-4, Dec. 22, 1854, p.188, c.4, p.189, cs.1-3, Dec. 29, 1854, p.197, cs.34, p.198, cs.1-2, Mar. 2, 1855, p.269, cs.1-3, Nov. 9, 1855, p.148, cs.1-4; Grinstein, *New York City*, 231, 238 ff.; Tarshish, "American Judaism," 61, 286; *Jew. Rev.*, 2:187-88; Carl Russell Fish, *The Rise of the Common Man, 1830-1850* (N.Y., 1927), 256.

11. Grinstein, *New York City*, 244; Fierman, "Jewish Education," 188; *Asmonean*, Nov. 30, 1849, p.45, c.3; Beard, *Rise of Am. Civilization*, 1:810-11; Ellis, *Am. Catholicism*, 52-55; Schlesinger, *Rise of the City*, 160 ff.; Cubberley, *Public Education*, 163 ff.; Morison, *History*, 531-32; Cole, *Irrepressible Conflict*, 205 ff.; Glazer, *American Judaism*, 34.

12. Fein, *Baltimore*, 122; *Jew. Rev.*, 2:189; "Annual Report of the Commissioner of the Bureau of Education, 1870," in San Francisco *Hebrew*, Mar. 17, 1871; Pilch, *Hist. Jew. Ed.*, 39; *AI*, Dec. 8, 1854, p.174, cs.2-4.

13. Gartner, *Jewish Ed. in the U.S.*; Goldberg, "Hist. Am. Jew. Ed.," 77-78; *Asmonean*, May 23, 1851, p.37, cs.1-2. Isaac Harby conducted a private school in New York City for a few months in 1828. It is not intended to document all Jewish private schools in the United States during this period. The following references may be consulted with profit: Marcus, *AJWD*, 146-47; Grinstein, *New York City*, 242 ff., 565, n.34; *Jew. Rev.*, 2:52 ff.; Pilch, *Hist. Jew. Ed.*, 39; Fierman, "Jewish Education," 129 ff., 136 ff.; *PAJHS*, 27:499-500, 29:129 ff., 42:53-54; Tarshish, "American Judaism," 292-93; Dushkin, *Jew. Ed. in NYC*, 49-50; Benjamin, *Three Years*, 1:229-31; *AI*, June 23, 1865, p.416, cs.2-3; *RIJHN*, 5:298; *Occ.*, 18(The Advertiser):1-2; Fein. *Baltimore*, 69; Glanz, *The German Jew in America*, no.1101; *Kiev Festschrift*, 199, no. 138; Brickner, "Jew. Com. of Cin.," 135; Fierman, "Some Higher Educational Efforts," 19 ff.; B.H. Gotthelf, Louisville, to I.L., Phila., Nov. 15, 1852, copy in Marcus Collections; Auerback, "San Francisco Jewry," 16, 19, for *The Gleaner*, Sept. 16, 28, 1859, p.5, Oct. 12, 1860, p.4; Goldberg, "Elem. Jew. Ed.," 16 ff.; Goldberg, "Hist. Am. Jew. Ed.," 72 ff.; *American Jews' Annual for 5649 A.M.* (1888-89), 62.

14. Lipman, *Soc. Hist. of Jews in England*, 47; Grinstein, *New York City*, 242-47; Wise, *Reminiscences*, 212; *PAJHS*, 27:55; *Occ.*, 1:104-5, 3:224-25; *Deborah*, Mar. 22, 1867, p.146, cs.1-3; Beard, *Rise of Am. Civilization*, 1:812; Levine, *Am. Jew. Bibliography*, no.27; *Jew. Rev.*, 2:52 ff.; *Kiev Festschrift*, 200, no.145; Fierman, "Jewish Education," 151 ff.

15. Benjamin, *Three Years*, 1:229-31; Goldberg, "Elem. Jew. Ed.," 18-19; Auerback, "San Francisco Jewry," 16 ff., for *The Gleaner*, Oct. 12, 1860, p.4; *Asmonean*, Dec. 14, 1849, p.61, c.2; Brickner. "Jew. Com. of Cin.," 144; *Occ.*, 1:200-1.

16. *Jew. Rev.*, 2:49 ff., 53, 194; Goldberg, "Hist. Am. Jew. Ed.," 72 ff.; Grinstein, *New York City*, 242-43, 253 ff.; *Occ.*, 5:316-17, 8:424-26; Fierman, "Some Higher Educational Efforts," 19; Korn, *Eventful Years*, 42 ff.; Philipson, *Max Lilienthal*, 1 ff.; "Lilienthal, Max," *JE, UJE, EJ, DAB*.

17. *PAJHS*, 29:130 ff., 34:123 ff., 42:53, 57, 61, 64, n.62; Blum, *Baltimore*, 16; Fein, *Baltimore*, 68 ff.; Benjamin, *Three Years*, 1:304; *Essex Story*, 31 ff.; Grinstein, *New York City*, 231 ff., 243 ff.; *Jew. Rev.*, 2:47, 191; R. & E., *Charleston*, 150; *Gartner, Jew. Ed. in the U.S.*, 85-86; *Fifty Years Work of the H.E.S.*, 27 ff.; Tarshish, "American Judaism," 283, 287; Dushkin, *Jew. Ed. in NYC*, 464 ff.

18. *PAJHS*, 29:132 ff., 42:55 ff.; Tarshish, "American Judaism," 286-88; *AI*, Jan. 14, 1859, p.220, c.1; *JQR*, 12:563 ff., 575; Fein, *Baltimore*, 122-23; Blum, *Baltimore*, 16; *Proceedings of the Commemorative Celebration . . . Hebrew Sunday Schools in America* (Phila., 1888); Marcus, *Memoirs*, 1:214, 281-88; Goldberg, "Hist. Am. Jew. Ed.," 86 ff.; "San Francisco," *UJE*; P. & K., *Tourist's Guide*, 29; Korn, *Eventful Years*, 42 ff.; Fierman, "Jewish Education," 181, 188; Todes, "Jewish Education in Philadelphia," 112 ff.; *Occ.*, 1:38-40; Brickner, "Jew. Com. of Cin.," 144-45; Dushkin, *Jew. Ed. in NYC*, 50 ff.; *AJA*. 8:66-67.

19. Cole, *Irrepressible Conflict*, 209; Sweet, *Story of Religion in America*, 362 ff.; Cubberley, *Public Education*, 245 ff.; Grinstein, *New York City*, 251 ff., 427-29; Pilch, *Hist. Jew. Ed.*, 42 ff.; Lander, "Jewish Religious Education," 6-7; M.E. Levy, N.Y.C., to Sam Myers, Norfolk, Oct. 18, Oct. 30, Nov. 1, 1818, copies in AJAr; Korn, *Eventful Years*, 199 ff.; *AJHQ*, 52:313, 317-19; Gartner, *Jew. Ed. in U.S.*, 47-49; *Occ.*, 1:301-307, 555-56, 2:249 ff., 3:21 ff., 136 ff., 168, 4:469-78, 6:433 ff.; *Fifty Years Work of the H.E.S.*, 20-22; *Asmonean*, Dec. 21, 1849, p.69, c.1, Jan. 4, 1850, p.85, c.2, Jan. 25, 1850, p.108, c.3, p.109, c.1; *AI*, Dec. 8, 1854, p.175, c.2, Nov. 16, 1855, p.156, cs.1-3, Nov. 23, 1855, p.165, cs.2-4; Minutes, B'nai Yeshurun, Cincinnati, Nov. 6, 1858; Brickner, "Jew. Com. of Cin.," 138-39; *American Jews' Annual for 5650 A.M.* (1889-90), 90, 96; Michael, "Cincinnati," 90-92; Plaut, *Reform Judaism*, 51-52; Fierman, "Some Higher Educational Efforts," 14 ff., 22-23; Tarshish, "American Judaism," 214-15; Glanz, *The German Jew in America*, no.1144; Curti, *American Thought*, 265 ff.; Heller, *Isaac M. Wise*, 273 ff.

20. L.C. Moïse, *Biograghy of Isaac Harby with an Account of The Reformed Society of Israelites of Charleston, S.C.* (n.p.,1931). 63; Marcus, *Memoirs*, 1:247; B. & B., *JOUS*, 2:437-39; *PAJHS*, 42:55, 50:79 ff.; *University of Rochester Library Bulletin*, 14:1 ff.; "Tuska," *UJE*; Simon Tuska, *Stranger in the Synagogue* (Rochester, 1854).

21. Morris A. Gutstein, *A Priceless Heritage: The Epic Growth of Nineteenth Century Chicago Jewry* (N.Y., 1953), 300-1; Robert Miller, "The *Asmonean*, 1855-1856" (HUC term paper, n.d.), 6; Curti, *American Thought*, 355 ff.; Ernst, *Immigrant Life*, 142-43; Lyons & De Sola, *Jewish Calendar*, 166; *PAJHS*, 48:234-35; *AI*, Jan. 5, 1855, p.206, c.4; Grinstein, *New York City*, 193 ff., 195, 200 ff.; Glanz, *Milieu*, 38-39; *Jewish Year Book*, 1915, 254; *Occ.*, 14:257-58; Max Rosenberg and Arthur Marmor, *Temple Beth El: A Centennial History of Beth El Congregation Serving Northern Virginia Since 1859* (Alexandria?, 1959?), 1; Fierman, "Some Higher Educational Efforts," 12-13. For antebellum Jewish youth and adult literacy societies and associations in the United States, in Boston, Albany (Jews and Gentiles here were in the same organization), New York City, Newark, Philadelphia, Baltimore, Buffalo, Cleveland, Cincinnati, Louisville, New Orleans, St. Louis, and San Francisco, see: *Commentary*, 15:495; Tarshish, "American Judaism," 299 ff., lxxxiii, n.655; Wise, *Reminiscences*, 106-7; *AZJ*, Apr. 23, 1855, pp.219-20, Oct. 29, 1855, p.565; *Essex Story*, 45 ff.; Morais, *Philadelphia*, 162 ff.; Blum, *Baltimore*, 25 ff.; *PAJHS*, 37:221 ff.; Goodman, *Documentary Story*, 5 ff.; Benjamin, *Three Years*, 1:53, 229; *American Jews' Annual for 5649 A.M.* (1888-89), 61-62; "San Francisco," *JE*, 11:35. This list is not intended to be complete.

22. Marcus, *Memoirs*, 1:239 ff.; Grinstein, *New York City*, 202-3.
23. Lyons & De Sola, *Jewish Calendar*, 166; Grinstein, *New York City*, 193 ff., 198 ff., 560, n.12; Goodman, *Documentary Story*, 6, 11; *PAJHS*, 37:221 ff.; Meites, *Chicago*, 148-49; Blum, *Baltimore*, 25; *Essex Story*, 45; *Asmonean*, Dec. 14, 1855, p.67, c.2; Tarshish, "American Judaism," 299 ff.; Benjamin, *Three Years*, 1:229; Brickner, "Jew. Com. of Cin.," 288; Fierman, "Some Higher Educational Efforts," 12; *AZJ*, Apr. 23, 1855, pp.219-20, Oct. 29, 1955, p.565; *Programme of the First Anniversary Celebration of the Mendelssohn Literary Association of Chicago* (May 14, 1857), copy in Marcus Collections.
24. Circular of Touro Literary Institute, New York, Jan. 22, 1855, copy in Marcus Collections; *Constitution and By- Laws of the Hebrew Literary Association of Philadelphia* (Phila., 1856); Goodman, *Documentary Story*, 7-12; *PAJHS*, 37:221 ff.; *Essex Story*, 45; *Sinai*, 1:47-50, 67 ff.; Grinstein, *New York City*, 193-97, 560, n.12; Tarshish, "American Judaism," 299-300.
25. *AZJ*, Jan. 1, 1847, p.27, June 7, 1847, pp.364-66; for Hebraists in the colonial period see Marcus, *CAJ*, 3:Index sub "Education, Jewish"; *Judaism*, 3:396-97; Grinstein, *New York City*, 14, 220-21, 252-53, 283, 486, 488, n.8, 521, 567, n.61; Shearith Israel, Minutes of Trustees, N.Y., Oct. 31, 1849, p.16; James Seixas and Dr. D.L.M. Peixotto taught Hebrew to the Mormons, (see *United States Jewry*, 1:Index sub "Seixas, James Joshua" and "Peixotto, D.L.M.") and Simon Tuska taught it to Christians at Union Theological Seminary. Schappes, *DHJUS*, 373 ff.; Auerback, "San Francisco Jewry," 30, for the *Gleaner*, June 3, 1857; E. & L., *Richmond*, 141; J.M. Netter, *Shelabim min Ha-yam* (Vienna, 1860); Joseph Levy, Cleveland, to I.L., Phila., Thursday, parashat ekev (Aug. 1852), Leeser Papers, copy in Marcus Collections; *Occ.*, 10:305 ff.; *AI*, Jan. 5, 1855, p.207, c.1; Kraut and Fox, *Completion of Independence*, 364; Rogson, "Isaac Leeser"; Gartner, *Cleveland*, 56.
    The following is a list, in no sense exhaustive, of antebellum knowledgeable Hebraists: Isaac M. Wise, Max Lilienthal, A. Rice, D. Einhorn, M. Raphall, S.M. Isaacs, B. Illowy, I. Kalisch, S. Morais, Henry A. Henry, Abraham Joseph Ash, Benjamin Szold, Samuel Adler, Bernard Felsenthal, Samuel Hillel Isaacs. Their biographies are found in the standard Jewish encyclopedias; some of them are in the *DAB*. In addition, Grinstein lists Simeon Abraham, Emanuel Goldsmith, Hermann Felsenheld, C. Nussbaum, Joseph N. Oettinger, S. Poppers, and Jacob J.M. Falkenau. Others worthy of note are Ignas Kunreuther of Chicago, Isaac Strouse of Albany and Pottsville, Simon Cohen Noot of New York, Jacob De Sola Mendes of Richmond, P.(?) Davidsohn, of New York. For them see Meites, *Chicago*, 45, and letters to Isaac Leeser, Phila., Leeser Papers, copies in Marcus Collections as follows: Strouse, Albany, Nov. 15, 1849, Strouse, Pottsville, July 14, 1858; Noot, 24 Tebet 5601 (1841); Mendes, Iyyar, 1851; Davidsohn, Jan. 12, 1858. In addition Hebrew letters appeared not infrequently in the *Occident*. "Joshua ben Mordecai Falk Ha-Kohen," *JE*; S. Wininger, *Grosse Juedische National-Biographie, u.s.w.* (n.p., n.d.), 2:217.
26. Lipman, *Soc. Hist. of Jews in England*, 35-36; *PAJHS*, 48:239; *R*, nos.353 ff.; "America, Judaism in," *JE*, 1:516-17; Levine, *Am. Jew. Bibliography*, 1-23; *Studies in Bibliography and Booklore*, 5:135-36; Glanz, *The German Jew in America*, nos.1158, 2302; *Kiev Festschrift*, 188 ff., nos.61-199; *EIAJH*, 220-45; Marcus, *Jewish Americana*, 75 ff., nos.169-227; Grinstein, *New York City*, 219; Morais, *Eminent Israelites*, 149-53, 252-55; Michael, "Cincinnati," 102; Morais, *Philadelphia*, 329-31; Octavia Harby Moses, *A Mother's Poems* (n.p., 1915); Markens, *Hebrews*, 97; "Carvalho," *UJE*; *American Heritage*, 27:49 ff.
27. "Raphall, Morris Jacob," *JE*.
28. For Joshua I. Cohen, see *United States Jewry*, 1:Index; Cyrus Adler, *Catalogue of a Hebrew Library . . . Joshua I. Cohen. etc.* (Privately Printed, Baltimore, 1887).
29. Elzas, *Jews of S.C.*, 145, n.72, 194; R. & E., *Charleston*, 105, 293-94, n.167; Stern, *FAJF*, 169; "Vindiciae Judaeorum," Mss., Phillips Papers, L.C.; *Southern Quarterly Review*,

5(1844):312-60; Cecil Roth, *A Life of Menasseh ben Israel, Rabbi, Printer, and Diplomat* (Phila., 1934), 303-4; Lucien Wolf, *Menasseh ben Israel's Mission to Oliver Cromwell, etc.* (London, 1901), see appendix for *Vindiciae Judaeorum* (1656); Wolf, *Yates and Samuel Families*, 24 ff.

30. Cole, *Irrepressible Conflict*, 216-17; Curti, *American Thought*, 350, 355, 363 ff.; *Kiev Festschrift*, 191, no.84; *AI*, Nov. 23, 1855, p.165, cs.2-4; Grusd, *B'nai B'rith*, 29, 36-37, 48-49; Lucius L. Solomons, *Historical Sketch of B'nai B'rith* (n.p., n.d.), 4; *National Jewish Monthly*, Sept. 1968, p.14; *Menorah*, 1:12 ff.; Grinstein, *New York City*, 203, 252-53; *JM*, Jan. 5, 1866, p.4, c.4, p.5, c.1, June 1, 1866, p.1, cs.3-4, p.2, c.1; Circular of Touro Literary Institute, January 22, 1855, copy in Marcus Collections.

31. Sweet, *Story of Religion in America*, 350 ff.; Circular of the Jewish Publication Society, Dec. 10, 1845, copy in Marcus Collections; "Jewish Publication Society of America, The," *UJE*; "American Jewish Publication Society," *JE*; Schappes, *JIUS*, 77-78; *Occ.*, 2:517 ff., 3:35-37, 10:237 ff.; *Jewish Book Annual*, 3:4 ff., 7:89 ff.; Korn, *Eventful Years*, 45-46; Tarshish, "American Judaism," 216-17.

32. *R*, no.258; Grinstein, *New York City*, 218 ff., 282 ff.; S.C. Noot, N.Y.C., to I.L., Phila., 17 Shebat 5609 (1849), copy in Marcus Collections; *AJA*, 20:163-68; for the Frank publications see Levine, *Am. Jew. Bibliography*, p.96, 1-23, see particularly nos.27, 144, 150-52, 171, 197, 229; Isidor Bush, St. Louis, to I.L., Phila., May 6, 1857, copy in Marcus Collections; *RIJHN*, 5:295.

33. May, *Isaac M. Wise*, 150, 333; *Kiev Festschrift*, 192, no.91; Glanz, *The German Jew in America*, no.1048; *Occ.*, 1:214-16, 263-64, 515-16; Schappes, *DHJUS*, 287 ff.; Morris, *EAH*, 616; *PAJHS*, 26:270-73; "Periodicals," *JE*, 9:616 ff.; letters to I.L., Phila.: Joseph Jonas, Cincinnati, Sept.6, 1845, L. Cohen, Dalton, Ga., Jan. 6, 1857, E. Wolff, Eagle Pass, Texas, Dec. 31, 1850, copies in Marcus Collections; *AJA*, 8:66-67, 74-75; R. & E., *Charleston*, 298-99, n.185; Glanz, *Milieu*, 46-47; Heller, *Isaac M. Wise*, 661; Tarshish, "American Judaism," lxxxvii, n.684; Grinstein, *New York City*, 214 ff.; Prospectus, *Israel's Herald* (N.Y., 1849), in German, copy in AJAr; Michael, "Cincinnati," 99-100; Morais, *Eminent Israelites*, 221-23; Meyer Waxman, *A History of Jewish Literature* (4 vols., 2d ed., N.Y., 1960), 4:1088 ff.; Korn, *Eventful Years*, 39 ff.; Friedman, *Pilgrims*, 163 ff., 409-11; Levine, *Am. Jew. Bibliography*, no.666.

34. *AZJ*, June 7, 1847, pp.364-66; Grinstein, *New York City*, 253-57; *AI*, Mar. 2, 1855, p.269, cs.1-3, Jan. 14, 1859, p.220, c.1, June 20, 1973, p.4, c.5, p.5, cs.1-2; Beard, *Rise of Am. Civilization*, 1:766; Cole, *Irrepressible Conflict*, 242.

35. Grinstein, *New York City*, 174-192; "Tikkun," *JE*; Goldberg, *Major Noah*, 189 ff.; *PAJHS*, 31:153; Tarshish, "American Judaism," 316 ff.

36. Grinstein, *New York City*, 200-3; Glanz, *Milieu*, 25, 32-33, 36-37; Benjamin, *Three Years* 2:281; Swichkow & Gartner, *Milwaukee*, 55 ff.; Adler & Connolly, *Buffalo*, 17; Fein, *Baltimore*, 75; Ernst, *Immigrant Life*, 128-29; Ginsberg, *Jews of Virginia*, 41.

37. Marcus, *CAJ*, 2:1022 ff.; Cole, *Irrepressible Conflict*, 200; Brickner, "Jew. Com. of Cin.," 286-88; *JSS*, 31:82 ff.; Grinstein, *New York City*, 202-3, 205; Glanz, *Milieu*, 42; Benjamin, *Three Years*, 1:304, 312; Blum, *Baltimore*, 29; Fein, *Baltimore*, 130 ff.; for Portuguese prejudice see letter to Leeser, unsigned, undated, probably in 1840's, discussing Portuguese prejudice against Germans, probably published in the *Occident*, copy in Leeser papers in Marcus Collections; Mercantile Club Minutes (Philadelphia), Mss., AJAr.

38. Brickner, "Jew. Com. of Cin.," 286; Swichkow & Gartner, *Milwaukee*, 56; Glanz, *Milieu*, 34; Benjamin, *Three Years*, 1:312.

39. Benjamin, *Three Years*, 1:304; Mercantile Club Minutes (Philadelphia), Feb. 18, 1855, Mss., AJAr; Morais, *Philadelphia*, 51-52, 252-54.

40. Grinstein, *New York City*, 205, 559, n. 48; Glanz, *Milieu*, 23, 32, 38-39, 42; *PAJHS*, 40:135 ff.

CHAPTER TWELVE

REJECTION OF JEWS, 1840–1860

1. Stokes & Pfeffer, *Church and State*, 78; *AJA*, 10:14 ff.; *AI*, Mar. 22, 1861, p.300, c.4, p.301, c.1; *PAJHS*, 16:64 ff.

2. Schaff, *Church and State*, 128 ff.; Ephraim Frisch, "Is the United States a Christian Nation?: A Legal Study," paper read before the So. Rabbinical Assoc., Nashville, Tenn., Dec. 25, 1906; Stokes, *Church and State*, 3:868; *American State Papers* (1949), 253, 552 ff.; Morais, *Philadelphia*, 261; E. & L., *Richmond*, 117-18; Morison, *History*, 459; *PAJHS*, 9:160 ff.; Swichkow & Gartner, *Milwaukee*, 43-44; May, *Isaac M. Wise*, 206 ff.; *RIJHN*, 1:235; *Occ.*, 2:496 ff., 6:403 ff.; R. & E., *Charleston*, 111 ff.; *Asmonean*, Nov. 2, 1855, p.20, c.1; Karff, "Anti-Semitism," 13-18.

3. *The Pennsylvania Magazine of History and Biography*, 94: 308-9; Billington, *Protestant Crusade*, 157-58; Myers, *Bigotry*, 164; *AI*, Nov. 26, 1858, p.165, c.4, p.166, c.1; Wish, *Society and Thought*, 1:317; *American State Papers* (1949), see index under "Bible reading in public schools."

4. *PAJHS*, 5:202, 9:162-63, 10:136-37, 11:104, 107, 12:87 ff.; *American State Papers*(1949), see index sub "Sunday," especially 228, 232-33, 248-49; R. & E.. *Charleston*, 110-11; Morison, *History*, 459; Cole, *Irrepressible Conflict*, 254-55; Billington, *Protestant Crusade*, 404; E. & I.., *Richmond*, 117-18; *AI*, May 11, 1855, p.345, cs.1-4, p.346, cs.1-4; Karff, "Anti-Semitism," 2 ff.; *Occ.*, 6:413-14, 13:123-32, 558-59; *AJA*, 12:15 ff.; Vorspan & Gartner, *Los Angeles*, 15; *AJYB*, 10(1908-1909):152 ff.

5. Tarshish, "American Judaism," 153; Wise, *Reminiscences*, 217 ff.; Marcus, *Memoirs*, 1:18-19; Karff, "Anti-Semitism," 34; Myers, *Bigotry*, 172; Korn, *Eventful Years*, 58 ff.; *PAJHS*, 27:510, 47:6; *AI*, July 22, 1859, p.23, c.1; June 22, 1860, p.402, c.3.

6. Marcus, *Jews in the Medieval World*, 38; for Lilienthal's letter, see Cincinnati *Daily Times*, Apr. 11, 1860; Cincinnati *Daily Commercial*, April 12, 1860, p.2, c.1; *Occ.*, 18:23; *AI*, Jan. 29. 1869, p.4, cs.1-5; Brickner, "Jew. Com. of Cin.," 311-13; Philipson, *Max Lilienthal*, 99; May, *Isaac M. Wise*, 377, wrote that Purcell forbade Catholics to sing in Jewish choirs. This seems to be an unauthenticated variant of the Lilienthal-Purcell incident which is documented.

7. Marcus, *AJWD*, 102; Billington, *Protestant Crusade*, 185, 208, 217, n. 88, 234, 322, 409, 437 ff.; Stokes & Pfeffer, *Church and State*, 225 ff., 233-34, 237; Schappes, *DHJUS*, 252 ff., 631, n.5, 634, n.15; "Levin, Lewis Charles," *DAB*; Lewis C. Levin, Phila., to John Campbell, et al., Phila., Oct. 3, 1848, Pa. Hist. Soc.; Lewis C. Levin, Phila., to Daniel Webster, Wash., D.C.(?), Apr. 25, 1851, Webster Collection, vol.x, LC; Myers, *Bigotry*, 141 ff., 179 ff., 200 ff.; *PAJHS*, 49:238, n.39; May, *Isaac M. Wise*, 240 ff.; Morison, *History*, 482, 590 91; Fein, *Baltimore*, 88-89; *AJA*, 11:176 ff.; Curti, *American Thought*, 316; Wish, *Society and Thought*, 1:319; Schappes, *JIUS*, 78-82; Stokes, *Church and State*, 3:867-70 (1830-1860); Ellis, *Am. Catholicism*, 287, sub 1844, 1853, 1855; "Catholicism in the United States," *DAH* (1942); Cole, *Irrepressible Conflict*, 142 ff., 247; *Bulletin of the Cincinnati Historical Society*, 22:240 ff.; Korn, *Eventful Years*, 58 ff.; Carl Wittke, *We Who Built America* (N.Y., 1939), 494; Karff, "Anti-Semitism," v-vi; *AI*, July 20, 1855, p.12, cs.1-3; Sept. 21, 1855, p.85, c.4, p.86, c.1; Oct. 5, 1855, p.102, cs.1-3; *Asmonean*, Aug. 8, 1856, p.132, c.1.

8. Schappes, *DHJUS*, 286 ff., 293; Leeser, *Discourses*, 10:130-31, 12:597-604, 13:85-86, 14:148-49, 18:307; Myers, *Bigotry*, 132; B.H. Gotthelf, Louisville, to I.L., Phila., Apr. 4, 1853, enclosing an undated newspaper clipping from the Louisville *Journal*, copy in Marcus Collections; Swichkow & Gartner, *Milwaukee*, 23-24; *PAJHS*, 11:158 ff., 47:5; Marcus, *CAJ*, 1:367, 471, 2:888, 3:1127, 1561, n.25; Fein, *Baltimore*, 63-74; "Hershel, Clemens," *DAB*; "Jew," "Sheeny," (verb), OED; Fleishaker, "Illinois-Iowa Jewish

Community," 21; Irving J. Sloan, *The Jews in America, 1621-1970* (N.Y., 1971), 24; Vorspan & Gartner, *Los Angeles*, 15-16; *JSS*, 6:18; Wolf, *Yates and Samuel Families*, 25-26; Selzer, *"Kike,"* 32 ff.; "Boston," *UJE*, 2:481; "Levy, Uriah Phillips," *UJE*; Marcus, *Memoirs*, 1:103; *Bulletin of History and Philosophical Society of Ohio*, 19:209-10; Arthur G. King, Cincinnati, to JRM, Aug. 12, 1961, Marcus Collections; Edward Zane Carrol Judson, *The Mysteries and Miseries of New York* (N.Y.,1848), glossary.

 9. Labatt, New Orleans, to I.L., Phila., Oct. 27, 1852, Leeser Papers, copy in Marcus Collections; *AZJ*, May 14, 1842, p.294; *Asmonean*, Oct. 20, 1854, p.6, cs.3-4; Korn, *Eventful Years*, 60-68; *PAJHS*, 22:96-97; Fleishaker, "Illinois-Iowa Jewish Community," 25; Myers, *Bigotry*, 208.

10. *PAJHS*, 25:12-13, 101; Marcus, *CAJ*, 1:452; *Asmonean*, Nov. 13, 1857, p.37, c.4; *AI*, Sept. 22, 1854, p.85, cs.1-3, Jan. 14, 1859, p.220, c.1, Sept. 13, 1872, p.8, c.2-3; Schappes, *DHJUS*, 641-42; Wise, *Reminiscences*, 16; H. Didimus, *New Orleans as I Found It* (N.Y., 1845), 49.

11. *National Anti-Slavery Standard*, Feb. 17, 1842, p.148, cs.2-3, March 29, 1849, p.176, cs.1-2. These columns are reprints from the London press; *YA*, 6:132; *Der Orient* (1841), 15:116-18; Wilkes-Barre *Farmer and Journal*, Aug. 27, 1845, Sept. 10, 1845, copies in Marcus Collections; *AI*, June 27, 1856, p.413, cs.3-4, p.414, c.1.

12. Selzer, *"Kike,"* 18-19, 22-23, 32-39; *AI*, Mar. 1, 1858, p.292, cs.1-2, July 22, 1859, p.23, c.1, Nov. 18, 1859, p.158, cs.1-2, Dec. 9, 1859, p.180, cs.2-3, June 22, 1860, p.402, c.3; Glanz, *Studies*, 143 ff.; *American Jews' Annual for 5649 A.M.* (1888-89), 52-53; *PAJHS*, 40:347-48, 47:6; *JM*, July 16, 1858, p.10, cs.2-3, p.11, c.1.

13. Karff, "Anti-Semitism," iv; *PAJHS*, 22:96-97; "Anti-Semites," *JE*, 1:642; Benjamin, *Three Years*, 2:227 ff.

14. *PAJHS*, 9:163, 11:8.

15. Rutman, "Swiss-American Treaty," 36-37; Schappes, *DHJUS*, 315-24; *PAJHS*, 11:8-10, 27:507-8; *Sinai*, 2:662 ff.; Morais, *Philadelphia*, 260-61; "United States," *JE*, 12:356-57; *Occ.*, 8:613-15.

16. *PAJHS*, 11:15, 36:311; Korn, *Eventful Years*, 90-93; Weldler-Steinberg, *Geschichte der Juden*, 2:79; Rutman, "Swiss-American Treaty," 1-9.

17. Rutman, "Swiss-American Treaty," iii-iv, 8, 26, 29, 30-39, 56; *PAJHS*, 11:13-15, 21-23, 30 ff., 46-47, 36:299 ff.; Weldler-Steinberg, *Geschichte der Juden*, 2:48 ff., 61, 64, 70, 73-4, 82; Karff, "Anti-Semitism," 55; *Der Israelitische Volkslehrer*, 8:135-36; Elzas, *Leaves*, First Series, 1:3; *TJHSE*, 10:207 ff.; May, *Isaac M. Wise*, 215 ff.; Schappes, *DHJUS*, 315 ff., 649, n.5.

18. *Occ.*, 15:291 ff., 18:310; *PAJHS*, 11:21 ff., 27 ff., 36:299 ff., 48:243, n.217; "Appleton, John," *DAB*; Rutman, "Swiss-American Treaty," 40-51, 57; *Sinai*, 3:1023 ff.; "United States," *JE*, 12:356-57; Karff, "Anti-Semitism," 43 ff.; Swichkow & Gartner, *Milwaukee*, 24-25; Meites, *Chicago*, 59 ff.; *Asmonean*, Nov. 6, 1857, p.28, cs.3-4, p.29, cs.1-2; *AI*, July 31, 1857, p. 26, cs.3-4, p. 27, c.1; Aug. 7, 1857, p.33, c.1, p.34, cs.2-3; Aug. 14, 1857, p.41, c.1, p.42, c.1; Aug. 21, 1857, p.52, cs.1-3; Oct. 2, 1857, p.100, cs. 3-4, p.101, cs.1-2.

19. May, *Isaac M. Wise*, 127-28, 213; Rutman, "Swiss-American Treaty," 49 ff., 54-55; *PAJHS*, 11:30 ff., 33-34, 36:299 ff.; Wallach, *"Sinai,"* 3:553-55; Schappes, *DHJUS*, 321-24; Washington *Union*, Nov. 5, 1857, clipping in P. Phillips Papers, L.C.; *Asmonean*, Nov. 6, 1857, p.28, cs.3-4, p.29, cs.1-2, Nov. 20, 1857, p.45, c.2, Dec. 11, 1857, p.68; *AI*, Dec. 4, 1857, p.169, cs.1-3.

20. "United States," *JE*, 12:357; Wallach, *"Sinai,"* 3:553- 55; *PAJHS*, 11:37, 44-45, 49, 36:299 ff.; Rutman, Swiss-American Treaty," 71-106; Records of the Department of State, Diplomatic Dispatches, Switzerland, vol.1 (April 12, 1853-Dec. 26, 1854), NA.

21. "Alexander II," *UJE*; *Occ.*, 15:296-97; Records of the Department of State, Diplomatic Dispatches, Zurich, vol.2 (Jan. 25, 1858-Oct. 30, 1863), NA; *PAJHS*, 9:52, 11:50.

22. "Godefroi, Michael H.," *JE*; Francis Newton Thorpe (ed.), *The Federal and State Constitutions, Colonial Charters, and Other Organic Laws of . . . the United States of America* (7 vols., Washington, D.C., 1906-1909), 4:2491-92; "Aargau," *JE*; Records of the Department of State, Diplomatic Dispatches, Switzerland, vol. 6(July 2, 1861-Oct. 16, 1865), NA; *TJHSE*, 10:207 ff., 218-19; *Occ.*, 15:296-97, 20:211-12, 24:191-92; *PAJHS*, 11:44 ff., 49-52, 36:309-11; Rutman, "Swiss-American Treaty," iv, 105 ff.

23. *Occ*, 24:191-92; Elbogen, *Cent. of Jewish Life*, 32-33; Michael, "Cincinnati," 154-62; Edwin M. Borchard, *The Diplomatic Protection of Citizen Abroad or, The Law of International Claims*, (N.Y., 1927); *AI*, Jan. 5, 1855, p.270, c.1; Karff, "Anti-Semitism," 43 ff.; Temkin, "Isaac Mayer Wise," 558 ff.; Wolf, *The Jewish Question*, 65-68, 73-75; Heller, *Isaac M. Wise*, 319.

24. Paul Rieger, *Juden in Rome* (Berlin, 1895), 382; "Pope," *JE*; "Mortara Case," *New Catholic Encyclopedia*; Michael, "Cincinnati," 162 ff.; *AI*, Jan. 7, 1859, p.212, cs.1-4, p.213, cs.1-3; Roth, *Personalities*, 156 ff.

25. Wolf, *Sir Moses Montefiore*, 172 ff.; H.E., *Leiden*, 123- 24; Korn, *Mortara*, 132 ff., 136 ff.; see above for Lilienthal letter to Archbishop Purcell of Cincinnati; Marcus, *CAJ*, 1:451; Grinstein, *New York City*, 430 ff.

26. Korn, *Mortara*, 59, 95, 101, 111, 115, 120-21, 135, 143; Swichkow & Gartner, *Milwaukee*, 26.

27. "Mortara Case," *JE*; "Deutsch, Ignaz," *EJ*; Max Grunwald, *Vienna* (Phila., 1936), 350-53; Sigmund Mayer, *Die Wiener Juden, u.s.w.* (Wien, 1918), 369-70.

28. Wolf, *Sir Moses Montefiore*, 172-88; Paul Goodman, *Moses Montefiore* (Phila., 1925), 104-10; Korn, *Mortara*, 72, 157.

29. The greatest of Americans wrote congratulatory letters to Montefiore on the occasion of his centenary. Copies of some are found in AJAr. *Occ.*, 16:450 ff., 492 ff.; Korn, *Mortara*, 28; Schappes, *DHJUS*, 675, n.10, 676, n.14; *AI*, Sept. 17, 1858, p.85, c.1, Oct. 22, 1858, p.126, cs.1-3, Nov. 19, 1858, p.157, c.4, Aug. 26, 1859, p.62, cs.1-2; *JE*, Aug. 13, 1858, p. 29, c.1.

30. Korn, *Mortara*, 23, 26-27, 36-37, 41, 47, 59-60, 68, 72-75; *JM*, Oct. 15, 1858, p.68, cs. 1-2, Dec. 31, 1858, p.154, cs.2-3; Grinstein, *New York City*, 430 ff.; *Occ.*, 16:492 ff.; *AI*, Jan. 21, 1859, p.228, cs. 1 3; *Proceedings of the San Francisco Meeting*, 4, 8; Marcus, *CAJ*, 1:450; Albert Warwick Werline, *Church and State in Maryland* (So. Lancaster, Mass., 1948), 60; *American Jews' Annual for 5649 A.M.* (1888-89), 63 ff.

31. *AI*, Dec. 17, 1858, p.188, cs.1-2, May 27, 1859, p.373, c.4; Korn, *Mortara*, 38; *Jewish Forum*, 38:14-15; *Fourth Annual Report of the Association for the Relief of Jewish Widows and Orphans of New Orleans*, Mar. 27, 1859, 20-21, AJAr; *Asmonean*, Feb. 8, 1850, p.125, c.3; *Occ.*, 17:5; news item sent to I.L., Phila., dated Jan. 4, 1859, New Orleans, copy in Marcus Collections; Grinstein, *New York City*, 160; unidentified Detroit Jewish newspaper clipping, n.d., copy in Marcus Collections.

32. Schappes, *JIUS*, 85; *Occ.*, 16:492 ff.; Korn, *Mortara*, 43 ff., 46 ff., 56, 68 ff., 92-93; *AI*, Jan. 7, 1859, p.212, cs.1-4, p.213, cs.1-3, Feb. 11, 1859, p.253, c.3, Apr. 15, 1859, p.326, c.1; Benjamin, *Three Years*, 1:234-35; *American Jews' Annual for 5649 A.M.* (1888-89), 63 ff.

33. Korn, *Mortara*, 30-31, 40 ff., 50 ff., 61-66, 72, 78, 81-82, 90 ff., 157; *JM*, Dec. 17, 1858, p.138, cs.1-3, p.139, c.1, Dec. 31, 1858, p.154, cs.2-3, p.155, c.1; Schappes, *DHJUS*, 674, n.6; Fein, *Baltimore*, 105-6.

34. *AI*, Jan. 7, 1859, p.212, cs.1-4, p.213, cs.1-3; Schappes, *DHJUS*, 674, n.6; Wallach, *"Sinai,"* 3:564-70; *Occ.*, 16:450 ff., 492 ff., 536-42; *JM*, Dec. 17, 1858, p.140, cs.1-2; Korn, *Mortara*, 38-39, 67, 79, 158-59; Temkin, "Isaac Mayer Wise," 568 ff.; Michael, "Cincinnati," 162 ff.

35. "Mortara Case," *JE, UJE, EJ*; Korn, *Mortara*, 4, 159 ff.; Schappes, *DHJUS*, 676, n.14; Wolf, *Sir Moses Montefiore*, 182-83.

CHAPTER THIRTEEN

DEFENSE: THE BOARD OF DELEGATES OF AMERICAN ISRAELITES

1. Grinstein, *New York City*, 430 ff.; Tarshish, "American Judaism," 219; Hansen, *Atlantic Migration*, 167-68; *JM*, June 17, 1859, p.180, cs.1-2, June 24, 1859, p.188, cs.1-2, July 22, 1859, p.20, cs.1-2; *PAJHS*, 29:84; *AJYB*, 19(1917-1918):106 ff.
2. Grinstein, *New York City*, 409, 424-26, 435 ff., 446-47; *PAJHS*, 48:224 ff.; Ernst, *Immigrant Life*, 272, n.24; J. Bizart, Strasbourg, to Samuel Adler, N.Y., Feb. 14, 1871, copy in Marcus Collections.
3. A. Lindo, Kingston, Jamaica, to the president of Mikveh Israel, Phila., Mar. 8, 1844. Attached: Resolutions and Minutes of a protest meeting held in Kingston, Mar. 7, 1844 (Printed), copy in Marcus Collections; Grinstein, *New York City*, 416-18, 425-26; *HUCA*, 2:425; *PAJHS*, 29:88, 49:39 ff.; *National Anti-Slavery Standard*, Sept. 11, 1851, p.64, cs.1-3; *AI*, Apr. 13, 1855, p.318, cs.1-4, p.319, cs.1-4; *Occ.*, 11:1 ff., 24:229 ff.; *Brooklyn Jewish Center Review*, Feb. 1954, pp.12, 27; Heller, *Temple Sinai*, 10; Jacob Ezekiel, Richmond, to I.L., Phila., May 9, 1853, Michael Light, N.Y.C., to I.L., Phila., Aug. 25, 1853, copies in Marcus Collections; Huhner, *Judah Touro*, 67, 99-100, 132, 172, n.40; "China," *JE*, 4:35; "Halevy, Joseph," *EJ*.
4. Charleston *Courier*, May 10, 1824: An Appeal of Franklin Moses for Palestine. Moses later became chief justice of the state of South Carolina. Reference is found in B. Elzas to J.D. Eisenstein, N.Y.C., Nov. 8, 1905, Elzas papers, NYHS; Grinstein, *New York City*, 441 ff.; *JSS*, 5:115 ff.; *PAJHS*, 24:250, 29:98-99, 36:7; Lewis Abraham, Cincinnati, to I.L., Phila., Oct. 9, 1849, copy in AJAr; Circular Letter: S.M. Isaacs, N.Y., to Jews of the United States, Kislev 15, 5614(1852), unprinted, copy in Marcus Collections; *Occ.*, 12:324-25; *MGWJ*, 3:284 ff.; Shinedling, *West Virginia Jewry*, 3:1330; Auerback, "San Francisco Jewry," 15, for the *Gleaner*, Apr. 2, 1858, p.4; Fein, *Baltimore*, 53; Ernst, *Immigrant Life*, 272, n.24; Isaac Rivkind, *Me-Korat Hizonim* (*Kobez ha yovel shel histadrut ha-mizrahi: ba-Amerika*) (N.Y., 1936); Phila. *Jewish Exponent*, Dec. 3, 1854; *AI*, Nov. 19, 1858, p.156, c.4, p.157, cs.1-2.
5. *PAJHS*, 27:185 ff., 48:217; Korn, *Eventful Years*, 199-200; Leeser, *Discourses*, 2:251; Grinstein, *New York City*, 421 ff.; I.L., Phila., to Z. Rehine, Baltimore, Ab 3rd 5601, (July 21, 1841), copy in Marcus Collections; R. & E., *Charleston*, 142; Tarshish, "American Judaism," 205 ff.; Grusd, *B'nai B'rith*, 20; *AJA*, 2:21 ff.; *Occ.*, 1:265 ff., 457 ff., 2:196; Schappes, *JIUS*, 73; Philipson, *Max Lilienthal*, 46 ff.; *AZJ*, Jan. 1, 1847, pp.20-27.
6. Korn, *Eventful Years*, 27 ff.; Tarshish, "American Judaism," 206 ff., 209 ff.; Grinstein, *New York City*, 395 ff., 421-25; *AJA* 2:21-46; *Occ.*, 6:308, 313-21, 7:41-2, 137 ff., 139-49, 203 ff., 258 ff., 267 ff., 433 ff.; Leeser, "Circular," on the need for a union, Adar 5, 5609 (Feb. 28, 1849), Phila., copy in AJAr; "New York City," *UJE*, 8:187.
7. *Occ.*, 6:614 ff., 7:433 ff., 440-41; Korn, *Eventful Years*, 35 ff.; Tarshish, "American Judaism," 208 ff.; New York *Sun*, Aug. 11, 1849; Grinstein, *New York City*, 423 ff., 436 ff.
8. *Occ.*, 6:421 ff., 508 ff., 529 ff., 563 ff., 604, 7:41 ff., 94 ff., 134 ff., 203 ff., 247 ff., 258 ff., 433 ff., 8:599 ff., 10:236 ff.; Lebeson, *Pilgrim People*, 314-15; Tarshish, "American Judaism," 205 ff.; Korn, *Eventful Years*, 35 ff.; *AJA*, 2:21 ff.; *PAJHS*, 48:217 ff., 49:16 ff.; Grinstein, *New York City*, 423 ff., 448 ff.; Leeser, "Circular," Phila., Adar 5, 5609 (Feb. 28, 1849), copy in AJAr; Joshua Lazarus, Charleston, to I.L., Phila., Apr. 10, 1849, copy in Marcus Collections.
9. Tarshish, "American Judaism," 219 ff.; Allen Tarshish, "Board of Delegates of American Israelites (1859-1878)" (rabbinical thesis, H.U.C., 1932); *JM*, Apr. 1, 1859, p.100, c.3, p.101, c.1, June 24, 1859, p.188, cs.1-2, Aug. 4, 1865, p.36, c.3; Rutman, "Swiss-American Treaty," 63; *PAJHS*, 29:84, 111 ff., 48:224-25; *Proceedings of the Board of Dele-*

gates of American Israelites, etc. (New York, 1860); Grinstein, *New York City*, 430 ff.; H.S. Linfield, *Statistics of Jews and Jewish Organizations . . . 1850-1937* (N.Y., 1939), 15, 30-31; *Occ.*, 6:308, 312-21; 7:433 ff., 19:503; Circular letter of Henry L. Hart, president, BDAI, Jan. 9, 1863, copy in Marcus Collections; "Board of Delegates of American Israelites," *UJE*; "Evangelical Alliance," *Oxford Dictionary of the Christian Church.*

10. *JM*, June 24, 1859, p.188, cs.1-2, July 1, 1859, p.196, cs.1-3, July 22, 1859, p.20, cs.1-2; *Jewish Chronicle*, Mar. 1, 1861, p.6, c.3, Aug. 18, 1865, p.4, cs.1-3; *PAJHS*, 29:79, 112, 48:224-27, 49:16 ff.; *AZJ*, Nov. 11, 1892, pp.542-44; Grinstein, *New York City*, 433-34, 437-38; *AI*, May 13, 1859, p.357, c.4, Jan. 27, 1860, p.236, cs.1-2, Jan. 3, 1862, p. 212, c.3, Feb. 6, 1863, p.244, cs.1-3, Aug. 16, 1867, p.4, cs.4-5, p.5, c.1; Wallach, *"Sinai,"* 3:556 ff., 590-95; Tarshish, "American Judaism," 222-23, 228; Abraham J. Duker, "Efforts to Establish an Overall Jewish Body in the United States," typescript, copy in Marcus Collections; *Occ.*, 19:503 ff.; *Sinai*, 5:47-54.

11. "Isaacs, Samuel Myer," *JE, UJE*; Morais, *Eminent Israelites*, 153-57; Tarshish, "American Judaism," 226-27.

12. Tarshish, "American Judaism," 224-26, 229; *PAJHS*, 29:75 ff., 81, 103-09, 49:22-25.

13. *PAJHS*, 29:101-2, 115, 36:102 ff., 49:27-29.

14. *JSS*, 22:132; Henry Steele Commager (ed.), *Documents of American History* (7th ed., N.Y., 1936), 236-37; Grinstein, *New York City*, 435; Cyrus Adler & Aaron M. Margalith, *With Firmness in the Right: American Diplomatic Actions Affecting Jews, 1840-1945* (N.Y., 1946), xxiii, 30 ff.; *PAJHS*, 27:147, 29:87-89, 36:19-35; "United States," *JE*, 12:357, *UJE*, 10:350; "Morocco," *JE*; Shindling, *West Virginia Jewry*, 3:1332-33; Wolf, *Sir Moses Montefiore*, 185; Auerback, "San Francisco Jewry," for the *Gleaner*, Feb. 24, 1860, p.4, Mar. 9, 1860, p.5; *Studies in Bibliography and Booklore* (1961), 134, no.156: Printed Circular: "Portuguese Congregation Mickveh Israel," Philadelphia, appealing for funds for Moroccan Jewish refugees at Gibraltar, Dec. 25, 1859.

15. *PAJHS*, 29:85-86, 89, 98 ff., 115, 36:7, 348 ff., 37:95 ff., 49:26-27; Circular of BDAI, "Relief for Palestine," Dec. 1866, AJHS, copy in Marcus Collections; "Free Sons of Israel," *EJ*.

16. *PAJHS*, 36:171 ff., 179 ff., 182, 187, 189, 193-205.

17. *PAJHS*, 29:91, 36:173-77, 194; *Zion*, 30:220-23; *Menorah*, 15:462 ff.; M.S. Isaacs, Secretary, BDAI, N.Y. to H. Fish, Washington, D.C., Jan. 31, 1870, Hamilton Fish letter files, vol. 67, LC.

18. *PAJHS*, 24:2, et passim, 29:92 ff., 36:5-7, 205 ff.; "Servia," *JE*.

19. Tarshish, "American Judaism," 416 ff.; *PAJHS*, 24:25 ff., 102 ff., 138, 29:92-98, 36:99 ff.; *AJYB*, 19(1917-1918): 133 ff.; "Rumania," *EJ*, 14:388-89; Wolf, *The Jewish Question*, 18 ff., 24.

20. Grusd, *B'nai B'rith*, 75; Wolf, *Sir Moses Montefiore*, 184; *PAJHS*, 24:1 ff., 25-29, 29:93 ff., 36:99 ff.; "Peixotto, Benjamin Franklin," *JE, UJE*; Morais, *Eminent Israelites*, 267 ff.; M.S. Isaacs, Secretary, BDAI, N.Y., to Hamilton Fish, Washington, D.C., July 6, 1870, with enclosed clipping from Vienna *Freie Presse*, Hamilton Fish letter files, v. 68, LC.

21. *PAJHS*, 17:200 ff., 24:14 ff., 24, 29 ff., 32 ff., 39, 102 ff., 120 ff., 29:92-97, 109 ff., 36:102 ff.

22. *PAJHS*, 24:39 ff., 69-70, 29:97-98, 110, 114 ff., 36:112 ff.; Wolf, *The Jewish Question*, 23-36.

23. "Board of Delegates of American Israelites," *UJE, EJ*; "Roumania," *UJE*, 9:257; "Rumania," *EJ*, 14:389-90; *PAJHS*, 36:115 ff.

24. "Board of Delegates of American Israelites," *UJE*; Tarshish, "American Judaism," 226; *PAJHS*, 29:111 ff., 49:31.

25. Tarshish, "American Judaism," 228-29; R. & E., *Charleston*, 165. General References for BDAI: *AI*, May 13, 1859, p.357, c.4, p.358, c.1, Jan. 3, 1863, p.212, c.3, Feb. 6, 1863, p.244, cs.1-3, June 29, 1877, p.5, cs.3-5; *Occ.*, 8:599 ff., 19:503 ff.; Benjamin,

Three Years, 1:109; *Jewish Chronicle*, June 15, 1860, p.6, c. 3, Aug. 18, 1865, p.4, cs.1-3; Schappes, *JIUS*, 72-3; *JM*, Sept. 10, 1858, p.45, cs.1-2, Apr. 1, 1859, p.100, c.3, p.101, c.1, June 17, 1859, p.180, cs. 1-2, June 24, 1859, p.188, cs.1-2, July 1, 1859, p.196, cs.1-3, July 22, 1859, p.20, cs.1-2, July 29, 1859, p.28, cs.1-2; Sachar, *Modern Jewish History*, 178-79; Leo J. Stillpass, "The Board of Delegates of American Israelites from Record of the *Jewish Messenger* of 1858-1859" (HUC term paper, 1942); Michael Light, N.Y., to I.L., Phila., Aug. 25, 1853, German in Hebrew script, copy in Marcus Collections; Leo J. Stillpass, "The Attitude of Isaac M. Wise Toward the Board of Delegates as Reflected in the volumes of the *Israelite*" (HUC term paper, 1942); Elbogen, *Cent. of Jewish Life*, 66 ff.; M. & M., *History*, 688-90; Theodore Levy, "Board of Delegates of the Israelites of the United States, Minute Book, 1859-1860" (HUC term paper, n.d.); Leeser, "Circular," Phila., Adar 5, 5609 (Feb. 28, 1849); J. Bizart, Strasbourg, to Samuel Adler, N.Y., Feb. 14, 1871, copy in Marcus Collections; Circular, Myer S. Isaacs, Secretary, BDAI, N.Y., Feb. 15, 1865, printed, copy in Marcus Collections; Circular, Henry L. Hart, president, BDAI, Jan. 9, 1863, copy in Marcus Collections.

CHAPTER FOURTEEN
AMERICAN JEWRY, 1840–1860: A SUMMARY

1. *AJA*, 6:6 ff; Korn, *German-Jewish Intellectual Influences*, 1 ff.
2. Korn, *German-Jewish Intellectual Influences*, 8-9, 17, n.3.
3. Grinstein, *New York City*, 223-24.
4. Vorspan & Gartner, *Los Angeles*, 20-22.
5. Grinstein, *New York City*, 170-73, 391, 404-6; *AZJ*, June 7, 1847, pp.364-66.
6. Tarshish, "American Judaism," 65-66.

INDEX

Aaron, Sam ("Lucky Jew Kid"), 179
Aaronsburg, Pa., 188
Abeles, Ark., 64
Abilene, Kans., 134, 149
Abolitionism, 213, 236, 263, 279, 299
Abraham, Simeon, 245
Abrahams, Levi, 162
Abrams, Chapman, 91
Abrams, L., 157
Abrams, Susman, 54
Acculturation. *See* Americanization and acculturation
Achdut Vesholom Congregation (Fort Wayne), 197
Acoma Indians, 171
Actors, 229
Adair, James, 60
Adams, John Quincy, 287
Adams Express Co., 247
Adath Joseph Congregation (St. Joseph, Mo.), 105
Adler, Cyrus, 65
Adler, Felix, 231
Adler, Henry, 320
Adler, Moses, 142
Adler, Samuel (father of Cyrus Adler), 65
Adler, Samuel (rabbi of Temple Emanu-El), 231, 243, 253, 264, 307, 334
Adler, Sarah Sulzberger (Mrs. Samuel Adler), 65
Adrian, Mich., 91, 92
Adult education, 264, 266-268
Advertisements, 29, 153, 215, 224, 237, 285, 287
Agassiz, Louis, 50
Agricultural colonies, 44-45
Ahabat Israel Congregation (Richmond, Va.), 29

Ahavat Ahim Congregation (Bangor, Maine), 54
Akron, Ohio, 39, 48
Alaska, 59-61
Alaska Commercial Co., 117
Albany, Ga., 36
Albany, N.Y., 46, 50, 186, 189, 275, 282
Albany, Oreg., 125
Alberquerque, N.Mex., 139, 170, 174, 175
Alder Gulch, Mont., 154
Alexander, Idaho, 160
Alexander, Moses, 105, 159-160, 164
Alexander II (Russian tsar), 295
Alexandria, La., 71, 189
Alexandria, Va., 29, 79, 262
Alexandria Literary Society, 262
Allentown, Pa., 25
Allgemeine Zeitung des Judenthums, 19
Alliance, Ohio, 39
Alliance Israélite Universelle, 308, 313, 317, 318, 323, 324
Allis Chalmers Co., 87
Alpena, Mich., 93
Alsatian Jews, in U.S., 11, 61, 62, 69, 71, 86, 104, 116, 153, 211, 319
Altheimer, Ark., 64, 66
Altheimer, Louis, 65
Altheimer Dry Goods Co., 66
Altman, Henry, 135
Altoona, Pa., 25
Ambassadors. *See* Diplomatic and consular officials
Amberg, Jacob, 170
Americana collectors, 112
American and Commercial Advertiser (Baltimore), 299
American Bible Society, 269

387